2009

CHILDREN'S WRITER'S & ILLUSTRATOR'S MARKET®

Alice Pope, Editor

WRITER'S DIGEST BOOKS
CINCINNATI, OH

Editorial Director, Writer's Digest Books: Jane Friedman
Managing Editor, Writer's Digest Market Books: Alice Pope

Children's Writer's & Illustrator's Market Web page: wwww.cwim.com
Writer's Market Web site: www.writersmarket.com
Writer's Digest Web site: www.writersdigest.com
F+W Publications Bookstore: http://fwbookstore.com

Distributed in Canada by Fraser Direct
100 Armstrong Ave.
Georgetown, ON, Canada L7G 5S4
Tel: (905) 877-4411

Distributed in the U.K. and Europe by David & Charles
Brunel House, Newton Abbot, Devon, TQ12 4PU, England
Tel: (+44) 1626 323200, Fax: (+44) 1626 323319
E-mail: postmaster@davidandcharles.co.uk

Distributed in Australia by Capricorn Link
P.O. Box 704, Windsor, NSW 2756, Australia
Tel: (02) 4577-3555

Distributed in New Zealand by David Bateman Ltd.
P.O. Box 100-242, N.S.M.C., Auckland 1330, New Zealand
Tel: (09) 415-7664, Fax: (09) 415-8892

Distributed in South Africa by Real Books
P.O. Box 1040, Auckland Park 2006, Johannesburg, South Africa
Tel: (011) 837-0643, Fax: (011) 837-0645
E-mail: realbook@global.co.za

ISSN: 0897-9790
ISBN-13: 978-1-58297-549-8
ISBN-10: 1-58297-549-3

Cover design by Claudean Wheeler
Interior design by Clare Finney
Production coordinated by Greg Nock

Attention Booksellers: This is an annual directory of F+W Publications. Return deadline for this edition is December 31, 2009.

Contents

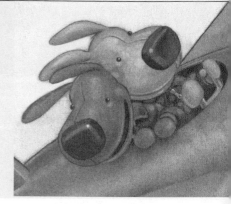

© 2008 Dan Andreasen

© 2008 Kelly Murphy

THE MARKETS

RESOURCES

© 2008 Marla Frazee

INDEXES

From the Editor

Last night as I put my son Murray to bed we read Maurice Sendak's *Where the Wild Things Are* (which is one of the select few picture books he loves that does not star cars, trucks, or construction equipment). After I read the book to him a few times he insisted on reading it aloud himself. The look on his face as he flipped through the pages spouting his unique version of the text was priceless. He was so amused and proud of himself and full of joy.

In editor Allyn Johnston's interview with herself she poses the question, *What is a picture book, anyway?* (Turn to page 31 for her answer). To me, picture books are stories perfectly meshed with works of art. They are funny or quiet or goofy or educational. They are enchanting. They are lasting. "Picture books have a pulse to them," author Barbara Kanninen (page 254) says.

For the past few years I've been reading a lot of YA novels—things like Scott Westerfeld's Uglies series (see page 156) and Jay Asher's *Thirteen Reasons Why* (see page 348)—and I've neglected picture books a bit. I'd been hearing that the picture book market was flat, that publishers weren't as interested in them, that it was harder than ever to break in. Maybe I've neglected picture book a little in *Children's Writer's & Illustrator's Market*, too. But not in this edition.

Dozens of debut authors answered the call on my blog for First Books candidates—and tons were first-time picture book authors and illustrators. This year's First Books (page 133) is all picture books, all featuring anthropomorphic animals—gay guinea pigs headed to the altar, an iguana who takes a vacation, a princess-eating baby dragon, and a gloomy fish (who's brought to life in sulky perfection by Dan Hanna—a detail from his cover illustration for *The Pout-Pout Fish* is above).

If you write picture books, you'll be inspired by First Books; Allyn Johnston's piece; Lisa Wheeler's article on great opening lines (page 37) (Murray also loves Lisa's book *Bubble Gum, Bubble Gum*); Sue Bradford Edwards' piece on authors and illustrators dividing details (page 44); an Insider Report with author Michelle Meadows, whose first picture book was plucked from the slush pile; and others. If you don't write picture books, there are plenty of features within these pages that cover everything—young chapter books (page 74), graphic novels (pages 83), anchoring dialogue (page 61), creating characters (page 55), YA fiction (page 78), and much more.

It was picture books that re-awakened my love of children's literature (as an adult). And aren't they everyone's first (book) love? "Whenever I am working on a picture book," says Allyn Johnston, "I try to remain as mindful as I can of the actual experience an adult and a child will have reading it together. I think of the shared feelings of connectedness they'll have as they listen to the story—as much for a raucous book as for a quiet one." It's thrilling to share that with Murray. And I'm happy to share a lot of picture book love with you in this book. I hope it helps you to introduce your own work (picture book or otherwise) to the world's many tiny readers.

Alice Pope
alice.pope@fwpubs.com
http://cwim.blogspot.com

How to Use This Book

As a writer, illustrator, or photographer first picking up *Children's Writer's & Illustrator's Market*, you may not know quite how to start using the book. Your impulse may be to flip through the book and quickly make a mailing list, then submit to everyone in hopes that someone will take interest in your work. Well, there's more to it. Finding the right market takes time and research. The more you know about a company that interests you, the better chance you have of getting work accepted.

We've made your job a little easier by putting a wealth of information at your fingertips. Besides providing listings, this directory includes a number of tools to help you determine which markets are the best ones for your work. By using these tools, as well as researching on your own, you raise your odds of being published.

USING THE INDEXES

This book lists hundreds of potential buyers of freelance material. To learn which companies want the type of material you're interested in submitting, start with the indexes.

Names Index

This index lists book and magazine editors and art directors as well as agents and art reps, indicating the companies they work for. Use this index to find company and contact information for individual publishing professionals.

Age-Level Index

Age groups are broken down into these categories in the Age-Level Index:

- **Picture books or picture-oriented material** are written and illustrated for preschoolers to 8-year-olds.
- **Young readers** are for 5- to 8-year-olds.
- **Middle readers** are for 9- to 11-year-olds.
- **Young adults** is for ages 12 and up.

Age breakdowns may vary slightly from publisher to publisher, but using them as general guidelines will help you target appropriate markets. For example, if you've written an article about trends in teen fashion, check the Magazines Age-Level Index under the Young Adult subheading. Using this list, you'll quickly find the listings for young adult magazines.

Subject Index

But let's narrow the search further. Take your list of young adult magazines, turn to the Subject Index, and find the Fashion subheading. Then highlight the names that appear on

Find a handy pull-out bookmark, a quick reference to the icons used in this book, right inside the front cover.

both lists (Young Adult and Fashion). Now you have a smaller list of all the magazines that would be interested in your teen fashion article. Read through those listings and decide which ones sound best for your work.

Illustrators and photographers can use the Subject Index as well. If you specialize in painting animals, for instance, consider sending samples to book and magazine publishers listed under Animals and, perhaps, Nature/Environment. Since illustrators can simply send general examples of their style to art directors to keep on file, the indexes may be more helpful to artists sending manuscripts/illustration packages who need to search for a specific subject. Always read the listings for the potential markets to see the type of work art directors prefer and what type of samples they'll keep on file, and obtain art or photo guidelines if they're available through the mail or online.

Photography Index

In this index you'll find lists of book and magazine publishers that buy photos from freelancers. Refer to the list and read the listings for companies' specific photography needs. Obtain photo guidelines if they're offered through the mail or online.

USING THE LISTINGS

Many listings begin with one or more symbols. Refer to the inside covers of the book for quick reference and find a handy pull-out bookmark (shown at left) right inside the front cover.

Many listings indicate whether submission guidelines are available. If a publisher you're interested in offers guidelines, get them and read them. The same is true with catalogs. Sending for and reading catalogs or browsing them online gives you a better idea of whether your work would fit in with the books a publisher produces. (You should also look at a few of the books in the catalog at a library or bookstore to get a feel for the publisher's material.)

Especially for artists & photographers

Along with information for writers, listings provide information for illustrators and photographers. Illustrators will find numerous markets that maintain files of samples for possible future assignments. If you're both a writer and an illustrator, look for markets that accept manuscript/illustration packages and read the information offered under the **Illustration** subhead within the listings.

If you're a photographer, after consulting the Photography Index, read the information under the **Photography** subhead within listings to see what format buyers prefer. For example, some want 35mm color transparencies, others want black and white prints. Note the type of photos a buyer wants to purchase and the procedures for submitting. It's not uncommon for a market to want a résumé and promotional literature, as well as tearsheets from previous work. Listings also note whether model releases and/or captions are required.

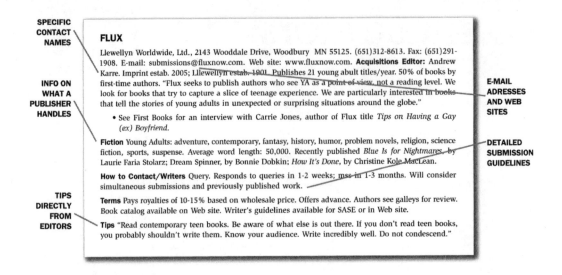

SPECIFIC CONTACT NAMES

INFO ON WHAT A PUBLISHER HANDLES

TIPS DIRECTLY FROM EDITORS

FLUX

Llewellyn Worldwide, Ltd., 2143 Wooddale Drive, Woodbury MN 55125. (651)312-8613. Fax: (651)291-1908. E-mail: submissions@fluxnow.com. Web site: www.fluxnow.com. **Acquisitions Editor:** Andrew Karre. Imprint estab. 2005; Llewellyn estab. 1901. Publishes 21 young adult titles/year. 50% of books by first-time authors. "Flux seeks to publish authors who see YA as a point of view, not a reading level. We look for books that try to capture a slice of teenage experience. We are particularly interested in books that tell the stories of young adults in unexpected or surprising situations around the globe."

• See First Books for an interview with Carrie Jones, author of Flux title *Tips on Having a Gay (ex) Boyfriend.*

Fiction Young Adults: adventure, contemporary, fantasy, history, humor, problem novels, religion, science fiction, sports, suspense. Average word length: 50,000. Recently published *Blue Is for Nightmares*, by Laurie Faria Stolarz; Dream Spinner, by Bonnie Dobkin; *How It's Done*, by Christine Kole MacLean.

How to Contact/Writers Query. Responds to queries in 1-2 weeks; mss in 1-3 months. Will consider simultaneous submissions and previously published work.

Terms Pays royalties of 10-15% based on wholesale price. Offers advance. Authors see galleys for review. Book catalog available on Web site. Writer's guidelines available for SASE or in Web site.

Tips "Read contemporary teen books. Be aware of what else is out there. If you don't read teen books, you probably shouldn't write them. Know your audience. Write incredibly well. Do not condescend."

E-MAIL ADRESSES AND WEB SITES

DETAILED SUBMISSION GUIDELINES

Especially for young writers

If you're a parent, teacher, or student, you may be interested in Young Writer's & Illustrator's Markets. The listings in this section encourage submissions from young writers and artists. Some may require a written statement from a teacher or parent noting the work is original. Also watch for age limits.

Young people should also check Contests & Awards for contests that accept work by young writers and artists. Some of the contests listed are especially for students; others accept both student and adult work. These listings contain the phrase **open to students** in bold. Some listings in Clubs & Organizations and Conferences & Workshops may also be of interest to students. Organizations and conferences which are open to or are especially for students also include **open to students**.

Quick Tips for Writers & Illustrators

I f you're new to the world of children's publishing, buying *Children's Writer's & Illustrator's Market* may have been one of the first steps in your journey to publication. What follows is a list of suggestions and resources that can help make that journey a smooth and swift one:

1. Make the most of *Children's Writer's & Illustrator's Market*. Be sure to read How to Use This Book on page 2 for tips on reading the listings and using the indexes. Also be sure to take advantage of the articles and interviews in the book. The insights of the authors, illustrators, editors, and agents we've interviewed will inform and inspire you.

2. Join the Society of Children's Books Writers and Illustrators. SCBWI, more than 19,000 members strong, is an organization for both beginners and professionals interested in writing and illustrating for children. They offer members a slew of information and support through publications, a Web site, and a host of Regional Advisors overseeing chapters in almost every state in the U.S. and in a growing number of locations around the globe (including France, Canada, Japan, and Australia). SCBWI puts on a number of conferences, workshops, and events on the regional and national levels (many listed in the Conferences & Workshops section of this book). For more information, contact SCBWI, 8271 Beverly Blvd., Los Angeles CA 90048, (323)782-1010, or visit their Web site: www.scbwi.org.

3. Read newsletters. Newsletters, such as *Children's Book Insider, Children's Writer*, and the *SCBWI Bulletin*, offer updates and new information about publishers on a timely basis and are relatively inexpensive. Many local chapters of SCBWI offer regional newsletters as well. (See Helpful Books & Publications on page 364 for contact information on the newsletters listed above and others. For information on regional SCBWI newsletters, visit www.scbwi .org and click on "Publications.")

4. Read trade and review publications. Magazines like *Publishers Weekly* (which offers two special issues each year devoted to children's publishing and is available on newsstands), *The Horn Book*, and *Booklinks* offer news, articles, reviews of newly-published titles, and ads featuring upcoming and current releases. Referring to them will help you get a feel for what's happening in children's publishing.

5. Read guidelines. Most publishers and magazines offer writer's and artist's guidelines that provide detailed information on needs and submission requirements, and some magazines offer theme lists for upcoming issues. Many publishers and magazines state the availability of guidelines within their listings. Send a self-addressed, stamped envelope (SASE) to publishers who offer guidelines. You'll often find submission information on publishers' and magazines' Web sites.

6. Look at publishers' catalogs. Perusing publishers' catalogs can give you a feel for

Getting Started

their line of books and help you decide where your work might fit in. If catalogs are available (often stated within listings), send for them with a SASE. Visit publishers' Web sites, which often contain their full catalogs. You can also ask librarians to look at catalogs they have on hand. You can even search Amazon.com by publisher and year. (Click on "book search" then "publisher, date" and plug in, for example, "Lee & Low" under "publisher" and "2006" under year. You'll get a list of Lee & Low titles published in 2006, which you can peruse.)

7. Visit bookstores. It's not only informative to spend time in bookstores—it's fun, too! Frequently visit the children's section of your local bookstore (whether a chain or an independent) to see the latest from a variety of publishers and the most current issues of children's magazines. Look for books in the genre you're writing or with illustrations similar in style to yours, and spend some time studying them. It's also wise to get to know your local booksellers; they can tell you what's new in the store and provide insight into what kids and adults are buying.

8. Read, read, read! While you're at that bookstore, pick up a few things, or keep a list of the books that interest you and check them out of your library. Read and study the latest releases, the award winners, and the classics. You'll learn from other writers, get ideas, and get a feel for what's being published. Think about what works and doesn't work in a story. Pay attention to how plots are constructed and how characters are developed or the rhythm and pacing of picture book text. It's certainly enjoyable research!

9. Take advantage of Internet resources. There are innumerable sources of information available on the Internet about writing for children (and anything else you could possibly think of). It's also a great resource for getting (and staying) in touch with other writers and illustrators through listservs, blogs, social networking sites and e-mail, and it can serve as a vehicle for self-promotion. (Visit some authors' and illustrators' sites for ideas. See Useful Online Resources on page 367 for a list of Web sites.)

10. Consider attending a conference. If time and finances allow, attending a conference is a great way to meet peers and network with professionals in the field of children's publishing. As mentioned above, SCBWI offers conferences in various locations year round. (See www.scbwi.org and click on "Events" for a full conference calendar.) General writers' conferences often offer specialized sessions just for those interested in children's writing. Many conferences offer optional manuscript and portfolio critiques as well, giving you a chance for feedback from seasoned professionals. See the Conferences & Awards section for information on SCBWI and other conferences. The section features a Conferences & Workshops Calendar to help you plan your travel.

11. Network, network, network! Don't work in a vacuum. You can meet other writers and illustrators through a number of the things listed above—SCBWI, conferences, online. Attend local meetings for writers and illustrators whenever you can. Befriend other writers in your area (SCBWI offers members a roster broken down by state)—share guidelines, share subscriptions, be conference buddies and roommates, join a critique group or writing group, exchange information, and offer support. Get online—sign on to listservs, post on message boards and blogs, visit social networking sites and chatrooms. (The Institute of Children's Literature offers regularly scheduled live chats and open forums. Visit www.institutechildren slit.com and click on Scheduled Events. Also, visit author Verla Kay's Web site, www.verlaka y.com, for information on workshops. See Useful Online Resources on page 367 for more information.) Exchange addresses, phone numbers, and e-mail addresses with writers or illustrators you meet at events. And at conferences, don't be afraid to talk to people, ask strangers to join you for lunch, approach speakers and introduce yourself, or chat in elevators and hallways.

12. Perfect your craft and don't submit until your work is its best. It's often been said that a writer should try to write every day. Great manuscripts don't happen overnight;

there's time, research, and revision involved. As you visit bookstores and study what others have written and illustrated, really step back and look at your own work and ask yourself—honestly—*How does my work measure up? Is it ready for editors or art directors to see?* If it's not, keep working. Join a critique group or get a professional manuscript or portfolio critique.

13. Be patient, learn from rejection, and don't give up! Thousands of manuscripts land on editors' desks; thousands of illustration samples line art directors' file drawers. There are so many factors that come into play when evaluating submissions. Keep in mind that you might not hear back from publishers promptly. Persistence and patience are important qualities in writers and illustrators working toward publication. Keep at it—it will come. It can take a while, but when you get that first book contract or first assignment, you'll know it was worth the wait. (For proof, read First Books on page 133.)

Getting Started

Before Your First Sale

I f you're just beginning to pursue your career as a children's book writer or illustrator, it's important to learn the proper procedures, formats, and protocol for the publishing industry. This article outlines the basics you need to know before you head to the post office with your submissions.

FINDING THE BEST MARKETS FOR YOUR WORK

Researching publishers thoroughly is a basic element of submitting your work successfully. Editors and art directors hate to receive inappropriate submissions; handling them wastes a lot of their time, not to mention your time and money, and they are the main reason some publishers have chosen not to accept material over the transom. By randomly sending out material without knowing a company's needs, you're sure to meet with rejection.

If you're interested in submitting to a particular magazine, write to request a sample copy or see if it's available in your local library or bookstore. For a book publisher, obtain a book catalog and check a library or bookstore for titles produced by that publisher. Most publishers and magazines have Web sites that include catalogs or sample articles (Web sites are given within the listings). Studying such materials carefully will better acquaint you with a publisher's or magazine's writing, illustration, and photography styles and formats.

Most of the book publishers and magazines listed in this book offer some sort of writer's, artist's, or photographer's guidelines for a self-addressed, stamped envelope (SASE). Guidelines are also often found on publishers' Web sites. It's important to read and study guidelines before submitting work. You'll get a better understanding of what a particular publisher wants. You may even decide, after reading the submission guidelines, that your work isn't right for a company you considered.

SUBMITTING YOUR WORK

Throughout the listings, you'll read requests for particular elements to include when contacting markets. Here are explanations of some of these important submission components.

Queries, cover letters, & proposals

A query letter is a no-more-than-one-page, well-written piece meant to arouse an editor's interest in your work. Many query letters start with leads similar to those of actual manuscripts. In the rest of the letter, briefly outline the work you're proposing and include facts, anecdotes, interviews, or other pertinent information that give the editor a feel for the manuscript's premise—entice her to want to know more. End your letter with a straightforward request to write or submit the work, and include information on its approximate length, date it could be completed, and whether accompanying photos or artwork are available.

In a query letter, think about presenting your book as a publisher's catalog would present it. Read through a good catalog and examine how the publishers give enticing summaries of their books in a spare amount of words. It's also important that query letters give editors a taste of your writing style. For good advice and samples of queries, cover letters, and other correspondence, consult *Formatting & Submitting Your Manuscript*, Second Edition, by Cynthia Laufenberg and the editors of *Writer's Market* and *How to Write Attention-Grabbing Query & Cover Letters*, by John Wood (both Writer's Digest Books).

For More Info

- **Query letters for nonfiction.** Queries are usually required when submitting nonfiction material to a publisher. The goal of a nonfiction query is to convince the editor your idea is perfect for her readership and that you're qualified to do the job. Note any previous writing experience and include published samples to prove your credentials, especially samples related to the subject matter you're querying about.

- **Query letters for fiction.** More and more, queries are being requested for fiction manuscripts. For a fiction query, explain the story's plot, main characters, conflict, and resolution. Just as in nonfiction queries, make the editor eager to see more.

- **Cover letters for writers.** Some editors prefer to review complete manuscripts, especially for picture books or fiction. In such cases, the cover letter (which should be no longer than one page) serves as your introduction, establishes your credentials as a writer, and gives the editor an overview of the manuscript. If the editor asked for the manuscript because of a query, note this in your cover letter.

- **Cover letters for illustrators and photographers.** For an illustrator or photographer, the cover letter serves as an introduction to the art director and establishes professional credentials when submitting samples. Explain what services you can provide as well as what type of follow-up contact you plan to make, if any. Be sure to include the URL of your online portfolio if you have one.

- **Résumés.** Often writers, illustrators, and photographers are asked to submit résumés with cover letters and samples. They can be created in a variety of formats, from a single page listing information to color brochures featuring your work. Keep your résumé brief, and focus on your achievements, including your clients and the work you've done for them, as well as your educational background and any awards you've received. Do not use the same résumé you'd use for a typical job application.

- **Book proposals.** Throughout the listings in the Book Publishers section, publishers refer to submitting a synopsis, outline, and sample chapters. Depending on an editor's preference, some or all of these components, along with a cover letter, make up a book proposal.

A *synopsis* summarizes the book, covering the basic plot (including the ending). It should be easy to read and flow well.

An *outline* covers your book chapter by chapter and provides highlights of each. If you're developing an outline for fiction, include major characters, plots and subplots, and book length.

Sample chapters give a more comprehensive idea of your writing skill. Some editors may request the first two or three chapters to determine if she's interested in seeing the whole book.

Manuscript formats

When submitting a complete manuscript, follow some basic guidelines. In the upper-left corner of your title page, type your legal name (not pseudonym), address, and phone number. In the upper-right corner, type the approximate word count. All material in the upper corners should be single-spaced. Then type the title (centered) almost halfway down that page, the word "by" two spaces under that, and your name or pseudonym two spaces under "by."

The first page should also include the title (centered) one-third of the way down. Two spaces under that type "by" and your name or pseudonym. To begin the body of your manuscript, drop down two double spaces and indent five spaces for each new paragraph. There should be one-inch margins around all sides of a full typewritten page. (Manuscripts with wide margins are more readable and easier to edit.)

Set your computer to double-space for the manuscript body. From page two to the end of the manuscript, include your last name followed by a comma and the title (or key words of the title) in the upper-left corner. The page number should go in the top right corner. Drop down two double spaces to begin the body of each page. If you're submitting a novel, type each chapter title one-third of the way down the page. For more information on manuscript formats, read *Formatting & Submitting Your Manuscript*, by Cynthia Laufenberg and the editors of *Writer's Market* (Writer's Digest Books). SCBWI members and nonmembers can refer to their publication *From Keyboard to Printed Page: Facts You Need to Know*. Visit their Web site www.scbwi.org and click on "Publications."

For More Info

Picture book formats

The majority of editors prefer to see complete manuscripts for picture books. When typing the text of a picture book, don't indicate page breaks and don't type each page of text on a new sheet of paper. And unless you are an illustrator, don't worry about supplying art. Editors will find their own illustrators for picture books. Most of the time, a writer and an illustrator who work on the same book never meet or interact. The editor acts as a go-between and works with the writer and illustrator throughout the publishing process. *How to Write and Sell Children's Picture Books*, by Jean E. Karl (Writer's Digest Books), offers advice on preparing text and marketing your work.

For More Info

If you're an illustrator who has written your own book, consider creating a dummy or storyboard containing both art and text, and then submit it along with your complete manuscript and sample pieces of final art (color photocopies or computer printouts—never originals). Publishers interested in picture books specify in their listings what should be submitted. For tips on creating a dummy, refer to *How to Write and Illustrate Children's Books and Get Them Published*, edited by Treld Pelkey Bicknell and Felicity Trotman (North Light Books), or Frieda Gates' book, *How to Write, Illustrate, and Design Children's Books* (Lloyd-Simone Publishing Company).

Writers may also want to learn the art of dummy making to help them through their writing process with things like pacing, rhythm, and length. For a great explanation and helpful hints, see *You Can Write Children's Books*, by Tracey E. Dils (Writer's Digest Books).

Mailing submissions

Your main concern when packaging material is to be sure it arrives undamaged. If your manuscript is less than six pages, simply fold it in thirds and send it in a #10 (business-size) envelope. For a SASE, either fold another #10 envelope in thirds or insert a #9 (reply) envelope which fits in a #10 neatly without folding.

Another option is folding your manuscript in half in a 6×9 envelope, with a #9 or #10 SASE enclosed. For larger manuscripts, use a 9×12 envelope both for mailing the submission and as a SASE (which can be folded in half). Book manuscripts require sturdy packaging for mailing. Include a self-addressed mailing label and return postage.

If asked to send artwork and photographs, remember they require a bit more care in packaging to guarantee they arrive in good condition. Sandwich illustrations and photos between heavy cardboard that is slightly larger than the work. The cardboard can be secured by rubber bands or with tape. If you tape the cardboard together, check that the artwork doesn't stick to the tape. Be sure your name and address appear on the back of each piece of art or each photo in case the material becomes separated. For the packaging, use either a manila envelope, a foam-padded envelope, brown paper, or a mailer lined with plastic air bubbles. Bind nonjoined edges with reinforced mailing tape and affix a typed mailing label or clearly write your address.

Mailing material first class ensures quick delivery. Also, first-class mail is forwarded for one year if the addressee has moved, and it can be returned if undeliverable. If you're concerned about your original material safely reaching its destination, consider other mailing options, such as UPS or certified mail. If material needs to reach your editor or art director quickly, use overnight delivery services.

Remember, companies outside your own country can't use your country's postage when returning a manuscript to you. When mailing a submission to another country, include a self-addressed envelope and International Reply Coupons, or IRCs. (You'll see this term in many listings in the Canadian & International Book Publishers section.) Your postmaster can tell you, based on a package's weight, the correct number of IRCs to include to ensure its return.

If it's not necessary for an editor to return your work (such as with photocopies), don't include return postage. You may want to track the status of your submission by enclosing a postage-paid reply postcard with options for the editor to check, such as "Yes, I am interested," "I'll keep the material on file," or "No, the material is not appropriate for my needs at this time."

Some writers elect to include a deadline date. If you don't hear from the editor by the specified date, your manuscript is automatically withdrawn from consideration. Because many publishing houses and companies are overstocked with material, a minimum deadline should be at least three months.

Unless requested, it's never a good idea to use a company's fax number or e-mail address to send manuscript submissions. This can disrupt a company's internal business. Some publishers and magazines, however, may be open to e-mail submissions. Study the listings for specifics and visit publishers' and publications' Web sites for more information.

Keeping submission records

It's important to keep track of the material you submit. When recording each submission, include the date it was sent, the business and contact name, and any enclosures (such as samples of writing, artwork, or photography). You can create a record-keeping system of your own or look for record-keeping software in your area computer store.

Keep copies of articles or manuscripts you send together with related correspondence to make follow-up easier. When you sell rights to a manuscript, artwork, or photos, you can "close" your file on a particular submission by noting the date the material was accepted, what rights were purchased, the publication date, and payment.

Often writers, illustrators, and photographers fail to follow up on overdue responses. If you don't hear from a publisher within their stated response time, wait another month or so and follow up with a note asking about the status of your submission. Include the title or description, date sent, and a SASE for response. Ask the contact person when she anticipates making a decision. You may refresh the memory of a buyer who temporarily forgot about your submission. At the very least, you'll receive a definite "no" and free yourself to send the material to another publisher.

Simultaneous submissions

If you opt for simultaneous (also called "multiple") submissions—sending the same material to several publishers at the same time—be sure to inform each editor to whom you submit that your work is being considered elsewhere. Many editors are reluctant to receive simultaneous submissions but understand that for hopeful writers and illustrators, waiting several months for a response can be frustrating. In some cases, an editor may actually be more inclined to read your manuscript sooner if she knows it's being considered by another publisher. The

Society of Children's Book Writers and Illustrators cautions writers against simultaneous submissions. They recommend simultaneously submitting to publishers who state in their submission guidelines that they accept multiple submissions. In such cases, always specify in your cover letter that you've submitted to more than one editor.

It's especially important to keep track of simultaneous submissions, so if you get an offer on a manuscript sent to more than one publisher, you can instruct other publishers to withdraw your work from consideration.

AGENTS & ART REPS

Most children's writers, illustrators, and photographers, especially those just beginning, are confused about whether to enlist the services of an agent or representative. The decision is strictly one that each writer, illustrator, or photographer must make for herself. Some are confident with their own negotiation skills and believe acquiring an agent or rep is not in their best interest. Others feel uncomfortable in the business arena or are not willing to sacrifice valuable creative time for marketing.

About half of children's publishers accept unagented work, so it's possible to break into children's publishing without an agent. Some agents avoid working with children's books because traditionally low advances and trickling royalty payments over long periods of time make children's books less lucrative. Writers targeting magazine markets don't need the services of an agent. In fact, it's practically impossible to find an agent interested in marketing articles and short stories—there simply isn't enough financial incentive.

One benefit of having an agent, though, is it may speed up the process of getting your work reviewed, especially by publishers who don't accept unagented submissions. If an agent has a good reputation and submits your manuscript to an editor, that manuscript will likely bypass the first-read stage (which is generally done by editorial assistants and junior editors) and end up on the editor's desk sooner.

When agreeing to have a reputable agent represent you, remember that she should be familiar with the needs of the current market and evaluate your manuscript/artwork/photos accordingly. She should also determine the quality of your piece and whether it is saleable. When your manuscript sells, your agent should negotiate a favorable contract and clear up any questions you have about payments.

Keep in mind that however reputable the agent or rep is, she has limitations. Representation does not guarantee sale of your work. It just means an agent or rep sees potential in your writing, art, or photos. Though an agent or rep may offer criticism or advice on how to improve your work, she cannot make you a better writer, artist, or photographer.

Literary agents typically charge a 15 percent commission from the sale of writing; art and photo representatives usually charge a 25 to 30 percent commission. Such fees are taken from advances and royalty earnings. If your agent sells foreign rights to your work, she will deduct a higher percentage because she will most likely be dealing with an overseas agent with whom she must split the fee.

Be advised that not every agent is open to representing a writer, artist, or photographer who lacks an established track record. Just as when approaching a publisher, the manuscript, artwork, or photos and query or cover letter you submit to a potential agent must be attractive and professional looking. Your first impression must be as an organized, articulate person.

For listings of agents and reps, turn to the Agents & Art Reps section. For additional listings of art reps, consult *Artist's & Graphic Designer's Market*; for photo reps, see *Photographer's Market*; for more information and additional listings of agents see *Guide to Literary Agents* (all Writer's Digest Books).

Running Your Business

The Basics for Writers & Illustrators

A career in children's publishing involves more than just writing skills or artistic talent. Successful authors and illustrators must be able to hold their own in negotiations, keep records, understand contract language, grasp copyright law, pay taxes, and take care of a number of other business concerns. Although agents and reps, accountants and lawyers, and writers' organizations offer help in sorting out such business issues, it's wise to have a basic understanding of them going in. This article offers just that—basic information. For a more in-depth look at the subjects covered here, check your library or bookstore for books and magazines to help you. We also tell you how to get information on issues like taxes and copyright from the federal government.

CONTRACTS & NEGOTIATION

Before you see your work in print or begin working with an editor or art director on a project, there is negotiation. And whether negotiating a book contract, a magazine article assignment, or an illustration or photo assignment, there are a few things to keep in mind. First, if you find any clauses vague or confusing in a contract, get legal advice. The time and money invested in counseling up front could protect you from problems later. If you have an agent or rep, she will review any contract.

Sources for Contract Help

Writers organizations offer a wealth of information to members, including contract advice:

Society of Children's Book Writers and Illustrators members can find information in the SCBWI publication Answers to Some Questions About Contracts. Contact SCBWI at 8271 Beverly Blvd., Los Angeles CA 90048, (323)782-1010, or visit their Web site: www.scbwi.org.

The Authors Guild also offers contract tips. Visit their Web site, www.authorsguild.org. (Members of the guild can receive a 75-point contract review from the guild's legal staff.) See the Web site for membership information and application form, or contact The Authors Guild at 31 E. 28th St., 10th Floor, New York NY 10016, (212)563-5904. Fax: (212)564-5363. E-mail: staff@authorsguild.org. Web site: www.authorsguild.org.

A contract is an agreement between two or more parties that specifies the fees to be paid, services rendered, deadlines, rights purchased, and for artists and photographers, whether original work is returned. Most companies have standard contracts for writers, illustrators, and photographers. The specifics (such as royalty rates, advances, delivery dates, etc.) are typed in after negotiations.

Though it's okay to conduct negotiations over the phone, get a written contract once both parties have agreed on terms. Never depend on oral stipulations; written contracts protect both parties from misunderstandings. Watch for clauses that may not be in your best interest, such as "work-for-hire." When you do work-for-hire, you give up all rights to your creations.

When negotiating a book deal, find out whether your contract contains an option clause. This clause requires the author to give the publisher a first look at her next work before offering it to other publishers. Though it's editorial etiquette to give the publisher the first chance at publishing your next work, be wary of statements in the contract that could trap you. Don't allow the publisher to consider the next project for more than 30 days and be specific about what type of work should actually be considered "next work." (For example, if the book under contract is a young adult novel, specify that the publisher will receive an exclusive look at only your next young adult novel.)

For More Info

(For more information about SCBWI, The Authors Guild, and other organizations, turn to the Clubs & Organizations section and read the listings for the organizations that interest you.)

Book publishers' payment methods

Book publishers pay authors and artists in royalties, a percentage of either the wholesale or retail price of each book sold. From large publishing houses, the author usually receives an advance issued against future royalties before the book is published. Half of the advance amount is issued upon signing the book contract; the other half is issued when the book is finished. For illustrations, one-third of the advance should be collected upon signing the contract; one-third upon delivery of sketches; and one-third upon delivery of finished art.

After your book has sold enough copies to earn back your advance, you'll start to get royalty checks. Some publishers hold a reserve against returns, which means a percentage of royalties is held back in case books are returned from bookstores. If you have a reserve clause in your contract, find out the exact percentage of total sales that will be withheld and the time period the publisher will hold this money. You should be reimbursed this amount after a reasonable time period, such as a year. Royalty percentages vary with each publisher, but there are standard ranges.

Book publishers' rates

According to figures from the Society of Children's Book Writers and Illustrators, first-time picture book authors can expect advances of $2,000-3,000; first-time picture book illustrators' advances range from $5,000-7,000; text and illustration packages for first-timers can score $6,000-8,000. Rates go up for subsequent books: $3,500-5,000 for picture book text; $7,000-10,000 for picture book illustration; $8,000-10,000 for text and illustration. Experienced authors can expect higher advances. Royalties for picture books are generally about five percent (split between the author and illustrator) but can go as high as ten percent. Those who both write and illustrate a book, of course, receive the full royalty.

Advances for hardcover novels and nonfiction can fetch authors advances of $4,000-6,000 and 10 percent royalties; paperbacks bring in slightly lower advances of $3,000-5,000 and royalties of 6-8 percent.

As you might expect, advance and royalty figures vary from house to house and are affected by the time of year, the state of the economy, and other factors. Some smaller houses may not even pay royalties, just flat fees. Educational houses may not offer advances or offer smaller amounts. Religious publishers tend to offer smaller advances than trade publishers. First-time writers and illustrators generally start on the low end of the scale, while established and high-profile writers are paid more. For more information SCBWI members can request or download SCBWI publication ''Answer to Some Questions About Contracts.'' (Visit www.scbwi.org.)

Pay rates for magazines

For writers, fee structures for magazines are based on a per-word rate or range for a specific article length. Artists and photographers have a few more variables to contend with before contracting their services.

Payment for illustrations and photos can be set by such factors as whether the piece(s) will be black and white or four-color, how many are to be purchased, where the work appears (cover or inside), circulation, and the artist's or photographer's prior experience.

Remaindering

When a book goes out of print, a publisher will sell any existing copies to a wholesaler who, in turn, sells the copies to stores at a discount. When the books are ''remaindered'' to a wholesaler, they are usually sold at a price just above the cost of printing. When negotiating a contract with a publisher, you may want to discuss the possibility of purchasing the remaindered copies before they are sold to a wholesaler, then you can market the copies you purchased and still make a profit.

KNOW YOUR RIGHTS

A copyright is a form of protection provided to creators of original works, published or unpublished. In general, copyright protection ensures the writer, illustrator, or photographer the power to decide how her work is used and allows her to receive payment for each use.

Essentially, copyright also encourages the creation of new works by guaranteeing the creator power to sell rights to the work in the marketplace. The copyright holder can print, reprint, or copy her work; sell or distribute copies of her work; or prepare derivative works such as plays, collages, or recordings. The Copyright Law is designed to protect work (created on or after January 1, 1978) for her lifetime plus 70 years.

If you collaborate with someone else on a written or artistic project, the copyright will last for the lifetime of the last survivor plus 70 years. The creators' heirs may hold a copyright for an additional 70 years. After that, the work becomes public domain. Works created anonymously or under a pseudonym are protected for 120 years, or 95 years after publication. Under work-for-hire agreements, you relinquish your copyright to your ''employer.''

Copyright notice & registration

Some feel a copyright notice should be included on all work, registered or not. Others feel it is not necessary and a copyright notice will only confuse publishers about whether the material is registered (acquiring rights to previously registered material is a more complicated process).

Although it's not necessary to include a copyright notice on unregistered work, if you don't feel your work is safe without the notice, it is your right to include one. Including a copyright notice—© (year of work, your name)—should help safeguard against plagiarism.

Registration is a legal formality intended to make copyright public record, and it can help you win more money in a court case. By registering work within three months of publication or before an infringement occurs, you are eligible to collect statutory damages and attorney's fees. If you register later than three months after publication, you will qualify only for actual damages and profits.

Ideas and concepts are not copyrightable, only expressions of those ideas and concepts. A character type or basic plot outline, for example, is not subject to a copyright infringement lawsuit. Also, titles, names, short phrases or slogans, and lists of contents are not subject to copyright protection, though titles and names may be protected through the Trademark Office.

You can register a group of articles, illustrations, or photos if it meets these criteria:

- the group is assembled in order, such as in a notebook
- the works bear a single title, such as "Works by (your name)"
- it is the work of one writer, artist, or photographer
- the material is the subject of a single claim to copyright

It's a publisher's responsibility to register your book for copyright. If you've previously registered the same material, you must inform your editor and supply the previous copyright information, otherwise, the publisher can't register the book in its published form.

For More Info

For more information about the proper way to register works and to order the correct forms, contact the U.S. Copyright Office, (202)707-3000. The forms available are TX for writing (books, articles, etc.); VA for pictures (photographs, illustrations); and PA for plays and music. For information about how to use the copyright forms, request a copy of Circular I on Copyright Basics. All of the forms and circulars are free. Send the completed registration form along with the stated fee and a copy of the work to the Copyright Office.

For specific answers to questions about copyright (but not legal advice), call the Copyright Public Information Office at (202)707-3000 weekdays between 8:30 a.m. and 5 p.m. EST. Forms can also be downloaded from the Library of Congress Web site: www.copyright.gov. The site also includes a list of frequently asked questions, tips on filling out forms, general copyright information, and links to other sites related to copyright issues. For members of SCBWI, information about copyrights and the law is available in their publication: Copyright Facts for Writers.

The rights publishers buy

The copyright law specifies that a writer, illustrator, or photographer generally sells one-time rights to her work unless she and the buyer agree otherwise in writing. Many publications will want more exclusive rights to your work than just one-time usage; some will even require you to sell all rights. Be sure you are monetarily compensated for the additional rights you relinquish. If you must give up all rights to a work, carefully consider the price you're being offered to determine whether you'll be compensated for the loss of other potential sales.

Writers who only give up limited rights to their work can then sell reprint rights to other publications, foreign rights to international publications, or even movie rights, should the opportunity arise. Artists and photographers can sell their work to other markets such as paper product companies who may use an image on a calendar, greeting card, or mug. Illustrators and photographers may even sell original work after it has been published. And there are a number of galleries throughout the U.S. that display and sell the original work of children's illustrators.

Rights acquired through the sale of a book manuscript are explained in each publisher's contract. Take time to read relevant clauses to be sure you understand what rights each contract is specifying before signing. Be sure your contract contains a clause allowing all rights to revert back to you in the event the publisher goes out of business. (You may even want to have the contract reviewed by an agent or an attorney specializing in publishing law.)

The following are the rights you'll most often sell to publishers, periodicals, and producers in the marketplace:

First rights. The buyer purchases the rights to use the work for the first time in any medium. All other rights remain with the creator. When material is excerpted from a soon-to-be-published book for use in a newspaper or periodical, first serial rights are also purchased.

One-time rights. The buyer has no guarantee that she is the first to use a piece. One-time permission to run written work, illustrations, or photos is acquired, then the rights revert back to the creator.

First North American serial rights. This is similar to first rights, except that companies who distribute both in the U.S. and Canada will stipulate these rights to ensure that another North American company won't come out with simultaneous usage of the same work.

Second serial (reprint) rights. In this case, newspapers and magazines are granted the right to reproduce a work that has already appeared in another publication. These rights are also purchased by a newspaper or magazine editor who wants to publish part of a book after the book has been published. The proceeds from reprint rights for a book are often split evenly between the author and his publishing company.

Simultaneous rights. More than one publication buys one-time rights to the same work at the same time. Use of such rights occurs among magazines with circulations that don't overlap, such as many religious publications.

All rights. Just as it sounds, the writer, illustrator, or photographer relinquishes all rights to a piece—she no longer has any say in who acquires rights to use it. All rights are purchased by publishers who pay premium usage fees, have an exclusive format, or have other book or magazine interests from which the purchased work can generate more mileage. If a company insists on acquiring all rights to your work, see if you can negotiate for the rights to revert back to you after a reasonable period of time. If they agree to such a proposal, get it in writing.

Note: Writers, illustrators, and photographers should be wary of ''work-for-hire'' arrangements. If you sign an agreement stipulating that your work will be done as work-for-hire, you will not control the copyrights of the completed work—the company that hired you will be the copyright owner.

Foreign serial rights. Be sure before you market to foreign publications that you have sold only North American—not worldwide—serial rights to previous markets. If so, you are free to market to publications that may be interested in material that's appeared in a North American-based periodical.

Syndication rights. This is a division of serial rights. For example, if a syndicate prints portions of a book in installments in its newspapers, it would be syndicating second serial rights. The syndicate would receive a commission and leave the remainder to be split between the author and publisher.

Subsidiary rights. These include serial rights, dramatic rights, book club rights, or translation rights. The contract should specify what percentage of profits from sales of these rights go to the author and publisher.

Dramatic, television, and motion picture rights. During a specified time, the interested party tries to sell a story to a producer or director. Many times options are renewed because the selling process can be lengthy.

Display rights or electronic publishing rights. They're also known as ''Data, Storage, and Retrieval.'' Usually listed under subsidiary rights, the marketing of electronic rights in this era of rapidly expanding capabilities and markets for electronic material can be tricky. Display rights can cover text or images to be used in a CD-ROM or online, or they may cover use of material in formats not even fully developed yet. If a display rights clause is listed in your contract, try to negotiate its elimination. Otherwise, be sure to pin down which electronic rights are being purchased. Demand the clause be restricted to things designed to be read only. By doing this, you maintain your rights to use your work for things such as games and interactive software.

STRICTLY BUSINESS

An essential part of being a freelance writer, illustrator, or photographer is running your freelance business. It's imperative to maintain accurate business records to determine if you're making a profit as a freelancer. Keeping correct, organized records will also make your life easier as you approach tax time.

When setting up your system, begin by keeping a bank account and ledger for your business finances apart from your personal finances. Also, if writing, illustration, or photography is secondary to another freelance career, keep separate business records for each.

You will likely accumulate some business expenses before showing any profit when you start out as a freelancer. To substantiate your income and expenses to the IRS, keep all invoices, cash receipts, sales slips, bank statements, canceled checks, and receipts related to travel expenses and entertaining clients. For entertainment expenditures, record the date, place, and purpose of the business meeting, as well as gas mileage. Keep records for all purchases, big and small. Don't take the small purchases for granted; they can add up to a substantial amount. File all receipts in chronological order. Maintaining a separate file for each month simplifies retrieving records at the end of the year.

Record keeping

When setting up a single-entry bookkeeping system, record income and expenses separately. Use some of the subheads that appear on Schedule C (the form used for recording income from a business) of the 1040 tax form so you can easily transfer information onto the tax form when filing your return. In your ledger include a description of each transaction—the date, source of income (or debts from business purchases), description of what was purchased or sold, the amount of the transaction, and whether payment was by cash, check, or credit card.

Don't wait until January 1 to start keeping records. The moment you first make a business-related purchase or sell an article, book manuscript, illustration, or photo, begin tracking your profits and losses. If you keep records from January 1 to December 31, you're using a calendar-year accounting period. Any other accounting period is called a fiscal year.

There are two types of accounting methods you can choose from—the cash method and the accrual method. The cash method is used more often: You record income when it is received and expenses when they're disbursed.

Using the accrual method, you report income at the time you earn it rather than when it's actually received. Similarly, expenses are recorded at the time they're incurred rather than when you actually pay them. If you choose this method, keep separate records for "accounts receivable" and "accounts payable."

Satisfying the IRS

To successfully—and legally—work as a freelancer, you must know what income you should report and what deductions you can claim. But before you can do that, you must prove to the IRS you're in business to make a profit, that your writing, illustration, or photography is not merely a hobby.

The Tax Reform Act of 1986 says you should show a profit for three years out of a five-year period to attain professional status. The IRS considers these factors as proof of yourprofessionalism:

- accurate financial records
- a business bank account separate from your personal account
- proven time devoted to your profession
- whether it's your main or secondary source of income
- your history of profits and losses
- the amount of training you have invested in your field
- your expertise

If your business is unincorporated, you'll fill out tax information on Schedule C of Form

1040. If you're unsure of what deductions you can take, request the IRS publication containing this information. Under the Tax Reform Act, only 30 percent of business meals, entertainment and related tips, and parking charges are deductible. Other deductible expenses allowed on Schedule C include: car expenses for business-related trips; professional courses and seminars; depreciation of office equipment, such as a computer; dues and publication subscriptions; and miscellaneous expenses, such as postage used for business needs.

If you're working out of a home office, a portion of your mortgage interest (or rent), related utilities, property taxes, repair costs, and depreciation may be deducted as business expenses—under special circumstances. To learn more about the possibility of home office deductions, consult IRS Publication 587, Business Use of Your Home.

The method of paying taxes on income not subject to withholding is called "estimated tax" for individuals. If you expect to owe more than $500 at year's end and if the total amount of income tax that will be withheld during the year will be less than 90 percent of the tax shown on the current year's return, you'll generally make estimated tax payments. Estimated tax payments are made in four equal installments due on April 15, June 15, September 15, and January 15 (assuming you're a calendar-year taxpayer). For more information, request Publication 533, Self-Employment Tax.

The Internal Revenue Service's Web site (www.irs.gov) offers tips and instant access to IRS forms and publications.

For More Info

Social Security tax

Depending on your net income as a freelancer, you may be liable for a Social Security tax. This is a tax designed for those who don't have Social Security withheld from their paychecks. You're liable if your net income is $400 or more per year. Net income is the difference between your income and allowable business deductions. Request Schedule SE, Computation of Social Security Self-Employment Tax, if you qualify.

If completing your income tax return proves to be too complex, consider hiring an accountant (the fee is a deductible business expense) or contact the IRS for assistance. (Look in the White Pages under U.S. Government—Internal Revenue Service or check their Web site, www.irs.gov.) In addition to offering numerous publications to instruct you in various facets of preparing a tax return, the IRS also has walk-in centers in some cities.

Insurance

As a self-employed professional, be aware of what health and business insurance coverage is available to you. Unless you're a Canadian who is covered by national health insurance or a full-time freelancer covered by your spouse's policy, health insurance will no doubt be one of your biggest expenses. Under the terms of a 1985 government act (COBRA), if you leave a job with health benefits, you're entitled to continue that coverage for up to 18 months—you pay 100 percent of the premium and sometimes a small administration fee. Eventually, you must search for your own health plan. You may also choose to purchase disability and life insurance. Disability insurance is offered through many private insurance companies and state governments. This insurance pays a monthly fee that covers living and business expenses during periods of long-term recuperation from a health problem. The amount of money paid is based on the recipient's annual earnings.

Before contacting any insurance representative, talk to other writers, illustrators, or photographers to learn which insurance companies they recommend. If you belong to a writers' or artists' organization, ask the organization if it offers insurance coverage for professionals. (SCBWI has a plan available to members in certain states. Look through the Clubs & Organizationssection for other groups that may offer coverage.) Group coverage may be more affordable and provide more comprehensive coverage than an individual policy.

Six Reasons To Quit Writing

(& One Reason You Shouldn't)

by Donna Gephart

Writing is hard work.

Not ditch-digging, fire-fighting, cancer-curing hard work, but hard. So hard you might entertain thoughts of quitting.

Go ahead.

In fact, I'll give you six good reasons why you should put down your pen, turn off your computer and do something more "practical."

Then I'll give you one vital reason you mustn't quit. (Hint: That reason enables us to push beyond the frustration inherent in this pursuit.)

1) You're not good enough.

Nothing will send you running from your keyboard faster than comparing yourself to another writer. Don't. We have different voices, abilities and gifts to offer.

Be aware of the competition, of course, but don't base your worth on it. Your story isn't less valuable because it hasn't won a major award (yet).

Don't worry if someone appears to write better, faster or more creatively than you. Simply write (and rewrite) the best story you can.

Those feelings of inadequacy intensify when we work alone. And writing is a lonely profession. To counter this, write in coffee shops or libraries once in awhile. Go on message boards and join the blogging community. Attend a conference. Join a critique group. Spend time with friends and family. Just don't do these things to the exclusion of writing.

The best way to avoid loneliness is to become absorbed in the world of your characters. Let them keep you company during your writing hours. Someday, those same characters might provide an afternoon's companionship for an otherwise lonely young reader.

2) It takes too long to become successful.

It's often said that if you want to succeed in the field of writing, prepare for a decade-long apprenticeship. That's 10 years of reading voraciously, writing and revising . . . and dreaming.

My husband once told me, "You're not running a race. It's not about publishing one book. You're building a career here. It's a full-blown marathon."

So, lace up your sneakers and take a deep breath because it is indeed a marathon of

---

DONNA GEPHART's novel, *As If Being 12¾ Isn't Bad Enough, My Mother Is Running for President* (Delacorte Press) is available wherever books are sold. To learn more, visit www.donnagephart.com.

creating, revising and marketing your work. If you want to make a career of writing for children, be prepared for the long haul.

As Eddie Cantor once said, "It takes 20 years to make an overnight success."

J.K. Rowling spent a year on welfare while she sent her book about the boy wizard to agents and publishers. After that year, an agent finally took her on. It took him another four rejections from publishers before he got Rowling a modest advance from Bloomsbury, U.K.

And we know how Rowling's patience and persistence led to one of the greatest "happily ever after" stories in the history of children's publishing.

3) You don't have time to write.

The late Linda Smith wrote picture books like *Mrs. Biddlebox* and novels while caring for her eight children.

Newbery Medal winner, Christopher Paul Curtis wrote during his breaks at the assembly line at Fischer Body Plant in Flint Michigan between hanging car doors.

Eventually, Curtis' wife supported him and their two children while he spent each day (for eight hours) writing a novel at the public library. It took him a bit more than a year (because it takes a long time), but the result was *The Watsons Go to Birmingham—1963*, a Newbery honor winner. His next book, *Bud, Not Buddy*, won the Newbery.

Best-selling novelist, Mary Higgins Clark, widowed with five young children, wrote from five to seven every morning. It took her three years to write a biography of George Washington that was published, but sunk without a trace. It took another three years of early-morning writing to produce *Where Are the Children?* which launched a wildly successful career.

After hearing people tell her they'd love to write, but can't find the time, she labeled that the "as soon as . . ." syndrome. As soon as the kids are grown, the dog dies, etc.

There will never be a perfect time to write. Do it anyway. Make dates with yourself. Turn off the TV. Want it more than you want other things and you will find the time.

4) You're afraid you'll fail.

You will fail.

Sorry to break it to you, but failure is inherent in any successful endeavor because we need to risk in order to succeed. Every time we put pen to paper, we fail to achieve the perfect vision in our mind's eye.

In her brilliant book, *Bird by Bird: Some Instructions on Writing and Life*, Anne Lamott gives you permission to write "shitty first drafts." Of course you can write "shitty first drafts," because every writer knows a good book isn't written—it's rewritten.

A writing friend of mine, Donald Vaughan, once said, "It's a whole lot easier to revise a bad page than a blank page." Amen!

Literary agent, Jeff Herman, says, "No rejection is fatal until the writer walks away from the battle leaving dreams and goals behind."

Incidentally, fear of failure isn't the only stumbling block for some writers. Some freeze in the face of success. When they get close to reaching their goals, the prospect is so frightening, they can't proceed. Don't be one of those people. When you come close to reaching your goals, grab for them with gusto.

Banish fear of failure (or success) from your thought process. Writing is hard enough without that particular form of self-sabotage.

As Harlan Ellison once said, "The great secret of writing is not becoming a writer, it's *staying* a writer."

5) Rejections are too painful.

No one likes to have his or her work rejected. But it happens to even highly successful writers. And often, the reason your work was passed up has nothing to do with the work itself.

The editor may have just purchased a book about a similar subject.

Your work might not fit with the editor's current goals for her list.

There might not be enough money in the budget to acquire all the stories an editor would like.

The list goes on.

If there's not a specific reason for your rejection—a form letter—the only thing you can do is keep writing, revising and sending it out. Join a critique group. Members can catch errors and help make your story the best it can be before it lands on the desk of an agent or editor.

If you're lucky enough to get a personal response to your work, decide if the comment makes sense, and if it does, use it to improve your writing before sending it out again.

Look at every rejection slip as tangible evidence that you're doing the courageous work of writing, revising and sending it out. Each rejection slip is merely a brick on your path to success.

Jack London's character, Martin Eden (in a novel of the same name), succumbed to multiple rejections and gave up just before success arrived. Luckily, Jack London didn't succumb to the same despair as his character. Mr. London received six hundred rejection slips before he sold his first story. *Six hundred!* If he hadn't persevered beyond those rejections, we wouldn't have such masterpieces today as "White Fang" and "Call of the Wild."

Don't let rejections deter you, especially if you're getting personal responses and encouragement. Success might be right around the corner, but if you quit, you'll never know.

I was so discouraged by numerous rejections (mostly personal responses) that I decided to give up writing. Being so close yet not making it was painful. I loved books. I loved kids.

Inspirational Rejection Stories

- Ellen Jackson's picture book, *Cinder Edna*, was rejected more than 40 times before she sold it. The hardcover version went on to sell more than 150,000 copies. Ms. Jackson shares some of those rejection letters at her Web site: www.ellenjackson.net/work11.htm.

- *A Wrinkle in Time*, by Madeleine L'Engle, was rejected by 26 publishers before editors at Farrar, Straus & Giroux enthusiastically accepted it. That novel won the Newbery Medal in 1963 and has sold over eight million copies.

- Dr. Seuss' *And to Think That I Saw It on Mulberry Street* was rejected by 27 publishers. The 28th publisher, Vanguard Press, sold six million copies of the book.

- Shel Silverstein's *The Giving Tree* was rejected by a Simon & Schuster editor with a letter that included this comment: "I'm sorry, but I don't think you're going to find a publisher for it." *The Giving Tree* went on to sell more than two million copies for Harper & Row and launched Shel Silverstein's career as one of history's bestselling authors of children's books.

- The following work was described as "very dull" by a reader's report. It was also depicted as "a dreary record of typical family bickering, petty annoyances and adolescent emotions." *The Diary of a Young Girl*, by Anne Frank, was turned down by 15 publishers before Doubleday published it in 1952. More than 30 million copies are in print, making it one of the best-selling books in history.

I decided I'd become a children's librarian. After an interview for the job, I was told I was an excellent candidate, but they chose someone else. That particular rejection turned into an opportunity. I used my time to write another novel.

You'll read about what happened with that novel in the next section.

6) Someone says you should quit.

Few people pursue their writing dreams without having at least one naysayer tell them it's hopeless. Sometimes that person is a parent, a teacher or even a friend.

My naysayer was my stepbrother. Since he, too, was a writer and nearly a decade older, I respected his opinion.

In college, I timidly sent him a few pieces I'd written, which he promptly critiqued and returned. He also quizzed me on my knowledge of children's literature, which at the time was abysmally deficient.

To save me future despair, I suppose, he sent a letter stating I should give up writing. "You will never, ever be a writer."

His words crushed me. I gave up writing ambitions I'd fostered since I was eight.

For a while. I have a writer's soul. Words seeped through the cracks in the wall I'd erected. Eventually, I found my way back to writing.

In Ralph Keyes' book, *The Writer's Book of Hope: Getting from Frustration to Publication*, he refers to these naysayers as goads. Keyes says you should thank these people because often, they spur you on to prove them wrong.

He tells the story of a writer whose college professor told him he should give up writing. That writer then sent every book he'd ever published to that professor as a tangible "I told you so."

Patricia MacLachlan (*Sarah, Plain and Tall*) was warned by a high school teacher that she should seek another profession because writing wouldn't be it.

Naysayers often pretend to have your best interest at heart, but have ulterior motives or

A Reading List to Keep You Writing

Here are books for writers that inspire, educate and encourage:

- *The Courage to Write: How Writers Transcend Fear* and *The Write's Book of Hope: Getting from Frustration to Publication*, by Ralph Keyes
- *The Forest for the Trees: An Editor's Advice to Writers*, by Betsy Lerner
- *Five Pages a Day: A Writer's Journey*, by Peg Kehret
- *Bird by Bird: Some Instructions on Writing and Life*, by Anne Lamott
- *The Right to Write: An Invitation and Initiation into the Writing Life*, by Julia Cameron
- *Story: Substance, Structure, Style and the Principles of Screen Writing*, by Robert McKee
- *On Writing: A Memoir of the Craft*, by Stephen King
- *Writing Magic: Creating Stories that Fly*, by Gail Carson Levine

as if being 12³/₄ isn't bad enough, my mother is running for president!

DONNA GEPHART

It took Donna Gephart about a year to complete her novel *As If Being 12¾ Isn't Bad Enough, My Mother Is Running for President*. Delacorte published Gephart's book in February 2008.

severe cases of self-doubt. Besides, who has a crystal ball and knows which of us will make it and which will falter?

When someone tells you that you can't or shouldn't pursue your dream of writing, let that comment spur you on to do exactly that.

The great pleasure in life is doing what people say you cannot do. —Walter Bagehot.

Remember when I didn't get that job as a children's librarian?

Shortly after that, I began working on a short story about a shy, gawky girl whose mother is too busy for her because she's running for president. That story received a lot of encouragement from members of my critique group. With their thoughtful suggestions, I turned that story into a novel about Vanessa Rothrock, klutzy spelling bee champ who wants nothing more than to be out of the spotlight, playing a game of Scrabble with her mom—the governor of Florida, and quite possibly, the next president of the United States. As my novel progresses, Vanessa receives threatening letters in her locker at school and has to find the courage to thwart an assassination attempt.

Tina Wexler, a literary agent at I.C.M., loved Vanessa's quirky voice, and offered me revision suggestions.

Determined (beyond all reason) to sell this novel, I spent four months researching and revising according to her excellent suggestions.

Wexler loved the revisions and sent *As If Being 12³/₄ Isn't Bad Enough, My Mother is Running for President* to seven publishers. "It might take a few months until we hear anything," she warned. (Writing takes a long time.)

Three weeks later, she called. "Are you sitting down?"

I was standing, folding laundry. (Very glamorous, I know.)

"No, but tell me anyway." I clutched the doorframe.

"We got an offer on your novel, but another house is also interested. I'll get back to you."

And I'll get back to that as soon as I make my final point: There is one very important reason *not* to quit writing.

1) You have unflappable determination to persevere through every obstacle and reach your goal of having a successful writing career.

No one and nothing can put a big enough obstacle in your path if you want it bad enough to put in the sweat equity (revisions) and work through inevitable frustrations.

Hemingway said he rewrote the ending to Farewell to Arms 39 times. *Thirty-nine times!*

So, if you're willing to ignore the naysayers (including the one inside your head), realize failure is part of the process and work like you've never worked on anything before, your writer's story may have the same happy ending as mine.

Delacorte Press bought my novel, *As If Being 12³/₄ Isn't Bad Enough, My Mother Is Running for President*, and has supported me every step of the way with both revisions and promotion.

If I'd given into my many temptations to quit, I would never have known the elation of selling my first novel for children and looking hopefully toward my writing future.

Like the very characters we create, writers struggle through both external and internal obstacles. Here's to proceeding on that journey with as much hope, faith, joy and tenacity as humanly possible.

And here's to *your* future writing successes!

What's In?
What's Out?

An Expert Panel Talks Trends

by Darcy Pattison

You've finished your latest project and you're tossing around ideas about what to work on next. Your mind turns to book stores, book clubs, royalty statements. And you wonder if there's a way to predict what books will sell well next year. What's in? What's out? What's up-and-coming? What's clichéd?

The many perspectives of publishing

I went searching for the answers to these questions and talked to an agent, a bookseller, a librarian, a teen, several middle grade readers—and a writer. As might be expected, each section of the publishing world has a different perspective, and, of course, each of the individuals is expressing his/her opinion, which might differ greatly from others in his/her field.

Agents, editors and writers are concerned about creating books, creating and breaking trends, and staying one step ahead. Representing the agents is **Alyssa Eisner Henkin**, a literary agent who specializes in children's and young adult books at Trident Media Group (www.tridentmediagroup.com). **Stephen Mooser**, co-founder and president of the Society of Children's Bookwriters and Illustrators (www.scbwi.org) speaks for the writers' perspective.

Representing the booksellers' point-of-view is **Kristen McLean**, Executive Director of The Association of Booksellers for Children (www.abfc.com). Booksellers are the here-and-now people, concerned with what titles are selling well right now; but they have one foot in the past as they stock the classics and one step in the future as they struggle to decide what front list titles to stock. Booksellers support and hand-selling can dramatically impact a title's sales.

Librarians are mostly concerned with current and past books, as their calling in life is to archive our culture and from that vast archive, meet the current reading needs of their patrons. From A Fuse8 Production blog (go to www.slj.com, click on Blogs) comes the opinions of **Elizabeth Bird**, librarian with The New York Public Library system.

Seth Cassel, teen and co-webmaster of Flamingnet.com, a book review Web site, represents the teen take on books. He is joined by several anonymous-to-protect-their-privacy middle grade readers who review for his Web site. These readers are definitely grounded in

DARCY PATTISON, an author of both picture books and novels, has been published in eight languages. Her books include *Nineteen Girls and Me* (Philomel), *Searching for Oliver K. Woodman* (Harcourt), and *The Journey of Oliver K. Woodman* (Harcourt). Her books have been recognized for excellence by starred reviews in *Kirkus* and *BCCB*, and many awards. She is also the author of two books on writing: a teacher resource book, *Paper Lightning: Prewriting Activities to Spark Creativity* (Cottonwood) and a workbook for intermediate to advanced novelists, *Novel Metamorphosis: Uncommon Ways to Revise* (Mims). Read her Revision Notes blog at www.darcypattison.com.

the here-and-now, but they run two or three years behind the agents' point of view, because it takes so long to publish a book. As part of their education, kids must read classics and older books—and they find treasures there—but, these days, they have cash to spend at bookstores for the new titles. They can make or break a trend.

WHAT'S IN?

Zombies, paranormal stories, graphic novels, reality-based fantasy, romance, diary and school stories about cliques and gangs, sports stories, picture books, easy readers, teen stories.

Bird starts off tongue-in-cheek by noting that 2006 was the year of sentient cheese. "In 2007, it was situations where a mouth was covered over with flesh (gross, but true)." In other trends, zombies—the new vampires—join other paranormal offerings of ghosts, seances, seers and spiritualism. Graphic novels are definitely in if they are child-friendly.

For younger kids, McLean says picture books and early readers are strong. For teens, Cassel says fantasy is still strong, but not overblown fantasy. He prefers fantasies about teens who lead ordinary lives, but have some interesting twist. Some faith-based books do well, too. Opinions from the middle grade crowd vary widely, as they list these as popular topics: romance; fantasy; diary and school stories about cliques and gangs; sports stories; vampires; realistic stories of fiction or romance; teen problems; and graphic novels, especially manga.

19 Girls and Me

Darcy Pattison ILLUSTRATED BY Steven Salerno

© Little, Brown and Company Books for Young Readers. Reprinted with permission.

The main character in Darcy Pattison's *19 Girls and Me* is John Hercules Po—the lone boy in his kindergarten class. "Readers will have almost as much fun with this title as these energetic and happy classmates have together," says *School Library Journal*.

Looking to the future, Henkin sees a better market for middle grade and tween stories. She echoes the teens and middle graders in looking for reality-based fantasy, school based stories, and graphic novels. She agrees with McLean that younger illustrated fiction is on the way up.

WHAT'S OUT

Vampires, chick-lit, Harry Potter rip-offs, science fiction, historical fiction, classics, religion, dead parents.

Henkin is still looking for chick-lit, but not stories based in New York City; look instead, for regional chick-lit. For picture books, she finds birthday and tooth fairy stories hard to sell. Booksellers have trouble selling explicit YA titles, too. McLean appreciates teen titles that push the envelope, or are edgy, because they sell well. But titles that have to be shelved away from the main YA titles because of X-rated material are much harder to sell. Also hard to sell are YA titles with parents who are dead, dying of cancer, abusive, gone, etc.

In the library, Bird is getting tired of dragons, urban fairy literature, and big fat fantasy Harry Potter rip-offs. Cassell is also tired of fantasy with non-human creatures, or the overused fantasy creatures such as dragons or witches. The middle grade readers add vampires to the list, as well as different species of people at special magical schools. Other topics top on their

Tired List are girly boyfriend problem books, science fiction, classics, religion, true love stories, adventure quests, self-help books and wizards. One reviewer is especially tired of school stories where a girl is bullied, someone stands up for her and the bully gets in trouble.

ARE THERE TABOO TOPICS?

When Susan Patron's book won the 2006 Newbery for *The Higher Power of Lucky*, there was a huge ruckus over the use of the word ''scrotum'' on the first page. Are there topics that are taboo, or should be avoided, for different age levels?

''Lice'' is the only topic McLean could think of as inappropriate for the picturebook crowd. For middle grade, she's more serious when she says to avoid graphic sex. Bird personally feels that torture has no place in children's books. For these two age levels, everyone urged common sense.

For the teen audience, however, everyone agreed the field is wide open. Bird says ''how the material is presented'' is important and McLean makes that thought more specific when she says she looks for ''authentic treatments of a topic.''

The teens weigh in with their own perspective. Cassel says inappropriate topics are sex, drugs and gruesome violence. One middle grade reviewer says, ''As long as the person reading it is mature then there are no problems.'' Another adds, ''We are at that point in our lives where we are most curious about those topics, so reading about them gives us more knowledge about the subjects.'' And another takes a balanced approach: ''Most topics are appropriate as long as they do not overwhelm the reader or become the focus of the story. For example, the purpose of a novel should not be sex. Religion should also not be overwhelming if the target audience is not devout.''

WHAT WOULD YOU LIKE TO SEE PUBLISHED?

Our panel wasn't shy in speaking about books they'd love to see published. Henkin says reading historical fiction is what drew her into publishing, so she'd like to see a renewed interest the genre. Parents, she notes, are also looking for picture books for the pre-school child who is too young for the short-chapter Clementine books, by Sara Pennypacker, but has outgrown The Pigeon books, by Mo Willems. Picture books with longer text seem to fit that bill.

As a librarian who tries to balance a collection, Bird has strong opinions on the holes she sees in children's literature. ''I'd like to see published more fantasy with characters who aren't white. Sorry, but there it is,'' she says. ''And no, I don't want to see 'the black Harry Potter' or 'the Asian Harry Potter'.'' She also mentions other under-represented areas: ethnic characters, strong female characters, and gay families where it's not the point of the story. Manga is prevalent for teens, she points out, but titles which extend graphic novels toward younger ages would be welcome. For nonfiction, she'd like to see more attention paid to book design and illustrations.

One of the middle grade reviewers says, ''Although there are many vampire books, I would like to see more of them if they are like Stephanie Myers'. It might also be interesting if an author combined different people, like pirates and vampires, and made a story of how they interact with each other.'' Another adds, ''I would like to see some good, new science fiction that has a decent plot and could revive the genre.''

''A BEACON IN THE MUD''

Did you notice that in all the discussion above one voice was missing? Mooser, the writer, refused to say what's in or what's out. ''In the end,'' he writes, ''it is the manuscript that will sell the book. Write the very best you can. Your manuscript has to stand out. It has to be something fresh and unique.''

We knew that before we started this discussion, didn't we? It's fun to read about trends,

Titles Recommended by the Panel

Most of the panel agreed with Kristen McLean, "I'm not sure what topics I'd like to see published, because what I most like is to be surprised by originality."

Our agent's picks
- *The Night Tourist*, by Katherine Marsh; *Amaranth*, by Julie Berry (reality-based fantasy)
- *My Life in Pink and Green*, by Lisa Greenwald (school-based story + enviroment)
- *Ivy and Bean*, by Annie Barrows and *Diary of a Wimpy Kid*, by Jeff Kinney (younger middle grade)
- *Peaches*, by Jodi Lynn Anderson and *Dairy Queen*, by Catherine Murdock (regional chick-lit)
- *Fancy Nancy*, by Jane O'Conner and *Pinkalicious*, by Victoria Kann (character-driven, franchise-minded picture books)
- *The Luxe*, by Anna Godberson and *Hattie Big Sky*, by Kirby Larson (historical fiction)
- *Hero*, by Perry Moore (unusual topic—a homosexual superhero)
- *Ringside 1925*, by Jen Bryant (evolutionary theory); novels by Susan Shaw (rape and abuse); novels by Alex Sanchez (teens struggling with sexuality); *Emma Jean Lazarus Fell Out of a Tree*, by Lauren Tarshis (death of parent); (all hard or controversial topics done well)

Our writer's picks
- *Millicent Min, Girl Genius*, by Lisa Yee (new take on characters)
- New take on story, taut writing: *Thirteen Reasons Why*, by Jay Asher (suicide)
- Unique approach and dazzling execution: *The Arrival*, by Shaun Tan (wordless graphic novel)
- Humor: *Maxwell's Magic Mix-up*, by Linda Ashman (picturebook), *Clementine*, by Sara Pennypacker (middle grade novel)

Our bookseller's picks
- *Thirteen Reasons Why*, by Jay Asher (YA, suicide)
- *Fan Boy and Goth Girl*, by Barry Lyga (YA, fantasizing about a school shooting)
- *The Red Tree*, by Sean Tan (picture book, childhood depression)
- *Pink*, by Nan Gregory (picture book—not getting what you desperately want)
- *The Astonishing Life of Octavian Nothing*, by MT Anderson (YA—slavery in colonial America)
- *Alabama Moon*, by Watt Key (middle grade, being raised by survivalists in the woods)
- *Dairy Queen*, by Catherine Murdock (teen novel with strong teen content, but no X-rated stuff)
- *Thirteen Little Blue Envelopes*, by Maureen Johnson; *Notes from a Midnight Driver*, by Jordan Sonnenblick; *Memoirs of a Teenage Amnesiac*, by Gabrielle Sabin (all teen novels with refreshingly bright YA novels with plenty of appeal)

Our librarian's picks
- *We are the Ship: The Story of the Negro League Baseball*, by Kadir Nelson (unusual subject and interesting illustration for a nonfiction topic)
- *The Rabbits*, by John Marsden and *Rose Blanche*, by Robert Innocenti (picture books not for little kids, but adult readers)

Our YA reader/reviewer's picks
- *The Ear, the Eye, and the Arm*, by Nancy Farmer; *Ender's Game*, by Orson Scott Card; Harry Potter novels by J.K. Rowling (all favorite books with plausible human world, that is somehow different)

Our middle grade readers/reviewers' picks
- The Twilight saga, by Stephanie Meyer (absolutely amazing vampire series) and The Eragon series by Christopher Paolini (fantasy) (stories that surprise and go beyond expectations)
- *Attack and Bride of the Soul Sucking Brain Zombies/Bride of the Soul Sucking Brain Zombies*, by Brett Hartinger (zombies); *The God of Mischief*, by Paul Bajoria (twins solving a murder mystery); and *Story Time*, by Edward Bloor (horror inside one of America's smartest schools)
- *Grief Girl*, by Erin Vincent; Harry Potter series (great writing)

NOVEL
Metamorphosis

Uncommon
Ways
to
Revise

Darcy Pattison

Foreword by Kirby Larson,
author of the 2007 Newbery Honor Book
Hattie Big Sky

Darcy Pattison's *Novel Metamorphosis* is based on the Novel Revision Retreat coordinated by the author after 12 years of dieting a wrting conference. The book is hands-on, offering plenty of writing and brain storming-space, to help writers take their fresh ideas and mold them into strong novels.

fun to stay up with our culture and our times, but in the end, we must write our own stories. "When something knocks my socks off it's always because of one of the following things: an amazing and honest voice, an off-beat premise, emotional authenticity, a timeless adventure, or unflinching love of a character on the part of an author, especially if the character is flawed," says McLean. "These kind of books can only be written from a deeply personal and consistent place, a place of immersion. True originality stand on its own, and it requires a heroic leap of faith to stop worrying about market issues. Originality shines like a beacon in the mud."

In an informal poll of writers, the most common rejection letters read something like this: "While the writing is strong, the story just doesn't stand out in today's crowded market." For all the panel, it holds true that originality trumps everything else. Originality is the spark that stands out in the crowd. To succeed, make this your mantra: Originality is imperative.

What this discussion of trends will tell you—the writer—is what's been done before. Ignore the categories of what's in and what's out. Ignore what others would like to see published. Instead, ask yourself these questions: What's not on any of these lists anywhere? What could I write and no one else could write? What intrigues me, puzzles me, makes me cry, makes me mad, stirs up passion in my heart? Of those, what do I want to write and how can I write it in a way that is original?

Bird says it this way, "If there are 500 books out there on the subject of women dressing up like boys to go to war, do you truly feel you can add something to the dialogue if you write the 501st?"

Mooser offers five examples of directions the originality might take: a surprisingly new take on character (*Millicent Min, Girl Genius*, by Lisa Yee); taut writing (*Thirteen Reason's Why*, by Jay Asher); a unique approach and dazzling execution (*The Arrival*, by Shaun Tan); original humor in a picture book (*Maxwell's Magic Mix-up*, by Linda Ashman); or original humor in a middle grade novel (*Clementine*, by Sara Pennypacker) "These books signal the debut of a unique voice," he says. "If it takes you a year to come up with a fresh idea or character it's worth it because your book will sell if you can pull it all together and produce a strong manuscript."

One of the middle grade reviewers offers this advice to writers: "Add a lot of twists and think to yourself, what you would expect to happen and either end the story there and create a sequel or don't do quite the opposite but make it something the readers can be outraged by or really touched by. Twists to a story are what really affect people. Get a little creative in your topics. No one wants the same story line twice. Think of something in your life that could be unique to yourself and twist it. Or something that everyone goes through and twist it."

Mooser adds one final clichéd, but true statement: "Be persistent. It may take you years, but if you work hard, read a lot and study the market, you will succeed. I've seen it happen literally hundreds of times."

A Long-time Editor Talks Picture Books

by Allyn Johnston

Allyn Johnston is the vice president and publisher of a small, west-coast imprint of Simon & Schuster. She began her career at Clarion Books and Putnam Books for Young Readers, and then returned to her home state of California in 1986, where she worked at Harcourt Children's Books for 22 years, rising to the position of editor in chief, until she was laid off in a cost-cutting measure following a takeover in March, 2008.

Worried about her mental state post-dismissal, the concerned editor of *Children's Writer's & Illustrator's Market* begged Allyn to sit down and ask herself some questions about her first love as an editor: picture books.

AJ: What is a picture book, anyway?

AJ: Well, in the most basic, classic, and very best sense, I suppose you could say it is a story for young children told in both text and illustrations that unfolds over 32 printed pages that are sewn together at the spine and housed within hard cardboard covers. And this story, when read aloud, will cast a spell around all who are present to hear it and look at it, and, with luck, will go straight into their hearts and never be forgotten.

Damn. That's intimidating, huh?

AJ: Why do you think you are good at editing them?

AJ: My coziest memories from early childhood involve being read to by the cherished adults in my life—my mom, my dad, my grandfather, my adored elderly babysitter, Mrs. Clark. Many things about those times together remain vivid in my mind: their voices, the quietly turning pages, the soft texture of the paper, the gentle cadence of the language, even the yellow velvet of my grandfather's reading chair and the light glinting off of his glasses. . . .

So if I am, in fact, good at editing picture books, I completely believe it's because of the power of these intense childhood memories—and of the quality of the books: *Ferdinand* and *Ping* and *Peter Rabbit* and *One Morning in Maine* and *Goodnight, Moon* and *Over and Over* and *Mr. Rabbit and the Lovely Present* and *The Country Bunny and the Little Gold Shoes*, among many, many others. Whenever I am working on a picture book, I try to remain as mindful as I can of the actual experience an adult and a child will have reading it together.

ALLYN JOHNSTON began as vice president and publisher of her Simon & Schuster imprint at the end of March, 2008 after 22 years with Harcourt. Her new imprint focuses on picture books and middle-grade fiction. Over the years, she's worked with Lois Ehlert, Marla Frazee, Mem Fox, Jane Dyer, Debra Frasier, Avi, Cynthia Rylant, and Ursula K. LeGuin, among other talented authors and illustrators.

A Couple of Boys Have the Best Week Ever, by Marla Frazee, a book for slightly older children, is a terrific example of how the picture-story says one thing, the word-story says another, and together they deliver unexpected—and hilarious—results.

I think of the shared feelings of connectedness they'll have as they listen to the story—as much for a raucous book as for a quiet one.

I try to have those thoughts inform all of my decisions—especially about pacing, and most especially about that Mother of All Page Turns: the one from pages 30-31 to page 32. That's the most important part of a picture book, the place where the arrow goes right into the reader and listener, and that's where I want the book to have its strongest emotional impact.

AJ: What do you think are the most common mistakes people make when they are trying to create picture books?

AJ: Too long; no rhythm; too much description; too heavy-handed and message-driven; terrible alliterative rhyme; no awareness of the page-turn; illustrations that are merely decorative and can't sustain a narrative; no narrative arc in words or pictures; and worst of all, no emotional center.

And did I say that if you don't read as many picture books as humanly possible, you're doomed?

AJ: What sort of process do you engage in when you are editing picture books?

AJ: I feel that picture books are more like poems than anything else, so it's especially important to me to be aware of every single detail in them. Each syllable, each line break, each sentence's placement on the page and where those critical page-turns occur—all of these are massively important. I often say when speaking to aspiring picture-book writers that one of the most informative things they could do for their story is take it and break it out into a little 32-page book dummy. No pictures are necessary at this point! What's needed is a quiet, thoughtful ear to the experience of reading through the text while the page-turns unfold to see if it flows in a lyrical, spare, emotionally-true way.

I do this myself. Since I am so conscious of picture books as physical objects that depend on rhythm, pacing, page-turns and, to quote Mem Fox, "perfect words in perfect places," I spend a ton of time throughout the process with physical dummies that are often ones I make myself, paging back-and-forth and forth-and-back, pondering the way everything works together. I also read them aloud—seriously. There's nothing quite like hearing the story spoken to point out slow or wordy or confusing spots.

And of course then there are the illustrations—which are equally important! As much of the storytelling responsibility lies with them as it does with the words. The artist has to figure out how each picture will follow another seamlessly, expanding and deepening the narrative, and carrying the story threads through from beginning to end. I've long thought of picture books as miniature theater pieces, with the page-turns creating an ever-unfolding stage on which the

© 2008 Lois Ehlert. Reprinted with permission of Harcourt Children's Books.

Lois Ehlert's genius with color and design paired with her spare, witty, completely child-centered poems shine in her generous collection *Oodles of Animals*.

action takes place. Thinking of them in this way—and keeping it in mind during the editorial process—often helps clarify places in both text and art that need revision.

AJ: Do you work differently with different authors and illustrators?

AJ: Yes, I most definitely do.

With an Australian writer who hates writing, I spend my own money to fly to her house so I can force her to sit in front of her computer and work—when she's not cooking delicious Mediterranean meals or demanding that we zip down the road for yet another incredible latte. With an author/illustrator from Pasadena, my son and I drive up from San Diego so that he and her son can ride bikes, eat banana waffles, and play video games—all while she and I sit at the picnic table by the fountain on her porch and try to figure out what's not quite working in her latest dummy. And then there's the Minnesota one who has the most perfect screened-in-porch-among-the-trees imaginable. When I go to her house in the non-winter months (and why would I go any other time?), I pretty much require that all editing—or talking, for that matter—occurs out there within two feet of the couch (where I am permanently located).

What I'm really saying is if it's late-night phone calls from my totally-out-of-minutes cell phone, wandering Wisconsin farmers markets to observe dog-obedience behavior, or sitting around on some hotel-room floor (I know, gross!) surrounded by scissors and paper and a glue stick, hey, that's my job—and I am constantly amazed at the brilliant ideas and solutions people come up with during these sorts of unorthodox moments.

AJ: How would you describe the most important thing you do as a picture book editor?

AJ: In 2003, I was asked with little-to-no warning to speak to a group visiting from Harcourt's Orlando Finance Department on this very subject. (The Children's Books Department was

Ten Little Fingers and Ten Little Toes, a collaboration between Mem Fox and Helen Oxenbury, is a stellar example of how text and illustrations in a book for very young children can combine to deliver a truly emotionally powerful reading experience.

based in San Diego, so we didn't really know these serious, money-oriented people very well.) The whole experience was rather deer-in-the-headlights for me, so afterward I successfully blocked it out—until recently when I found my notes in an old file. I shouldn't admit this, but I found what I'd written gave me chills:

"Authors and illustrators are our most important resource. Without them none of us would be here. Our primary job in the editorial department is to maintain—and build—strong, trusting, collaborative relationships with them so they keep bringing their projects to us. And when those projects are wonderful, great. The editorial development process is relatively smooth. But when talented folks bring us weaker ideas—or ideas that don't quite make sense yet—we must try our best to help them figure out how to make the project work and to coax it out of them without being discouraging.

I think our biggest role, then, is to believe in our authors and illustrators, to believe great things can happen."

(Speaking of believing, can you believe I said that to a conference room full of finance guys?)

Related to that is my conviction that a key part of my job is to ask the sorts of questions that help people figure out what they are most trying to say. (This, by the way, goes for working with writers of every genre, not just picture books.) If I had to boil down everything I do as an editor into one sentence, I really would say, "Ask questions." Though I suppose I could add "provocative and inspiring" to that if I were feeling expansive.

One of the toughest things to keep in mind for editors, especially at the fragile early stage when a book might be merely an elusive fragment of an idea, is how deeply and personally writers and artists must lose themselves in their story so they can pull it out of thin air. When they are at last brave enough to share stuff, we have to summon the focus to go with them into their process and not leave them hanging—even if we have to say hard things. Ack! Hard things, as well all know—even when delivered in a timely manner—can shut down the creative spirit right quick. So this question-asking is a delicate skill, not for the faint of heart.

AJ: What, besides trying to get any work done when you have to spend three quarters of your life in meetings, do you think is the toughest part of being an editor?

AJ: It'd say it's figuring out how to hold my center so I can consistently respond in a thoughtful and rigorous way to everyone I work with, both in and out of house. I have to be brave about trusting my intuition, about taking chances, and putting myself on the line if I believe in the integrity of a project or—even harder—if I don't.

It is a precarious place, that swaying bridge between the corporate and the creative, and every editor must figure out their own way to balance there. It falls to us to draw lines around the places where the ideas of those with whom we work can safely flourish, and it gets more and more difficult to help keep those true working places sacred.

AJ: You have worked in your native California, away from the east-coast publishing hub, for most of your career. How has that informed what you do?

AJ: Because I'm from Malibu and grew up on the beach, I don't necessarily see what I do or how I approach things as different in a Californian sort of way; it's just the way I am. I surf. I don't like to wear shoes in the house. I hate to do expense reports. I don't always do my best work while sitting at a 9-to-5 office desk. (Actually, I never do.) I have been criticized for years by corporate supervisors for being too emotionally engaged with the creative people with whom I work.

These things obviously inform the way I approach the editorial process (well, perhaps not the surfing or the lack of shoes . . .). But as I said, none of this seems different to me.

But any number of people have told me they think my west-coast and beach orientation make what I bring to the whole process unique.

I don't know if they're right. I think it's probably just because I'm a Pisces.

AJ: What do you imagine as the legacy for the picture books you've edited?

AJ: Last March, right before I was fired from Harcourt after 22 years, I spoke at the 12th Annual Charlotte S. Huck Children's Literature Festival. Over the course of the conference's two days, speaker after speaker—including me—got up and began their talks with slides of adored childhood books that they credited with not only bringing them to where they are today as writers, illustrators, or editors, but—more importantly—with helping shape them as people.

If any of the books I have had the privilege of editing in my career could have that sort of impact on a person's life, then I'd consider that a dream legacy.

Wouldn't you?

Picture Books Edited by Allyn Johnston

- *Ten Little Fingers and Ten Little Toes*, by Mem Fox, illustrated by Helen Oxenbury
- *A Couple of Boys Have the Best Week Ever*, by Marla Frazee
- *Oodles of Animals*, by Lois Ehlert
- *Wangari's Trees of Peace*, by Jeanette Winter
- The Mr. Putter and Tabby books by Cynthia Rylant, illustrated by Arthur Howard
- *Snow*, by Cynthia Rylant, illustrated by Lauren Stringer
- *Miss Alaineus: A Vocabulary Disaster*, by Debra Frasier
- *Mrs. Spitzer's Garden*, by Edith Pattou, illustrated by Tricia Tusa

Articles & Interviews

Great Opening Lines in Picture Books

by Lisa Wheeler

Some people have the patience to date leisurely, taking their own sweet time to meet and get to know their potential partners. Reading a novel is like marathon dating . . . although first impressions are important, readers tend to give the book several pages if not chapters to win their affection. A picture book reader, on the other hand, is a speed dater. As a picture book author, you must make every moment count, starting from that ever-important first line.

In other words, make a good first impression or prepare to get dumped.

Readers often pick up a picture book because of an eye-catching cover or interesting title. Unless you are also an illustrator, you have no control over the art. Therefore, you have to assume that sending your picture book to a publisher is a blind date.

How will you impress an editor if you can't *wow* him with your looks?

Start with a great pick-up line.

FACE-TO-FACE

Fragility was a solid piece of work.

This is the first line of the book, *Hurty Feelings*. It *doesn't* hurt that the Lynn Munsinger's art depicts Fragility as an irresistible hippopotamus. But the author, Helen Lester, had no control over how Fragility would look. Describing her as a 'solid piece of work' made this date extremely attractive. I was immediately curious how Fragility would look and act. I bought the book on the spot and I am betting the editor who acquired it did, too.

Face-to-face opening lines let readers know *who* they are dating.

Here are three examples of *face-to-face* opening lines:

> Officer Buckle knew more safety tips than anyone else in Napville.
> —*Officer Buckle and Gloria*, by Peggy Rathmann

> Otis was a very fine pig.
> —*Otis*, by Janie Bynum

LISA WHEELER has published over 20 children's books (all containing first lines!) She has written picture books in rhyme and prose, poetry books, and an easy readers series. Her awards include, the Michigan Mitten for *Old Cricket* (illustrated by Ponder Goembel), Missouri Building Blocks for *Bubble Gum, Bubble Gum* (illustrated by Laura Huliska-Beith), and the Texas Blue Bonnet for *Seadogs: An Epic Ocean Operetta* (illustrated by Mark Siegel). She lives and writes in a little town just south of Detroit.

Sure, she was little, but Beatrice loved riddles and tricks and she could think fast on her feet.
—*Clever Beatrice*, by Margaret Willey

Fast introductions are always appreciated by readers and editors, and face-to-face opening lines are an upfront way to get your story started.

Q&A: MARGARET WILLEY
Why is it so important for readers to "meet" Beatrice in the opening line of your story?
The line, "Sure, she was little, but . . ." had been in my mind since the earliest conception of the character of Beatrice. I wanted to establish her right away as a little person who would not let the fact that she was little stop her from being very present, very memorable—the sort of little girl people notice and appreciate right away. Heather Solomon really got on board with her popping-off-the-page first image of Beatrice, an illustration which was also chosen for the cover.

I think I set the stage for Beatrice to have an over-the-top adventure and for the reader to completely go along with it.

THE FLIRT
Flirtatious opening lines give readers more than just a pretty face. With a flirty first line, you get a sneak peak at things to come.

Here are few:

Before Julius was born, Lilly was the best big sister in the world.
—*Julius Baby of the World*,
by Kevin Henkes

The night Max wore his wolf suit and made mischief of one kind and another his mother called him "WILD THING!" and Max said "I'LL EAT YOU UP!"
—*Where the Wild Things Are*, by Maurice Sendak

Very Boring Alligator came one day to play, but he stay-stay-stayed and HE WOULDN'T GO AWAY.
—*Very Boring Alligator*, by Jean Gralley

Notice that the authors not only introduce you to the main character, but immediately set up a problem which hooks your interest. If you flirt with your reader at the beginning of the date, be prepared to deliver. A firey build-up will fizzle if you're all talk and no action.

Q&A: JEAN GRALLEY
When a writer sets readers up with a "flirty" opener, how can she maintain that first attraction?
For picture books, the significance of first lines (and second lines and third . . .) can't be over-estimated, but I'll add this. If the illustration takes a turn from the expected, does a little dance or play against the words, even deadpan lines become dynamite. To make this happen a writer doesn't need to be an illustrator. But the writer *does* need a "picture book mind." That's a mindset that anticipates a word-picture juxtaposition, welcomes it, and, in fact, prepares psychic space for it. It makes room for a look in the eye, a shift in posture, a certain tone of voice to deliver the words. We know from real life how compelling that can be."

Here's another layer to the analogy. We illustrators know when writers have left that psychic space for us and it's a great come-on! It invites us to engage with our very best. Asa writer/

illustrator, I love exploring that extra-dimensional thinking with writers. Writers—know that when you write with the restraint of a true "picture book mind," it entices your illustrators, as well as your readers.

SET THE MOOD

Remember the game Mystery Date? You never knew what type of guy was standing behind that door. This shouldn't happen with your picture book. A serious book about death should not open with a light bouncy rhyme. Likewise, a silly book shouldn't start off with serious tones. This is like promising your date a trip to Paris and taking her to Chuck E. Cheese.

Consider this opening:

> My pa was a man who dreamed
> of standing alone in an open field
> where the only shadow he could
> see was his own.
> —*A Packet of Seeds*, by
> Deborah Hopkinson

Author/illustrator Jean Gralley feels that first lines are of utmost importance, but, after a flirty opener, the book must deliver—and illustrations can help accomplish this. "If the illustration takes a turn from the unexpected, does a little dance or plays against the words, even deadpan becomes dynamite," she says.

Where is this particular date taking you? I highly doubt you're headed to Disney World. This beautiful opening is quiet and serious. The cadence of the first line suggests a slowly unfolding story and the picture it paints is solemn. This opening line promises a buggy ride rather than a turn on the tilt-o-whirl.

Now try this:

> Bella Lagrossi was the messiest monster in Booville.
> —*Boris and Bella*, by Carolyn Crimi.

This face-to-face opening line promises some fun to come. With a character named Bella Lagrossi and a town called Booville, chances are you're headed for a laugh-out-loud good time.

Q&A: CAROLYN CRIMI
Do you ever have trouble staying true to the mood of your story? How do you fix it?

Sometimes I read one of my stories and realize that something is wrong, but I can't pinpoint exactly what it is. When this happens I study the very first paragraphs and the very last paragraph of the story. Have I delivered the goods? Does my last line answer the question that was brought up in the first line? Have I taken a wrong turn somewhere? It all boils down to this: Your story must be about One True Thing. Every detail, every phrase, must support that One True Thing. If your story is off, it usually means that either you don't know that the One True Thing is, or you have taken a detour along the way.

AN AIR OF MYSTERY

Did you ever meet someone and just *know* that there was more to this mysterious stranger than meets then eye? Didn't you want to stick around and find out what it was?

Articles & Interviews

Some picture book authors do the same thing with an opening line. Even when the book is not a mystery, an opening that leaves readers with a big question makes them turn the page.

Here are three examples of the Mysterious Stranger opening:

> The day Helen gave Martha dog her alphabet soup, something unusual happened.
> —*Martha Speaks*, by Susan Meddaugh

> One evening a little white egg bounced off a farm cart and cracked open.
> —*Fox and Fluff*, by Shutta Crum

> The Christmas Crocodile didn't mean to be bad, not really.
> —*The Christmas Crocodile*, by Bonny Becky.

What unusual thing happened to Martha? What was in that egg that cracked open? And what was did that crocodile do that was so bad? We must know!

Q&A: BONNY BECKER
When you began writing *The Christmas Crocodile*, was the opening line a mystery?

Illustration © 2006 Kurt Cyrus.

Lisa Wheeler's *Mammoths on the Move* starts with a "where are we going?" opening. "Since the book is about an extinct animal, I needed to set a time and place for the reader," she says. The book begins "Fourteen thousand years ago, the north was mostly ice and snow."

Finding the opening line to *The Christmas Crocodile* was definitely a mystery. It took me years, including a rhyming version of the story that began: "There once was a Christmas Crocodile—a crocka-a crocka-a crocka-dile."

What I love about the line I ended up with is that I think it goes straight to the heart of any little kid. I mean, what kid doesn't mean to be bad, not really?

It's interesting that you call it a "mystery opening." I never thought of it that way. For the longest time the opening line was, "Alice Jayne found the Christmas Crocodile under the tree on Christmas Eve." I can see now that's a mystery opening, too. What's a Christmas Crocodile? But it doesn't do much more than that.

"The Christmas Crocodile didn't mean to be bad, not really," does so much more

for me. Not just: What's a Christmas Crocodile? But how was he bad? Why was he bad even if he didn't mean to be? What happened because he was bad? I guess if there's a lesson here, it's to work in character, not just situation.

LOCATION, LOCATION, LOCATION
One of the first questions you might ask a date is, *Where are we going?* Sometimes first lines of a picture book are like a GPS tracking system in a vehicle: They let the reader know exactly where they are, or where they're headed.

It took Bonny Becker several years of revising the opening line of *The Christmas Crocodile* (including some not-stellar rhyming) before she settled on the perfect beginning—one that offered a bit of a mystery. "What I love about the line I ended up with is that I think it goes straight to the heart of any little kid," she says. "I mean, what kid doesn't mean to be bad, not really?"

Illustration © David Smalls. Reprinted with permission.

On a knotty little hill, in a dreary little funk, Mrs. Biddlebox rolled over on the wrong side of her bunk.
—*Mrs. Biddlebox*, by Linda Smith

After the war, there was little left in the tiny Dutch town of Olst.
—*Boxes for Katja*, by Candace Flemming

Upon a salt-licked island shore stands a lady folks adore.
—*Liberty's Journey*, by Kelly DiPucchio

This type of opening sets the stage and gives readers a sense of place. Now that you know where you're headed, you can sit back and enjoy the ride.

Q&A: KELLY DIPUCCHIO

Not only does *Liberty's Journey* set the stage right from the start, but your books *Bed Hogs* and *Dinosnores* begin by establishing a setting. Why do you think these "Where are we going?" openers work so well?

I didn't realize that I used this technique at the beginning of so many stories until you pointed it out! I think setting the stage is just a natural component of story telling. It helps me as a writer to know where the journey begins, just as much as it helps the reader to get a sense of time and place. Once I wrap my brain around the setting and the problem, the characters' actions will naturally follow. So, in stories where location, time, and/or movement are somehow connected to the character's problem, establishing a sense of place at the beginning is a nice way of inviting your reader to take the journey with you.

YOU'RE SO FRESH!

What's a nice girl like you doing in a place like this?

That's a moldy-oldie pickup line you hope to never hear again.

The equivalent in picture books might be:

"Long ago and far away . . ." or *"Once upon a time . . ."* or *"Long before you were born . . ."*

Try to keep your opening line fresh. Give the readers something they don't expect, something they've never seen before.

Here are some fresh pickup lines:

> Aunt Nancy didn't turn cartwheels when Cousin Lazybones come to visit.
> —*Aunt Nancy and Cousin Lazybones*, by Phyllis Root

> On August 1, 1815, when Angelica Longrider took her first gulp of air on this earth, there was nothing about the baby to suggest that she would become the greatest woodswoman in Tennessee.
> —*Swamp Angel*, by Anne Isaacs

> Arnie turned out to be just the kind of doughnut he thought he'd be—chocolate-covered with bright-colored candy sprinkles.
> —*Arnie the Doughnut*, by Laurie Keller

These fresh opening lines make me want to invite these books back to my place for a cozy seat by the fire.

Q&A: LAURIE KELLER

Did you write several opening lines for *Arnie the Doughnut* before you settled on the one you used?

The answer is Yes! First of all, I just started jotting down all sorts of things about this doughnut who didn't want to be eaten. I wrote some little jokes to include, doughnut puns, etc. But after that I focused on Mr. Bing (who had a number of different names before I settled on Mr. Bing). I had several paragraphs about him—where he lived, where he worked, his schedule, his hobbies, his morning ritual of eating doughnuts. And I kept writing the same thing over and over. Finally, I realized I didn't need any of that stuff and that any important things about Mr. Bing would be revealed along the way. So I canned all of that and focused on Arnie (who also had many different name before he became Arnie.) I played around with different sections of the story before going to the beginning. Once I did, I went through several tries before coming up with the line I used:

- Douglas was not an ordinary dog. In fact, he wasn't really a dog at all—he was a doughnut.
- Douglas officially became a doughnut at 4:27 in the morning. He caught a glimpse of himself in the reflection of the bakery window. "Oh, look at me. I'm fancier than I could have ever imagined!"
- Daryl was a chocolate-covered doughnut with coconut sprinkles. He had 11 brothers and sisters. They all lived in a try and were born only seconds apart.
- Arnie was made at precisely 4:27 a.m. He went to the cooling rack then and was dunked in chocolate.
- At 4:27 in the morning before the sun came up, Arnie, a glob of dough, was rolled into a ring and dropped into a vat of boiling oil. That probably doesn't sound like fun to most people, but to Arnie it was a dream come true.

• Hi. My name is Arnie. I'm a chocolate-frosted doughnut with coconut sprinkles. Look how I'm neatly frosted on one side and dry and clean on the other. This is so when I sit down I don't leave brown stains on things.

Uggh! I think that last line about the brown stains finally knocked some sense into me! That was my last line attempt before I came up with the opening line I used in the book.

DON'T APPEAR DESPERATE

What if your blind date showed up with a bouquet of flowers, chocolates, a teddy bear, and a list of his favorite baby names?

Whoa buddy! Slow down.

Liken that to your first line. What if in a desperate attempt to impress an editor, you try to cram too much in? The result could be disastrous.

Good first lines, like good first dates, lead to a second and a third, etc. You'll have plenty of time to impress your reader. Save some of the goodies for later.

Whether you prefer a face-to-face meeting, a little flirting, or even an air of mystery, the result is the same. Your pick-up line should be so seductive that your reader cannot resist the temptation to stick around for more.

And that is a match made in publishing heaven.

Authors & Illustrators

Dividing Details in Picture Books

by Sue Bradford Edwards

t seems simple. A picture book is the sum of two parts, the text and the illustrations. The author and illustrator each depend on the other to carry part of the story.

It seems simple.

But, it's not.

"This is one of the most difficult and intangible parts of picture book making, and what makes the picture-book form so unique: The factual and emotional information in the book does not come solely from the words. All we writers, illustrators, and editors of picture books are on a quest we cannot accomplish alone: to marry the words and pictures perfectly, inextricably," say Arthur A. Levine Books editor Cheryl Klein in her presentation *Words, Wisdom, Art and Heart: Making a Picture-Book Cookie.*

Successfully completing a picture book means bringing together the work of a diverse group of professionals, each of whom will shape the story until it sings. For this to happen, the author must first understand which details come from the text and which details fall under the control of the illustrator.

YOURS OR MINE?

Dividing the detail is pretty straightforward. If it's visual, it probably belongs to the illustrator. This means that you can describe your character's appearance, their school, or their yard in visual detail if and only if it is vital to the story.

Is the visual detail in your manuscript truly vital to the plot? Or is it just the way you laid the story down after imagining it one scene at a time? Many writers, myself included, imagine their story scene by scene, like a movie. "When you are writing picture books, it's helpful to have a picture in your head, but there's a point you need to let that go," says Charlesbridge Associate Editor Randi Rivers.

Illustrations are visual, so illustrators get most of the visual detail. So what! Writers get everything else. "All sensory details except visual are my territory. I get to use sound effects, onomatopoeia, strong smells, textural details such as smooth or rough, and tastes when appropriate. I especially love the kinesthetic details, how it feels to move in space, I can add by using the right verbs," says author Darcy Pattison. Used effectively sound, smell, taste, texture and movement impact everything from character to setting.

SUE BRADFORD EDWARDS works to leave room for the illustrations from her office in St. Louis, Missouri. You can find her nonfiction in a variety of testing and educational publications, *Children's Writer* newsletter, and the *St. Louis Post-Dispatch*. Visit her web site at www.suebradfordedwards.com.

MORE THAN SKIN DEEP

Characterization can easily sound like an APB: "Be on the lookout for a 5-year-old male. He is slender with brown hair and green eyes. He was last seen wearing a denim jacket." While picture book readers need these details, they normally get them not from the text but from the illustrations.

"Visual characterization—what the characters look like, what their expressions are—will be shown in the illustrations," says Klein. "The text supplies verbal and behavioral characterization. Who a character is, as seen in her words and actions."

This encourages the author to show the character in more meaningful ways. "How are you envisioning the character when you write the story? Do you know that she has brown hair and wears a yellow coat or do you know she's funny and afraid of spiders?" asks Rivers. "In other words, don't rely solely on a physical description to get across who she is unless the description has something to do with a plot point."

This is why author Lisa Wheeler includes a brief visual description for her animal characters. "I let the reader know up front which type of animal I am writing about when I am using anthropomorphism," she says. "But I steer clear of specifics on clothing, colors, etc. For instance, I might say the character has a hat, if a hat if important to the plot, but it is best to leave it up to the illustrator as to what kind of hat." Thus she lays down what the character *is* but leaves as much visual control as possible to the illustrator.

It is up to the author to seize the opportunity to lay out habits, likes and dislikes that create depth of character. This allows the illustrator to add another layer by bringing in the visual detail. Characters thus deeply drawn stride through the world of their stories.

YOU ARE HERE

As with the characters themselves, even without visual detail, the writer maintains surprising control over the manuscript's setting. Although the writer may not determine if the character's house is blue or white, he or she does establish where the story takes place. City or country. Gym or playground. Past or present. The author not only selects the setting, but is the first to describe it. "What does it smell like? What do you hear?" asks Rivers. "Use the senses that can't be captured in the illustration."

Not only do these specifics anchor the story in a specific place, carefully chosen, they establish the mood of the story. "By careful selection of specific details, I can create the story's mood," says Pattison. "For example, think about how you would describe a playground and create a happy versus a scary mood. It's the same playground; the difference is in the selection of details. Illustrators only get the left-over visual stuff and, actually, I dictate a lot for them by the careful selection of action words and by creating moods."

The skilled author does this without inflating the word count. "I would never say in my text, 'The dark clouds hung overhead and the flowers began bending in the breeze.' That kind of description is told through the illustration and it would be a waste of space to say it in the text," says author/illustrator Todd Aaron Smith. If the main character must face a bully on the playground, perhaps the slide is hulking or looming. A playground where a birthday party is held may have a glimmering slide and singing swings. "The text helps in achieving the emotional content of the story," says Smith, "and the illustrations are for visually conveying these emotions."

Once established by the author, the illustrator heightens the mood by selecting which details to illustrate. "A good illustration shows the highest point of emotional interest and active tension in a scene," says Klein. "Suppose a text reads, 'Cheryl ran through the park, leaped across the ravine, somersaulted through the daffodils, stood up, and started running again. But the man was still behind her.' But in a picture book, the illustrator has to choose—

and so he'd probably go with the point where Cheryl was leaping across the ravine, because that's the moment with the most tension and excitement."

For the illustrator to do this well, the writer must include a variety of action and emotion. "It is important to give the illustrator enough action and emotion to illustrate. Don't squeeze it all in the beginning. You need to do it spread after spread after spread," says author/illustrator Joan Holub. "Move from place to place, even if it's two places and you go back and forth. For instance, in *Skippyjon Jones*—you see a lot of different aspects of his room as setting."

Picture Books to Check Out

One of the best ways to learn what details the writer brings to a story as compared to the illustrator is to study picture books. Study them. Don't just read them casually. "Read a picture book without looking at the illustrations," says Charlesbridge Associate Editor Randi Rivers, "and then go back and look at the illustrations but don't read the story. What do you get each time? Can you see what the illustrator added and the author didn't say?"

Be careful which books you study, however. "Be aware that author/illustrators write different sorts of stories than just authors. The author/illustrator can leave out much more text than you'll be able to," says author Darcy Pattison. "When I write the same type of abbreviated story, I get rejections that say, *This is too slight. This needs to be fleshed out more.* Explanations in the cover letter aren't the same as a sample illustration. So, when you study picture books as models for how to write, look for those written by authors and illustrated by someone else. Of course, if you're an author-illustrator, then study those picture books by author-illustrators."

Here is a list to start you on your way.

Books by an Author/Illustrator
- Barbara Berger's *Grandfather Twilight*
- Lauren Child's Clarice Bean books
- Anna Dewdney's *Llama, Llama Red Pajama*
- Laura McGee Kvasnosky's Zelda and Ivy books
- Nina Laden's *The Night I Followed the Dog*
- Peggy Rathman's *Officer Buckle and Gloria*.
- Maurice Sendak's *Where the Wild Things Are*

Books by an Author and a Separate Illustrator
- Jessica Clerk's *The Wriggly, Wriggly Baby*, illustrated by Laura Rankin
- Doreen Cronin's *Click Clack Moo: Cows that Type*, illustrated by Betsy Lewin
- Lois Grambling's *Can I Bring My Pterodactyl to School, Ms. Johnson?*, illustrated by Judy Love
- Mary Ann Hoberman's *Seven Silly Eaters*, illustrated by Marla Frazee
- David LaRochelle's *The End*, illustrated by Richard Egielski
- Reeve Lindbergh's *The Day the Goose Got Loose*, illustrated by Steven Kellogg
- Darcy Pattison's *The Journey of Oliver K. Woodman* and *Searching for Oliver K. Woodman*, illustrated by Joe Cepeda
- Rick Walton's *Bertie Was a Watchdog*, illustrated by Arthur Robbins; *So Many Bunnies*, illustrated by Paige Miglio; *A Very Hairy Scary Story*, illustrated by David Clark; and *Just Me and 6000 Rats*, illustrated by Mike Gordon and Carl Gordon

TESTING FOR BALANCE

Details of smell, taste, touch and sound. Details selected to show mood and emotion. Varied action. How can the author be sure she's selected the right details and distributed them evenly through the text?

"Look at every line of your story, every word, and make sure it wouldn't be better represented in the illustrations," says author Rick Walton. "Make sure that it needs to be in the text for the story to work."

One tool can help the author judge pacing and analyze a manuscript line by line. "Make a test dummy," says Holub. "That will show you so quickly if there is too much text on one spread and not enough on another." Study the manuscript one spread at a time to evaluate your details and how they work to establish tone and mood.

If a spread is wordy, this may be a place to trim. "Make cuts in places where you have lots of description and see if the story still flows," says Wheeler. "It probably flows better! Any word or line that does not move the story forward is probably expendable. Beware of 'stage directions' in your story. This is one of those things that we tend to miss when revising our picture books. Your text doesn't have to tell readers that 'Billy opened the door, stepped onto the porch, walked down the sidewalk and headed to town.' In a picture book just say, 'Billy headed to town.' The artist will take care of the rest. "

Study your text spread by spread. Do you have sensory detail? Action? Emotion? Details carefully chosen give subtle cues that influence the illustrator in creating his or her work.

CHANGING FOR THE BETTER

Now that we've examined how authors influence illustration, it's time to look at the reverse, when the illustration influences the text. Although it isn't the case with every picture book, an illustrator's work can mean making changes to the text.

At times, this happens because details that originally appeared in the text have been duplicated in the illustrations. "With a mystery I recently edited, there were certain things that had to appear in the illustrations," says Rivers. Once the details appeared in the illustrations, the author could remove them from the text, and Rivers asked for cuts. "I've done that with most of the books I've edited because the tendency is for tighter texts," she says. "It's important to keep things in the text until you see what the illustrator is going to pick to illustrate."

Making cuts this late in the picture book process is an art. "Look for things that don't influence the voice or the humor. Taking out words can help with pacing and the emotion," says Rivers. "If you want to build drama, sometimes you want the text to be shorter and punchier."

Sometimes the editor asks the author to alter the text to match the illustrator's specialty. "My editor once came to me and asked if we could change the characters in one of my books from kids into bunnies, because they'd found an illustrator who did cute bunnies," says Walton. "I made the change, adapted the text appropriately, and it became my best selling book, *So Many Bunnies*."

Changes may also be requested because the illustrator has contradicted certain textual details. The decision to go against the text usually comes about when details as established in the text would yield a sub-standard illustration. "In one book, I described a truck as being gray and a toad as being brown. The finished art was vibrant, with a blue truck and green toad. I went back and rewrote my rhyme accordingly," says Wheeler. "I wouldn't have added those color details except that, for meter and rhyme, they were words that served a purpose. When the colors got changed, I realized that it was a good choice by the illustrator to keep with the vibrancy of the book. Changing rhyming text is never easy, but in this case, it was worthwhile."

This give and take between writer and illustrator marries the text and the illustration to form a seamless picture book. For this give and take to take place, the author must have faith. "You have to trust that the illustrator will put as much into the book as you have," says Rivers. "They are just as smart, funny and witty, but they will show this visually in a way that complements your text."

This faith allows the author to hand over the control the illustrator needs to truly create. "You want the illustrator to feel like it is a true collaboration, that it is as much their book as yours," says Walton. "If they do, they will put more effort into the work, make the work their own, add dimensions that will make the book richer, better, more successful."

Pattison agrees and hopes that each illustrator she works with will bring her characters to life for generations of kids. This level of collaboration can happen only where both creative parties have the space to shine. In a picture book, this means handing visual details to the illustrator and using all else to the greatest possible effect.

Illustration Notes

Tempted to include detailed illustration notes with your text?

"There is a long debate about whether authors can include visual notes—things the illustrations should include that do not belong in the text," says Arthur A. Levine Books editor Cheryl Klein. "Editors dislike it because, I must tell you, it often feels like if you give an author a visual inch, he will take a mile. He will describe shot angles. He will write character descriptions. And obviously the only thing keeping him from illustrating this book is the fact that he can't draw. So if you can avoid having visual notes, do."

If you still want to include illustration notes, Charlesbridge Associate Editor Randi Rivers has a request. "Type the manuscript with the notes and give it to a friend to read aloud. You'll see how they lose the thread of the story," she says. "When I lose interest in the story, I don't read it all the way through." If an editor can't follow your story from beginning to end, you've just botched a potential sale.

There are times when illustration notes *are* needed. "If the visual action is essential to the story, describe that action in your cover letter or at the appropriate point in the story, briefly," says Klein. "Then let the rest of the manuscript stand on its own."

Respect the expertise the illustrator brings to the job and an editor may ask for illustration notes. "*Noah's Square Dance* is a danceable square dance," says Rick Walton, "and my editor requested that I, with the help of my wife who is more logical than I am, prepare notes that showed where each of the characters would be in the dance sequence. This helped the illustrator place the characters in the scenes."

Even with illustration notes, the picture book remains a collaboration.

Getting Rid of the Dull Stuff

by Kathleen Duey

THE ASSIGNMENT

There is no right or wrong way to write a novel. Methods vary. But the primary task of any fictionalist is to draw readers into the story on the first page and keep them immersed in it all the way to the end of the book. The audience doesn't matter—pre-K, early readers, middle graders, tweens, teens, adults, editors, reviewers, award committees—the assignment doesn't change. Genre doesn't matter either—contemporary, historical, mystery, fantasy, science fiction, humor, serious YA literature—the goal is to keep the reader reading; make the book impossible to put down. How? It's simple (which is not a synonym for easy). Make the story compelling and keep it moving—physically and emotionally. And skip the dull stuff.

WHAT'S DULL?

The list is long and wide. Big chunks of narrative, even if the reader needs the information it carries, can be dull. Dialogue, if it is over-long, strained, or burdened with authorial baggage, can be tedious. Description, even if it is graceful and poetic, can be deadweight if it's misplaced, too long, or convoluted. Confusing scenes can be deadly dull; forced rereading annoys most readers. A single-minded focus on action, at the expense of emotion, logic, and nuance, can irritate rather than thrill. But these missteps aren't deal-breakers for most readers, if the story works. And that's the Big If.

As readers we all know this to be true: We often put up with flawed writing technique if the story compels us. As writers we must remember that the reverse *isn't* true: Brilliant writing can't save a poorly constructed story.

SO. ABOUT THAT STORY . . .

Q: What makes a story impossible to put down?

A: Good novels have emotionally engaging characters who are causing/experiencing a believable chain of increasingly dramatic events capped by a compelling climax, followed by an ending that leaves readers feeling whatever the writer meant for them to feel.

Oh, how many times have we all read that last sentence in one form or another? It is so obviously true. But it can be so hard to see that elegant structural arc once we are immersed

KATHLEEN DUEY writes for children, tweens, teens, and adults. Book One of her dark YA fantasy trilogy, *A Resurrection of Magic: Skin Hunger*, was a 2007 National Book Award finalist, a Cybil's short list title, and featured in critical journals including *Locus*. The second title, *Sacred Scars*, is slated for Spring 2009. All projects erratically blogged at http://kathleenduey.blogspot.com.

in the word-by-word process of writing, blinded by the scene-trees that make up the plot-forest. Our stories, as we add one word at a time, can so easily spin out of control, stall, circle, wilt, ricochet, tangle . . . and then we can only revise them, over and over, sometimes only making things worse.

FINDING YOUR WAY

We have all heard writers try to summarize the book they are working on—and fail. It all too often sounds into something like this:

"A 17-year-old boy named Al is at Penn Station in New York City with a girlfriend and she gets shot. She's really more just a friend, but she has an ex-boyfriend who harasses her. Al is trying to help her avoid the guy and back him off. It isn't the ex who shoots her. Al flips out when it happens. He has ADHD and an anger problem, so he's always in trouble at school. His mother doesn't deal with him very well and his father is never around. Al tries to warn the girl, but she isn't facing him so he can't. Seeing her fall devastates him—she is the only person he can really talk to. They're at the station waiting for Al's uncle to come in. He runs a school for the deaf—that's where Al worked when he learned to sign and . . . Wait. Did I tell you the girl is deaf? And Al's father is an undercover cop. He shows up at the hospital. I'm not sure where it goes from there, yet . . ."

This kind of promising jumble is all too familiar to most writers—we hear it in our minds as plots are born. Stories *are* confusing. So many events, so many connections. Where does the story start? At the beginning? Al's ADHD has effected his ability to have friends, lifelong. His loneliness is the basis of his bond with the deaf girl. The reader really needs to know that they met in grade school, in a special needs classroom, and that Al begged his uncle for the summer job so he could learn how to communicate with her.

But can you spend 100 pages following these two from grade school until their late teens when the actual story takes place? You could. Should you? Is there a way to figure out a riveting story arc before the twelfth draft?

For me, structure begins with imagining. I write a few scenes down, try to hear the protagonist's voice, them go fishing in the Great Beyond for more interesting stuff. I see two people arguing in a grocery store, read a story about a UFO convention, see a stray white cat, have a run-in with an old friend, all the usual random stuff that sparks and feeds stories. It can take a week or 10 years, but when I think I have the basis for a story, I try to imagine the scenes that will be pivotal in telling it.

To identify the milestones—the pivotal moments—ask this question: "Could the story work without this scene (or another one that accomplishes the same emotional and physical result)?" If the answer is yes, the scene might be important. It might touch the reader's heart and enrich the novel. But it isn't a milestone.

In almost all conventionally structured stories, there's a line-up of milestone events, separated by scenes that reveal the characters' backstory, traits, and ongoing growth, etc. These scenes pull the readers in, deepening their interest and building tension as the next milestone approaches. Each milestone leaves the protagonist changed, each one moves the story forward.

Milestones can be close together or spaced farther apart in the book, but they always have a causal relationship. Remove any one of these pivotal events, or change it substantially, and it is likely that the once logical progression alters or falters. The book will then need revision. That might be exactly what the story needs. Or not. The milestones will help you think it through.

FINDING MILESTONES

Some writers like to outline in detail before they begin. They pore over numbered chapters, imagining them in detail, revising the outline many times before they begin to write. Others,

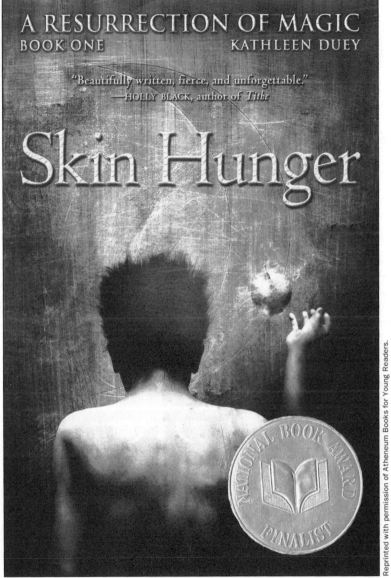

A RESURRECTION OF MAGIC
BOOK ONE   KATHLEEN DUEY

"Beautifully written, fierce, and unforgettable."
—HOLLY BLACK, author of *Tithe*

Skin Hunger

NATIONAL BOOK AWARD FINALIST

Reprinted with permission of Atheneum Books for Young Readers.

The Horn Book found no dull stuff in Kathleen Duey's National Book Award Finalist, *Skin Hunger*: "Duey sweeps readers up in the page-turning excitement, making this one of the more promising fantasy series beginnings in recent memory." The second book in Duey's A Resurrection of Magic trilogy, *Sacred Scars*, is a Spring '09 release from Atheneum.

to use Jane Yolen's description of her own method, "fly into the mist." Many of us lie somewhere in between. Outlines don't work for me. I make milestone lists—sometimes with as few as two or three scenes listed to start with. From there I fly-into-the-mist until I get bogged, then I work with the list again expanding it, until I can fly again: Repeat as needed.

A milestone list can be useful before you begin, as you go, after the first draft is complete, or at any other point in your work that makes sense to you. Writing it can take weeks, days, or minutes. Rewriting it is almost inevitable. But every version will get closer to the basic, no-frills progression of both the pivotal events and essential emotional arcs of your characters.

Pondering the list helps you focus on the skeleton of the story, the bare bones upon which all else depends. And the milestones are inherently the most dramatic, emphatic, indispensable scenes in your story—the opposite of dull—deserving of your very careful attention in the first draft, and thereafter.

MARY'S MILESTONES: AN EXAMPLE

Backstory: The protagonist, Mary Grove, 13, is restless and miserably unhappy. She lost her mother when she was eight. She has since acted as a parent to five brothers while their bitter, strict father struggles with poverty on their depression era farm. Her oldest brother is 15, rebellious. The others younger than Mary. Her life is an endless round of chores. There is never enough food, or anything else.

Partial milestone list:

1. Mary finds the entrance to an abandoned root cellar behind her family's farm house when she is planting an oak sapling to commemorate the anniversary of her mother's death. The cellar is like a small room, quiet, private, safe. Mary re-camouflages the planked door with the pile of brush that hid it from sight all along. She tells the first of many lies to hide her discovery when her father questions her half-hour absence.

2. Mary steals away and hides in the secret root cellar when her father is angry, shouting at her oldest brother. Often, if he rebels and argues, then walks away, their father takes it out on Mary. But this time, by the time she comes out, her father has calmed down.

3. Mary buries her makeshift diary (an old scrapbook of her mother's with a few dozen blank pages) beneath the dirt floor of the cellar.

4. Using candles to light the cellar, Mary writes her anger and despair in her diary, straight and true. It sharpens her discontent.

5. One day, she hears her father passing close to the hidden door, and she decides to bury the diary deeper, close to the earthen rear wall. Digging, she uncovers a flour sack full of coins and dollar bills. She reburies it and her diary in the far corner, and tells no one. How can she explain finding the money to her father without telling him about her refuge?

6. Mary has an argument with her overworked father and runs to hide in the secret cellar. She discovers her oldest brother frantically digging in the dirt floor. He doesn't see her and she slips back out, bereft. Her secret place isn't hers alone. And the money is his? How? It has to be ill-gotten. She is afraid, paralyzed emotionally.

7. One Sunday Mary stares at the coins and dollar bills in the offering basket, then watches her brother closely. He takes a quarter before he passes it on. She is ashamed of him, but she understands his desperation. She shares it.

8. Mary finally confronts her brother. He says the money is his; he'll use it to leave the farm and their father—whom he hates. She persuades him to stay, for the sake of their younger siblings. He finally promises to stay one more year.

9. Mary begins to steal from the offering plates, too. A dime the first time. A nickel the second. She sits where her father can't see her. Her brother does, and he winks.

10. Meeting in the root cellar, Mary and her brother decide to wait two years, then leave together. Mary clings to her newfound hope, daydreaming about a different life.

11. One Sunday, the pastor's sermon is about stealing. He asks the parishioners to make right any thefts, large or small, they might have committed. Mary is panicked that someone has noticed them stealing. Her brother says the pastor means to scare people. He knows how poor many of them are. She wants to return the money. He says he will think about it.

12. Mary's brother disappears without leaving a note—taking all of the money with him. She is heart-smashed at his betrayal and the sudden absence of hope. Her father is devastated at his departure, too. The younger boys can't help plow yet. Mary hates the idea of being alone with her father's surliness. Her refuge becomes a place to weep.

13. Her father discovers her in the cellar is furious at her deceit, he forbids her to leave the house.

You get the idea. A milestone list isn't a complete story outline, nor is it a chapter list. It charts the protagonist's journey without including subplots, minor characters, or the tension-building incidents that will connect and strengthen the milestones. It's a dot-to-dot drawing of the book, showing you a clear path, a general shape. How you space the dots, and what you add between them will give your readers many more reasons to keep reading. You can leave out the dull stuff in the connective scenes, too.

Between the dots: dialogue
When characters speak, they should sound like themselves, and they should say things that they would say if they were real, using language they would really use. They should stick to the topics they would really discuss. If you ''hear'' your characters talking to the reader, reciting backstory or other information you want the reader to know, instead of talking to each other, consider other ways to inform the reader and let the characters interact and stay true to themselves. If you can do that, your dialogue will not be dull.

Between the dots: description
Description can slow your story if you overuse it or misplace it. Repetition is dull, too. You don't need to tell the reader it's a two-story house if your character runs up the stairs to her bedroom. Placement is key. Most readers get annoyed when the author's descriptions come long after their own imaginations have produced an image. Who cares what the kitchen sink looks like, unless it's heart-shaped, pink, cracked or . . .? Describe what is unique, interesting, revelatory of your characters, their lives, their moods. Try adding description to the flow of action: Kary bent to pick up her sister, then crossed the room to sit on the stained blanket that almost covered the couch. Freeing her long black ponytail from Tilda's busy fingers, Kary listened to the clanging of pots and pans. Her mother was cooking? Why?

Between the dots: backstory
Backstory is a major dullness trap. Let's say you need the readers to know your teen protagonist has been tormented by a bully since third grade so they'll feel his despair when another bully comes onstage. How do you deliver the information to the reader? Dialogue is tricky as a backstory vehicle. Would he talk about it? Maybe. But trumping up a scene in which he confides the depth of his pain to someone is likely to be more forced than touching. A bit of narration can serve, or the character's thoughts, which are usually much juicier.

Backstory—narration: Sanders leaned against the cold brick. His sophomore year of high school was going to be better than his freshman year. Much better. Thomas Pain had moved away. He had been the classic bully from fourth grade on, consistently mean, always alert for opportunities to humiliate Sanders. Thomas had been especially fond of the trash-can-dunk, but the hallway-trip was a favorite, along with the ever popular ''sharing'' of cookies and sandwiches at lunch.

Backstory—character thoughts: Sanders leaned against the cold brick, watching the jocks maneuver around the geeks sitting on the steps. The tat-and-pierce-tribe was staking out their usual oak tree on the far edge of the lawn. The band kids were circled, glancing at each other, barely talking. Sophomore year was about to begin. Sanders took a long slow breath. He felt odd, too light, like gravity wasn't quite working this morning. For the first time since fourth grade, he would be free to eat his own lunch. He wouldn't have bruises to hide from his parents tonight. Thomas Pain was in Cincinnati, far, far away, at his new school, shoving new victims into trash cans. Sanders felt himself smile. That felt odd, too. Good. But odd.

SHINE, SHINE, SHINE

Dullness can be avoided, it can be revised until it shines, it can be replaced with attention-riveters that suit your intent and your story, from silk-soft-subtle to straight-up whammo. Creepy-intriguing mystery, spit-your-milk funny, those precious connections between friends—whatever you write, all the tools of the trade are in your toolbox. Use them bravely. If there are enough riveting books, maybe kids will keep reading. And that would be wonderful.

Why Milestones?

I stumbled onto the idea of listing pivotal scenes when I was creating and writing middle grade series. It was a desperate time-saving experiment—I had ten books to write that year, and no time to outline thoroughly. Milestone lists are both rigid—and pliable—enough to help with plot development, synopses, and can provide an ongoing interactive map for works in progress.

Creating Memorable Characters

by Cecil Castellucci

Remember how your mom and dad always told you that eating spinach or doing chores would build character? Or being on a sports team? Or learning how to not be a sore loser? There are all these things, all these choices in our lives that we make when we are growing up (and when we are already grown) that build our character as people. In my opinion it's the same when you are writing a book; a memorable character is always the goal. Because sure, whatever, plot is important, it's the what of the book, but you can't fall in love with it. You can fall in love with a character! Character is the why of the book.

In kids' lit, we gots lots of character. Perhaps it's because in kids lit we are capturing the imagination of readers who are willing to go anywhere with us and believe that anything and any one is possible. A boy wizard with a scar on his forehead? Sure! A red headed girl who can lift a horse over her head? OK! A mouse who can read, likes soup and saves a princess? Of course! A girl who makes her Q's look like a cat? That's right. A girl who wears striped tights and carries around a rag doll? She's the coolest. I'm not saying that our characters are better, or more memorable than those in adult fiction, I'm just proposinging that our characters are a bit more colorful. In kids lit we can explore the absurd. We can go anywhere and do anything. Even in our realistic fiction, we can be a little fantastical or allegorical and because of that, I've noticed that many a grown up will cite a favorite character from a book they read when they were young as being most memorable.

Just think about it. Just off the top of your head. You think of yours and I'll name some of mine. (See Books With Memorable Characters sidebar on page 57 for a list I came up with.)

Whether you are starting off with a cool premise, a character whose voice won't let you go, or a plot that is as solid as going from A to Z, there is always a way to get in deeper with your characters to make them stand out, sing loud and fluff out their colorful selves a little better.

CECIL CASTELLUCCI has published three novels for young adults, *Boy Proof*, *The Queen of Cool* and *Beige* all with Candlewick Press. She also wrote the graphic novel *The PLAIN Janes*, illustrated by Jim Rugg, which was the launch title for DC Comics new Minx line of graphic novels for young adults. In 2008 she has a short story in Wizards of the Coast's *Magic in the Mirrorstone* anthology and an essay in Bloomsbury's *First Kiss: Then Tell* anthology, as well the graphic novel sequel *Janes in Love*. Upcoming in 2009 and beyond are two books for younger readers, a picture book *Grandma's Gloves* and an early chapter book *Odd Duck*, as well as a new YA novel. Her books have been on ALA's BBYA, Quick Pick for Reluctant Readers, Great Graphic Novels for Teens lists as well as the NYPL books for the Teen Age and the Amelia Bloomer list. In addition to writing books, she writes plays, makes movies and occasionally rocks out. She lives in Los Angeles, California. For more information go to www.misscecil.com.

Like they say, write what you know.

And who do you know best? You.

When I first moved to Los Angeles, I was an indie rock girl working at Epitaph Records, which was punk rock central. I felt totally like an outsider. My neighborhood was filled with southern California punk rock legends. They were in bands. They looked cool as pie. They had excellent vintage cars. They had tattoos everywhere. They had Betty Page hair. They collected cool things, like skulls, or action figures, or antique medical equipment. They were out at rock shows. They were at yoga. They were at the café.

Next to all of them, I felt like I was boring, bland, and *beige*. On top of that, I was living in Hollywood and I didn't want to write movies, I wanted to write *books*.

Based on this personal experience, I came up with the character of Katy, the main character in *Beige*.

I wanted Katy to be someone who was observing Los Angeles from an outsiders point of view from the inside. Katy is a part of the mainstream, but the world she's plopped into is an alternative one. I liked the tension of that, but that's also too simple. Usually we concern ourselves with the things that make sense for a character, but often we as people in the real world don't make sense, and that is what makes us so interesting. We are not summed up neatly as one thing. So, you want to create tension in your character, and you want it to be something that stands out.

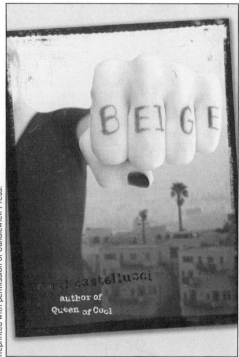

Reprinted with permission of Candlewick Press.

"[Cecil] Castellucci gives a fresh spin to the familiar exciled-teen plot by mixing details of the L.A. punk scene with memorable characters and witty dialogue," says *Booklist* about *Beige*. Castellucci drew on her own experience as a transplant to L.A. as she created her main character Katy.

Maybe it's my acting background—but in acting, we were always taught that we have the whole world inside of us. I am every woman. You are every man. And I believe that that is true and that we do house all those different kinds of people within us: The excellent me. The terrible me. The mean girl me. The queenly me. The shy me. The loud me. The happy me. The loving me. The capable me. The helpless me.

Think about it.

Can you see that in yourself? Ask yourself: How do I act the same or differently when I deal with my doctor? My mother in law? My best friend? My sibling? My partner? My boss? My workers? My clients? My butcher? My dance instructor? My child? My friends family?

I know that I have walked into a room and felt as though I were the coolest girl in the world and then walked into another room and felt as though I were the biggest loser. That's why I wrote the book *The Queen of Cool*. I wondered how a person could be the coolest in one situation and the lamest in another.

Look at your own fabulous self for inspiration! You are a big mish mash of contradictions. For example, you might love opera and also have a mohawk. Or you might be

Books With Memorable Characters

MIDDLE GRADE

Character	Book	Author
Harry Potter	Harry Potter (1-7)	J.K. Rowling
Pippi Longstocking	Pippi Longstocking Series	Astrid Lundgren
Ged	Earthsea Triology	Ursula K LeGuin
Ramona Quimby	Ramona Series	Beverly Cleary
Sheila	Otherwise Known as Sheila the Great	Judy Blume
Winnie	Tuck Everlasting	Natalie Babbit
Opal	Because of Winn Dixie	Kate DiCamillo
Desperaux	The Tale of Desperaux	Kate DiCamillo
Sara	The Little Princess	Frances Hodgson Burnett
Julie	Julie of the Wolves	Jean Craighead George
Millicent Min	Millicent Min, Girl Genius	Lisa Yee
Taran	The Chronicles of Prydain	Lloyd Alexander
Anne	Anne of Green Gables	L.M. Montgomery
Laura	Little House on the Prarie	Laura Ingalls Wilder
Ender	Ender's Game	Orson Scott Card
Elias	Ninjas, Piranhas and Galileo	Greg Leitich Smith
Adam	Adam Canfield of The Slash	Michael Winerip

YOUNG ADULT

Character	Book	Author
Cyd Charrisse	Gingerbread	Rachel Cohn
Holden Caufield	Catcher in the Rye	J.D. Salinger
Jerry	The Chocolate War	Robert Cormier
Egg	Boy Proof	Cecil Castellucci
Melinda	Speak	Laurie Halse Anderson
Kaye	Tithe	Holly Black
Clary	City of Bones	Cassandra Clare
Marisol	Hard Love	Ellen Wittlinger
Gen	Attolia Series	Meghan Whalen Turner
Octavian	The Astonishing Life of Octavian Nothing	M.T. Anderson
Bobby	First Part Last	Angela Johnson
Arnold Spirit	The Absolutely True Diary of a Part Time Indian	Sherman Alexie
Colin	An Abundance of Katherines	John Green
Gemma	A Great and Terrible Beauty	Libba Bray
Paul	Boy Meets Boy	David Levithan
Joe	Totally Joe	James Howe
Ruby	The Boyfriend List	E. Lockhart
Virgina	The Earth, My Butt and Other Big Round Things	Carolyn Mackler
Death	The Book Thief	Markus Zusak
Battle	Empress of the World	Sara Ryan
Quince	Tantalize	Cynthia Leitich Smith
Livy Two	Gentle's Holler	Kerry Madden
Reason	Magic or Madness	Justine Larbalestier

Articles & Interviews

a gourmet cook who loves a late night fast food drive-thru burger. Or you might be a ballet dancing sports freak.

Try a spiraling exercise. First, take a blank piece of paper and write a word that is definitely one hundred percent your character and what she likes in the middle. I'll use Katy, from *Beige*.

QUIET

Then, draw a line from that word and free associate.

WINDOW

Then again and again and again six or seven times.

BIRD

TREE

TREE HOUSE

BACKYARD

TENT

CAMPING

Reprinted with permission of Candlewick Press.

boy proof

Cecil Castelucci

Cecil Castellucci's debut novel *Boy Proof* offers a main character who is "refreshingly unique and impossible to forget," according to one Amazon.com customer review. Castellucci named her character Victoria; Victoria named herself Egg after her favorite sci-fi character.

See. I learn something new about Katy and what she might like. Camping has nothing specifically to do with loving quiet, and not music, but it actively does. People who camp like to get away. But it's not a detail I might have thought of for her. But it makes total sense.

Try it with your own character and you'll find that the sixth or seventh thing bubbled out from your first word is something, probably an interesting detail, that you can use in creating your character and fleshing her out to be real.

What's in a name? Everything.

Names inform the reader who a character is and how they move in the world.

Sometimes a name can be totally ordinary and dull, but the character can be anything but ordinary. Take Harry Potter for example, he's an extraordinary boy, he's the boy who lived, but his name is ordinary and he is just trying to be ordinary even though he's caught up in events bigger than himself. Sometimes you get a character with a unique name, like Reason Cansino from *Magic or Madness*. If she doesn't do magic, she will lose her reason. Her name

Authors on Creating Characters

Here are some pearls of wisdom from authors whose characters we love!

"I think to create a memorable character you need to isolate the character's 'unique perspective' (particularly on the relevant thematic or other matter at hand) and how he arrived at that perspective. This means you may have to create a lot of background on the character even if it doesn't make it into the actual written text."

—Greg Leitich Smith

"To stay true to a character, you'll serve him/her well by trying not to judge them. Let your characters screw up, live and love and learn. Trust them."

—Rachel Cohn

"I'd say, since I write fantasy, that for me a memorable character is one who reacts believably and relatably no matter how fantastic the circumstances s/he is surrounded by. Memorable characters are the ones who feel emotionally true."

—Cassandra Clare

"In order to avoid stereotypes, start your character from his/her core, that place in which we're all the same, then layer on the ways in which your character is unique, like putting an onion back together."

—Ellen Wittlinger

"I may spend a week, or even two, developing my characters before I even write the first word of a novel. It's sort of like just sitting in a room talking to people. You don't go anywhere. But then, once you start writing the book, suddenly you and your characters are out and about—and then the fun starts."

—Lisa Yee

"When a character suddenly graces your door and offers to come in, make sure you are open to whom he or she is. Don't try to make them something they aren't, for they can vanish as easily as they appeared."

—Angela Johnson

"Shared humor may well require the highest level of empathy. If a protagonist can make you laugh, then the character has presented her perspective in a way that rang true, surprised and delighted you. I try to infuse my characters with humor that flows naturally from their personalities and the situation. It may seem counterintuitive to think about humor when your hero is facing death or worse, but laughter doesn't only brighten already light-hearted situations. It also can deflect pain, heal, and keep the drama from slipping into melodrama."

—Cynthia Leitich Smith

"A Tennessee Pearl of Wisdom? Maybe or maybe not, but my advice is to go back to childhood and listen hard to memories . . . write them down stream of conscious. . . . and find the voice in the memories. Livy Two was waiting for me to find her in Appalachia even though I'd lived in eight states and moved all the time . . . The voices of Tennessee and North Carolina stuck, and though I had all ages of characters to pick from, Livy Two's voice was the strongest. So listen to your memories and your past, and don't forget to play like a kid all over again today—long walks, wasting time, being silly, dressing up the dog, feeding the hermit crab . . . The more we play and the more we listen, the more we open up our hearts to characters and stories and most important of all—to each other."

—Kerry Madden

Articles & Interviews

binds her to the story. Or how about Livy Two in *Gentle's Holler*. Her name comes with a history, she's the Olivia that lived.

In *Boy Proof* and in *Beige*, my main characters have nicknames. In Boy Proof Victoria calls herself Egg after the main character of the movie that she's obsessed with. The movie is a post apocalyptic film and the character of Egg is a tough no nonsense end of the world survivor. Victoria, who has a shield around herself and her soft heart shields herself with the name to feel stronger. In *Beige*, Lake Suck calls Katy Beige because she thinks she's boring. Lake Suck is the daughter of Sam Suck, the leader of the band for which Katy's dad is the drummer. Lake has attitude and Suck is not her real last name, it's her punk last name.

Try this exercise. Make a list of every single nickname you've ever had. Every single one. Even if that name is Loser. Or Snotnose. Or Hooters. Whatever. List every World of Warcraft name you've had. Every screen name. Every love muffin name. Dig deep. Go back to what your grandma called you. What your nickname was in first grade. What you call yourself secretly. List them down.

Got it? Good. Now look it over and pick a few choice ones out. Think about who gave you that name and how that name made you feel.

Now write it down. It can be a poem, a free verse, a paragraph, whatever.

I bet you have something beautiful. And I bet you know more about that character (even if it is yourself). This is a reminder that you can get a lot of information out about someone in a paragraph. And sometimes it can make a beautiful first line or first paragraph.

Or the idea for a new book.

Your character is like a bird. A plane. A Superman.

One thing that I've found is that all great characters share a little something with my favorite superhero, Superman.

When you think of your character, think of Superman. He has five things that every great character needs.

- **A special skill/superpower**—Superman can fly, go faster than a speeding bullet, leap tall buildings.
- **A weakness/flaw**—Kryptonite. Lois Lane.
- **An enemy**—Lex Luthor
- **Something he loves**—Lois Lane. His parents.
- **A special place**—Fortress of Solitude

Don't believe me? Try it out! Do it with your own favorite memorable character or plug in some of the ones I've picked out for you. Miss Piggy, Pippi Longstocking, Harry Potter, Frodo, Oliver Twist, Anne Shirley, Cinderella, you get the idea.

- **A special skill/superpower**—
- **A weakness/flaw**—
- **An enemy**—
- **Something he loves**—
- **A special place**—

Now try it on your own character! Exercises like these can help your characters reveal themselves to you. And the more you learn about them the more complex, interesting—and memorable—they'll become.

Anchoring Dialogue for Stronger Fiction

by Kirby Larson

Some invitations arrive engraved on luscious Italian card stock. Some come via phone. Others pop up in e-mail in-boxes. But the most irresistible invitations of all appear on the page, between quotation marks.

We call it dialogue. It's a way for readers to feel like they're right there, leaning against a locker as Josh and Kevin argue about who was to blame for the rotten grade on their group science project; or out in the woods as Cami and Emma keep one other's spirits up when they get separated from the rest of their Girl Scout troop. Perhaps this strong connection to dialogue is complexly tied to human development; after all, oral traditions existed long before the written word. Perhaps it's as simple as the notion that human beings are basically busy bodies who like to know the inside scoop. I love the way Gary Provost in *Make Every Word Count*, puts it: "Dialogue is the chocolate-covered munchies of fiction reading."

Since, at the most basic level, stories are about people, dialogue keeps our story-people front and center. Their conversation reminds us that no matter what the setting or situation— deep in the back woods (*Alabama Moon*, by Watt Key), in an eerily familiar future (*Feed*, by M.T. Anderson), or living in a car (*How to Steal a Dog*, by Barbara O'Connor)—the characters we're reading about are people, like us. Dialogue is an important story-telling component because it engages the reader, advances the plot, conveys emotion and brings our characters to life as unique individuals.

Most writers have no problem incorporating dialogue in their work, and countless books explore writing effective, meaningful dialogue. I particularly like Gary Provost's thoughts in *Make Every Word Count* and Elizabeth George's *Write Away*. Find a book on the craft of writing that speaks to you and study what it says about *how* to write dialogue. That's not my purpose here.

The reason I put together this piece is that I've seen many manuscripts so focused on creating characters' conversations that they missed something very basic. It's what I call "anchoring."

KIRBY LARSON went from history-phobe to history fanatic thanks to a snippet of a story about her great-grandmother homesteading in eastern Montana. That bit of family lore inspired her to write *Hattie Big Sky*, a young adult historical novel, which is a 2007 Newbery Honor Award and Montana Book Award winner, as well as a Junior Library Guild selection, a Borders Original Voices title, a Barnes & Noble Teen Discover title, a *School Library Journal* Best Book and a *Book Links* Lasting Connections, in addition to being nominated for several state reading/Children's Choice awards. A nonfiction picture book, *Two Bobbies: A True Tale of Hurricane Katrina, Friendship and Survival* (Walker), co-authored with Mary Nethery and illustrated by Jean Cassels, is due out in August 2008. She is recently retired from the faculty of the Whidbey Writers Workshop MFA program and is a frequent presenter at writing conferences.

Consider this exchange below:

"Trish, get your stuff off there."
"Make me, Anne."
"I'm telling."
"Oh, I am so scared," responded Trish.
"You'll be scared if I do this."

We get a vague sense of these characters—two girls engaged in the eternal "keep your stuff on your side of the room" argument. And it's not all that difficult to follow who's saying what.

Carefully anchored dialogue added to the engaging storytelling in Kirby Larson's Newbery Honor Winning historical novel *Hattie Big Sky*. Says *Booklist* in a starred review: "Writing in figurative language that draws on nature and domestic detail to infuse her story with the sound, smells, and sights of the prairie, she creates a richly textured novel full of memorable characters."

But where are they saying it? Are they arguing in a bedroom in Lincoln, Nebraska in 1954? A space ship circling Mars in 2097? A cabin at summer camp on Whidbey Island? Are they sisters? Friends? Forced-upon-each-other-roommates? While we don't want to spoon-feed our readers, we also don't want them navigating blindly through too many unknowns. The reader won't know how to make meaning from this bit of dialogue because it's adrift in a sea of limitless possibilities. Visual media may get away with talking heads but we writers can't.

Years ago, I learned to sew from my grandmother. She taught me that a key step in assembling a garment is basting the pieces together as you go. Basting a bodice front to a bodice back, for example, keeps the two pieces from slipping around when you go to stitch up the sides, guaranteeing straight, accurate seams (at least, when my grandmother manned the treadle. I did a lot of ripping out in those days). It turns out the concept of basting is useful for writers, too. Instead of conversation floating around on the page, we can anchor it with **character stage action**, **narrative threads**, **setting details** and appropriate **speech tags**. Anchoring is basting for writers: it tacks conversations into place in a story, allowing the reader get the most out of carefully crafted dialogue.

CHARACTER STAGE ACTION

Put on your director's hat to move the characters around on the stage of your story. Where are the girls in relation to one another? What behaviors does Anne engage in to emphasize her point? What nonverbal communication does Trish use to convey her lack of concern over Anne's issues? What are they *doing* while they're in that space together? Pretend you've got a camera rolling on your characters in each scene. Film's expensive: make what they do count. In *Harmless*, Dana Reinhardt provides a perfect example of stage action. Emma's big brother, Silas, isn't too pleased with some of the kids she's started to hang out with, specifically a boy named DJ:

> "[DJ's] cool." I still hadn't ever talked to DJ but I wanted Silas to think I knew him. I wanted Silas to know I had a life; that my circle was expanding. "He's older. He's a senior."
> Silas bounced his basketball a few times on the floor. Then he started bouncing it off the wall. He fixed his eyes on me. "Well, all I can say is be careful."
> I now ask myself why I didn't listen to Silas when I have to admit, strange as it sounds, I don't think he's ever been wrong about anything.
> But I didn't listen. Instead I grabbed the basketball from him. "What's that supposed to mean?"

Notice how Reinhardt uses the basketball and how each sibling handles it to pack an emotional punch. There is a harder edge, a harder sound, when a ball's bounced off a wall than on the floor. This nuance leaves no doubt in the reader's mind about Silas' feelings about DJ. And Emma's defiance is vividly conveyed when she grabs the basketball away from Silas.

A character's actions can also help convey personality traits as well as emotions. In a scene early on in *A Crooked Kind of Perfect*, Linda Urban nails Zoe Elias' mother's personality during a visit to the school for career day. Mom is a controller for the state and she explains her job by handing out a nickel to this kid, a dime to that, covering the classroom, all the while chatting with the students, asking their names, etc. Then Mom returns to the front of the room:

> "In any organization there are distractions. Personalities. Drama. It is a controller's job to ignore these distractions and focus exclusively on the money," said my mom.

Then, with her eyes closed so we wouldn't think she was cheating, my mom said, "Lily, quarter. Buckley, nickel. Colton, quarter. Ashley, dime." She named every single kid in the class and said exactly which coin she gave them. "I got them all right, yes?" asked Mom and we all said yes and clapped. Mrs. Trimble said, "Thank you very much," and started telling my mom how much we all enjoyed her talk. My mom interrupted her.

"Before I go," Mom started. And my stomach started aching and my hands started sweating and I knew that every kid in class was about to hate me.

"Before I go," she repeated, "I'll need you to pass those coins up to the front of your rows. Every penny counts. That is fiscal responsibility."

Through this mother's presentation for career day, we know exactly what kind of person—or at least, employee—she is. This was no amusing authorial parlor trick but a carefully choreographed ballet of action and words to shed insight into a key player in Zoe's story.

NARRATIVE THREADS

Sometimes effective dialogue is stitched together with narrative to more fully anchor the reader in the story. In the example just above, Urban's sentence, "And my stomach started aching

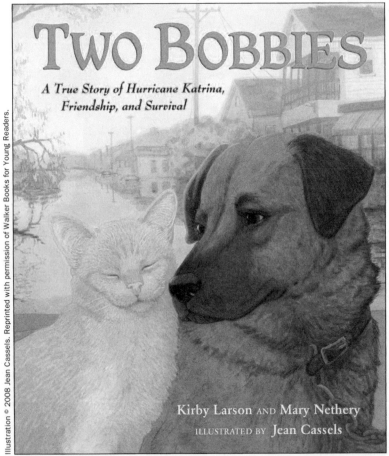

Kirby Larson's two trips to help with Hurricane Katrina clean up sparked the idea for *Two Bobbies: A True Story of Hurricane Katrina, Friendships, and Survival.* "It's been a sheer joy to write the book with my good friend Mary Nethery," says Larson. "She and I are the human equivalents of the two Bobbies!"

and my hands started sweating and I knew that every kid in the class was about to hate me,'' is pure narrative but without it to link Mom's snippets of dialogue asking for the coins to be returned, we wouldn't fully understand Zoe's upset and embarrassment at this point.

Narrative threads worked to add texture to this bit of dialogue from my novel, *Hattie Big Sky*. Hattie is riding with her neighbors, the Muellers, out to her homestead for the first time. On the way, young Chase points out a wolf in the distance.

> "Are—," I cleared my throat. "Are wolves a problem here?"
>
> "I'm not afraid of wolves," said Chase. "I'd shoot one if it came too close."
>
> "Have you ever had to? Shoot one?" I asked. Nowhere in that vast array of purchases from Mr. Hanson was a gun. Maybe Uncle Chester had one lying around. Not that'd I'd know how to use it.

The narrative cues the reader that Hattie is nowhere as ready as she thinks she is for her homestead adventure. She's made some major purchases at Mr. Hanson's general store but the question is raised in the reader's mind—and Hattie's—about whether she's bought the right items for her kit. This leads to a bigger question: in what other ways is Hattie unprepared?

SETTING DETAILS

Think zoom lens rather than telephoto here. You'll want to include details that give a sense of the specific place in which the conversation is taking place. Jerome Stern (*Making Shapely Fiction*) says it this way: "A brown Naugahyde chair with a long gash in its seat can establish an interior. Big nostrils can make a person. Give one vivid detail, and readers will build the rest." If a conversation is taking place in the bedroom, mention the quilt or stuffed rabbit in the corner. If it's taking place on a space ship, describe the REM-pod; if taking place at summer camp, work in the rusted cot springs. My body's never been to the southern backwoods, but my mind spent several engrossing days there when Watt Key plunked me down under a red oak tree with his *Alabama Moon*. In this excerpt, Moon has gone to check out a cabin being built near the shelter where he and his survivalist father live, instead of picking mulberries as instructed:

> Pap was sitting outside, weaving a basket from muscadine vine when I walked up. I stood in front of him, ready to tell him why I didn't have any mulberries, but he didn't ask me about them or anything else.
>
> Finally I said, "They're puttin' walls on that lodge, Pap."
>
> His fingers stopped and he looked up at me. "I don't ever want you goin' near it again."
>
> "But it's not even finished."
>
> "I don't care. You heard what I said."

Now, I don't know what muscadine vine is, but I can visualize the place where it grows and where a rough acting and talking man would be weaving it into a basket.

Later in the story, Moon goes to stay with Hal Mitchell and his father, who live in slightly more civilized but equally rough conditions. Key doesn't tell us that, however. He carefully selects details to anchor us in that specific setting, weaving those details into both the narrative and the words the characters speak:

> They showed me a mattress I could sleep on in Hal's room and said it was the best they had to give me. The little wiener dog was already lying on it, and she looked at me like she wasn't giving up her spot.
>
> "She gonna get mad at me?"

"Naw," Hal said. "Just scoot her over. She'll get under the covers with you at night. She likes gettin' under things and crawlin' in holes. Daddy had to get her out of an armadillo hole last week. She was down there for two days."

"She get it?"

"Hell, yeah, she got it," Mr. Mitchell said. "Them dogs is crazy. She got dead squirrels lyin' all over the yard like dishrags."

Clues like the improper grammar, the dropped "gs" and the fact that the dog gets stuck in an armadillo hole are as good as GPS in helping the reader home in on where this scene is happening. But you also get a sense of this very *particular* place from the fact that the only spot for Moon to sleep is a mattress previously commandeered by a dog, one that no doubt smells like dead animals, to boot. Particularly delicious is the irony of Mr. Mitchell's comparing the dead squirrels in the yard to dishrags, an item I don't picture him using much.

SPEECH TAGS

Even in an emotion-packed scene, rely on those old standards: "said" and "asked." To paraphrase Mark Twain, "If you catch a speech tag, kill it." Resist the temptation to write, *"Trish, get your stuff off there," said Anne angrily;* or *"Make me," replied Trish sarcastically.* Read the snippet of dialogue here from Barbara O'Connor's *How to Steal a Dog.* Georgina and her little brother Toby have stolen a neighbor's dog, Willy, and have him hidden in an old shack. A homeless man, Mookie, has set up camp outside the shack:

"Is he a bum? Toby said.

"I don't know." I sat on the step beside Willy and let him root around inside the paper bag. He pulled out a chunk of bagel and gobbled it down.

"I bet he is," Toby said.

I stroked Willy's head while he ate the rest of the scraps I had brought him. (Except a slice of tomato. He just sniffed at that.)

"Don't you think he's a bum?" Toby said.

"How should I know?" I snapped.

The saids in this paragraph slide right down our gullets because we are so caught up in the exchange between the kids and what's going on with Willy. Notice how O'Connor uses just one speech tag here—"snapped." The selective use of this tag makes it stand out, adding to our understanding of Georgina's frustration.

Trust that the emotion of a scene, the words the characters use, and the way you anchor the dialogue will inform the reader about the emotional content of what's being said. Dole out those speech tags like a strict teacher hands out praise.

Not to press this metaphor too far, but the above examples should clarify for you how anchoring allows readers to get their sea legs—or story legs—for smooth sailing through your story.

Let's get back to our girls. Here's one way to anchor their conversation:

"Trish, get your stuff off there." Anne pointed at her bed. "Now."

"Make me."

"I'm telling."

"Oh, I am so scared." Trish slowly turned the page in the latest issue of *People.*

Anne started for the door. Something caught her eye. "You'll be scared if I do this," she said, picking up the empty Band Aid tin where her sister stashed her pot.

The words the girls use in each dialogue example are virtually the same. But now we're in their world as they have this argument. We can see them moving around "on stage," as well as hear them. We're in that bedroom as Trish taunts Anne and pushes her to an act of retaliation.

Take at look at the story you're working on. Do you have sections of dialogue that are adrift at sea? Anchor them with character stage action, narrative threads, specific setting details and appropriate speech tags and you may find yourself full steam ahead toward publication.

Bringing History to Life for Young Readers

by Brandon Marie Miller

THE PEP TALK

OK—I'm a history geek. I read biographies as a kid, majored in history in college, and today I write history for young people. No—don't turn the page! Don't shrug off history as dusty textbooks crammed with useless facts.

Instead, think of history as the greatest story of all. Fiction has nothing on history for tales of courage, sacrifice, redemption, cruelty, and betrayal. As writers of history we have the chance to inspire our readers with stories of people who have struggled, overcome great odds, and made a contribution to our human spirit. It's no coincidence that ''story'' is right there in the word history.

Surprisingly, history is fluid and changing. Today's scholarship and research offer more inclusive stories of people and cultures than ever before. Writers tackle subjects once overlooked or taboo. Common folk, and how they lived, shares space with the famous and infamous.

RESEARCH

Research is the bedrock of history writing. Simply put—it's hard to be interesting when you don't know anything. So before you write a word, begin the hunt for information. But beware! Research is time consuming, often challenging, and sometimes downright frustrating. So take your time, because without in-depth research you'll fail to give life to your subject.

I like to start broad to gain an overall picture of the time I'm writing about. Then, I delve more into details, noting where holes and questions arise. When I began researching *Declaring Independence, Life During the American Revolution* I realized how the eight-year struggle affected many groups, each in their own way—Patriots/rebels, Loyalists/Tories, men and women, soldiers and civilians, African Americans (both enslaved and free), and Native Americans. I needed to examine everyone's stories!

Through my years of doing historical research for book projects, I've developed a number of practices that help me find the information I'm looking for and keep it organized.

BRANDON MARIE MILLER's history books for young people have been honored by the National Council for the Social Studies, the International Reading Association and the New York Public Library, among others. Her books include *George Washington for Kids, His Life and Times*; *Declaring Independence, Life During the American Revolution*; *Good Women of a Well-Blessed Land, Women's Lives in Colonial America*; *Growing up in Revolution and the New Nation*; and *Dressed for the Occasion, What Americans Wore 1620-1970*. She grew up in Park Forest, Illinois, graduated from Purdue University, and now calls Cincinnati, Ohio home. She talks about history and writing at school visits and conferences. Visit www.brandonmariemiller.com.

First of all, I turn to books offering in-depth and scholarly research. I usually purchase the books I know I'll grab often as a main source. Be sure to use the most up-to-date or current books, magazine articles, and scholarly journals you can find. Don't overlook older titles considered "classics" on the subject. And scour the bibliographies and notes at the back of recent books seeking further sources you can track down.

It's also helpful to create a working relationship with your local reference librarian or an online expert on your subject. They can answer questions and point you toward more information.

When seeking out reference materials, look for primary sources, materials actually written or used during the time period

"Although most children's biographies of Washington convey the facts of his life as a youth, a military man, and a public servant," says *Booklist* of Brandon Marie Miller's *George Washington for Kids*, "this book offers a well-written account of these topics, spiced with details providing insight into his personality."

about which you are writing. Find historic papers, letters, journals, and newspapers online or compiled into books. Libraries have period newspapers, census reports and other documents on microfilm. Visit state historical societies and libraries to work from the original documents.

Non-written materials are also helpful, often necessary, for studying past eras—materials like photographs, paintings, tools, maps and clothing. For *Good Women of a Well-Blessed Land, Women's Lives in Colonial America*, I laced into a replica of an 18th century corset (or stays). Each tug of the strings took me back a step in time—it changed how I stood, sat, moved, breathed.

Also reach for books and articles written by archaeologists, botanists, anthropologists, historians of oral traditions, and art historians. All help recreate past eras and cultures that left few, if any, written records.

When doing historical research, nothing tops seeing things for yourself. If possible, pack your bags and go! There are many types of museums and historic sites—both large and small—offering a wealth of information on the past including art, daily life, period clothing and furniture, society, farming, education, trades, ship building. So, soak up the ambience, snap photographs, purchase books and pamphlets, post cards, CDs of period music. Experts at museums and historic sites love their subjects and most will happily share information and little known tidbits.

Can't travel? Virtual tours of historic homes and museum collections let you research from the comfort of home. Also check out Web sites for the National Park Service, the National Archives, and the Library of Congress. And television programs appearing on networks like National Geographic, PBS, the History Channel, and Discovery Channel can often be purchased or downloaded as transcripts.

Keeping track of the facts

When researching history you must absolutely keep track of where you find every fact, quote and story. Book title, author, publisher, date of publication, and page number, please.

Many writers live by the rule that a fact or quote must appear in at least three sources. However, beware of mistaken information simply repeated in book after book. And it's even worse on the Internet! Try to verify your facts as carefully as possible, but just because something appears often doesn't guarantee correctness.

Every writer has her own system of note taking and organization, so experiment, borrow ideas, and discover what works best for you. Some writers create computer documents and files using a program like Microsoft OneNote. They sit at the computer, a book held opened before them, and type their notes directly into their files. Files set up as chapters organize the notes. Computer notes can be printed out or cut and pasted into your manuscript.

I'd like to move into the 21st century when it comes to note taking, but so far I've written eight books using not-very-high-tech 4×6 note cards. (At least I'm not using a quill pen and parchment, right?) I try to write only one quote, topic, etc. per card. Each card has a number on it that corresponds to that reference book's number in my bibliography. I also record on each card the page number where I found the information. My chapters take shape as I stack the cards into piles of similar topics. I arrange each pile by putting the information in order. As I type my manuscript I flip through my ordered cards, which makes the writing much easier.

It's also helpful to keep a plastic bin or large binder to hold accumulated photocopies of book pages, photographs, printed Web pages (this helps because Web sites often change or disappear), pamphlets and newspaper articles. These are usually highlighted and annotated. While you're at it, copy the title page of a book and staple it to your photocopied pages.

Keep a running bibliography of sources including books, scholarly journals, Web sites, and documentary videos. For library books, keep a note of the call number in case you have to go back to the source. I also draw up a simple chapter-by-chapter outline as a guidepost for where I need to go and what I need to cover. This outline usually changes as I begin writing—some topics shift to different chapters or sections.

WRITING

Writing history for younger readers presents some challenges. They possess little prior knowledge of history and a limited vocabulary. Writers wrestle with how to present basic background information. It helps to select very focused topics young readers can understand or relate to. A simple account of a journey west on the Oregon Trail carries familiar themes of moving to a new home, family travel, foods, chores, all in an exciting setting. You have fewer words to work with, so make every one convey information and energy.

The number one rule of writing history is that your information must be presented in a clear, lively and well-organized manner. The details, quotes and anecdotes uncovered during your research will illuminate the reader's journey into the past.

Many books start with a short scene of an exciting or life-changing event, then back track to tell the rest of the story in chronological fashion. Look for themes you can carry throughout the book and by all means, use humor when appropriate.

It can be helpful to break the writing down into smaller segments and write in ''scenes.'' Many history books are designed with the chapters made up of smaller subsection, so think like this as you write.

History is a distant land

While people of the past felt the same raw emotions we experience—jealousy, joy, ambition, desire—the societies they lived in are very different from our reader's time. History is a distant land, with different sounds, sights, and sensibilities. As writers, we must place events in context with background information to set the stage. Explain the situation; offer facts and period perspectives.

Even with difficult issues such as slavery, avoid judging past societies and cultures. While Thomas Jefferson illuminated the American Revolution's ideals with the words ''all men are created equal,'' he remains a citizen of his 18th century Virginia class and society. His words did not apply to the slaves he owned or to the fact that only white male property owners could vote.

Another consideration is that language has changed over time. Words we no longer use and varying spellings of words present problems. In the past, sometimes an "s" was written as a symbol looking like an "f" People often capitalized words throughout a sentence. I usually leave the original spelling of a word and add a note to readers explaining there were no uniform, common forms of spelling at the time—people just wrote words as they sounded.

Sentences from past centuries are often longer and more complicated than present day usage. When writing for younger readers, paraphrase quotes using a few words from the original. Simplify long quotes using ellipses—just be sure you don't change the meaning of the original quote.

Putting the modern definition of a word in brackets is helpful to the reader if the meaning is not clear within the context of your sentence.

Let people of the past speak for themselves

I've used quotes from letters, diaries, newspapers, legal documents, advertisements, and song lyrics—whatever I can find. One topic discussed in *Good Women* is that a 17th or 18th century female's sole purpose was to marry and bear children. A woman who failed in this duty bore the shameful stigma of "old maid." One period newspaper characterized 18th century sentiments better than I ever could:

> "An old maid is one of the most cranky, ill-natured, maggotty, peevish . . . good for nothing creatures. . . . [She] enters the world to take up room, not to make room for others."

I have to admit words like "maggotty" and "peevish" would never have crossed my keyboard!

Your whole book can't be simply a string of quotes, however. Let your research help you tell the story. Give examples. Pick out details. In *George Washington for Kids, His Life and Times*, I wrote about 22- year-old Washington's first battle, a short skirmish that embarrassed Great Britain and helped spark the French and Indian War. Few people in 1754 felt the young colonist's actions destined him for any kind of fame or greatness! Luckily I had Washington's own words describing the events of May 27, 1754. Washington wrote:

> "I left a guard there to defend it [his camp], and with the rest of my men began to march through a heavy rain, with the night as black as pitch and by a path scarcely wide enough for a man. We were often astray for 15 of 20 minutes before we could find the path again, and often we would jostle each other without being able to see. We continued our march all night long, and about sunrise we arrived at the camp of the Indians, where, after holding council with the Half King, we decided to strike jointly."

In the preface I wrote:

> The rain pounded down, the night black as pitch. Through darkness the Virginia militia soldiers struggled to find a path. They crashed through trees, lost their way, stumbled into one another in the Pennsylvania wilderness. At daybreak they reached the camp of Native American leader Half King and his warriors. Half King and the militia leader, a newly appointed lieutenant colonel at age 22, agreed to strike an encampment of French soldiers in a ravine a few miles away.

I don't believe in making up dialogue or placing real people in fictional scenes. That is best left to historical fiction, but not in nonfiction. Sometimes no one knows what really happened. Say so and then give some ideas as to what historians think might have happened. That's part of the mystery of history.

Revision

As with any writing, revise, revise, and revise again until you've said exactly what you wanted and every word gleams. Now is the time to double-check quotes, sources, and information. I type the source citation into my manuscript at the end of every quote. This comes out before I send the final manuscript to the publisher, but the information is all there if I need it. Be sure you can supply these sources if asked.

Ask yourself if you've given enough examples, used enough quotes—or too many, that bog down the writing? Is the material in the right order, or is the manuscript stronger if you move those three paragraphs around and maybe switch those sentences? Is there a cause and effect—this happened and so that happened?

You'll have stacks of research. Don't think you can use it all. Every writer must pick and choose. This is why no two people will ever write the same book, even if they are writing about the same subject.

After months of research and writing you know your subject like an old friend, so you might gloss over explanations or background you take for granted but your reader still needs. Try to read your work like someone coming to it for the first time or ask a writing group for feedback.

SUBMITTING HISTORY

Using market guides, Internet and publishers catalogs explore what's being published, both stand-alone books and series titles—see where you can offer a great idea.

Books

Publishers usually require a detailed outline (a paragraph for each chapter works well) and one to three sample chapters for a book proposal. Also include a bibliography of sources you've used or plan to use. Let the editor know how your book will be different from others already on the shelf. Perhaps your book coincides with an important upcoming anniversary of an historical event. Maybe you've targeted an age group different from other books on the subject. Does your book look at an event from a fresh historical perspective? Will your book

Resources for History Writers

- Read some of the best authors writing history for young people today, especially Russell Freedman, Jim Murphy, and James Cross Giblin, all perennial top award winners.

- A few helpful books include *Creative Nonfiction: Researching and Crafting Stories of Real Life*, by Philip Gerard; and *Writing Creative Nonfiction: Fiction Techniques for Crafting Great Nonfiction*, by Theodore A. Rees Cheney.

- Check out the Nonfiction for Kids listserv, where you can question and comment about anything related to writing history and other nonfiction topics. NFforkids-subscribe@yahoogroups.com.

offer readers more primary source material than other books? Give the editor a sound idea, a taste of your writing style, and above all, let passion for your subject infuse your proposal.

Magazines

History is full of little fascinating stories that help illuminate a larger historical subject. These little gems work great for magazine articles, which usually run less than 800 words, and require a fine focus. Many magazines prefer to see a complete manuscript. The Cobblestone group of magazines, however, features monthly themes and requires a query letter, outline and bibliography related to an upcoming theme. Check back issues or indexes to see what topics a magazine has already covered.

AND IN THE END . . .

History offers something of interest to everyone. Set your sights on a great human story—a true story. Inspire young people to explore the world and their own emotions as they journey to that far away land of time and place called history.

My Journey Into Young Chapter Books

by Lynn E. Hazen

Here was my situation—I had two books published, a picture book and a middle grade novel. My unfinished YA novel was taking all my time and creative writing energy. So I didn't need the distraction of yet another story idea in new genre—but it's hard to ignore your muse when inspiration comes calling.

I was returning from a field trip to our neighborhood library with my preschool class when a young girl's shoe fell off right in the middle of the crosswalk. The teacher holding her hand didn't notice, so the girl hopped, leaving her shoe behind, all the way across the busy intersection. Without missing a beat, a boy behind her deftly scooped up her shoe, carried it to the curb, and knelt to help her put it back on. The event was quick, completely unexpected, had a key moment of tension, and an emotionally satisfying "aha" feeling at the end. All good elements for a story. It reminded me of the glass slipper scene in *Cinderella*, only better because this scene was funnier and more spontaneous. Inspired to try to capture the spunk of the hopping shoeless girl and her charming friend, I thought of the title—*Cinder Rabbit*—even before we arrived back at preschool.

That evening I sat down to write. But write what? I had a title, a quick scene followed by an "aha" moment, and . . . and . . . nothing else.

I *did* have lots of questions. Were my characters bunnies? We've all heard "No more talking bunnies!" OK, humans then in a school-related story? But with *Cinder Rabbit* as my title, how would I accomplish that? And would this be a picture book or a book with chapters? What genre would best suit my story? Forget about what genre—what story? I only had a title and an idea, but I hadn't captured a single word on paper!

Fingers poised, no words written, self-doubt rising, I thought, *I can't write!* But my fingers finally started moving and several hours later I had a creative, fun, and messy first draft.

Many revisions later I had several characters, a story problem (or two or three) and unfolding events on paper. My critique group knows all too well how many times my characters flip-flopped from bunnies to humans to bunnies as I wrote and rewrote my story. Not only did my characters' mammal species change, so did my genre. At first I aimed for a

---

LYNN E. HAZEN'S middle grade novel, *Mermaid Mary Margaret*, was hailed "a winner" by *Kirkus Reviews*. She has written a picture book, *Buzz Bumble to the Rescue*; two young chapter books, *Cinder Rabbit* and *Seymour's Snail Trail* (Henry Holt 2008 and 2009); and a young adult novel, *Shifty* (Tricycle Press, 2008). She earned an M.F.A. in Education and graduated from Vermont College with an M.F.A. in Writing for Children and Young Adults. She lives with her family in San Francisco. Visit her Web sites, www.LynnHazen.com and www.CinderRabbit.com, and her blog, www.LynnHazenImaginaryBlog.blogspot.com.

picture book, happy with the colorful language options available to me because picture books are meant to be read aloud by
adults. But my story was getting longer—
too long for a picture book, and I found myself writing Chapter One, Chapter Two . . .
Maybe it would be a beginning reader, but
my *Cinder Rabbit* story seemed beyond the
limited word count, and simple repetitive
language and structure found in typical beginning readers. (See the 2008 *Children's
Writer's & Illustrator's Market* for a great
discussion by JoAnn Early Macken on *Writing for Beginning Readers*).

I still wasn't sure of my genre, but in
my creative process, I discovered that my
characters were bunnies attending Grand
Rabbits Elementary School, putting on the
play of *Cinder Rabbit*. The star of the play
must lead her class in the Bunny Hop, but
when a classmate laughs at her, she forgets
how to hop! Her tagline is, *I can't hop!*
Hmm, does her performance anxiety sound
familiar? You guessed it—the heart of my
bunny character was me—fingers poised
over keyboard that first evening trying to
capture story and thinking, *I can't write!*

Lynn E. Hazen   Illustrated by Elyse Pastel

Illustration © 2008 Elyse Pastel

The idea for Lynn Hazen's *Cinder Rabbit* came to her
while observing a preschool shoe-falling-off incident,
but beyond the title, for a time Hazen was stuck, "fingers poised over keyboard. . . thinking *I can't write!*"
she says. After much work on her characters and plot,
Hazen discovered her story *and* her genre—young
chapter books.

When an editor asked me if I'd be interested in revising another picture book manuscript,
Seymour's Snail Trail, into a possible young chapter book, I of course said yes. In the meantime, I sent her my too-long-to-be-a-picture-book and too-complex-to-be-an-early-reader version of *Cinder Rabbit*. Fast forward, imagine more revisions, and hooray, Henry Holt is publishing both *Cinder Rabbit* and *Seymour's Snail Trail*.

What did my book turn out to be? A young chapter book. So, is there a clear distinction
between beginning readers and young chapter books? Who are the readers of these books?
Is the young chapter books genre your genre, too? Read on.

Young chapter books vs. beginning readers

Anastasia Suen, author of 106 children's books, says the question she's asked most is this:
When does a beginning reader become a young chapter book? This happens, she says, when
the art no longer supports all of the text. "Look at an easy reader like *Frog and Toad*, by
Arnold Lobel. The writer doesn't describe everything in the scene because the child can see
it in the art. The text is mainly action and dialogue. All of this changes in a chapter book. In
Knights of the Kitchen Table, a chapter book by Jon Scieszka, there isn't art on every page.
Words describe the scenes. Adding description to the action and dialogue makes the stories
much longer."

San Francisco children's librarian Kathleen Keeler says there are really no hard and fast
rules for determining whether a title is a beginning reader or a young chapter book. "Many
beginning readers have chapters so that is not a deciding factor. I estimate that beginning
readers are usually 2,000 words or less (usually less) and that the sentences in beginning
readers stand alone rather than being organized into paragraphs (which results in a lot of

white space on the page which is less intimidating to new readers than paragraphs),'' says Keeler. ''In addition the plots are simpler in beginning readers, with the protagonist grappling with a single problem per book (or per chapter when each chapter is a stand-alone story). Chapter books may have multi-layered plots and problems, and even subplots.'' Still, it can be hard to tell the difference since both easy readers and chapter books have chapters. ''You can see the difference between an easy reader with chapters and a chapter book by putting two book pages side by side,'' says Suen. ''The easy reader page has color art and a large font. A chapter book page has black and white (or grayscale) art and a smaller font.''

A knowledgeable children's bookseller notes that a big difference between beginning readers and chapter books is that the art in beginning readers is essential for the young reader—that it is usually a literal visual translation of the text in order to help the beginning reader decode the words. The art in chapter books on the other hand is more decorative or entertaining and is not meant to help the reader decode the words. And most young chapter books' illustrations are in black and white such as in the popular Ivy and Bean and Junie B. Jones series (one exception being the colorful illustrations in the Mercy Watson young chapter book series by Kate di Camillo).

Who reads young chapter books?

And just who is the audience for young chapter books? How old are they? What are their grade levels? ''When, as a children's librarian, I introduce children and their caregivers to our beginning readers, I explain that readers are for children Kindergarten to third grade roughly and that the young chapter books (we call them younger reading titles) are from second through fourth grade,'' says Keeler. ''Working in the public library, I want to list a broad range of ages since I don't want to insult an older child reading at a younger reader level. For average to good readers, though, I would estimate that most children outgrow beginning readers in first or second grade and that solid readers like reading chapter books in second, third and sometimes fourth grade.''

Chapter book series are something young readers love. ''Children learning to read (which applies to beginning readers and chapter books both) gravitate towards series,'' says Keeler. ''Reading a new title in a series that they have already succeeded with gives them extra confidence and pleasure in the reading experience. Because of this, I think providing series to children as they learn and solidify their reading skills is even more important than with older children reading longer middle grade juvenile fiction.''

"One of the things that I hear most often from teachers and librarians is that they want more early chapter books, not only to help them teach children the basic skills but also to get children excited about reading,'' says Henry Holt Senior Editor Reka Simonsen. ''And the ALA's recent creation of the Geisel Award certainly supports this. On the other hand, there still doesn't seem to be a very big market for hardcover chapter books. Perhaps that's why the larger houses with established easy-reader programs tend to publish those books in paperback first, and tend to do series.''

My bookseller friend notes that children at this stage love series such as A-Z Mysteries, Cam Jansen, Junie B. Jones, Mercy Watson, The Magic Treehouse, and more.

And there are many other examples of great young chapter books and chapter book series out there. ''I love the Good Knight books by Shelley Moore Thomas, which are on the younger, just-beginning-to-read end of the spectrum,'' says Simonsen. ''And of course Arnold Lobel's Frog and Toad books set the gold standard. For more experienced readers, I think the Ivy and Bean books by Annie Barrows and the Clementine books by Sara Pennypacker are terrific.''

If you're curious about reading levels, word and page counts of various books, Amazon. com offers a useful feature—"Text Stats.'' Listed under the ''Inside This Book'' section on a book's Amazon page (following "Product Details"), "Text Stats" reveals not only how many pages the finished book has, but also the number of words, sentences, words per sentence, and various readability indexes.

At RenLearn.com there is a nifty search tool outlining the interest level, book level, word count and number of pages in many children's books, as well as various awards, booklists, and groupings. (From RenLearn.com, click on "store," then "quiz search," then search for a particular title or author).

While it might be useful and fun to see these text stats and reading levels on Amazon or RenLearn, my advice is that once you click around a bit, once you've immersed yourself in reading favorite titles, just forget about specific word counts and reading levels. Instead stay focused on the heart of your story. Aim for accessibility by creating a strong story with interesting, fun, and emotionally real characters.

"When I'm writing a first draft, I try not to get too hung up on word length or classifications like 'chapter book' or 'reader,'" says Deborah Underwood, author of 12 children's books including the popular *Pirate Mom*. "Once the story's in place, if it feels more like an easy reader, I can simplify the vocabulary and sentence structure. If it feels more like a chapter book, I can add subplots. It seems to me that editors are primarily concerned with finding strong stories."

Tips for Writing Chapter Books

- Keep your eyes, ears, and heart open to your muse, no matter how busy you are with other projects or genres.

- Talk to booksellers, librarians, teachers, and children to discover the best young chapter books you can find, especially award-winners such as those selected for the Theodor Seuss Geisel Award (chosen by the American Library Association).

- Cruise the Internet. Familiarize yourself with the wide range of word counts, page numbers, readability levels, and formats of young chapter books, and perhaps sign up for an online class.

- After completing the activities in the two previous tips and immersing yourself in all things young chapter book, promptly forget about it all and capture the heart of your story. Focus on the inspiration and ideas that originally drew you to write.

- Revise, keeping in mind the elements that make the best story for any age reader: a unique voice, tight writing, strong characters, humor, heart, story tension and conflict, surprise, emotionally satisfying "aha" moments, and a perfect ending.

- If you ever find yourself poised at the keyboard, fingers hovering, thinking as I did: *I can't write!* just keep those fingers hovering, until they're moving again capturing a messy, fun, and creative first draft.

- If your muse takes you there, give it a try. Young chapter books might be your genre, too.

YA Fiction

A Matter of Perspective

by Andrew Karre

In college, I had a history professor who proclaimed that in order to understand the medieval worldview, we had to rid ourselves of the modern notion that the sun will always rise tomorrow. Unless we could believe for a moment in the idea that each morning the odds of apocalypse or sunrise were about even, we would never be able to grasp medieval man. We needed to be able to believe temporarily that some misfortune might indeed herald the literal end of the world and that the "future" was something to be viewed with great skepticism and trepidation. It is a matter not just of a shift in perspective, but of a radical shortening of perspective, and it has far-reaching consequences for how people see the world.

And what in the world does this have to do with writing young adult fiction? A lot, I'd say. As an editor, I regularly suggest that adult writers of fiction for teenagers—fiction of any YA subgenre—adopt a very similar approach in order to occupy their teenage characters, who are as different from them as modern man is from medieval. To borrow from that professor, in order to write YA, you must banish from your minds any notion that adolescence is a golden age, and that one day when you grow up you'll look back fondly on its quaint trials and tribulations as the best years of your life; instead, you must believe for a moment that any number of its catastrophes, despite what you mothers might have said, are actually the end of the world.

I believe that YA fiction is a genre concerned with teenage perspective. Whatever else they might do, authors who write in the mystery genre concern themselves with well crafted and entertaining solutions to murders; fantasy authors focus on creating elaborate imaginary worlds full of forces not found in mundane life; similarly, I think that YA authors must always be consumed with capturing and portraying teenage perspective. Keeping this in mind at all times helps authors of any subgenre of teen fiction (fantasy, historical, "literary," romance, mystery, or anything else you can imagine) have a solid foundation for the voices and stories of their characters. It's this approach, I think, that separates appealing YA fiction from stories about teenagers.

You might well ask why this is necessary at all. Why do authors need an "approach" to the books they write? Can't authors just tell stories? Isn't that the main thing? Of course, anyone can simply tell stories and hope for an audience, but as an editor, my job is to help authors participate in the book business successfully, something that authors and publishers do on the

ANDREW KARRE has been the acquiring editor for Flux, the young adult imprint of Llewellyn Worldwide, Ltd., since its launch in 2006. He has acquired and edited more than 40 young adult novels for Flux, and particularly enjoys working with debut novelists. He lives in St. Paul, Minnesota with his wife and son. He blogs at fluxnow.blogspot.com.

marketplace's terms (given the book you're holding right now, this shouldn't be a surprise). And in my experience this requires more than some storytelling skill, more than a tale that the young people in your life have liked and encouraged you to publish. What I'm trying to do here is define that "more." In the manuscripts I read that are good stories but that are somehow not irresistible or resonant as YA novels, I find that the problem is almost always perspective, the point of view the author occupies as she tells her character's story. It's not a matter of language or plot or pacing. An author can master teenage slang and imagine a clever teen scenario and tell it at break-neck speed, but if she is looking at that story across years of post-adolescent experience, from an adult perspective, it will be evident in, among other things, the voice. Voice can make the hair on the back of my neck stand up when it's done well, and I believe it is what ultimately makes a book viable in the young adult marketplace.

It's my experience as well that some authors approach YA novels as educational tools. This approach may seem intuitive, especially if you're coming from children's book categories concerned with the development of reading skills. All I can say in answer to this is that it's a common approach but I think it underestimates the sophistication of the majority of the audience and, from a business standpoint, I believe it is a recipe for failure in the marketplace. As a for-profit book editor, my concern is books that teens will want to read in order to entertain themselves, not to improve their reading comprehension or to learn something (though both may well happen coincidentally).

I hope you'll see in what follows something that will help you to refine the voices of your teen characters and their stories, and ultimately to write books likely to appeal to a variety of readers who are interested in teenage experience, never mind just readers between 12 and 18.

TEEN VS. ADULT PERSPECTIVES: MUSIC

What does good young adult genre writing look like? And maybe just as importantly, what *doesn't* it look like? Before I talk about books, a couple of well-known rock songs about teenagers illustrate nicely what I do and don't mean by the YA genre. One is John Mellencamp's "Jack and Diane," a song featuring two sixteen year olds. The other is Nirvana's "Smells Like Teen Spirit," a song generally accepted to be an anthem of '90s adolescence. (If you're not familiar with the lyrics of these popular songs by Mellencamp and Nirvana's Curt Cobain, they're easily found on the Internet.)

The differences between these two songs are pretty striking, but before I go into them, I want to point out that I intend no value judgment here. Both songs were hits, have endured in the popular entertainment marketplace, and presumably reflect their writer's intentions. Mellencamp's song follows a classic formula all the way to a polished finished product. It starts with a heavy dose of American teenage cliché (football stars, back seats, James Dean, sex, etc.) and then chases it with a sentimental adult admonition to "hold on to 16 as long as you can" because adulthood is coming. It's a story about teenagers and it even addresses teenagers rhetorically, but its final impression is of an adult saying something like "enjoy this while you can."

Given that, try to imagine taking the song's raw material (the characters and the situations) and its perspective (backward-looking nostalgia) and forming them into an interesting YA novel. Sure, there's a story with teenagers and they're even doing naughty, edgy things (that's good, right?), but where's the teenage voice? At a minimum, the song's wistful, nostalgic final note is really hard to imagine from a teenage perspective or in the voice of a first-person 17-year-old narrator. This is because an adult perspective has processed the story and its characters. It explicitly looks back on Jack and Diane over years of adulthood, and this is evident in the song itself.

Now, what about "Smells Like Teen Spirit"? I won't try to explain what this song is about—I'm not sure it's possible or desirable to do so. There are no discernable storylines this time, but I do think it's easy to get a sense of the song's adolescent emotional core amidst a tangle of unprocessed imagery. Longing, boredom, and social awkwardness all fight their way through "guns," "mosquitoes," and "well, whatever, never mind." In fact, the inscrutability, liquid quality of the lyrics is the key thing to notice. It's what places the song's perspective within teenage experience rather than outside it. Unlike "Jack and Diane," this song is unprocessed by experience and offers no comforting long-term perspective on being a bored, horny, and awkward teenager. Its voice doesn't seem to be tainted by adult distance (Cobain and Mellencamp were both in their twenties when they wrote these songs, by the way). Instead, it captures the *feeling* of being 16, unmitigated by the comforting notion that someday you won't be 16 and it won't be so "hard to find the, well, whatever, never mind." There's even an ominous note of fatality and uncertainty about the what's coming next that feels achingly teenage in "Our little group has always been / And always will until the end." The voice of this song isn't thinking about the future as part of progression; it's scared of the future, period. Now imagine the novel you could write from this raw material. Where's the story, you might ask. I have no idea, but that's less important than you might imagine because I'm sure it would have strong teenage voice (and a good story is almost always lurking near a good voice).

The difference between these songs is almost entirely in perspective. Forget the superficial differences—that's just subgenere. What makes one song YA and the other song something else is how they look at teenage life. If you look back at your teenage years perched on adult observation tower, you will gain perspective that might not be welcome if your goal is to write YA of any kind. You will probably write a John Mellencamp song—possibly a very good one. You will tend to contextualize and minimize the pain of, for example, prom night humiliation, or you'll chuckle inwardly at how hard it was to talk to a boy. You'll take suffering as part of a progression, a series of indignities that continued through your twenties and on to proper adulthood. You'll do the same with the teenage triumphs. If you look back across years of life to what made you happy when you were 14, it will very likely seem quaint or, worse, painfully shallow, and your writing will betray this.

On the other hand, if, by some magical means, you are able to fit yourself with blinders that make every perspective-providing experience since you were 16 disappear (at least from your writing), if you are actually able to truly "hold on to 16," then you'll roll your eyes when a parent says "it's not the end of the world." Teenage joys and indignities won't seem small in comparison to anything; they'll be completely incomparable. You won't chuckle much, but you may laugh out loud or be deadly serious. Nothing will be processed or contextualized and lots of things won't make sense or form a coherent narrative. You will look to the future with urgent skepticism and concern if you do so at all. And, fortunately, your writing will also betray all of this, and readers will eat it up.

TEEN VS. ADULT PERSPECTIVES: BOOKS

Now, let's see what these approaches look like in a couple of fine, commercially successful novels. I can't think of a better example of a Mellencamp approach than Lorrie Moore's beautiful short novel *Who Will Run the Frog Hospital* (an adult novel according to the book trade). In fact, Moore manages to say everything I'm trying to say in this whole article in about half a page at the beginning of the novel. She perfectly sums up adolescence at the moment versus adolescence remembered (emphasis is mine):

> My childhood had no narrative; it was all just a combination of air and no air: waiting for life to happen, the body to get big, the mind to grow fearless. There were no stories, no ideas, not really, not yet. Just things unearthed from elsewhere and propped up later to help the mind get around. *At the time, however, it was*

liquid, like a song—nothing much. It was just a space with some people in it.
But one can tell a story anyway.
One can get a running start, then begin, do it, and be done.

Moore's narrator, Berie, is looking back on her childhood—mainly her teens—across more than a decade of largely disappointing adulthood. It is from that perspective that she forms a story out of her storyless adolescence. Berie admits in the next sentence that "things stiffen and shift in memory, become what they never were before," but that's all right here. Moore's book isn't YA and she's not really telling a pure teenage story, not trying to capture the flavor of her adolescent voice as it actually was; she's hoping to understand her adulthood as it is.

The "stiffening" effect of memory, of looking backward, as Moore describes it is what separates "Jack and Diane" from "Smells Like Teen Spirit," what separates "a story about teens" from a "YA story." The first uses memory to form adolescence ("waiting for life to happen") into a story that culminates in adulthood; the second consciously suppresses the stiffening effect of memory to keep things fluid and to give a sense of narrativelessness "waiting for life to happen" ("Oh well, whatever, never mind," as Cobain says).

In fact, I'd say Moore's observation that in childhood "There were no stories, no ideas, not really, not yet. Just things unearthed from elsewhere and propped up later to help the mind get around" nicely sums up not only the lyrics of "Smells Like Teen Spirit" but a great deal of what good contemporary teen writers are trying to capture.

On that note, I'd like to look at some contemporary YA. Peter Cameron's *Someday This Pain Will Be Useful to You* is, in my mind, a tremendously good YA *genre* novel (and my source for a very useful and applicable quote from Ovid's *Amores*) and a good example of a short, teenage perspective. Cameron's narrator, 18-year-old James Sveck, is a character not only in an intensely personal kind of pain (what adults condescendingly and reductively call "teen angst"), but he is also extremely skeptical about the future. College is the next part of the progression of his life as the son of wealthy Manhattan parents—at least that's what everyone expects. James isn't so sure, though, as he tells his grandmother in this passage:

> "It's hard for me to explain why I don't want to go [to college]. All I can say is that there's nothing about going that appeals to me. I don't want to be in that kind of social environment, I've been with people my own age all my life and I don't really like them or seem to have much in common with them, and I feel that anything I want to know I can learn from reading books—basically that's what you do in college anyway—and I feel I can do that on my own and not waste all that money on something I don't think I need or want."

Here is a teenage character absolutely terrified of the idea of the future (not to mention pretty sick of the present). If he does what's expected of him, he feels like it will be the end of the world and he's trying, desperately, to explain this to everyone without cracking up completely (he doesn't always succeed). By the time you read this speech of James' at the end of the first third of the book, Cameron has you so thoroughly entranced by James' voice, by his seriousness and his suffering, that instead of rolling your eyes at what he's saying (which is, from an adult perspective, pretentious nonsense and overreaction), you are struck by the intensity of the pain he's feeling *even if you can't relate to it anymore as an adult.* You know that if his grandmother were to smile, pat his hand, and say, "Oh, James, someday this pain will be useful to you," James' world would end. Cameron's perspective on his character is short and entirely within teenage James, with no hint of adult context, softening, or nostalgia. We are carried along by James' voice, as he does almost the exact opposite of what adult Berie does in Moore's book (tell a story and fit things into a progression to adulthood). Throughout the book, numerous adults ask James to tell a certain story, to explain himself, to put things in perspective—to grow up—and he always resists. Even if this book— or any book like it—ends hopefully, with a character at peace with growing up, its success hinges on the pleasure readers take in the unflinching intensity of teenage perspective up to the final resolution.

So what does all this really mean to a writer trying to write or revise her own YA project into a form that's viable in what is now a very hot market for young adult manuscripts? By now it should be clear that I think perspective is the cornerstone of the young adult genre, but it should also be said that because the young adult genre is primarily a function of point of view, it welcomes a huge variety of styles and stories—and, by extension, audiences. If you look carefully at books from the Gossip Girl series to *The Astonishing Life of Octavian Nothing* to *Harry Potter and the Deathly Hallows,* you'll find perspectives that look at the world from within teenage experiences—very different teenage experiences in very different worlds, but teenage all the same. These are all character-driven stories, and whether the characters are Blair and Serena or Octavian or Harry, they ring true as teenagers, without looking backward, without nostalgia, and with serious regard for the idea that what happens in adolescence just might be the end of the world. And as a result, I think, these books have found and maintained audiences. To put it another way, regardless of whether the pain might be useful someday, what matters is that it's painful *now*—and that's what's interesting.

Children's Graphic Novels

Formatting & Submitting Proposals

by Mac McCool

Until just a few years ago, children in the U.S. who wanted quality graphic novels had very few options. Yet, an ocean away, the most popular series in France and Belgium, like Tintin and Asterix, continued to appeal to all ages and to sell by the 10 of millions. For decades in Japan, the very young all the way to the very old had been reading mangas (Asian comics), many exceeding hundreds of pages and crafted by large teams of artists.

Now, thanks in large part to the critical success of masterpiece graphic novels like Art Spiegelman's *Maus* and to the commercial success of mangas in the U.S., publishers of all stripes are looking with a fresh eye at an art form once derided as too cute, cartoony, or "just for kids!" And many writers and artists are expressing the passion and the ambition to bring to this generation of children the same tradition of creativity and perfection found in picture books to graphic novels. By examining the types of children's graphic novel publishers, their editorial and art direction practices, the experience of active graphic novel writers and artists, and emerging trends, this article will jumpstart your submission process.

CHILDREN'S GRAPHIC NOVEL LANDSCAPE

Today, two very different types of publishers produce children's graphic novels: comics publishers and children's book publishers. They distinguish each other through their editorial philosophies, production practices, sales channels, and methods of paying creators. Although we are witnessing a convergence between these two types of publishers, the gap between them has been so marked for so long that any aspiring graphic novel creator should study them both to see which offers the best fit.

Comics publishers

Since the 1960s, the philosophies and editorial programs at North American comics publishing houses have remained narrowly defined and slow to react to outside innovation, especially for the "big two," Marvel (Spider-Man) and DC Comics (Superman). Smaller publishers, such as Dark Horse and Image Comics, have proven somewhat more nimble and original in order to compete. Still, all these publishers continue to produce and derive most of their

MAC McCOOL had his first comics strips published at age 16. He grew up in France, where they take graphic novels just as seriously as we treat children's book in the U.S. He champions the art of the graphic novel, especially for children's graphic novels, at conferences and universities across the country (SCBWI, San Diego Comic-Con, University of Central Florida, UCLA Extension, Calstate Fullerton, and more). On his Web site, www.macmcool.com, he shares his art, learning tips, and industry resources for publishing children's graphic novels.

Mac McCool created *Arizona*, "a short graphic novel about friendship, family and Arizona's cultural and natural wonders," as a promotional piece. Page four of *Arizona*, above, offers a great example of the varying ways art and text can be showcased within frames for maximum effect. Read the full graphic novel at www.macmccool.com.

revenues from their mainstay: superheroes and their licensing. Teenage boys and young men have long constituted the largest block of this audience. In this part of the industry, the creative production process often involves a tight division of labor with a writer, a penciler, an inker, a letterer, and a colorist. While many creators have made a living working for the larger of these comics publishers, the "big two" in particular tend to hold a tight grip on their properties, frequently employing creators in work-for-hire agreements. Because of decades of experience, editors and art directors often have high visual storytelling acumen, a fact reflected in their tendency to favor and deliver extravagant yet well-designed art which appeals to first-time buyers over quality writing which sustains long-term customers. Diamond Comic Distributor holds a quasi-monopoly over the distribution of this industry segment, with a network of independent comics retail stores.

Thanks in large part to the recent teen craze for mangas supplied mainly by Tokyopop and Viz, traditional U.S. comics publishers are now adjusting their programs to include more titles for children and girls. In fact, Image Comics, which prides itself in leaving all the rights to the material it publishes to its creators, has long courted a younger audience, and now seems more committed to this age group with graphic novels such as the award-winning all-ages epic tale, *Lions, Tigers, and Bears*, by Mike Bullock and Jack Lawrence. Staying closer to its readers' core age range, DC Comics recently launched the Minx imprint to target YA readers with more "emo" and chick lit titles from established creators such as writer Cecil Castellucci (*The Plain Janes*) and artist-writer Derek Kim Kirk (*Good as Lily*).

Small comics companies and even alternative comics publishers have also expanded their collections with comics for younger readers. Top Shelf Productions has received Eisner awards for its first wordless series for emerging readers, *Owly* by Andy Runton, and for the stand-alone Spiral Bound by Aaron Renier. SLG Publishing, mostly known for its goth comic books for teens has partnered with Disney to issue new interpretations of animated classics and TV series such as *Wonderland* (based on *Alice in Wonderland*), *Tron*, and *Gargoyles*, written and illustrated by fresh talent, such as Tommy Kovac.

In the American manga world, Tokyopop is aggressively seeking homegrown talent now that it and manga competitor, Viz, have translated most of the best Asian properties into English. Papercutz, a new publishing house connected through one of its founders, Terry Nantier, to comics publisher, NBM, is applying the fast-paced visual and narrative style of mangas to graphic novel adaptations of classic American series like Nancy Drew and The Hardy Boys.

Children's book publishers

Best known for their picture and chapters books, children's book publishers have also been launching graphic novel titles and imprints. The first significant developments occurred in 2005. Scholastic then laid the foundations for its pioneering graphic novel imprint, Graphix, with wise bets: an elegant repackaging of the well-established *Bone*, by Jeff Smith, and the graphic novel adaptations of The Baby-Sitters Club drawn by Raina Telgemeier and of Goosebumps drawn by several artists. Graphix is now expanding its line with new series such as Kazu Kibuishi's Amulet. In contrast, Random House's initial foray into children's graphic novels in that same year consisted of one series, Babymouse, by Matthew and Jennifer Holm, smartly designed to fit the bookstore shelves of chapter books for young reader. Due to its success, we may anticipate more such series from Random and other publishers.

Since 2007, just about every U.S. children's book publisher has been developing its own children's graphic novels, even if they have not all publicized their efforts and experiments. At Candlewick Press, Executive Editor Mary Lee Donovan introduced what she called a "graphic storybook," with *Sticky Burr*, by John Lechner, a story for young independent readers, which blends picture-book-like spreads with comics pages. With the series *Joey Fly, Private Eye* by writer Aaron Reynolds and illustrator Brian M. Weaver, Henry Holt has respected the customary picture book approach of keeping the editing of the manuscript separate from the art direction, even if more communication between the writer and artist had to take place than with a typical picture book. Meanwhile, Simon & Schuster has shadowed the traditional American comic book process with a high division of labor by employing veteran writers, artists, letterers, and colorists from the superheroes field for the teen horror graphic novel

© 2007 Gene Luen Yang. Reprinted with permission.

Gene Luen Yang's *American Born Chinese* is the first graphic novel to win a major book award, earning the Michael L. Printz Award in 2007. It was a National Book Award finalist, among a host of other honors.

anthology, *Dead High Yearbook*. At Harcourt, the award-winning *Bow-Wow* came together when cartoonist Mark Newgarden and graphic designer and children's book illustrator Megan Montague Cash combined their expertise to design an ultra-clear, humoristic, wordless graphic novel for emerging readers. Hyperion, having its own rich history with comics thanks to its Disney legacy, has branched out into non-fiction, and more specifically into biographies, written and directed by seasoned alternative comic artists like James Sturm (*Satchel Paige*) and Jason Lutes (*Houdini*) paired with young artists. Hyperion is also adapting successful chapter book series into graphic novels (*Artemis Foul*, *W.I.T.C.H.*) and launching new series for younger readers like Kean Soo's *Jellaby*. Last, let's not forget even more innovative formal experiments, like Brian Selznick's Caldecott-winning cinematic novel, The Invention of Hugo Cabret, with its sequences of spreads that evoke highly rendered movie storyboards.

Educational publishers too are riding the graphic novel wave. Capstone Press and Lerner Publishing have each created graphic novel imprints, respectively Stone Arch Books and Graphic Universe. Their titles, emphasizing action and heroic storylines, appeal primarily to reluctant readers, and more precisely, to boys grades 2nd through 8th. In order to conform to curriculum standards, most of their graphic novel manuscripts originate from in-house concepts. With educational publishers, writers and artists generally agree to work-for-hire, a notable difference from the advance and royalty system commonly practiced with trade publishers.

Finally, some more autonomous imprints and brand new publishers focus solely on graphic novels. With its first titles reaching the market in 2006, First Second, an imprint of Holtzbrinck, raised the bar on quality of content and of production, with a catalog balancing children's and mature graphic novels culled from local and international talent. Although First Second's book dimensions stay close to those of the pocket-sized mangas, its editorial vision has a more European flair. In just a few years, First Second has collected an impressive list of awards thanks to such smartly crafted stories as Gene Luen Yang's *American Born Chinese*. Françoise Mouly and Art Spiegelman, who edited the Little Lit hardbound comics volumes long before children's graphic novels became popular, have recently launched their own publishing venture, Toon Books, for emerging readers.

FORMATTING A GRAPHIC NOVEL PROPOSAL

So you want to draft a proposal for a children's graphic novel?

The first question is: can you draw? If not, brace yourself for a bigger challenge. Because sequential art is such a visual medium, most publishers prefer to look at more than just a manuscript at this point. However, do not feel discouraged.

A handful of publishers will consider your writing alone. For example, *The Plain Janes* writer Cecil Castellucci recounts that Minx Editor Shelly Bond approached her because Bond was specifically looking for writers who had penned YA content appealing to teenage girl readers. Likewise, if you follow the Marvel and Dark Horse guidelines, their editors may ask for your writing. Moreover, some agents who evaluate literary prose as well as graphic novels, such as Kelly Sonnack from the Sandra Dijkstra Literary Agency, will look at graphic novel manuscripts alone.

To improve your odds, demonstrate you understand that dialogues, captions, and onomatopoeias are the only text your reader will see. These deserve the highest level of craft. Conversely, any other bit of text you write will only concern the creative team. Thus, outside of dialogues and captions, Sonnack advises that writers "should concentrate only on describing the action and information necessary for the reviewer to understand the story, and not go into hyper-detail. For example, I would need to know that there is a monster sneaking out of the closet in Jane's room in order to understand why she's screaming in the next panel. But, I probably would not need to know whether his hand is on the doorknob or on the side of the doorframe *unless* this is integral to the following of the plot."

Writing for comics also implies a rigorous economy of words. Keep in mind that pictures do much of the talking, as Castellucci acknowledges in her back-and-forth collaboration with artist, Jim Rugg: "once I get his thumbnails [based on my first script version], I revise the script. I remove text and try to make it sparer because usually the artwork says everything and the text I've written is redundant." On average, U.S. comics include about 80 words per page and 6 to 7 panels per page, with some panels including no words. With graphic novels for beginning readers, these totals fall further, ultimately leading to wordless stories like *Bow Wow* or *Owly*.

To date, the industry has no standard manuscript format. However, because of the abundance of dialogues in graphic novels, using a format similar to screenplays is a good place to start (Graphix, First Second, and Holt are comfortable with this approach). DC Comics has a tradition of using a "full script" format where the writer also includes panel-by-panel descriptions of key visual elements, suggestions for shots, staging, and "more importantly emotions," says Castellucci.

Another approach consists in "boarding" the scenes, with panels containing various degrees of textual notations and sketches. Some writers will only include text in their panels, such as Jennifer Holm when she drafts the first version of her scripts for Babymouse, which her editor and her artist brother, Matthew Holm, then review.

When a writer or artist fills the panels with not only text but crude yet legible sketches, and systematically positions them on paper to suggest a first draft of the composition of each page, you have "breakdowns." Think of breakdowns as a cousin of picture book dummies. Most breakdowns look like sequences of panels inhabited by stick figures, minimal drawings, lines of dialogue, and occasional annotations. In other words, most writers draw well enough to produce breakdowns! Whereas editing breakdowns is less efficient than revising a script, because you cannot just copy and paste panels in a layout without having to reorganize the entire page or a sequence of pages, breakdowns will make your editor, artist, and yourself aware of a sense of space and of narrative timing absent in screenplay formats. In fact, if you are new to writing graphic novels, creating breakdowns after having penned your script will improve your understanding of the medium. Publishers such as Candlewick Press and most art directors like Cecilia Yung at Penguin favor looking at breakdowns during the review process.

Besides your breakdowns or your manuscript (partial or full, depending on the length of your graphic novel), what else should you include in your proposal? Senior Editor at Penguin, Tim Travaglini, voices a commonly shared attitude: "the more material pulled together the better, bearing in mind that it will need to be art directed from scratch and thus any work done prior to acquisition may likely need to be re-done."

Kazu Kibuishi, who in addition to authoring *Amulet*, edits the popular *Flight* and *Flight Explorer* graphic novel anthologies, goes much further: ''the very best way to put together a proposal is to finish the book before showing it around!'' He arrived at his opinion after observing for himself and with his peers how producing a graphic novel is a long-term, labor intensive, and often lonely commitment that many artists struggle to complete. Moreover, with so many editors and art directors new to this art form, comic artists who have some years of experience may have more informed and practical judgment. However, ''second to [a finished book],'' Kibuishi recommends your proposal ''have a clear and concise story treatment (1-2 pages) and at least five sample pages of final artwork.''

By the highly acclaimed author of *Boy Proof* and *The Queen of Cool*

THE PLAIN JANES

CECIL CASTELLUCCI
and JIM RUGG

Cover illustration © 2007 Jim Rugg. Reprinted with permission of Minx.

The Plain Janes, written by Cecil Castellucci and illustrated by Jim Rugg, was the title that launched DC Comic graphic novel imprint Minx in 2007. A second Janes title, *Janes in Love*, is a September 2008 Minx release.

Whereas almost every professional contacted for this article agreed that proposals should include sample finished pages, only a few of them, such as Image Comics, ask for a synopsis or treatment as part of a proposal. Associate Agent Jamie Weiss Chilton at the Andrea Brown Literary Agency says she likes to have a big picture view which the synopsis provides as well as breakdowns and a minimum of 5 finished pages. In the case of assembling the proposal for *The Plain Janes*, Castellucci had to put together ''a pitch line, a synopsis and character arcs'' with the help of her editor. Although Dan Santat defines himself first as an ''illustrator at large,'' he found that writing a chapter-by-chapter outline, in addition to a synopsis for his upcoming graphic novel, *The Domesticated Four*, clarified for him and his editor the structure of the story, and that it streamlined his process. Matthew Holm, the artist on Babymouse, also notes that ''if all goes well, the editor will in turn have to pitch your book to her bosses, and you want to give her enough ammo to do so, enough material so that she can explain to an even more time-strapped audience what your book is all about.''

As for the sample finished pages, they should look the way you envision them in your published graphic novel. On the low end, many editors wish to see 5 to 6 pages, with some asking as many as 10 to 20 (Top Shelf). Remember to never send originals. As with a picture book dummy, it helps reviewers if they can see a sizeable section of your graphic novel, even if you only turn in breakdowns in addition to the sample final pages. This stack of pages will flesh out your narrative vision, sense of page composition, panel staging, and story timing. Finally, in order to complete your proposal, some publishers, such as Graphix and First Second, ask for character sheets.

WHAT THE FUTURE MAY BRING

For a 2007 issue of *Kite Tales* (and SCBWI regional newsletter), I wrote that creating a children's graphic novel these days was like ''heading for the Wild West.'' With this segment of the publishing industry still so new and unpredictable, opportunities and challenges abound. Mary Lee Donovan, Executive Director at Candlewick Press echoes this view: "I think we're just so fortunate to be witnesses to and participants in the evolution of this format; I expect we're just at the tip of the iceberg, and have yet to be delighted by the utterly new and surprising twists that known and still-unknown creators are certain to add to the mix. And we'll see artists from other industries entering the field of children's book making. Outsiders and rebels and renegades are always a thrill to be around; they're the ones who start revolutions by throwing out the old rules. Hang on to your hats!" Thus, for folks who would rather shape the future than follow standards set by pioneers, this is your time!

However, don't delay. We are already seeing predictable new trends. For instance, while many imprints seeking to build their collections accept unsolicited graphic novel proposals (Graphix, Putnam, Philomel, Bloomsbury USA, Henry Holt), a few already will not consider them (First Second, Candlewick Press). To address this challenge, more professional agents are seeking quality graphic novels. Right now, as Santat says, "the process in comics, as opposed to illustrating/writing picture books is largely in the control of the artist/writer, even more so than the editor or art director." However, it won't be long before editors and art directors master the ropes of shaping and revising a graphic novel, and play a more active role. Some publishers may even create new staff positions for professionals who possess the right mix of literary and visual storytelling savvy to midwife graphic novels. By then, we will most likely have clearer submission standards and more established conventions for formatting manuscripts and proposals.

If all these changes bewilder you, keep your eye on the bigger picture. As Donovan concludes, "the editor is still looking for originality of vision, creative use of format, mastery in both textual and visual elements. You don't need a degree in cinema or comic-book-making to create a graphic book, but you still need to know how to create memorable characters and you still need to know how to tell a great story in both words and pictures."

Fiction Inspired by Reality

Put Some Life in Your Work

by JoAnn Early Macken

Water poured past me, splashing and roaring. The river pulled my feet out from under me, threatening to sweep me downstream. I couldn't comprehend how I had landed on the branch. I couldn't hold into it, either.

My husband and I had taken our two sons on a spring canoe trip down the Buffalo River. Rain had raised the water to a dangerous level, and the pace of the rushing river made us all nervous. We decided to find a campsite and wait until the water level dropped.

Before we reached the site, the river took a sharp turn, and we swerved into a clump of trees. The canoe my husband and I were paddling flipped over. The water's force pinned the canoe against the trees. Food and gear floated out and tumbled downstream.

My husband stood in chest-deep water, grabbed my shoulders, and slid me over to the tree trunk, where I clung as water gushed past. He straightened the boys' canoe, which was taking on water, and shoved it toward the bank. He retrieved a backpack from our canoe. I grabbed a paddle that floated by, and we swam to shore.

The four of us spent a long, cold night outside with no tent and only two sleeping bags. Unable to sleep, I replayed the accident in my mind, trying to understand what happened and figure out how I could have avoided it. Finally, I started writing. By firelight, I filled page after page with details.

Nearly 24 hours after we capsized, a ranger found us. She told us horrifying stories about people who had not been so lucky. Four days later, an outfitter with the necessary equipment and expertise pulled our damaged canoe from the trees. Bruised and sorry, we drove home, not sure whether we would ever paddle again.

I knew I had to write about the experience. I wanted to turn my notes into a middle-grade novel. But I made many unsuccessful attempts before I figured out how. Some lucky coincidences helped the process.

REVELATION!

At the time, I was writing a biography of author Gary Paulsen. I studied Paulsen's work to see how he included his own experiences in his stories. In his autobiographical *Caught by the Sea: My Life on Boats*, Paulsen describes learning to sail by heading out alone on the ocean. When a storm hits, he loses control of the boat and ends up 250 miles away. In his

JOANN EARLY MACKEN is the author of *Flip, Float, Fly: Seeds on the Move*; *Sing-Along Song*; the forthcoming *Waiting Out the Storm*; and more than one hundred nonfiction books for the school and library market. She speaks to children and adults about poetry and writing. Visit her web site at www.joannmacken.com.

novel *The Voyage of the Frog*, 14-year-old David inherits a sailboat and sails off alone. A storm hits, he loses control of the boat, and he ends up 250 miles away. What a revelation! Events from our lives can turn into stories! That example gave me hope.

In my novel *Nothing but Water*, I stepped far enough away from the facts to make the narrator a 13-year-old girl. But every draft I wrote turned out flat. The unfortunate narrator was merely an observer who watched her parents struggle to survive. She had a stake in the story, but it was her parents' story. I had to find a way to make it hers.

The book *Turning Life into Fiction*, by Robin Hemley, helped me recognize the options for using my own experiences in fiction. Hemley says, "Either you write a story based on something that happened to you, or you write a largely imagined story, with snippets from your own life woven into the basic fabric of the story."

Aha! I had been trying to write what happened instead of imagining what might have been. I began to ask myself, What if? What if the narrator and her younger brother were left alone on the riverbank? What if they had to survive on their own? How could I remove the parents from the scene and allow that to happen? After months of agonizing and uncounted drafts, I finally found a solution: What if the father rescues the kids first? Then what if the water pulls the mother downriver, and he takes the remaining canoe to follow her? Leaving the kids alone in the wilderness gave my story a whole new life.

For a while. Later, I realized the plot still needed help. After their father left, all the kids had to do was sit tight and wait to be rescued. My writing group gently agreed with me: readers would be bored. I had to let go of reality and imagine the rest of the story.

STEP BY STEP

The next book that struck me was Patricia Reilly Giff's *A House of Tailors*. Thirteen-year-old Dina leaves Germany in 1870 to live with her uncle's family in Brooklyn. She misses her family, especially her sister, and she hates her sewing job. Eventually, she comes to love her new family and home and find work she enjoys. She is delighted to learn that her sister will join her in America.

In an Afterword, Giff explains that the story is based on her great-grandmother's life. Many details are true, but the sister never left Germany. She may have been killed by Nazis. Reading that Afterword made me realize that it's possible to give a sad story a happy ending—or a boring story a more exciting one.

Again, I asked myself, What if? What if the passive kids in my story decided to act instead of waiting to be rescued? I had to make them leave their comfortable campsite, creating more problems for themselves.

Turning Life into Fiction reminds us not to worry so much about what happened—that kind of focus creates a memoir, not a story. Besides, the facts might not be as believable as the story you invent. As Patricia Polacco's grandmother said about stories she told, "Of course it's true, but it may not have happened." Fiction can be more honest—more to the point—than the reality that inspired it.

INSPIRATION

Everything we write comes from somewhere. People, places, and things I know and care about show up again and again in my stories and poems. I can't help it. Sometimes they surprise me.

My son Jimmy, who is always singing, inspired my picture book *Sing-Along Song*. Other sources are less obvious. My sisters and I grew up singing, too. A Quaker hymn called "How Can I Keep from Singing?" helped me express my feelings about music and the glorious spring that cheered me after a difficult winter. My father had died, and I poured my memories of him and my childhood into my work. My sister Judy contributed the word "delish." I still

JoAnn Early Macken's novel about her perilous canoe trip is currently under consideration. Her recent title *Flip, Flat, Fly* (Holiday House), chronicles another kind of journey, the ingenious travel methods employed by seeds on their way to the soil.

hear her coaxing a toddler with baby food whenever I read that line. Inspiration is all around us—we just have to pay attention.

Once while visiting a friend, I was tickled to hear her call her son "Buttercup." That term of endearment stuck with me and landed in another picture book, *Waiting Out the Storm*. That text, a conversation between a mother and child, was my response to the terrible events of September 11, 2001. I wanted to reassure kids that they—and all of us—would somehow be OK.

Cynthia Lord wrote the 2007 Newbery Honor book *Rules*, the story of a 12-year-old girl with an autistic brother. Lord, who has an autistic son, said the idea came from a question her daughter asked when she was about 10 years old. "She came to me and said, 'Mom, how come I never see families like mine in books and on TV?' I went looking for books for her that included families with disabled children and I was dismayed to find most of those books were very sad. Sadness is part of living with someone with a severe disability, but it's only one part. It's also funny, heartwarming, inspiring, disappointing, frustrating. . . it is everything that it is to love anyone. So on some level, I wrote *Rules* to be the book my daughter found missing."

Mary Ann Rodman's novel *Jimmy's Stars* features an 11-year old girl whose brother is drafted during World War II. "The whole story had its genesis in a drawer of letters I found when my grandmother died," Rodman says. Her grandmother had sent weekly letters to her eight children, five of whom were in the service. They all answered her, and they all wrote to each other, too. "What really struck me were the letters from my youngest aunt," Rodman says. The girl was 13 when her brother joined the Merchant Marines. Although many details in the story came from real life, Rodman invented others. "What is true," she says, "is the heart of the story, the love and trust between a brother and sister."

Dori Chaconas wrote *Pennies in a Jar*, a picture book about a boy whose father is serving overseas during World War II. "I was a pre-TV child," Chaconas says. "We spent many summer hours on our big front porch. It became our playroom by day and a gathering place for adults and children in the evening. I remember the street horses vividly, and how my dad, a farm boy transplanted to the city, loved to watch them. That was the kernel that inspired the story, and the plot grew from there."

RESEARCH AND REMEMBERING

Chaconas relied mostly on her memory to write the story. "I didn't have to do much research about the WWII home front because I was a kid during that time and have many clear memories of it," Chaconas says. "I did do some fact checking once the main story was written, but mostly to verify that my perception of what went on was accurate and not a child's interpretation or faulty memory."

Kimberly Willis Holt remembered an exciting childhood experience. "One summer, my grandfather swapped an old truck for a Shetland pony. My cousins, sister, and I gathered in the pasture to take turns on Buster. I got to go first. The saddle wasn't tight enough, so after I mounted, it slid to the side with me holding the saddle horn.

"When we finally got the saddle adjusted, Buster wouldn't budge—until my grandfather cut a switch from a tree. Then Buster took off with me grasping the horns, but not the reins. He took me on a wild ride, narrowly missing trees and the barbed wire fence." She used that incident in her novel *Piper Reed, Navy Brat*. "If you're a writer," she says, "childhood humiliation can pay off later."

What if you don't remember? Rodman considers herself lucky because she had help. "Nearly all of my mother's family worked at the downtown Kauffman's Department Store in the pre-war years, and had endless details they shared about what it was like to work in a big city department store in those times. . . . I could call any one of them at any time and ask 'Did Kauffman's have elevators or escalators? How much was a trolley token in 1943?' And they always knew, God bless 'em."

FAMILY LEGACIES

Gretchen Woelfle, author of *Jeannette Rankin: Political Pioneer*, has written several stories based on family history. "I added characters and subplots and even changed the ending of one story," Woelfle says. "One family member objected to the change, but the story, not the history, won out."

Woelfle's story "Sail by the Moon," published in *Cricket* and *Stories from Where We Live: The North Atlantic Coast*, won the SCBWI Magazine Merit Award. "It came from a story told to me by my father-in-law about his father, Chester, who was 'the fastest iceboater on Damariscotta Lake' in Maine. Chester once took a timid neighbor out for a sail that terrified the neighbor." Woelfle developed the story from that tidbit. "I set the story in 1892 when the real Chester was 11 years old. I began with him building an iceboat with his father while hiding his fear of sailing alone for the first time. This inner conflict is tested when Chester delivers the neighbor safely home, then responds skillfully to a dangerous situation. I didn't make him the fastest iceboater, but invented an earlier part of his life using the anecdote with the fearful neighbor."

Family records and mementos can be invaluable resources. "I enjoy writing fiction rooted in real life because it gives my stories a starting point and helps create authenticity," says author Carmela Martino. "My middle-grade novel *Rosa, Sola* is based on events that happened when I was 10. However, while working on the novel, I discovered I had big gaps in memory. I ended up having to research my own story. I dug through family photos and school pictures. I drew maps of our old house and neighborhood. I journaled about family traditions. This research helped me reconnect with what it felt like to be the 10-year-old daughter of Italian immigrants, and what it was like to grow up in Chicago in the 1960s."

REAL CHARACTERS

Because some of the events in *Rosa, Sola* were traumatic, Martino had to distance herself from the narrator so she could tell the story objectively. "I had to keep reminding myself that Rosa was not me, even though we shared similar experiences," Martino says. "Then I found a black and white photograph in an old book to represent Rosa. Whenever I needed to get inside her character, I'd gaze at the picture and ask myself, What would Rosa do, think, or feel in this situation? That helped a great deal."

We can base characters not only on people we know but also on composites of several people. Rodman gives us a perfect example from *Jimmy's Stars*: "Aunt Toots is a true amalgamation. Her name came from a male distant relative who died on D-Day, her personality from a distant cousin on my father's side of the family who had a good heart but zero tact, and her looks from my across-the-street neighbor." Wow.

So don't be afraid to rely on people you know to create your characters. I once heard author Richard Peck say, "When you're a writer, you can give yourself the grandmother you wish you had."

THE SUM OF THE DETAILS

How do you choose which memories to keep? Let go of any that don't move the story forward. Imagine others that work better. Author Carolyn Marsden collaborates with people who have spent their childhoods in foreign countries. "In order to create fiction from this raw material, to transform it into art," she says, "I move events around in time, add or delete characters, invent dialogue, and create scenes. For example, in *The Buddha's Diamonds*, I invented my protagonist's family; in my upcoming book set in Rhodesia, I dreamed up the events wherein Evan betrays an African from the Mission; and in a current project set in postwar Italy, I'm telescoping 10 years of experience into two years. When I'm finished, my collaborators often don't recognize their own lives!"

The Buffalo River story? It barely resembles what happened to us, although the setting is realistic. A year after our accident, we made a triumphant return with a patched-up canoe and camped at the spot where we capsized. I took pictures and notes to strengthen my novel, now under consideration. My fingers are crossed.

And I just received a treasure-trove of family stories from a relative who shares my interest in genealogy. I can't wait to dig in.

Ghostwriting Fiction

Providing the Spark

by Sara Grant

When most people hear the term ghostwriting, they think of the unnamed writers who secretly pen celebrity autobiographies. But in the children's book market, ghostwriters help create some of the most well-known series fiction for children, including Nancy Drew, Hardy Boys, Rainbow Magic, Sweet Valley High and Warriors. Opportunities abound in the children's book market for prolific, creative, competent writers with minimum ego and maximum flexibility. Ghostwriting can be a training ground and a lucrative career option for fiction writers.

"Ghostwriters have been around as long as commercial series fiction," says Kate Angelella, assistant editor at Simon & Schuster imprint Aladdin Paperbacks. "I couldn't say for sure when the idea was first conceived, but I do know that Carolyn Keene never existed, and neither did Franklin W. Dixon of Hardy Boys fame. The very first books of those two series—which first came out in the 1930s—were ghostwritten."

Series fiction continues to be popular in the children's market where loyal readers prefer to return again and again to familiar characters or trusted formulas. Consider the success of Goosebumps, Lemony Snicket and Harry Potter. Some series endeavor to produce multiple books a year to feed the voracious appetites of their readers. The sometimes grueling deadlines to maintain a popular series can be overwhelming for one writer. Or a writer may lose interest in a series before readers tire of reading it or publishers tire of publishing it.

"Working with a book packager gives the publisher control of the schedule and relieves them of the editorial process," says Ben Baglio, co-founder and owner of Working Partners Ltd, a U.K.-based book packager developing best-selling series—such as Rainbow Magic and Warriors—for top U.S. and U.K. children's publishers. Baglio started working in the book packaging industry more than 20 years ago. "A series can continue as long as it makes commercial sense for the publisher."

Top publishers also use ghostwriters for movie and TV tie-ins and to create new titles for beloved characters, such as Strawberry Shortcake, Angelina Ballerina and Dick and Jane. They may also hire writers to work behind the scenes to help write books outlined by prolific well-known authors.

According to Samantha Schutz, editor, licensed publishing Grosset & Dunlap and Price Stern Sloan, freelance writers allow her to quickly tap into unexpected trends, for example,

SARA GRANT is a published author, freelance writer and editor for Working Partners, a UK-based book packager focusing on series fiction for children. Her publication credits include stories in *Spider* and *Pockets* children's magazines. She earned a master's degree in creative and life writing at Goldsmiths College, University of London.

when High School Musical exploded as a teen phenomenon. "All of a sudden there are all these young stars who kids want to know more about," says Schutz, whose imprint published a series of "pop bios" for High School Musical stars in a matter of months.

THE MORE THE MERRIER

Why do publishers turn to book packagers and ghostwriters to create fiction? The strength of ghostwriting stems from its collaborative progress. At a book packager like Working Partners the process starts with an idea from the owners, managing director or an editor. That idea is then brainstormed by up to a dozen Working Partners editors. The concept is developed and reworked among a smaller team until the organization is satisfied with the storyline and series concept.

"The strength of our creative process is that it's a community," says Baglio. "I don't think that the collaborative process stamps out the individual creative process. There is room for individuality."

Publishers and book packagers supply the plot and characters. Some provide detailed storylines. For example, a book packager may provide a 1,500-word synopsis for a 4,000-word book or a 10,000-word storyline for a 40,000 word book. Other publishers ask the authors to suggest storylines based on established characters or submit book ideas with a specific focus: a Christmas book for Strawberry Shortcake, for example.

At Penguin, almost everything published by Grosset & Dunlap is written by a freelance writer or written in house. They create books based on TV shows, movies and established characters. When writing movie or TV tie-ins, the author will receive an advance copy of the show and be asked to translate what they see into written text. "Some people think it's easy, but it's a skill to take the 3D into the 2D," says Schutz.

Author Micol Ostow should know. In addition to her growing list of original titles, including *Emily Goldberg Learns to Salsa* and *Crush du Jour*, she has ghostwritten for several well-known series and TV tie-in books. "I loved working on *Fearless* because as a teenager, I was a huge fan of Sweet Valley High," Ostow says. "So it was an enormous honor to be ghostwriting as Francine Pascal. And of course, as a major Buffy junkie, it was a great to be able to contribute to the third edition of *The Watcher's Guide*."

FINDING THE VOICE

In many cases writers must "try out" to ghostwrite a series. Selected writers will be given the characters and storyline and asked to write a few chapters of the book. As with any audition, this work is unpaid.

"Ghostwriting is particularly challenging because writers have to adapt to a voice which has been predetermined," says Angelella. "There are amazing writers out there who have a difficult time ghostwriting because they have to conform to a very specific voice and overall tone."

For new series or characters, writers must bring a unique and age-appropriate voice to the storyline. "We look for the same thing in ghostwriters as we do in all writers—a unique voice, dynamic characters, vivid descriptions," says Sara Shandler, executive editor for Alloy Entertainment, a creative think tank that develops and produces original books, television series and feature films. "There are definitely bonus points if you make us laugh—a good sense of humor always stands out in a crowd."

And working from a storyline isn't necessarily a drawback, according to Tui Sutherland, author of the Avatars trilogy and *This Must be Love*, among others. "One of the fun parts of ghostwriting is working with someone else's outline. I love coming up with my own stories, but things go faster when the whole plot is already laid out for you. Then you can really focus on details like character quirks or funny dialogue to keep it interesting."

Usually when a ghostwritten book is published, the name of a fictitious author will appear on the cover. Author names may be chosen for memorablity or so the book will appear on bookshelves next to similar books. Some publishers will include an acknowledgement to the writer in the book, but the copyright will remain with the publisher or book packager where the idea and plot originated and/or where the license for a character or series is owned.

Aladdin Paperbacks hires ghostwriters to work on established series such as Nancy Drew, Hardy Boys and variations thereof. "There are a few reasons we like to use ghostwriters for certain projects," says Angelella. "For a series like Nancy Drew, the name Carolyn Keene is the name that has always been attached. People see the name and they associate it with the series. We also tend to publish those series with a regularity that would be difficult for just one writer to maintain. With ghostwriters, we can have several writers working on several projects all at the same time."

THE BOTTOM LINE

Why consider ghostwriting? For the pragmatic, professional writer, the main advantage is a guaranteed paycheck. Ghostwriters receive a flat fee, which can range from several hundred to several thousand dollars based on the scope of the project and the experience of the writer. Writers may have to sign contracts that restrict them from working on similar topics and disclosing their contribution to a book.

Working Partners also shares a percent of the royalties it receives from publishers with the author. If a series succeeds, the author will see additional income. "Some of our writers have made in excess of six figures in royalties," says Chris Snowdon, managing director of Working Partners. "They are a small in number but they've worked on successful series and on a number of books."

Susan Cohen, a literary agent at Writers House, only encourages her writers to consider ghostwriting when the right opportunity comes along. "It shouldn't keep them from doing their own work," Cohen says. "And it's often necessary income for them to be able to spend time on projects they're writing 'on spec' in hopes that it will get published."

Emma Carlson Berne has earned a living as a freelance writer since she finished graduate school. She has written nonfiction series and edited anthologies for many years and has recently started ghostwriting series fiction for Alloy Entertainment. She works on three or four projects at a time, all of which are under contract. "I don't do any of my own writing. This is the writing I've always done. It's hard for me to get around to doing work that I don't have a contract for."

Sutherland, on the other hand, fits ghostwriting assignments around her own published fiction. "I like to keep busy, and I prefer to always be working on something, so I look for other projects to fill in the times when my editor has my manuscript or we're waiting for the next publication," says Sutherland. "It's also easier to support myself that way, rather than relying on the one book a year I can publish under my own name."

ON THE JOB TRAINING

For up-and-coming writers, ghostwriting can offer valuable feedback in what's normally a solitary endeavor. Once selected, a writer may have several rounds of editing and revision. Some companies that ask ghostwriters to audition also offer detailed feedback to writers who submit samples and aren't selected. "We have a responsibility to develop the writers we work with on a regular basis and new writers," says Snowdon. Working Partners editors provide feedback on any requested sample they receive. "We absolutely have the responsibility to train them. We possibly give too much feedback but it is an investment we should be making in our writers."

Cohen agrees. "It can be a good thing to do at the beginning of one's career, to get practice just doing a novel and being edited," says Cohen. "And if it's something they feel they can

Ghostwriting Do's and Don'ts

Ghostwriting isn't for everyone. Several industry experts shared their list of do's and don'ts for succeeding as a ghostwriter:

Do your research. Agent Susan Cohen of Writers House encourages her writers to read as much material as the publisher or packager can give them. Read any published books in the series and study the series "bible"—a document detailing the nuts and bolts of the series—if one exists.

Check your ego. "You must put your ego aside when you ghostwrite," says full-time freelance writer Emma Carlson Berne. "I don't find it difficult. You see it as a book you are sharing with other people. Everyone needs each other."

Respect deadlines. Catherine Hapka works with a number of publishers and book packagers at a time so juggling deadlines can be challenging. "If one project gets delayed for some reason, it can impact other projects I have in the pipeline," she says. "You have to be prepared for that and make it work."

Be flexible. Author Tui Sutherland says, "In a work-for-hire project, the editor/publisher is usually looking for someone who will take direction and fit well within an existing pattern, so it's important to be adaptable, open-minded, and most of all, agreeable."

Remain true to the storyline. "You really have to be able to work in a frame work," Berne says. "Some editors will welcome your suggestions but others will have a storyline approved by the publisher. It's a hard balance to keep your emotional distance *and* invest yourself but that's where the best writing happens."

Relinquish control. "The main thing I would look for in a new project is people who I trust and would be happy to work with," Sutherland says, "because in ghostwriting you really have to step back a lot more and let the editor make the final decisions. They know what's right for the series and how to make the voice match the previous books. I'm very lucky with all my editors, because they are very smart, very serious about their projects, and very good at critiquing my work without making me feel like an idiot."

Be creative. Fleshing out a storyline with memorable characters, vivid settings, and sparkling dialogue takes a unique brand of creativity. Ghostwriting fiction means turning the *Cliff Notes* of a story into a book readers can't put down—and that takes talent.

do quickly and easily, it can be a good gig. But they should not do it if they're going to resent this type of work, or don't like the books."

BUILDING YOUR RÉSUMÉ

Writers need every advantage to rise above the slush pile. Ghostwriting can open the door to publishers and be a springboard for a writer's original book. Snowdon encourages writers to use ghostwriting to launch their own writing careers. "Their agents can speak to the publishers who publish their Working Partners titles and pitch the writer's manuscripts," says Snowdon. According to Shandler, some of Alloy Entertainment's best-known and best-selling authors started out as ghostwriters.

EXPERIMENTATION

Catherine Hapka's résumé looks like a who's who of series fiction. She's written nearly 150 books for nearly 20 different children fiction series and 24 separate TV, movie or licensed character projects. Mysteries, horses, magic, ghosts, teen angst, Disney characters, she ghost-written about it all.

"One of the biggest benefits is the variety," Hapka says. "I've really learned a lot over the years by taking on all different age groups, topics, types of books, etc. It keeps things interesting. I also get to work with a lot of really cool people and read scripts way before the movies come out."

Hapka has been ghostwriting full time for 11 years. Before that she was a children's book editor in New York City. At the time of the interview, she was working on a series of tie-in novels for Disney's *National Treasure* movies. Hapka also has had her original work published, including a chapter book series called *The Sleepover Squad*.

GETTING STARTED

Most publishers and book packagers are eager to find new talent who write well, work fast and have a unique voice that breathes life into their projects. "We find our writers in all kinds of ways—friends, colleagues, agents, recommendations from other writers," says Shandler. "Recently, one of our editors struck up a conversation with a woman sitting next to her on their Boston-bound bus. Three months later, she's ghostwriting a book."

Successful ghostwriters tend to have lots of repeat business. "A lot of publishers have their favorite freelancers," says Schutz. "We have several people who can just do anything. They become our go-to people."

To get started, visit publisher and book packager Web sites. Send a résumé or, if applicable, submit an online application. Include your interests, hobbies and areas of expertise. Many editors will look for writers with a passion for the series setting or subject, such as cats, horses, history, or vampires, for example.

Ghostwriters may start out anonymous, but good ghostwriters won't stay a secret for long.

Articles & Interviews

Intensive Publisher Research

by Deanna Caswell

After collecting enough form rejections to wallpaper our bathrooms, my critique partner and I were weary. We wondered if we would ever understand this business. It felt like we had better odds of being simultaneously struck by lightning than either of us getting a career in children's literature off the ground. I just knew that if an editor would talk to me, interact with me about my writing, I could become A Really Decent Writer . . . eventually. But, as we all know, that doesn't happen without good writing *and* good targeting. So, after a great deal of teeth-gnashing and e-mail whining, we buckled down and revisited the basics:

- Don't send your picture book to a company that publishes cookbooks. *Check.*
- Buy a *Children's Writer's & Illustrator's Market* and learn to use it. *No kidding, it's falling apart from overuse.*
- Read each company's catalog and see what they publish. *Seriously?*

I knew which companies had published my favorite picture books. Wasn't that enough? My crit partner already was deep in the monumental task of "getting to know the list" of each of the 35 publishers we'd been hounding with our unwanted submissions, but I was resistant. It seemed like more work than should be expected. I wasn't an agent and I had no desire to be one. I not-so-secretly hoped that it really was all "a numbers game," that my statistically inevitable moment was fast approaching, and that my crit partner was wearing off her fingerprints in futility. Yes, I was lazy. But, after a few more stacks of letters from "The Editors" arrived, set askew on the page, and pockmarked with what I imagined was the photocopied evidence of some poor intern's blueberry crumble muffin, I gave in. Sigh. It was time to put in the effort. A lot of effort.

The immediate response was *ink* from publishers. A pen in an editor's hand actually came in contact with a sheet of paper addressed to me! (Well, "addressed" might be an exaggeration. It was a redacted form rejection, but still!) Mark McVeigh, bless his heart, gave me my Very First Ink. He crossed out "Dear Author" and wrote "Deanna." He wrote the name of my manuscript at the top and crossed out "The Editors" at the bottom. He signed it with his initials "MM." I was ecstatic. From that point on, I rarely got a form rejection. I got rejected

DEANNA CASWELL secretly dreams of being a ballerina someday. But, being a graceless, 5'10" 32-year-old with an excessive affinity for all things salty and a deep, abiding hatred for high-waisted tights. . . it's probably never going to happen. So, she has poured her fancy into her debut picture book. In *First Ballet* (Hyperion), she uses poetic imagery and sparse language to capture a young child's excitement and wonder as she watches her first ballet.

all the time, of course, but with comments! I was finally getting the feedback I desperately needed to improve. And I did improve, quickly. In under two years, I went from crumb-Xeroxed form rejections, to personal comments and letters, to an accomplished agent and two picture book contracts.

Before we buckled down, we were already doing some things correctly. We weren't sending picture books to cookbook publishers. We owned a *Children's Writer's & Illustrator's Market* and learned to use it, especially the subject index. In fact, when I use it, that's the first place I go. (I may love the press and success of a certain company, but if they don't publish what I write, then my odds of getting in there are negligible.) If I write humor, I need to know what companies buy humor. If I write multicultural, I need to know which companies characterize their books as multicultural. If I write both, I need to generate a list for each. Once we had the list of people who said they printed what we write, we read their full entries. A children's writer never really finishes with the *Children's Writer's & Illustrator's Market*, but there comes a stopping point when it is marked up sufficiently and/or stuffed with enough post-it notes and loose-leaf notebook paper to say that we have a pretty good list of companies we want publishing our books.

And we did. We already had our dream list (affectionately named The Snob List). We'd had it for months and had been snubbed three times over by everyone on it! Now we needed to Get To Know The List. My crit partner was too impatient to wait for catalogs and I was too lazy to search every publisher's Web site. Our tool of choice was Amazon.com. Through Amazon Advanced Search, we could generate lists of books according to a single publisher/imprint, for a single year. We suspected that houses like Farrar, Straus & Giroux who bought *Shrek* 20 years ago might not be buying those kinds of manuscripts today. We wanted to know what a given publisher had put out this year and last year before we spent energy learning about anything else they'd done. That would tell us what they'd been buying from authors for the last four years.

Amazon.com offers searches restricted to its book section. If this option is chosen, an Advanced Search tab appears at the top of the page. Clicking on it produces a form with a dozen blanks. If I am interested in researching trade, hardcover picture books and am interested in Abrams, I would type "Abrams" in the publisher blank, change the format to "Hardcover," choose a reader age of "4-8 years," and set the publication date for "During 2007." Leaving everything else alone or empty and clicking Search generates a list of every hardcover picture book Abrams published in the last year.

The book reviews on Amazon quickly told us what each book was about, if it was in rhyme, if it was funny, multicultural, taught a lesson, if it was a fairytale, fractured or traditional, a song rewrite, etc. We picked about ten buzz words to describe different aspects of books like: funny, light lesson, heavy lessons, rhyme, song, rewrite, serious, fluff, or educational. We wanted to know about the manuscripts they were buying from unknowns, so we read the reviews for each of the books on the list, skipping any book that was licensed, a sequel, a reprint, a novelty book, or written by a celebrity, an author/illustrator, or a perennial author. We listed out the titles that remained and read each with our buzz words in mind, recording our findings. You can't tell a book by it's cover, but you can certainly tell if it's something in your ballpark by the review!

By the time we reached the end of the list, we had a much better idea of the "character" of each house and what kind of manuscripts they would buy from an unknown and put the time in to hunt down an illustrator. But the realizations didn't set in until we started counting. At the time, we were both writing mostly fun, anthropomorphic. For each house, we counted how much rhyme they published. We asked how many anthropomorphic books were light lessons or pure fun or heavy, like ducks with cerebral palsy. We found ourselves saying things like, "This house only bought two funny manuscripts and both were author/illustrator! Everything else is nonfiction. No wonder they wouldn't talk to us!"

We had been so wrong about the companies we'd been subbing. There were whole lists that we said, "I have nothing that would interest these people!" There were others that we felt we could have written any number of books on the list, but we had never submitted a manuscript to that company. After getting a good overview of each house's tendencies, we went back to the *Children's Writer's & Illustrator's Market* to see how the publishers categorized themselves and compared that to the books they published this year. We were shocked!

Charlesbridge and Abrams were both listed under humor. And they both belonged there, but Charlesbridge would probably never publish a book about tinkling monkeys and Abrams did! If we'd written a knee-slapper about learning fractions, we'd be more on track for Charlesbridge. And some companies that we'd be submitting to as "funny" companies hadn't bought any humor in ages. But they had funny licensed material that landed them in the category!

Armed with this new perspective on publishers and a dog-eared, post-it filled *Children's Writer's & Illustrator's Market*, we went to the library and read all of the books that we felt favored our style. The ability to mention exactly what about X book reminded us of our own work seemed to go a long way toward receiving a personal response. I'm quite sure, given my free-association style of thinking that some submission readers would have never made the connections I did between my work and the books I mentioned, but I wasn't as interested in being their opinion-twin as much as showing that I had put effort and thought into my submission. I tried to speak to them as a group of people that had produced material I identified with.

Each house has a personality, just like people. What is funny to one, is rude to another. What is educational to one, is heavy-handed to another, but they may have characterized themselves using the same words. By conducting your publisher research this way, you will no longer be submitting into a black hole. You will have well-earned confidence and be able to write effective query letters.

EXTRA CREDIT

Now, at this point in the process, I'd say that the critical work is done. Sending well-targeted material to the submissions editor will get attention (and got my crit partner her first contract), however, if you want, you can get fancy and try targeting individual editors. There is a big debate among writers whether it's more effective to send material to General Submissions or to Mr. Editor, specifically. First of all, submission editors do a good job. They know better than we do where to funnel the material. But, you may think sending it to a specific editor will get you farther. We did both and both worked well.

To research editors, we felt we first needed to find out if they were still working where we last saw them. Some years it seems all the editors are changing positions, so it was important to know where each one was currently working to avoid sending submissions to the trash can beside an empty desk. There was no sense in building an editor list from scratch and I was way too chicken to call the front desk at each house and verify my list. We found that the best option was to make alterations to the entries in our poor, long-suffering *Children's Writer's & Illustrator's Market* volumes.

The first stop was www.underdown.org/chchange.htm. Harold Underdown lists most of the children's publishing moves for the past 18 months. We started at the beginning just to make sure we caught everyone. The second stop was www.vistacomp.com/pub_moves/pub_moves.html. This site chronicles the moves for the whole publishing industry, so we scanned the entries for anything mentioning the children's department for the companies on

Summary of Our Research System

1 Read everything in *Children's Writer's & Illustrator's Market* about companies who publish what you like to write.

2 Choose a tentative list of houses based on your preferences, gut reactions, and beliefs.

3 Profile this year's book list for each house, skipping material that doesn't fit your situation. (Author/illustrator, celebrity, licensed, etc.)

4 Make a note of all books that you feel are similar to your work and go read them. Write brilliant letters to the submissions editor and immediately proceed to step six—or—do the Extra Credit below.

5 Pore over the responses, dissecting every word and gabbing about it to your writer friends.

6 Send out more work.

Step 4—Extra Credit
- Make a current editor list for each house using *Children's Writer's & Illustrator's Market*, www.underdown.org/chchange.htm, and www.vistacomp.com/pub_moves/pub_moves.html.

- Check out the "Edited By" publication at SCBWI.org, www.robinfriedman.com, Amazon, and your writing community to find specific editorial credits and preferences.

- Google if you have to.

- Make a note of all books (edited by people working at houses on your list) that you feel are similar to your work and go read them.

- Write brilliant letters to Mr. Editor.

Articles & Interviews

our list. Any mentions of promotions or hiring in other areas of the company were skipped. We focused exclusively on people exiting or entering the editorial department of a given company. Between these two Web sites, we kept an editorial move list that stayed months ahead of any of our other resources.

Next we wanted to collect information about individual editor's tastes and preferences. We felt that the best information about an editor was the list of books they'd edited. Just like an individual publisher, an editor could say, "I like humor," but their definition of that word may be quite different from ours.

We used five basic resources to research editors. The first stop was www.robinfriedman.com. Robin has put together a large collection of interviews with editors discussing their past and present works. Gold mine!

Second, as members of SCBWI, we had access to a great publication, "Edited By: A House By House Listing of Editorial Credits." Even if an individual editor was no longer at the same house, the list of books they'd helped create told us a great deal about how that person might react to our work.

The third resource was Amazon. We plugged individual editors into the general search box. Out popped all mentions they'd received in acknowledgments (i.e., "Thanks to my dear editor, Jane Doe") and, surprisingly, several editors had written their own books.

The fourth source, and possibly the most important, was our friends. Our writer pals were spread out all over the United States and we each were active in different areas of the writing community. Some were active on Verla's Boards. Some attended lectures. Others liked weekend workshops. So, together, we amassed a great deal of information. The last resource was good old Google. Some editors were so new that there was no track record. Some books weren't listed in our other resources and we just *knew* that whoever edited that book would love something we'd written, so we Googled the titles with additions like "edited by" or "editor."

I cut and pasted all of this information into a spreadsheet by house. We read the reviews on Amazon, noting which ones leaned toward anything we'd written. Then, we headed back to the library and got familiar with those books.

In the end we'd compiled a huge list of editors, their submission preferences, their past work, and what they said about their preferences in interviews. Those details, combined with the current character of the publishing house gave us a *person* to contact, not just a name on a list. We had finally gone beyond "Ooo, her name sounds like a nice person who likes puppy stories," to "Mr. Editor said in an interview two years ago that he wants adventure and historical fiction, but his house hasn't ever published anything like that. They clearly support his history interest, but through their nonfiction offerings. And oddly, he seems to have edited a lot of song rewrites."

The most important thing to remember in all of this, is to not get hung up on the One Perfect Submission. Searching for the golden bullet is a wild goose chase that ends with a frustrated writer. There are factors and unknowns that we as writers can't possibly nail down, but the submission process (read: rejection process) is where we learn the business. At least, it's where I learned the business. I truly believe that if I hadn't gone through this process, if I hadn't written and submitted dozens of manuscripts, if I hadn't pored over a hundred responses, I don't believe I would have produced the manuscripts that have finally made it. Additionally, I have a confidence in talking about the field that I wouldn't have had otherwise and an affection for editors I've never met whose comments and encouragement helped me get my career off the ground. You've already got the *Children's Writer's & Illustrator's Market* in your hands. So you're off to a great start. So roll up your sleeves and dig into the Internet for the rest. Good luck in your researching—may you learn helpful things from your rejections!

Is An Agent Essential?

Agent & Editors Weigh In

by Alma Fullerton

There's always a lot of agent talk among children's writers. The Big Question: Is it necessary to have an agent to get published? The answer varies depending on who you ask, who you are, and what you're trying to get published.

Here you'll hear from editors and agents and get their opinions on whether you should pursue an agent. Agents talk about what they like in an editor. Editors talk about what they like in an agent. Agents talk about what they like in an author. And an agent gives some advice specifically for illustrators and author-illustrators.

Reka Simonsen is a senior editor at Henry Holt Books for Young Readers, where she edits everything from picture books to young adult novels. Titles she has edited include *The Golden Dream of Carlo Chuchio*, by Lloyd Alexander; *Glass Slipper, Gold Sandal: A Worldwide Cinderella*, by Paul Fleischman with illustrations by Julie Paschkis; *The Poet Slave of Cuba*, by Margarita Engle with art by Sean Qualls; *The Hollow Kingdom*, by Clare Dunkle; *The Truth About Sparrows*, by Marian Hale; and the Melvin Beederman Superhero series by Greg Trine. Before joining Holt, she edited coffee table books, assisted with college textbooks, and worked at New York's premier children's bookstore, Books of Wonder.

Cheryl Klein is a senior editor at Arthur A. Levine Books, where she started her career as an editorial assistant in 2000. Some of the books she has edited or co-edited include *Millicent Min, Girl Genius*, by Lisa Yee; *Food for Thought*, by Saxton Freymann; *My Senator and Me: A Dog's-Eye View of Washington, D.C.*, by Edward Kennedy, illustrated by David Small; *The Light of the World: The Life of Jesus for Children*, by Katherine Paterson, illustrated by Francois Roca; *The Book of Everything*, by Guus Kuijer; and *A Curse Dark as Gold*, by Elizabeth C. Bunce. She also served as the continuity editor on the last three Harry Potter books. Please visit her Web site at www.cherylklein.com.

Edward Necarsulmer began his journey working with a specialist firm on the floor of the New York Stock Exchange. He went on to do a summer roving internship at Random House. After graduating from college in 2001, he realized he wanted to be where he could help the "authors voice" be heard. Soon after he worked for a brief stint in the Children's Department at Sterling Lord Literistic, he then worked as an assistant as well as assistant-

ALMA FULLERTON has published three young adult novels *In the Garage*, *Walking on Glass*, and *Libertad* (Fall 08). Her first chapter book *Claude Hyder—Master of Disguise* will be released Spring '09. Poet, author, freelance writer and public speaker, she holds writing workshops for teens and adults both online and in person. She also posts writing articles and interviews with authors, editors and agents on her website and online journals www.almafullerton-.com. She currently resides in Ontario, Canada with her husband and two daughters.

agent to legendary Children's literary agent, Marilyn E. Marlow of Curtis Brown. Ltd. After her death in 2003, Edward moved over to McIntosh & Otis where he remains as the head of the children's department.

Rebecca Sherman graduated from Northwestern University as an English Major, worked at a dot.com for a year, and set out for New York. A friend of the family told Rebecca to send a letter and résumé to her friend at Writers House. Two days later, she interviewed with Susan Cohen and became her assistant in September of 2001. A few years later, she became a junior agent (continuing to assist Susan while taking on my own clients). In May 2006, she was promoted to Senior Agent.

Read on for insights from these industry insiders—and whether you decide to query an agent or not remember to always stay true to your own vision, your own story, and yourself. Write the story you need to write.

Reka Simonsen
Senior Editor
Henry Holt Books for Young Readers

Do you think a writer needs an agent to get published?
I think a lot depends on a writer's personality. If a writer is a real go-getter and feels comfortable with the ups and downs of the submission process, then she might not benefit that much from having an agent. But someone who feels shy about submitting her work might find an agent very helpful. Of course, an agent is an absolutely necessity if a writer wants to submit to a house that does not accept unsolicited submissions.

What qualities do you like in an agent?
I appreciate agents who send me good manuscripts! That sounds obvious, but you'd be surprised how often I see agented submissions that are quite average, at best. The agents that I have the best relationships with are real readers and have done their homework—they have a good sense of my taste and of what my company does and does not publish, and they know the market. They also know when to step in to advocate for their client and when to step back to allow the editor and author to form a good working relationship.

What advice can you offer to writers pursuing agents?
Do your research! Before you approach an agent, look at her client list, see what publishing companies have signed her clients, see what kinds of books she likes to represent, ask all the other writers you know what they have heard about that agent, and if you can, try to talk to some of the authors the agent represents. You need to be sure that your agent is legitimate, since there are some people out there who call themselves agents but don't have any publishing connections. And you need to be sure that you and your agent see eye-to-eye about the things that are important to you.

Cheryl Kelin
Senior Editor
Arthur A. Levine Books

Do you think a writer needs an agent to get published?
No, I don't think it's necessary for a writer to have an agent in the children's book world—there are enough other ways to make contact with editors (open submissions policies, conferences, online) that you don't need representation to get your foot in the publication door. Having an agent offers three definite advantages: 1) It cuts down research time, as the agent

should know what editors are and aren't right for your work; 2) It will substantially cut down on an editor's response time to your manuscript, as editors usually read and respond to agented submissions first, and 3) If the book gets bought, it will ensure that you have someone looking out for your interests and advising you on all the arcana of book contracts.

What qualities do you like in an agent?
Good agents know editors have their hands full with manuscripts in process, books in publication, new submissions, old submissions, sales conferences, design notes, copyediting, you name it—so they make *my* job easy by providing me with all the information I'd need to take a project to Acquisitions Committee. This includes a biography of the author, with attention paid to prior book publications and publicity hooks; ideas for comparison titles (realistic ones—you can't compare every retold fairy tale to *Ella Enchanted*); and sometimes even good selling copy—not that I can't write that myself, but it's useful to have it already laid out for me!

Some agents have also recently begun including a date by which they want to hear about any interest, which is actually really useful, because it means that you don't automatically lose a project if you don't drop everything and read it right now. . . . It takes some of the pressure off, and allows for a more thoughtful and pleasurable reading experience.

I would rather not deal with agents who don't play fair—if they aren't upfront about whether a manuscript is a multiple submission.

Edward Necarsulmer
Director, Children's Department
McIntosh & Otis

Does a writer need an agent to get published?
More and more publishers are closing their doors to unsolicited submissions but an agent is not essential to getting published, especially if you write early readers, nonfiction, or work for hire. With that type of work an agent wouldn't necessarily be able to improve the standard contract—and I wouldn't feel comfortable taking 15% on those. For sure, there are going to be projects that will need an agent's guidance but for first time authors, especially for picture books, an agent is not 100% imperative.

What questions should a writer ask a potential agent?
Ask if the agent is a member of the AAR (The Association of Authors' Representatives). To be inducted into the AAR you need to have done a certain amount of deals with major publishing houses and you need to agree to follow the AAR's code of ethics.

Ask if they have a foreign rights department i.e., I handle foreign rights for my clients personally, attending the Bologna Book Fair annually. Also ask if they have an in-house movie/film/television/audio/stage department.

Ask about an in house adult agent that can rep any adult books you may write.

It's very important to ask about the agency agreements. Ask about clauses in written contracts. Watch for the interminable agency agreement (not a good thing).

Ask about response time to their clients, especially with regard to communication.

What are your feelings about the children's market right now?
I think it's in a great place. There's always going to be comments about what's dead and what's hot. I find that to be all totally inconsequential. If you write something superlative in any genre, it will be published. As with any business that is driven by a free market economy, in my humble opinion, book publishing is to some degree cyclical like anything else.

What advantages do agents give to already published writers?

Better deals—better contracts and better terms. It's the agent's job to be up on the publishing scene and know the editors' likes and dislikes so they can place things correctly. It's not just enough to make a sale but to find an ongoing home for the writer. Of course the trend is to have multiple houses but I prefer to divide them into genres. The agent would know when and how appropriately to shop all the different ancillary rights as well. He/she can also act as a conduit between the author and editor if need be. Sometimes he has to explain the publisher's position to the author as well as, of course, the author's position to the publisher.

What kind of manuscripts would you like to see more of?

Comedy, middle grade and middle grade mysteries, nonfiction with a really distinct hook. I recently sold a book to Walker & Co. called *How They Croaked* about how famous people died. I'm a big music fan so I've sold musician bios (bios with great non-linear twists) to Viking; Little, Brown; and Clarion. On the other hand, I have been seeing (and this could just be me) all too many uber self-conscience voices, first person in-the-head narratives where nothing seems to actually transpire for kids. I'd prefer to see more straight third person. As any editor or agent will tell you, there are, of course, always exceptions. Again, the strength of the voice and the writing are the most important factors.

Do you have any advice to writers who are asked for revisions from an editor and/or agent?

Don't revise for an editor or agent in a way that will make you feel uncomfortable revising. Don't change your vision for the prospect of getting an agent or for a sale. It's all about the right fit. I would say do the revisions, but only do the revisions you agree with. If the editor/agent still passes then your manuscript is not the right fit for that person. The last thing I want when I ask for revisions is for an author to publish a book they never intended to publish. Nevertheless, feedback, especially from editors (who are the most qualified to discuss craft) is entirely useful and can be a fantastic resource, even if the publisher is not outright offering to publish the book.

Besides the obvious, what are some things authors can do that make them the best clients?

Honesty and communication are the number one things for me. Mutual respect. Treat me like a person—I try to treat all my clients like they are my only author.

Passive aggression is the number one way you can be sure I'll end our relationship. If you don't like the way I've handled something or don't think I'm responding quickly enough, say so. Don't just send me an e-mail that says: 'What's going on over there?'

Do you represent illustrators as well?

Yes I do, although I do represent fewer illustrators than writers right now, that's a part of the business that I'm looking to expand. I'd be more likely to take on an author/illustrator for picture book than just a picture book writer.

Rebecca Sherman
Senior Agent
Writers House

What are your feelings about the children's book market right now? How do you see the market changing in the future?

I think the market for YA remains strong and the market for younger work continues to rebuild its strength after a period of weakness. 2007 was a particularly interesting year for illustrated books. Not only did a graphic novel win the Printz award, and a wordless picture book win the Caldecott, we saw the publication of books like *The Invention of Hugo Cabret* [which won the Caldecott in 2008], *The Arrival*, and *The Wall*. I think the market will embrace new formats for illustrated books in the near future.

What advantages do agents give authors/illustrators?

The relationship with an agent is beneficial because it allows the client to focus on the creative elements of being an author/illustrator. Having a career as an author/illustrator is not just about being able to have a book published.

Working with an agent allows for stronger deals, solid contracts reviewed by those who can compare to contracts for other clients, the ability to reserve and license subsidiary rights, and much more. Simply, an agent is an industry insider whose job is to be your advocate with the backing of her entire agency.

What kind of things would you like to see more of?

I would love to see more stories with multicultural characters (protagonists and supporting cast) wherein race is not the conflict. I don't think we see enough "slice of life" stories from diverse view points.

Will you represent both illustrators for trade projects and educational projects?

I represent an illustrator for trade book projects and any subsidiary rights that come from those contracts. I do not represent clients for educational illustration or editorial illustration as these are not my areas of expertise. I want to work with clients who see their careers in children's books. If they want to do a bit of other illustration work on the side, I believe they can handle those projects on their own, and I wouldn't want to take commission.

Do you have established relationships with editors who prefer author/illustrators?

I have established relationships with many editors. Now that illustrated books are successful for a range of age groups, there are few editors who wouldn't be interested in author/illustrators. However, there are certain editors and publishers that I seem to work with over and over. Certain editors have come to know my client list more than others, and in turn I'm more accustomed to working with them.

Would you be willing to help work with an illustrator to strengthen the written part of manuscripts before they go to an editor?

I'm more than willing to work with all clients editorially. I think it's important to send out the strongest submissions possible, so I'm happy to do rounds of revisions with novelists, picture book author/illustrators, etc. I find that editorial advice is particularly helpful to pre-published clients and those looking for a new home. With potential clients, I almost always go through a round of revisions with them before offering representation. Selling a book by an author/illustrator is easier than selling the text of an illustrated book alone or waiting for an editor to find the perfect manuscript for one of my illustrator clients. However, not every illustrator is an author. I want to make clear that it's not a problem if a potential client or client is a very strong illustrator who does not want to write as well.

How would you like author/illustrators to present their dummies to you?

Potential clients who intend to write and illustrate should send me a submission with a query letter that includes a link to an online portfolio and a snail-mailed dummy with a complete text and sketches and one full color spread (because this is the kind of package that I would send to an editor when submitting an author/illustrator's work). [Note: For Sherman's submission guidelines and preferred illustrator style check her Publisher's Marketplace page to see her client list.]

Do you do anything differently in the way you represent your illustrators than you do with your authors?

For author clients, I pitch specific projects. For illustrators who are open to illustrating others' texts, it is important that I familiarize those at publishing houses with a client's work, directing them to an online portfolio, so that they think of my client when they acquire texts that need to be illustrated.

School Visit's from a Librarian's Perspective

by Lisa Mullarkey

During my eight years as a school librarian, I've hosted more than 25 author and illustrator visits for our annual Wizards of Words week-long celebration. The opportunity for children to meet and ask questions of their heroes—the wizards behind the pens and paintbrushes—is a powerful gift for a school to give its student body.

With so many speakers to choose from, how do I pick those who would reinforce or spark students' love of reading and awaken their inner muse? Like most gifts, I know one size doesn't fit all and like all good shoppers, I'll search for months to find the perfect one. Before I shopped, I reviewed my obvious must-haves:

- A book/author/illustrator/topic kids are buzzing about. When I see and feel their passion, I want to fan the fire and spread their enthusiasm throughout the school.
- Curriculum connections: Sadly, there's little wiggle room for "extras" these days. I don't want to add to a teacher's workload but, instead, enrich the existing curriculum. If the book doesn't have an overt connection, I'll look for character education themes, and, of course, it will always correlate with any literacy curriculum when focusing on the writing process.
- Books/speakers that the children will want to read and revisit again. Although our annual Wizard of Words celebration spans a week, the ripple effect was felt throughout the year and often extended into the next.
- I want to immerse the school-wide community into the visit. Can I include the computer, art, gym, and music teachers? The reading specialist?

Once I have a clear idea of what type of book/author/illustrator I want, it's time to shop for that perfect fit. Will it be you?

Online shopping: No Web site? No deal!

Online shopping is popular because it's convenient and quick—so that's where I shop for authors. I feel so strongly that a presenter must have a Web site that I won't host anyone who doesn't. Why is a Web site important and neccesary?

LISA MULLARKEY is the author of *Splashing by the Shore* (Gibbs Smith) and the early chapter book series, Katharine the *Almost* Great, to be published in January 2009 by ABDO Publishing. She's currently writing four nonfiction cheerleading books for Enslow Publishers for release in 2010. During her years as teacher and children's librarian, she hosted dozens of author and illustrator visits in her library. She now writes fulltime and enjoys doing author visits of her own. Visit her Web site, www.lisamullarkey.com.

First, it makes my job easier. Librarians juggle teaching, collection development, and manage the media center among other tasks. Clicking around your site gives immediate information about whether you'd be a good fit for our program. Also, I prep the kids for your visit. Instead of creating new material, I prefer to use yours. I'll head straight to your "About Me" section for my introductory lesson. And easy access to you by all is crucial since I involve the entire school-wide community in your visit. Many teachers use your Web site in their lessons as well and parents are given your Web site to review book titles—it gets them more vested in and excited about your visit which in turn gets their kids even more excited.

Web content that can increase your chances of getting booked

- Include every book you've worked on since you never know what a librarian's needs are. A colleague booked an author—not because of his popular series, but because of his *Blues Clues* books: She needed someone to visit with pre-school handicapped classes.
- Fun facts about you that will help the kids connect with you as soon as they "meet" you.
- Pictures! Kids especially get a kick out of seeing pictures of you at their age.
- Mention everything you have to offer. Audio books? Curriculum Guides? Reader's Theater Scripts? Are your books on Accelerated Reader lists? Do you have Battle of the Books questions? Does your program involve songs? Flannel boards? Puppets? Seeing what's offered helps with my planning and decision-making. (Once booked, speakers often send a packet that expands on Web site content or includes postcards, bookmarks, etc.)
- Include fun ideas for your visit. Do you have recipes the cafeteria can make for lunch? A game perfect for gym class? Craft examples?
- Offer references. No matter who you are, I call three people to make sure you've delivered what was promised. It once saved me from booking a popular author due to her "diva-like" behavior.

Tip: To get visitors to your Web site, give a shout out to the school before your visit. To keep them coming back, post pictures/letters/drawings you receive from students after your visit. This goes for speaking engagements, too. Many authors prefer to take pictures from behind the students so none are recognizable—thus lessening the need for parental permission before posting on the web.

Big box shopping

Why are super stores popular? It's one-stop shopping, of course. Where else can you buy diamonds, dining room furniture, and diapers all in one store? Make your Web site or author packet a little bit like Costco: Offer something for everyone. Hopefully, the librarian won't feel the need to look anywhere else. Maybe I'm looking for a K-2 presenter but hope to include a session for fifth graders. Can you handle it? Do you only write picture books? Novels for grades 3-5? No worries! Market yourself.

Let's say you're a picture book writer for the K-2 market. Here are examples of how you can broaden your appeal to a K-8 school:

- Develop a program that focuses on buddy classes. Could eighth graders work with a Kindergarten buddy class? Get creative! Have older kids use Reader's Theater Scripts to act out your book for younger students.
- Offer writing workshops/art programs. To have kids actually be invited to work side by side with presenters? Divine! Think buddy classes here, too: younger students can illustrate stories written by older students.
- Not every school has a librarian. A "What's Hot in Children's Books" session, talks on award-winning books, or storytelling might be desirable.
- Discuss available writing market for kids.

- Offer PTO/Parent talks
- Zero in on your book: Cookbook? Offer to cook with students. Sports-related? Offer to ref or play a game in gym. The possibilities are endless.

Budget: avoid sticker shock

While it's a personal decision, I advise against listing your honorarium on your Web site. Don't let a potential school click off your site because of budget constraints. After you reel them in with your offerings, prove you're affordable no matter what your fee and show them how to help offset costs.

Do you live in California and the school is in New Jersey? Airfare prices can be intimidating and are often a deal breaker. Suggest asking parents to donate Frequent Flyer Miles.

Explain the power of book sales: Order books at a 40% discount from the publisher and sell at retail price keeping the profit to offset the cost of the visit. You often earn $6 a book. Fourteen of my visitors have been *free*. But since each school is different, you can safely say it will help defray the cost of your visit.

Direct them to applications for Grants or Title 1 Funds.

Cha-ching: Triple your sales

When I inherited the WOW program, I wanted to expand it to include 3-4 visitors at a time. I needed to increase book sales. With a few simple changes, sales tripled. Authors and illustrators were thrilled! Here's what worked for me:

Step One: I ditched the order form supplied in the author/illustrator packet. I'm always surprised at how little information it conveyed about the speaker and book(s). You need to toot your own horn a bit. (See Sample Order form on page 115.)

Step Two: I added books that were "outside" the age range of the intended audience. For example, I included books that were YA even though I was a K-5 librarian. Of course I had a "disclaimer" and full description of the novel. Parents were often eager to purchase them for older children at home. We sold dozens of Kimberly Willis Holt's *Keeper of the Night* and made over $250 on that title.

Step Three: I bought extra copies of the presenter's books to have on hand. I encourage presenters to bring or ask the school to get extra books—always. They'll sell. Now that I'm a visiting author, I bring and sell at least 35 extra books per visit. I once had an author bring 100 books and he

After hosting dozens of authors as a school librarian, Lisa Mullarkey, here posing with her Gibbs Smith title *Splashing on the Shore*, illustrated by Debra Dixon, now visits schools herself.

sold all of them. If the school had provided those extra books, that would have been $600 dollars that would have been used to offset the cost of his visit.

Step Four: I held contests. Nothing builds excitement like winning something. I asked the PTO to donate books for prizes. The more potential winners, the more excitement contests generate.

Step Five: I asked the PTO to donate a book to each class or grade level.

Step Six: I specifically invited the PTO board members and my library volunteers to the presentation as a way of thanking them for the work they did throughout the year. Once I had a PTO member stop by to watch a speaker's first grade presentation. Although she had a fifth grader, she bought twenty(!) copies of his books for her nieces and nephews. Many of the visitors will purchase your book.

A word about contests:

If you're a prolific author and wish the kids would read more of your books prior to your visit, this contest idea may be worth mentioning to your host. Teachers appreciate the tip because no one wants an author to hold up a book, ask if anyone has read it, and get no response. When Dan Gutman asked to have lunch with ten students, I knew I needed a contest that would excite the kids, determine who had lunch with him, and help me (by exposing them to more of his books) out as well. Six months prior to his visit, I announced the rules: Anyone reading five or more of his books over the next six months (which included summer break) would earn a ticket for the lunch drawing. I also offered audio books during lunch/recess periods that counted toward the total. The results: 368 kids entered the contest. His sales were through the roof and no matter what book he mentioned, dozens of hands shot into the air.

Last-minute shopping

Even savvy shoppers resort to last minute shopping once in a while. Sometimes a speaker cancels last minute or new funds are discovered and need to be spent by a specific date, putting a school in the position of looking for an author on short notice. Be the person fresh in the host's mind and at the top of their file folder. How? Send a yearly e-mail/snail mail letter to the librarian. Douglas Florian mailed me his information six years in a row before the time was right to book him. And when a nonfiction author became ill and canceled a week before his visit, who did I call? A new author who had sent me her packet a few weeks prior.

Loyal customers

As a shopper, once I find a store or product (you!) I'm happy with, I want to experience it again. As a visiting author or illustrator, you want repeat business. By the time you pack up to leave, I know whether or not I hope to have you return. How can you nail down an exact date?

- Write a thank you note. If you enjoyed your visits and were impressed with the students and staff members, say so. Tell the principal too.
- Keep track of the year/grade levels you visited so you know when the next visit's possible. If it's a K-2 school, you'll know to contact them again when the current kinder-gartners graduate.
- Before you leave, offer the librarian an opportunity to book you for a future date at your current rate. If you're just starting out, this could work in your favor. When librarians visit your site and see a school has already *re*booked you, it adds credibility to your performance.

Sample Order Form

Adds credibility.

Gives a sense of
what I'm about.

Always include
your Web site.

Adds credibility
to the series.

Highlights the
party planning
chapter for land-
locked kids.

American Girl is
popular...might help
sales!

Articles & Interviews

AN AUTOGRAPHED BOOK!!!

Splashing by the Shore was the editor's pick
in the July/August *Nick Jr.* Magazine

Children's Author Lisa Mullarkey will visit our school on
Thursday, September 27th. If you'd like to purchase a book,
return the order form and a check by Friday, September 13th.
Lisa donates 10% of all book sales (as well as 10% of her
honorarium) to the Robert Packard Center for ALS (Lou
Gehrig's disease) Research.

Visit www.lisamullarkey.com for more information.

SPLASHING by the SHORE: Hit the beach with the newest
addition to the successful Outdoor Activity Series published
by Gibbs Smith. (Over 200,000 books have been sold in this
series!) From sand games to water relays, science experiments to beach-themed crafts and recipes, this book is the
perfect companion to bring with you when you're headed to
the beach. Not going to the shore? Turn your house into the
ultimate beach party destination with the creative ideas
featured in this book. So, catch a wave and get your very
own autographed copy. (Illustrated by Debra Dixon who
also illustrated American Girl's *Party Secrets*).

I'd like _____ copies of *Splashing by the Shore* at $9.95 each.

Autograph book(s) to: _____

Using a book order form like this one for her own book *Splashing by the Shore* helped librarian Lisa Mullarkey
triple book sales for authors visiting her school during their annual week-long Wizards of Words celebration.

- Follow-up with the other librarians in the district reminding them of your recent visit and desire to come to their school.

No refunds allowed!

While most librarians are thrilled with their guests, there are some things to remember that will keep you from being the "gift" people wish they could return.

First, always be courteous and polite. Don't complain that you're tired of visiting schools. You may have presented hundreds of times but it's your first time with us. Taking your lunch out to your car is not a way to make friends. Granted, down time is a must—but schedule it separately from lunch if the staff plans on eating with you.

Telling a joke or two above the kids heads thrown in for the teachers is fine. More than that? It's time to rethink your intended audience.

It's okay to discuss a difficult year or a bad experience you had in school. Kids will appreciate your honesty. However, don't continuously bash teachers or schools throughout your presentation. You're with committed teachers and impressionable kids. Offer hope. Balance out your negative experience with a positive one.

Finally, although it's the teacher's job to control her class, you still need to be in command of your audience. Are kids talking over you? We can spot an unpolished presentation a chalkboard eraser away.

Regifting

Regifting is often considered taboo in its traditional form, but if the visit goes well, I know I've given a valuable, meaningful gift to the children: You. I'm happy to pass your name on so other children can reap the benefits of your gifts as well.

Making Your Web Site Educator-Friendly

by Cynthia Leitich Smith

Who will visit your author or illustrator Web site? Young readers may be your ultimate target audience, but educators—teachers, university professors, and school librarians—are on the forefront of efforts to connect books and kids. What's more, they're using the Internet more than ever to help them make purchasing decisions.

"It is professional librarians and educators who are most likely to specifically seek out information about authors and illustrators and ways to use children's books in educational and group settings," says author and former school librarian Toni Buzzeo. "Teachers and librarians continue to discover and value books, even when the books are no longer on the front list. They look for books that connect with writing and literature topics. They value books long after they've appeared in the publisher's catalog or a review source."

Buzzeo adds that librarians are likewise interested in paperbacks and that teachers sometimes seek paperbacks that can be purchased for full class study.

Many teachers build their own classroom libraries. Some use their own money. Others apply for grants or get donations from parents and other community members.

"We've heard reports that many media specialists can only buy books for the media center if these books are requested by teachers," says publicist Vicki Palmquist of Winding Oak, an agency offering promotional services to authors and illustrators. "This puts a lot of book-buying power in the hands of teachers."

Organizations such as the National Council of Teachers of English (NCTE), the International Reading Association (IRA), the National Science Teachers Association (NSTA), the National Council for the Social Studies (NCSS), and the American Library Association (ALA), as well as their state and district affiliates, are highly influential.

Each publishes journals and Web sites that highlight authors, illustrators, and youth literature. In addition, they sponsor prestigious award programs, a few of which can prompt thousands—even hundreds of thousands—of sales.

Publicist Susan Raab of Raab Associates emphasizes a Web site is one way that authors

CYNTHIA LEITICH SMITH is the award-winning author of *Jingle Dancer*, *Indian Shoes*, and *Rain Is Not My Indian Name*. Her more recent titles are *Santa Knows*, *Tantalize*, and *Eternal*. She is a member of faculty at the Vermont College M.F.A. program in Writing for Children and Young Adults. Her Web site, www.cynthialeitichsmith.com, was named one of the top 10 Writer Sites by *Writer's Digest* and an ALA Great Web site for Kids. Her Cynsations blog at cynthialeitichsmith.blogspot.com was listed as among the top two read by the children's/YA publishing community in the SCBWI "To Market" column.

and illustrators can raise their awareness in this market so their books have a better chance of being considered for awards.

As librarian Sharron L. McElmeel notes, "What could be more credible than the author's own site providing information about a book?"

So, how do you make your Web site educator-friendly?

First, cover the basics. It's better to start with a small, well-designed site and build thoughtfully over time than to upload several unorganized and incomplete pages.

Remember that this is your "professional face" to prospective readers. Kid-friendly and colorful may work. Cutesy and homemade won't. When in doubt, err on the side of easy navigation, clean lines, and a limited color palette. Wait until the site is ready before uploading. "Under construction" signs suggest a lack of commitment. On the flip side, think twice before adding cutting edge technology. Freezing your visitors' computer screens won't help you (or your book) win any new readers.

One question is whether the focus of the site should be you or your debut book itself. Your byline is your brand. In today's crowded market, it will be enough of a challenge for readers to learn your name. When it comes to awareness-raising, you don't want to have to start over with each new title. If you're planning a long-term career, first launch an author/illustrator site and then consider a book-specific site as a supplemental marketing tool. For example, although we both have official author sites, my co-author Greg Leitich Smith and I decided to launch www.santa-knows.com to promote our picture book, *Santa Knows*. "The real marketing window for a holiday book is only open for a couple of months," he explains. "You have to look for any opportunity to maximize outreach."

One exception to the author-site-first guideline would be in the case of a book series. Before you take on the job of launching a series tie-in site, however, check first to see if your publisher is willing to provide one for you.

Ideally, your site should launch at about the same time review copies are sent, usually six months prior to publication. Each new book listing should be added to the site on the same schedule. But it's never too late to promote a book in print.

If budget allows, research the possibility of hiring a Web designer. The time saved and professional results may well be worth the money. A handful of designers even specialize in children's-YA book creator sites. Ask established published authors and illustrators in your local writing community or on listservs for recommendations.

In the alternative, investigate pre-formatted options. The Authors Guild, for example, offers such sites to members for nominal fees.

"I chose the Authors Guild as host because they're inexpensive, it's a good organization, and they use a convenient template without bells and whistles that a simple-minded person such as I can update in seconds," says author Leda Schubert (www.ledaschubert.com).

What to include on your site

At a minimum, include a brief biography and your photograph along with basic publication information (cover art, title, author, illustrator, publisher, publication date, target audience age range, and ISBN). The cover art should be large enough to see clearly and, if possible, include a link to a larger, high-resolution image. Clear titles for each page, emphasizing the title and author/illustrator names, will help facilitate search engines. So will choosing your name as the URL. "A name like supercoolwriter.com is not going to be as easily discovered by someone looking for you as cynthialeitichsmith.com," says Anne Irza-Leggat, educational marketing supervisor at Candlewick Press.

Links to the publisher's Web site and/or the sites of your co-creators also are helpful and courteous.

Market Yourself As A Speaker

Your Web site can help sell you as a speaker to school groups.

Publicist Susan Raab of Raab Associates says, "For many authors and illustrators, schools have a significant impact on their careers because they offer opportunities for doing school visits, workshops, and other events that provide substantial income separate from the revenue any given book brings in."

You may want to create a separate "events" page, which includes information on your school visits and young author workshops. School visits are made up of one to five classroom or auditorium presentations during the regular class schedule. Young author workshops may be distinguished in that they take place on weekends or after school and the students involved are participating by choice.

In each case, include information on the types of programs you offer.

According to Anne Irza-Leggat, educational marketing supervisor at Candlewick Press, it's important to include: (a) whether you do donation events; (b) your rates; (c) the number of programs you're willing to do in a day; and (d) any preferences when it comes to student age range and audience size.

Author Tanya Lee Stone (www.tanyastone.com) provides an "About Tanya" section, which includes three different lengths of biographies, links to interviews with her, links to articles and reviews she's written, speaking information, and downloadable photos. "These things have really helped people access the information they need," she says, "especially when inviting me as a speaker or having students learn more about an author."

But not all author/illustrator visits occur in "real space." Chat technology has made it possible for speakers to participate in an online question-and-answer session with classroom groups. Supply the same information to planners as you would for an in-person visit as well as any specific technological requirements.

Finally, the page should include information on ordering your books. Many publishers offer related pages on their own sites that can be easily linked for a complete overview.

Children's-YA author Tanya Lee Stone (www.tanyastone.com) offers a printer-friendly, comprehensible title list of her books. She explains, "This was a suggestion I got from a librarian who commented that she's surprised more authors don't have their own complete list somewhere."

Beyond the basics, offer visitors a taste of each book. Consider including an excerpt or interior illustration or link to these on your publisher's site, if provided.

Keep in mind that copyright law applies to the Internet. Authors should request permission from illustrators to highlight an example of their interior art. Illustrators should request authors' permission to feature text excerpts.

Include award listings and review excerpts as they arise. Those from established print journals and/or blurbs from well-known authors or youth literature experts tend to be the most persuasive. Moreover, reviews, too, are subject to copyright and may not be wholly reproduced without permission. Use short quotes, and link to the source Web site.

Keeping this information up-to-date is critical. Interior links should always be in working order. The occasional exterior link may be unavoidable, but do your best to keep these current. New books should be added promptly. Such maintenance will preserve the site's credibility and effectiveness as a promotional tool.

Offer teachers and school librarians reasons to share your book with students.

"If your book has good curricular tie-ins, it pays to make that obvious on your site," says children's author-poet Hope Vestergaard (www.hopevestergaard.com).

Curriculum guides and related activities are especially sought after. These may include discussion questions and links to curriculum-related sites.

"I was a teacher," explains young adult author Gail Giles, "and I know I'd pick up a book that has a teacher's guide before a book that didn't—if the books were essentially equal."

Buzzeo adds, "Content standard based curriculum activities are much appreciated. Teachers do not have time to teach things simply for the fun of it anymore in this age of standardized testing. Thoroughly familiarize yourself with national and state content standards before writing support material." She recommends hiring a member of the educational, library, and children's writing community to write guides.

Children's author and reading expert Tracie Vaughn Zimmer not only is available for hire. She also posts the guides she writes to her own site (www.tracievaughnzimmer.com), offering a "directory" that attracts visitors.

"Since most of my visitors are teachers," Vaughn says, "I decided to appeal directly to them. Teachers are visual people (think bulletin boards and their wonderful bright classrooms) so my directory is like a bulletin board with all the beautiful book covers speaking for themselves. I can feature new guides this way too."

She adds that dividing the books into age categories (along with one for poetry) makes the directory easier to navigate.

"I also don't add a lot of design to the guides themselves," Vaughn says, "so that teachers can use as little ink and paper necessary (both often on stingy little budgets) and just dive into activities and lessons with their students."

Teacher guides may be augmented by background on the crafting of the book.

"If authors and illustrators will provide information about process, research, and revision that applies to specific titles, they will help educators adopt them more readily," Palmquist says.

Question-and-answer interviews might touch on such subjects as the author's and/or illustrator's background in the field, inspiration behind the book, required research, challenges in bringing the story to life, the revision process, and themes.

This same information could also be shared in a story-behind-the-story article.

"I think the 'How I Wrote It' section is part of the educator's extended experience for the class or reader," says Giles (www.gailgiles.com). "I put it there to enhance the reading experience and make it really easy for the teacher to use the book in the classroom."

Such Q&A interviews and articles may be further supplemented with bibliographies of books or other resources used for research in writing the story.

Librarian Sharon McElmeel encourages a global approach—making your focus wider than just yourself and your own book(s). "The 'online presence' should not be merely a sales site but rather should give more than take. The idea is to introduce you as an author/illustrator to more educators, and educators will find your site more often if you are gracious and include the titles and authors of other books that might be collaborative reading material."

Consider the author's/illustrator's expertise and each book for special opportunities. These are limited only by the site creator's imagination.

Children's nonfiction author Fred Bortz (www.fredbortz.com) offers a set of "Ask Dr. Fred" questions that includes suggestions for asking good science questions. He says, "I get an average of 30 to 50 visitors per day who are wondering why Pluto isn't a planet anymore."

Debut author Rebecca Stead's novel *First Light* (www.firstlightbook.com) takes place in

Q&A With a Web Designer

Lisa Firke of Hit Those Keys: Creative Encouragement, Copy Editing, Web Design (www.hitthosekeys.com) specializes in the design of children's and young adult book author sites.

What do you think makes a good author site? What elements are essential?
Perhaps the most important thing is something the average site visitor never sees—the underlying markup and coding. (The most engaging content in the world won't be appreciated if it shows up mangled or not at all.)

Second, the purpose of the site should be clear from the first glance. It's about a person, an author, and that author's work. It should look particular and unique and it should suit the person it's about.

Third, a site shouldn't be too fancy for its own good. Links should look like links, and sections of the site should have clear labels. Think of it this way: as a writer you work hard to make your meanings clear and valuable. Your Web site should reflect the same kind of care.

What considerations do you recommend to authors in selecting a designer?
Start with personal preference: Do you *like* the designer's other work? (Check for credits on sites you like to locate designers). Sound out the designer. Do you feel comfortable describing what you want and asking questions about how things are done? Hire someone you can talk to, whose taste and judgment you trust.

Look to hire someone who is at ease with HTML and CSS and who can tell the difference between the "golden section" (a design principle) and the "golden arches" (the ugly but well-known branding of a fast food chain).

Consider the practical: what can you afford? Think about this carefully. What's cheapest up front might not be best. A poorly-made, cookie-cutter site won't serve you well. Budget carefully, but avoid stinting on costs. Fees vary widely, but a professional will give you an estimate up front.

What mistakes do you see in author sites as you're surfing the Web?
A lot of author sites fall into this tricky abyss where the site looks both mass-produced *and* amateurish—certainly not what you want.

Pitfalls include:
- Problems with type: text that's too large or too small for comfortable reading; too many different font styles; large blocks of italic or all-capped text.
- Problems with color and/or graphics: jaggy images; jarring color combinations; busy backgrounds; unnecessary or distracting animated effects; "school picture"-ish author head shots.
- Problems with performance: slow-loading pages; confusing navigation; content that's inaccessible to visitors with disabilities.
- Problems with copy: gross spelling or grammatical errors; or key information falls "below the fold" (the first span of the screen before it becomes necessary to scroll down).

What advice do you have for do-it-yourself-ers?
Take your time and keep it simple. If you're not intimidated by technology, it can be fun. Invest in a few good tools and references and learn to use them.

Greenland. One character's father researches climate change. Another character lives in an imagined world within the ice cap. "I wrote a Q&A fact sheet with input from scientists, interviewed a guy about what it's really like to dig snow pits (and why) and posted links to educational sites," Stead says. "I also put in some bits of history/science that inspired me—about sled dogs, Volkswagen's secret testing ground in Greenland, oak trees, etc."

Readers' theater adaptations of picture books, short stories, and chapters are popular with classroom groups. These work best with dialogue-heavy texts.

Coloring pages also are an option for illustrated books. Again, authors should obtain permission from illustrators before making art available for this purpose.

Children's author-illustrator Katie Davis' site (www.katiedavis.com) includes activity sheets and games made with a program called Puzzlemaker. "I can input specific words from my books," she says, "and they'll get imported into a crossword puzzle."

Recipes tend to attract traffic from teachers and parents alike.

"My 'Hairy Toe Cookies' is one of the biggest entry pages to my site . . . a lot from teachers at Halloween time," says Shutta Crum (www.shuttacrum.com), author of *Who Took My Hairy Toe?* (Albert Whitman, 2001).

Ultimately, your author site should be a reflection of your creative and professional self, a place to celebrate books and writing, and a way of reaching young readers and their champions. Educators are such heroes. Design and maintain your site to offer them all the encouragement and support they need to integrate your books into their schools.

A King's Legacy

*Five Champions on Winning the
Coretta Scott King Award*

by Kelly Milner Halls

Launched in 1969 by librarians Mabel McKissick and Glyndon Flynt Greer and publisher John Carroll, the Coretta Scott King Award called for a new public awareness. It asked the world of children's literature to herald and bring to the forefront books about African American people and experiences. Brown vs. Board of Education had overturned the segregation of schools 15 years earlier. But the diversity of books had not kept pace with the diversity of the students they were meant to serve.

This award, named for Dr. Martin Luther King's window (and Greer's good friend) was a determined attempt at correcting that inequity—an effort to shed a shining light on the rich history of this nation's African American population including the skilled writers who chose to bring those stories to life. But it wasn't always an easy road.

According to E.J. Josey, past president of the American Library Association, "there were those who opposed the establishment of a minority award." But Josey harbored the fledgling award under the ALA's Social Responsibilities Round Table. And despite opposition, the Coretta Scott King Award became the official award of the SRRT in 1979.

Now a branch of the ALA's Ethnic Multicultural Information Exchange Round Table (EMIERT), the CSK awards—given each January at the ALA Midwinter Conference—celebrate and encourage "the artistic expression of the African American experience." And recipients are among the nation's finest professionals.

How do winning authors feel about the endowment, which includes a plaque and a $1,000 cash prize? We caught up with five recipients—**Christopher Paul Curtis** (*Bud, Not Buddy*, 2000); **Sharon Draper** (*Copper Sun*, 2007; *Forged by Fire*, 1998); **Nikki Grimes** (*Bronx Masquerade*, 2003); **Angela Johnson** (*The First Part Last*, 2004; *Heaven*, 1999; *Toning the Sweep*, 1994); and **Julius Lester** (*Days of Tears*, 2006)—and asked them about their CSK Award experience. Their answers, as you'll soon discover, paint a vibrant picture of their prowess and their pride.

What was your reaction when you discovered you'd received the Coretta Scott King Award?

Christopher Paul Curtis: It's almost a cliché, but I was very surprised and pleased. In my readings before I won the award I always used It as a guide for what would be a good quality book, so to win the CSK was most pleasing.

KELLY MILNER HALLS has been a full-time freelance writer for the past 20 years. Her work has appeared in the *Chicago Tribune*, the *Washington Post*, the *Atlanta Journal Constitution*, *Writer's Digest*, *Highlight for Children*, *DIG*, *Ask*, *Teen PEOPLE* and dozens of other publications. She has nearly 30 published children's books including the award winning *Tales of the Cryptids*, *Dinosaur Parade* and *Albino Animals*. She lives in Spokane, WA with two daughters, two dogs, too many cats and a four-foot iguana.

Sharon Draper: I've been fortunate enough to receive the award four times. The first was when I received what was then called the Genesis Award (Now called the John Steptoe New Talent Award) for *Tears of a Tiger*. I was the first person to receive it and nobody knew exactly what it was, but it was clear it was really significant. The second time was for *Forged by Fire* in 1998 when it won the full literary award. The third time was for *The Battle of Jericho*, which was an Honor book, and most recently for *Copper Sun*, which was also awarded the full literary award. Getting that phone call on a chilly January morning is *always* a real thrill.

Nikki Grimes: I was both surprised and excited. I had just about given up hope of every winning it. Which just goes to show that one should never give up!

Angela Johnson: I have been thrilled each time that I have won the Coretta Scott King. I believe with most people there are always a myriad of emotions when you are informed that you've won any award. I am always astounded. I always seem to experience shock, joy and temporary incredulous pessimism (always believing someone has made a mistake and shall be calling me back to say so).

Julius Lester: Well, it was a Sunday night and I was watching *Law & Order: CI*, which can be very complicated. When the phone rang, I almost didn't answer because I was concentrating on the plot. But, annoyed, I answered, and then there was a woman telling me that *Day of Tears* had been awarded the CSK Award. Part of me was in disbelief and part of me wanted to get back to the show. It took several days before the news really sank in.

How has that award impacted your career as a writer?

Curtis: I think any award that has a reputation as solid as the CSK can only help a writer's career. It means more people will look at your work.

Draper: I believe that because of the awards doors have been opened for me, and opportunities given to me that I might not have received otherwise.

Grimes: The CSK award raises the profile of any book it honors. It guarantees the book will go to paperback, which, of course, extends the life of the book, keeping it in print longer than it might otherwise be. Most importantly, though, it encourages the winners to continue to pursue excellence in their chosen field. It has done all of those things for me.

Johnson: The Coretta Scott King Award is always easily recognizable and I am sure it has impacted my career positively. People tend to feel a bit more comfortable buying award-winning books I suppose because they feel they have already been vetted.

Lester: Given that I've published more than 40 books since 1968, I don't think the award has had that great an impact on my career. My very first children's book, *To Be a Slave*, received a Newbery Honor Award in 1969. That had a much greater impact on my career, coming as it did at the beginning of the career. However, the CSK Award has meant that many more children will read *Day of Tears* than might have otherwise. For that reason, I am very grateful the book received such an honor.

Why is the Coretta Scott King Award important to the realm of literature for young readers?

Curtis: Since there are relatively few books published which are written by, for or about African Americans, the award is particularly important to highlight those of special merit.

Draper: Young adult literature is often overlooked and undervalued by the general public and awards like the CSK offer veracity, dignity and respect to the field.

Grimes: Multicultural literature is an important tool for preparing young readers to live in a diverse society. Awards like the CSK and the Belpre shine a light on some of the best of those books. Without the attention that comes from such awards, many a teacher, librarian, or reading specialist would miss out on these titles.

Johnson: The award successfully opens avenues for more children to read multicultural literature.

Lester: The CSK Award is important because it brings greater attention to books that might otherwise have been ignored. The award gives the imprimatur of the American Library Association to these books, and ALA is highly respected among librarians and teachers.

What doors does the award open that might not otherwise be available to you?

Curtis: Once again, the award gives an author exposure which is one of the most important aspects of a writing career.

Draper: Writing opportunities. Speaking opportunities. Increased connection with librarians and teachers and publishers.

Johnson: The CSK award has indeed opened doors for me. The writing world does take notice of awards. But I must say that when I walk through those doors I am always greeted kindly as a writer and not just an award winner.

Lester: I don't think of the award as being for me. The award is for the book, and because the book is a CSK award winner, many libraries will feel that they have to have at least one copy on the shelves. Without the award, their purchase of the book would be seen as an option. With the award, purchasing the book becomes necessary.

What qualities have you noticed each of the award books have in common, if any?

Curtis: Speaking generally, the CSK award seems to take notice of books that portray African American life in a positive and uplifting way.

Grimes: It is difficult to answer this question without sounding vain or self-serving, but I would hope that each of us has broken ground in some way, or that we have contributed something substantial to the world of children's literature by and about African Americans.

Johnson: Happily, as far as I know, the only thing any of the King award books have in common is that their protagonists are African American. Like all other literature the characters are unique to each story, and by virtue of the books winning the CSK award I would take for granted that the stories are extremely well written, engaging, but speak to children or young adults of all cultures.

Lester: I don't read children's literature simply because I do not want to be unconsciously influenced by what someone else might be doing. So, I've not read any of the other award books.

When you wrote your story, did the award ever cross your mind as a possibility?

Curtis: No. I think it would be both foolish and counter-productive to try to write toward an award. The author needs to focus all of his or her attention on telling a good story.

Draper: I write for young people, not for awards. A writer can go crazy trying to out-think and out-write an award committee. I just write. The awards are icing on the cake.

Grimes: You can't write a book to win an award. Your focus has got to be telling the story you want to tell, reaching the audience you want to reach, and crafting the best book possible. Awards are gravy.

Johnson: I never write books with winning an award in mind. Anyone who does will more than likely be disappointed. I write because a character or plot has engaged me and needs a life in fiction.

Lester: Yes. I knew the story was a powerful one and that I had written the story in a form that was different. So, the idea crossed my mind. Then again, like most writers, I think anything I write should be given every prize available.

How important is your public speaking to advancing your books? Is it more impactful than the award?

Curtis: I'm really not sure which is more impactful, the award or the speaking. They really go hand in hand in advancing and promoting the books.

Draper: When people hear me speak about a certain title, they generally buy the book. It's the personal connection that makes the difference.

Grimes: The Caldecott and the Newbery are probably the only awards that substitute for the exposure an author gets from speaking tours. The CSK award can certainly make an author more appealing as a speaker, but, at this point, it simply does not have the same cache as the Caldecott and the Newbery.

Johnson: As a rule I don't do much public speaking, but the little that I do may or may not have that much impact on advancing my books. I usually go places that have had my books around for years. I've been at the writing thing for a while. But I would hope that I've excited the few kids I've spoken to.

Lester: I haven't done much public speaking since the year 2000. I have never been one to do much publicity about my books. Doing so takes time from writing and other things. I know that publishers expect writers to do a lot of publicity when their books come out. That's the norm now. But when I got published for the first time back in 1968, that was not the norm. I have done publicity, however, and was never convinced that I sold very many books as a result. However, if Oprah asked me to come on her show, that would be an entirely different story.

Do awards get kids more excited about reading? Or are they aimed at adults who work with young people?

Curtis: I really believe the awards are aimed more at adults. They are in effect a seal of approval that says, ''A knowledgeable group of professionals has read this and think it's worth your while to do the same.''

Draper: Kids don't care about awards. They care about good stories (with great covers, by the way) that keep them spellbound. Adults who work with young people care about awards because it can help them make decisions about which books to offer to students.

Johnson: Yes I think that children do get excited about awards. They tend to correlate awards with success and quality. Of course they usually think of awards in terms of television, glitz and screaming throngs. It makes me smile. But when I do speak to kids I always stress that the work of writing is my true award. For most writers it must be so as many of us will never win anything so we must always work hard and be true to our craft.

Awards can also be helpful tool for librarians and educators who are inundated with hundreds of titles a year and are looking for quality books for children on limited budgets.

Lester: The strange thing about writing children's books is that we write for people who don't buy books. We need the parents, librarians and teachers to bring the books to the attention of children. Awards certainly help in that process. I would think that awards mean much more to adults. However, there are awards given in many states to books chosen by children. I've had books nominated for a number of these and received one from the state of Nebraska and another from school children in Detroit.

What advice do you have for new writers hoping to follow in your footsteps?

Curtis: First, write everyday. Second, have fun with your writing. Third, be patient with yourself. And finally, once you learn how to tell a story, ignore all the rules and develop your own style.

Draper: Write what's in your heart. Write it well. Keep your audience first in your mind, and read what you have written through their eyes, not yours.

Grimes: Write the best book you can. At the end of the day, you can't worry about awards. You can't write to win an award, so why try? What matters is creating a story from your heart, crafting a work that will reach your audience, that will move them in some way, that will elevate them, that will inspire them, that will touch their hearts. If that book you write wins you an award, that's wonderful, but it's gravy. Your job as a writer is to write what's true, to spin a story that will take the reader on an unforgettable journey. Do that well and you have your reward—no matter what.

Johnson: I tell future writers I meet to read, read, read. I believe they need to get a sense of voice and place in other's writing. I also tell them to ask themselves when writing—is their story true? For even if you are writing fantasy or science fiction your characters and plots can be fantastic but must follow the same concepts of any good literature. But the most important thing is not to pander in the craft. Write from your heart, soul and any muse that happens upon you.

Lester: My advice to writers is fairly simple. First, read, read, read. One cannot expect to write without having a good knowledge of what has been written. Also, reading helps you identify what writing styles appeal to you, which don't, subject matter that engages you. Two, write. I learned a lot about putting words together from the copious letters I used to write as well as the journal I kept. Three, rewrite, rewrite, rewrite. Writing is very hard work and you have to put in a lot of work to make the words say what you want them to say, to make a sentence sound like you want it to sound. I rewrite constantly. There are some pages in books that I rewrote 25 times. Four, maybe my footsteps are not the ones to follow. Perhaps there is another writer whose footsteps fit one better. Or, maybe not even a writer. I've probably been more influenced by music and art than other writers.

Where do you keep your award?

Curtis: The award hangs in a place of honor in my library.

Draper: I have a display case in my living room which proudly shows my various awards as well as my glass apple collection. I have over a hundred crystal and hand-blown glass apples.

Grimes: My CSK award and honors share a wall in my office. That wall serves as inspiration, pushing me to continue striving for excellence in everything that I write.

Johnson: My Coretta Scott King awards are at my parent's home where they smile at them every time they pass them—I'm sure.

Lester: Hmmm. Interesting question. I have no idea where it is, and let me explain. As I stated before, I don't think of the award as being mine. The award is for the book; I know that I wrote the book but I don't think of the award as being mine. What brings me joy is seeing the CSK Award Medal on the cover of the book. And that's where the award belongs.

Sherman Alexie

Elevating—and Shaking Up—YA

by Kelly Milner Halls

Shattering expectations has come naturally for 2007 National Book Award winning author Sherman Alexie.

As an infant born with a hydrocephalic brain condition, he survived surgery experts thought would kill him. As a young boy with a prognosis of mental retardation, he read and understood parts of Steinbeck's *The Grapes of Wrath* at five. As a teenager on the Spokane Indian Reservation, he enrolled in different public school because he thought it would offer him a better education.

Much of Alexie's early life experience is reflected in *The Absolutely True Diary of a Part-Time Indian*, his NBA Young People's Literature title, published by Little, Brown and Company in 2007. The brilliant balance between heartbreak and humor is fictionalized, but chock full of the realities that made Sherman Alexie the storyteller he is today.

Though he never dreamed of being an author in those early days at Reardon High School, Alexie admits he was inspired to write and read well by an exceptional English teacher. "She had done her masters on the John F. Kennedy assassination," Alexie remembers. It was a topic his father had also discussed with great interest. That common link, along with the pantheon of literature she offered, formed a connection that remains today.

"She has cameos in all my books," Alexie says. "There is usually someone named Dorothy, in tribute to her."

If writing wasn't always his life's goal, what was? Alexie admits, he wanted to be a doctor. "I think a lot of smart poor kids have that goal," he says, "especially smart poor brown kids, because it's one of the most prestigious careers. And I was really sick as a kid, so being a pediatrician was the dream."

An aversion to dead bodies forced Alexie to rethink his medical aspirations and led him to a poetry workshop at Washington State University in Pullman. Thanks to the keen instincts of WSU professor Alex Kuo who taught the workshop (and who remains one of Alexie's closest friends), a bright new path almost immediately revealed itself.

"On the first day of class, Alex handed me this anthology, *Songs from This Earth on Turtles Back*," Alexie says, "And I was blown away." Edited by Joseph Bruchac, the collection of

KELLY MILNER HALLS has been a full-time freelance writer for the past 20 years. Her work has appeared in the *Chicago Tribune*, the *Washington Post*, the *Atlanta Journal Constitution*, *Writer's Digest*, *Highlight for Children*, *DIG*, *Ask*, *Teen PEOPLE* and dozens of other publications. She has nearly 30 published children's books including the award winning *Tales of the Cryptids*, *Dinosaur Parade* and *Albino Animals*. She lives in Spokane, WA with two daughters, two dogs, too many cats and a four-foot iguana.

poetry by contemporary American Indians authors introduced Alexie to a new vision. To his delight, Alexie discovered almost any topic could be transformed into legitimate poetry—almost any theme could apply.

"I wrote my first poems and turned them in the second week of class," Alexie remembers. With Kuo's guidance and encouragement, those early poems became Alexie's debut poetry collection, *The Business of Fancydancing*, published in 1991. The same year, he won the Washington State Arts Commission Poetry Fellowship, based on his obvious potential.

Wellpinit, Washington's native son was a star on the rise, and critics took note of his

Reprinted with permission of Little, Brown and Company Books for Young Readers.

Sherman Alexie's first book for young readers, *The Absolutely True Diary of a Part-Time Indian*, won the National Book Award in 2007. Says *School Library Journal* of Alexie's main character, 14-year-old Arnold Spirit (in a starred review): "The teen's determination to both improve himself and overcome poverty, despite handicaps of birth, circumstance, and race, delivers a positive message in a low-key manner."

creative prowess and at least two common threads. They recognized Alexie had an intuitive, even instinctual way with words. Fellow Washington author Chris Crutcher calls it, "a brilliance that can't be learned, but simply is." And they saw that his authenticity was crystal clear.

Though he may not have known it as his career began, Alexie was destined to break stereotypes. And he continues to do so as an author—most recently of young adult literature.

Apart from a short flirtation with alcohol in college, Alexie's rise to recognition has been an exceptionally good one. He grew up on the Spokane Indian Reservation where poverty was the norm, but his family was in tact, and he says, "we were never the poorest people on the block."

But Alexie was keenly aware of the struggles in close proximity. "Nothing went wrong for me in a major way," he admits, "but things went wrong for the people I loved—my friends, my family, and my tribe." The pain and loneliness he felt and witnessed gave birth to a writer's voice that was universally true.

Spokane reporter, Dan Webster, who watched the author's rise from the hometown bleachers says public speaking helped sell the brilliance of the writer.

"That's what really made the difference," Webster says, "his ability to read his own work. He has a great stage presence. In the early years, he would actually play his own characters, especially Thomas Builds a Fire. And those of us who had the privilege of seeing him hone his stuff at Auntie's Bookstore in the 1980s were extremely fortunate."

Drawn from his short story collection, The Lone Ranger and Tonto Fistfight in Heaven (1994), Thomas Builds a Fire was a reservation storyteller, largely ignored by his neighbors until he held the postmaster hostage. The colorful character defended himself in court with a string of remarkable stories, including a past life recollection of being a pony—the lone survivor of a horse herd massacre. Even in prison, his stories made him well known.

The same short story collection was adapted as Alexie's first screenplay and critically acclaimed film called Smoke Signals in 1998 staring Adam Beach (best known for his work in NBC's Law & Order, Special Victims Unit, and the 2007 HBO mini-series Bury My Heart at Wounded Knee). Like Alexie, Beach grew up on the reservation, a member of the Lake Manitoba First Nation.

Thousands of readers who have shared reporter Webster's experience agree. Alexie is warm and engaging in his public presentations. He seems at home and at ease in any setting. But Alexie says the opposite is often true.

"When I'm on," he admits, "I'm actually highly uncomfortable. That's why I turn to humor. If you start making people laugh, it not only makes them feel better, it takes the pressure off. But the truth is, I'm very much an introvert. Aside from my kids and my wife, I spend most of my time alone. Most serious writers I know are the same."

That uneasy feeling is central to most of Alexie's fiction—including his teenage protagonists. But of his first 17 published works—11 books of poetry, three short story collections, and three novels (not to mention two screenplays)—none were considered young adult. Only his most recent novel, The Absolutely True Diary of a Part-Time Indian was marketed for kids.

What set The Absolutely True Diary of a Part-Time Indian apart? According to Alexie, the answer is almost nothing. "I've always written about young men," he says, "and a lot of books about teenagers. So YA is not a big subject matter leap for me. But what sets this book apart as YA is the fact that the protagonist is not looking back. It's not told in past tense, but rather in the now."

He does say the first three drafts were more like his work for adult readers. But the editorial revisions were relatively minor. "There was a slightly different vocabulary," he says, "a slightly different sentence structure. And I think in general, YA is more driven by the narrative

Sherman Alexie Reading List

Though Sherman Alexie burst onto the young adult literature scene in 2007, his body of work spans almost two decades. His bibliography is listed below to make exploration of his craftsmanship a little easier. For reviews, excerpts and other information about Sherman Alexie, see his website at www.shermanalexie.com.

- *The Business of Fancy Dancing* (poetry, 1991)
- *I Would Steal Horses* (poetry, 1993)
- *Old Shirts & New Skins* (poetry, 1993)
- *First Indian on the Moon* (poetry, 1993)
- *The Lone Ranger and Tonto Fistfight in Heaven* (short stories, 1993)
- *Seven Mourning Songs for the Cedar Flute I Have Yet to Learn to Play* (poetry, 1993)
- *Reservation Blues* (novel, 1995)
- *Water Flowing Home* (poetry, 1996)
- *Indian Killer* (novel, 1996)
- *The Summer of Black Widows* (poetry, 1996)
- *The Man Who Loves Salmon* (poetry, 1998)
- *Smoke Signals* (screenplay, 1998)
- *The Toughest Indian in the World* (short stories, 2000)
- *One Stick Song* (poetry, 2000)
- *The Business of Fancydancing* (screenplay, 2003)
- *Ten Little Indians* (short stories, 2003)
- *Il powwow della fine del mondo* (poetry, 2005)
- *Dangerous Astronomy* (poetry, 2005)
- *Flight* (novel, 2007)
- *The Absolutely True Diary of a Part-Time Indian* (YA novel, 2007)

than the lyrical. But my writing style has always been narrative driven. So YA just meant fewer semicolons.''

Even if his other books were written for adults, teens were anything but unfamiliar. "Teachers had used my books in high school classrooms for years," he admits. So that part wasn't unusual. What was unique was the young adult literature promotional realm—the American Library Association, International Reading Association and National Council of Teachers of English gatherings and their reaction to Alexie's presentations.

What was the key distinction that set YA events apart from adult events? "Other young adult writers show up," he says. "That simply doesn't happen in the adult world. YA authors, teachers and librarians are not afraid to be fans. And there is much less artifice.''

Dealing with young people, Alexie says, ''forces people to be more nakedly emotional; more honest about your teen experience and more willing to carry that experience forward into the rest of their lives. A part of me is always 16, so I can certainly understand that.''

He is also overwhelmed by the positive reaction to his work, especially *The Absolutely True Diary of a Part-Time Indian* and the National Book Award honor. ''There is nothing better than seeing a kid fall in love with my books. It reminds me of how I fell in love with books when I was their age.

''I'm like a virgin again,'' he continues. ''I've had a long and really successful career, but this book has made it all new again. I went to the gym the other day, and a couple of guys came up to me and said, 'You've hit the big time.' In truth, I was already there, but this new enthusiasm is an amazing luxury I'm very happy about.''

Was the National Book Award a surprise? ''It was,'' he says. ''When I got the call, I vomited a little bit in lamb. I had lamb for dinner, and threw up a little. Then my wife and my kids starting kissing me, and all I could think was they were kissing lamb vomit.''

Spokane reporter Dan Webster, however, saw the honor coming. ''Since they created the Young Adult category, the book was a natural winner,'' he says. ''If you've read it, and you're familiar with Sherman's life, there's not much in the first half that surprises you. It's barely veiled memoir, both better and worse than what he really went through. But just at that point, the book becomes an impassioned plea for tolerance and compassion that can't help but move you.''

Can other writers mimic Alexie's success? They can, he says, but only by creating a path of their own.

''You shouldn't have to think or worry about the respect of others,'' he says, ''But you should pay attention to your audience. Listen to what they are saying. In terms of the National Book Award, it was interesting because there was less coverage. In the traditional literary blogs, no one talks about YA books. I found that amusing, but I always knew the real test would be the kids and the librarians.

That audience offered ample feedback, even if press outlets came up short. And that's okay with Alexie. ''You don't write YA for canonization,'' he says. ''You write YA because it's so immediate and so alive. A book—*your* book—can be life altering for a kid out there, and you can't say the same about adult literature. In YA, you're reaching people when they are just figuring things out.''

And according to Alexie, it just doesn't get any better than that.

First Books

Debut Picture Books
Authors & Illustrators

by Meg Leder

What do a gay guinea pig, an iguana on vacation, a princess-eating baby dragon, and a sulky fish have a common?

While the question sounds like it may be the set-up to a complicated and probably not-very-good joke, the answer is much more simple: all four have come to life in brilliant new picture books—*Uncle Bobby's Wedding* (Putnam); *Cesar Takes a Break* (Sterling); *Hush, Little Dragon* (Abrams); and *The Pout-Pout Fish* (Farrar, Straus & Giroux).

The four animals have some other things in common: All were created by first-time authors—**Sarah Brannen**, **Susan Collins Thoms**, **Boni Ashburn**, and **Deborah Diesen**—who describe the experience of their acceptance calls as "unreal," "amazing," "happy," and "I was floating all day. To tell the truth, I am still floating." (First-time illustrator **Dan Hanna** adds to their experiences: "It was like I was in Heaven.") All four characters were also dreamed up by people who value critique groups, know that it takes persistence to get published, and find quite a bit of joy in reading themselves.

There are some differences, too. Two were inspired by the lives of children around them—Brannen decided to write *Uncle Bobby's Wedding* based on her niece's desire to be a flower girl; Ashburn found the spark for *Hush, Little Dragon* after singing one too many lullabies to her kids. One was based on a real-life animal—Thoms wrote *Cesar Takes a Break* after hearing about a renegade iguana at a local elementary school. And *The Pout-Pout Fish* was based on children *and* the animal world: Diesen and her son discovered that the expression you make when you're pouting looks like fish lips, and illustrator Hanna found the prototype for the Pout-Pout fish while diving.

One thing they do share: All four characters will leave children coming back to their stories again and again, in the process creating devoted readers who will be ready for each of their creators' next book, and the next, and the next . . .

Sarah S. Brannen
Uncle Bobby's Wedding
(Putnam)
www.sarahbrannen.com

For artist Sarah Brannen, the idea for her first book—a story about a guinea pig wedding—originated in part thanks to a

---

MEG LEDER is an editor at Perigee Books. Her writing has appeared in *Cincinnati Magazine*, *Writer's Digest*, and *The Bellingham Review*.

persistent family member: her niece. "When my youngest niece was around five or six, she started dropping heavy-handed hints that it would be nice if I got married," she says. "It wasn't that she was thinking of my happiness, but that she wanted to be a flower girl. It seemed like a very common wish for little girls, so I started thinking about doing some kind of wedding story in which a little girl ended up being a flower girl."

Brannen began imagining the character who would become Chloe—the little girl guinea pig in *Uncle Bobby's Wedding* who's worried that when her favorite uncle gets married, she won't be special to him anymore—around the same time same-sex marriage was legalized in Massachusetts. "The news was full of stories of people marrying with such intense joy— people who had never thought they would be allowed to marry, finally being able to fully commit to a life together. It was very moving, and it just occurred to me, one spring day, to make the couple in my story both men."

And so, *Uncle Bobby's Wedding* was born. In the book, which Brannen wrote and illustrated, Chloe gets to know her Uncle Bobby's friend Jamie—the three go to the ballet, have ice cream sodas, try sailing, and toast marshmallows together—agrees to be their flower girl, and learns that she'll always be special to her Uncle Bobby and her new Uncle Jamie.

The book literally exudes happiness and delight, from the charming moment Jamie imitates the ballet dancer and Chloe laughs so hard "she got soda up her nose," to the joyous wedding reception, filled with guinea pigs dancing under a full moon. It's evident that the sense of happiness comes from Brannen herself, as the book represents a homecoming to her true love—illustrating.

As an art student at Harvard and University of Pennsylvania, Brannen was "always happiest doing drawings and watercolors that might be considered 'illustrations,'" she says. "However, in college and graduate school, if a professor called your work an illustration, it was criticism amounting to an insult."

"I knew I was never as happy painting as I was illustrating. Even taking my illustrations out and looking at them made me happy, when I was struggling with my 'real' work. It took far too long for me to listen to what my heart was telling me."

But in 2001, she did listen and began pursing children's illustration seriously. Along with that came an interest in writing as well. "I just did it to teach myself the basics, but I found that I enjoyed it as much as illustrating, and it's wonderful to be able to create the whole book, story and pictures together."

Brannen mailed her first book dummy in March 2002, sending out several other books as well as illustration samples over the next three years. In 2005, she got a break: an agent. "A friend of mine was interested in Karen Klockner and I was looking for an agent. Karen sounded perfect, so I sent her some work and we e-mailed a few times." Klockner, the mother of a figure skater, was interested in a book Brannen had proposed on figure skater Johnny Weir, and offered to represent it. "As we worked together on that, we both decided that we should formalize the relationship and I officially signed with Transatlantic Literary Agency," Brannen says. She wrote *Uncle Bobby's Wedding* that summer and fall. (Incidentally, figure skater Johnny Weir named the main character of *Uncle Bobby's Wedding*.)

While Brannen is usually drawn to a particular story because she wants to do illustrations for it, with *Uncle Bobby's Wedding*, writing the story came first. "I did a lot of drafts in the beginning. I would finish one draft, think about it, and then begin a new one without even looking at the earlier one."

A big part of the revision involved getting the story line just right. "I tried a number of different approaches to the gay aspect of the story—I felt like I was walking on eggshells, trying to avoid being didactic and to stay away from anything that might be disturbing to anyone," she says. "I knew it was a sweet story about a little girl and her uncle, but it was also a story about a very grown-up issue—two people deciding to spend their lives together—and it was tricky to frame it completely from the child's point of view."

Brannen attributes part of the finished story's success to her online writing group, Yellapalooza. "We've been in existence for over five years now, and we've become a close, trusting group," she says. In particular, the group provided her with one of *Uncle Bobby's* first readers, fellow member Lisa Kopelke. "I'm so grateful to have been able to talk to her as I was working on the early drafts. She was a big help working out the plot."

Unlike the books Brannen submitted on her own, once she signed up with Klockner, she didn't submit a dummy for *Uncle Bobby's Wedding*, just a few character sketches. Klockner met with Putnam editor Timothy Travaglini in New York, and the rest, as they say, is history. "He saw a character sketch I had done for *Uncle Bobby's Wedding* and loved it," Brannen says. "My

While the Uncle Bobby in *Uncle Bobby's Wedding* is marrying his same-sex (guinea pig) partner, "the issue of same-sex marriage is incidental to the plot," say *Publishers Weekly*. But instead the book "straight forwardly addresses the fear of being replaced when a loved one marries." Sarah S. Brannen both wrote and illustrated this debut picture book.

agent told him there was a book and he asked to see it. She sent it to him, he read it, took it to the publisher the next day and they made an offer that night. Amazing!"

When Brannen got the news, she wasn't as surprised as one might expect. "I was very happy, but I was so sure the book would be published that it almost wasn't a surprise. In a way, I was more excited when I finished it, because I just *knew* it was good."

She was surprised, however, that Putnam wanted her to illustrate the book as well; from the get-go, *Uncle Bobby's Wedding* had been all about the story for her. "I wasn't even sure I was the best person to illustrate the book," she says. "When my agent told me that Putnam had made an offer, my first question was, 'Do they want me to illustrate it too?' I couldn't believe they did!"

Working with Travaglini and Putnam Art Director Cecilia Yung proved to be a smooth process for Brannen. She finalized the manuscript with Travaglini, who she describes as "very sweet and kind." He encouraged Brannen to expand the wedding at the end of the book, and once the manuscript was finalized, she worked on a thumbnail dummy, on which Travaglini and Yung both provided feedback. "Cecilia suggested only a few minor changes," Brannen says. "Throughout the process, she always tried to help me realize my vision and never imposed her own."

After she integrated the initial comments, Brannen did a full-sized dummy, received another round of comments from Travaglini and Yung, and then prepared the finished art. "There wasn't much time for the finished art and the schedule was pretty tight, but fortunately Cecilia only asked for two tiny changes," Brannen says. "They sent proofs which I was, for the most part, delighted with. The whole process was very easy, except for the deadline."

The book was published in March 2008, and Brannen and Putnam set the groundwork by spreading the word in advance about *Uncle Bobby's Wedding*. "My editor sent F&Gs to lots of booksellers and reviewers," she says. "Since my book has a special target audience, gay families, I sent postcards and e-mails to gay community centers and Unitarian Universalist churches, and contacted gay magazines and newspapers. I had several book-signings set up around the release of the book, and I hope to do some readings at Family Pride events this summer."

Later in the summer, Brannen's next book is due out: *The ABC Book of American Homes*, by Michael Shoulders. Brannen illustrated the nonfiction picture book, which she describes as "about the different kinds of places Americans call home, from Apartment to Farmhouse to Pueblo to a Yurt!" Of the process, she says, "There are some aspects of children's book illustration which are very much a craft, and illustrating someone else's story requires a lot of discipline. I had a huge amount of leeway in the book I did for Charlesbridge; however, I did an educational book in 2006 for which I was instructed minutely what to show. It was interesting. Making something sing, in spite of restrictions, is satisfying, although never as fulfilling as illustrating your own story."

In the meantime, Brannen is busy working on more stories, trying, as she says, "to come up with another story good enough to find a publisher." For Brannen, that means finding a story with as much joy as *Uncle Bobby's Wedding*. "To make a book irresistible to an editor, it needs to have heart."

Susan Collins Thoms
Cesar Takes a Break
(Sterling)
www.susancollinsthoms.com

Christmas of 2007 brought writer Susan Collins Thoms her "best Christmas present ever."

"On Christmas Eve, the doorbell rang and I went out to find a package on the front porch and a UPS truck driving away. I thought maybe there was a gift I had forgotten that I had ordered, and I would have to wrap another present," she says. "I opened the envelope and there was my first bound copy of *Cesar Takes a Break*, with a note from my editor. I didn't even know it was on the way. I had tears in my eyes."

For the journalist of 25 years, getting a copy of her first book was a childhood dream come true. "Like so many writers, I loved reading as a child. My three favorite things to do as a child were: read books, bake cookies, and climb trees. And, of course, reading so many stories made me want to write my own. I was going to be a writer. I couldn't imagine doing anything else."

Thoms' path to writing children's books was paved by her parents, both of whom were great story tellers. "My mom told me a lot of stories about her childhood, growing up in a family of 11 kids during the Depression. And my mother saw stories in everyday life. She was a very compassionate soul who connected easily with others. She could meet a stranger and, in no time, know their life story—and be offering words of encouragement or support," Thoms says. "And my dad is great at entertaining a crowd with a good story."

Thoms inherited this love of storytelling, and after getting a Master's degree in journalism, reported for 10 years in Pennsylvania, Ohio, and Michigan. "I loved reporting," she says. "It was like having a license to ask questions. I covered a wide range of topics, including medicine, courts, schools, and crime. I met so many interesting people who shared their stories with me." (She does add, however, that "publishing a picture book was just as hard— if not harder—than any reporting assignment.") After her stint reporting, she became a copy editor, and has been one for the past 15 years.

Throughout her years of journalism, Thoms wrote some fiction and a little poetry. While she didn't try to get anything published, she did realize she loved writing fiction. "Life was just much more interesting when I wrote fiction. I looked at the world with new eyes,'' she says. ''I saw characters, dilemmas, and details that would be great for a story. And it was just plain fun to write stories where I could make up all the facts and not just report the opinions and experiences of others.''

Thoms' love of literature led her to a University of Michigan Children's Literature class, taught by Joan Blos, Newbery award-winning author of *A Gathering of Days*. Thoms credits Blos with opening her eyes to what she calls the ''wonder of picture books.'' She says, ''I remember being so impressed by the way words and pictures came together to tell a story. And it seemed to me that writing a picture book was as difficult as writing a poem. You really have to make each word count.''

However, it wasn't until years later, after Thoms had children of her own, that she started trying to write for children. ''When my youngest started school, I started writing picture books. By then, after reading a million stories to my kids, I had fallen in love with picture

Cover illustration © 2008 Rogé. Reprinted with permission of Sterling Publishing Co., Inc.

After years as a reporter, debut author Susan Collins Thoms got the idea for *Cesar Takes a Break* from a real-life incident when Cesar, the class pet iguana at her son's school, went missing. The book, written in journal style, recounts Cesar's adventures during his vacation exploration of the school he calls home.

books.'' And it was through her son David that Thoms first got the spark of the idea that would become *Cesar Takes a Break*.

"An iguana in my son David's fourth-grade classroom escaped during spring break. The teacher had come into school every day during vacation to take care of him, but the day the kids returned to school, Cesar was gone,'' she says. "The teacher and other school staff searched frantically for five days for Cesar. We were all worried about what happened to him and if he would ever be found. That Friday, my son David spotted Cesar peeking his head out from behind the wall. David was the hero for the day.''

At the time, her son was supposed to write a story for a children's writing workshop. Thoms encouraged him to write about Cesar, but David opted for a different subject. Thoms, however, couldn't stop thinking about Cesar. "It seemed to me Cesar had decided to take his own spring break. Maybe he was miffed about the kids leaving him for a week. He thought he would leave them for a week and see how they liked it,'' she says. "I couldn't stop playing with Cesar's story in my head. I had too much fun imagining why Cesar left, where he went and what he did. So I wrote Cesar's story.''

Written in journal form, *Cesar Takes a Break* tells readers about Cesar's adventures during his spring break week, from his trip to the cafeteria to meet a guinea pig named Sassy (they spend time toasting under the French-fry heat lamps) to visiting other class pets and playing hockey in the teacher's lounge. In the end, Cesar turns down the chance to leave the school, deciding instead to stay with the kids, a decision Thoms made because she loves books "that celebrate all the wonderful things schools have to offer.''

Once she seized upon the idea of writing Cesar's story, Thoms began researching iguanas. "Cesar is a hockey-playing, blues-singing, dancing, fun-loving creature—not exactly a text-book iguana,'' she says. "But I also wanted Cesar to ring true as far as basic iguana behaviors, so I did some research to find out what iguanas eat and how they act. I got books from the library, consulted reptile Web sites, talked to iguana owners and interviewed people who worked in pet stores.''

Along with the research, Thoms spent time revising to get her final draft in place. "I love to write a first draft straight through, when the ideas are bubbling in my brain, without stopping too much to revise. But I also am big on revising. I could fill a small room with all my old drafts of *Cesar*.''

Thoms is part of an online critique group that has also helped her hone her writing skills, and in particular, Cesar's story. "My online crit group has been invaluable. It's wonderful to have someone read your story closely, challenge the big and small issues, and push you to make the story stronger,'' she says. "I don't follow all my crit partners' suggestions and I don't expect them to follow all of mine—it's still important to keep your own vision for your story. But I owe my critique partners a huge debt for all the mistakes they have caught and good suggestions they have made.''

Thoms also owes a debt to her journalism experience, from which she was able to draw upon extensively when writing Cesar's story. "In both cases, you need to tell the story simply, clearly, concisely and in an interesting way,'' she says. "Neither picture books nor news-papers are 'required reading.' You have to grab your readers' interest and give them a reason to keep reading.'' Thoms also credits journalism with helping her develop a thick skin when it comes to having her work edited. "Even when I think a story is perfect, I know some editor somewhere is just going to have to tinker with it. In the case of *Cesar Takes a Break*, I prefer to think of my editor's 'tinkering' as 'tender loving care.' ''

Thoms met her editor, Meredith Mundy Wasinger, at an SCBWI conference. "She critiqued an early draft of Cesar for me. She had lots of suggestions and questions, but she also seemed very enthusiastic about the story,'' Thoms says. "I ended up revising the story twice for her before she offered to publish it.''

When the offer came in, Thoms was thrilled. Her editor called and read her all the comments made by colleagues during the editorial meeting. "It was so fun to hear all those wonderful comments. I was floating all day," she says. "To tell the truth, I am still floating."

The path to publication has been very smooth, including the process of working with her illustrator Roge. "I was pleasantly surprised to have lots of input. "My editor asked what kind of illustrations I envisioned for the story before an artist was chosen," she says. "I got to see early sketches and was encouraged to comment on them. I think that's pretty rare, especially for new authors. I love Roge's work—I love his colors, the energy and personality in his illustrations. He has brought so much to Cesar's story."

Now that *Cesar* is published, Thoms will spend the next few months participating in book signings and doing school visits, starting with the school where the original Cesar escaped on spring break. Perhaps when she's there, she'll be inspired to find her next book idea: "With luck," she says, "new adventures for Cesar!"

Boni Ashburn
Hush, Little Dragon
(Abrams)
www.boniashburn.com

The inspiration for Boni Ashburn's first book came from something she thought she could improve: the lyrics to a lullaby. "'Hush, Little Baby' was my twins' favorite lullaby and I had to sing it to them *every* night," she says. "To me, the lyrics are inane. What do a mockingbird, a garden swing, a 'looking glass' that breaks, and a diamond ring have to do with a baby?"

After repeatedly singing it, Ashburn decided to write her own version, one that made sense and would appeal to kids. "I played around with different animals (two-syllable ones, of course) and when *dragon* popped into my head, I thought, 'Now what would make a baby dragon happy?' For Ashburn, the answer was immediate: " 'A princess to eat!' That would not only be deliciously evil, but it would also rid the world of a few of the princesses with which my daughter was completely obsessed."

Thus began *Hush, Little Dragon*. A riff on the popular lullaby, it features a mother dragon singing her baby dragon to sleep, listing all the different foods she'll give her baby, from a princess and magician, to a mean old queen and three musketeers. With its charming, dark humor and quirky take on the traditional, the book is sure to appeal to kids, something Ashburn strives for when writing.

"I enjoy picture books that don't talk down to kids, that don't preach or underestimate kids and their sense of humor," she says. "I also wanted to write books that I knew *my* kids would enjoy (and that I would enjoy sharing with them)—offbeat humor, twisty endings, with playful language that's fun to read out loud."

For Ashburn, parody was a natural starting place, making the best of her instincts as a writer, as well as appealing to kids' natural curiosity. "Re-invention, when well-done, is genius. I love fractured fairy tales and re-written songs with new lyrics. I write a lot of them," she says. "Kids like what is familiar to them (at least mine do) and when they recognize the tune or framework or plotline, I think they are more open to, and interested in, new concepts and content, new twists. The familiar rhythm of the song draws them in, but they love to point out things that are the same and notice what's different."

Ashburn spends a lot of time thinking out her ideas before she gets started writing. "I brainstorm a lot when I begin a new idea. I might have a few words that strike me, or a subject I want to tackle or a song I think would be fun to rewrite. The idea really has to brew for a while before I can start writing. When I do start then, it goes pretty fast because I already know a lot of what I want to write,'' she says.

Cover illustration © 2008 Kelly Murphy.

Boni Ashburn's debut picture book *Hush, Little Dragon* is a take on a familiar lullaby "Hush, Little Baby"—with a dark twist. In Ashburn's version, a mommy dragon lists all the foods she'll give her baby to eat, like a magician, a mean old queen, and a princess, thus ridding the world of a few princesses, "with which my daughter was completely obsessed," she says.

Revision, she admits, is not her strong suit. "I'd say it's a big weakness of mine. Once I commit a manuscript to paper, it's hard for me to 're-vision' it unless I have some external direction." For Ashburn, that external direction comes from a few trusted critique friends and her critique partner, author Deanna Caswell, who she describes as "the yin to my yang."

"She'll be the first to tell you I almost never take her specific advice," Ashburn says, "but she has a way of getting me to think about my manuscripts in a new way that always leads me to the perfect solution for whatever problem I'm having."

Caswell isn't the first writer whose advice Ashburn hasn't taken. While writing *Hush, Little Dragon*, she was in several critique groups, all of whom suggested to Ashburn that the material was too dark for a picture book, and that she should tone it down or take a different angle. Ashburn held strong. "I didn't exactly get defensive," she says, "but I went with my gut because I felt that other people could appreciate what I had written—I just had to find them."

Ashburn credits these differing opinions with helping her see the "other" side's viewpoint. "I'm sure some people will agree with my crit group when they read *Hush*. Some will say it *is* too dark," she says. "But I think most kids are sophisticated enough to realize that *if* there were dragons, they would naturally have to eat *something* . . . and hey, a food chain is a food chain. It's a natural part of life, even if grown-ups don't like to talk about it."

Ashburn believes critique groups are critical in teaching beginning writers how to do exactly what she did: trust her gut. "In the beginning, as a writer, you are looking for validation. Are you a 'good' writer? Are your ideas good? Are your stories good?" she says. "I was very unsure of everything! A crit group gives you a community, but also a reference point. You can say, 'Wow, I have so much to learn!' or 'Wow, my manuscript sounds more like a 'book' than this one I'm critting does,' or you can realize, 'Wow, they understand structure so much better than I do. I need to really work on that.' You learn how to look at other peoples' work critically, and how to do the same to your own."

Trusting her gut when it came to *Hush, Little Dragon*, Ashburn began sending it out for review. "I submitted *Hush* to one publisher in May 2005. It took them four months to send me a form rejection. Then, I queried three publishers. Two went to specific editors at their houses, but at Abrams I didn't have any good research on specific editors, so I sent it to the 'Submissions Editor,' " she says. "Almost one month later, I received a request from an editor, Maggie Lehrman, at Abrams. It was my first ever request from a query!" Ashburn and Lehrman talked, and two weeks later, Ashburn received an offer.

Ashburn describes working with her editor as "the icing on the cake." Not only did the editing process go smoothly, but Ashburn was invited to offer suggestions and see the illustrator's sketches, which doesn't always happen in the picture book process. Kelly Murphy's finished illustrations are beautiful and funny, capturing the right tone and humor without making the book scary.

Now that the book is published, Ashburn has been concentrating on building her Web site and blog. While she doesn't love the promotion end of things, she's "hoping it will come as things develop." Also coming as things develop is her second book with Abrams, a companion to *Hush* tentatively titled *Over at the Castle*. In the meantime, she'll be "writing and submitting and writing and submitting." She'll also be practicing what she preaches to all authors: "intelligent but tenacious persistence."

"Learn absolutely everything you can about the children's writing business and make publication your goal and do not stop until you achieve that goal. Seriously. Research, read, learn, do. And keep at it."

Deborah Diesen
The Pout-Pout Fish
(Farrar, Straus & Giroux)
www.deborahdiesen.com

For Deborah Diesen, the inspiration for her first published picture book came from her son. "My young son was having a pouty afternoon, and I was doing a little good-natured teasing of him. Pretty soon we were both making funny faces and laughing," she says. "A college roommate of mine used to refer to a pout as a small ledge (as in, 'Hey, you've got a little knick-knack shelf going there'), so my son and I got to sticking our lower lips out in an exaggerated fashion to make shelves. Then we started making fish faces. Pretty soon we'd combined the two and become pout-pout fish. That was the spark: I started writing the story the same day."

The result is *The Pout-Pout Fish*, a magical picture book that details the life of a gloomy fish who believes his face is in a permanent pout. All that changes, however, when he meets a beautiful silver fish who gives him a kiss. Suddenly, his pout turns into a smile, and declares himself a "kiss-kiss" fish, meant to spread "cheery-cheeries" all over the place.

The book is written in rhyme—not an easy writing style to master, but one that suits Diesen's writing style. "One of the reasons I like to write in rhyme is because of the constraints that writing in rhyme puts on a story. When I don't write in rhyme, the writing experience feels a little like wandering around in a huge castle—there are so many rooms, I'm not sure where I should go; it leaves me more than a little prone to aimless wandering," she says. "In a rhyming story structure, the square footage is smaller and the floor plan is clear, so it's easier for me to settle in and make the place uniquely my own."

Diesen's earliest writing—a poem about a butterfly—was composed in rhyme, when she was in third grade. "It was," she says, "the start of a long period of poetry writing, all in rhyme, mostly around simple themes (colors, friendship, and animals)." A few years later, she later moved on to a novel, an effort she describes as "a thinly-disguised rip-off of the Laura Ingalls Wilder books (my favorite at the time)."

While many children aspire to be writers, what made the difference for Diesen—what made her believe that she could be a "Real Writer"—was the response she received: "The reason I remember writing that butterfly poem was due to my Mom's response. Not only did she like the poem, but she encouraged me to put a date on it, because she told me that writers always date their drafts," she says. "My laboriously written *Little House on the Prairie* rip-off was warmly received by my school librarian, who even gave me written comments on it. And later, in junior high, my creative writing teacher laughed so hard at a story I had written about a disastrous cooking episode that she had tears in her eyes."

Diesen wrote throughout her high school years but put it aside when she got older, comparing the pursuit to being an astronaut: "a common and at-the-time-reasonable childhood aspiration, but not something that most of us really go on to become." However, when she became a parent, she started thinking about writing again.

"There's nothing like chronic sleep deprivation and stress to catalyze some major rethinking of who you are and what you're meant to be doing, and if you happen to be reading children's books aloud for hours every day as you're going through that stress," she says, "there's a good likelihood that at some point you'll say aloud (in a burst of joyful enthusiasm), 'I could write a children's book.' "

Once again, what made the difference for Diesen was the reaction she received: "My kids *loved* my stories, and though of course this is no indicator of quality (my elder son went through a stage during which his favorite read-aloud was the bus schedule; this helped me stay humble about his enthusiasm for my writing), it did encourage me a little."

Her next steps were, for Diesen, the most critical on her path to publication: she joined

The Pout-Pout Fish

Deborah Diesen   Pictures by Dan Hanna

Cover illustration © 2008 Dan Hana. Reprinted with permission of Farrar, Straus & Giroux.

After a total of 100 rejections for various projects, Deborah Diesen's debut rhyming picture book *The Pout-Pout Fish*, was accepted by Farrar, Straus & Giroux. Along with her persistence, Diesen's critique group played a part in her publishing debut. "A tough critique is the first step in making a great manuscript," she says.

SCBWI and found a good critique group. In the process, she says, she'd unofficially done the most important thing: "I'd allowed myself to think of myself as a Children's Book Writer."

The critique group Diesen joined—what she calls the WBCG (World's Best Critique Group)—has been crucial to both her development as a writer and her developing manuscripts. "We all have a strong commitment to one another, so we want each other's writing to be the best it can be. This motivates us to be honest. Kind, but honest. Flat prose and plot flaws are pounced upon, because a tough critique is the first step in making a great manuscript," she says.

Diesen leaves her critique sessions with ideas on how to improve her manuscripts and encouragement for getting started—both of which she, quite literally, wouldn't trade for anything. "If a magical genie popped out of a bottle and offered me the gift of Writing Fame and Fortune, with just one catch—that I'd have to drop out of my critique group—I'd tell the genie to take a hike. (Of course, that wouldn't stop me from hoping for a genie who'd make me a better offer. . . .)"

While a silver fish helped the Pout-Pout fish to turn his day around, for Diesen, the inspiration she needed came when she won the SCBWI Barbara Karlin award. "In the summer of 2004, I was very down on my writing. What little writing I was doing seemed flat, and the only thing that was developing was my stack of rejection letters," she says. However, on a particularly bad summer day ("One of my children had been up a lot during the previous night, so I was in a fatigue fugue state made even more intense by the heat of the afternoon,") Diesen received a call telling her she won the award. It was another key moment in her writing career. "The manuscript that received the award has not yet found a home, but the award itself gave me a real boost. It gave me confidence in my writing and renewed my desire to keep at it."

The desire to keep at it paid off when, in October 2004, Diesen got a call from then FSG editor Robbie Mayes, offering a home for *The Pout-Pout Fish*. Diesen had received eleven previous rejection letters for *Pout-Pout* when the book finally found a home. After the book was accepted, she went through and counted her complete stack of rejection letters. "I had about a dozen stories I was submitting, and the sum total of all my rejections to date was exactly 100," she says. "So if my experience is any indication, the rejection-acceptance ratio runs about 100:1."

Unfortunately, soon after the book was signed, Diesen's editor left FSG. Without an editor for half a year, she worried the book would become a "homeless orphan and somehow never be published after all." During that time, however, the Editorial Director at FSG Books for Young Readers gave Diesen encouragement, and in February 2006, she was assigned her new editor, Janine O'Malley, who "got to work right away on finding an illustrator, and the wheels of publishing motion got moving again for Mr. Fish."

The illustrator, Dan Hanna, completed the work during 2006, and in February 2007, Diesen got to see a complete set of pages: "What a moment, opening the envelope and *seeing* Mr. Fish and his friends. I couldn't have asked for better illustration."

Now, Diesen's working on spreading the word about *Pout-Pout,* planning school and library visits as well as story time programs and building a Web site that includes an interactive site for kids. The Web site also serves another purpose: keeping Diesen writing. "This year I set formal writing goals for myself and went so far as to post them on my Web site," she says. "It remains to be seen if the public posting helps me stick to my goals or if I'll end up regretting my foolishness . . ."

With another picture book on the way, the wonderfully titled *The Barefooted, Bad-Tempered Baby Brigade* (Tricycle Press), it sounds like Diesen won't have anything to regret—she's doing a pretty good job of sticking to her goals and becoming the writer she's wanted to be ever since third grade.

Dan Hanna
The Pout-Pout Fish
(Farrar, Straus & Giroux)
www.bluebellylizard.com

During his 10 years in the animation industry, Dan Hanna's worked on animating an orange dog, a space monkey, a one-handed worm, a chain-smoking nun, M&M's, stomach acid, blue men, Sinbad, a spotted elephant, flopping fish, lizards, assorted flying creatures, a cranky critic, a Canadian bulldog, and a German elf, to name just a few. Now he can add children's book illustrator to the résumé, and a pouting fish to an already-eclectic list.

As the illustrator for Deborah Diesen's *The Pout-Pout Fish*, the 6'1" Hanna (who's now "standing a bit taller" since the book is out) came up with the goofy and magical illustrations that detail the life of the Pout-Pout fish, a grumpy guy who, after receiving a kiss of his own, happily starts kissing everyone he meets and in the process, turns his frown upside down.

Hanna can relate to Mr. Fish's joyous epiphany. When he got the call from FSG editor Janine O'Malley, saying he'd been chosen to illustrate Deborah Diesen's book, he was ecstatic. "I was sitting in a cafe, pouting to myself when I received the call," he says. "My pout immediately turned upside down and I went around kissing everyone."

For Hanna, the call was the hard-earned result of a lot of patient and persistent pitching of his own children's book ideas. "I had sent a couple of dummies to Janine O'Malley over the years and had just sent a third. She wrote me to say she loved it and that it had made everyone laugh—but ultimately she was unable to convince enough people and it was rejected," he explains. "However, she asked me if I'd consider illustrating someone else's text. I can't remember exactly what I said but *I do* remember what *I did not* say. And what *I did not* say was 'only if you say pretty please.' A couple of months later she asked me to do a test image for *The Pout-Pout Fish* and then shortly after that I received 'The Phone Call.' "

Illustrating picture books is a natural extension of Hanna's talent and an outlet for his sense of humor, both of which were honed during his time working in the animation world.

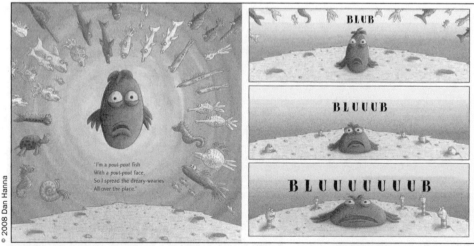

Dan Hanna's experience as both an animator and a diver came in handy as he completed illustrations for his debut picture book *The Pout-Pout Fish*. His main character, inspired by a sad looking little fish he saw during a dive, comes to life in this spread including sequential art.

"As a kid, I loved Disney's *Fantasia* and their animated version of *The Jungle Book*," he says. "I went to lots of animation festivals, did animation in high school, and then after college (and many years of work as a computer programmer) I saved up money to go to an art school (CalArts) and study animation. This led to computer animation work in San Francisco where I worked on mostly advertising and web based animation."

The crash of the dotcom industry changed Hanna's path when the animation company he worked for went out of business. He seized the time off as an opportunity to explore writing for kids. "I had saved up some money so I decided to pursue my dream of writing and illustrating a children's picture book," he says. "I made a deal with myself to go as long as my savings held out."

Even though Hanna started out just trying to write, he ended up creating illustrations for his stories, and it's what he ultimately ended up getting hired for—with *The Pout-Pout Fish*. He's found the illustration process as wonderful as his work in animation. "One of my favorite parts of the animation process is the brain-storming, writing and design work that's done at the beginning of a project. Building the world. Coming up with the story and characters," he says. "Trying to put together a picture book gives me the same kind of joy."

Once Hanna was selected for the job, he didn't work directly with Diesen. "Deborah and I were kept in separate padded cells and we could only communicate using an elaborate system of grunts and groans," he jokes. "Actually we didn't communicate at all until after the illustrations were done. From what I understand, editors generally discourage communication between an author and illustrator. I think this is to allow an illustrator the freedom to interpret the words without being burdened by any prior expectations."

He did, however, work extensively with the editor and FSG's art director in shaping the illustrations. "Janine gave me complete freedom to come up with stuff. Most of my early sketches were rejected—but with terrific constructive feedback. I'd do a bunch of sketches, post them on my Web site and then proceed based on her feedback and that of the art director," he says. "I cringe when I look back at some of my earlier sketches. I'm tremendously thankful that I was pushed to reach beyond those early attempts." Hanna also credits his critique group with helping him get to the final illustrations.

While Hanna recognizes the importance of revision, he's quick to caution illustrators about

Dan Hanna says he got "terrific constructive feedback" from his editor and art director at FSG as he worked on the illustrations for *The Pout-Pout Fish*, such as this spread featuring an octopus interacting with the title character. "I cringe when I look back at some of my earlier sketches," he says, "I'm tremendously thankful that I was pushed to reach beyond those early attemps."

overworking illustrations, and consequently sucking the charm out of them. "When I was about five, I remember my dad laying in a brick walkway from the street to our front door. He'd slap a trowel full of cement down and then drop in a brick and quickly knock it into place. I said, 'Dad, you're not lining the bricks up very straight.' He looked at me, wiped the sweat from his forehead and smiled. 'Dan, that's where the charm is, in those crooked lines.'

While the five-year-old Hanna didn't understand what that meant, he keenly recognizes the wisdom of that approach now. "I've often scribbled something that made me laugh. Then, after I 'cleaned it up,' the humor/magic would disappear," he says.

Not only does Hanna recognize the importance of the "crooked line" in his own work, he finds inspiration in similar artists, illustrators he describe as masters of "loose charm": William Steig, Gary Larson, Shel Silverstein, Mordicai Gerstein, and Edward Gorey. "Long ago I bought a book of Gary Larson's *Farside* comics," he says. "In this particular book he showed what his original drawings looked like (before he refined them) and it was an epiphany for me. They were just a bunch of messy scribbles which looked just like my messy scribbles! That was a great inspiration."

Not only has Hanna brought his own loose charm to *Pout-Pout*, he's also brought to the project his experience as a diver. "The ocean is filled with natural pouters. I remember one deep dive where there was a large ship wreck and a tall mast-like spire that rose from the ship's deck," he says. "On the tip of that spire was a little basket and within that basket sat a small

Hanna's Tips for Getting Published

- Join SCBWI and learn all you can about what you're trying to do.
- Join a critique group.
- Do what I did! Get laid off and then grasp desperately at a childhood dream.
- Become a celebrity first. I can't emphasize this enough. If only I'd thought of it when I was younger.
- Believe in reincarnation. It's the only way you'll have the time to be able to do everything you want to do.
- Check your spam! My editor Janine's initial e-mail was buried in the bulk/ spam folder of my e-mail account. If I hadn't taken the time to wade through all those body part enhancement offers then I would have deleted Janine's e-mail without ever seeing it! As a bonus, I also hooked up with a rich sultan who wanted me to help transfer his fortune to an American bank account. Sometimes spam isn't spam—it's caviar!
- Take a scuba diving class.
- Don't suck the charm out of things by overworking them. A successful squiggle is a very sublime, fragile thing that is easily destroyed by giving it too much attention.
- And finally, follow Alfred Hitchcock's advice when he won the Lifetime Achievement award at the Oscars many years ago. He stood up very solemnly and everyone was expecting a terrific speech. Instead, his voice trembled a bit and all he said was, "stay out of jail."

pudgy fish with the saddest pout I've ever seen. He sat there, wallowing in his dark gloom, looking out over that rusting hulk. That little guy was my model for The Pout-Pout Fish.''

The real-life model for the Pout-Pout fish will soon find himself in more than just the pages of a book. Hanna has helped Diesen with publicity and marketing for the title, creating related bookmarks, business cards, cootie-catchers, fish sticks, and trading cards. On top of that, he's putting the fish on coffee mugs, T-shirts, bibs, and more, and, of course, creating some animated clips.

He also jokes about starting a guerrilla promotion group. "I plan to create an organization called FOS (Face Out Society)—a subversive group of children's book authors, illustrators and friends who will visit bookstores throughout the world and discretely turn deserving books Face Out—ideally obscuring a less deserving celebrity book in the process.

"Hanna's eager to continue with illustrating and, eventually, illustrate *and* write his own book. *The Pout-Pout Fish* is just the beginning. "I feel like now, after many years, I finally have my big toe in the door. My next goal is to slip my entire foot in and then I'll really have some leverage," he says. "Maybe some day I'll squeeze my head in the door and then I'll be able to see what's going on in there.''

Book Publishers

There's no magic formula for getting published. It's a matter of getting the right manuscript on the right editor's desk at the right time. Before you submit it's important to learn publishers' needs, see what kind of books they're producing and decide which publishers your work is best suited for. *Children's Writer's & Illustrator's Market* is but one tool in this process. (Those just starting out, turn to Quick Tips for Writers & Illustrators on page 5.)

To help you narrow down the list of possible publishers for your work, we've included several indexes at the back of this book. The **Subject Index** lists book and magazine publishers according to their fiction and nonfiction needs or interests. The **Age-Level Index** indicates which age groups publishers cater to. The **Photography Index** indicates which markets buy photography for children's publications. The **Poetry Index** lists publishers accepting poetry.

If you write contemporary fiction for young adults, for example, and you're trying to place a book manuscript, go first to the Subject Index. Locate the fiction categories under Book Publishers and copy the list under Contemporary. Then go to the Age-Level Index and highlight the publishers on the Contemporary list that are included under the Young Adults heading. Read the listings for the highlighted publishers to see if your work matches their needs.

Remember, *Children's Writer's & Illustrator's Market* should not be your only source for researching publishers. Here are a few other sources of information:

- The Society of Children's Book Writers and Illustrators (SCBWI) offers members an annual market survey of children's book publishers for the cost of postage or free online at www.scbwi.org. (SCBWI membership information can also be found at www.scbwi.org.)
- The Children's Book Council Web site (www.cbcbooks.org) gives information on member publishers.
- If a publisher interests you, send a SASE for submission guidelines or check publishers' Web sites for guidelines *before* submitting. To quickly find guidelines online, visit The Colossal Directory of Children's Publishers at www.signaleader.com.
- Check publishers' Web sites. Many include their complete catalogs that you can browse. Web addresses are included in many publishers' listings.
- Spend time at your local bookstore to see who's publishing what. While you're there, browse through *Publishers Weekly* and *The Horn Book*.

SUBSIDY & SELF-PUBLISHING

Some determined writers who receive rejections from royalty publishers may look to subsidy and co-op publishers as an option for getting their work into print. These publishers ask writers to pay all or part of the costs of producing a book. We strongly advise writers and illustrators to work only with publishers who pay them. For this reason, we've adopted a policy not to include any subsidy or co-op publishers in *Children's Writer's & Illustrator's Market* (or any other Writer's Digest Books market books).

If you're interested in publishing your book just to share it with friends and relatives, self-publishing is a viable option, but it involves time, energy, and money. You oversee all book production details. Check with a local printer for advice and information on cost or check online for print-on-demand publishing options (which are often more affordable).

Whatever path you choose, keep in mind that the market is flooded with submissions, so it's important for you to hone your craft and submit the best work possible. Competition from thousands of other writers and illustrators makes it more important than ever to research publishers before submitting—read their guidelines, look at their catalogs, check out a few of their titles and visit their Web sites.

ADVICE FROM INSIDERS

For insight and advice on getting published from a variety of perspectives, be sure to read the Insider Reports in this section with authors **Scott Westerfeld** (page 156), **Katherine Applegate** (page 170), **Marissa Doyle** (page 184), **Michelle Meadows** (page 202), and **Natalie Rompella** (page 216).

Information on book publishers listed in the previous edition but not included in this edition of *Children's Writer's & Illustrator's Market* may be found in the General Index.

⚏ HARRY N. ABRAMS BOOKS FOR YOUNG READERS

115 W. 18th St., New York NY 10011. (212)519-1200. Web site: www.abramsyoungreaders.com. **Publisher, Children's Books:** Howard W. Reeves.

- Abrams title *365 Penguins*, by Jean-Luc Fromental, illustrated by Joelle Jolivel, won a Boston Globe-Horn Book Picture Book Honor Award in 2007. See First Books on page 133 for an interview with Boni Ashburn, author of Abram's title *Hush, Little Dragon*.

Fiction/Nonfiction Picture books, middle readers, young adult.
How to Contact/Writers Submit complete ms for picture book; for longer works, submit a query with SASE. Responds in 6 months only with SASE. Mail only; no email. Will consider multiple submissions.
Illustration Illustrations only: Do not submit original material; copies only. Contact: Chad Beckerman.

⚏ ABSEY & CO.

23011 Northcrest Dr., Spring TX 77389. (281)257-2340. Fax: (281)251-4676. E-mail: abseyandco@aol.com. Web site: www.absey.com. New York address: 45 W. 21st Street, Suite 5, New York NY 10010. (212)277-8028. (Send mss to Spring TX address only.) **Publisher:** Edward Wilson. "We are looking for education books, especially those with teaching strategies based upon research, for children's picture books and Young Adult fiction. We haven't done much with nonfiction." Publishes hardcover, trade paperback and mass market paperback originals. Publishes 5-10 titles/year. 50% of books from first-time authors; 50% from unagented writers.
Fiction "Since we are a small, new press, we are looking for good manuscripts with a firm intended audience." Recently published *Stealing a Million Kisses* (board book); *Adrift* (YA fiction).
How to Contact/Writers Fiction: Query with SASE. Does not consider simultaneous submissions. Responds to queries in 3 months. No e-mail submissions. "We do not download from unknown sources."
Illustration Reviews ms/illustration packages. Send photocopies, transparencies, etc.
Photography Reviews ms/photo packages. Send photocopies, transparencies, etc.
Terms Pays 8-15% royalty on wholesale price. Publishes book 1 year after acceptance of ms. Manuscript guidelines for #10 SASE.
Tips "Absey publishes a few titles every year. We like the author and the illustrator working together to create something magical. Authors and illustrators have input into every phase of production."

ALADDIN PAPERBACKS/SIMON PULSE PAPERBACK BOOKS

1230 Avenue of the Americas, 4th Floor, New York NY 10020. (212)698-2707. Fax: (212)698-7337. Web site: www.simonsays.com. **Vice President/Associate Publisher, Aladdin:** Ellen Krieger; Vice President/Editorial

Director, Simon Pulse: Bethany Buck; Mark McVeigh, Editorial Director (Aladdin); Liesa Abrams, senior editor (Aladdin); Jennifer Klonsky, executive editor (Pulse); Michelle Nagler, Senior Editor (Pulse). **Manuscript Acquisitions:** Attn: Submissions Editor. **Art Acquisitions:** Karin Paprocki, Aladdin; Russell Gordon, Simon Pulse. Paperback imprints of Simon & Schuster Children's Publishing Children's Division. Publishes c. 250 titles/year.

- Aladdin publishes reprints of successful hardcovers from other Simon & Schuster imprints as well as original beginning readers, chapter books, and middle grade single title and series fiction and is looking for graphic fiction and nonfiction. They accept query letters with proposals for originals. Simon Pulse publishes original teen series and single title fiction, as well as reprints of successful hardcovers from other Simon & Schuster imprints. They accept query letters for originals.

Fiction Recently published Robin Hill School beginning reader series (Julia Richardson, editor); Nancy Drew and the Clue Crew chapter book series (Molly McGuire, editor); Pendragon middle grade series (Julia Richardson, editor); Edgar & Ellen middle grade series (Ellen Krieger, editor).

ALASKA NORTHWEST BOOKS

Imprint of Graphic Arts Center Publishing Co., P.O. Box 10306, Portland OR 97296-0306. (503)226-2402. Fax: (503)223-1410. E-mail: editorial@gacpc.com. Web site: www.gacpc.com. **Executive Editor:** Tim Frew. Imprints: Alaska Northwest Books. Publishes 3 picture books/year; 1 young reader/year. 20% of books by first-time authors. "We publish books that teach and entertain as well as inform the reader about Alaska or the western U.S. We're interested in wildlife, adventure, unusual sports, inspirational nature stories, traditions, but we also like plain old silly stories that make kids giggle. We are particular about protecting Native American story-telling traditions, and ask that writers ensure that it's clear whether they are writing from within the culture or about the culture. We encourage Native American writers to share their stories."

Fiction Picture books, young readers: adventure, animal, contemporary, fantasy, history, humor, multicultural, nature/environment, poetry. Middle readers, young adult/teens: adventure, animal, anthology, contemporary, history, humor, multicultural, nature/environment, suspense/mystery. Average word length: picture books—500-1,000; young readers—500-1,500; middle readers—1,500-2,000; young adults—35,000. Recently published *Seldovia Sam and the Wildfire Rescue*, by Susan Woodward Springer, illustrated by Amy Meissner (ages 6-10, early chapter book); *Ten Rowdy Ravens*, by Susan Ewing, illustrated by Evon Zerbetz (age 5 and up, humor); *Berry Magic*, by Teri Sloat and Betty Huffmon, illustrated by Teri Sloat (age 6 and up, legend).

Nonfiction Picture books: animal. Young readers: animal, multicultural, sports. Middle readers, young adults/teens: animal, history, multicultural, nature/environment, sports, Alaska- or Western-themed adventure. Average word length: picture books—500-1,000; young readers—500-1,500; middle readers—1,500-2,000; young adults—35,000. Recently published *Big-Enough Anna: The Little Sled Dog Who Braved the Arctic*, by Pam Flowers and Ann Dixon, illustrated by Bill Farnsworth (5 and up); *Recess at 20 Below*, by Cindy Lou Aillaud (ages 6-10).

How to Contact/Writers Fiction: Submit complete ms for picture books or submit outline/synopsis and 2 sample chapters for YA novels. Nonfiction: Submit complete ms for picture books or submit 2 sample chapters for YA nonfiction chapter books. Responds to queries/mss in 3-5 months. Publishes book 2 years after acceptance. Will consider simultaneous submissions.

Illustration Works with 4-5 illustrators/year. Uses color artwork only. Reviews ms/illustration packages from artists. Submit ms with dummy or scans of final art on CD. Contact: Tricia Brown. Illustrations only: Query with résumé, scans on CD. Responds only if interested. Samples not returned; samples filed.

Photography Buys stock and assigns work. "We rarely illustrate with photos—only if the book is more educational in content." Photo captions required. Uses color and 35mm or 4×5 transparencies. Submit cover letter, résumé, slides, portfolio on CD, color promo piece.

Terms Pays authors royalty of 5-7% based on net revenues. Offers advances (average amount: $2,000). Pays illustrators royalty of 5-7% based on net revenues. Pays photographers royalty of 5-7% based on net revenues. Sends galleys to authors; dummies to illustrators. Originals returned to artist at job's completion. Book catalog available for 9×12 SASE and $3.85 postage; ms, art, and photo guidelines available for SASE. All imprints included in a single catalog. Catalog available on Web site.

Tips "As a regional publisher, we seek books about Alaska and the West. We rarely publish YA novels, but are more interested in the pre-school to early reader segment. A proposal that shows that the author has researched the market, in addition to submitting a unique story, will get our attention."

ALL ABOUT KIDS PUBLISHING

9333 Benbow Drive, Gilroy CA 95020. (408)846-1833. Fax: (408)846-1835. E-mail: lguevara@aakp.com. Web site: www.aakp.com. **Acquisitions:** Linda Guevara. Publishes 3-5 picture books/year; 3-5 chapter books/year. 80% of books by first-time authors.

Fiction Picture books, young readers: adventure, animal, concept, fantasy, folktales, history, humor, nature, poetry, suspense/mystery. Average word length: picture books—450 words. Recently published *Dillan McMil-*

lan, Please Eat Your Peas, by David Schneider (picture book); *The Titanic Game*, by Mike Warner (chapter book).

Nonfiction Picture books, young readers: activity books, animal, biography, concept, history, nature. Average word length: picture books—450 words. Recently published *Shadowbox Hunt: A Search & Find Odyssey*, by Laura L. Seeley (picture book).

How to Contact/Writers Fiction: Submit complete ms. Nonfiction: Submit complete ms for picture books; outline synopsis and completer ms for young readers. Responds to mss in 3 months. Publishes a book 2-3 years after acceptance. Manuscript returned with SASE only.

Illustration Works with 5-10 illustrators/year. Reviews ms/illustration packages from artists. Submit ms with dummy or ms with 2-3 pieces of final art. Contact: Linda Guevara, editor. Illustrations only: Arrange personal portfolio review or send résumé, portfolio and client list. Responds in 3 months. Samples returned with SASE; samples filed.

Photography Works on assignment only. Contact: Linda Guevara, editor. Model/property releases required. Submit portfolio, résumé, client list.

Terms Pays author royalty. Offers advances (average amount: $1,000). Pays illustrators by the project (range: $3,000 minimum) and/or royalty of 3-5% based on retail price. Pays photographers by the project (range: $500 minimum) or royalty of 5% based on wholesale price. Sends galleys to authors; dummies to illustrators. All imprints included in a single catalog. Writer's, artist's and photographer's guidelines available for SASE and on Web site.

Tips "Submit only one manuscript at a time. Not accepting submission until July 2008. Please check our Web site for guidelines before submitting."

AMERICAN GIRL PUBLICATIONS

8400 Fairway Place, Middleton WI 53562-2554. (608)836-4848. Fax: (608)836-1999. Web site: www.americangirl.com. **Manuscript Acquisitions:** Submissions Editor. Publishes 30 middle readers/year. 10% of books by first-time authors. Publishes fiction and nonfiction for girls 8-12.

Fiction: American Girls publishes 2-3 titles per year for its Girl of the year character and 3 mystery titles per year for its historical characters. American Girl does not accept ideas or manuscripts.

Nonfiction Middle readers: activity books, arts/crafts, cooking, history, hobbies, how-to self help, sports. Recently published *A Smart Girl's Guide to Friendship Troubles*, by Patti Kelley Crisswell, (ages 8 and up; self-help); *Paper Punch Art*, by Laura Torres (ages 8 and up; craft); *Quiz Book 2*, by Sarah Jane Brian, illustrated by Debbie Tilley (ages 8 and up; activity).Also publishes *American Girl* magazine. See the listing for *American Girl* in the Magazines section.

How to Contact/Writers Nonfiction: Submit well-focused concepts for activity, craft or advice books. "Proposals should include a detailed descripton of your concept, sample chapters or spreads and lists of previous publications. Complete manuscripts also accepted." Responds in 3 months. Will consider simultaneous submissions.

Illustration Works with 10 illustrators/year. Reviews ms/illustration packages from artists. Illustrations only: Query with samples. Contact: Art Director. Responds only if interested. Samples not returned.

Photography Buys stock and assigns work. Submit cover letter, published samples, promo piece.

Terms Pays authors royalty or work purchased outright. Pays illustrators by the project. Pays photographers by the project. Sends galleys to authors; dummies to illustrators. Originals returned to artist at job's completion. Book catalog available for 8½×11 SAE and 4 first-class stamps. All imprints included in a single catalog.

AMULET BOOKS

Abrams Books for Young Readers, 115 W. 18th St., New York NY 10001. (212)229-8000. Web site: www.hnabooks.com. Estab. 2004. Specializes in trade books, fiction. **Manuscript Acquisitions:** Susan Van Metre, executive editor. **Art Acquisitions:** Chad Beckerman, art director. Produces 6 middle readers/year, 6 young adult titles/year. 10% of books by first-time authors.

Fiction Middle readers: adventure, contemporary, fantasy, history, science fiction, sports. Young adults/teens: adventure, contemporary, fantasy, history, science fiction, sports, suspense. Recently published *The Sisters Grimm: The Fairy-Tale Detectives*, by Michael Buckley (mid-grade series); *ttyl*, by Lauren Miracle (YA novel); *The Hour of the Cobra*, by Maiya Williams (middle grade novel).

How to Contact/Writers Fiction: Query. Responds to queries in 2-3 months. Publishes book 18-24 months after acceptance. Considers simultaneous submissions.

Illustration Works with 10-12 illustrators/year. Uses both color and b&w. Query with samples. Contact: Chad Beckerman, art director. Samples filed.

Photography Buys stock images and assigns work.

Terms Offers advance against royalties. Illustrators paid by the project . Author sees galleys for review.

Illustrators see dummies for review. Originals returned to artist at job's completion. Catalog available for 9×12 SASE and 4 first-class stamps.

☠ ATHENEUM BOOKS FOR YOUNG READERS

Imprint of Simon & Schuster Children's Publishing Division, 1230 Avenue of the Americas, New York NY 10020. (212)698-2715. Web site: www.simonsayskids.com. Estab. 1960. **Publisher:** Vice President, Associate Publisher Emma D. Dryden. **Acquisitions:** Ginee Seo, editorial director, Ginee Seo Books; Caitlyn Dlouhy, editorial director; Susan Burke, editor; Jordan Brown, associate editor; Carol Chou, editorial assistant. **Art Acquisitions:** Ann Bobco, executive art director. Publishes 20-30 picture books/year; 20-25 middle readers/year; 15-25 young adult titles/year. 70% of books by first-time authors; 60% from agented writers. "Atheneum publishes original hardcover trade books for children from pre-school age through young adult. Our list includes picture books, chapter books, mysteries, biography, science fiction, fantasy, graphic novels, middle grade and young adult fiction and nonfiction. The style and subject matter of the books we publish is almost unlimited. We do not, however, publish textbooks, coloring or activity books, greeting cards, magazines or pamphlets or religious publications."

- Atheneum title *November Blues*, by Sharon M. Draper, won a Coretta Scott King Author Honor Award in 2008. See A King's Legacy on page 123 for an interview with Draper. Atheneum title *Let It Shine*, by Ashley Bryan, won the Coretta Scott King Illustrator Award in 2008.

Fiction Recently published *Someday*, by Alison McGhee, illustrated by Peter Reynolds (picture book); *Trucks Roll!*, by George Ella Lyon, illlustrated by Craig Frazier (picture book); *Mr. Pusskins*, by Sam Lloyd (picture book); *Olivia Helps With Christmas*, by Ian Falconer (picture book); *Middle School Is Worse Than Meatloaf*, by Jennifer L. Holm, illustrated by Elicia Castaldi (illustrated middle grade); *Touching Snow*, by M. Sindy Felin (debut teen novel); *Edward's Eyes*, by Patricia Maclachlan (middle grade novel); *November Blues*, by Sharon Draper (teen novel); *The Mysterious Edge of the Heroic World*, by E. L. Konigsburg (middle grade novel).

Nonfiction Recently published *Race*, by Marc Aronson.

How to Contact/Writers Send query letters with SASE for picture books; send synopsis and first 3 chapters or first 30 pages with SASE for novels. Responds to queries in 1-2 months; requested mss in 3-4 months. Publishes a book 24-36 months after acceptance. Will consider simultaneous queries from previously unpublished authors and those submitted to other publishers, "though we request that the author let us know it is a simultaneous query." Please do not call to query or follow up.

Illustration Works with 40-50 illustrators/year. Send art samples résumé, tearsheets to Ann Bobco, Design Dept. 4th Floor, 1230 Avenue of the Americas, New York NY 10020. Samples filed. Responds to art samples only if interested.

Terms Pays authors in royalties of based on retail price. Pays illustrators royalty or by the project. Pays photographers by the project. Original artwork returned at job's completion. Manuscript guidelines for #10 SAE and 1 first-class stamp.

Tips "Atheneum has a 40+ year tradition of publishing distinguished books for children. Study our titles."

Ⓐ AVON BOOKS/BOOKS FOR YOUNG READERS

1350 Avenue of the Americas, New York NY 10019. (212)261-6500. Fax: (212)261-6668. Web site: www.harperc hildrens.com.

- Avon is not accepting unagented submissions. See listing for HarperCollins Children's Books.

AZRO PRESS

PMB 342, 1704 Llano St. B, Santa Fe NM 87505. (505)989-3272. Fax: (505)989-3832. E-mail: books@azropress.c om. Web site: www.azropress.com. Estab. 1997. Specializes in trade books, fiction. **Writers contact:** Gae Eisenhardt. Produces 3-4 picture books/year; 1 young reader/year. 75% of books by first-time authors. "We like to publish illustrated children's books by Southwestern authors and illustrators. We are always looking for books with a Southwestern look or theme."

Fiction Picture books: animal, history, humor, nature/environment. Young readers: adventure, animal, hi-lo, history, humor. Average word length: picture books—1,200; young readers—2,000-2,500. Recently published *Tis for Tortilla*, by Jody Alpers, ill by Celeste Johnson; *Cactus Critter Bash*, by Sid Hausman; *Cute As A Button*, by Jeff della Penna, ill by Nicole Blau.

Nonfiction Picture books: animal, geography, history. Young readers: geography, history.

How to Contact/Writers Accepts international submissions. Fiction/nonfiction: Query or submit complete ms. Responds to queries/mss in 3-4 months. Publishes book 1½-2 years after acceptance. Considers simultaneous submissions.

Illustration Accepts material from international illustrators. Works with 3 illustrators/year. Uses color artwork only. Reviews ms/illustration packages. Reviews work for future assignments. Query with samples. Submit samples to illustrations editor. Responds in 3-4 months. Samples not returned. Samples not filed.

Terms Pays authors royalty of 10% based on wholesale price. Pays illustrators by the project ($2,000) or royalty of 5%. Author sees galleys for review. Illustrators see dummies for review. Originals returned to artist at job's completion. Catalog available for #10 SASE and 3 first-class stamps. Offers writer's guidelines for SASE. See website for artist's, photographer's guidelines.

Tips ''We are not currently accepting new manuscripts. Please see our Web site for acceptance date.''

☐ BANCROFT PRESS

P.O. Box 65360, Baltimore MD 21209. (410)358-0658. Fax: (410)637-7377. E-mail: bruceb@bancroftpress.com. Web site: www.bancroftpress.com. **Manuscript Acquisitions:** Bruce Bortz, publisher. **Art Acquisitions:** Bruce Bortz, publisher. Publishes 1 middle reader/year; 2-4 young adult titles/year.

Fiction Middle readers, young adults: adventure, animal, contemporary, fantasy, humor, multicultural, problem novels, religion, science fiction, special needs, sports, suspense/mystery. Average word length: middle readers—40,000; young adults—50,000. Recently published *Finding the Forger: A Bianca Balducci Mystery*, by Libby Sternberg (ages 10 and up); *The Reappearance of Sam Webber*, by Jonathon Scott Fuqua (ages 10 and up); *Jake: The Second Novel in the Gunpowder Trilogy*, by Arch Montgomery (ages 13 and up); *Like We Care*, by Tom Matthews (ages 15 and up).

Nonfiction Middle readers, young adults: animal, biography, concept, health, history, multicultural, music/ dance, nature/environment, reference, religion, science, self help, social issues, special needs, sports, textbooks.

How to Contact/Writers Fiction/nonfiction: Submit complete ms or submit outline/synopsis and 3 sample chapters. Responds to queries/mss in at least 6 months. Publishes book 18 months after acceptance. Will consider e-mail submissions, simultaneous submissions or previously published work.

Terms Pays authors royalty of 8% based on retail price. Offers advances (average amount: $1,000-3,000). Sends galleys to authors. Catalog and ms guidelines available on Web site.

Tips ''We advise writers to visit our Web site and to be familiar with our previous work. Patience is the number one attribute contributors must have. It takes us a very long time to get through submitted material, because we are such a small company. Also, we only publish 4-6 books per year, so it may take a long time for your optioned book to be published. We like to be able to market our books to be used in schools and in libraries. We prefer fiction that bucks trends and moves in a new direction.We are especially interested in mysteries and humor (especially humorous mysteries).''

BANTAM DELACORTE DELL BOOKS FOR YOUNG READERS

Random House Children's Books, 1745 Broadway, Mail Drop 9-2, New York NY 10019. (212)782-9000. Web sites: www.randomhouse.com/kids, www.randomhouse.com/teens. Imprints of Random House Children's Books. 75% of books published through agents. Publishes middle-grade and young adult fiction.

How to Contact/Writers Unsolicited mss are only being accepted as submissions to either the Delacorte Dell Yearling Contest for a First Middle-Grade Novel or Delacorte Press Contest for a First Young Adult Novel. See Web site for rules and guidelines or make a written request addressed to either contest and include a SASE. Query letters for novels are accepted when addresses to a specific editor and must be accompanied by a SASE for response. No e-mail queires.

BAREFOOT BOOKS

2067 Massachusetts Ave., 5th Floor, Cambridge MA 02140. Web site: www.barefootbooks.com. **Manuscript/ Art Acquisitions:** U.S. editor. Publishes 35 picture books/year; 10 anthologies/year. 35% of books by first-time authors. ''At Barefoot Books, we celebrate art and story that opens the hearts and minds of children from all walks of life, inspiring them to read deeper, search further, and explore their own creative gifts. Taking our inspiration from many different cultures, we focus on themes that encourage independence of spirit, enthusiasm for learning, and sharing of the world's diversity. Interactive, playful and beautiful, our products combine the best of the present with the best of the past to educate our children as the caretakers of tomorrow.www.barefoot books.com.''

Fiction Picture books, young readers: animal, anthology, concept, folktales, multicultural, nature/environment, poetry, spirituality. Middle readers, young adults: anthology, folktales. Average word length: picture books—500-1,000; young readers—2,000-3,000; anthologies—10,000-20,000. Recently published *The Prince's Bedtime*, by Joanne Oppenheim; *The Hare and the Tortoise*, by Ranjit Bolt; *Elusive Moose*, by Clare Beaton.

How to Contact/Writers Fiction: Submit complete ms for picture books; outline/synopsis and 1 sample story for collections. Responds in 4 months if SASE is included. Will consider simultaneous submissions and previously published work.

Illustration Works with 20 illustrators/year. Uses color artwork only. Reviews ms/illustration packages from artists. Send query and art samples or dummy for picture books. Illustrations only: Query with samples or send promo sheet and tearsheets. Responds only if interested. Samples returned with SASE.

Terms Pays authors royalty of 5% based on retail price. Offers advances. Sends galleys to authors. Originals returned to artist at job's completion. Book catalog available for SAE and 5 first-class stamps; ms guidelines available for SASE.

Tips ''We are looking for books that inspire and are filled with a sense of magic and wonder. We also look for strong stories from all different cultures, reflecting the ways of the individual culture while also touching deeper human truths that suggest we are all one. We welcome playful submissions for the very youngest children and also anthologies of stories for older readers, all focused around a universal theme. We encourage writers and artists to visit our Web site and read some of our books to get a sense of our editorial philosophy and what we publish before they submit to us. Always, we encourage them to stay true to their inner voice and artistic vision that reaches out for timeless stories, beyond the momentary trends that may exist in the market today.''

BARRONS EDUCATIONAL SERIES

250 Wireless Blvd., Hauppauge NY 11788. Fax: (631)434-3723. E-mail: waynebarr@barronseduc.com. Web site: www.barronseduc.com. **Manuscript Acquisitions:** Wayne R. Barr, acquisitions manager. **Art Acquisitions:** Bill Kuchler. Publishes 20 picture books/year; 20 young readers/year; 20 middle readers/year; 10 young adult titles/year. 25% of books by first-time authors; 25% of books from agented writers.

Fiction Picture books: animal, concept, multicultural, nature/environment. Young readers: adventure, multicultural, nature/environment, fantasy, suspense/mystery. Middle readers: adventure, fantasy, multicultural, nature/environment, problem novels, suspense/mystery. Young adults: problem novels. Recently published *Night at the Museum*, by Leslie Goldman; *Renoir and the Boy in the Long Hair*, by Wendy Wax.

Nonfiction Picture books: concept, reference. Young readers: biography, how-to, reference, self help, social issues. Middle readers: hi-lo, how-to, reference, self help, social issues. Young adults: reference, self help, social issues, sports.

How to Contact/Writers Fiction: Query via e-mail with no attached files. No snail mail. Nonfiction: Submit outline/synopsis and sample chapters. ''Nonfiction Submissions must be accompanied by SASE for response.'' Responds to queries in 2 months; mss in 4 months. Publishes a book 1 year after acceptance. Will consider simultaneous submissions.

Illustration Works with 20 illustrators/year. Reviews ms/illustration packages from artists. Query first; 3 chapters of ms with 1 piece of final art, remainder roughs. Illustrations only: Submit tearsheets or slides plus résumé. Responds in 2 months.

Terms Pays authors royalty of 10-14% based on net price or buys ms outright for $2,000 minimum. Pays illustrators by the project based on retail price. Sends galleys to authors; dummies to illustrators. Book catalog, ms/artist's guidelines for 9×12 SAE.

Tips Writers: ''We publish preschool storybooks, concept books and middle grade and YA chapter books. No romance novels.'' Illustrators: ''We are happy to receive a sample illustration to keep on file for future consideration. Periodic notes reminding us of your work are acceptable.'' Children's book themes ''are becoming much more contemporary and relevant to a child's day-to-day activities, fewer talking animals. We have a great interest in children's fiction (ages 7-11 and ages 12-16) dealing with modern problems.''

BENCHMARK BOOKS

Imprint of Marshall Cavendish, 99 White Plains Rd., Tarrytown NY 10591. (914)332-8888. Fax: (914)332-1888. E-mail: mbisson@marshallcavendish.com. Web site: www.marshallcavendish.us. **Manuscript Acquisitions:** Michelle Bisson. Publishes about 300 young reader, middle reader and young adult books/year. ''We look for interesting treatments of only nonfiction subjects related to elementary, middle school and high school curriculum.''

Nonfiction Most nonfiction topics should be curriculum related. Average word length: 4,000-20,000. All books published as part of a series. Recently published First Americans (series), Family Trees (series), Bookworms (series).

How to Contact/Writers Nonfiction: ''Please read our catalog or view our Web site before submitting proposals. We only publish series. We do not publish individual titles.'' Submit outline/synopsis and 1 or more sample chapters. Responds to queries/mss in 3 months. Publishes a book 2 years after acceptance. Will consider simultaneous submissions.

Photography Buys stock and assigns work.

Terms Buys work outright. Sends galleys to authors. Book catalog available online. All imprints included in a single catalog.

BICK PUBLISHING HOUSE

307 Neck Rd., Madison CT 06443. (203)245-0073. Fax: (203)245-5990. E-mail: bickpubhse@aol.com. Web site: www.bickpubhouse.com. **Aquisitions Editor:** Dale Carlson. ''We publish psychological, philosophical,

scientific information on health and recovery, wildlife rehabilitation, living with disabilities, teen psychology and science for adults and young adults.''

Nonfiction Young adults: nature/environment, religion, science, self help, social issues, special needs. Average word length: young adults—60,000. Recently published *In and Out of Your Mind* (teen science); *Who Said What?* (philosophy quotes for teens); *What are You Doing with Your Life?*, by J. Krishnamurti (philosophy for teens); *The Teen Brain Book*, by Dale Carlson.

How to Contact/Writers Fiction: Submit outline/synopsis and 3 sample chapters. Nonfiction: Submit outline/synopsis or outline/synopsis and 3 sample chapters. Responds to queries/mss in 2 weeks. Publishes book 1 year after acceptance. Will consider simultaneous submissions and previously published work.

Illustration Works with 1 illustrator/year. Uses b&w artwork only. Reviews ms/illustration packages from artists. Submit sketches of teens or science drawings. Contact: Dale Carlson, president. Illustrations only: Query with photocopies, résumé, SASE. Responds in 2 weeks. Samples returned with SASE.

Terms Pays authors royalty of 5-10%. Pays illustrators by the project (range: up to $1,000). Sends galleys to authors; dummies to illustrators. Book catalog available for SASE with 1 first-class stamp; writer's guidelines available for SAE. Catalog available on Web site.

Tips ''Read our books!''

BIRDSONG BOOKS

1322 Bayview Rd., Middletown DE 19709. (302)378-7274. E-mail: Birdsong@BirdsongBooks.com. Web site: www.BirdsongBooks.com. **Manuscript & Art Acquisitions:** Nancy Carol Willis, president. Publishes 1 picture book/year. ''Birdsong Books seeks to spark the delight of discovering our wild neighbors and natural habitats. We believe knowledge and understanding of nature fosters caring and a desire to protect the Earth and all living things. Our emphasis is on North American animals and habitats, rather than people.''

Nonfiction Picture books, young readers: activity books, animal, nature/environment. Average word length: picture books—800-1,000. Recently published The Animals' Winter Sleep, by Lynda-Graham Barber (age 3-6, nonfiction picture book); *Red Knot: A Shorebird's Incredible Journey*, by Nancy Carol Willis (age 6-9, nonfiction picture book); *Raccoon Moon*, by Nancy Carol Willis (ages 5-8, natural science picture book); *The Robins In Your Backyard*, by Nancy Carol Willis (ages 4-7, nonfiction picture book).

How to Contact/Writers Nonfiction: Submit complete manuscript package with SASE. Responds to mss in 3 months. Publishes book 2-3 years after acceptance. Will consider simultaneous submissions (if stated).

Illustration Accepts material from residents of U.S. Works with 1 illustrator/year. Reviews ms/illustration packages from artists. Send ms with dummy (plus samples/tearsheets for style). Illustrations only: Query with brochure, résumé, samples, SASE, or tearsheets. Responds only if interested. Samples returned with SASE.

Photography Uses North American animals and habitats (currently North American animals in winter dens). Submit cover letter, résumé, promo piece, stock photo list.

Tips ''We are a small independent press actively seeking manuscripts that fit our narrowly defined niche. We are only interested in nonfiction, natural science picture books or educational activity books about North American animals and habitats. Our books include several pages of back matter suitable for early elementary classrooms. Mailed submissions with SASE only. No e-mail submissions or phone calls, please. Cover letters should sell author/illustrator and book idea.''

BLOOMING TREE PRESS

P.O. Box 140934, Austin TX 78714. Estab. 2000. (512)921-8846. Fax: (512)873-7710. E-mail: email@bloomingtreepress.com. Web site: www.bloomingtreepress.com. **Publisher:** Miriam Hees; Madeline Smoot, senior editor, children's division; Judy Gregerson, editor, children's division, Meghan Dietsche, associate editor, children's division; Kay Pluta, accociate edtior, children's division; Bradford Hees, senior editor, graphic novels/comics. **Art Acquisitions:** Regan Johnson. ''Blooming Tree Press is dedicated to producing high quality book for the young and the young at heart. It is our hope that you will find your dreams between that pages of our books.''

Fiction Picture books: adventure, animal, contemporary, fantasy, folktales, history, humor, multicultural, religion, science fiction, special needs, sports. Young readers: adventure, animal, contemporary, fantasy, folktales, history, humor, multicultural, rcligion, science fiction, special needs, sports, suspense. Middle readers: adventure, animal, anthology, contemporary, fantasy, folktales, history, humor, multicultural, poetry, religion, science fiction, suspense. Young adults/teens: adventure, animal, anthology, contemporary, fantasy, folktales, history, humor, religion, science fiction, suspense. Average word length: picture books—500-1,000; young readers—800-9,000; middle readers—25,000-40,000; young adult/teens: 40,000-70,000. Recently published *Jessica McBean, Tap Dance Queen*, by Carole Gerger, illustrated by Patrice Barton (chapter book about teasing); *One-Eyed Jack*, by Paula Miller, illustrated by Chris Forrest (mid-grade about a boy and his dog in 1880s Montana); *Summer Shorts*, by multiple authors and illustrators (mid-grade stories about summer); Kichi in Jungle Jeopardy, by Lila Guzman, illustrations by Regan Johnson (middle grade about a talking dog in the Mayan temples.

Nonfiction Picture Books: biography, cooking, geography, history, self help, social issues, special needs, sports.

Scott Westerfeld

'Solve your problems on the page'

I f you think the characters in Scott Westerfeld's books have adventurous lives, then you should meet the author himself. As if writing and publishing 10 books since 2004 isn't enough, Westerfeld also works as an educational software designer and a success-ful composer for modern dance. And he somehow still finds time to travel with his wife back and forth across the globe between New York and Sydney, Australia—the two cities he calls home.

Prior to writing for a young adult audience, Westerfeld wrote science fiction novels for a more mature market. His first success creating a series was with Succession in 2003. He then used this experience inventing extensive plots to create two YA trilogies, Midnight-ers and Uglies, whose sequels were published almost simultaneously between 2005 and 2007.

When you first began writing *Uglies*, did you imagine your characters would lead you into a series?

I always knew the story would unfold over more than a single book. I began the idea aware that my characters would overthrow the world's established order in the end—I just didn't know how. I'm primarily a science fiction and fantasy writer, genres that thrive in the series format. After all, once you've created an entire alternate world, you might as well play in it for a while. *Uglies* sold from an outline that covered all three novels in the series. Of course, tales grow in the telling, and the third book turned out very different from its original outline. For me, writing a series is about building a landscape, a place full of tension and drama that lends itself to all the extensions that take place over several books. The setting becomes a character so to speak.

With that said, a trilogy can be a big commitment to make for both writers and publish-ers, because first books don't always sell and later books usually have to be bought unseen. Trilogies and longer series often need sustained support to succeed. For these reasons, publishers nowadays often see trilogies as more of an economic gamble and shy away from taking them on. Back when advances in the young adult market were modest, that level of commitment wasn't considered nearly as risky as it is now. Today's field is much more expansive and expensive to compete in, and this kind of environment doesn't encourage risk taking.

You once said in an interview that new writers need to, "Write 'til it hurts." How has this phrase been true in your experience?

Writing is the best way to learn how to write—the same goes for playing basketball, paint-ing, cooking and being successful in just about anything. Yet so many young writers grasp at any solution other than putting the pen to paper. For example, many young writers have asked me what to do when they get contradictory advice from their writing groups. I think the answer is obvious: Write it both ways and decide which way is better. Then create a third and a fourth version and see if either of these directions are stronger than the first two. My best advice—solve your problems on the page. Persistence is the only virtue I've seen consistently rewarded in this business.

What is your writing process like?

I write every day. I start by editing the previous three days' work and then dive into writing a fresh a thousand words or so. The editing portion of the day leads my brain back into the

The thrilling fourth book in the UGLIES series

EXTRAS
SCOTT WESTERFELD
NEW YORK TIMES BESTSELLING SERIES

Jacket photo © 2007 Howard Pyle. Reprinted with permission of Simon Pulse, an imprint of Simon & Schuster.

Scott Westerfeld's Uglies series (Simon Pulse) started out as a trilogy—*Uglies*, *Pretties*, *Specials*. *Extras*, published in 2007, picks up where *Specials* left off but features new characters wending their way through Westerfeld's distopian future.

world and minds of my characters. Editing also helps me gather momentum for when I reach the dreaded blank space. For me, more dramatic levels of output—10,000 word days—may feel exhilarating, but they ultimately do more damage than good, because I am frequently left with a mass of words that are unfocused. In my experience, slow and steady wins the race.

Also, I only write one novel at a time, and I try to do as little as possible outside that novel. Paying bills, seeing friends—all of it suffers. I would call this single-mindedness. Novels are massive documents, after all, and to make room for them in your head, you're going to have to clear out other things that are distracting. No one will care in a hundred years that you didn't shave today.

It also helps that my wife, Justine, is a writer. When she and I are in full writing mode, we read our work to each other every few days. It's great to get feedback while the words are still "soft" I find it very useful to say the words out loud to another listening ear. In fact, Justine often challenges me to take plot paths that are much more difficult and taxing than the ones I might have chosen on my own. After all, she doesn't have to do the work.

What changes or trends do you see happening in the YA market?

The best thing about this market is that it's growing in all directions. As I write this, the *New York Times* chapter book list includes science fiction, fantasy, novel-length poetry, contemporary realism, historical fiction, nonfiction, and even a comic. That's seven out of 10 books with distinct genres. Therefore, my advice to young writers would be not to worry about categories—just write well.

Having said that, we're living in a golden age of nonfiction and I personally would like to try my hand at it in the future. I've tackled multiple genres in the fiction world, but I have an entire nonfiction book in my mind that I plan to write, once I get the time. There are many nonfiction writers whose techniques I admire, like Eric Larson, author of *Devil in the White City*. I hope to perfect some of these practices and adapt them for a YA audience.

What are the benefits of having an agent?

My first few adult books were represented, but sadly my agent retired. She and I had worked so well together that I was unsure if anyone could fill her big shoes, so I decided to go it alone. I spent four years without an agent, which I regret, because it took a considerable amount of energy away from my actual writing and left me without guidance.

What do I mean by guidance? Well, if you're writing a cat story, wouldn't you rather submit your manuscript to an editor with a big cat poster in her office? A good agent knows which editors have cat posters in their offices, so you don't waste time headed in the wrong direction. It's that simple.

Like many writers, it took you almost 10 years to get your first book published. How did you use your writing talent in the meantime?

I worked as an editor, an indexer, a software designer, and a gopher at a small packaging house. All of these jobs helped me in different ways to become a better writer. In my opinion, working in the industry (as a librarian, agent, editor, or bookseller) seems really essential. I also acted as a ghost writer before I published my own book. I found that writing in someone else's voice was great practice. It gave me the space to play and develop my craft without revealing as much of myself. For many writers, honing these skills without immediate personal exposure is a real benefit.

—Rebecca Ward

Young Readers: animal, biography, careers, cooking, geography, history, music/dance, religion, science, self help, social issues, special needs, sports. Middle Readers: biography, cooking, geography, history, how-to, music/dance, religion, science, self help, social issues, sports. Young Adults/Teens: biography, careers, cooking, geography, history, hobbies, music/dance, religion, science, self help, social issues, sports.

How to Contact/Writers Fiction: Query. Nonfiction: submit outline/synopsis and 3 sample chapters. Responds to queries in 1-3 months; mss in 3-4 months. Publishes ms 18-36 months after acceptance. Will consider simultaneous submissions.

Illustration Works with 6-20 illustrators/year. Reviews ms/illustration packages. Send manuscript with dummy and sample art. Contact: Regan Johnson, publisher. Illustration only: Query with samples to Regan Johnson, publisher. Samples not returned; sample filed.

Terms Pays authors royalty of 10% depending on the project. Pays illustrators by the project. Authors see galleys for review; illustrators see dummies. Send e-mail with mailing address for catalog. Writer's guidelines on Web site.

Tips ''Send a crisp and clean one-page query letter stating your project, why it is right for the market, and a little about yourself. Write what you know, not what's 'in.' Remember, every great writer/illustrator started somewhere. Keep submitting . . . don't ever give up.''

BLOOMSBURY CHILDREN'S BOOKS

Imprint of Bloomsbury PLC, 175 Fifth Avenue, Suite 315, New York NY 10010. (646)307-5858. Fax: (212)982-2837. E-mail: bloomsburykids@bloomsburyusa.co. Web site: www.bloomsbury.com/usa. **Contact:** Manuscript Submissions or Art Department. Specializes in fiction, picture books. Publishes 15 picture books/year; 10 young readers/year; 20 middle readers/year; 25 young adult titles/year. 25% of books by first-time authors.

- Bloomsbury Children's Books will no longer respond to unsolicited manuscripts or art submissions. They say: ''Please include a telephone and e-mail address where we may contact you if we are interested in your work. Do not send a self-addressed stamped envelope. We regret the inconvenience, but unfortunately, we are too understaffed to maintain a correspondence with authors. We will continue to accept unsolicited manuscripts but we can contact you only if we are interested in acquiring your work.''

Fiction Picture books: adventure, animal, contemporary, fantasy, folktales, history, humor, multicultural, poetry, suspense/mystery. Young readers: adventure, animal, anthology, concept, contemporary, fantasy, folktales, history, humor, multicultural, suspense/mystery. Middle readers: adventure, animal, contemporary, fantasy, folktales, history, humor, multicultural, poetry, problem novels. Young adults: adventure, animal, anthology, contemporary, fantasy, folktales, history, humor, multicultural, problem novels, science fiction, sports, suspense/mystery. Recently published *Ruthie and the Not-So Teeny Tiny Lie*, by Laura Rankin (picture books); *The Salamander Spell*, by E.D. Baker (middle reader); *Book of a Thousand Days*, by Shannon Hale (young adult fantasy). ''All Bloomsbury Children's Books submissions are considered on an individual basis. Please note that we do accept simultaneus submissions but please be courteous and inform us if another house has made an offer on your work.''

Illustration ''Writers: There is no need to send art with a picture book manuscript. Artists should submit art with a picture book manuscript. Artist should submit art samples separately to the attention of the Art Department. We do not return art samples. Please do not send original art!''

Terms Pays authors royalty or work purchased outright for jackets. Offers advances. Pays illustrators by the project or royalty. Pays photographers by the project or per photo. Sends galleys to authors; dummies to illustrators. Originals returned to artist at job's completion. Writer's and art guidelines available on Web site: www.bloomsburyusa.com/FAQ.

Tips ''Spend a lot of time in the bookstore and library to keep up on trends in market. Never send originals. We are not liable for artwork or manuscript submissions. Do not send a SASE, as we are no longer responding to submissions. Please address all submissions to the attention of Manuscript Submissions. Please make sure that everything is stapled, paper clipped, or rubber-banded together. We do not accept e-mail or CD/DVD submissions. Be sure your work is appropriate for us. Familiarize yourself with our list by going to bookstores or libraries.''

BOYDS MILLS PRESS

815 Church St., Honesdale PA 18431. Web site: www.boydsmillspress.com. Estab. 1990. Imprints: Calkins Creek Books, Front Street, Wordsong. 5% of books from agented writers. ''We publish a wide range of quality children's books of literary merit, from preschool to young adult.''

Fiction Ages 0-18: adventure, contemporary, humor, multicultural, rhyming. Picture books: all kinds. Multicultural themes include any story showing a child as an integral part of a culture and which provides children with insight into a culture they otherwise might be unfamiliar with.

Nonfiction All levels: nature/environment, history, science. Picture books, young readers, middle readers: animal, multicultural. Does not want to see reference/curricular text.

How to Contact/Writers Fiction/nonfiction: Submit complete ms or submit through agent. Label package "Manucript Submission" and include SASE. Responds in 3 months.

Illustration Works with 25 illustrators/year. Reviews ms/illustration packages from artists. Submit complete ms with 1 or 2 pieces of art. Illustrations only: Query with samples best suited to the art (postcard, 8½×11, etc.). Label package "Art Sample Submission." Responds only if interested. Samples returned with SASE. Samples filed. Originals returned at job's completion.

Photography Assigns work.

Terms Authors paid royalty or work purchased outright. Offers advances. Illustrators paid by the project or royalties; varies. Photographers paid by the project, per photo, or royalties; varies. Manuscripts/artist's guidelines available on Web site.

Tips "Picture books with fresh approaches, not worn themes, are our strongest need at this time. Check to see what's already on the market and on our Web site before submitting your story. Prose fiction for middle-grade through young adult should be submitted to Boyds Mills imprint Front Street—see Front Street listing for submission information. Poetry for all ages should be submitted to Boyds Mills Wordsong imprint—see Wordsong listing for submission information. Historical fiction and nonfiction about the United States for all ages should be submitted to Calkins Creek Books—see Calkins Creek listing for submission information."

BRIGHT RING PUBLISHING, INC.

P.O. Box 31338, Bellingham WA 98228. (360)592-9201. Fax: (360)592-4503. E-mail: maryann@brightring.com. Web site: www.brightring.com. **Editor:** MaryAnn Kohl.

- Bright Ring is no longer accepting manuscript submissions.

CALKINS CREEK BOOKS

Boyds Mills Press, 815 Church St., Honesdale PA 18431. Web site: www.calkinscreek.com. Estab. 2004. "We aim to publish books that are a well-written blend of creative writing and extensive research which emphasize important events, people, and places in U.S. history."

Fiction All levels: history. Recently published *Blue*, by Joyce Moyer Hostrtter (ages 10 and up, historical fiction); *Booth's Daughter*, by Raymond Wemmlinger (ages 10 and up, historical fiction).

Nonfiction All levels: history. Recently published *The Printer's Trail*, by Gail Jarrow (ages 10 and up, nonfiction chapter book); *American Slave, American Hero*, by Laurence Pringle (ages 8 and up, nonfiction picture book); *Jeannette Rankin: Political Pioneer*, by Gretchen Woelfle (ages 10 and up, nonfiction biography).

How to Contact/Writers Accepts international submissions. Fiction: Submit outline/synopsis and 3 sample chapters. Nonfiction: Submit outline/synopsis and 3 sample chapters. Considers simultaneous submissions. Responds in 3 months.

Illustration Accepts material from international illustrators. Works with 25 (for all Boyds Mills Press imprints) illustrators/year. Uses both color and b&w. Reviews ms/illustration packages. For ms/illustration packages: Submit ms with 2 pieces of final art. Submit ms/illustration packages to Tim Gillner, art director. Reviews work for future assignments. If interested in illustrating future titles, query with samples. Submit samples to Tim Gillner, art director.

Photography Buys stock images and assigns work. Submit photos to: Tim Gillner, art director. Uses color or b&w 8×10 prints. For first contact, send promo piece (color or b&w).

Terms Authors paid royalty or work purchased outright. Offers advances. Illustrators paid by the project or royalties; varies. Photographers paid by the project, per photo, or royalties; varies. Manuscripts/artist's guidelines available on Web site.

Tips "Read through our recently-published titles and review our catalog. When selecting titles to publish, our emphasis will be on important events, people, and places in U.S. history. Writers are encouraged to submit a detailed bibliography, including secondary and primary sources, and expert reviews with their submissions."

CANDLEWICK PRESS

99 Dover St., Somerville MA 02144. (617)661-3330. Fax: (617)661-0565. E-mail: bigbear@candlewick.com. Web site: www.candlewick.com. **Manuscript Acquisitions:** Karen Lotz, publisher; Liz Bicknell, editorial director and associate publisher; Joan Powers, editorial director; Mary Lee Donovan, executive editor; Sarah Ketchersid, senior editor; Deborah Wayshak, executive editor; Andrea Tompa, associate edtior; Katie Cunningham, associate editor; Kaylan Adair, associate editor; Kate Fletcher, associate editor; Jennifer Yoon, associate editor. **Art Acquisitions:** Anne Moore. Publishes 160 picture books/year; 15 middle readers/year; 15 young adult titles/year. 5% of books by first-time authors. "Our books are truly for children, and we strive for the very highest standards in the writing, illustrating, designing and production of all of our books. And we are not averse to risk."

- Candlewick Press is not accepting queries and unsolicited mss at this time. Candlewick title *Good Masters! Sweet Ladies! Voices from a Medieval Village*, by Amy Schlitz, won the John Newbery Medal in 2008. Their title *Twelve Rounds to Glory: The Story of Muhammad Ali*, by Charles R. Smith Jr., illustrated by Bryan

Collier, won a Coretta Scott King Author Honor Award in 2008. Their title *The Astonishing Life of Octavian Nothing*, by M.T. Anderson won the Boston Globe-Hornbook Award for Fiction and Poetry in 2007.

Fiction Picture books: animal, concept, contemporary, fantasy, history, humor, multicultural, nature/environment, poetry. Middle readers, young adults: contemporary, fantasy, history, humor, multicultural, poetry, science fiction, sports, suspense/mystery. Recently published *The Astonishing LIfe of Octavian Nothing, Traitor to the Nation: Volume One: The Pox Party by M.T. Anderson* (young adult fiction); *Surrender*, by Sonya Hartnett (young adult fiction); *Good Masters! Sweet Ladies! by* Laura Amy Schlitz, illustrated by Robert Byrd (middle grade poetry collection), *Drangonolgy*, by Ernest Drake; Encyclopedia Prehistorica: *Dinosaurs*, by Robert Sabuda and Matthew Reinhart.

Nonfiction Picture books: concept, biography, geography, nature/environment. Young readers: biography, geography, nature/environment. Recently published *Twelve Rounds to Glory : The Story of Muhammad Ali* by Charles R. Smith Jr., illustrated by Bryan Collier.

Illustration Works with approx. 40 ill ustrators/year. ''We prefer to see a range of styles from artists along with samples showing strong characters (human or animals) in various settings with various emotions.'' Receives unsolicited illustration packages/dummies from artists. Color or b&w copies only, please; no originals. Illustrations only: Submit color samples to Art Resource Coordinator. Samples returned with SASE; samples filed.

Terms Pays authors royalty of $2\frac{1}{2}$-10% based on retail price. Offers advances. Pays illustrators $2\frac{1}{2}$-10% royalty based on retail price. Sends galleys to authors; dummies to illustrators. Pays photographers $2\frac{1}{2}$-10% royalty. Original artwork returned at job's completion.

CAPSTONE PRESS INC.

151 Good Counsel Dr., P.O. Box 669, Mankato MN 55438. Fax: (888)262-0705. Web site: www.capstone-press.com. Book publisher. **Contact:** Kay M. Olson. Imprints: A+ Books, Pebble Books, Edge Books, Blazers books, Snap Books, Capstone High-Interest Books, Fact Finders, First Facts, Pebble Plus, You Choose Books. ''Capstone Press books provide new and struggling readers with a strong foundation on which to build reading success. Our nonfiction books are effective tools for reaching readers, with precisely-leveled text tailored to their individual needs.''

- Capstone Press does not accept unsolicited manuscripts.

Nonfiction Publishes only nonfiction books. All elementary levels: animals, arts/crafts, biography, geography, health, history, hobbies, science, and social studies.

How to Contact/Writers Does not accept submissions. Do not send mss. Instead, send query letter, résumé, samples of nonfiction writing to be considered for assignment, and references

Terms Authors paid flat fee. Buys all rights.

Tips ''See website prior to sending query letter.''

CAROLRHODA BOOKS, INC.

A division of Lerner Publishing Group, 241 First Ave. N., Minneapolis MN 55401. Web site: www.lernerbooks.c om. **Contact:** Zelda Wagner, submissions editor. Estab. 1969. Publishes hardcover originals. Averages 8-10 picture books each year for ages 3-8, 6 fiction titles for ages 7-18, and 2-3 nonfiction titles for various ages.

- Starting in 2007, Lerner Publishing Group no longer accepts submissions to any of their imprints except for Kar-Ben Publishing.

How to Contact/Writers ''We will continue to seek targeted solicitations at specific reading levels and in specific subject areas. The company will list these targeted solicitations on our Web site and in national newsletters, such as the SCBWI Bulletin.''

CARTWHEEL BOOKS, for the Very Young

Imprint of Scholastic Inc., 557 Broadway, New York NY 10012. (212)343-4804. Web site: www.scholastic.com. Estab. 1991. Book publisher. Vice President/Editorial Director: Ken Geist. **Manuscript Acquisitions:** Grace Maccarone, executive editor; Cecily Kaiser, executive editor. **Editorial Assistant:** Erika Lo. **Art Acquisitions:** Daniel Moreton, executive art director. Publishes 15-20 picture books/year; 10-20 easy readers/year; 40-45 novelty/concept/board books/year.

Fiction Picture books, young readers: humor, seasonal/holiday, humor, family/love. Average word length: picture books—100-500; easy readers—100-1,500.

Nonfiction Picture books, young readers: seasonal/curricular topics involving animals (polar animals, ocean animals, hibernation), nature (fall leaves, life cycles, weather, solar system), history (first Thanksgiving, MLK Jr., George Washington, Columbus). ''Most of our nonfiction is either written on assignment or is within a series. We do not want to see any arts/crafts or cooking.'' Average word length: picture books—100-1,500; young readers—100-2,000.

How to Contact/Writers Cartwheel Books is no longer accepting unsolicited mss. All unsolicited materials will be returned unread. Fiction/nonfiction: For previously published or agented authors, submit complete ms.

Responds to mss in 6 months. Publishes a book within 2 years after acceptance. SASE required with all submissions.

Illustration Works with 30 illustrators/year. Reviews illustration packages from artists. Illustrations only: Query with samples; arrange personal portfolio review; send promo sheet, tearsheets to be kept on file. Contact: Executive Art Director. Responds in 6 months. Samples returned with SASE; samples filed. Please do not send original artwork.

Photography Buys stock and assigns work. Uses photos of kids, families, vehicles, toys, animals. Submit published samples, color promo piece.

Terms Pays advance against royalty or flat fee. Sends galley to authors; dummy to illustrators. Originals returned to artist at job's completion.

Tips ''With each Cartwheel list, we seek a pleasing balance among board books and novelty books, hardcover picture books and gift books, nonfiction, paperback storybooks and easy readers. Cartwheel seeks to acquire projects that speak to young children and their world: new and exciting novelty formats, fresh seasonal and holiday stories, curriculum/concept-based titles, and books for beginning readers. Our books are inviting and appealing, clearly marketable, and have inherent educational and social value. We strive to provide the earliest readers relevant and exciting books, that will ultimately lead to a lifetime of reading, learning, and wondering. Know what types of books we do. Check out bookstores or catalogs to see where your work would fit best.''

☐ ☑ CHARLESBRIDGE

85 Main St., Watertown MA 02472. (617)926-0329. Fax: (617)926-5720. E-mail: tradeeditorial@charlesbridge.com. Web site: www.charlesbridge.com. Estab. 1980. Book publisher. **Contact:** Trade Editorial Department. Publishes 60% nonfiction, 40% fiction picture books and early chapter books. Publishes nature, science, multicultural, social studies and fiction picture books.

- Charlesbridge title *Hello, Bumblebee Bat,* written by Darrin Lunde, illustrated by Patricia J. Wynne, won a Theodor Seuss Geisel Award in 2008.

Fiction Picture books and chapter books: &quotStrong, realistic stories with enduring themes.'' Considers the following categories: adventure, concept, contemporary, health, history, humor, multicultural, nature/environment, special needs, sports, suspense/mystery. Recently published *The Searcher and Old Tree,* by David Mcphail; *Not so Tall for Six,* by Dianna Hutts Aston; *Wiggle and Waggle,* by Caroline Arnold; *Rickshaw Girl,* by Mitali Perkins.

Nonfiction Picture books: animal, biography, careers, concept, geography, health, history, multicultural, music/dance, nature/environment, religion, science, social issues, special needs, hobbies, sports. Average word length: picture books-1,000. Recently published *Trout are made of trees,* by April Pulley Sayre; *Hello, Bumblebee Bat,* by Darrin Lunde; *Teeth,* by Sneed B. Collard Iii; *Life on Earth-and Beyond: An Astrobiologist's Quest,* by Pamela S. Turner.

How to Contact/Writers Send ms as exclusive submission for three months. Responds only to mss of interest. Full mss only; no queries.

Illustration Works with 5-10 illustrators/year. Uses color artwork only. Illustrations only: Query with samples; provide résumé, tearsheets to be kept on file. &quotSend no original artwork, please.'' Responds only if interested. Samples returned with SASE; samples filed. Originals returned at job's completion.

Terms Pays authors and illustrators in royalties or work purchased outright. Manuscript/art guidelines available for SASE. Exclusive submissions only.

Tips ''Charlesbridge Publishes picture books and transitional 'bridge books' (books ranging from early readers to middle-grade chapter books. We look for fresh and engaging voices and directions in both fiction and nonfiction.''

CHELSEA HOUSE PUBLISHERS, an imprint of Infobase Publishing

Facts on File, 132 West 31st Street, 17th Floor, New York, New York 10001. (800)322-8755. Fax: (917)339-0326. E-mail: jciovacco@factsonfile.com@chelseahouse.com. Web site: www.chelseahouse.com. Specializes in nonfiction chapter books. **Manuscript Acquisitions:** Laurie Likoff, editorial director; Justine Ciovacco, managing editor. Imprints: Chelsea Clubhouse; Chelsea House. Produces 150 middle readers/year, 150 young adult books/year. 10% of books by first-time authors.

How to Contact/Writers ''All books are parts of series. Most series topics are developed by in-house editors, but suggestions are welcome. Authors my query with résumé and list of publications.''

☐ CHICAGO REVIEW PRESS

814 N. Franklin St., Chicago IL 60610. (312)337-0747. Fax: (312)337-5110. E-mail: frontdesk@chicagoreviewpress.com. Web site: www.chicagoreviewpress.com. **Manuscript Acquisitions:** Cynthia Sherry, publisher. **Art Acquisitions:** Allison Felus, managing editor. Publishes 4-5 middle readers/year; 2-3 young adult titles/year. 33% of books by first-time authors; 30% of books from agented authors. ''Chicago Review Press publishes

high-quality, nonfiction, educational activity books that extend the learning process through hands-on projects and accurate and interesting text. We look for activity books that are as much fun as they are constructive and informative.''

Nonfiction Young readers, middle readers and young adults: activity books, arts/crafts, multicultural, history, nature/environment, science. ''We're interested in hands-on, educational books; anything else probably will be rejected.'' Average length: young readers and young adults—144-160 pages. Recently published *Amazing Rubber Band Cars*, by Michael Rigsby (ages 9 and up); *Don't Touch That!*, by Jeff Day M.D. (ages 7 to 9); and *Abraham Lincoln for Kids*, by Janis Herbert (ages 9 and up).

How to Contact/Writers Enclose cover letter and no more than table of contents and 1-2 sample chapters; prefers not to receive E-mail: queries. Send for guidelines. Responds to queries/mss in 2 months. Publishes a book 1-2 years after acceptance. Will consider simultaneous submissions and previously published work.

Illustration Works with 6 illustrators/year. Uses primarily b&w artwork. Reviews ms/illustration packages from artists. Submit 1-2 chapters of ms with corresponding pieces of final art. Illustrations only: Query with samples, résumé. Responds only if interested. Samples returned with SASE.

Photography Buys photos from freelancers (''but not often''). Buys stock and assigns work. Wants ''instructive photos. We consult our files when we know what we're looking for on a book-by-book basis.'' Uses b&w prints.

Terms Pays authors royalty of $7\frac{1}{2}$-$12\frac{1}{2}$% based on retail price. Offers advances of $3,000-6,000. Pays illustrators by the project (range varies considerably). Pays photographers by the project (range varies considerably). Original artwork ''usually'' returned at job's completion. Book catalog/ms guidelines available for $3.

Tips ''We're looking for original activity books for small children and the adults caring for them—new themes and enticing projects to occupy kids' imaginations and promote their sense of personal creativity. We like activity books that are as much fun as they are constructive. Please write for guidelines so you'll know what we're looking for.''

CHILDREN'S BOOK PRESS

965 Mission St., Suite 425, San Francisco CA 94103. Web site: www.childrensbookpress.org. **Acquisitions:** Dana Goldberg. ''Children's Book Press is a nonprofit publisher of multicultural and bilingual children's literature. We publish contemporary stories reflecting the traditions and culture of minorities and new immigrants in the United States. Our goal is to help broaden the base of children's literature in this country to include stories from the African-American, Asian-American, Latino/Chicano and Native American communities. Stories should encourage critical thinking about social and/or personal issues. These ideas must be an integral part of the story.''

Fiction Picture books: contemporary, history, multicultural, poetry. Average word length: picture books—750-1,500.

Nonfiction Picture books, young readers: multicultural.

How to Contact/Writers Submit complete ms to Submissions Editor. Responds to mss in roughly 4 months. ''Please do not inquire about your manuscript. We can only return/respond to manuscripts with a SASE.'' Publishes a book 1-2 years after acceptance. Will consider simultaneous submissions.

Illustration Works with 4-5 illustrators/year. Uses color artwork only. Reviews ms/illustration packages from artists. Send ms with 3 or 4 color photocopies. Illustrations only: color copies only, no original artwork. Responds in 8-10 weeks. Samples returned with SASE.

Terms Original artwork returned at job's completion. Book catalog available; ms guidelines available via Web site or with SASE.

Tips ''Vocabulary level should be approximately third grade (eight years old) or below. Keep in mind, however, that many of the young people who read our books may be 9, 10, or 11 years old or older. Their life experiences are often more advanced than their reading level, so try to write a story that will appeal to a fairly wide age range. We are especially interested in humorous stories and original stories about contemporary life from the multicultural communities mentioned above by writers *from* those communities.''

☐ CHRISTIAN ED. PUBLISHERS

P.O. Box 26639, San Diego CA 92196. (858)578-4700. Web site: www.ChristianEdWarehouse.com. Book publisher. **Acquisitions:** Janet Ackelson, assistant editor; Carol Rogers, managing editor; Angela Lee, production coordinator. Publishes 80 Bible curriculum titles/year. ''We publish curriculum for children and youth, including program and student books and take-home papers—all handled by our assigned freelance writers only. Do not send unsolicited manuscripts.''

Fiction Young readers: contemporary. Middle readers: adventure, contemporary, suspense/mystery. ''We publish fiction for Bible club take-home papers. All fiction is on assignment only. Do not send unsolicited manuscripts.''

Nonfiction Publishes Bible curriculum and take-home papers for all ages. Recently published *All-Stars for Jesus*, by Lucinda Rollings and Laura Gray, illustrated by Aline Heiser (Bible club curriculum for grades 4-6); *Honeybees Classroom Activity Sheets*, by Janet Miller and Wanda Pelfrey, illustrated by Ron Widman (Bible club curriculum for ages 2-3).

How to Contact/Writers Fiction/nonfiction: Query. Responds to queries in 5 weeks. Publishes a book 1 year after acceptance. Send SASE for guidelines or contact Christian Ed. at cgast@cehouse.com.

Illustration Works with 6-7 illustrators/year. Query by e-mail. Contact: Angela Lee, production coordinator (alee@cehouse.com). Responds in 1 month. Samples returned with SASE.

Terms Work purchased outright from authors for 3¢/word. Pays illustrators $11-15/page. Book catalog available for 9 × 12 SAE and 4 first-class stamps; ms and art guidelines available for SASE or via e-mail.

Tips "Read our guidelines carefully before sending us a manuscript or illustrations. Do not send unsolicited manuscripts. All writing and illustrating is done on assignment only and must be age-appropriate (preschool-6th grade)."

CHRONICLE BOOKS

680 Second St. San Francisco CA 94107. (415)537-4400. Fax: (415)537-4415. Web site: www.chroniclekids.com. Book publisher. **Acquisitions:** Victoria Rock, founding publisher & editor-at-large; Traci Todd, editor; Andrea Menotti, editor; Julie Romeis, editor; Melissa Manlove, assistant editor. Publishes 50-60 (both fiction and nonfiction) books/year; 5-10% middle readers/year; young adult nonfiction titles/year. 10-25% of books by first-time authors; 20-40% of books from agented writers.

Fiction Picture books, young readers, middle readers, young adults: "We are open to a very wide range of topics." Recently published *Wave* by Suzy Lee (all ages, picture book); Ivy and Bean (series), by Annie Barrows, illustrated by Sophie Blackall (ages 6-10, chapter book).

Nonfiction Picture books, young readers, middle readers, young adults: "We are open to a very wide range of topics." Recently published *Delicious: The Life & Art of Wayne Thiebaud*, by Susan Rubin (ages 9-14, middle grade).

How to Contact/Writers Fiction/nonfiction: Submit complete ms (picture books); submit outline/synopsis and 3 sample chapters (for older readers). Responds to queries in 1 month; will not respond to submissions unless interested. Publishes a book 1-3 years after acceptance. Will consider simultaneous submissions, as long as they are marked "multiple submissions." Will not consider submissions by fax, e-mail or disk. Do not include SASE; do not send original materials. No submissions will be returned; to confirm receipt, include a SASP.

Illustration Works with 40-50 illustrators/year. Wants "unusual art, graphically strong, something that will stand out on the shelves. Fine art, not mass market." Reviews ms/illustration packages from artists. "Indicate if project *must* be considered jointly, or if editor may consider text and art separately." Illustrations only: Submit samples of artist's work (not necessarily from book, but in the envisioned style). Slides, tearsheets and color photocopies OK. (No original art.) Dummies helpful. Résumé helpful. Samples suited to our needs are filed for future reference. Samples not suited to our needs will be recycled.Queries and project proposals responded to in same time frame as author query/proposals."

Photography Purchases photos from freelancers. Works on assignment only.

Terms Generally pays authors in royalties based on retail price, "though we do occasionally work on a flat fee basis." Advance varies. Illustrators paid royalty based on retail price or flat fee. Sends proofs to authors and illustrators. Book catalog for 9 × 12 SAE and 8 first-class stamps; ms guidelines for #10 SASE.

Tips "Chronicle Books publishes an eclectic mixture of traditional and innovative children's books. We are interested in taking on projects that have a unique bent to them-be it subject matter, writing style, or illustrative technique. As a small list, we are looking for books that will lend us a distinctive flavor. We are also interested in growing our ficition program for older readers, including chapter books, middle grade, and young adult projects."

☑ CLARION BOOKS

215 Park Ave. S., New York NY 10003. (212)420-5889. Web site: www.clarionbooks.com. **Manuscript Acquisitions:** Dinah Stevenson, publisher; Virginia Buckley, contributing editor; Jennifer Wingertzahn, editor; Marcia Leonard, editor. **Art Acquisitions:** Joann Hill, art director.

- Clarion title *The Wednesday Wars*, by Gary D. Schmidt, won a Newbery Honor Medal in 2008.

Fiction Recently published *The Wonderful Thing About Hiccups*, by Cece Meng, illustrated by Janet Pedersen (ages 4-7, picture book); *The Wednesday Wars*, by Gary D. Schmidt (ages 10-148, historical fiction).

Nonfiction Recently published *Who Was First? Discovering the Americas*, by Russell Freedman (ages 9-12, history).

How to Contact/Writers Fiction and picture books: Send complete mss. Nonfiction: Send query with up to 3 sample chapters. Must include SASE. Will accept simultaneous submissions if informed. "Please no e-mail queires or submissions."

Illustration Send samples (no originals).

Terms Pays illustrators royalty; flat fee for jacket illustration. Pays royalties and advance to writers; both vary. Guidelines available on Web site.

CLEAR LIGHT PUBLISHERS

823 Don Diego, Santa Fe NM 87505. (505)989-9590. Fax: (505)989-9519. Web site: www.clearlightbooks.com. **Acquisitions:** Harmon Houghton, publisher. Publishes 4 middle readers/year; 4 young adult titles/year.

Nonfiction Middle readers and young adults: multicultural, American Indian and Hispanic only.

How to Contact/Writers Fiction/nonfiction: Submit complete ms with SASE. "No e-mail submissions. Authors supply art. Manuscripts not considered without art or artist's renderings." Will consider simultaneous submissions. Responds in 3 months. Only send *copies*.

Illustration Reviews ms/illustration packages from artists. "No originals please." Submit ms with dummy and SASE.

Terms Pays authors royalty of 10% based on wholesale price. Offers advances (average amount: up to 50% of expected net sales within the first year). Sends galleys to authors.

Tips "We're looking for authentic American Indian art and folklore."

CONCORDIA PUBLISHING HOUSE

3558 S. Jefferson Ave., St. Louis MO 63118. (314)268-1187. Fax: (314)268-1329. Web site: www.cph.org. **Contact:** Peggy Kuethe. **Art Director:** Norm Simon. "Concordia Publishing House produces quality resources that communicate and nurture the Christian faith and ministry of people of all ages, lay and professional. These resources include curriculum, worship aids, books, and religious supplies. We publish approximately 30 quality children's books each year. We boldly provide Gospel resources that are Christ-centered, Bible-based and faithful to our Lutheran heritage."

Nonfiction Picture books, young readers, young adults: Bible stories, activity books, arts/crafts, concept, contemporary, religion. "All books must contain explicit Christian content." Recently published *Three Wise Women of Christmas*, by Dandi Daley Mackall (picture book for ages 6-10); *The Town That Forgot About Christmas*, by Susan K. Leigh (ages over 5-9, picture book); *Little Ones Talk With God* (prayer book compilation, aged 5 and up).

How to Contact/Writers Submit complete ms (picture books); submit outline/synopsis and samples for longer mss. May also query. Responds to queries in 1 month; mss in 3 months. Publishes a book 2 years after acceptance. Will consider simultaneous submissions. "Absolutely no phone queries."

Illustration Works with 20 illustrators/year. Illustrations only: Query with samples. Contact: Norm Simon, art director. Responds only if interested. Samples filed.

Terms Pays authors royalties based on retail price or work purchased outright ($750-2,000). Manuscript guidelines for 1 first-class stamp and a #10 envelope. Pays illustrators by the project.

Tips "Do not send finished artwork with the manuscript. If sketches will help in the presentation of the manuscript, they may be sent. If stories are taken from the Bible, they should follow the Biblical account closely. Liberties should not be taken in fantasizing Biblical stories."

Ⓐ JOANNA COTLER BOOKS

HarperCollins Children's Books. 1350 Avenue of the Americas, New York NY 10019. Web site: www.harperchildrens.com. **Senior Vice President and Publisher:** Joanna Cotler. Senior Editor: Karen Nagel. Assistant Editor: Alyson Day. Publishes literary and commercial fiction and nonfiction. Publishes 6 picture books/year; 5 middle readers/year; 2 young adult titles/year. 15% of books by first-time authors.

Fiction Recently published *Psyche in a Dress*, by Francesca Lia Block; *I'm dirty*, by Kate McMullan, illustrated by Jim McMullan; *Grandfather's Dance*, by Patricia MacLachlan.

How to Contact/Writers Only interested in agented material.

Illustration Will review ms/illustration packages. Reviews work of illustrators for possible future assignments. Contact: Alison Day, assistant editor. Sample are not kept on file.

Terms Illustrators see dummies for review. Originals returned to artist at job's completion.

Ⓒ COTTONWOOD PRESS, INC.

109-B Cameron Drive, Fort Collins CO 80525. Estab. 1986. (907)204-0715. Fax: (907)204-0761. E-mail: cottonwood@cottonwoodpress.com. Web site: www.cottonwoodpress.com. Specializes in educational material. **President:** Cheryl Thurston. Cottonwood Press strives "to publish material that are effective in the classroom and help kids learn without putting them to sleep, specializing in materials for grades 5-12." Publishes 4 middle reader and young adult book/year. 60% of books by first-time authors.

Nonfiction Middle readers: textbooks. Young Adults/Teens: textbooks. Recently published: *Un-Journaling: daily writing exercises that are NOT personal, NOT introspective, NOT boring!*, by Dawn DiPrince, illustrated by

Cheryl Miller Thurston; *Singuini: noodling around with silly songs*, by Heather Stenner and Cheryl Miller Thurston; *Phunny Stuph: Proofreading exercises with a sense of humor*, by M.S. Samston.

How to Contact/Writers Nonfiction: Submit complete manuscript. Responds to queries in 2 weeks; mss in 2 months. Publishes a book 6 months-1 year after acceptance. Will consider simultaneous submissions if notified.

Terms Pay royalty of 10-15% based on net sales.

Tips ''It is essential that writers familiarize themselves with our Web site to see what we do. The most successful of our authors have used our books in the classroom and know how different they are from ordinary textbooks.''

CREATIVE EDUCATION

Imprint of The Creative Company, P.O. Box 227, Mankato MN 56001. (800)445-6209. Fax: (507)388-2746. **Manuscript Acquisitions:** Aaron Frisch. Publishes 5 picture books/year; 20 young readers/year; 30 middle readers/year; 40 young adult titles/year. 5% of books by first-time authors.

Fiction Picture books, young readers, middle readers, young adult/teens: adventure, animal, anthology, contemporary, folktales, history, nature/environment, poetry, sports. Average word length: 1,500. Recently published *The Adventures of Pinocchio*, by Carlo Collodi, illustrated by Roberto Innocanti (ages 10-adult); *A Was an Apple Pie*, illustrated by Etienne Delessert (ages 5-adult); *Galileo's Universe*, by J. Patrick Lewis, illustrated by Tom Curry (ages 12-adult).

Nonfiction Picture books, young readers, middle readers, young adults: animal, arts/crafts, biography, careers, geography, health, history, hobbies, multicultural, music/dance, nature/environment, religion, science, social issues, special needs, sports. Average word length: young readers—500; middle readers—3,000; young adults—6,500. Recently published *My First Look At Science*, by Melissa Gish (age 7, young reader); *The Wild World of Animals*, by Mary Hoff (age 11, middle reader); *Martin Luther King, Jr.*, by Jennifer Fandel (age 14, young adult/teen).

How to Contact/Writers Fiction: Submit complete ms. Nonfiction: Submit outline/synopsis and 2 sample chapters. Responds to queries in 3 months; mss in 3 months. Publishes book 2 years after acceptance. Do not accept illustration packages.

Photography Buys stock. Contact: Tammi Stoffel, photo editor. Model/property releases not required; captions required. Uses b&w prints. Submit cover letter, promo piece. Ms. and photographer guidelines available for SAE.

Tips ''We are primarily a nonfiction publisher and are very selective about fiction picture books, publishing five or fewer annually. Nonfiction submissions should be in series (of 4, 6, or 8), rather than single.''

CRICKET BOOKS

Carus Publishing Company, 70 East Lake St., Suite 300, Chicago IL 60601. Web site: www.cricketmag.com. **Art Acquisitions:** John Sandford.

- Cricket books has a moratorium on manuscripts. Queries from agents and authors who have worked with Cricket Books are still welcome. Direct queries to Jenny Gillespie. Watch Web site for updates.

How to Contact Not accepting unsolicited mss. See Web site for details and updates on submissions policy.

Illustration Works with 4 illustrators/year. Use color and b&w. Illustration only: Submit samples, tearsheets. Contact: John Sanford. Responds only if interested. Samples returned with SASE; sample filed.

Tips ''You may consider submitting your manuscript to one of our magazines, as we sometimes serialize longer selections and always welcome age-appropriate stories, poems, and nonfiction articles.''

DARBY CREEK PUBLISHING

7858 Industrial Pkwy., Plain City OH 43064. (614)873-7955. Fax: (614)873-7135. E-mail: info@darbycreekpublis hing.com. **Manuscript/Art Acquisitions:** Tanya Dean, editorial director. Publishes 10-15 children's books/year.

- Darby Creek does not publish picture books.

Fiction Middle readers, young adult. Recently published *The Warriors*, by Joseph Bruchac (ages 10 and up); *Dog Days*, by David Lubar (ages 10 and up); *Four Things My Geeky-Jock-of-a-Best-Friend Must Do in Europe*, by Jane Harrington.

Nonfiction Middle readers: biography, history, science, sports. Recently published *Albinio Animals*, by Kelly Milner Halls, illustrated by Rick Spears; *Miracle: The True Story of the Wreck of the Sea Venture*, by Gail Karwoski.

How to Contact/Writers Accepts international material only with U.S. postage on SASE for return; no IRCs. Fiction/nonfiction: Submit publishing history and/or résumé and complete ms for short works or outline/synopsis and 2-3 sample chapters for longer works, such as novels. Responds in 6 weeks. Does not consider previously published work.

Illustration Illustrations only: Send photocopies and résumé with publishing history. ''Indicate which samples we may keep on file and include SASE and appropriate packing materials for any samples you wish to have returned.''

Terms Offers advance-against-royalty contracts.

Tips ''We like to see nonfiction with a unique slant that is kid friendly, well researched and endorsed by experts. We're interested in fiction or nonfiction with sports themes for future lists. No series, please. We do not publish picture books of any kind.''

MAY DAVENPORT, PUBLISHERS

26313 Purissima Rd., Los Altos Hills CA 94022-4539. (650)947-1275. Fax: (650)947-1373. E-mail: mdbooks@eart hlink.net. Web site: www.maydavenportpublishers.com. **Acquisitions:** May Davenport, editor/publisher. Publishes 1-2 picture books/year; 2-3 young adult titles/year. 99% of books by first-time authors. Seeks books with literary merit. ''We like to think that we are selecting talented writers who have something humorous to write about today's unglued generation in 30,000-50,000 words for teens and young adults in junior/senior high school before they become tomorrow's 'functional illiterates.' We are interested in publishing literature that teachers in middle and high schools can use in their Language Arts, English and Creative Writing courses. There's more to literary fare than the chit-chat Internet dialog and fantasy trips on television with cartoons or humanoids.'' This publisher is overstocked with juvenile books.

Fiction Young readers, young adults: contemporary, humorous fictional literature for use in English courses in junior-senior high schools in U.S. Average word length: 40,000-60,000. Recently published *Charlie and Champ*, by Alysson Wagoner (a fun way to learn phonics coloring book, ages 5-7); *Suriving Sarah, the Sequel: Brown Bug & China Doll*, by Dinah Leigh (novel set in post-WWII Manhattan, ages 15-18);*The Lesson Plan*, by Irvin Gay (about an illiterate black boy who grows up to become a teacher, ages 15-18); *A Life on the Line*, by Michael Horton (about a juvenile delinquent boy who recovers from his past abusive life heroically, ages 15-18); *Making My Escape*, by David Lee Finkle (about a young boy who daydreams movie-making in outer space to escape unhappy family life, ages 12-18); *Matthew Livingston and the Prison of Souls*, by Marco Conelli (about a high-tech solution to a crime, ages 12-18).

Nonfiction Teens: shocking pathway choices. Recently published *The Runaway Game*, by Kevin Casey (a literary board game of street life in Hollywood, ages 15-18).

How to Contact/Writers Fiction: Query. Responds to queries/mss in 3 weeks. Mss returned with SASE. Publishes a book 6-12 months after acceptance.

Illustration Works with 1-2 illustrators/year. ''Have enough on file for future reference.'' Responds only if interested. Samples returned with SASE; samples filed. Originals returned at job's completion.

Terms Pays authors royalty of 15% based on retail price; negotiable. Pays ''by mutual agreement, no advances.'' Pays illustrators by the project (range: $75-350). Guidelines free on request with SASE.

Tips ''Write stories with teen narrators and sharing digital camera/computer activities which today's teenages can relate to. Entertain teenagers who don't, won't, or can't read English, won't read printed pages so your book will be useful to teachers in high schools nationwide.''

DAWN PUBLICATIONS

12402 Bitney Springs Rd., Nevada City CA 95959. (530)274-7775. Web site: www.dawnpub.com. Book publisher. Co-Publishers: Muffy Weaver and Glenn J. Hovemann. **Acquisitions:** Glenn J. Hovemann. Publishes works with holistic themes dealing with nature. ''Dawn Publications is dedicated to inspiring in children a deeper appreciation and understanding of nature.''

Fiction Picture books exploring relationships with nature. No fantasy or legend.

Nonfiction Picture books: animal, nature/environment. Prefers ''creative nonfiction.''

How to Contact/Writers Query or submit complete ms by email (enclose self-addressed stamped envelope for reply) or by email to submission@dawnpub.com (with title and your name in the subject line, ms inserted into the body of the email or attached as a Word document only). Responds to queries/mss in 3 months.

Illustration Works with 5 illustrators/year. Will review ms/illustration packages from artists. Query; send ms with dummy. Illustrations only: Query with samples, résumé.

Terms Pays authors royalty based on net sales. Offers advance. Book catalog and ms guidelines available online.

Tips Looking for ''picture books expressing nature awareness with inspirational quality leading to enhanced self-awareness. Does not publish anthropomorphic works; no animal dialogue.''

DIAL BOOKS FOR YOUNG READERS

Penguin Young Readers Group, 345 Hudson St., New York NY 10014. Web site: www.penguin.com. Vice President and Publisher: Lauri Hornik. **Acquisitions:** Liz Waniewski, editor; Alisha Niehaus, editor; Jessica Garrison, associate editor. **Art Director:** Lily Malcom. Publishes 30 picture books/year; 2 young readers/year; 8 middle readers/year; 12 young adult titles/year.

Fiction Picture books, young readers: adventure, animal, fantasy, folktales, history, humor, multicultural, poetry, sports. Middle readers, young adults: adventure, fantasy, folktales, history, humor, multicultural, poetry, problem novels, science fiction, sports, mystery/adventure. Recently published *Emma-Jean Lazarus Fell Out of a Tree*, by Lauren Tarshis (agent 10-14); *On the Wings of Heroes*, by Richard Peck (ages 10 and up); *The Rules of Survival*, by Nancy Werlin (ages 14 and up); *The Little Red Hen*, by Jerry Pinkney (ages 3-7); *I'm the Biggest Thing in the Ocean*, by Kevin Sherry (ages 3-6).

Nonfiction Will consider query letters for submissions of outstanding literary merit. Picture books, young readers, middle readers: biography, history, sports. Young adults: biography, history, sports. Recently published *A Strong Right Arm*, by Michelle Y. Green (ages 10 and up); *We the Kids*, by David Catrow (ages 5 and up).

How to Contact/Writers "Due to the overwhelming number of unsolicited manuscripts we receive, we at Dial Books for Young Readers have had to change our submissions policy: As of August 1, 2005, Dial will no longer respond to your unsolicited submission unless interested in publishing it. Please do not include SASE with your submission. You will not hear from dial regarding the status of your submission unless we are interested, in which case you can expect a reply from us within four months. We accept entire picture book manuscripts and a maximum of 10 pages for longer works (novels, easy-to-reads). When submitting a portion of a longer work, please provide an accompanying cover letter that briefly describes your manuscript's plot, genre (i.e. easy-to-read, middle grade or YA novel), the intended age group, and your publishing credits, if any."

Illustration "Art samples should be sent to attn: Dial Design and will not be returned without SASE. Never send original art. Please do not phone, fax, or email to inquire after your art submission."

Terms Pays authors and illustrators in royalties based on retail price. Average advance payment varies. Catalogue available for 9×12 envelope with four 37¢ stamps. "This is one way to become informed as to the style, subject matter, and format of our books."

Tips "Because confirmation postcards are easily separated from or hidden within the manuscript, we do not encourage you to include them with your submission. Please send only one manuscript at a time. Never send cassettes, original artwork, marketing plans, or faxes and do not send submissions by e-mail. Please know that we only keep track of requested manuscripts; we cannot track unsolicited submissions due to the volume we receive each day, so kindly refrain from calling, faxing or e-mailing to inquire after the status of an unsolicited submission as we will be unable to assist you. If you have not received a reply from us after four months, you can safely assume that we are not presently interested in publishing your work."

ⒶDK PUBLISHING

375 Hudson St., New York NY 10014. Web site: www.dk.com. **Acquisitions:** submissions editor. "DK publishes photographically illustrated nonfiction for children ages 4 and up."

• DK Publishing does not accept unagented manuscripts or proposals.

ⒶDOG-EARED PUBLICATIONS

P.O. Box 620863, Middletown WI 53562-0863. (608)831-1410. Fax: (608)831-1410. E-mail: field@dog-eared.com. Web site: www.dog-eared.com. **Art Acquisitions:** Nancy Field, publisher. Publishes 2-3 middle readers/year. 1% of books by first-time authors. "Dog-Eared Publications creates action-packed nature books for children. We aim to turn young readers into environmentally aware citizens and to foster a love for science and nature in the new generation.

Nonfiction Middle readers: activity books, animal, nature/environment, science. Average word length: varies. Recently published *Discovering Black Bear*, by Margaret Anderson, Nancy Field and Karen Stephenson, illustrated by Michael Maydak (middle readers, activity book); *Leapfrogging Through Wetlands*, by Margaret Anderson, Nancy Field and Karen Stephenson, illustrated by Michael Maydak (middle readers, activity book); *Ancient Forests*, by Margaret Anderson, Nancy Field and Karen Stephenson, illustrated by Sharon Torvik (middle readers, activity book).

How to Contact/Writers Nonfiction: **Currently not accepting unsolicited mss.**

Illustration Works with 2-3 illustrators/year. Reviews ms/illustration packages from artists. Submit query and a few art samples. Illustrations only: Query with samples. Responds only if interested. Samples not returned; samples filed. "Interested in realistic, nature art!"

Terms Pays authors royalty based on wholesale price. Offers advances (amount varies). Pays illustrators royalty based on wholesale price. Sends galleys to authors. Originals returned to artist at job's completion. Brochure available for SASE and 1 first-class stamp or on Web site.

DUTTON CHILDREN'S BOOKS

Penguin Group (USA), 345 Hudson St., New York NY 10014-4502. (212)414-3700. Web site: www.penguin.com/youngreaders and www.DuttonWritersRoom.com. **Acquisitions:** Stephanie Owens Lurie (picture books, middle-grade fiction); Lucia Monfried (picture books, middle-grade fiction); Maureen Sullivan (books for all ages with distinct narrative style); Julie Strauss-Gabel (literary, contemporary young adult fiction); Sarah Shumway (commercial young adult fiction). **Art Acquisitions:** Sara Reynolds, art director. Publishes approximately 50%

fiction—fewer picture books, mostly YA and mid-grade novels. 10% of books by first-time authors.

 • Dutton is open to query letters only, must include SASE for response.

Fiction Picture books: adventure, animal, history, humor, multicultural, nature/environment, contemporary. Young readers: adventure, animal, contemporary, fantasy. Middle readers: adventure, animal, contemporary, fantasy, history, multicultural, nature/environment. Young adults: adventure, animal, contemporary, fantasy, history, multicultural. Recently published *Skippyjon Jones and the Big Bones*, by Judy Schachner (picture book); *Antsy Does Time*, by Neal Shusterman (middle grade); *Paper Towns*, by John Green (young adult).

Nonfiction Picture books. Recently published *The Wolves are Back*, by Jean Craighead George.

How to Contact/Writers Query with SASE only. Does not accept unsolicited mss. Responds to queries in 3-6 months. Will consider simultaneous submissions.

Illustration Works with 40-60 illustrators/year. Reviews ms/illustration packages from artists. Query first. Illustrations only: Query with samples; send résumé, portfolio, slides—no original art please. Responds to art samples only if interested. Samples returned with SASE; samples filed. Original artwork returned at job's completion.

Terms Pays authors royalty of 5-10% based on retail price or outright purchase. Ms guidelines for SASE. Pays illustrators royalty of 5% based on retail price unless jacket illustration—then pays by flat fee. Pays photographers by the project or royalty based on retail price.

Tips "Avoid topics that appear frequently. Illustrators: "We would like to see samples and portfolios from potential illustrators of picture books (full color), young novels (b&w) and jacket artists (full color)." Dutton is actively building its fiction lists. Humor welcome across all genres.

⬭ EDCON PUBLISHING GROUP

30 Montauk Blvd., Oakdale NY 11769. (631)567-7227. Fax: (631)567-8745. Web site: www.edconpublishing.com. **Manuscript Acquisitions:** Editor. Publishes 6 young readers/year, 6 middle readers/year, 6 young adult titles/year. 30% of books by first-time Looking for educational games and nonfiction work in the areas of math, science, reading and social studies.

Fiction Recently adapted/published *A Christmas Carol*; *Frankenstein*; *Around the World in 80 Days*; *The Picture of Dorian Grey*.

Nonfiction Grades K-12 though primarily 6-12 remedial.

How to Contact/Writers Submit outline/synopsis and 1 sample chapter. Publishes book 6 months after acceptance. Will consider simultaneous submissions. Submission kept on file unless return is requested. Include SASE for return.

Illustration Buys b&w and color illustrations and computerized graphic art. Send postcards, samples, links to Web site. Mailed Submissions kept on file, not returned.

Terms Work purchased outright from authors for up to $1,000. Pays illustrators by the project (range: $100-$500). Catalog available at Web site www.edconpublishing.com.

⬭ EDUCATORS PUBLISHING SERVICE

Division of School Specialty Publishing, P.O. Box 9031, Cambridge MA 02139-9031. (617)547-6706. Fax: (617)547-3805. E-mail: epsbooks@epsbooks.com. Web site: www.epsbooks.com. **Manuscript Acquisitions:** Charlie Heinle. **Art Acquisitions:** Julie Webster, managing editor. Publishes 30-40 educational books/year. 50% of books by first-time authors.

How to Contact/Writers Responds to only if interested. Publishes book 6-12 months after acceptance. Will consider e-mail submissions, simultaneous submissions, previously published work. See website for submission guidelines.

Illustration Works with 12-18 illustrators/year. Reviews ms/illustration packages from artists. Query. Illustrations only: Query with samples; send promo sheet. Responds only if interested. Samples not returned; samples filed.

Photography Buys stock and assigns work. Submit cover letter, samples.

Terms Pays authors royalty of 5-12% based on retail price or work purchased outright from authors. Offers advances. Pays illustrators and photographers by the project. Sends galleys to authors. Book catalog free. All imprints included in a single catalog. Catalog available on Web site.

Tips "We accept queries from educators writing for the school market, primarily in the reading and language arts areas, grades K-8, with a focus on struggling readers. We are interested in materials that follow certain pedagogical constraints (such as decodable texts and leveled readers) and we would consider queries and samples from authors who might be interested in working with us on ongoing or future projects."

⬭ EDUPRESS, INC.

W5527 State Road 106, Ft. Atkinson WI 53538. (920)563-9571. Fax: (920)563-7395. E-mail: edupress@highsmith.com. Web site: www.edupressinc.com. **Manuscript Acquisitions:** Elizabeth Bowie, product development manager. "Our mission is to create products that make kids want to go to school!"

Katherine Applegate

A career that's a journey in reinvention

A uthor Katherine Applegate has been writing and publishing for nearly two decades and has conquered numerous genres with success. Lately she's reinvented her writing self, moving on from best-selling series like Animorphs and Everworld to see her first novel in verse, her first picture book, and her first middle-grade series hit bookstores.

Here Applegate traces her career from ghostwriting to series writing to today; talks about her recent and upcoming projects; and offers advice to both budding series writers and authors interested in jumping genres.

You've written sci-fi series, romance series, a mid-grade novel in verse, a historical picture book . . . it seems as though there are half a dozen little writers living in your brain. How have you managed to be so diverse?
"Managed to be so diverse" has such a nice ring to it, suggesting I actually had a deliberate career plan! But the truth is, I served a long writing apprenticeship, taking work where it came and trying new projects to see what I could pull off. Very often, I've worked in tandem with my husband, Michael Reynolds (who is currently publishing, as "Michael Grant," a young adult series entitled Gone with HarperCollins), and that's pushed us both to expand our writing boundaries. It's great fun to write for different ages and in multiple genres, but I do think there's a down side. It's harder for publishers to "brand" you, and harder for booksellers and readers to know what to expect from you next. If you write a fun, "light" series, can you really be a Serious Writer, too?

Going from writing series of books to working on projects with spare text such as a picture book and a novel in verse seems like a big adjustment. Was this difficult? Refreshing? Exciting?
Absolutely exhilarating! Getting that first draft down is always a struggle for me, but I love to edit, to tweak, to play with words, and that's especially important when space is at a premium. I suppose it's like the difference between a string quartet and a symphony: You can convey huge amounts of information either way, but the delivery will be wildly different. For me, the discipline imposed by form is strangely liberating.

You've been writing—and publishing—for a long time. When did you start writing for young readers? Can you tell me about your initial path to publication?
I've been writing for 18 years or so. At some point, post-college—way post college—I realized I made a lousy waitress/plant waterer/toilet cleaner, and I needed to get a respectable job. (Writing was at least semi-respectable.) But I was timid about taking the

leap, afraid of failing, I suppose. So I started out as a ghostwriter for a middle-grade series called "Sweet Valley Twins." I believe I wrote something like 17 of those.

Eventually I started writing my own series, but still with a book packager. Again, it was good on-the-job training, but a downside was that I had to surrender a lot of control over what happened with series once I had launched them. There are series I created that continued long after my involvement. And sometimes a series will be repackaged and relaunched and I don't find out about it until after it's happened.

Eventually I moved past the packager years and started doing things like Animorphs and Everworld. Now, in what I think of as phase three of my career, I'm writing very different things altogether. I love series, but there's a real luxury in writing a book with a beginning, a middle, and an end!

I'm interested in what led you to write your novel in verse *Home of the Brave*. Why did you take this journey with Kek and why did it lend itself to free verse?
I'd been living in Minneapolis, a perfect city with with decidedly imperfect weather. There'd been a large contingent of refugees moving to Minneapolis around that time, many from sub-Saharan Africa, and I could not begin to imagine how they could deal with the challenges of a new language and a new culture while simultaneously enduring the endless search for lost mittens. It seemed impossibly brave to me.

I tried parts of the novel as both prose and free verse, reading sections aloud to see what seemed to work. In the end, I felt that using free verse helped convey the challenges

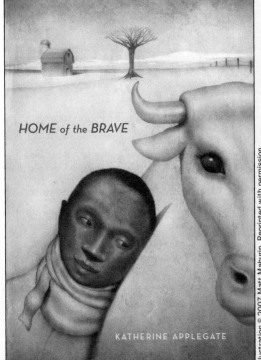

Katherine Applegate's novel in verse *Home of the Brave* (Feiwel & Friends) is the story of Sudanese immigrant Kek and his adjustment to life in Minnesota. "Precise, highly accessible language evokes a wide range of emotions and simultaneously tells an initiation story," says *Publishers Weekly*. "A memorable inside view of an outsider."

Kek faced as he learned a new language. The book was tremendous fun to research and to write, and I'm very proud of it.

Your wildly popular Animorphs series features characters who morph into animals. Your latest books, *Home of the Brave* and *The Buffalo Storm*, feature young main characters who undergo huge transition as they relocate. What draws you to explore Big Change, be it turning from a human into a dolphin, or moving from Sudan to the U.S.?

Change is the one constant in a child's life. It's also the one constant in fiction. Besides, it's great fun to walk a character through a life-transforming transition. He does all the heavy lifting. All I have to do is watch what happens, write it down and take the credit.

Your Web site tells visitors that your two latest books feature brave kids. In an interview you said, "It's up to kids to save the world." You seem to have a true admiration for young people—is that part of the reason you write for them?

Absolutely. They're a tremendously discerning audience. They can sniff out a lie the way my Labrador can sniff out a half-eaten bagel two blocks away. They're tough, but they're not cynical. They're honest. And they truly want to change the world.

Tell me about Roscoe Riley Rules, your upcoming chapter book series.

Roscoe Riley Rules is a new book series targeted for beginning readers. I'd been looking for a fun easy-to-read series that would appeal to my six-year-old son, and when I couldn't find something that quite fit the bill, I decided to try my hand at writing one.

Roscoe is an irrepressible first-grader who, despite always trying to do the right thing, inevitably finds himself breaking the rules. In the first book, that rule turns out to be "We Do Not Glue Our Friends to Chairs." This reading level looks deceptively easy, but I've discovered it's tough to juggle the need for accessible vocabulary, short sentences, and kid-friendly humor!

What's your advice for writers interested in writing series?

First and foremost, be sure your idea needs to be a series. Could it be told just as well in a single, freestanding novel? Does it lend itself to episodic treatment? Remember that writing a book series is a little like entering into a marriage. You're going to be spending a lot of time with your characters. Do you like them enough to return for repeat visits?

Naturally, from a publisher's point of view, a series represents a bigger investment in time and money. Because the stakes are higher, you're going to have to deliver a compelling idea in a convincing package.

What's your advice for writers interested in changing genres?

Be prepared for a certain amount of resistance from publishers and readers. But don't let that stop you—it's too much fun! It will bring new depth and possibility to all your work. As always, before you make the leap, read everything in the new genre that you can get your hands on.

Then read some more.

And some more.

—*Alice Pope*

How to Contact/Writers Nonfiction: Submit complete ms. Responds to queries/mss in 3 months. Publishes book 1-2 years after acceptance.

Illustration Query with samples. Contact. Contact: Sandra Harris, product development manager. Responds only if interested. Samples returned with SASE.

Photography Buys stock.

Terms Work purchased outright from authors. Pays illustrators by the project. Book catalog available at no cost. Catalog available on Web site.

Tips ''We are looking for unique, quality supplemental materials for Pre-K through eighth grade. We publish all subject aread in many different formats, including games. Our materials are intended for classroom and home schooling use.''

EERDMAN'S BOOKS FOR YOUNG READERS

An imprint of Wm. B. Eerdmans Publishing Co., 2140 Oak Industrial Dr. NE, Grand Rapids, MI 49505 (616) 459-4591. Fax: (616) 776-7683. E-mail: youngreaders@eerdmans.com. Web site: www.eerdmans.com/youngre aders. We are an independent book packager/producer. **Writers contact:** Acquisitions Editor. **Illustrators contact:** Gayle Brown, art director. Produces 16 picture books/year; 3 middle readers/year; 3 young adult books/year. 10% of books by first-time authors. ''We seek to engage young minds with words and pictures that inform and delight, inspire and entertain. From board books for babies to picture books, nonfiction, and novels for children and young adults, our goal is to produce quality literature for a new generation of readers. We believe in books!''

Fiction: Picture books: animal, concept, contemporary, folktales, history, humor, multicultural, nature/environment, poetry, religion, special needs, social issues, sports, suspense. Young readers: animal, concept, contemporary, folktales, history, humor, multicultural, poetry, religion, special needs, social issues, sports, suspense. Middle readers: adventure, contemporary, history, humor, multicultural, nature/environment, problem novels, religion, social issues, sports, suspense. Young adults/teens: adventure, contemporary, folktales, history, humor, multicultural, nature/environment, problem novels, religion, sports, suspense. Average word length: picture books—1,000; middle readers—15,000; young adult—45,000. Recently published *Four Feet, Two Sandals*, by Karen Lynn Williams and Khadra Mohammed, illustrated by Doug Chayka (picture book, ages 7-10); *Cotton ball Colin*, by Jeanne Willis, illustrated by Tony Ross (picture book, ages 4-9); *Always with You*, by Ruth VanderZee; illustrated by Ronald Himler (picture book, ages 8-12); *Ethan, Suspended*, by Pamela Ehrenberg (middle reader fiction, ages 11-14) .

Nonfiction Middle readers: biography, history, multicultural, nature/environment, religion, social issues. Young adults/teens: biography, history, multicultural, nature/environment, religion, social issues. Average word length: middle readers—35,000; young adult books—35,000. Recently published *C.S. Lewis: The Man Behind Narnia*, by Beatrice Gormley.

How to Contact/Writers: We only consider submissions sent *exclusively* to Eerdmans. YA and middle reader fiction: Please send query, synopsis, and 3 sample chapters. Responds to exclusive queries/mss in 3-5 months. ''We no longer acknowledge or respond to unsolicited manuscripts. Exceptions will be made only for exclusive submissions marked as such on outside envelope.''

Illustration Accepts material from international illustrators. Works with 10-12 illustrators/year. Uses color artwork primarily. Reviews work for future assignments. If interested in illustrating future titles, send promo sheet. Submit samples to Gayle Brown, art director. Samples not returned. Samples filed.

Terms Offers advance against royalties. Author sees galleys for review. Illustrators see proofs for review. Originals returned to artist at job's completion. Catalog available for 8×10 SASE and 4 first-class stamps. Offers writer's guidelines for SASE. See Web site for writer's guidelines. (www.eerdmans.com/youngreaders/submit.h tm).

Tips ''Find out who Eerdmans is before submitting a manuscript. Look at our website, request a catalog, and check out our books.''

FACTS ON FILE

132 W. 31st St., New York NY 10001. (212)967-8800. Fax: (212)967-9196. E-mail: editorial@factsonfile.com. Web site: www.factsonfile.com. Estab. 1941. Book publisher. Editorial Director: Laurie Likoff. **Acquisitions:** Frank Darmstadt, science and technology/nature; Andrew Gyory, American history and cultural studies; Jeff Soloway, language and literature; Owen Lancer, world studies; Jim Chambers, arts, health and entertainment. ''We produce high-quality reference materials for the school library market and the general nonfiction trade.'' Publishes 25-30 young adult titles/year. 5% of books by first-time authors; 25% of books from agented writers; additional titles through book packagers, co-publishers and unagented writers.

Nonfiction Middle readers, young adults: animal, biography, careers, geography, health, history, multicultural, nature/environment, reference, religion, science, social issues and sports.

How to Contact/Writers Nonfiction: Submit outline/synopsis and sample chapters. Responds to queries in 10 weeks. Publishes a book 10-12 months after acceptance. Will consider simultaneous submissions. Sends galleys to authors. Book catalog free on request. Send SASE for submission guidelines.

Terms Submission guidelines available via Web site or with SASE.

Tips ''Most projects have high reference value and fit into a series format.''

⊠ FARRAR, STRAUS & GIROUX INC.

19 Union Square W., New York NY 10003. (212)741-6900. Fax: (212)633-2427. Web site: www.fsgkidsbooks.com. Estab. 1946. Book publisher. Imprints: Frances Foster Books, Melanie Kroupa Books. Children's Books Editorial Director: Margaret Ferguson. **Manuscript Acquisitions:** Margaret Ferguson, editorial director; Frances Foster, Frances Foster Books; Melanie Kroupa, Melanie Kroupa Books; Beverly Reingold, executive editor; Wesley Adams, executive editor; Janine O'Malley, Senior editor. **Art Director:** Robbin Gourley, art director, Books for Young Readers. Publishes 40 picture books/year; 30 middle grade books/year; 10 young adult titles/year. 5% of books by first-time authors; 20% of books from agented writers.

- Farrar/Frances Foster title *The Wall: Growing Up Behind the Iron Curtain*, by Peter Sís, won a Caldecott Honor Medal in 2008. Farrar/Melanie Kroupa title *Rex Zero and the End of the World*, by Tim Wynne-Jones, won a Boston Globe-Horn Book Fiction and Poetry Honor Award in 2007. Farrar/Frances Foster title *Dreamquake: Book Two of the Dreamhunter Duet*, by Elizabeth Knox, won a Michael L. Printz Honor Award in 2008. See First Books on page 133 for interviews with Deborah Diesen and Dan Hanna, author and illustrator of FSG title *The Pout-Pout Fish*.

Fiction All levels: all categories. ''Original and well-written material for all ages.'' Recently published *Harlem Hustle*, by Janet McDonald; *So Sleepy Story*, by Uri Shulevitz.

Nonfiction All levels: all categories. ''We publish only literary nonfiction.''

How to Contact/Writers Fiction/nonfiction: for novels, query with outline/synopsis and 3 sample chapters; for picture books send complete ms. Do not fax or e-mail submissions or queries. Responds to queries/mss in 3 months. Publishes a book 18 months after acceptance. Will consider simultaneous submissions.

Illustration Works with 30-60 illustrators/year. Reviews ms/illustration packages from artists. Submit ms with 1 example of final art, remainder roughs. Do not send originals. Illustrations only: Query with tearsheets. Responds if interested in 2 months. Samples returned with SASE; samples sometimes filed.

Terms ''We offer an advance against royalties for both authors and illustrators.'' Sends galleys to authors; dummies to illustrators. Original artwork returned at job's completion. Book catalog available for 9 × 12 SASE with $1.95 postage; ms guidelines for SASE1 first-class stamp, or can be viewed at www.fsgkidsbooks.com.

Tips ''Study our catalog before submitting. We will see illustrator's portfolios by appointment. Don't ask for criticism and/or advice—due to the volume of submissions we receive, it's just not possible. Never send originals. Always enclose SASE.''

⬚ ⬚ FIVE STAR PUBLICATIONS, INC.

P.O. Box 6698, Chandler AZ 85246-6698. (480)940-8182. Fax: (480)940-8787. E-mail: art@fivestarpublications.com. Web sites: www.FiveStarPublications.com, www.LittleFivestar.com, www.FiveStarLegends,com, www.FiveStarSleuths.com, www.SixPointsPress.com. **Art Acquisitions:** Sue DeFabis. Publishes 7 middle readers/year.

Nonfiction Recently published *Tic Talk Book: Living with Tourette Syndrome*, by Dylan Peters, illustrated by Zachary Wendland (www.TicTalkBook.com); *Alfie's Bark Mitzvah*, by Shari Cohen, songs by Cantor Marcello Gindlin, illustrated by Nadia Komorova (www.AlfiesBarkMitvah.com).

How to Contact/Writers Nonfiction: Query.

Illustration Works with 3 illustrators/year. Reviews ms/illustration packages from artists. Query. Illustrations only: Query with samples. Responds only if interested. Samples filed.

Photography Buys stock and assigns work. Works on assignment only. Submit letter.

Terms Pays illustrators by the project. Pays photographers by the project. Sends galleys to authors; dummies to illustrators.

FLASHLIGHT PRESS

3709 13th Ave., Brooklyn NY 11218. (718)288-8300. Fax: (718)972-6307. E-mail: editor@flashlightpress.com. Web site: www.flashlightpress.com. Estab. 2004. **Editor:** Shari Dash Greenspan. Publishes 2-3 picture books/year. 25% of books by first-time authors.

Fiction Picture books: contemporary, humor, multicultural. Average word length: 1,000. Recently published: *Grandpa for Sale*, by Dotti Enderle and Vicki Sansum, illustrated by T. Kyle Gentry (ages 4-8, picture book); *Getting to Know Ruben Plotnick*, by Roz Rosenbluth, illustrated by Maurie J. Manning (ages 5-9, picture book); *Alley Oops*, by Janice Levy, illustrated by Cynthia B. Decker (ages 5-9, picture book); *Carla's Sandwich*, by Debbie Herman, illustrated by Sheila Bailey (ages 4-8, picture book).

How to Contact/Writers Query by e-mail only. ''Do not send queries or manuscripts by mail.'' Responds to queries in 1 week; mss in 1 month. Publishes a book 2 years after acceptance.

Illustration Works with 2-3 illustrators/year. Uses color artwork only. Query by e-mail with link to online portfolio. Contact: Shari Dash Greenspan, editor.

Terms Pays authors and illustrators royalty of 10% based on wholesale price. Offers advance of $500-1,000. Catalog available through IPG (Independent Publishers Group). E-mail to request catalog or view on Web site.

FLUX

Llewellyn Worldwide, Ltd., 2143 Wooddale Drive, Woodbury MN 55125. (651)312-8613. Fax: (651)291-1908. E-mail: submissions@fluxnow.com. Web site: www.fluxnow.com. **Acquisitions Editor:** Andrew Karre. Imprint estab. 2005; Lllewelyn estab. 1901. Publishes 21 young abult titles/year. 50% of books by first-time authors. "Flux seeks to publish authors who see YA as a point of view, not a reading level. We look for books that try to capture a slice of teenage experience. We are particularly interested in books that tell the stories of young adults in unexpected or surprising situations around the globe."

● See Flux editor Andrew Karre's article YA Fiction on page 78.

Fiction Young Adults: adventure, contemporary, fantasy, history, humor, problem novels, religion, science fiction, sports, suspense. Average word length: 50,000. Recently published *Blue Is for Nightmares*, by Laurie Faria Stolarz; *Dream Spinner*, by Bonnie Dobkin; *How It's Done*, by Christine Kole MacLean.

How to Contact/Writers Query. Responds to queries in 1-2 weeks; mss in 1-3 months. Will consider simultaneous submissions and previously published work.

Terms Pays royalties of 10-15% based on wholesale price. Offers advance. Authors see galleys for review. Book catalog available on Web site. Writer's guidelines available for SASE or in Web site.

Tips "Read contemporary teen books. Be aware of what else is out there. If you don't read teen books, you probably shouldn't write them. Know your audience. Write incredibly well. Do not condescend."

FREE SPIRIT PUBLISHING

217 Fifth Ave. N., Suite 200, Minneapolis MN 55401-1299. (612)338-2068. Fax: (612)337-5050. E-mail: acquisitions@freespirit.com. Web site: www.freespirit.com. Publishes 25-30 titles/year for pre-K through 12, educators and parents. "Free Spirit is the leading publisher of learning tools that support young people's social and emotional health, helping children and teens to think for themselves, succeed in life, and make a difference in the world."

● Free Spirit does not accept fiction, poetry or storybook submissions.

How to Contact/Writers Accepts nonfiction submissions from prospective authors or through agents." Please review catalog and author guidelines (both available online) before submitting proposal." Reponds to queries in 4-6 months. "If you'd like material returned, enclose an SASE with sufficient postage." Write or e-mail for catalog and submission guidelines before sending submission. Accepts queries only—not submissions—by e-mail.

Illustration Works with 5 illustrators/year. Submit samples to creative director for consideration. If appropriate, samples will be kept on file and artist will be contacted if a suitable project comes up. Enclose SASE if you'd like materials returned.

Photography Submit samples to creative director for consideration. If appropriate, samples will be kept on file and photographer will be contacted if a suitable project comes up. Enclose SASE if you'd like materials returned.

Terms Pays authors royalty based on net receipts. Offers advance. Pays illustrators by the project. Pays photographers by the project or per photo.

Tips "We do not publish fiction, poetry or picture storybooks, books with animals or mythical characters, books with religious content, or single biographies, autobiographies or memiors. Free Spirit prefers books written in a practical, pshycologically sound, and positive style."

FREESTONE/PEACHTREE, JR.

Peachtree Publishers, 1700 Chattahoochee Ave., Atlanta GA 30318-2112. (404)876-8761. Fax: (404)875-2578. E-mail: hello@peachtree-online.com. Web site: www.peachtree-online.com. **Acquisitions:** Helen Harriss. Publishes 4-8 young adult titles/year.

● Freestone and Peachtree, Jr. are imprints of Peachtree Publishers. See the listing for Peachtree for submission information. No e-mail or fax queries or submissions, please.

Fiction Picture books: animal, folktales, health, history, humor, multicultural, nature/environment, special needs, sports. Young readers: history, humor, health, multicultural, sports. Middle readers: adventure, contemporary, history, humor, multicultural, problem novels, sports, suspense/mystery. Young adults/teens: adventure, contemporary, history, humor, multicultural, problem novels, sports, suspense/mystery. Recently published *Martina the Beautiful Cockroach*, by Carmen Agra Deedy, illustrated by Michael Austin(ages 4-8, picture book); *The Last Polar Bears*, written and illustrated by Harry Horse (ages 7-10; early reader); *The Sorta Sisters*, by Adrian Fogelin (ages 8-12, middle reader); *Giving Up the Ghost*, By Sheri Sinykin (ages 12-16, young adult).

Nonfiction Picture books, young readers, middle readers, young adults: history, sports. Picture books: animal, health, multicultural, nature/environment, science, social issues, special needs.

How to Contact Responds to queries/mss in 6 months.

Illustration Works with 10-20 illustrators/year. Responds only if interested. Samples not returned; samples filed. Originals returned at job's completion.

Terms Pays authors royalty. Pays illustrators by the project or royalty. Pays photographers by the project or per photo.

☙ FRONT STREET

Imprint of Boyds Mills Press, 815 Church Street, Honesdale, PA 18431 Web site: www.frontstreetbooks.com. Publishes20-25 titles/year. "We look for fresh voices for children and young adults. Titles on our list entertain, challenge, or enlighten, always employing novel characters whose considered voices resonate."

• Front Street title *Keturah and Lord Death*, by Martine Leavitt, was a 2007 National Book Award Finalist. Their title *One Whole and Perfect Day*, by Judith Clarke won a Michael L. Printz Honor Book Award in 2008.

Fiction Recently published *I'm Being Stalked by a Moonshadow*, by Doug MacLeod; *Runaround*, by Helen Hemphill; *Baby*, by Joseph Monninger.

How to Contact/Writers Fiction: Submit cover letter and complete ms if under 30 pages; submit cover letter, 1 or 2 sample chapters and plot summary if over 30 pages. Label package "Manuscript Submission." Include SASE with submissions if you want them returned. "We try to respond within three months."

Illustration "Send sample illustrations. Label package 'Art Sample Submission.' "

Terms Pays royalties.

▣ FULCRUM PUBLISHING

4690 Table Mountain Drive, Suite 100 Golden CO 80403. (303)277-1623. Fax: (303)279-7111. Web site: www.fulcrum-books.com. **Manuscript Acquisitions:** T. Baker, acquisitions editor.

Nonfiction Middle and early readers: activity books, multicultural, nature/environment.

How to Contact/Writers Submit complete ms or submit outline/synopsis and 2 sample chapters. Responds to queries in 3 weeks; mss in 3 months.

Illustration Works with 2 illustrators/year. Reviews ms/illustration packages from artists. Send ms with dummy or submit ms with 3 pieces of final art. Send résumé, promotional literature and tearsheets. Contact: Ann Douden. Responds only if interested. Samples not returned; samples filed.

Photography Works on assignment only.

Terms Pays royalty based on wholesale price. Offers advances. Pays illustrators by the project or royalty based on wholesale price. Originals returned to artist at job's completion. Book catalog available for 9 × 12 SAE and 77¢ postage; ms guidelines available for SASE. Catalog available on website.

Tips "Research our line first. We are emphasizing science and nature nonfiction. We look for books that appeal to the school market and trade. Be sure to include SASE."

LAURA GERINGER BOOKS

Imprint of HarperCollins Publishers, 1350 Avenue of the Americas, New York NY 10019. Web site: www.haperchildrens.com. **Manuscript and Art Acquisitions:** Laura Geringer. Publishes 3 picture books/year; 6 young readers/year; 4 middle readers/year; 3 young adult titles/year. 15% of books by first-time authors.

Fiction Picture books, young readers: adventure, folktales, humor, multicultural, poetry. Middle readers: literary, adventure, fantasy, history, humor, poetry, suspense/mystery. Young adults/teens: literary, adventure, fantasy, history, humor, suspense/mystery. Average word length: picture books—500; young readers—1,000; middle readers—25,000; young adults—40,000. Recently published *If You Give a Pig a Party*, by Laura Numeroff, illustrated by Felicia Bond (ages 3-7); *So B.It*, by Sarah Weeks, (ages 10 and up); *Down the Rabbit Hole*, by Peter Abrahams (ages 10 and up).

How to Contact/Writers Only interested in agented material.

Illustration Works with 8 illustrators/year. Reviews ms/illustration packages from artists. Send ms with dummy and 3 pieces of final art. Illustrations only: Query with color photocopies. Contact: Laura Geringer, publisher. Responds only if interested. Samples returned with SASE.

Terms Book catalog available for 11 × 9 SASE and $2 postage; all imprints included in a single catalog.

GIBBS SMITH, PUBLISHER

P.O. Box 667, Layton UT 84041. (801)544-9800. Fax: (801)544-5582. E-mail: duribe@gibbs-smith.com. Web site: www.gibbs-smith.com. **Manuscript Acquisitions:** Suzanne Taylor, vice president and editorial director (children's activity books). **Art Acquisitions:** Jennifer Grillone. Book publisher; co-publisher of Sierra Club Books for Children. Imprint: Gibbs Smith. Publishes 2-3 books/year. 50% of books by first-time authors. 50%

of books from agented authors. "We accept submissions for picture books with particular interest in those with a Western (cowboy or ranch life style) theme or backdrop."

● Gibbs Smith is not accepting fiction at this time.

Nonfiction Middle readers: activity, arts/crafts, cooking, how-to, nature/environment, science. Average word length: picture books—under 1,000 words; activity books—under 15,000 words. Recently published *Hiding in a Fort*, by G. Lawson Drinkard, illustrated by Fran Lee (ages 7-12); *Sleeping in a Sack: Camping Activities for Kids*, by Linda White, illustrated by Fran Lee (ages 7-12).

How to Contact/Writers Nonfiction: Submit an outline and writing samples for activity books; query for other types of books. Responds to queries/mss in 2 months. Publishes a book 1-2 years after acceptance. Will consider simultaneous submissions. Manuscript returned with SASE.

Illustration Works with 2 illustrators/year. Reviews ms/illustration packages from artists. Query. Submit ms with 3-5 pieces of final art. Illustrations only: Query with samples; provide résumé, promo sheet, slides (duplicate slides, not originals). Responds only if interested. Samples returned with SASE; samples filed.

Terms Pays authors royalty of 2% based on retail price or work purchased outright ($500 minimum). Offers advances (average amount: $2,000). Pays illustrators by the project or royalty of 2% based on retail price. Sends galleys to authors; color proofs to illustrators. Original artwork returned at job's completion. Book catalog available for 9×12 SAE and $2.30 postage. Manuscript guidelines available—e-mail duribe@gibbs-smith.com.

Tips "We target ages 5-11. We do not publish young adult novels or chapter books."

Ⓐ DAVID R. GODINE, PUBLISHER

9 Hamilton Place, Boston MA 02108. (617)451-9600. Fax: (617)350-0250. Web site: www.godine.com. Estab. 1970. Book publisher. Publishes 1 picture book/year; 1 young reader/year; 1 middle reader/year. 10% of books by first-time authors; 90% of books from agented writers. "We publish books that matter for people who care."

● This publisher is no longer considering unsolicited manuscripts of any type.

Fiction Picture books: adventure, animal, contemporary, folktales, nature/environment. Young readers: adventure, animal, contemporary, folk or fairy tales, history, nature/environment, poetry. Middle readers: adventure, animal, contemporary, folk or fairy tales, history, mystery, nature/environment, poetry. Young adults/teens: adventure, animal, contemporary, history, mystery, nature/environment, poetry. Recently published *Little Red Riding Hood*, by Andrea Wisnewski (picture book); *The Merchant of Noises*, by Anna Rozen, illustrated by François Avril.

Nonfiction Picture books: alphabet, animal, nature/environment. Young readers: activity books, animal, history, music/dance, nature/environment. Middle readers: activity books, animal, biography, history, music/dance, nature/environment. Young adults: biography, history, music/dance, nature/environment.

How to Contact/Writers Only interested in agented material. Query. Include SASE for return of material.

Illustration Only interested in agented material. Works with 1-3 illustrators/year. "Please do not send original artwork unless solicited. Almost all of the children's books we accept for publication come to us with the author and illustrator already paired up. Therefore, we rarely use freelance illustrators." Samples returned with SASE.

Tips "E-mail submissions are not accepted. Always enclose a SASE. Keep in mind that we do not accept unsolicited manuscripts and that we rarely use freelance illustrators."

Ⓐ GOLDEN BOOKS

1745 Broadway, New York NY 10019. (212)782-9000. **Editorial Directors:** Courtney Silk, color and activity; Chris Angelilli, storybooks; Dennis Shealy, novelty. **Art Acquisitions:** Tracey Tyler, executive art director.

● See listing for Random House-Golden Books for Young Readers Group.

How to Contact/Writers Does not accept unsolicited submissions.

Fiction Publishes board books, novelty books, picture books, workbooks, series (mass market and trade).

GRAPHIA

Houghton Mifflin Company, 222 Berkeley St., Boston MA 02116. (617)351-5000. Web site: www.graphiabooks.com. **Manuscript Acquisitions:** Julia Richardson. "Graphia publishes quality paperbacks for today's teen readers, ages 14 and up. From fiction to nonfiction, poetry to graphic novels, Graphia runs the gamut, all unified by the quality of writing that is the hallmark of this imprint."

Fiction Young adults: adventure, contemporary, fantasy, history, humor, multicultural, poetry. Recently published: *The Off Season*, by Catherine Murdock; *Come in from the Cold*, by Marsha Qualey; *Breaking Up is Hard to Do*, with stories by Niki Burnham, Terri Clark, Ellen Hopkins, and Lynda Sandoval; *Zahrah the Windseeker*, by Nnedi Okorafot-Mbachu.

Nonfiction Young adults: biography, history, multicultural, nature/environment, science, social issues.

How to Contact/Writers Query. Responds to queries/mss in 3 months. Will consider simultaneous submissions and previously published work.

Illustration Do not send original artwork or slides. Send color photocopies, tearsheets or photos to Art Dept. Include SASE if you would like your samples mailed back to you.

Terms Pays author royalties. Offers advances. Sends galleys to authors. Catalog available on Web site (www.houghtonmifflin.com).

GREENE BARK PRESS

P.O. Box 1108, Bridgeport CT 06601-1108. (203)372-4861. Fax: (203)371-5856. E-mail: greenebark@aol.com. Web site: www.greenebarkpress.com. **Acquisitions:** Thomas J. Greene, publisher. Publishes 1-6 picture books/ year; majority of books by first-time or repeat authors. "We publish only quality fictional hardcover picture books for children. Our stories are selected for originality, imagery and color. Our intention is to fire-up a child's imagination, encourage a desire to read in order to explore the world through books."

Fiction Picture books, young readers: adventure, fantasy, humor. Average word length: picture books—650; young readers—1,400. Recently published *Edith Ellen Eddy*, by Julee Ann Granger; *Hey, There's a Gobblin Under My Throne*, by Rhett Ranson Pennell.

How to Contact/Writers Responds to queries in 3 months; mss in 6 months; must include SASE. No response without SASE. Publishes a book 18 months after acceptance. Will consider simultaneous submissions. Prefer to review complete mss with illustrations.

Illustration Works with 1-2 illustrators/year. Uses color artwork only. Reviews ms/illustration packages from artists. Submit ms with 3 pieces of final art (copies only). Illustrations only: Query with samples. Responds in 2 months only if interested. Samples returned with SASE; samples filed. Originals returned at job's completion.

Terms Pays authors royalty of 10-12% based on wholesale price. Pays illustrators by the project (range: $1,500-3,000) or 5-7% royalty based on wholesale price. No advances. Sends galleys to authors; dummies to illustrators. Manuscript guidelines available for SASE or per e-mail request.

Tips "As a guide for future publications look to our latest publications, do not look to our older backlist. Please, no telephone, e-mail or fax queries."

GREENHAVEN PRESS

Imprint of the Cengage Gale, 27500 Drake Road, Farmington Hills MI 48331. E-mail: mary.lavey@cengage.com. Web site: www.gale.com/greenhaven. **Acquisitions:** Mary Lavey. Publishes 220 young adult academic reference titles/year. 50% of books by first-time authors. Greenhaven continues to print quality nonfiction anthologies for libraries and classrooms. Our well known Opposing Viewpoints series is highly respected by students and librarians in need of material on controversial social issues.

  • Greenhaven accepts no unsolicited manuscripts. All writing is done on a work-for-hire basis. Also see listing for Lucent Books.

Nonfiction Young adults (high school): controversial issues, social issues, history, literature, science, environment, health. Recently published (series): Issues That Concern You; Writing the Critical Essay: An Opening Viewpoint Guide; Introducing Issue with Opposing Viewpoints; Social Issues in Literature; and Perspectives on Diseases and Disorders.

How to Contact/Writers Send query, résumé, and list of published works by e-mail.

Terms Work purchased outright from authors; write-for-hire, flat fee.

Ⓐ 🅥 GREENWILLOW BOOKS

1350 Avenue of the Americas, New York NY 10019. (212)261-6500. Web site: www.harpercollinschildrens.com. Book publisher. Imprint of HarperCollins. Vice President/Publisher: Virginia Duncan. **Art Acquisitions:** Paul Zakris, art director. Publishes 40 picture books/year; 5 middle readers/year; 5 young adult books/year. "Greenwillow Books publishes picture books, fiction for young readers of all ages, and nonfiction primarily for children under seven years of age."

  • Greenwillow Books is currently accepting neither unsolicited manuscripts nor queries. Unsolicited mail will not be opened and will not be returned. Call (212)261-6627 for an update. Greenwillow title *Escape!: The Story of the Great Houdini*, by Sid Fleischman, won a Boston Globe-Horn Book Nonfiction Honor Award in 2007.

Illustration Art samples (postcards only) should be sent in duplicate to Paul Zakris and Virginia Duncan.

Terms Pays authors royalty. Offers advances. Pays illustrators royalty or by the project. Sends galleys to authors.

Ⓐ GROSSET & DUNLAP PUBLISHERS

Penguin Group (USA), 345 Hudson St., New York NY 10014. Web site: http://us.penguingroup.com/youngreaders. Estab. 1898. **Acquisitions:** Debra Dorfman, president/publisher. Publishes 175 titles/year. "Grosset & Dunlap publishes children's books that show children reading is fun with books that speak to their interests and are affordable so children can build a home library of their own. Focus on licensed properties, series, readers and novelty books."

Fiction Recently published series: Camp Confidential; Hank Zipper; Katie Kazoo; Dish; Dragon Slayers' Academy; Nancy Drew. Upcoming series: Pirate School; The Misadventure of Benjamin Bartholomew Piff. Licensed series: Angelina Ballerina; Strawberry Shortcake; Charlie & Lola; Dick & Jane (brand). Also published the Clear & Simple Workbook series.

Nonfiction Young readers: nature/environment, science. Recently published series: All Aboard Reading sereis; Who Was . . .? series.

How to Contact/Writers "We do not accept e-mail submissions. Unsolicited manuscripts witll receive a response in 6-8 weeks."

🖸 GRYPHON HOUSE

P.O. Box 207, Beltsville MD 20704-0207. (301)595-9500. Fax: (301)595-0051. E-mail: kathyc@ghbooks.com. Web site: www.gryphonhouse.com. **Acquisitions:** Kathy Charner, editor-in-chief.

Nonfiction Parent and teacher resource books, textbooks. Recently published *Reading Games*, by Jackie Silberg; *Primary Art*, by MaryAnn F. Kohl; *Teaching Young Children's with Autism Spectrum Disorder*, by Clarissa Willis; *The Complete Resource Book for Infants*, by Pam Schiller. "At Gryphon House, our goal is to publish books that help teachers and parents enrich the lives of children from birth through age eight. We strive to make our books useful for teachers at all levels of experience, as well as for parents, caregivers, and anyone interested in working with children."

How to Contact/Writers Query. Submit outline/synopsis and 2 sample chapters. Responds to queries/mss in 6 months. Publishes a book 18 months after acceptance. Will consider simultaneous submissions, e-mail submissions.

Illustration Works with 4-5 illustrators/year. Uses b&w realistic artwork only. Illustrations only: Query with samples, promo sheet. Responds in 2 months. Samples returned with SASE; samples filed.

Photography Buys photos from freelancers. Buys stock and assigns work. Submit cover letter, published samples, stock photo list.

Terms Pays authors royalty based on wholesale price. Offers advances. Pays illustrators by the project. Pays photographers by the project or per photo. Sends edited ms copy to authors. Original artwork returned at job's completion. Book catalog and ms guidelines available via website or with SASE.

Tips "Send a SASE for our catalog and manuscript guidelines. Look at our books, then submit proposals that complement the books we already publish or supplement our existing books. We are looking for books of creative, participatory learning experiences that have a common conceptual theme to tie them together. The books should be on subjects that parents or teachers want to do on a daily basis."

HACHAI PUBLISHING

527 Empire Blvd., Brooklyn NY 11225. (718)633-0100. Fax: (718)633-0103. E-mail: info@hachai.com. Web site: www.hachai.com. **Manuscript Acquisitions:** Devorah Leah Rosenfeld, submissions editor. Publishes 4 picture books/year; 1 young reader/year; 1 middle reader/year. 75% of books published by first-time authors. "All books have spiritual/religious themes, specifically traditional Jewish content. We're seeking books about morals and values; the Jewish experience in current and Biblical times; and Jewish observance, Sabbath and holidays."

Fiction Picture books and young readers: contemporary, historical fiction, religion. Middle readers: adventure, contemporary, problem novels, religion. Does not want to see fantasy, animal stories, romance, problem novels depicting drug use or violence. Recently published *Let's Go Visiting*, written and illustrated by Rikki Benenfeld (ages 2-5, picture book); *What Else Do I Say*, by Malky Goldberg, illustrated by Patti Argoff (ages 1-2, lift-the-flap book); *Way Too Much Challah Dough*, by Goldie Shulman, illustrated by Vitaliy Romanenko (ages 3-6, picture book); *Faigy Finds the Way*, by Batsheva Brandeis (ages 7-10, short chapter book).

Nonfiction Recently published *The Invisible Book*, by Bracha Goetz, illustrated by Patti Agroff; *My Jewish ABC's*, by Draizy Zelcer, illustrated by Patti Nemeroff (ages 3-6, picture book); *Shadow Play*, by Leah Pearl Shollar, illustrated by Pesach Gerber (ages 3-6, picture book); *Much Much Better*, by Chaim Kosofsky, illustrated by Jessica Schiffman (ages 5-8).

How to Contact/Writers Fiction/nonfiction: Submit complete ms. Responds to queries/mss in 6 weeks.

Illustration Works with 4 illustrators/year. Uses primary color artwork, some b&w illustration. Reviews ms/illustration packages from authors. Submit ms with 1 piece of final art. Illustrations only: Query with samples; arrange personal portfolio review. Responds in 6 weeks. Samples returned with SASE; samples filed.

Terms Work purchased outright from authors for $800-1,000. Pays illustrators by the project (range: $2,000-4,000). Book catalog, ms/artist's guidelines available for SASE.

Tips "Write a story that incorporates a moral, not a preachy morality tale. Originality is the key. We feel Hachai publications will appeal to a wider readership as parents become more interested in positive values for their children."

Ⓐ 🐛 HARCOURT CHILDREN'S BOOKS

Imprint of Houghton Mifflin Harcourt Children's Book Group, 215 Park Ave South, New York NY 10003. Web site: www.harcourtbooks.com. **Senior Vice President and Publisher:** Betsy Groban. **Associate Publisher:** Jennifer Haller. 20% of books by first-time authors; 50% of books from agented writers. "Harcourt Children's Books publishes hardcover picture books and fiction only."

● Harcourt Children's Books no longer accepts unsolicited manuscripts, queries or illustrations. Recent Harcourt titles *Tails*, by Matthew Van Fleet; *Leaf Man*, by Lois Ehlert; *The Great Fuzz Frenzy*, by Janet Stevens and Susan Steven Crummel; *How I Became a Pirate* and *Pirates Don't Change Diapers*, by Melinda Long, illustrated by David Shannon; and *Frankenstein Makes a Sandwich*, by Adam Rex, are all New York Times bestsellers. Harcourt title *Jazz Baby*, by Lisa Wheeler, illustrated by R. Gregory Christie, won a Theodor Seuss Geisel Award in 2008. See Lisa Wheeler's article Great Opening Lines in Picture Books on page 37.

How to Contact/Writers Only interested in agented material.

Illustration Only interested in agented material.

Photography Works on assignment only.

Terms Pays authors and illustrators royalty based on retail price. Pays photographers by the project. Sends galleys to authors; dummies to illustrators. Original artwork returned at job's completion.

Ⓐ 🐛 HARPERCOLLINS CHILDREN'S BOOKS

1350 Avenue of the Americas, New York NY 10019. (212)261-6500. Web site: www.harperchildrens.com. Book publisher. President and Publisher: Susan Katz. Associate Publisher/Editor-in-Chief: Kate Morgan Jackson. Associate Publisher, Fiction: Elise Howard. Editorial Directors: Margaret Anastas, Barbara Lalicki, Maria Modugno, Phoebe Yeh. **Art Acquisitions:** Martha Rago or Barbara Fitzsimmons, director. Imprints: HarperTrophy, HarperTeen, EOS, HarperFestival, Greenwillow Books, Joanna Cotler Books, Laura Geringer Books, Katherine Tegen Books.

● HarperCollins Children's Books is not accepting unsolicited and/or unagented manuscripts or queries. "Unfortunately, the volume of these submissions is so large that we cannot give them the attention they deserve. Such submissions will not be reviewed or returned." HarperTempest title *The White Darkness*, by Geraldine McCaughrean, won the Michael L. Printz Award in 2008. HarperTeen *Title Repossessed*, by Judith Clarke, won a Printz Honor Award in 2008.

Fiction Publishes picture, chapter, novelty, board and TV/movie books.

How to Contact/Writers Only interested in agented material.

Illustration Art samples may be sent to Martha Rago or Stephanie Bart-Horvath. **Please do not send original art.** Works with over 100 illustrators/year. Responds only if interested. Samples returned with SASE; samples filed only if interested.

Terms Art guidelines available for SASE.

🖸 HAYES SCHOOL PUBLISHING CO. INC.

321 Pennwood Ave., Wilkinsburg PA 15221-3398. (412)371-2373. Fax: (800)543-8771. E-mail: chayes@hayespub.com. Web site: www.hayespub.com. Estab. 1940. **Acquisitions:** Mr. Clair N. Hayes. Produces folders, workbooks, stickers, certificates. Wants to see supplementary teaching aids for grades K-12. Interested in all subject areas. Will consider simultaneous and electronic submissions.

How to Contact/Writers Query with description or complete ms. Responds in 6 weeks. SASE for return of submissions.

Illustration Works with 3-4 illustrators/year. Responds in 6 weeks. Samples returned with SASE; samples filed. Originals not returned at job's completion.

Terms Work purchased outright. Purchases all rights.

HEALTH PRESS NA INC.

P.O. Box 37470, Albuquerque NM 87176-7479. (505)888-1394 or (877)411-0707. Fax: (505)888-1521. E-mail: goodbooks@healthpress.com. Web site: www.healthpress.com. **Acquisitions:** Editor. Publishes 4 young readers/year. 100% of books by first-time authors.

Fiction Picture books, young readers: health, special needs. Average word length: young readers—1,000-1,500; middle readers—1,000-1,500. Recently published *The Girl With No Hair*, by Elizabeth Murphy-Melas, illustrated by Alex Hernandez (ages 8-12, picture book); *The Peanut Butter Jam*, by Elizabeth Sussman-Nassau, illustrated by Margot Ott (ages 6-12, picture book).

Nonfiction Picture books, young readers: health, special needs, social issues, self help.

How to Contact/Writers Submit complete ms. Responds in 3 month. Publishes a book 9 months after acceptance. Will consider simultaneous submissions.

Terms Pays authors royalty. Sends galleys to authors. Book catalog available.

HENDRICK-LONG PUBLISHING COMPANY

10635 Tower Oaks, Suite D, Houston TX 77070. (832)912-READ. Fax: (832)912-7353. E-mail: hendrick-long@w orldnet.att.net. **Acquisitions:** Vilma Long, vice president. Publishes 4 young readers/year; 4 middle readers/ year. 20% of books by first-time authors. Publishes fiction/nonfiction about Texas of interest to young readers through young adults/teens.

Fiction Young readers, middle readers: history books on Texas and the Southwest. No fantasy or poetry.

Nonfiction Young readers, middle readers: history books on Texas and the Southwest, biography, multicultural. ''Would like to see more workbook-type manuscripts.''

How to Contact/Writers Fiction/nonfiction: Query with outline/synopsis and sample chapter. Responds to queries in 5 months. Publishes a book 18 months after acceptance. No simultaneous submissions. Include SASE.

HOLIDAY HOUSE INC.

425 Madison Ave., New York NY 10017. (212)688-0085. Fax: (212)421-6134. Web site: www.holidayhouse.com. Estab. 1935. Book publisher. **Vice President/Editor-in-Chief:** Mary Cash. **Acquisitions:** Acquisitions Editor. **Art Director:** Claire Counihan. Publishes 35 picture books/year; 3 young readers/year; 15 middle readers/year; 8 young adult titles/year. 20% of books by first-time authors; 10% from agented writers. Mission Statement: ''To publish high-quality books for children.''

Fiction All levels: adventure, contemporary, fantasy, folktales, ghost, historical, humor, literary, multicultural, school, suspense/mystery, sports. Recently published *Jazz*, by Walter Dean Myers, illustrated by Christopher Myers; *Keeper of Soles*, by Teresa Bateman, illustrated by Yayo; *Freedom Walkers*, by Russell Freedman.

Nonfiction All levels, but more picture books and fewer middle-grade nonfiction titles: animal, biography, concept, contemporary, geography, historical, math, multicultural, music/dance, nature/environment, religion, science, social issues.

How to Contact/Writers Send queries only to editor. Responds to queries in 3 months; mss in 4 months. ''If we find your book idea suits our present needs, we will notify you by mail.'' Once a ms has been requested, the writers should send in the exclusive submission, with a SASE, otherwise the ms will not be returned.

Illustration Works with 35 illustrators/year. Reviews ms illustration packages from artists. Send ms with dummy. Do not submit original artwork or slides. Color photocopies or printed samples are preferred. Responds only if interested. Samples filed.

Terms Pays authors and illustrators an advance against royalties. Originals returned at job's completion. Book catalog, ms/artist's guidelines available for a SASE.

Tips ''We need books with strong stories, writing and art. We do not publish board books or novelties. No easy readers.''

HENRY HOLT & COMPANY

175 Fifth Ave, New York NY 10010. Unsolicited Manuscript Hotline: (646)307-5087. Web site: www.HenryHoltK ids.com. Submissions Web site: www.HenryHoltKids.com/submissions.htm. **Manuscript Acquisitions:** Laura Godwin, vice president and publisher of Books for Young Readers; Christy Ottaviano, editorial director, Christy Ottaviano Books; Reka Simonsen, senior editor; Kate Farrell, editor. **Art Acquisitions:** Patrick Collins, art director. Publishes 30-35 picture books/year; 6-8 chapter books/year; 10-15 middle readers/year; 8-10 young adult titles/year. 15% of books by first-time authors; 40% of books from agented writers. ''Henry Holt and Company Books for Young Readers is known for publishing quality books that feature imaginative authors and illustrators. We tend to publish many new authors and illustrators each year in our effort to develop and foster new talent.''

- New imprint Holt Christy Ottaviano Books will publish approximately 20 books per year ranging from preschool picture books to middle-grade and young adult fiction, as well as some nonfiction. Of particular interest—picture books: humor; curriculum-focused; books that explore childhood milestones and feelings; nature; history. Middle grade and young adult fiction: adventure; mystery; urban fantasy; coming of age; historical; commercial and edgy YA fiction. Submission policy: agents only and by author/illustrator referral.

Fiction Picture books: animal, anthology, concept, folktales, history, humor, multicultural, nature/environment, poetry, special needs, sports. Middle readers: adventure, contemporary, history, humor, multicultural, special needs, sports, suspense/mystery. Young adults: contemporary, humor, multicultural, mystery, historical.

Nonfiction Picture books: animal, arts/crafts, biography, concept, geography, history, hobbies, multicultural, the arts, nature/environment, sports. Middle readers, young readers, young adult: biography, history, multicultural, sports.

How to Contact/Writers Fiction/nonfiction: Submit complete ms, Attn: Submissions; ''no SASE please.'' Responds in 4-6 months only if interested, otherwise mss are not returned or responded to. Will not consider simultaneous or multiple submissions.

Illustration Works with 50-60 illustrators/year. Reviews ms/illustration packages from artists. Random samples OK. Illustrations only: Submit tearsheets, slides. Do *not* send originals. Responds to art samples only if interested. Samples filed but not returned. If accepted, original artwork returned at job's completion. Portfolios are reviewed every Monday.

Terms Pays authors/illustrators royalty based on retail price. Sends galleys to authors; proofs to illustrators.

🅜 HOUGHTON MIFFLIN CO.

Children's Trade Books, 222 Berkeley St., Boston MA 02116-3764. (617)351-5000. Fax: (617)351-1111. E-mail: childrens_books@hmco.com. Web site: www.houghtonmifflinbooks.com. **Manuscript Aquisitions:** Submissions Coordinator; Betsy Groban, publisher; Margaret Raymo, editorial director; Ann Rider, senior editor; Mary Wilcox, franchise director, Julia Richardson, paperback director; Kate O'Sullivan, senior editor, Monica Perez, editor; Erica Zappy, associate editor. **Art Acquisitions:** Sheila Smallwood, creative director. Imprints include Clarion Books, Sandpiper and Graphia. Averages 60 titles/year. Publishes hardcover originals and trade paperback reprints and originals. "Houghton Mifflin gives shape to ideas that educate, inform, and above all, delight."

- Houghton title *Tracking Trash: Flotsam, Jetsam, and the Science of Ocean Motion*, by Loree Griffin Burns, won a Boston Globe-Horn Book Nonfiction Honor Award in 2007.

Fiction All levels: all categories except religion. "We do not rule out any theme, though we do not publish specifically religious material." Recently published *Princess Ben*, by Catherine Gilbert Murdock (ages 12 and up, YA novel); *Farm Friends*, by Anna Roan (ages 3-6, picture book); *Hogwash*, by Arthur Geisert (ages 4-8, picture book).

Nonfiction All levels: all categories except religion. Recently published *Sisters & Brothers*, by Steven Jenkins (picture book, all ages); *The Mysterious Universe*, by Ellen Jackson (ages 10 and up);

How to Contact/Writers Fiction: Submit complete ms on unfolded white paper. Nonfiction: Submit outline/synopsis and sample chapters. Responds within 4 months only if interested—do not send self-addressed stamped envelope.

Illustration Works with 60 illustrators/year. Reviews ms/illustration packages from artists. Manuscript/illustration packages or illustrations only: Query with samples (colored photocopies are fine); provide tearsheets. Responds in 4 months. Samples returned with SASE; samples filed if interested.

Terms Pays standard royalty based on retail price; offers advance. Illustrators paid by the project and royalty. Manuscript and artist's guidelines available with SASE.

HUNTER HOUSE PUBLISHERS

P.O. Box 2914, Alameda CA 94501-0914. (510)865-5282. Fax: (510)865-4295. E-mail: acquisitions@hunterhouse .com. Web site: www.hunterhouse.com. **Manuscript Acquisitions:** Jeanne Brondino. Publishes 0-1 nonfiction titles for teenage women/year. 50% of books by first-time authors; 5% of books from agented writers.

Nonfiction Young adults: self help, health, multicultural, violence prevention. "We emphasize that all our books try to take multicultural experiences and concerns into account. We would be interested in a self-help book on multicultural issues." Books are therapy/personal growth-oriented. Does *not* want to see books for young children, fiction, illustrated picture books, autobiography. Published *Turning Yourself Around: Self-Help Strategies for Troubled Teens*, by Kendall Johnson, Ph.D.; *Safe Dieting for Teens*, by Linda Ojeda, Ph.D.

How to Contact/Writers Query; submit overview and chapter-by-chapter synopsis, sample chapters and statistics on your subject area, support organizations or networks and marketing ideas. "Testimonials from professionals or well-known authors are crucial." Responds to queries in 3 months; mss in 6 months. Publishes a book 18 months after acceptance. Will consider simultaneous submissions.

Terms Payment varies. Sends galleys to authors. Book catalog available for 9×12 SAE and $1.25 postage; ms guidelines for standard SAE and 1 first-class stamp.

Tips Wants teen books with solid, informative material. "We do few children's books. The ones we do are for a select, therapeutic audience. No fiction! Please, no fiction."

🅐 🅜 HYPERION BOOKS FOR CHILDREN

114 Fifth Ave., New York NY 10011-5690. 914-288-4100 . Fax: (212)633-4833. Web site: www.hyperionbooksfor children.com. **Manuscript Acquisitions:** Editorial Director. **Art Director:** Anne Diebel. 10% of books by first-time authors. Publishes various categories.

- Hyperion title *Knuffle Bunny Too: A Case of Mistaken Identity*, by Mo Willems, won a Caldecott Honor Award in 2008. Their title *There is a Bird on Your Head!*, also by Mo Willems, won the Theodor Seuss Geisel Award in 2008. Their title *Clementine*, by Sara Pennypacker, illustrated by Marla Frazee, won a Boston Globe-Horn Book Fiction and Poetry Award in 2007.

Fiction Picture books, young readers, middle readers, young adults: adventure, animal, anthology (short stories), contemporary, fantasy, folktales, history, humor, multicultural, poetry, science fiction, sports, suspense/mystery. Middle readers, young adults: commercial fiction. Recently published *Emily's First 100 Days of School*, by Rosemary Wells (ages 3-6, *New York Times* bestseller); *Artemis Fowl*, by Eoin Colfer (YA novel, *New York Times* bestseller); *Dumpy The Dump Truck*, series by Julie Andrews Edwards and Emma Walton Hamilton (ages 3-7).
Nonfiction All trade subjects for all levels.
How to Contact/Writers Only interested in agented material.
Illustration Works with 100 illustrators/year. "Picture books are fully illustrated throughout. All others depend on individual project." Reviews ms/illustration packages from artists. Submit complete package. Illustrations only: Submit résumé, business card, promotional literature or tearsheets to be kept on file. Responds only if interested. Original artwork returned at job's completion.
Photography Works on assignment only. Publishes photo essays and photo concept books. Provide résumé, business card, promotional literature or tearsheets to be kept on file.
Terms Pays authors royalty based on retail price. Offers advances. Pays illustrators and photographers royalty based on retail price or a flat fee. Sends galleys to authors; dummies to illustrators. Book catalog available for 9×12 SAE and 3 first-class stamps.

IDEALS CHILDREN'S BOOKS AND CANDYCANE PRESS

Imprint of Ideals Publications, 2636 Elm Hill Pike, Suite 120, Nashville TN 37214. Web site: www.idealsbooks.com. **Manuscript Acquisitions:** Submissions. **Art Acquisitions:** Art Director. Publishes 10 picture books/year; 40 board books/year. 50% of books by first-time authors.
Fiction Picture books: animal, concept, history, religion. Board books: animal, history, nature/environment, religion. Average word length: picture books—1,500; board books—200.

ILLUMINATION ARTS

P.O. Box 1865, Bellevue WA 98009. (425)644-7185. Fax: (425)644-9274. E-mail: liteinfo@illumin.com. Web site: www.illumin.com. **Acquisitions:** Ruth Thompson, editorial director.
Fiction Word length: Prefers under 1,000, but will consider up to 1,500 words. Recently published *Just Imagine*, by John M. Thompson and George M. Schultz, illustrated by Wodin; *Mrs. Murphy's Marvelous Mansion*, by Emma Perry Roberts, illustrated by Robert Rogalski.
How to Contact/Writers Fiction: Submit complete ms. Responds to queries in 3 months with SASE only.No electronic or CD submissions for text or art. Publishes a book 1-2 years after acceptance. Will consider simultaneous submissions.
Illustration Works with 3-5 illustrators/year. Uses color artwork only. Reviews ms/illustration packages from artists. Query or send ms with dummy. Illustrations only: Query with color samples, résumé and promotional material to be kept on file or returned with SASE only. Responds in 3 months with SASE only. Samples returned with SASE or filed.
Terms Pays authors and illustrators royalty based on wholesale price. Book fliers available for SASE.
Tips "Read our books and follow our guidelines. Be patient. The market is competitive. We receive 2,000 submissions annually and publish 2-3 books a year. Sorry, we are unable to track unsolicited submissions."

IMPACT PUBLISHERS, INC.

P.O. Box 6016, Atascadero CA 93423-6016. (805)466-5917. Fax: (805)466-5919. E-mail: info@impactpublishers.com. Web site: www.impactpublishers.com. **Manuscript Acquisitions:** Melissa Froehner, children's editor. **Art Acquisitions:** J. Trumbull, production. Imprints: Little Imp Books, Rebuilding Books, The Practical Therapist Series. Publishes 1 young reader/year; 1 middle reader/year; 1 young adult title/year. 20% of books by first-time authors. "Our purpose is to make the best human services expertise available to the widest possible audience. We publish only popular psychology and self-help materials written in everyday language by professionals with advanced degrees and significant experience in the human services."
Nonfiction Young readers, middle readers, young adults: self-help. Recently published *Jigsaw Puzzle Family: The Stepkids' Guide to Fitting It Together*, by Cynthia MacGregor (ages 8-12, children's/divorce/emotions).
How to Contact/Writers Nonfiction: Query or submit complete ms, cover letter, résumé. Responds to queries in 12 weeks; mss in 3 months. Will consider simultaneous submissions or previously published work.
Illustration Works with 1 illustrator/year. Uses b&w artwork only. Reviews ms/illustration packages from artists. Query. Contact: Children's Editor. Illustrations only: Query with samples. Contact: Sharon Skinner, production manager. Responds only if interested. Samples returned with SASE; samples filed. Originals returned to artist at job's completion.
Terms Pays authors royalty of 10-12%. Offers advances. Pays illustrators by the project. Book catalog available for #10 SAE with 2 first-class stamps; ms guidelines available for SASE. All imprints included in a single catalog.
Tips "Please do not submit fiction, poetry or narratives."

Marissa Doyle

History, mystery, romance & magic

Growing up in Massachusetts—a place where "history is everywhere"—might be behind Marissa Doyle's love of the past. Doyle majored in history and archaeology at Bryn Mawr College in Pennsylvania, and is a devoted nonfiction reader. And from all the history books she's read, she's learned that "quite often, real life is far stranger than any fiction."

It makes sense, then, that Doyle, a self-described history geek, writes historical fiction. Her first book, *Bewitching Season* (Henry Holt), set in Victorian England, blends history with magic, mystery, and romance, resulting in an intoxicating cocktail of a story. Main character Persephone and her twin Penelope prepare for their coming-out season. Persy, however, would rather study magic with their governess, Ally, than bother with social functions. Then Ally goes missing, nicely thickening the plot. Throw in a handsome neighbor, a love potion, a little brother, a nefarious wizard and a soon-to-be-crowned Queen Victoria and you've got a page-turner. "This wonderfully crafted debut novel braids several very different story lines into an utterly satisfying whole," says *Booklist* in a starred review. ". . . Doyle takes as much care with characters (even minor ones) as with story details."

Doyle says she got her first book contract the old-fashioned way. "I wrote a lot, entered writing contests for feedback, researched agents and sent them query letters, and went to conferences and pitched to them," she says. Then, in spring 2005, she queried Emily Sylvan Kim at Writers House. Kim requested Doyle's full manuscript for *Bewitching Season*. But when she hadn't heard back by late summer, Doyle assumed Kim wasn't interested—until she read on www.agentquery.com that Kim had opened Prospect Agency (www.prospectagency.com). "So I took a chance and e-mailed her and said that I guessed she'd been busy over the summer with the new agency, and could I resubmit my story to her. She e-mailed back that she'd been about to contact me." A week later Doyle signed with Kim, and within three months she had a two-book deal with Henry Holt for *Bewitching Season* and its sequel, *Twice Bewitched*, which focuses on Pen and is a spring 2009 release.

Here Doyle talks magic, history, romance, research, publishing, and promotion. To learn more about her, visit Doyle's Web site, www.marissadoyle.com. To learn more about being a teen in the 19th century, visit her blog, www.nineteenteen.blogspot.com.

Your debut novel is historical romance with a bit of magic thrown in. Considering your education background, the historical element in your writing makes sense. Where does the magic element come from? (Do you dabble?)
Dabbling? No—I'm pretty much an all-round agnostic though I have had a few experiences that make me feel there's more to the world than what we perceive with our five senses.

I'm not sure where the magic in *Bewitching Season* comes from, but everything I write seems to have some element of magic or fantasy in it to a greater or lesser degree. I have always been a lover of science fiction and fantasy, though, and grew up reading Susan Cooper and Madeleine L'Engle and Evangeline Walton. In fact, I still have the first chapter book I ever read, which was a book called *The Little Witch*. Which might explain things, come to think of it.

And magic and historical settings just seem to go together. For me, fiction with magical elements in it just seems more believable set in any time before World War II because it's distant and foreign and pre-modern/pre-technology enough to somehow "work." It's much easier to suspend your disbelief about magic or other supernatural elements when they're happening on the foggy, gas-lit streets of Victorian London than when they're in the sodium-lamp-lit, automobile-choked streets of today.

Historical fiction seems like a unique challenge. One must incorporate a lot of accurate historical details while still telling a compelling story. How did you handle this?

Oh dear. This is going to sound dreadfully smug, but it *wasn't* hard. I am an utter, unashamed history geek. I've been reading historical fiction and serious historical nonfiction since about age eight after I saw *The Six Wives of Henry VIII* on Masterpiece Theatre and then found the book on which it was based on a bookshelf in my house. Before I'd ever

Is magic the life for a lady?

BEWITCHING SEASON

Marissa Doyle

Reprinted with permission of Henry Holt & Company.

"In her debut, [Marissa] Doyle offers a heart-throbbing romance full of magic and royal court intrigue," says *Kirkus* of *Bewitching Season*, which is the first in Doyle's two-book deal with Henry Holt. "Fans of historical mysteries will find this a page turner."

thought about writing historical fiction I'd been reading books on British and French and American history for three decades. I get excited about a new biography or social history the way other people get excited about the latest Janet Evanovitch or John Grisham novel. After absorbing that much history, it sort of becomes a part of you so that you *can* concentrate on the story . . . the history part just comes naturally. That's not to say that I don't check up on historical factoids and minutiae all the time while writing—but most of the people and dates and events are already there in my head.

Naturally, my conversation at cocktail parties can be rather strange.

One thing that is very important to me when writing historical fiction is to try to be as true as I possibly can to the mindset of the period. I intensely dislike historical fiction that is simply 21st century people in period costume, with 21st century values and mores. So when I wrote about Persy and Pen, I didn't want to fall into the "I don't care if women in this time and place don't do this—I'm going to be spunky and break the rules and seek to fulfill my dreams!" trap. I wanted to be very careful to make them products of their time and social class, yet still have them be accessible to modern teen readers. Maybe there was a little unconscious didacticism there . . . or maybe not so unconscious. I do hope readers will absorb how different it was to be a female then and understand how the world has changed for the better in that respect.

Any tips you could offer on research for historical fiction? How did you keep track of your facts (for example, all the details of the twins' various party outfits)?

Because of my history geekiness (geekism?), I prefer research books to online research, though I use both. What I love to do is pore through the bibliography of good general histories to find more specific books on topics that interest me or that I need more information on. For example, I found dozens of treasures in the bibliographies of Daniel Pool's *What Jane Austen Ate and Charles Dickens Knew* and Kristine Hughes' *The Writer's Guide to Everyday Life in Regency and Victorian England* that I was able to find on eBay or through Alibris. And I use lots and lots of Post-it tags to mark useful bits as I go through my books— I'll scribble a word or two on them to help identify the useful information on that page. I think the fact that my writing room is also our spare bedroom is important—I have a bed to spread all my research books out on, sorted into piles . . . this pile for books on clothes, that one for etiquette books, that one for biographies of Victoria . . . so I know where all my references are and can go to them immediately if I need a bit of knowledge in a hurry. Having a strong visual memory—remembering what book you ran across something interesting in—helps a lot too.

As for keeping track of details like the twins' clothes? I *have* twin daughters. You just learn to remember who has what outfits . . . or where which daughter left her shoes after she got home from school yesterday. And again, being history-geekoid and having a strong visual memory helps. But if I weren't, I'd probably keep hand-written lists on my desk, which is something I do when I have details that I want to go back and work into a story after it's done.

Enough about history—let's talk romance. I enjoyed the scenes in *Bewitching Season* between Persy and Lochinvar. There are a lot of classic romance elements going on in your story: misunderstandings, obstacles, despair, longing, stolen kisses. Great stuff! Why did you choose to write romance for a YA audience and not for adults?

That's a really good question . . . and the answer is originally, I thought I *was* writing romance for adults. I started out my writing career by joining the RWA (Romance Writers of America), which is an outstandingly supportive organization for new writers and has some of most publishing-savvy people I've ever met in it, so I started writing romances. Except I always found myself more interested in my heroines and the journeys they were making rather than in their relationships with the heroes. I decided this was a personal failing and did my best to correct it by entering a bazillion writing contests held by the various chapters within RWA in order to get feedback on my work. At first I tanked, but then I started placing and winning. But no romance editors who read my entries seemed terribly interested in requesting them. Then one day I got a packet of my entries and score sheets back from a contest that I had entered with the first 25 pages of *Bewitching Season*, and one judge wrote, "This story seems more like a Young Adult novel than a romance." Ding ding ding! It was like lights started flashing and bells ringing. Of course! I could write young adult books, and then it would be perfectly acceptable for me to concentrate on my heroine's journey—and part of that journey could still be Getting the Guy.

Another reason I love writing YA romance is that the adult romance market these days really wants lots of graphic sensuality right there, up front—no gently closing bedroom doors. I have no problem with that . . . but I can't write it so save my life. It's very difficult to write about sex and not make it sound silly or repetitious. Believe me, I've tried—and when I read what I've written, I usually dissolve in giggles and hit delete. Sexual tension is another thing entirely. It's enormous fun to write sexual tension—and what is likely to be more rife with it than a YA story with romantic elements? But sex, no matter how romantic and loving and fulfilling? Nope. Not me.

Is your second upcoming novel is still in progress? Can you give me a teaser?

Actually, *Twice Bewitched* is done and I'm expecting revisions back soon from my editor. It's Pen's story, set in Cork, Ireland, where she goes with Ally and Michael Carrighar to study magic and make up for the slacking off she's done in the past. So of course Irish political issues about home rule play a role. There's also more magic in it than in *Bewitching Season*, probably because I utilized threads of Irish/Celtic folklore and mythology in the plot. There's a hero who happens to be the illegitimate son of Queen Victoria's "wicked" uncle, the King of Hanover, whom some people suspected at this time of plotting against the new queen since he would be heir to the British throne until she married and had children. Oh yes—and there's also a drunken clurichaun (a type of leprechaun from southern Ireland) who lives in the cellar and is befriended by Pen.

The pub date for *Bewitching Season* was moved up to spring '08 causing you to leave the Class of 2k7 for the Class of 2k8. Were there any other surprises during the publishing process?

Well, all of it was new. I've been afraid of annoying my long-suffering editor and her assistant, but they've both been very gracious about answering my newbie questions, and having an agent like Emily who knows the industry well helps. I guess my chief surprise is that in a lot of ways, publishing is still rather an old-fashioned business and moves at a statelier pace than most other industries.

How has your membership in the Class collectives benefited you as a first-time author?

It has made a huge difference, because I'm never alone—I can get onto our listserv and ask a question or share good or bad news, and all my classmates will understand or be able to help. We're all going through this journey together, so we're very supportive of each other. And seeing what other class members are doing for their own promotion is very educational, so that I'm doing, or at least considering doing, promotional activities that I never would have done if I didn't have the class to look to for examples and help.

What do you have lined up as far as promotional efforts? Have you seen any reviews or gotten any feedback?

Well, as of the time I'm answering this question, it's three months until *Bewitching Season* is officially released. So I'm in the midst of setting up book signings both for myself and in conjunction with other 2k8 writers in the New England area, lining up some school visits, and preparing some panel appearances at conferences. A lot of it is beyond my usual comfort zone, but as I said above I have the Class of 2k8 (www.classof2k8.com) to thank for helping me learn to extend that zone.

Holt has been fabulous about sending review copies out. So far I've gotten reviewed by *Booklist*, which gave me a lovely starred review, and I'm waiting on tenterhooks for any others to come in. There has been a fair bit of quiet buzz going on about the book on the Internet, which I attribute to being a part of 2k8, to my MySpace presence, and to being an active participant on Verla Kay's Children's Writer's and Illustrator's Chat Board. I hope it turns into good reviews on the many wonderful teen book review sites and blogs out there.

I also co-host a blog, Nineteenteen (www.nineteenteen.blogspot.com), with fellow 2k8 member Regina Scott, a Regency Romance writer-turned-YA author. Its focus is on how people like the characters in our books lived—a sort of behind the scenes look at life as an upper class young woman in the first half of the nineteenth century. I wasn't at all sure about blogging, but doing it with a partner cuts down on the work, and I'm actually having a lot of fun with it.

What advice would you offer to unpublished writers?

Write every day if you possibly can, and when you finish a story, start another. When you're done with that one, start a third. I think you learn a lot more writing several different stories than focusing on polishing just your first.

Join a critique group and/or take writing classes. You will not only learn a lot and improve your writing, but also get used to the idea of letting other people read your words.

Join an organization like SCBWI and read the chatboards, because that's where you learn about the industry and how it works. Once you've done steps one and two and three, *then* start researching and submitting—but not before. You want your writing (and yourself) as ready for prime time as possible once you start submitting.

Finally, don't let initial rejection keep you from continuing to learn and grow as a writer.

—*Alice Pope*

JOURNEY STONE CREATIONS

3533 Danbury Rd., Fairfield OH 45014. Estab. 2004. (513)860-5616. Fax: (513)860-0176. E-mail: pat@jscbooks. com (submissions). E-mail: danelle@jscbooks.com (art dept.). Web site: www.jscbooks.com. Publishes mass market and trade fiction and nonfiction, Christian, educational and multicultural material. **Editor:** Patricia Stirnkorb; **Creative Director:** Danelle Pickett. Publishes 40 or more titles/year. 90% of books by first-time authors. Strives to "engage children in the love of reading, while entertaining and educating."

Fiction Picture books: adventure, animal, contemporary, history, humor, multicultural, nature/environment, poetry, religion, sports. Early readers: adventure, animal, contemporary, health, history, humor, multicultural, nature/environment, poetry, religion, sports, suspense. "We are not accepting middle readers at this time." Word length: picture books—1200 or less; Early readers—5,000 or less. Recently published *Stranger Danger*, by Patricia Stirnkorb, illustrated by Claudia Wolf (ages 7-12, childhood saftey); *Camp Limestone*, by Paul Kijinski (ages 10-16, middle reader); *Big Yellow School Bus*, by Sandi Eucks; (ages 3-6)

How to Contact/Writers Query or submit complete ms if less than 2,000 words. Reports on queires/mss in 4-6 weeks. Publishes a book up to 2 years after acceptance. Accepts simultaneous and electrionic submissions. "At this time we are only accepting picture books and early reader books with less than 5,000 words. We are reviewing books for publication 12-18 months away."

Illustration Work with 25 illustrators/year. Uses color artwork only. Will review ms/illustrations packages from illustrators. Query; submit ms with 2-3 pieces of final art. Contact: Danelle Pickett, creative director. Illustrations only: Query with samples. Send tearsheets or link to online portfolio. Contact: Danelle Pickett, creative director. Samples not returned, samples filed.

Terms Pays authors negotiable royalty based on wholesale price or work purchased outright. Pay illustrators by the project or negotiable royalty. Book catalog available on Web stie. Writer's/artist's guidelines available on Web site.

Tips "Make sure you submit only your best work. For writers, if it is not letter perfect, we don't want to see it. Review our guidelines."

☐ KAEDEN BOOKS

P.O. Box 16190, Rocky River, OH 44116-6190. E-mail: lstenger@kaeden.com. Web site: www.kaeden.com. **Contact:** Lisa Stenger, Editor. Kaeden Books produces high-quality children's books for the educational market.

Fiction Stories with humor, surprise endings and interesting characters suitable for the education market. "Must have well-developed plots with clear beginnings, middles and endings. No adult or religious themes." Word count range: 25-2,000.

Nonfiction Unique, interesting topics, supported with details and accurate facts. Word count range :25-2000.

How to Contact/Writers Submit complete ms; include SASE. Do not send originals. Respond within 1 year. For complete guidelines see www.kaeden.com. No phone calls please.

Illustrators Work with 8-10 illustrators per year. Looking for samples that are appropriate for children's literature. Submit color samples no larger than 8½×11. Samples kept on file. Responds only if interested. "No originals, disks or slides please." Samples not returned.

Terms Work purchased outright from authors. Pays royalties to previous authors. Illustrators paid by project (range: $50-150/page).

Tips "We are particularly interested in humorous stories with surprise endings and beginning chapter books."

KAR-BEN PUBLISHING, INC.

A division of Lerner Publishing Group, 241 First Ave. No., Minneapolis, MN 55401. (612)332-3344. Fax: (612)332-7615. E-mail: editorial@karben.com. Web site: www.karben.com. **Manuscript Acquisitions:** Joni Sussman, director. Publishes 10-15 books/year (mostly picture books); 20% of books by first-time authors. All of Kar-Ben's books are on Jewish themes for young children and families.

Fiction Picture books: adventure, concept, folktales, history, humor, multicultural, religion, special needs; must be on a Jewish theme. Average word length: picture books—1,000. Recently published *A Grandma Like Yours / A Grandpa Like Yours*, by Andrea Warmflash Rosenbaum, illustrated by Barb Bjornson; *It's Tu B'Shevat*, by Edie Stoltz Zolkower, illustrated by Richard Johnson.

Nonfiction Picture books, young readers: activity books, arts/crafts, biography, careers, concept, cooking, history, how-to, multicultural, religion, social issues, special needs; must be of Jewish interest. Recently published *Paper Clips—The Making of a Children's Holocaust Memorial*, by Peter and Dagmar Schroeder (ages 8-12); *It's Purim Time*, by Latifa Berry Kropf, photos by Tod Cohen (ages 1-4); *Where Do People Go When They Die?*, by Mindy Avra Portnoy, illustrated by Shelly O. Haas (ages 5-10).

How to Contact/Writers Submit complete ms. Responds to queries/mss in 6 weeks. Publishes a book 24-36 months after acceptance. Will consider simultaneous submissions.

Illustration Works with 6-8 illustrators/year. Prefers "four-color art in any medium that is scannable." Reviews illustration packages from artists. Submit sample of art or online portfolio (no originals).

Terms Pays authors royalties of 3-5% of net against advance of $500-1,000; or purchased outright. Original artwork returned at job's completion. Book catalog free on request. Manuscript guidelines on Web site.

Tips Looks for "books for young children with Jewish interest and content, modern, nonsexist, not didactic. Fiction or nonfiction with a Jewish theme can be serious or humorous, life cycle, Bible story, or holiday-related. In particular, we are looking for stories that reflect the ethnic and cultural diversity of today's Jewish family."

☑ ALFRED A. KNOPF AND CROWN BOOKS FOR YOUNG READERS

Imprint of Random House Children's Books, 1745 Broadway, New York NY 10019. (212)782-9000. Web site: www.randomhouse.com/kids. See Random House and Delacorte and Doubleday Books for Young Readers listings. Book publisher. "We publish distinguished juvenile fiction and nonfiction for ages 0-18."

- Knopf title *Your Own, Sylvia: A Verse Portrait of Sylvia Plath*, by Stephanie Hemphill, won a Michael L. Printz Honor Award in 2008.

How to Contact/Writers No query letters, accompanying SASE or reply postcard. Send full picture book mss up to 25 pages plus a 1-page synopsis for longer works. "Please let us know if it is a multiple submission. If we are interested, we will reply withing 6 months of receipt of the manuscript." Address envelope to: Acquisitions Editor, Knopf & Crown/Books for Young Readers, Random House, 1745 Broadway, 9-3, New York, NY 10019.

Illustration Contact: Isabel Warren-Lynch, executive director, art & design. Responds only if interested. Samples returned with SASE; samples filed.

Terms Pays illustrators and photographers by the project or royalties. Original artwork returned at job's completion.

Ⓐ KNOPF, DELACORTE, DELL BOOKS FOR YOUNG READERS

Imprint of Random House Children's Book, Division of Random House, Inc., 1745 Broadway, New York NY 10019. (212)782-9000. Web site: www.randomhouse.com/kids. Book publisher.

- See listings for Random House/Golden Books for Young Readers Group, Delacorte and Doubleday Books for Young Readers, Alfred A. Knopf and Crown Books for Young Readers, and Wendy Lamb Books.

How to Contact/Writers Not seeking manuscripts at this time.

Illustration Contact: Isabel Warren-Lynch, executive director, art & design. Responds only if interested. Samples returned with SASE; samples filed.

Terms Pays illustrators and photographers by the project or royalties. Original artwork returned at job's completion.

KRBY CREATIONS, LLC

P.O. Box 327, Bay Head NJ 08742. Fax: (815)846-0636. E-mail: info@KRBYCreations.com. Web site: www.KRBYCreations.com. Estab. 2003. Specializes in children's picture books for the trade, library, specialty retail, and educational markets. **Writers contact:** Kevin Burton. 40% of books by first-time authors.

Fiction Recently published *The Snowman in the Moon*, by Stephen Heigh (picture book); *Mulch the Lawnmower*, by Scott Nelson (picture book); *My Imagination*, by Katrina Estes-Hill (picture book).

How to Contact/Writers Fiction/nonfiction: Writers *must* request guidelines by e-mail prior to submitting mss. See Web site. Submissions without annotation found in guidelines will not be considered. Responds to e-mail queries in 1 week; mss in 1-3 months. Publishes book 1 year after acceptance. Considers simultaneous submissions.

Illustrators Detailed contact guidelines available on Web site. Illustrator terms negotable. Pays advance plus royalties for experienced Illustrators. Avoids work-for-hire contracts. 40-60% of illustrators are first-time children's picture book published.

Terms Pays authors royalty of 6-15% based on wholesale price. Catalog on Web site. Offers writer's guidelines by e-mail.

Tips "Submit as professionally as possible; make your vision clear to us about what you are trying to capture. Know your market/audience and identify it in your proposal. Tell us what is new/unique with your idea. All writers submitting must first request guidelines by e-mail."

WENDY LAMB BOOKS

Imprint of Random House, 1745 Broadway, New York, NY 10019. Web site: www.randomhouse.com. **Manuscript Acquisitions:** Wendy Lamb. Receives 1,500-2,000 submissions/year. Publishes 12-15 novels/year for middle grade and young adult readers. WLB does not publish picture books at present. 15% of books by first-time authors and 10% unagented writers.

Fiction Recently published *Eyes of the Emporer*, by Graham Salisbury; *A Brief Chapter in My Impossible Life*, by Dana Reinhardt; *What They Found: Love on 145th Street*, by Walter Dean Myers; *Eleven*, by Patricia Reilly

Giff. Other WLB authors include Christopher Paul Curtis, Gary Paulsen, Donna Jo Napoli, Peter Dickinson, Marthe Jocelyn, Graham McNamee and Marcus Sedgwick.

How to Contact/Writers Query letter with SASE for reply. A query letter should briefly describe the book you have written, the intended age group, and your brief biography and publishing credits, if any. Please send the first 10 pages (or to the end of the chapter) of your manuscript. Our turn-around time is approximately 4 - 8 weeks.

LARK BOOKS

Sterling Publishing, 67 Broadway, Ashville NC 28801. (828)253-0467. Fax: (828)253-7952. E-mail: joe@larkboo ks.com. Web site: www.larkbooks.com. Specializes in nonfiction. **Writers contact:** Rose McLarney, children's books. **Illustrators contact:** Celia Naranjo, creative director. Produces 3-5 picture book/year. 70% of books by first-time authors. "Lark Books' philosophy is to produce high-quality, content-oriented nonfiction title for ages 0-18 with a focus on art, concept, picture books, humor, science, nature, fun and games, crafts, and activities."

Nonfiction All levels: activity books, animal, arts/crafts, cooking, hobbies, how-to, nature/environment, self help. Recently published *The Boo Boo Book*, by Joy Masoff (ages 0-5, board book); *My Very Favorite Art Book: I Love Collage*, by Jennifer Lipsey (ages 5-9, art instruction); *The Don't-Get-Caught Doodle Notebook*, by Susan McBride (ages 10-110, sneaky art instruction); *Pet Science: 50 Purr-Fectly Woof-Worthy Activities for You & Your Pets*, by Veronika Alice Gunter (ages 8-12, science/activity).

How to Contact/Writers Accepts international submissions. Fiction: Submit complete ms; accept only picture books. Nonfiction: Submit outline/synopsis and 1 sample chapter. Responds to queries in 3 weeks; mss in 3 months. Publishes book 1 year after acceptance. Considers simultaneous submissions, electronic submissions, previously published work.

Illustration Accepts material from international illustrators. Works with 7-10 illustrators/year. Reviews ms/ illustration packages. For ms/illustration packages: Send manuscript with dummy. Submit ms/illustration packages to Joe Rhatigan, senior editor. If interested in illustrating future titles, query with samples. Submit samples to Rose McLarney, children's books. Samples returned with SASE.

Terms Offers advance against royalties. Author sees galleys for review. Illustrators see dummies for review. Originals returned upon request. Catalog on Web site. See Web site for writer's guidelines.

Tips "Study the market you're writing for. Let me know why you think now is the right time to publish your book idea. I'm always on the lookout for strong writers with an expertise in an area (science, art, etc.), and even through we publish a lot of books that appeal to teachers and parents, these books are for the kids. Our books have a lot of humor in them as well as a lot of things to do and learn."

LEE & LOW BOOKS INC.

95 Madison Ave., New York NY 10016-7801. (212)779-4400. Fax: (212) 683-1894. E-mail: info@leeandlow.com. Web site: www.leeandlow.com. **Acquisitions:** Louise May, editor-in-chief; Jennifer Fox, senior editor. Publishes 12-14 children's books/year. 25% of books by first-time authors. Lee & Low Books publishes books with diverse themes. "One of our goals is to discover new talent and produce books that reflect the diverse society in which we live."

- Lee & Low Books is dedicated to publishing culturally authentic literature. The company makes a special effort to work with writers and artists of color and encourages new voices.

Fiction Picture books, young readers: anthology, contemporary, history, multicultural, poetry. "We are not considering folktales or animal stories." Picture book, middle reader: contemporary, history, multicultural, nature/environment, poetry, sports. Average word length: picture books—1,000-1,500 words. Recently published *Jazz Baby* by Carol Boston Weatherford, illustrated by Laura Freeman; *Home at Last* by Susan Middleton Elya, illustrated by Felipe Davalos.

Nonfiction Picture books: concept. Picture books, middle readers: biography, history, multicultural, science and sports. Average word length: picture books—1,500-3,000. Recently published *George Crum and the Saratoga Chip*, by Gaylia Taylor, illustrated by Frank Morrison by Lynne Barasch; *Rattlesnake Mesa*, by Ednah New Rider Weber, photographed by Richela Renkun.

How to Contact/Writers Fiction/nonfiction: Submit complete ms. No e-mail submissions. Responds in 4 months. Publishes a book 1-2 years after acceptance. Will consider simultaneous submissions. Guidelines on Web site.

Illustration Works with 12-14 illustrators/year. Uses color artwork only. Reviews ms/illustration packages from artists. Contact: Louise May. Illustrations only: Query with samples, résumé, promo sheet and tearsheets. Responds only if interested. Samples returned with SASE; samples filed. Original artwork returned at job's completion.

Photography Buys photos from freelancers. Works on assignment only. Model/property releases required. Submit cover letter, résumé, promo piece and book dummy.

Terms Pays authors advances against royalty. Pays illustrators advance against royalty. Photographers paid advance against royalty. Book catalog available for 9 × 12 SAE and $1.75 postage; ms and art guidelines available via Web site or with SASE.

Tips ''We strongly urge writers to visit our Web site and familiarize themselves with our list before submitting. Materials will only be returned with SASE.''

LEGACY PRESS

Imprint of Rainbow Publishers, P.O. Box 261129 San Diego CA 92196. (800)638-4428. Web site: www.rainbowp ublishers.com. Manuscript/Art Acquisitions: Editorial Department Publishes 3 young readers/year; 3 middle readers/year; 3 young adult titles/year. Publishes nonfiction, Bible-teaching books. '' We publish growth and development books for the evangelical Christian from a non-denominational viewpoint that may be marketed primarily through Christian bookstores.''

Nonfiction Young readers, middle readers, young adults: reference, religion. Recently published *Bill the Warthog—Full Metal Trench Coat*, by Dean Anderson, illustrated by Dave Carleson.

How to Contact/Writers Nonfiction: Submit outline/synopsis and 3-5 sample chapters. Responds to queries in 6 weeks; mss in 3 months. Publishes a book 36 months after acceptance. Will consider simultaneous submissions and previously published work.

Illustration Works with 5 illustrators/year. Reviews ms/illustration packages from artists. Submit ms with 5-10 pieces of final art. Illustrations only: Query with samples to be kept on file.

Terms Pays authors royalty or work purchased outright. Offers advances. Pays illustrators per illustration. Sends galley to authors. Book catalog available for business size SASE; ms guidelines for SASE.

Tips ''Get to know the Christian bookstore market. We are looking for innovative ways to teach and encourage children about the Christian life. No picture books please .''

LERNER PUBLISHING GROUP

241 First Ave. N., Minneapolis MN 55401. (612)332-3344. Fax: (612)332-7615. E-mail: info@lernerbooks.com. Web site: www.lernerbooks.com. **Manuscript Acquisitions:** Jennifer Zimian, nonfiction submissions editor; Zelda Wagner, fiction submissions editor. Primarily publishes books for children ages 7-18. List includes titles in geography, natural and physical science, current events, ancient and modern history, high interest, sports, world cultures, and numerous biography series.

- Starting in 2007, Lerner Publishing Group no longer accepts submission in any of their imprints except for Kar-Ben Publishing.

How to Contact/Writers ''We will continue to seek targeted solicitations at specific reading levels and in specific subject areas. The company will list these targeted solicitations on our Web site and in national newsletters, such as the SCBWI *Bulletin*.''

ARTHUR A. LEVINE BOOKS

Imprint of Scholastic, Inc., 557 Broadway, New York NY 10012. (212)343-4436. Fax: (212)343-4890. Web site: www.arthuralevinebooks.com. **Acquisitions:** Arthur A. Levine, editorial director; Cheryl Klein, senior editor. Publishes approximately 8 picture books/year; 8 full-length works for middle grade and young adult readers/ year. Approximately 25% of books by first-time authors.

Fiction Recently published *The Arrival*, by Shaun Tan (graphic novel); *The Nutcracker Doll*, by Mary Newell DePalma (picture book); *The Book of Time*, by Guillaume Prévost, trans. by William Rodarmor (novel);*The Spell Book of Listen Taylor*, by Jaclyn Moriarty (novel); and *Wilderness*, by Roddy Doyle (novel).

Nonfiction Recently published *The Secret World of Hildegard*, by Jonah Winter and Jeanette Winter (picture book); *Dizzy*, by Jonah Winter and Sean Qualls (picture book); and *The Adventures of Marco Polo*, by Russell Freedman and Bagram Ibatoulline (picture book).

How to Contact/Writers Fiction/nonfiction: Accepts queries only. Responds to queries in 1 month; mss in 5 months. Publishes a book 1½ years after acceptance.

Illustration Works with 8 illustrators/year. Will review ms/illustration packages from artists. Query first. Illustrations only: Send postcard sample with tearsheets. Samples not returned.

Ⓐ LITTLE, BROWN AND COMPANY BOOKS FOR YOUNG READERS

Hachette Book Group USA, 237 Park Ave, New York NY 10017. (212)364-1100. Fax: (212)364-0925. Web sites: www.lb-kids.com; www.lb-teens.com. **Senior Vice President, Publisher:** Megan Tingley. Editorial Director, Little, Brown Books for Young Readers (core hardcover and paperback list): Andrea Spooner. Editorial Director, Poppy (young women's commercial fiction imprint): Cynthia Eagan; Editorial Director, LB Kids (novelty and licensed books imprint): Liza Baker. Senior Editor: Jennifer Hunt. **Creative Director:** Gail Doobinin. Publishes picture books, board books, chapter books, novelty books, and general nonfiction and novels for middle and young adult readers.

- Little, Brown does not accept unsolicited mss or unagented material.

Fiction Picture books: humor, adventure, animal, contemporary, history, multicultural, folktales. Young adults: contemporary, humor, multicultural, suspense/mystery, chick lit. Multicultural needs include "any material by, for and about minorities." Average word length: picture books—1,000; young readers—6,000; middle readers—15,000- 50,000; young adults—50,000 and up. Recently published *The Gulps*, by Marc Brown, illustrated by Rosemary Wells; *Hug Time*, by Patrick McDonnel; *The Fabulous Bouncing Chowder*, by Peter Brown; *How to Twist a Dragon's Tale*, by Cressida Cowell; *Atherton*, by Patrick Carman; *Nothing But the Truth (and a Few White Lies)*, by Justina Chen Headley; *Story of a Girl*, by Sara Zarr; *Eclipse*, by Stephanie Meyer.

Nonfiction Middle readers, young adults: arts/crafts, history, multicultural, nature, self help, social issues, sports, science. Average word length: middle readers—15,000-25,000; young adults—20,000-40,000. Recently published *American Dreaming*, by Laban Carrick Hill; *Exploratopia*, by the Exploratorium; *Yeah! Yeah! Yeah!: The Beatles, Beatlemania, and the Music that Changed the World*, by Bob Spitz.

How to Contact/Writers Only interested in solicited agented material. Fiction: Submit complete ms. Nonfiction: Submit cover letter, previous publications, a proposal, outline and 3 sample chapters. Do not send originals. Responds to queries in 2 weeks. Responds to mss in 2 months.

Illustration Works with 40 illustrators/year. Illustrations only: Query art director with b&w and color samples; provide résumé, promo sheet or tearsheets to be kept on file. Does not respond to art samples. Do not send originals; copies only.

Photography Works on assignment only. Model/property releases required; captions required. Publishes photo essays and photo concept books. Uses 35mm transparencies. Photographers should provide résumé, promo sheets or tearsheets to be kept on file.

Terms Pays authors royalties based on retail price. Pays illustrators and photographers by the project or royalty based on retail price. Sends galleys to authors; dummies to illustrators.

Tips "In order to break into the field, authors and illustrators should research their competition and try to come up with something outstandingly different."

☐ LOLLIPOP POWER BOOKS

Imprint of Carolina Wren Press, 120 Morris Street, Durham NC 27701. (919)560-2738. Fax: (919)560-2759. E-mail: carolinawrenpress@earthlink.net. Web site: www.carolinawrenpress.org. **Manuscript Acquisitions:** Children's Book Editor. **Art Acquisitions:** Art Director. Publishes 1 picture book every three to four years. 50% of books by first-time authors. "Carolina Wren Press and Lollipop Power specialize in children's books that counter stereotypes or debunk myths about race, gender, sexual orientation, etc. We are also interested in books that deal with health or mental health issues—our two biggest sellers are *Puzzles* (about a young girl coping with Sickle Cell Disease) and *I like it when you joke with me, I don't like it when you touch me* (about inappropriate touching). Many of our children's titles are bilingual (English/Spanish)."

Fiction Average word length: picture books—500.

How to Contact/Writers Children's lit submissions are read February through April. (Illustrators may send samples any time.) Fiction: Submit outline/synopsis and 3 sample chapters. Responds to queries/mss in 6 months. Publishes book 3 years after acceptance. Will consider simultaneous submissions.

Illustrators We keep a file with artist samples, though we rarely can afford to use illustrators for our books. You are free to send samples to be included in this file. Reviews ms/illustration packages from artists. Submit ms with 5 pieces of final art. Illustrations only: Send photocopies, résumé, samples, SASE. Responds only if interested. Samples not returned; samples filed.

Terms Pays authors royalty of 10% minimum based on retail price or work purchased outright from authors (range: $500-$2,000). Pays illustrators by the project (range: $500-$2,000). Sends galleys to authors; dummies to illustrators. Originals returned to artist at job's completion. Catalog available on Web site.

LUCENT BOOKS

Imprint of Gale, 27550 Drake Road, Farmington Hills, MI 49331. E-mail: mary.lavey@cengage.com. Web site: www.gale.com/lucent. **Acquisitions:** Mary Lavey. Series publisher of educational nonfiction for junior high school and library markets.

- See also listing for Greenhaven Press.

Nonfiction Young adult circulating reference: current issues, diseases, drugs, biographies, geopolitics, history. Recently launched Crime Scene Investigations, and Hot Topics (both series). Recently published *Energy Alternatives*; *Hate Crimes*; *Human Papillomavirus*; *Malnutrition*; *Criminal Profiling*; *DNA Evidence*; *Tupac Shakur*; and *Zac Efron*.

How to Contact/Writers E-mail query with résumé or list of publications.

Terms Work purchased outright from authors; write-for-hire, flat fee.

Tips No unsolicited manuscripts.

MAGINATION PRESS

750 First Street, NE, Washington DC 20002-2984. (202)336-5618. Fax: (202)336-5624. Web site: www.maginatio npress.com. **Acquisitions:** Darcie Conner Johnston, managing editor. Publishes 4 picture books/year; 4 young readers/year; 2 middle readers/year; 1 young adult title/year. 75% of books by first-time authors. "We publish books dealing with the psycho/therapeutic resolution of children's problems and psychological issues with a strong self-help component."

- Magination Press is an imprint of the American Psychological Association.

Fiction All levels: psychological and social issues, self-help, health, multicultural, special needs. Picture books, middle readers. Recently published: *Samantha Jane's Missing Smile: A Story About Coping with the Loss of a Parent* by Julie Kaplow and Donna Pincus, illustrated by Beth Spiegel (ages 4-8); *Always My Grandpa: A Story for Children About Alzheimer's Disease* by Linda Scacco, illustrated by Nicole Wong.

Nonfiction All levels: psychological and social issues, self-help, health, multicultural, special needs. Picture books, young readers, middle readers; activity workbooks. Recently published: *Mind Over Basketball: Coach Yourself to Handle Stress*, by Jane Weierbach and Elizabeth Phillips-Hershey, illustrated by Charles Beyl (ages 8-12); *What to Do When You Dread Your Bed: A Kid's Guide to Overcoming Problems With Sleep*, by Dawn Huebner, illustrated by Bonnie Matthews (ages 6-12).

How to Contact/Writers Fiction/nonfiction: Submit complete ms. Responds to queries in 1-2 months; mss in 2-6 months. Will consider simultaneous submissions. Materials returned only with a SASE. Publishes a book 18-24 months after acceptance.

Illustration Works with 10-15 illustrators/year. Reviews ms/illustration packages. Will review artwork for future assignments. Responds only if interested, or immediately if SASE or response card is included. We keep samples on file.

How to Contact/Illustrators Illustrations only: Query with samples; a few samples and Web address are best. Original artwork returned at job's completion.

Photography Buys stock.

Terms Pays authors royalty of 5-15% based on actual revenues (net). Pays illustrators by the project. Book catalog and ms guidelines on request with SASE. Catalog and ms guidelines available on Web site.

MARGARET K. MCELDERRY BOOKS

Imprint of Simon & Schuster Children's Publishing Division, 1230 Avenue of the Americas, New York NY 10020. (212)698-7000. Web site: www.simonsayskids.com. **Publisher:** Vice President, Associate Publisher Emma D. Dryden. **Acquisitions:** Karen Wojtyla, executive editor; Lisa Cheng, associate editor; Sarah Payne, editorial assistant. **Art Acquisitions:** Ann Bobco, executive art director. Imprint of Simon & Schuster Children's Publishing Division. Publishes 12 picture books/year; 5-8 middle readers/year; 8-10 young adult titles/year. 10% of books by first-time authors; 50% of books from agented writers. "Margaret K. McElderry Books publishes original hardcover trade books for children from pre-school age through young adult. This list includes picture books, middle grade and teen fiction, poetry, and fantasy. The style and subject matter of the books we publish is almost unlimited. We do not publish textbooks, coloring and activity books, greeting cards, magazines, pamphlets, or religious publications."

Fiction All levels. "Always interested in publishing humorous picture books, original beginning reader stories, and strong poetry." Average word length: picture books—500; young readers—2,000; middle readers—10,000-20,000; young adults—45,000-50,000. Recently published *Bear Feels Sick*, by Karma Wilson, illustrated by Jane Chapman (picture book); *Birdsongs*, by Betsy Franco, illustrated by Steve Jenkins (picture book); *Hey Batta Batta Swing!*, by Sally Cook and Jim Charlton, illustrated by Ross MacDonald (picture book); *Questors*, by Joan Lennon (middle grade); *City of Bones*, by Cassandra Clare (debut teen); *America at War*, by Lee Bennett Hopkins, illustrated by Stephen Alcorn (poetry).

How to Contact/Writers Send query letters with SASE for picture books; send synopsis and first 3 chapters or first 30 pages with SASE for novels. Responds to queries in 1-2 month; mss in 3-4 months. Publishes a book 24-36 months after acceptance. Will consider simultaneous queries from previously unpublished authors and those submitted to other publishers, "though we request that the author let us know it is a simultaneous query." Please do not call to query or follow up.

Illustration Works with 20-30 illustrators/year. Query with samples, résumé, tearsheets. Contact: Ann Bobco, executive art director, Design Dept., 4th Floor. Samples filed. Responds only if interested.

Terms Pays authors royalty based on retail price. Pays illustrator royalty of by the project. Pays photographers by the project. Original artwork returned at job's completion. Manuscript guidelines for #10 SASE with one first-class stamp.

Tips "We're looking for strong, original fiction, especially mysteries and middle grade humor. We are always interested in picture books for the youngest age reader. Study our titles."

MEADOWBROOK PRESS

5451 Smetana Dr., Minnetonka MN 55343-9012. (952)930-1100. Fax: (952)930-1940. Web site: www.meadowbr ookpress.com. **Manuscript Acquisitions:** Submissions Editor. **Art Acquisitions:** Art Director. 20% of books by first-time authors; 10% of books from agented writers. Publishes children's poetry books, activity books, arts-and-crafts books and how-to books.
  • Meadowbrook does not accept unsolicited children's picture books, short stories or novels. They are primarily a nonfiction press. The publisher offers specific guidelines for children's poetry. Be sure to specify the type of project you have in mind when requesting guidelines, or visit their Web site.

Nonfiction Publishes activity books, arts/crafts, how-to, poetry. Average word length: varies. Recently published *Wiggleand Giggle Busy Book*, by Trish Kuffner (activity book); *My Teacher's in Detention*, by Bruce Lansky.
How to Contact/Writers Nonfiction: See guidelines on Web site before submitting. Responds only if interested. Publishes a book 1-2 years after acceptance. Will consider simultaneous submissions.
Illustration Works with 4 illustrators/year. Submit ms with 2-3 pieces of nonreturnable samples. Responds only if interested. Samples filed.
Photography Buys photos from freelancers. Buys stock. Model/property releases required.
Terms Pays authors royalt y of 5-7% based on retail price. Offers average advance payment of $1,000-3,000. Pays illustrators per project. Pays photographers by the project. Book catalog available for 5×11 SASE and 2 first-class stamps; ms guidelines and artists guidelines available for SASE.
Tips "Writers should visit our Web site before submitting their work to us. Illustrators should take a look at the books we publish to determine whether their style is consistent with ours. Writers should also note the style and content patterns of our books. No phone calls, please—e-mail us. We work with the printed word and will respond more effectively to your questions if we have something in front of us."

MERIWETHER PUBLISHING LTD.

885 Elkton Dr., Colorado Springs CO 80907-3557. (719)594-9916. Fax: (719)594-9916. E-mail: merpcds@aol.c om. Web site: www.meriwetherpublishing.com. **Manuscript Acquisitions:** Ted Zapel, comedy plays and educational drama; Rhonda Wray, religious drama. "We do most of our artwork in-house; we do not publish for the children's elementary market." 75% of books by first-time authors; 5% of books from agented writers. "Our niche is drama. Our books cover a wide variety of theatre subjects from play anthologies to theatrecraft. We publish books of monologs, duologs, short one-act plays, scenes for students, acting textbooks, how-to speech and theatre textbooks, improvisation and theatre games. Our Christian books cover worship on such topics as clown ministry, storytelling, banner-making, drama ministry, children's worship and more. We also publish anthologies of Christian sketches. We do not publish works of fiction or devotionals."
Fiction Middle readers, young adults: anthology, contemporary, humor, religion. "We publish plays, not prose-fiction." Our emphasis is comedy plays instead of educational themes.
Nonfiction Middle readers: activity books, how-to, religion, textbooks. Young adults: activity books, drama/ theater arts, how-to church activities, religion. Average length: 250 pages. Recently published *Acting for Life*, by Jack Frakes; *Scenes Keep Happening*, by Mary Krell-Oishi; *Service with a Smile*, by Daniel Wray.
How to Contact/Writers Nonfiction: Query or submit outline/synopsis and sample chapters. Responds to queries in 3 weeks; mss in 2 months or less. Publishes a book 6-12 months after acceptance. Will consider simultaneous submissions.
Illustration Works with 2 illustrators/year. Query first. Query with samples; send résumé, promo sheet or tearsheets. Samples returned with SASE.
Terms Pays authors royalty of 10% based on retail or wholesale price. Book catalog for SAE and $2 postage; ms guidelines for SAE and 1 first-class stamp.
Tips "We are currently interested in finding unique treatments for theater arts subjects: scene books, how-to books, musical comedy scripts, monologs and short comedy plays for teens."

MILET PUBLISHING LTD.

333 N. Michigan Ave., Suite 530, Chicago IL 60601. (312)920-1828. Fax: (312)920-1829. E-mail: info@milet.c om. Web site: www.milet.com. Estab. 1995. Specializes in trade books, nonfiction, fiction, multicultural material. **Writers contact:** Editorial Director. **Illustrators contact:** Editorial Director. Produces 30+ picture books, 2 middle readers/year. "Milet publishes a celebrated range of artistic and innovative children's books in English, as well as the leading range of bilingual children's books."
Fiction Picture books: adventure, animal, concept, contemporary, hi-lo, humor, multicultural, poetry. Young readers: adventure, animal, concept, contemporary, fantasy, hi-lo, multicultural, nature/environment, poetry. Middle readers: adventure, animal, contemporary, fantasy, multicultural, nature/environment, poetry, problem novels. Young adults/teens: contemporary, fantasy, multicultural, nature/environment, poetry, problem novels. Recently published *Telling Tales*, by Laura Hambleton & Sedat Turhan (ages 5-7, picture book); *Strawberry Bullfrog*, by Laura Hambleton, Sedat Turhan & Sally Hagin (agest 5-7, picture book); *Monkey Business*, by Laura

Hambleton, Sedat Turhan & Herve Tullet; *Bella Balistica and the African Safari*, by Adam Guillain (ages 8-12, novel).

Nonfiction All levels: activity books, animal, arts/crafts, concept, hi-lo, multicultural, nature/environment, social issues. language learning. Recently published *Starting English*, by Tracy Traynor & Anna Wilman (ages 14 and up); *English with Abby and Zak*, by Tracy Traynor & Laura Hambleton (ages 5-7).

How to Contact/Writers Accepts international submissions. Fiction/nonfiction: Submit outline/synopsis and 2-3 sample chapters. Responds to queries in 1 weeks; mss in 1-2 months. Publishes book 12-18 months after acceptance. Considers simultaneous submissions. "Please review the submissions page on our Web site, www. milet.com, for requirements on submitting your work. SASE must be included.

Illustration Accepts material from international illustrators. Works with 4-5 illustrators/year. Uses both color and b&w. Reviews ms/illustration packages. For ms/illustration packages: Submit ms with 2-3 pieces of final art. Reviews work for future assignments. If interested in illustrating future titles, send résumé, promo sheet, client list. Submit samples to Editorial Director. Samples returned with SASE.

Terms Authors paid all terms negotiated depending on type of project. Author sees galleys for review. Illustrators see dummies for review. Catalog on Web site. All imprints included in single catalog. See Web site for writer's, artist's guidelines.

Tips "Please check our list on our Web site to see if your work will be suitable. We are interested only in fresh, imaginative, non-traditional work."

MILKWEED EDITIONS

1011 Washington Ave. S., Suite 300, Minneapolis MN 55415-1246. (612)332-3192. Fax: (612)215-2550. E-mail: editor@milkweed.org. Web site: www.milkweed.org. **Manuscript Acquisitions:** Daniel Slager, publisher. Publishes 3-4 middle readers/year. 25% of books by first-time authors. "Milkweed Editions publishes with the intention of making a humane impact on society, in the belief that literature is a transformative art uniquely able to convey the essential experiences of the human heart and spirit. To that end, Milkweed Editions publishes distinctive voices of literary merit in handsomely designed, visually dynamic books, exploring the ethical, cultural, and esthetic issues that free societies need continually to address."

Fiction Middle readers: adventure, contemporary, fantasy, multicultural, nature/environment, suspense/mystery. Does not want to see anthologies, folktales, health, hi-lo, picture books, poetry, religion, romance, sports. Average length: middle readers—90-200 pages. Recently published *Perfect*, by Natasha Friend (contemporary); *The Linden Tree*, by Ellie Mathews(contemporary); *The Cat*, by Jutta Richter (contemporary/translation).

How to Contact/Writers Fiction: Submit complete ms. Responds to mss in 6 months. Publishes a book 1 year after acceptance. Will consider simultaneous submissions.

Illustration Works with 2-4 illustrators/year. Reviews ms/illustration packages from artists. Query; submit ms with dummy. Illustrations only: Query with samples; provide résumé, promo sheet, slides, tearsheets and client list. Samples filed or returned with SASE; samples filed. Originals returned at job's completion.

Terms Pays authors variable royalty based on retail price. Offers advance against royalties. Illustrators' contracts are decided on an individual basis. Sends galleys to authors. Book catalog available for $1.50 to cover postage; ms guidelines available for SASE or at Web site. Must include SASE with ms submission for its return.

☐ THE MILLBROOK PRESS

A division of Lerner Publishing Group, Inc., 241 First Avenue North Minneapolis, MN 5540. (800)328-4929. Fax: (800)332-1132. Web site: www.lernerbooks.com.

- Starting in 2007, Lerner Publishing Group no longer accepts submission in any of their imprints except for Kar-Ben Publishing.

How to Contact/Writers "We will continue to seek targeted solicitations at specific reading levels and in specific subject areas. The company will list these targeted solicitations on our Web site and in national newsletters, such as the SCBWI Bulletin."

MIRRORSTONE

Imprint of Wizards of the Coast, P.O. Box 707, Renton WA 98057. (425)254-2287. Web site: www.mirrorstonebo oks.com. **Manuscript and Art Acquisitions:** Nina Hess. Publishes 12 middle readers/year; 6 young adult titles/year. 25% of books by first-time authors. "We publish fantasy novels for young readers."

Fiction Young readers, middle readers, young adults: fantasy only. Average word length: middle readers—30,000-40,000; young adults—60,000-75,000. Recently published *A Practical Guide to Dragons*, by Lisa Trumbauer (ages 6 and up); *Time Spies: Secret in the Tower*, by Candice Ransom (ages 6 and up); *Hallomere: In the Serpent's Coils*, by Tiffany Trent (ages 12 and up).

How to Contact/Writers Fiction: Query with samples, writing credits. "No manuscripts, please." Responds to queries in 8-12 weeks. Publishes book 9-24 months after acceptance.

Illustration Works with 4 illustrators/year. Query. Illustrations only: Query with samples, résumé.

Terms Pays authors royalty of 4-6% based on retail price. Offers advances (average amount: $4,000). Pays illustrators by the project. Ms guidelines available on our Web site. All imprints included in a single catalog. Catalog available on Web site.

Tips Editorial staff attended or plans to attend ALA, BEA and IRA conferences.

MITCHELL LANE PUBLISHERS, INC.

P.O. Box 196, Hockessin DE 19707. (302)234-9426. Fax: (302)234-4742. E-mail: mitchelllane@mitchelllane.com. Web site: www.mitchelllane.com. **Acquisitons:** Barbara Mitchell, president. Publishes 80 young adult titles/year. "We publish nonfiction for children and young adults."

Nonfiction Young readers, middle readers, young adults: biography, multicultural. Average word length: 4,000-50,000 words. Recently published *Ashanti, Paris Hilton* (both Blue Banner Biographies); *Jamie Lynn Spears* (A Robbie Reader).

How to Contact/Writers Most assignments are work-for-hire.

Illustration Works with 2-3 illustrators/year. Reviews ms/illustration packages from artists. Query. Illustration only: Query with samples; send résumé, portfolio, slides, tearsheets. Responds only if interested. Samples not returned; samples filed.

Photography Buys stock images. Needs photos of famous and prominent minority figures. Captions required. Uses color prints or digital images. Submit cover letter, résumé, published samples, stock photo list.

Terms Work purchased outright from authors (range: $350-2,000). Pays illustrators by the project (range: $40-400). Sends galleys to authors.

Tips "Most of our assignments are work-for-hire. Submit résumé and samples of work to be considered for future assignments."

MORGAN REYNOLDS PUBLISHING

620 S. Elm St., Suite 223, Greensboro NC 27406. (336)275-1311. Fax: (336)275-1152. E-mail: editorial@morganreynolds.com. Web site: www.morganreynolds.com. **Acquisitions:** Sharon F. Doorasamy, acquisitions editor. Book publisher. Publishes 40 young adult titles/year. 50% of books by first-time authors. Morgan Reynolds publishes nonfiction books for juvenile and young adult readers. "We prefer lively, well-written biographies of interesting figures for our extensive biography series. Subjects may be contemporary or historical. Books for our Great Events series should take an insightful and exciting look at pivotal periods and/or events."

Nonfiction Middle readers, young adults/teens: biography, history. Average word length: 25-35,000. Recently published *No Easy Answers: Bayard Rustin and the Civil Rights Movement*, by Calvin Craig Miller; *Empire in the East: The Story of Genghis Khan*, by Earle Rice, Jr.; *The Mail Must Go Through: The Story of the Pony Express*, by Margaret Rau; *Nikola Tesla and the Taming of Electricity*, by Lisa J. Aldrich.

How to Contact/Writers First-time authors submit entire ms. Query; submit outline/synopsis with at least 2 sample chapters and SASE. Responds to queries in 6 weeks; mss in 2 months. Publishes a book 1-2 years after acceptance. Will consider simultaneous submissions.

Terms Pays authors negotiated price. Sends galleys to authors. Manuscript guidelines available at our Web site or by mail with SASE and 1 first-class stamp. Visit Web site for complete catalog.

Tips Does not respond without SASE. "Familiarize yourself with our titles before sending a query or submission, keeping in mind that we do *not* publish fiction, autobiographies, poetry, memoirs, picture books. We focus on serious-minded, well-crafted, nonfiction books for young adults that will complement school curriculums, namely biographies of significant figures." Editorial staff has attended or plans to attend the following conferences: ALA, TLA, PLA, FAME.

NEW VOICES PUBLISHING

Imprint of KidsTerrain, Inc., P.O. Box 560, Wilmington MA 01887. (978)658-2131. Fax: (978)988-8833. E-mail: rschiano@kidsterrain.com. Web site: www.kidsterrain.com. Estab. 2000. **Manuscript/Art Acquisitions:** Book Editor. Publishes 2 picture books/year. 95% of books by first-time authors.

Fiction Picture books, young readers: multicultural. Average word length: picture books—500; young readers—500-1,200. Recently published *Reaching Home*, by Ron Breazeale.

How to Contact/Writers Not accepting unsolicited manuscripts.

Illustration Works with 2 illustrators/year. Uses color artwork only. Reviews ms/illustration packages from artists. No unsolicited queries.

Terms Pays authors royalty of 10-15% based on wholesale price. Pays illustrators by the project or royalty. Sends galleys to authors. Offers writer's guidelines for SASE.

NORTH-SOUTH BOOKS

350 Seventh Ave., Suite 1400, New York NY 10001. (212)706-4545. Web site: www.northsouth.com. Imprint: Night Sky. U.S. office of Nord-Siid Verlag, Switzerland. Publishes 100 titles/year.

- North-South and its imprints do not accept queries or unsolicited manuscripts.

NORTHWORD BOOKS FOR YOUNG READERS

Imprint of T&N Children's Publishing international, 11571 K-Tel Dr., Minnetonka MN 55343. (982)933-7537. Web site: www.tnkidsbooks.com. Estab. 1984. Specializes in trade books, nonfiction. **Contact:** Submissions Editor. Produces 6-8 picture books/year; 2-4 board books/year; 4-6 young readers/year; 4 middle readers/year. 10-20% of books by first-time authors. NorthWord's mission is publish books for children that encourage a love for the natural world.''

Fiction Picture books: animal, concept, history, nature/environment, poetry—all nature-related. Young readers: animal, history, nature/environment, poetry—all nature-related. Average word length: picture books—500-1,000; young readers—1,000-4,000. Recently published *Papa Fish's Lullaby*, by Patricia Hubbell, illustrated by Susan Eaddy (ages 3-5, picture book); *What Does the Wind Say?*, by Wendi Silvano, illustrated by Joan Delehanty (ages 3-5, picture book); *Hungy Beasties*, by Neecy Twinem (ages 0-3, board book).

Nonfiction Activity books, animal, arts/crafts, biography, careers, concept, cooking, geography, history, hobbies, how-to, nature/environment, science, sports. Young readers: activity books, animal, arts/crafts, biography, careers, cooking, geography, history, hobbies, how-to, nature/environment, science, sports. Middle readers: activity books, animal, arts/crafts, biography, careers, cooking, history, hobbies, nature/environment, sports. Average word length picture books—500-1,000; young readers—1,000-4,000. Recently published *What Kinds of Seeds Are These?*, by Heidi Bee Roemer, illustrated by Olena Kassian (ages 5-8, nonfiction picture book); *The Seaside Switch*, by Kathleen V. Kudlinski, illustrated by Lindy Burnett (ages 5-8, nonfiction picture book); *Elephants*, by Jill Anderson (ages 3-6, Wild Ones series); *Rocky Mountains*, by Wayne Lynch (ages 8-11, Our Wild World Ecosystem series).

How to Contact/Writers Accepts international submissions. Submit complete mss for picture books. Nonfiction: Submit outline/synopsis. Responds to queries/mss in 3 months. Publishes book 2 years after acceptance. Considers simultaneous submissions, previously published work.

Illustration Accepts material from international illustrators. Works with 8-10 illustrators/year. Uses color artwork only. For ms/illustration packages: Send ms with dummy. Submit ms/illustration packages to Submission Editor. Reviews work for future assignments. If interested in illustrating future titles, query with samples. Submit samples to Submissions Editor. Responds in 3 months. Samples returned with SASE. Samples filed.

Photography Buys stock images. Submit photos to Submissions Editor. Looking for animal/nature photography. Model/property releases required. Photo captions required. Uses color prints. Prefers high resolution digital files. For first contact, send cover letter, client list, stock photo list, promo piece (color).

Terms Offers advance against royalties or flat fee. Pays illustrators royalty based on retail price or net receipts. Pays photographers by the project (range: $100). Author sees galleys for review. Illustrators see dummies for review. Originals returned to artist at job's completion. Catalog available for 9x11 SASE and $1.83 postage. Individual catalogs for imprints. Offers writer's, artist's guidelines for SASE; see Web site for guidelines.

Tips ''Read our material and mission and what we've recently published.''

☐ ONSTAGE PUBLISHING

190 Lime Quarry Road, Suite 106J, Madison AL 35601 35758-8962. (256)461-0661. E-mail: onstage123@knology .net. Web site: www.onstagepublishing.com. **Manuscript Acquisitions:** Dianne Hamilton. Publishes 2-4 middle readers/year; 1-2 young adult titles/year. 80% of books by first-time authors.

Fiction Middle readers: adventure, contemporary, fantasy, history, nature/environment, science fiction, suspense/mystery. Young adults: adventure, contemporary, fantasy, history, humor, science fiction, suspense/mystery. Average word length: chapter books—4,000-6,000 words; middle readers—5,000 words and up; young adults—25,00 and up. Recently published *Dorkman*, by Pearch Pearce & Story (a boy books for ages 12 and up); *Spies, Heroes: A Gander's Cove Mystery*, by Mary Ann Taylor (historical fiction for grades 3-5). ''We do not produce picture books.''

Nonfiction Query first; currently not producing nonfiction.

How to Contact/Writers Fiction: Send complete ms if under 20,000 words, otherwise send synopsis and first 3 chapters. Responds to queries/mss in 6-8 months. Publishes a book 1-2 years after acceptance. Will consider simultaneous submissions.

Illustration Reviews ms/illustration packages from artists. Submit ms with 3 pieces of final art. Contact: Dianne Hamilton, senior editor. Illustrations only: Arrange personal portfolio review. Responds in 6-8 weeks. Samples returned with SASE.

Photography Works on assignment only. Contact: Art Department. Model/property releases required; captions required. Uses color, 5×7, semi gloss prints. Submit cover letter, published samples, stock photo list.

Terms Pays authors/illustrators/photographers advance plus royalties. Sends galleys to authors; dummies to illustrators. Catalog available on Web site.

Tips ''Study our titles and get a sense of the kind of books we publish, so that you know whether your project is likely to be right for us.''

OOLIGAN PRESS

P.O. Box 751, Portland OR 97213. (503)725-9410. E-mail: ooliganacquisitions@pdx.edu. Web site: www.ooligan press.pdx.edu. Estab. 2001. **Contact:** Acquisitions Committee. "Ooligan Press is a general trade press at Portland State University. As a teaching press, Ooligan makes as little distinction as possible between the press and the classroom. Under the direction of professional faculty and staff, the work of the press is done by students enrolled in the Book Publishing graduate program at PSU. We are especially interested in works with social, literary, or educational value. Though we place special value on local authors, we are open to all submissions, including translated works and writings by children and young adults. We do not currently publish picture books, board books, easy readers, or pop-up books." 90% of books by first-time authors.

Fiction Middle readers, young adult: open to all categories. Recently published *Ricochet River*, by Robin Cody (YA novel).

Nonfiction Middle reader, young adult: open to all categories.

How to Contact/Writers Query with SASE or submit proposal package including 4 sample chapters, projected page count, intended audience, and marketing ideas. Prefers traditional mail, but will read unattached queries. Do not send proposal package by e-mail. Response to queries in 4-6 weeks. Publishes a book 18 months after acceptance. Will consider simultaneous submissions and previously published work.

Terms Pays negotiable royalty based on retail price. Authors see galleys for review. Book catalog and writer's guidelines available on Web site.

ORCHARD BOOKS

Imprint of Scholastic, Inc., 557 Broadway, New York NY 10012. (212)343-6782. Fax: (212)343-4890. Web site: www.scholastic.com. Book publisher. Editorial Director: Ken Geist. **Manuscript Acquisitions:** Lisa A. Sandell, senior editor. **Art Acquisitions:** David Saylor, creative director. "We publish approximately 50 books yearly including fiction, poetry, picture books, and young adult novels." 10% of books by first-time authors.

- Orchard is not accepting unsolicited manuscripts; query letters only.

Fiction All levels: animal, contemporary, history, humor, multicultural, poetry. Recently published *Children of the Lamp: The Day of the Djinn Warriors*, by P.B. Kerr; *Ten Things I Hate About Me*, by Randa Abdel-Fattah; *The Ruby Key*, by Holly Lisle; *I Lost My Kisses*, by Trudie Trewin, illustrated by Nick Bland; *A Pop-Up Guide to the Galaxy*, by Matthew Reinhart.

Nonfiction "We publish nonfiction very selectively."

How to Contact/Writers Query only with SASE. Responds in 3-6 months.

Illustration Works with 15 illustrators/year. Art director reviews ms/illustration portfolios. Submit "tearsheets or photocopies or Photostats of the work." Responds to art samples in 1 month. Samples returned with SASE. No disks or slides, please.

Terms Most commonly offers an advance against list royalties. Sends galleys to authors; dummies to illustrators. Original artwork returned at job's completion.

Tips "Read some of our books to determine first whether your manuscript is suited to our list."

OUR CHILD PRESS

P.O. Box 4379, Philadelphia PA 19118. Phone/fax: (610)308-8088. E-mail: ourchildpress@aol.com. Web site: www.ourchildpress.com. **Acquisitions:** Carol Perrott, president. 90% of books by first-time authors.

Fiction/Nonfiction All levels: adoption, multicultural, special needs. Published *Like Me*, written by Dawn Martelli, illustrated by Jennifer Hedy Wharton; *Is That Your Sister?*, by Catherine and Sherry Burin; *Oliver: A Story About Adoption*, by Lois Wichstrom.

How to Contact/Writers Query or submit complete ms. Responds to queries/mss in 6 months. Publishes a book 6-12 months after acceptance.

Illustration Works with 1-5 illustrators/year. Reviews ms/illustration packages from artists. Manuscript/illustration packages and illustration only: Query first. Submit résumé, tearsheets and photocopies. Responds to art samples in 2 months. Samples returned with SASE; samples kept on file.

Terms Pays authors royalty of 5-10% based on wholesale price. Pays illustrators royalty of 5-10% based on wholesale price. Original artwork returned at job's completion. Book catalog for business-size SAE and 67¢ postage.

◻ OUR SUNDAY VISITOR, INC.

200 Noll Plaza, Huntington IN 46750. (260)356-8400. Fax: (260)359-9117. Web site: www.osv.com. For guidelines: booksed@osv.com. **Acquisitions:** Jacquelyn Lindsey, Michael Dubruiel. **Art Director:** Tyler Ottinger. Publishes religious, educational, parenting, reference and biographies. OSV is dedicated to providing books, periodicals and other products that serve the Catholic Church.

- Our Sunday Visitor, Inc., is publishing only those children's books that tie in to sacramental preparation and Catholic identity. Contact the acquisitions editor for manuscript guidelines.

Nonfiction Picture books, middle readers, young readers, young adults. Recently published *Living the Ten Commandments for Children*, by Rosemarie Gortler and Donna Piscitelli, illustrated by Mimi Sternhagen.

How to Contact/Writers Query, submit complete ms, or submit outline/synopsis and 2-3 sample chapters. Responds to queries/mss in 2 months. Publishes a book 18-24 months after acceptance. Will consider simultaneous submissions, electronic submissions via disk or modem, previously published work.

Illustration Reviews ms/illustration packages from artists. Illustration only: Query with samples. Contact: Art Director. Responds only if interested. Samples returned with SASE; samples filed.

Photography Buys photos from freelancers. Contact: Acquisitions Editor.

Terms Pays authors royalty of 10-12% net. Pays illustrators by the project (range: $200-1,500). Sends galleys to authors; dummies to illustrators. Book catalog available for SASE; ms guidelines available for SASE.

Tips "Stay in accordance with our guidelines."

RICHARD C. OWEN PUBLISHERS, INC.

P.O. Box 585, Katonah NY 10536. (800)336-5588. Fax: (914)232-3977. Web site: www.rcowen.com. **Acquisitions:** Janice Boland, children's books editor/art director. 90% of books by first-time authors. We publish "child-focused books, with inherent instructional value, about characters and situations with which five-, six-, and seven-year-old children can identify—books that can be read for meaning, entertainment, enjoyment and information. We include multicultural stories that present minorities in a positive and natural way. Our stories show the diversity in America." Is not interested in lesson plans, or books of activities for literature studies or other content areas.

- Due to a high volume of submissions, Richard C. Owen Publishers are currently only accepting nonfiction pieces.

Nonfiction Picture books, young readers: animals, careers, hi-lo, history, how-to, music/dance, geography, multicultural, nature/environment, science, sports. Multicultural needs include: "Good stories respectful of all heritages, races, cultural—African-American, Hispanic, American Indian." Wants lively stories. No "encyclopedic" type of information stories. Average word length: under 500 words. Recently published *The Coral Reef*.

How to Contact/Writers Fiction/nonfiction: Submit complete ms and cover letter. Responds to mss in 1 year. Publishes a book 2-3 years after acceptance. See Web site for guidelines.

Illustration Works with 20 illustrators/year. Uses color artwork only. Illustration only: Send color copies/reproductions or photos of art or provide tearsheets; do not send slides or originals. Include SASE and cover letter. Responds only if interested; samples filed.

Terms Pays authors royalty of 5% based on net price or outright purchase (range: $25-500). Offers no advances. Pays illustrators by the project (range: $100-2,500). Pays photographers by the project (range: $100-2,000) or per photo ($100-150). Original artwork returned 12-18 months after job's completion. Book brochure, ms/artists guidelines available for SASE.

Tips Seeking "authentic nonfiction that has charm, magic, impact and appeal; that children living in today's society will want to read and reread; books with strong storylines, child-appealing characters, events, language, action. Write for the ears and eyes and hearts of your readers—use an economy of words. Visit the children's room at the public library and immerse yourself in the best children's literature."

PACIFIC PRESS

P.O. Box 5353, Nampa ID 83653-5353. (208)465-2500. Fax: (208)465-2531. E-mail: booksubmissions@pacificpress.com. Web site: www.pacificpress.com/writers/books.htm. **Manuscript Acquisitions:** Tim Lale. **Art Acquisitions:** Gerald Monks, creative director. Publishes 1 picture book/year; 2 young readers/year; 2 middle readers/year. 5% of books by first-time authors. Pacific Press brings the Bible and Christian lifestyle to children.

Fiction Picture books, young readers, middle readers, young adults: religious subjects only. No fantasy. Average word length: picture books—100; young readers—1,000; middle readers—15,000; young adults—40,000. Recently published *A Child's Steps to Jesus* (3 vols), by Linda Carlyle; *Octopus Encounter*, by Sally Streib; *Sheper Warrior*, by Bradley Booth.

Nonfiction Picture books, young readers, middle readers, young adults: religion. Average word length: picture books—100; young readers—1,000; middle readers—15,000; young adults—40,000. Recently published *Escape*, by Sandy Zaugg; *What We Believe*, by Seth Pierce.

How to Contact/Writers Fiction/nonfiction: Query or submit outline/synopsis and 3 sample chapters. Responds to queries in 3 months; mss in 1 year. Publishes a book 6-12 months after acceptance. Will consider e-mail submissions.

Illustration Works with 2-6 illustrators/year. Uses color artwork only. Query. Responds only if interested. Samples returned with SASE.

Photography Buys stock and assigns work. Model/property releases required.

Terms Pays author royalty of 6-15% based on wholesale price. Offers advances (average amount: $1,500). Pays illustrators royalty of 6-15% based on wholesale price. Pays photographers royalty of 6-15% based on wholesale price. Sends galleys to authors. Originals returned to artist at job's completion. Manuscript guidelines for SASE. Catalog available on Web site (www.adventistbookcenter.com).

Tips Pacific Press is owned by the Seventh-day Adventist Church. The Press rejects all material that is not Bible-based.

PACIFIC VIEW PRESS

P.O. Box 2897, Berkeley CA 94702. (510)849-4213. Fax: (510)843-5835. E-mail: pvpress@sprynet.com. Web site: www.pacificviewpress.com. **Acquisitions:** Pam Zumwalt, president. Publishes 1-2 picture books/year. 50% of books by first-time authors. "We publish unique, high-quality introductions to Asian cultures and history for children 8-12, for schools, libraries and families. Our children's books focus on hardcover illustrated nonfiction. We look for titles on aspects of the history and culture of the countries and peoples of the Pacific Rim, especially China, presented in an engaging, informative and respectful manner. We are interested in books that all children will enjoy reading and using, and that parents and teachers will want to buy."

Nonfiction Young readers, middle readers: Asia-related multicultural only. Recently published *Cloud Weavers: Ancient Chinese Legends*, by Rena Krasno and Yeng-Fong Chiang (all ages); *Exploring Chinatown: A Children's Guide to Chinese Culture*, by Carol Stepanchuk (ages 8-12).

How to Contact/Writers Query with outline and sample chapter. Responds in 3 months.

Illustration Works with 2 illustrators/year. Responds only if interested. Samples returned with SASE.

Terms Pays authors royalty of 8-12% based on wholesale price. Pays illustrators by the project (range: $2,000-5,000).

Tips "We welcome proposals from persons with expertise, either academic or personal, in their area of interest. While we do accept proposals from previously unpublished authors, we would expect submitters to have considerable experience presenting their interests to children in classroom or other public settings and to have skill in writing for children."

🗋 PARENTING PRESS, INC.

P.O. Box 75267, Seattle WA 98175-0267. (206)364-2900. Fax: (206)364-0702. E-mail: office@parentingpress. com. Web site: www.parentingpress.com. Estab. 1979. Book publisher. Publisher: Carolyn Threadgill. **Acquisitions:** Elizabeth Crary (parenting) and Carolyn Threadgill (children and parenting). Publishes 4-5 books/year for parents or/and children and those who work with them. 40% of books by first-time authors. "Parenting Press publishes educational books for children in story format—no straight fiction. Our company publishes books that help build competence in parents and children. We are known for practical books that build parenting skills and can be used successfully by parents, parent educators, teachers, and educators who work with parents. We are interested in books that help people feel good about themselves because they gain skills needed in dealing with others. We are particularly interested in material that provides 'options' rather than 'shoulds.'"

● Parenting Press's guidelines are available on their Web site.

Fiction Picture books: concept. Publishes social skills books, problem-solving books, safety books, dealing-with-feelings books that use a "fictional" vehicle for the information. "We rarely publish straight fiction." Recently published *What About Me? 12 Ways to Get Your Parent's Attention (Without Hitting Your Sister)*, by Eileen Kennedy-Moore, illustrated by Mits Katayama (a book offering children options for getting the attention they need in positive ways).

Nonfiction Picture books: emotional health, social skills building. Young readers: emotional health, social skills building books. Middle readers: emotional health, social skills building. No books on "new baby; coping with a new sibling; cookbooks; manners; books about disabilities (which we don't publish at present); animal characters in anything; books that tell children what they should do, instead of giving options." Average word length: picture books—500-800; young readers—1,000-2,000; middle readers—up to 10,000. Published *25 Things to Do When Grandpa Passes Away, Mom and Dad Get Divorced, or the Dog Dies*, by Laurie Kanyer, illustrated by Jenny Williams (ages 2-12).

How to Contact/Writers Query. Responds to queries/mss in 3 months, "after requested." Publishes a book 18 months after acceptance. Will consider simultaneous submissions.

Illustrations Works with 3-5 illustrators/year. Reviews ms/illustration packages from artists. "We do reserve the right to find our own illustrator, however." Query. Illustrations only: Submit "résumé, samples of art/drawings (no original art); photocopies or color photocopies okay." Responds only if interested. Samples returned with SASE; samples filed, if suitable.

Terms Pays authors royalty of 3-12% based on wholesale price. Pays illustrators 3-6% royalty based on wholesale price, or pays by the project ($250-3,000). Sends galleys to authors; dummies to illustrators.

Tips "Make sure you are familiar with the unique nature of our books. All are aimed at building certain 'people' skills in adults or children. Our publishing for children follows no trend that we find appropriate. Children need nonfiction social skill-building books that help them think through problems and make their own informed decisions. The traditional illustrated story book does not *usually* fit our requirements because it does all the thinking for the child."

Michelle Meadows

Write what you love to read

Picture book author Michelle Meadows has always loved poetry, but the birth of her son re-awakened that love. As she read to him she rediscovered the joy of both verse and children's literature—and began writing. She sold her first book, *The Way the Storm Stops* (Henry Holt) when her son was about two years old.

Meadows submitted that first manuscript on her own. These days she's represented "by the amazing Rosemary Stimola of the Stimola Literary Studio," she says. "Rosemary sold my second book, *Pilot Pups*, and my other forthcoming titles. Three weeks after submitting *Pilot Pups* to publishers, Rosemary called with good news. Multiple publishers had made an offer on the manuscript! The book will be published in May 2008 by Simon & Schuster."

A follow-up to *Pilot Pups*, *Biker Pups*, in which the Pups zoom through town as motorcycle cops, will be published by Simon & Schuster in 2009. Other upcoming titles feature a mouse who gets lost and some energetic pigs. Below Meadows talks about writing that first book; her love of rhyming poetry and anthropomorphic animal characters; and her soft spot for picture books. For more on Meadows and her forthcoming titles, visit her Web site, www.michellemeadows.com.

I love the story of how you wrote your first book, *The Way the Storm Stops*, after soothing your then 2-year-old son during a loud thunderstorm. Does life with your family often spark ideas?

Life with my family often sparks ideas. I get a lot of inspiration from experiences with my son. For example, he has always had a lot of stuffed animals on top of his bookshelf, along with toy airplanes and a helicopter. I wrote *Pilot Pups* after imagining that the toy dogs on top of his bookshelf climbed into an airplane and took off on a search and rescue mission.

You've said you pretty much wrote one draft of *Storm Stops*, sent it off, and it was pulled from the slush by Christy Ottaviano at Henry Holt. At that point were you thinking, This getting published thing is a snap?

I wrote *The Way the Storm Stops* in the middle of the night while the storm was still going on, and then I sent the manuscript off in the mail the next morning. But I definitely wasn't thinking that getting published would be easy! I think it was just a case where inspiration struck and the words rolled out of me quickly. I think that sometimes a story can come out quickly with a positive result. But on the flip side, there are plenty of things that I write quickly that don't turn out well. My agent helps me tell the difference. There have been times when I've written a manuscript quickly, and my agent has liked it and sold it. Other times, she might say: This one's not there yet; it needs more work.

How did you find your agent Rosemary Stimola who sold your subsequent books, including a 2-book auction deal with Simon & Schuster for *Pilot Pups*?

I saw Rosemary speak at an SCBWI conference in New York. I was really impressed with her knowledge of the industry. She has taught children's literature, she used to own a children's bookstore, and she's kind and considerate too. So she's like an editor and a cheerleader and a business woman all rolled into one.

I've heard many an editor discourage writers from both rhyme and anthropomorphic animals. You did both with success. Is there a secret?

I think it goes back to the importance of writing what you love to read. I have always been drawn to young, rhyming picture books about animals. There will certainly be some publishing houses that aren't interested in rhyming manuscripts or animal stories. I think writers should write what they love to read and then try to target submissions to publishing houses that have published similar books.

Why do animals make good picture book characters?

I love animals as picture book characters because they are cute and cuddly and they are often small—just like children. I think children like animals in picture books for these same reasons. Also, it's so much fun to see animals doing silly or unexpected things.

By Michelle Meadows
Illustrated by Dan Andreasen

Michelle Meadows' *Pilot Pups*, illustrated by Dan Andreasen (Simon & Schuster), was inspired by the collection of toys atop her son's bookcase. Says *School Library Journal*: "This book would be a great read-aloud in preschool storytime, not only because of the lively illustrations and amusing story, but also for its descriptive vocabulary."

You have an upcoming book about getting lost. Your first book dealt with a scary thunderstorm. Do you think of picture books as a way to help kids deal with their fears? Do you set out to do this?

I do think picture books can be a great way to help children deal with their fears. It usually happens that I come up with a story about something that is important to me. And then I might discover that I have created a book that could help others who may be dealing with the same issues.

When did writing picture books become an interest for you and when did it become a passion?

I have been interested in writing picture books ever since I was young. I remember thinking about it when I was in high school. And I have always been passionate about writing. I've enjoyed writing poems and stories as a young child, and I studied journalism in college. I started applying my passion for writing to picture books after my son was born and I was reading to him all the time.

You also studied in Spanish language in college. Have you considered incorporating Spanish into future picture books?

I haven't really considered it, but never say never! I definitely admire picture books that incorporate Spanish. One of the reasons I have been attracted to Spanish is because I think it's a beautiful language. I love the way it sounds. Much the way I love the sound of poetry.

You're interested in writing beginning readers. What appeals to you about writing for this age level? Have your writing interests been affected by what your son is reading as he gets older?

Now my son is reading middle-grade novels. But for now, I lean more toward the young side. In addition to loving rhyming picture books, I really enjoy beginning readers. Some of my favorites are the Wizard and Wart series by Janice Lee Smith and the Buzby series by Julia Hoban. So I am hoping that I can produce some entertaining beginning readers. I like the challenge of trying to come up with interesting stories that will keep new readers turning pages.

Your Web site is fairly simple but has a friendly voice and some wonderful images from your books. What were your goals when you created the site? What else have you done in the way of promotion?

With my Web site, my goals were to create a site that is easy to navigate and easy to read. A lot of people like to skim and scan on the Web, so I try to go lighter on text and heavier on the images. In addition to maintaining a Web site, I do school and library visits and participate in book festivals whenever I can.

Any tricks for engaging a young audience when you give presentations?

I really love interacting with children and talking with them about the writing process and the importance of books. I think the best way to engage them is to make presentations as interactive as possible. Anything you can do to bring the children up to the front with you and be a part of the presentations. I also bring lots of "show and tell" props to share with them.

What advice can you offer aspiring picture book writers?

Write the kind of books that you love to read. Attend SCBWI meetings where you can meet other writers and hear from editors. And look at rejection letters as part of a learning process. If you are getting personal comments from editors, see how you can apply those comments to your work.

—Alice Pope

PAULINE BOOKS & MEDIA

50 St. Paul's Ave., Jamaica Plain MA 02130-3491. (617)522-8911. E-mail: editorial@paulinemedia.com. Web site: www.pauline.org. **Acquisitions Editor:** Sr. Maria Grace Dateno, FSP. **Art Acquisitions:** Sr. Mary Joseph Peterson, FSP, art director. Publishes 2 picture books/year; 5 young readers/year; 3-5 middle readers/year; 1-2 young adult titles/year. 20% of books by first-time authors. "We communicate the Gospel message through our lives and all available forms of media, responding to the needs and hopes of all people in the spirit of St. Paul."

Nonfiction Picture books, young readers, middle readers, young adults: religion. Average word length: picture books—150-500; young readers—8,000-10,000; middle readers—15,000-25,000. Recently published *I Pray the Rosary!*, by Margaret Rose Scarfi (ages 6-9); *Holy Friends: Thirty Saints and Blesseds of the Americas*, by Diane Amadeo (ages 9-12); *Squishy: A Book About My Five Senses*, by Cherie B. Stihler (Ages 4-7).

How to Contact/Writers Nonfiction: Submit query letter with outline/synopsis and 3 sample chapters. Responds to queries in 2 months; mss in 4 months. Publishes book 2-3 years after acceptance. Will consider simultaneous submissions, electronic submissions via disk or modem.

Illustration Works with 20-35 illustrators/year. Uses color artwork only. Illustrations only: Send résumé, promotional literature, client list or tearsheets. Responds only if interested. Samples returned with SASE only or samples filed.

Terms Varies by project. Manuscript and art guidelines available by SASE or on Web site. Catalog available on Web site.

Tips "Please be sure that all material submitted is consonant with Catholic teaching and values. We generally do not accept anthropomorphic stories, fantasy or poetry."

Terms Pays authors royalty of 3-12% based on wholesale price. Pays illustrators 3-6% royalty based on wholesale price, or pays by the project ($250-3,000). Sends galleys to authors; dummies to illustrators.

Tips "Make sure you are familiar with the unique nature of our books. All are aimed at building certain 'people' skills in adults or children. Our publishing for children follows no trend that we find appropriate. Children need nonfiction social skill-building books that help them think through problems and make their own informed decisions. The traditional illustrated story book does not *usually* fit our requirements because it does all the thinking for the child."

PAULINE BOOKS & MEDIA

50 St. Paul's Ave., Jamaica Plain MA 02130-3491. (617)522-8911. E-mail: editorial@paulinemedia.com. Web site: www.pauline.org. **Acquisitions Editor:** Sr. Maria Grace Dateno, FSP. **Art Acquisitions:** Sr. Mary Joseph Peterson, FSP, art director. Publishes 2 picture books/year; 5 young readers/year; 3-5 middle readers/year; 1-2 young adult titles/year. 20% of books by first-time authors. "We communicate the Gospel message through our lives and all available forms of media, responding to the needs and hopes of all people in the spirit of St. Paul."

Nonfiction Picture books, young readers, middle readers, young adults: religion. Average word length: picture books—150-500; young readers—8,000-10,000; middle readers—15,000-25,000. Recently published *I Pray the Rosary!*, by Margaret Rose Scarfi (ages 6-9); *Holy Friends: Thirty Saints and Blesseds of the Americas*, by Diane Amadeo (ages 9-12); *Squishy: A Book About My Five Senses*, by Cherie B. Stihler (Ages 4-7).

How to Contact/Writers Nonfiction: Submit query letter with outline/synopsis and 3 sample chapters. Responds to queries in 2 months; mss in 4 months. Publishes book 2-3 years after acceptance. Will consider simultaneous submissions, electronic submissions via disk or modem.

Illustration Works with 20-35 illustrators/year. Uses color artwork only. Illustrations only: Send résumé, promotional literature, client list or tearsheets. Responds only if interested. Samples returned with SASE only or samples filed.

Terms Varies by project. Manuscript and art guidelines available by SASE or on Web site. Catalog available on Web site.

Tips "Please be sure that all material submitted is consonant with Catholic teaching and values. We generally do not accept anthropomorphic stories, fantasy or poetry."

PAULIST PRESS

97 Macarthur Blvd., Mahwah NJ 07430. Web site: www.paulistpress.com. Acquisitions: Children's Editor. Publishes 6-8 titles/year. 10% of books by first-time authors. "Our goal is to spread the good news about God's love. The demands of the market are always changing, but at the moment we are doing this from a Catholic perspective. You do not need to be Catholic to be published here. Some of our biggest writers and illustrators are not. But you must be willing to do the legwork and to get the details right."

Nonfiction "Few cold sumbissions are considered as many of our books are by repeat authors and illustrators. The very few books we consider are on explicitly Catholic doctrine, prayers, sacraments, or customs, all meant to be used in a catechetical setting. Activity book submissions must be writer/illustrator only. For examples see *My Catholic School Holiday Activity Book* and *Jesus Loves Me Activity Book*, both written and illustrated by Jennifer Galvin. Examples of other kinds of books are Child's Guide to the Stations of the Cross, by Sue Stanton, illustrated by Anne Catharine Blake; and *The Imitation of Christ for Children*, by Elizabeth Ficocelli with illustrations my Chris Sabatino.

How to Contact/Writers Send complete mss for short books; query, outline, and sample for longer works. No e-mail submissions. No pitching ideas over the phone. ''Query first because many topics are already in production or under contract.'' Include SASE. Responds in 4-6 months. Simultaneous submissions are OK.

Illustration Send non-returnable samples of your children's art, both color and b&w, or a link to your Web page showing the same. For activity books, send an outline and a few sample pages.

Terms Pays authors royalty of 4-8% based on net sales, depending on whether or not they are split between author and illustrator. Advance payment is $500, payable on publication. Illustrators sometimes receive a flat fee for spot illustrations.

Tips ''Our children's books have moved in new directions: We are no longer looking for picture book 'fiction,' even if the theme or characters are Catholic. Also, we are no longer looking for biographies for young people. As always, we do not want to see submissions with angels or animals as characters. No submissions on adoption, grandparents, death, pets, sharing, September 11, etc. No books in rhyme. No retelling of Bible stories. No books co-written or illustrated by relatives or friends. Always remember that, while our company has a spiritual mission, the company itself is a publisher like any other and must succeed financially in order to continue to spread our message. Send us only your best. Our repeat authors and illustrators are award-winning professionals who also work in the secular market but who return to Paulist Press time after time because of our mission. Please know our current books; please know our current market. Above all—surprise us.''

PEACHTREE PUBLISHERS, LTD.

1700 Chattahoochee Ave., Atlanta GA 30318-2112. (404)876-8761. Fax: (404)875-2578. E-mail: hello@peacht ree-online.com. Web site: www.peachtree-online.com. **Acquisitions:** Helen Harriss. **Art Director:** Loraine Joyner. Production Manager: Melanie McMahon Ives. Publishes 30-35 titles/year.

Fiction Picture books, young readers: adventure, animal, concept, history, nature/environment. Middle readers: adventure, animal, history, nature/environment, sports. Young adults: fiction, mystery, adventure. Does not want to see science fiction, romance.

Nonfiction Picture books: animal, history, nature/environment. Young readers, middle readers, young adults: animal, biography, nature/environment. Does not want to see religion.

How to Contact/Writers Fiction/nonfiction: Submit complete ms (picture books) or 3 sample chapters (chapter books) by postal mail only. Responds to queries/mss in 6-7 months. Publishes a book 1-2 years after acceptance. Will consider simultaneous submissions.

Illustration Works with 8-10 illustrators/year. Illustrations only: Query production manager or art director with samples, résumé, slides, color copies to keep on file. Responds only if interested. Samples returned with SASE; samples filed.

Terms ''Manuscript guidelines for SASE, visit Web site or call for a recorded message. No fax or e-mail submittals or queries please.''

☐ PELICAN PUBLISHING CO. INC.

1000 Burmaster St., Gretna LA 70053-2246. (504)368-1175. Web site: www.pelicanpub.com. **Manuscript Acquisitions:** Nina Kooij, editor-in-chief. **Art Acquisitions:** Terry Callaway, production manager. Publishes 19 young readers/year; 2 middle readers/year; 1 young adult title/year. 5% of books from agented writers. ''Pelican publishes hardcover and trade paperback originals and reprints. Our children's books (illustrated and otherwise) include history, biography, holiday, and regional. Pelican's mission is ''to publish books of quality and permanence that enrich the lives of those who read them.''

Fiction Young readers: history, holiday, multicultural and regional. Middle readers: Louisiana history. Multicultural needs include stories about African-Americans, Irish-Americans, Jews, Asian-Americans, and Hispanics. Does not want animal stories, general Christmas stories, ''day at school'' or ''accept yourself'' stories. Maximum word length: young readers—1,100; middle readers—40,000. Recently published *Witches' Night Before Halloween*, by Leslie Pratt Bannatyne(ages 5-8, holiday).

Nonfiction Young readers: biography, history, holiday, multicultural. Middle readers: Louisiana history, holiday, regional. Recently published *Mary Cassatt*, by Lois V. Harris (ages 5-8, biography).

How to Contact/Writers Fiction/nonfiction: Query. Responds to queries in 1 month; mss in 3 months. Publishes a book 9-18 months after acceptance.

Illustration Works with 10 illustrators/year. Reviews ms/illustration packages from artists. Query first. Illustrations only: Query with samples (no originals). Responds only if interested. Samples returned with SASE; samples kept on file.

Terms Pays authors in royalties; buys ms outright "rarely." Sends galleys to authors. Illustrators paid by "various arrangements." Book catalog and ms guidelines available on Web site or for SASE.

Tips "No anthropomorphic stories, pet stories (fiction or nonfiction), fantasy, poetry, science fiction or romance. Writers: be as original as possible. Develop characters that lend themselves to series and always be thinking of new and interesting situations for those series. Give your story a strong hook—something that will appeal to a well-defined audience. There is a lot of competition out there for general themes. We look for stories with specific 'hooks' and audiences, and writers who actively promote their work."

PHILOMEL BOOKS

Penguin Young Readers Group (USA), 345 Hudson St., New York NY 10014. (212)414-3610. Web site: www.penguin.com. **Manuscript Acquisitions:** submissions editor. **Art Acquisitions:** Katrina Damkoehler, design assistant. Publishes 18 picture books/year; 2 middle-grades/year; 2 young readers/year; 4 young adult titles/year. 5% of books by first-time authors; 80% of books from agented writers. "We look for beautifully written, engaging manuscripts for children and young adults."

Fiction All levels: adventure, animal, anthology, contemporary, fantasy, folktales, hi-lo, history, humor, poetry, sports, multicultural. Middle readers, young adults: problem novels, science fiction, suspense/mystery. No concept picture books, mass-market "character" books, or series. Average word length: picture books—1,000; young readers—1,500; middle readers—14,000; young adult—20,000.

Nonfiction Picture books, young readers, middle readers: hi-lo. "Creative nonfiction on any subject." Average word length: picture books—2,000; young readers—3,000; middle readers—10,000.

How to Contact/Writers "As of January 1, 2007, Philomel will no longer respond to your unsolicited submission unless interested in publishing it. Rejected submissions postmarked January 1, 2007, or later will be recycled. Please *do not* include a self-addressed stamped envelope with your submission. You will not hear from Philomel regarding the status of your submission unless we are interested in publishing it, in which case you can expect a reply from us within approximately four months. We regret that we cannot respond personally to each submission, but rest assured that we do make every effort to consider each and every one we receive."

Illustration Works with 20-25 illustrators/year. Reviews ms/illustration packages from artists. Query with art sample first. Illustrations only: Query with samples. Send résumé and tearsheets. Responds to art samples in 1 month. Original artwork returned at job's completion. Samples returned with SASE or kept on file.

Terms Pays authors in royalties. Average advance payment "varies." Illustrators paid by advance and in royalties. Sends galleys to authors; dummies to illustrators. Book catalog, ms guidelines free on request with SASE (9×12 envelope for catalog).

Tips Wants "unique fiction or nonfiction with a strong voice and lasting quality. Discover your own voice and own story and persevere." Looks for "something unusual, original, well-written. Fine art. The genre (fantasy, contemporary, or historical fiction) is not so important as the story itself and the spirited life the story allows its main character. We are also interested in receiving adolescent novels, current, contemporary fiction with voice."

▯ PIANO PRESS

P.O. Box 85, Del Mar CA 92014-0085. (619)884-1401. Fax: (858)755-1104. E-mail: pianopress@pianopress.com. Web site: www.pianopress.com. **Manuscript Acquisitions:** Elizabeth C. Axford, M.A, editor. "We publish music-related books, either fiction or nonfiction, coloring books, songbooks and poetry."

Fiction Picture books, young readers, middle readers, young adults: folktales, multicultural, poetry, music. Average word length: picture books—1,500-2,000. Recently published *Strum a Song of Angels*, by Linda Oatman High and Elizabeth C. Axford; *Music and Me*, by Kimberly White and Elizabeth C. Axford.

Nonfiction Picture books, young readers, middle readers, young adults: multicultural, music/dance. Average word length: picture books—1,500-2,000. Recently published *The Musical ABC*, by Dr. Phyllis J. Perry and Elizabeth C. Axford; *Merry Christmas Happy Hanukkah—A Multilingual Songbook & CD*, by Elizabeth C. Axford.

How to Contact/Writers Fiction/ nonfiction: Query. Responds to queries in 3 months; mss in 6 months. Publishes a book 1 year after acceptance. Will consider simultaneous submissions, electronic submissions via disk or modem.

Illustration Works with 1 or 2 illustrators/year. Reviews ms/illustration packages from artists. Query. Illustrations only: Query with samples. Responds in 3 months. Samples returned with SASE; samples filed.

Photography Buys stock and assigns work. Looking for music-related, multicultural. Model/property releases required. Uses glossy or flat, color or b&w prints. Submit cover letter, résumé, client list, published samples, stock photo list.

Terms Pays authors, illustrators, and photographers royalty of 5-10% based on retail price. Sends galleys to authors; dummies to illustrators. Originals returned to artist at job's completion. Book catalog available for #10 SASE and 2 first-class stamps. All imprints included in a single catalog. Catalog available on Web site.

Tips ''We are looking for music-related material only for any juvenile market. Please do not send nonmusic-related materials. Query first before submitting anything.''

PIÑATA BOOKS

Imprint of Arte Publico Press, University of Houston, 452 Cullen Performance Hall, Houston TX 77204-2004. (713)743-2843. Fax: (713)743-3080. Web site: www.artepublicopress.com. **Manuscript Acquisitions:** Dr. Nicholas Kanellos; Gabriela Baeza Ventura, executive editor. **Art Acquisitions:** Adelaida Mendoza, production manager. Publishes 6 picture books/year; 2 young readers/year; 5 middle readers/year; 5 young adult titles/year. 80% of books are by first-time authors. ''Arte Publico's mission is the publication, promotion and dissemination of Latino literature for a variety of national and regional audiences, from early childhood to adult, through the complete gamut of delivery systems, including personal performance as well as print and electronic media.''

Fiction Recently published *We Are Cousins/ Somos primos* by Diane Gonzales Betrand*; Butterflies on Carmen Street/ Mariposas en la calle Carmen* by Monica Brown*; and Windows into My World: Latino Youth Write Their Lives.*

Nonfiction Recently published *César Chávez: The Struggle for Justice/César Chávez: La Lucha Por La Justicia*, by Richard Griswold del Castillo, illustrated by Anthony Accardo (ages 3-7).

How to Contact/Writers Accepts material from U.S./Hispanic authors only (living abroad OK). Manuscripts, queries, synopses, etc. are accepted in either English or Spanish. Fiction: Submit complete ms. Nonfiction: Query. Responds to queries in 2-4 months; mss in 3-6 months. Publishes a book 2 years after acceptance. Will sometimes consider previously published work.

Illustration Works with 6 illustrators/year. Uses color artwork only. Reviews ms/illustration packages from artists. Query or send portfolio (slides, color copies). Illustrations only: Query with samples or send résumé, promo sheet, portfolio, slides, client list and tearsheets. Responds only if interested. Samples not returned; samples filed.

Terms Pays authors royalty of 10% minimum based on wholesale price. Offers advances (average amount $2,000). Pays illustrators advance and royalties of 10% based on wholesale price. Sends galleys to authors. Catalog available on Web site; ms guidelines available for SASE.

PINEAPPLE PRESS, INC.

P.O. Box 3889, Sarasota FL 34239. (941)739-2219. Fax: (941)739-2296. E-mail: info@pineapplepress.com. Web site: www.pineapplepress.com. **Manuscript Acquisitions:** June Cussen. Publishes 1 picture book/year; 1 young reader/year; 1 middle reader/year; 1 young adult title/year. 50% of books by first-time authors. ''Our mission is to publish good books about Florida.''

Fiction Picture books, young readers, middle readers, young adults: animal, folktales, history, nature/environment. Recently published *The Treasure of Amelia Island* by M.C. Finotti (ages 8-12).

Nonfiction Picture books: animal, history, nature/environmental, science. Young readers, middle readers, young adults: animal, biography, geography, history, nature/environment, science. Recently published *Those Magical Manatees* by Jan Lee Wicker and *Those Beautiful Butterflies* by Sarah Cussen.

How to Contact/Writers Fiction: Query or submit outline/synopsis and 3 sample chapters. Nonfiction: Query or submit outline/synopsis and intro and 3 sample chapters. Responds to queries/samples/mss in 2 months. Will consider simultaneous submissions.

Illustration Works with 2 illustrators/year. Reviews ms/illustration packages from artists. Query with nonreturnable samples. Contact: June Cussen, executive editor. Illustrations only: Query with brochure, nonreturnable samples, photocopies, résumé. Responds only if interested. Samples returned with SASE, but prefers nonreturnable; samples filed.

Terms Pays authors royalty of 10-15%. Pays illustrators royalties. Sends galleys to authors; dummies to illustrators. Originals returned to artist at job's completion. Book catalog available for 9×12 SAE with $1.06 postage; all imprints included in a single catalog. Catalog available on Web site at www.pineapplepress.com.

Tips ''Learn about publishing and book marketing in general. Be familiar with the kinds of books published by the publishers to whom you are submitting.''

PITSPOPANY PRESS

40 E. 78th St., #16D, New York NY 10021. (212)444-1657. Fax: (866)205-3966. E-mail: pitspop@netvision.net.il. Web site: www.pitspopany.com. Estab. 1992. Specializes in trade books, Judaica, nonfiction, fiction, multicultural material. **Manuscript Acquisitions:** Yaacov Peterseil, publisher. **Art Acquisitions:** Yaacov Peterseil, publisher. Produces 6 picture books/year; 4 young readers/year; 4 middle readers/year; 4 young adult books/year. 10% of books by first-time authors. ''Pitspopany Press is dedicated to bringing quality children's books of Jewish interest into the marketplace. Our goal is to create titles that will appeal to the esthetic senses of our readers and, at the same time, offer quality Jewish content to the discerning parent, teacher, and librarian.

While the people working for Pitspopany Press embody a wide spectrum of Jewish belief and opinion, we insist that our titles be respectful of the mainstream Jewish viewpoints and beliefs. Most of all, we are committed to creating books that all Jewish children can read, learn from, and enjoy.''

Fiction Picture books: animal, anthology, fantasy, folktales, history, humor, multicultural, nature/environment, poetry. Young readers: adventure, animal, anthology, concept, contemporary, fantasy, folktales, health, history, humor, multicultural, nature/environment, poetry, religion, science fiction, special needs, sports, suspense. Middle readers: animal, anthology, fantasy, folktales, health, hi-lo, history, humor, multicultural, nature/environment, poetry, religion, science fiction, special needs, sports, suspense. Young adults/teens: animal, anthology, contemporary, fantasy, folktales, health, hi-lo, history, humor, multicultural, nature/environment, poetry, religion, science fiction, special needs, sports, suspense. Recently published *Hayyim's Ghost*, by Eric Kimmel, illustrated by Ari Binus (ages 6-9); *The Littlest Pair*, by Syliva Rouss, illustrated by Hally Hannan (ages 3-6); *The Converso Legacy*, by Sheldon Gardner (ages 10-14, historial fiction).

Nonfiction All levels: activity books, animal, arts/crafts, biography, careers, concept, cooking, geography, health, history, hobbies, how-to, multicultural, music/dance, nature/environment, reference, religion, science, self help, social issues, special needs, sports.

How to Contact/Writers Accepts international submissions. Fiction/nonfiction: Submit outline/synopsis. Responds to queries/mss in 6 weeks. Publishes book 9 months after acceptance. Considers simultaneous submissions, electronic submissions.

Illustration Accepts material from international illustrators. Works with 6 illustrators/year. Uses color artwork only. Reviews ms/illustration packages. For ms/illustration packages: Submit ms with 4 pieces of final art. Submit ms/illustration packages to Yaacov Peterseil, publisher. Reviews work for future assignments. If interested in illustrating future titles, send promo sheet. Submit samples to Yaacov Peterseil, publisher. Samples returned with SASE. Samples not filed.

Photography Works on assignment only. Submit photos to Yaacov Peterseil, publisher.

Terms Pays authors royalty or work purchased outright. Offers advance against royalties. Author sees galleys for review. Originals returned to artist at job's completion. Catalog on Web site. All imprints included in single catalog. Offers writer's guidelines for SASE.

▢ THE PLACE IN THE WOODS

Different Books, 3900 Glenwood Ave., Golden Valley MN 55422-5307. (763)374-2120. Fax: (952)593-5593. **Acquisitions:** Roger Hammer, publisher/editor. Publishes 2 elementary-age titles/year; 1 middle reader/year; 1 young adult title/year. 100% of books by first-time authors. Books feature primarily diversity/multicultural/disability themes by first-time authors and illustrators.

Fiction All levels: adventure, animal, contemporary, fantasy, folktales, hi-lo, history, humor, poetry, multicultural, special needs. Recently published *Little Horse*, by Frank Minogue, illustrated by Beth Cripe (young adult fiction); *Smile, It's OK To Be You*, by Karen Foster French, illustrated by Susan Brados (grades preschool-8, self-esteem); *Mona & Friends in Land of Joan* (series), by Dawn Rosewitz (ages 5-11, adventure).

Nonfiction All levels: hi-lo, history, multicultural, special needs. Multicultural themes must avoid negative stereotypes. ''Generally, we don't publish nonfiction, but we would look at these.'' Recently published *African America*, by Roger Hammer, illustrated by Tacoumba Aiken (ages 12 and up, history); *American Woman*, by Roger Hammer, illustrated by Christie Nelson (history); *Hispanic America*, by Roger Hammer, illustrated by Paul Moran (history).

How to Contact/Writers Fiction/nonfiction: Submit complete ms. Responds to queries/mss in 1 month with SASE. ''No multiple or simultaneous submissions. Please indicate a time frame for response.''

Illustration Works with 4 illustrators/year. Uses primarily b&w artwork only. Reviews ms/illustration packages from authors. Query; submit ms. Contact: Roger Hammer, editor. Illustration only: Query with samples. Responds in 1 month. Include SASE. ''We buy all rights.''

Photography Buys photos from freelancers on assignment only. Uses photos that appeal to children. Model/property releases required; captions required. Uses any b&w prints. Submit cover letter and samples with SASE.

Terms Manuscripts purchased outright from authors ($250). Pays illustrators by the project ($10). Pays photographers per photo (range: $10-250). For all contracts, ''initial payment repeated with each subsequent printing.'' Original artwork not returned at job's completion. Guidelines available for SASE.

Tips ''Tell me about *who* you are, *how* you've come to be *where* you are, and *what* you want to accomplish. Don't waste our time telling me how good your work is it should speak for itself.''

PLAYERS PRESS, INC.

P.O. Box 1132, Studio City CA 91614-0132. (818)789-4980. **Manuscript Acquisitions:** Robert W. Gordon, vice president/editorial director. **Art Acquisitions:** Attention: Art Director. Publishes 7-25 young readers, dramatic plays and musicals/year; 2-10 middle readers, dramatic plays and musicals/year; 4-20 young adults, dramatic plays and musicals/year. 35% of books by first-time authors; 1% of books from agented writers. Players Press philosophy: "To create is to live life's purpose."

Fiction All levels: plays. Recently published *Play From African Folktales*, by Carol Korty (collection of short plays); *Punch and Judy*, a play by William-Alan Landes; *Silly Soup!*, by Carol Korty (a collection of short plays with music and dance).

Nonfiction Picture books, middle readers, young readers, young adults. "Any children's nonfiction pertaining to the entertainment industry, performing arts and how-to for the theatrical arts only." Needs include activity books related to theatre: arts/crafts, careers, history, how-to, music/dance, reference and textbook. Recently published *Scenery*, by J. Stell (How to Build Stage Scenery); *Monologues for Teens*, by Vernon Howard (ideal for teen performers); *Humorous Monologues*, by Vernon Howard (ideal for young performers); *Actor's Resumes*, by Richard Devin (how to prepare an acting résumé).

How to Contact/Writers Fiction/nonfiction: Submit plays or outline/synopsis and sample chapters of entertainment books. Responds to queries in 2 weeks; mss in 6 months-1 year. Publishes a book 10 months after acceptance. No simultaneous submissions.

Illustration Works with 2-6 new illustrators/year. Use primarily b&w artwork. Illustrations only: Submit résumé, tearsheets. Responds to art samples in 1 week only if interested. Samples returned with SASE; samples filed.

Terms Pays authors royalty based on wholesale price. Pays illustrators by the project (range: $5-1,000). Pays photographers by the project (up to $100); royalty varies. Sends galleys to authors; dummies to illustrators. Book catalog and ms guidelines available for 9 × 12 SASE.

Tips Looks for "plays/musicals and books pertaining to the performing arts only. Illustrators: send samples that can be kept for our files."

PRICE STERN SLOAN, INC.
Penguin Group (USA), 345 Hudson St., New York NY 10014. (212)414-3590. Fax: (212)414-3396. Estab. 1963. Web site: http://us.penguingroup.com/youngreaders. **Acquisitions:** Debra Dorfman, president/publisher. "Price Stern Sloan publishes quirky mass market novelty series for children's as well as licensed movie tie-in books.
● Price Stern Sloan does not accept e-mail submissions.

Fiction Publishes picture books and novelty/board books including Mad Libs and Movie and Television Tie-ins. "We publish unique novelty formats and fun, colorful paperbacks and activity books. We also publish the Book with Audio Series Wee Sing and Baby Loves Jazz." Recently published: Baby Loves Jazz Board Book With CD Series; New Formats In The Classic Mr. Men/Little Miss Series; Movie/TV tie-in titles Corbin Bleu: To The Limit; Happy Feet; Family Guy Mad Libs; Shrek the Third Mad Libs.

How to Contact/Writers Query. Responds to queries in 6-8 weeks.

Terms Work purchased outright. Offers advance. Book catalog available for 9 × 12 SASE and 5 first-class stamps; address to Book Catalog. Manuscript guidelines available for SASE; address to Manuscript Guidelines.

Tips "Price Stern Sloan pulbishes unique, fun titles."

PROMETHEUS BOOKS
59 John Glenn Dr., Amherst NY 14228-2119. (800)421-0351 Fax: (716)564-2711. E-mail: SLMitchell@prometheu sbooks.com. Web site: www.PrometheusBooks.com. **Acquisitions:** Steven L. Mitchell, editor-in-chief. Publishes 1-2 titles/year. 50% of books by first-time authors; 30% of books from agented writers. "We hope more books will be published that focus on real issues children face and real questions they raise. Our primary focus is to publish children's books with alternative viewpoints: humanism, free thought, moral values, critical reasoning, human sexuality, and independent thinking based upon science and reasoning, skepticism toward the paranormal. Our niche is the parent who seeks informative books based on these principles. We are dedicated to offering customers the highest-quality books. We are also committed to the development of new markets both in North America and throughout the world."

Nonfiction All levels: sex education, moral education, critical thinking, nature/environment, science, self help, skepticism, social issues. Average word length: picture books—2,000; young readers—10,000; middle readers—20,000; young adult/teens—60,000. Recently published *A Solstice Tree For Jenny*, by Karen Shrugg (ages 4 and up); *All Families Are Different*, by Sid Gordon (ages 7 and up); *Flat Earth? Round Earth?*, by Theresa Martin (ages 7 and up); *Humanism, What's That?* by Helen Bennett (ages 10 and up); *Dare To Dream* by Sandra McLeod Humphrey (ages 8 and up).

How to Contact/Writers Submit complete ms with sample illustrations (b&w). Responds to queries in 3 weeks; mss in 1-2 months. Publishes a book 12-18 months after acceptance. SASE required for return of ms/proposal.

Illustration Works with 1-2 illustrators/year. "We will keep samples in a freelance file, but freelancers are rarely used." Reviews ms/illustration packages from artists. "Prefer to have full work (ms and illustrations); will consider any proposal." Include résumé, photocopies.

Terms Pays authors royalty of 5-15% based on wholesale price and binding. "Author hires illustrator; we do not contract with illustrators." Pays photographers per photo (range: $50-100). Sends galleys to author. Book catalog is free on request.

Tips "We do not accept projects with anthropomorphic characters. We stress realistic children in realistic situations. "Books should reflect secular humanist values, stressing nonreligious moral education, critical thinking, logic, and skepticism. Authors should examine our book catalog and website to learn what sort of manuscripts we're looking for."

PUFFIN BOOKS

Penguin Group (USA), Inc., 345 Hudson St., New York NY 10014-3657. (212)414-3600. Web site: www.penguin.com/youngreaders. **Acquisitions:** Sharyn November, senior editor and editorial director of Firebird. Imprints: Speak, Firebird, Sleuth. Publishes trade paperback originals and reprints. Publishes 175-200 titles/year. Receives 600 queries and mss/year. 1% of books by first-time authors; 5% from unagented writers. "Puffin Books publishes high-end trade paperbacks and paperback originals and reprints for preschool children, beginning and middle readers, and young adults."

Fiction Picture books, young adult novels, middle grade and easy-to-read grades 1-3: fantasy and science fiction, graphic novels, classics. Recently published *Cindy Ella*, by Robin Palmer; *Walk of the Spirits*, by Richie Tankersley Cusick; *Just Listen*, by Sarah Dessen.

Nonfiction Biography, illustrated books, young children's concept books (counting, shapes, colors). Subjects include education (for teaching concepts and colors, not academic), women in history. "Women in history books interest us." **Illustration** Reviews artwork. Send color copies.

Photography Reviews photos. Send color copies.

How to Contact/Writers Fiction: Submit 3 sample chapters with SASE. Nonfiction: Submit 5 pages of ms with SASE. "It could take up to 5 months to get response." Publishes book 1 year after acceptance. Will consider simultaneous submissions, if so noted. Does not accept unsolicited picture book mss.

Terms Pays royalty. Offers advance (varies). Book catalog for 9 × 12 SASE with 7 first-class stamps; send request to Marketing Department.

Ⓐ PUSH

Scholastic, 557 Broadway, New York NY 10012-3999. Web site: www.thisispush.com. Estab. 2002. Specializes in fiction. Produces 6-9 young adult books/year. 50% of books by first-time authors. PUSH publishes new voices in teen literature.

- PUSH does not accept unsolicited manuscripts or queries, only agented or referred fiction/memoir.

Fiction Young adults: contemporary, multicultural, poetry. Recently published *Splintering*, by Eireann Corrigan; *Never Mind the Goldbergs*, by Matthue Roth; *Perfect World*, by Brian James.

Nonfiction Young adults: memoir. Recently published *Talking in the Dark*, by Billy Merrell; *You Remind Me of You*, by Eireann Corrigan.

How to Contact/Writers **Only interested in agented material.** Accepts international submissions. Fiction/nonfiction: Submit complete ms. Responds to queries in 2 months; mss in 4 months. No simultaneous, electronic, or previously published submissions.

Tips "We only publish first-time writers (and then their subsequent books), so authors who have published previously should not consider PUSH. Also, for young writers in grades 7-12, we run the PUSH novel Contest with the Scholastic Art & Writing Awards. Every year it begins in October and ends in March. Rules can be found on our Web site."

🌠 G.P. PUTNAM'S SONS

Penguin Putnam Books For Young Readers, 345 Hudson St., New York NY 10014. (212)414-3610. Web site: www.penguinputnam.com. **Manuscript Acquisitions:** Susan Kochan, associate editorial director; John Rudolph, senior editor; Timothy Travaglini, senior editor; Stacey Barney, editor. **Art Acquisitions:** Cecilia Yung, art director, Putnam and Philomel. Publishes 25 picture books/year; 15 middle readers/year; 5 young adult titles/year. 5% of books by first-time authors; 50% of books from agented authors.

- G.P. Putnam's Sons title *Feathers*, by Jacqueline Woodson, won a Newbery Honor Medal in 2008. See First Books on page 133 for an interview with Sarah S. Brannen, author and illustrator of Putnam title *Uncle Bobby's Wedding*.

Fiction Picture books: animal, concept, contemporary, humor, multicultural. Young readers: adventure, contemporary, history, humor, multicultural, special needs, suspense/mystery. Middle readers: adventure, contemporary, history, humor, fantasy, multicultural, problem novels, sports, suspense/mystery. Young adults: contemporary, history, fantasy, problem novels, special needs. Does not want to see series. Average word length: picture books—200-1,000; middle readers—10,000-30,000; young adults—40,000-50,000. Recently published *Leaves*, by David Ezra Stein (ages 4-8); *Faeries of Dreamdark: Blackbringer*, by Lainie Taylor (ages 10 and up).

Nonfiction Picture books: animal, biography, concept, history, nature/environment, science. Subjects must have broad appeal but inventive approach. Average word length: picture books—200-1,500. Recently published *The United Tweets of America*, by Hudson Talbott (ages 5 and up, 64 pages).

How to Contact/Writers Accepts unsolicited mss. No SASE required, as will only respond if interested. Picture books: send full mss. Fiction: Query with outline/synopsis and 10 manuscript pages. Nonfiction: Query with outline/synopsis, 10 manuscript pages, and a table of contents. Do not send art unless requested. Responds to mss within 4 months if interested. Will consider simultaneous submissions.

Illustration Write for illustrator guidelines. Works with 40 illustrators/year. Reviews ms/illustration packages from artists. Manuscript/illustration packages and illustration only: Query. Responds only if interested. Samples filed.

Terms Pays authors royalty based on retail price. Pays illustrators by the project or royalty based on retail price. Sends galleys to authors. Original artwork returned at job's completion.

Tips "Study our catalogs and get a sense of the kind of books we publish, so that you know whether your project is likely to be right for us."

RAINBOW PUBLISHERS

P.O. Box 261129, San Diego CA 92196. (858)668-3260. Web site: www.rainbowpublishers.com. **Acquisitions:** Editorial Department. Publishes 5 young readers/year; 5 middle readers/year; 5 young adult titles/year. 50% of books by first-time authors. "Our mission is to publish Bible-based, teacher resource materials that contribute to and inspire spiritual growth and development in kids ages 2-12."

Nonfiction Young readers, middle readers, young adult/teens: activity books, arts/crafts, how-to, reference, religion. Does not want to see traditional puzzles. Recently published More Bible Puzzles (series of 4 books for ages 8 and up).

How to Contact/Writers Nonfiction: Submit outline/synopsis and 3-5 sample chapters. Responds to queries in 6 weeks; mss in 3 months. Publishes a book 36 months after acceptance. Will consider simultaneous submissions, submissions via disk and previously published work.

Illustration Works with 2-5 illustrators/year. Reviews ms/illustration packages from artists. Submit ms with 2-5 pieces of final art. Illustrations only: Query with samples. Responds in 6 weeks. Samples returned with SASE; samples filed.

Terms For authors work purchased outright (range: $500 and up). Pays illustrators by the project (range: $300 and up). Sends galleys to authors. Book catalog available for 10×13 SAE and 2 first-class stamps; ms guidelines available for SASE.

Tips "Our Rainbow imprint carries reproducible books for teachers of children in Christian ministries, including crafts, activities, games and puzzles. Our Legacy imprint published titles for children such as devotionals, fiction and Christian living. Please write for guidelines and study the market before submitting material."

☐ Ⓐ RANDOM HOUSE-GOLDEN BOOKS FOR YOUNG READERS GROUP

Random House, Inc., 1745 Broadway, New York NY 10019. (212)782-9000. Estab. 1935. Book publisher. "Random House Books aims to create books that nurture the hearts and minds of children, providing and promoting quality books and a rich variety of media that entertain and educate readers from 6 months to 12 years." Publisher/Vice President: Kate Klimo. VP & Associate Publisher/Art Director: Cathy Goldsmith. **Acquisitions:** Easy-to-Read Books (step-into-reading and picture books), board and novelty books, fiction and nonfiction for young and mid-grade readers: Heidi Kilgras, Editorial Director. Stepping Stones: Jennifer Arena, Executive Editor. Middle grade and youbg adult fiction: Jim Thomas, Editorial Director. 100% of books published through agents; 2% of books by first-time authors.

- Random House-Golden Books does not accept unsolicited manuscripts, only agented material. They reserve the right not to return unsolicited material.

How to Contact/Writers Only interested in agented material. Reviews ms/illustration packages from artists through agent only. Does not open or respond to unsolicited submissions.

Terms Pays authors in royalties; sometimes buys mss outright. Sends galleys to authors. Book catalog free on request.

☐ RAVEN TREE PRESS, LLC

P.O. Box 11505, Green Bay WI 54307. (800)909-9901. (920)438-1607. Fax: (800)909-9901. E-mail: raven@raventreepress.com. Web site: www.raventreepress.com. Publishes 8-10 picture books/year. 50% of books by first-time authors. "We publish entertaining and educational bilingual materials for families in English and Spanish."

Fiction Picture books: K-3 focus. No word play or rhyme. Work will be translated into Spanish by publisher. Check Web site prior to any submissions for current needs. Average word length: 500.

How to Contact/Writers Check Web site for current needs, submission guidelines and deadlines.

Illustration Check Web site for current needs, submission guidelines and deadlines.

Terms Pays authors and illustrators royalty. Offers advances against royalties. Pays illustrators by the project or royalty. Originals returned to artist at job's completion. Catalog available on Web site.

Tips "Submit only based on guidelines. No e-mail of snail mail queries please. Word count is a definite issue, since we are bilingual." Staff attended or plans to attend the following conferences: BEA, NABE, IRA, ALA and SCBWI.

[N] RAZORBILL

Penguin Group, 345 Hudson St., New York NY 10014. Imprint estab. 2003. (212)414-3448. Fax: (212)414-3343. E-mail: razorbill@us.penguingroup.com. Web site: www.razorbillbooks.com. Specializes in fiction. **Acquisitions:** Laura Schechter, editorial assistant; Kristen Pettit, Lexa Hillyer, Jessica Rothenberg. Publishes 10 middle readers/year; 30 young adult titles/year. "This division of Penguin Young Readers is looking for the best and the most original of commercial contemporary fiction titles for middle grade and YA readers. A select quantity of nonfiction titles will also be considered."

Fiction Middle Readers: adventure, animal, contemporary, graphic novels, fantasy, humor, problem novels. Young adults/teens: adventure, animal, contemporary, fantasy, graphic novels, humor, multicultural, suspense. Average word length: middle readers—40,000; young adult—60,000. Recently published *Spud*, by John Van de Ruit (ages 12 and up, South Africa's fastest selling book); *Thirteen Reasons Why*, by Jay Asher (ages 14 and up, a suspenseful psychological thriller); *Those Girls*, by Sara Lawrence (ages 13 and up, a peek at the privileged lives of fabulous private school seniors).

Nonfiction Middle readers: activity books, arts/crafts, biography, cooking, health, how-to. Young adults/teens: biography, concept, health, how-to.

How to Contact/Writers Submit outline/synopsis and 3 sample chapters. Responds to queries/mss in approx. 8 weeks. Publishes a book 1-2 years after acceptance. Will consider e-mail submissions and simultaneous submissions.

Terms Offers advance against royalties. Authors see galleys for review. Catalog available online at www.razorbillbooks.com.

Tips "New writers will have the best chance of acceptance and publication with original, contemporary material that boasts a distinctive voice and well-articulated world. Check out www.razorbillbooks.com to get a better idea of what we're looking for."

[] [] RENAISSANCE HOUSE

Imprint of Laredo Publishing, Beverly Hills CA 90210. (800)547-5113. Fax: (310)860-9902. E-mail: laredo@renaissancehouse.net. Web site: www.renaissancehouse.net. **Manuscript Acquisitions:** Raquel Benatar. **Art Acquisitions:** Sam Laredo. Publishes 5 picture books/year; 10 young readers/year; 10 middle readers/year; 5 young adult titles/year. 10% of books by first-time authors.

Fiction Picture books: animal, folktales, multicultural. Young readers: animal, anthology, folktales, multicultural. Middle readers, young adult/teens: anthology, folktales, multicultural, nature/environment. Recently published *Isabel Allende, Memories for a Story* (English-Spanish, age 9-12, biography); *Stories of the Americas*, a series of legends by several authors (ages 9-12, legend).

How to Contact/Writers Submit outline/synopsis. Responds to queries/mss in 3 weeks. Publishes a book 1 year after acceptance. Will consider simultaneous submissions, e-mail submissions.

Illustration Works with 25 illustrators/year. Uses color artwork only. Reviews ms/illustration packages from artists. Send ms with dummy. Contact: Sam Laredo. Illustrations only: Send tearsheets. Contact: Raquel Benatar. Responds in 3 weeks. Samples not returned; samples filed.

Terms Pays authors royalty of 5-10% based on retail price. Pays illustrators by the project. Sends galleys to authors; dummies to illustrators. Originals returned to artist at job's completion. Book catalog available for 9×12 SASE and $3 postage. All imprints included in a single catalog. Catalog available on website.

THE RGU GROUP

P.O.Box 12770 Tempe AZ 85283. (480)736-9862. Fax: (480)736-9863. E-mail: info@theRGUgroup.com. Web site: www.theRGUgroup.com. **Manuscript/Art Acquisitions: Not Accepting Manuscripts at this time.**

Fiction Picture books, board books, young readers: adventure, animal, history, humor, multicultural, nature/environment. Recently published *Desert Night Shift—A Pack Rat Story*, by Conrad Storad, illustrated by Nathan Jensen (ages 4 and up); *A Wild and Wooly Night*, by Lorraine Lynch Geiger, illustrated by Sharon Vargo. Fiction may include non-fictional elements that complement the southwestern theme. Also will consider bilingual English/Spanish manuscripts.

[A] [Y] ROARING BROOK PRESS

175 Fifth Ave., New York NY 10010. (212)375-7149. **Manuscript/Art Acquisitions:** Simon Boughton, publisher. **Editorial Director, Neal Porter Books:** Neal Porter. **Executive Editor:** Nancy Mercado. **Senior Editor:** Dierdre Langeland. Publishes approximately 70 titles/year. 1% of books by first-time authors. This publisher's goal is "to publish distinctive high-quality children's literature for all ages. To be a great place for authors to be

published. To provide personal attention and a focused and thoughtful publishing effort for every book and every author on the list.''

• Roaring Brook Press is an imprint of MacMillan, a group of companies that includes Henry Holt and Farrar, Straus & Giroux. Roaring Brook is not accepting unsolicited manuscripts. Roaring Brook title *First the Egg*, by Laura Vaccaro Seeger, won a Caldecott Honor Medal and a Theodor Seuss Geisel Honor in 2008. Their title *Dog and Bear: Two Friends, Three Stories*, also by Laura Vaccaro Seeger, won the Boston Globe-Horn Book Picture Book Award in 2007.

Fiction Picture books, young readers, middle readers, young adults: adventure, animal, contemporary, fantasy, history, humor, multicultural, nature/environment, poetry, religion, science fiction, sports, suspense/mystery. Recently published *Dog and Bear*, by Laura Vaccaro Seeger; *Candyfloss*, by Jacqueline Wilson.

Nonfiction Picture books, young readers, middle readers, young adults: adventure, animal, contemporary, fantasy, history, humor, multicultural, nature/environment, poetry, religion, science fiction, sports, suspense/mystery.

How to Contact/Writers Primarily interested in agented material. Not accepting unsolicited mss or queries. Will consider simultaneous agented submissions.

Illustration Primarily interested in agented material. Works with 25 illustrators/year. Illustrations only: Query with samples. Do not send original art; copies only through the mail. Samples returned with SASE.

Photography Works on assignment only.

Terms Pays authors royalty based on retail price. Pays illustrators royalty or flat fee depending on project. Sends galleys to authors; dummies to illustrators, if requested.

Tips ''You should find a reputable agent and have him/her submit your work.''

SALINA BOOKSHELF, INC.

3120 N. Canden Court, Suite 4, Flagstaff, AZ 86004. (877)527-0070. Fax: (928)526-0386. E-mail: tmcconnell@sal inabookshelf.com. Web site: www.salinabookshelf.com. **Manuscript Acquisitions:** Tayloe McConnell. **Art Acquisitions:** Bahe Whitethorne, Jr. Publishes 10 picture books/year; 4 young readers/year; 1 young adult title/year. 50% of books are by first-time authors.

Fiction Picture books, young readers, middle readers, young adults: adventure, animal, contemporary, folktales, multicultural.

Nonfiction Picture books: multicultural. Young readers, middle readers, young adults: biography, history, multicultural.

How to Contact/Writers Fiction/nonfiction: Query or submit complete ms. Responds to queries in 1 month; mss in 2 months. Publishes a book 1 year after acceptance. Will consider simultaneous submissions and previously published work.

Illustration Works with 8 illustrators/year. Reviews ms/illustration packages from artists. Query. Illustrations only: Query with samples. Responds in 1 month. Samples returned with SASE; samples filed.

Photography Buys stock and assigns work.

Terms Pays authors royalty based on retail price. Offers advances (average amount varies). Pays illustrators and photographers by the project. Originals returned to artist at job's completion. Catalog available for SASE or on Web site; ms guidelines available for SASE.

Tips ''Please note that all our books are Navajo-oriented.''

⚑ SCHOLASTIC INC.

557 Broadway, New York NY 10012. (212)343-6100. Web site: www.scholastic.com. Arthur A. Levine Books, Cartwheel Books®, The Chicken House®, Graphix™, Little Scholastic™, Little Shepherd™, Michael di Capua Books, Orchard Books®, PUSH, Scholastic en español, Scholastic Licensed Publishing, Scholastic Nonfiction, Scholastic Paperbacks, Shcolastic Press, Scholastic Reference™, Tangerine Press®, and The Blue Sku Press® are imprints of Scholastic Trade Books Division. In addition, Scholastic Trade Books included Klutz®, a highly innovative publisher and creator of ''books plus'' for children.

• Scholastic title *The Invention of Hugo Cabret*, by Brian Selznick, won the Caldecott Medal in 2008.

SCHOLASTIC LIBRARY PUBLISHING

90 Old Sherman Turnpike, Danbury CT 06816. (203)797-3500. Book publisher. Vice President/Publisher: Phil Friedman. **Manuscript Acquisitions:** Kate Nunn, editor-in-chief. **Art Acquisitions:** Marie O'Neil, art director. Imprints: Grolier, Children's Press, Franklin Watts. Publishes more than 400 titles/year. 5% of books by first-time authors; very few titles from agented authors. Publishes informational (nonfiction) for K-12; picture books for young readers, grades 1-3.

Fiction Publishes 1 picture book series, Rookie Readers, for grades 1-2. Does not accept unsolicited mss.

Nonfiction Photo-illustrated books for all levels: animal, arts/crafts, biography, careers, concept, geography, health, history, hobbies, how-to, multicultural, nature/environment, science, social issues, special needs, sports. Average word length: young readers—2,000; middle readers—8,000; young adult—15,000.

How to Contact/Writers Fiction: Does not accept fiction proposals. Nonfiction: Query; submit outline/synopsis, résumé and/or list of publications, and writing sample. SASE required for response. Responds in 3 months. Will consider simultaneous submissions. No phone or e-mail queries; will not respond to phone inquiries about submitted material.

Illustration Works with 15-20 illustrators/year. Uses color artwork and line drawings. Illustrations only: Query with samples or arrange personal portfolio review. Responds only if interested. Samples returned with SASE. Samples filed. Do not send originals. No phone or e-mail inquiries; contact only by mail.

Photography Contact: Caroline Anderson, photo manager. Buys stock and assigns work. Model/property releases and captions required. Uses color and b&w prints; $2^1/_4 \times 2^1/_4$, 35mm transparencies, images on CD-ROM.

Terms Pays authors royalty based on net or work purchased outright. Pays illustrators at competitive rates. Photographers paid per photo. Sends galleys to authors; dummies to illustrators.

⚑ SCHOLASTIC PRESS

557 Broadway, New York NY 10012. (212)343-6100. Web site: www.scholastic.com. **Manuscript Acquisitions:** David Levithan, editorial director; Dianne Hess, executive editor (picture book fiction/nonfiction, 2nd-3rd grade chapter books, some middle grade fantasy that is based on reality); Tracy Mack, executive editor (picture book, middle grade, YA); Kara LaRue, executive editor (picture books, fiction/nonfiction, middle grade); Rachel Griffiths, editor: Jennifer Rees, associate editor (picture book fiction/nonfiction, middle grade, YA). **Art Acquisitions:** Elizabeth Parisi, art director, Scholastic Press; Marijka Kostiw, art director; David Saylor, creative director, all hardcover imprints for Scholastic. Publishes 60 titles/year. 1% of books by first-time authors.

- Scholastic Press title *Elijah of Buxton*, by Christopher Paul Curtis, won a Newbery Honor Medal and the Coretta Scott King Author Award in 2008. Their title *Henry's Freedom Box: A True Story from the Underground Railroad*, by Ellen Levine, illustrated by Kadir Nelson, won a Caldecott Honor Medal in 2008.

Fiction Looking for strong picture books, young chapter books, appealing middle grade novels (ages 8-11) and interesting and well written young adult novels.

Nonfiction Interested in "unusual, interesting, and very appealing approaches to biography, math, history and science."

How to Contact/Writers Fiction/nonfiction: "Send query with 1 sample chapter and synopsis. Don't call! Don't e-mail!" Picture books: submission accepted from agents or previously published authors only.

Illustrations Works with 30 illustrators/year. Uses both b&w and color artwork. Illustrations only: Query with samples; send tearsheets. Responds only if interested. Samples returned with SASE. Original artwork returned at job's completion.

Terms Pays advance against royalty.

Tips "Read *currently* published children's books. Revise, rewrite, rework and find your own voice, style and subject. We are looking for authors with a strong and unique voice who can tell a great story and have the ability to evoke genuine emotion. Children's publishers are becoming more selective, looking for irresistible talent and fairly broad appeal, yet still very willing to take risks, just to keep the game interesting."

SEEDLING PUBLICATIONS

520 E. Bainbridge St., Elizabethtown PA 17022. Web site: www.SeedlingPub.com. **Acquisitions:** Josie Stewart. 20% of books by first-time authors. Publishes books for classroom use only for the beginning reader in English. "Natural language and predictable text are requisite. Patterned text is acceptable, but must have a unique story line. Poetry, books in rhyme and full-length picture books are not being accepted. Illustrations are not necessary."

Fiction Young readers: adventure, animal, folktales, humor, multicultural, nature/environment. Does not accept texts longer than 16 pages or over 150-200 words. Average word length: young readers—100.

Nonfiction Young readers: animal, arts/crafts, biography, careers, concept, multicultural, nature/environment, science. Does not accept texts longer than 16 pages or over 150-200 words. Average word length: young readers—100.

How to Contact/Writers Fiction/nonfiction: Submit complete ms. Responds in 9 months. Publishes a book 1-2 years after acceptance. Will consider simultaneous submissions. Prefers e-mail submissions from authors or illustrators outside the U.S.

Illustration Works with 4-6 illustrators/year. Uses color artwork only. Reviews ms/illustration packages from artists. Submit ms with dummy. Illustrations only: Send color copies. Responds only if interested. Samples returned with SASE only; samples filed if interested.

Photography Buys photos from freelancers. Works on assignment only. Model/property releases required. Uses color prints and 35mm transparencies. Submit cover letter and color promo piece.

Terms Work purchased outright from authors. Pays illustrators and photographers by the project. Original artwork is not returned at job's completion. Catalog available on Web site.

Tips "See our Web site. Follow writers' guidelines carefully and test your story with children and educators."

Book Publishers

Natalie Rompella

*A teacher-turned-author on the
art and science of nonfiction*

Author Natalie Rompella is always on the lookout for ideas. She carries pen and paper with her, keeps a tape recorder in her car, and seems to keep a constant awareness of what's going on in the world around her, paying attention to anything that could spark some writing, whether she's exploring a nature preserve or sitting at the airport during a layover.

Rompella's natural curiosity comes with a love of science and math, and the education to back it up. She has a Masters in Education in Science Education. She's also worked at a nature museum. Her background led her to begin her writing career in the educational market writing science leveled readers. Her interest in the insect world led her to the publication of *Don't Squash That Bug! The Curious Kid's Guide to Insects*, a contract she got after sending Lobster Press a writing sample focused on insects at just the time they were looking to publish a book on the subject.

She followed up *Don't Squash That Bug!* with two books of science fair project ideas, *Science Fair Projects: Ecosystems*, and *Science Fair Projects: Chemistry* (both Heinemann Library) as well as another title with Lobster Press, *Famous Firsts: The Trendsetters, Groundbreakers, and Risk-Takers Who Got America Moving!* Next up is *Obsessive Compulsive Disorder: The Ultimate Teen Guide* (Scarecrow Press).

Below Rompella talks about writing and researching nonfiction and how her teaching experience helps her in her writing career. (She also talks about bugs.) To learn more about her and her books visit www.natalierompella.com (which includes an All About Insects section with fun bug-related links and book lists).

How did your first publication come about?

A friend was attending a workshop on writing for the educational market. At the time, I was more interested in writing picture books, but I decided to go to the workshop with her. It was a wonderful workshop; I ended up doing some writing samples and sending them to various educational developing houses. A company called me to write leveled readers for them—I ended up writing eight for them.

How does your experience as a teacher inform your writing? Do you write books you wish you had in your classroom? Do students' interests give you ideas?

I definitely think being a teacher has helped my writing. I do think about what kids would like to read about when I write, as well as about how different kids like different things. With my insect book, I felt that there would be some kids out there who would focus on the photos or fun facts and others who would enjoy learning the fancy order name of the insects.

Not only do I get ideas from students' interests, but also from some of the phrases that they say and the experiences they face. When I taught sixth grade in a middle school, I learned what a traumatic experience that first day is for many students because they weren't used to using lockers, switching classes, and having different teachers for different subjects. They had no idea what to expect, and it showed. I am presently working on some other manuscripts in which I try to capture that first-day-of-school moment.

Are there topics you think aren't covered enough when it comes to nonfiction books for young readers?

It's always surprising what topics there are books on. The problem is that often they aren't written in a way that's interesting to the reader. There also aren't always books on those topics that are written for a particular age level; they are often too high or too low in difficulty or in age appeal. This was often an issue for my students when I taught fifth grade.

How do you know so much about bugs? Do you have any favorites? Do your readers have any favorites?

I first became interested in insects after I saw a *National Geographic* magazine cover featuring insects. Before that, I hadn't ever noticed how insects looked like tiny works of art. I also love how there is such a wide variety of colors and sizes. My favorites are praying mantids, tree hoppers, true bugs, and weevils. And of course, summer wouldn't be the same without the sound of cicadas. My readers have favorites, too. Butterflies always

Lobster Press published Natalie Rompella's *Don't Squash That Bug!* after the author sent them writing samples. Rompella learned a lot about insects—like cockroaches, walking sticks, and giant millipedes—when she worked at a nature museum.

come out on top, as well as praying mantids. I have yet to meet someone whose favorite is a cockroach or a termite. (Although I have a pet Madagascar hissing cockroach.)

Can you offer some tips on doing research for nonfiction projects? What kinds of sources do you use? How do you keep things organized?

I suggest figuring out a system of organization before you begin your research. I sometimes write notes on notecards and write a key word for that card. That way I can sort them later by the key word. It's important to cite the title of the source, the author's name, the page number, and other bibliographic information.

I use a variety of sources: books, journals, magazines, newsletters, and reliable Internet sources. My favorite source to use, however, is an interview. I can get most any question answered and get firsthand information. This was especially helpful when I wrote my book on American famous firsts, because much of the information wasn't found in other sources. Besides, it was exciting to speak to the inventors, and I could be assured the information was accurate, since it was coming from a primary source. I had the privilege of speaking with George Nissen, the inventor of what would become the trampoline; the real surfing Gidget; and Bob Haro, a pioneer of BMX freestyle, to name a few.

You got to help your editor pick the photos used for *Don't Squash That Bug!*. Was this surprising? Tell me about the editorial process for that book.

It can be unusual to be asked to help with choosing an illustrator, but for *Don't Squash That Bug!*, I was given many photos to look through that the publisher sorted and re-searched, and then I decided which ones I thought would work in the book. Some of the photos were of bugs that weren't discussed in the text. These gave us the opportunity to have even more information, so then I came up with fun facts to use as the captions for those pictures. I believe it was actually harder to write the captions than the main text!

You consulted with an entomologist when writing the captions for *Don't Squash That Bug!* Any advice on how to find and how to approach experts?

I had met the entomologist years earlier when I was working at a nature museum in Chicago (he was a guest speaker). I had kept his business card because I had been working on a different insect book and had a question for him.

For *Famous Firsts*, I had to contact a lot of people. I would recommend finding the e-mail addresses or phone numbers for experts by contacting specialty magazines and organizations. It's surprising that almost any topic has a magazine and organization dedi-cated to it. For instance, to find someone to answer my skateboarding questions, I con-tacted various skateboard magazines, whose staff members then gave me the names of skateboard friends of theirs who are authorities on the subject. I found many helpful people this way, and, if someone didn't have an answer for me, he or she gave me the name of someone who did. This was also how I found the contact information for some of the originators of the activities.

You are a network rep for the SCBWI IL chapter. What's involved in that volunteer position? How has your involvement in SCBWI been beneficial?

I love helping out with SCBWI. Currently, I run a monthly meeting in the northwestern Chicago suburbs. Group members bring a manuscript they want feedback on. This is also a chance to talk about industry news and celebrate personal good news. I also try to help with larger events, such as the annual Illinois Prairie Writer's Day in November.

I believe my successes are directly a result of being involved in SCBWI. All my published works come from attending SCBWI events or networking with SCBWI members (I either heard about the company looking for certain topics or was given the company's name at an event). It is definitely a support group—I've never felt a sense of competition between children book writers. I also can't think of one event I've attended from which I didn't learn something new.

Tell me about your books on science fair ideas and what you do as a science fair consultant.

The two books I have on science fairs help children set up science fair projects. The books give suggestions for fun experiments that follow the scientific method. These ideas can be jumping-off points or can be followed very similarly. One book focuses on chemistry projects, while the other focuses on ecosystem projects.

As a science fair consultant, I can help students create an organized project. Schools require a science fair project have a certain formula they want students to follow. Some students feel overwhelmed by putting it together, or they spend too much time on the backboard. My job is to help them stay focused on the meat of the project while learning and having fun.

When I checked your Web site, your "For Writers" page on was not yet populated. What will you be offering writers who visit natalierompella.com?

I've just finished it. It is for writers (mainly adults) who are just getting started in writing for children. I have lists of great books for new writers, tons of helpful Web sites, and the names of books I think are well written. I also include a link to my blog, where I give writing exercises.

As a teacher I would imagine it's fairly easy for you to do book-related presentations for groups of young readers. Can you offer any tips on doing effective school visits?

I still get a little nervous doing presentations, even though I stand up in front of children daily as a teacher. What did help me is remembering that the children are just excited to see an author and are so much less judgmental than adults. They like hearing the behind-the scenes information about a book coming together. I try to have lots of things for the students to look at, and I get them involved as much as I can, such as by letting them wear feathery antennae or sharing how they would change a boring passage to "jazz it up."

What is your advice to unpublished writers interested in nonfiction books for young readers?

Start with a subject you are familiar with. Include more than the obvious facts. Chances are, if children are choosing the book to read, they already know a lot about that subject; they are wanting to know the nitty-gritty or crazy facts, so go the extra mile to find those facts. Read through published nonfiction books and find ones you like—figure out what you like about them. Nowadays, nonfiction books for kids have something quirky about them instead of just spitting out facts. Think about what will make your book special.

—Alice Pope

SHEN'S BOOKS

40951 Fremont Blvd., Fremont CA 94538. (510)668-1898. Fax: (510)668-1057. E-mail: info@shens.com. Web site: www.shens.com. Estab. 1986. Specializes in multicultural material. **Acquisitions:** Renee Ting, president. Produces 2 picture books/year. 50% of books by first-time authors.

Fiction Picture books, young readers: folktales, multicultural. Middle readers: multicultural. Recently published *The Wishing Tree*, by Roseanne Thong, illustrated by Connie McLennan (ages 4-8); *The Magical Monkey King*, by Ji-li Jiang (ages 7-10, chapter book); *Many Ideas Open the Way*, by Randy Snook (picture books of proverbs).

Nonfiction Picture books, young readers: multicultural. Recently published *Land of Morning Calm*, by John Stickler, illustrated by Soma Han (ages 7-12, picture book).

How to Contact/Writers Accepts international submissions. Fiction/nonfiction: Submit complete ms. Responds to queries in 1-2 weeks; mss in 6-12 months. Publishes book 1 year after acceptance. Considers simultaneous submissions.

Illustration Accepts material from international illustrators. Works with 2 illustrators/year. Uses color artwork only. Reviews ms/illustration packages. For ms/illustration packages: Send ms with dummy. Submit ms/illustration packages to Renee Ting, president. Reviews work for future assignments. If interested in illustrating future titles, query with samples. Submit samples to Renee Ting, president. Samples not returned. Samples filed.

Photography Works on assignment only. Submit photos to Renee Ting, president.

Terms Authors pay negotiated by the project. Pays illustrators by the project. Pays photographers by the project. Illustrators see dummies for review. Catalog on Web site.

Tips ''Be familiar with our catalog before submitting.''

SILVER MOON PRESS

381 Park Avenue South, Suite 1121,New York NY 10010. (212)802-2890. Fax: (212)802-2893. E-mail: mail@silvermoonpress.com. Web site: www.silvermoonpress.com. **Publisher:** David Katz. **Marketing Coordinator:** Karin Lillebo. Book publisher. Publishes 1-2 books for grades 4-6/year. 25% of books by first-time authors; 10% books from agented authors. Publishes mainly American historical fiction and books of educational value. Develops books which fit neatly into curriculum for grades 4-6. ''History comes alive when children can read about other children who lived when history was being made!''

Fiction Middle readers: historical, multicultural and mystery. Average word length: 14,000. Recently published *Liberty on 23rd Street*, by Jacqueline Glasthal; *A Silent Witness in Harlem*, by Eve Creary; *In the Hands of the Enemy*, by Robert Sheely; *Ambush in the Wilderness*, by Kris Hemphill; *Race to Kitty Hawk*, by Edwina Raffa and Annelle Rigsby; *Brothers of the Falls*, by Joanna Emery.

How to Contact/Writers Fiction: Query. Send synopsis and/or a few chapters, along with SASE. Responds to queries in 2 months; mss in 3 months. Publishes a book 1-2 years after acceptance. Will consider simultaneous submission or previously published work.

Illustration Works with 1-2 illustrators/year. Reviews ms/illustration packages from artists. Query. Illustrations only: Query with samples, résumé, client list. Responds only if interested. Samples returned with SASE; samples filed. Original artwork returned at job's completion.

Photography Buys photos from freelancers. Buys stock and assigns work. Uses archival, historical, sports photos. Captions required. Uses color, b&w prints; 35mm, $2\frac{1}{4} \times 2\frac{1}{4}$, 4×5, 8×10 transparencies. Submit cover letter, résumé, published samples, client list, promo piece.

Terms Pays authors royalty or work purchased outright. Pays illustrators by the project, no royalty. Pays photographers by the project, per photo, no royalty. Sends galleys to authors; dummies to illustrators. Book catalog available for $8\frac{1}{2} \times 11$ SAE and $1.11 postage.

Tips ''We do not accept biographies, poetry, or romance. We do not accept fantasy, science fiction, or historical fiction with elements of either. No picture books. Submissions that fit into New York State curriculum topics such as the Revolutionary War, Colonial times, and New York State history in general stand a greater chance of acceptance than those that do not.''

SIMON & SCHUSTER BOOKS FOR YOUNG READERS

1230 Avenue of the Americas, New York NY 10020. (212)698-7000. Fax: (212)698-2796. Web site: www.simonsayskids.com. **Manuscript Acquisitions:** Justin Chanda, associate publisher; David Gale, vice president, editorial director; Kevin Lewis, executive editor; Paula Wiseman, vice president, editorial director, Paula Wiseman Books. **Art Acquisitions:** Dan Potash, vice president, creative director. Publishes 95 books/year. ''We publish high-quality fiction and nonfiction for a variety of age groups and a variety of markets. Above all we strive to publish books that will offer kids a fresh perspective on their world.''

- Simon & Schuster Books for Young Readers does not accept unsolicited manuscripts. Queries are accepted via mail. Their title *Wolves*, by Emily Gravett, won a Boston Globe-Horn Book Picture Book Honor Award in 2007.

Fiction Picture books: animal, minimal text/very young readers. Middle readers, young adult: fantasy, adventure, suspense/mystery. All levels: contemporary, history, humor. Recently published *Orange Pear Apple Bear*, written and illustrated by Emily Gravett (picture book, ages 1-4); *Huge*, by Sasha Paley (young adult fiction, agest 13 and up).

Nonfiction Picture books: concept. All levels: narrative, current events, biography, history. "We're looking for picture book or middle grade nonfiction that have a retail potential. No photo essays." Recently published Insiders Series (picture book nonfiction, all ages).

How to Contact/Writers Accepting query letters only; please note the appropriate editor. Responds to queries/mss in 3-4 months. Publishes a book 2 years after acceptance. Will not consider simultaneous submissions.

Illustration Works with 70 illustrators/year. Do not submit original artwork. Editorial reviews ms/illustration packages from artists. Submit query letter to Submissions Editor. Illustrations only: Query with samples; samples filed. Provide promo sheet, tearsheets. Responds only if interested.

Terms Pays authors royalty (varies) based on retail price. Pays illustrators or photographers by the project or royalty (varies) based on retail price. Original artwork returned at job's completion. Manuscript/artist's guidelines available via Web site or free on request. Call (212)698-2707.

Tips "We're looking for picture books centered on a strong, fully-developed protagonist who grows or changes during the course of the story; YA novels that are challenging and psychologically complex; also imaginative and humorous middle-grade fiction. And we want nonfiction that is as engaging as fiction. Our imprint's slogan is 'Reading You'll Remember.' We aim to publish books that are fresh, accessible and family-oriented; we want them to have an impact on the reader."

Ⓐ SLEEPING BEAR PRESS

Imprint of Gale Group, 310 N. Main St., Suite 300, Chelsea MI 48118. (734)475-4411. Fax: (734)475-0787. Web site: www.sleepingbearpress.com. **Manuscript Acquisitions:** Heather Hughes. **Art Acquisitions:** Jennifer Bacheller, creative director. Publishes 30 picture books/year. 10% of books by first-time authors.

Fiction Picture books: adventure, animal, concept, folktales, history, multicultural, nature/environment, religion, sports. Young readers: adventure, animal, concept, folktales, history, humor, multicultural, nature/environment, religion, sports. Average word length: picture books—1,800. Recently published *Brewster the Rooster*, by Devin Scillian; *The Orange Shoes*, by Trinka Hakes Noble; *Yatandou*, by Gloria Whelan.

Nonfiction Average word length: picture books—1,800. Recently published *D is for Drinking Gourd: An African American Alphabet*, by E.B. Lewis.

How to Contact/Writers Fiction/nonfiction: Submit complete ms or proposal. "We do not return materials, so please only submit copies. SBP will contact you if interested." Publishes book 2 years after acceptance. Will consider e-mail submissions, simultaneous submissions.

Illustration Works with 30 illustrators/year. Uses color artwork only. Reviews ms/illustration packages from artists. Send ms with dummy. Illustrations only: "Send samples for our files. We will contact you if interested."

Terms Pays authors royalty. Offers advances. Pays illustrators royalty. Sends galleys to authors. Originals returned to artist at job's completion. Book catalog available. All imprints included in a single catalog. Catalog available on Web site.

Tips "Please review our book on line before sending material or calling." Editorial staff attended or plans to attend the following conferences: BEA, IRA, Regional shows, UMBE, NEBA, AASL, ALA, and numerous local conferences.

SMALLFELLOW PRESS

Imprint of Tallfellow Press, 9454 Wilshire BLVD., Suite 550, Beverly Hills, CA 90212. E-mail: tallfellow@pacbell.net. Web site: www.smallfellow.com. **Manuscript/Art Acquisitions:** Claudia Sloan.

• Smallfellow no longer accepts manuscript/art submissions.

STANDARD PUBLISHING

8805 Governor's Hill Drive, Suite 400, Cincinnati OH 45249. Web site: www.standardpub.com. Publishes resources that meet the church's needs in the area of children's ministry. Visit the publisher's Web site for writer's guidelines and current publishing objectives.

STARSEED PRESS

Imprint of HJ Kramer in joint venture with New World Library, P.O. Box 1082, Tiburon CA 94920. (415)435-5367. Fax: (415)435-5364. Web site: www.newworldlibrary.com. **Manuscript Acquisitions:** Jan Phillips. **Art Acquisitions:** Linda Kramer, vice president. Publishes 2 picture books/year. 50% of books by first-time authors. "We publish 4-color, 32-page children's picture books dealing with self-esteem and positive values, with a non-denominational, spiritual emphasis."

Fiction Picture books: self-esteem, multicultural, nature/environment. Average word length: picture books—

500-1,500. Recently published *Lucky Goose Goes to Texas*, by Holly Bea, illustrated by Joe Boddy (ages 3-10, picture book).

Nonfiction Picture books: multicultural, nature/environment.

How to Contact/Writers Fiction/nonfiction: Submit outline/synopsis. Responds to queries/mss in 10 weeks. Publishes a book 18 months after acceptance. Will consider simultaneous submissions, previously published work.

Illustration Works with 2 illustrators/year. Uses color artwork only. Illustrations only: Query with samples. Responds only if interested. Samples returned with SASE; samples filed.

Terms Negotiates based on publisher's net receipts. Split between author and artist. Originals returned to artist at job's completion. Book catalog available for 9×11 SAE with $1.98 postage; ms and art guidelines available for SASE. All imprints included in a single catalog.

STERLING PUBLISHING CO., INC.

387 Park Ave. S., 10th Floor, New York NY 10016-8810. (212)532-7160. Fax: (212)981-0508. E-mail: info@sterlingweb.com. Web site: www.sterlingpublishing.com. **Manuscript Acquisitions:** Frances Gilbert. **Art Acquisitions:** Karen Nelson, creative director. Publishes 10 picture books/year; 50 young readers/year; 50 middle readers/year; 10 young adult titles/year. 15% of books by first-time authors.

- See First Books on page 133 for an interview with Susan Collins Thoms, author of Sterling title *Cesar Takes a Break*.

Fiction Picture books.

Nonfiction Young readers: activity books, arts/crafts, cooking, hobbies, how-to, science. Middle readers, young adults: activity books, arts/crafts, hobbies, how-to, science, mazes, optical illusions, games, magic, math, puzzles.

How to Contact/Writers Nonfiction: Submit outline/synopsis, 1 sample chapter and SASE. Responds to queries/mss in 6 weeks. Publishes book 1 year after acceptance. Will consider simultaneous submissions, previously published work.

Illustration Works with 50 illustrators/year. Reviews ms/illustration packages from artists. Illustrations only: Send promo sheet. Contact: Karen Nelson, creative director. Responds in 6 weeks. Samples returned with SASE; samples filed.

Photography Buys stock and assigns work. Contact: Karen Nelson.

Terms Pays authors royalty or work purchased outright from authors. Offers advances (average amount: $2,000). Pays illustrators by the project. Pays photographers by the project or per photo. Sends galleys to authors; dummies to illustrators. Originals returned to artist at job's completion. Offers writer's guidelines for SASE. Catalog available on Web site.

Tips "We are primarily a nonfiction activities-based publisher. We have a small picture book list, but we do not publish chapter books or novels. Our list is not trend-driven. We focus on titles that will backlist well."

STONE ARCH BOOKS

7825 Telegraph Rd., Minneapolis MN 55438. (952)224-0514. Fax: (952)933-2410. Web site: www.stonearchbooks.com. **Acquisitions Editor:** Michael Dahl. **Art Director:** Heather Kindseth. Specializes in "high-interest, engaging fiction for struggling and reluctant readers, especially boys."

Fiction Young Readers, middle readers, young adults: adventure, contemporary, fantasy, hi-lo, humor, multicultural, science fiction, sports, suspense. Average word length: young readers—2,000; middle readers—5,000; young adults—7,000-10,000.

How to Contact/Writers Submit outline/synopsis and 3 sample chapters. Responds to mss in 8 weeks. Publishes a book 6-12 months after acceptance. Accepts e-mail submissions and simultaneous submissions.

Illustration Works with 35 illustrators/year. Used both color and b&w. Send manuscript with dummy. Contact: Heather Kindseth, art directorn. Samples not returned; samples filed.

Terms Work purchased outright from authors. Illustrators paid by the project. Book catalog available on Web site.

Tips "A 'high-interest' topic or activity is one that a young person would spend their free time on without adult direction or suggestion."

SYLVAN DELL PUBLISHING

Estab. 2004. E-mail: donnagerman@sylvandellpublishing.com. Web site: www.sylvandellpublishing.com. **Contact:** Donna German." The books that we publish are usually, but not always, fictional stories that relate to animals, nature, the environment, and science. All books should subtly convey an educational theme through a warm story that is fun to read and that will grab a children's attention. Each book has a 3-5 page "For Creative Minds" section in the back to reinforce the educational component of the book itself. This section will have a craft and/or game as well as "fun facts" to be shared by the parent, teacher, or other adult. Authors do not need to supply this information but may be actively involved in its development if they would like. Please read about our submission guidelines on our Web site.''

• Sylvan Dell only accepts electronic submissions.

Fiction Picture Books: animal, folktales, nature/environment. Word length—picture books: no more than 1500. Spring titles include: *In Arctic Waters* by Laura Crawford, illustrated by Ben Hodson; *ABC Safari*, written (first authored book) and illustrated by Karen Lee; *The Rainforest Grew All Around*, written by first-time author Susan K. Mitchell, illustrated by Connie McLennan; *Turtle Summer: A Journal for my Daughter*, written by NY Times bestselling adult novelist Mary Alice Monroe, photographs by Barbara Bergwerf; *Ocean Seasons*, by Ron Hirschi, illustrated by Kirsten Carlson; and *In My Backyard*, by first-time author Valarie Giogas, illustrated by Katherine Zecca.

How to Contact/ Writers Submit complete ms. Prefers to work with authors from the US and Canada because of marketing. Responds to mss in 3-4 months. Publishes a book about 2 years after acceptance. Accepts simultaneous submissions. Accepts electronic submissions only.

Illustration Works with 10 illustrators/year. Prefers to work with illustrators from the US and Canada. Uses color artwork only. Reviews ms/illustration packages from illustrators. Submit manuscript with 1-2 pieces of final art. Contact: Donna German. Illustrations only: submit Web link or 2-3 electronic images. Contact: Donna German. ''I generally keep submissions on file until I match the manuscripts to illustration needs.''

Terms Pays authors and illustrators step-up royalty of 7.5% based on wholesale price. Offers $1,000 advance. ''Authors and illustrators see PDFs of book as it goes to the printer. Any concerns or changes are dealt with then. We keep cover art and return all other art to illustrators.'' Catalog available on Web site. Writer's and artist's guidelines available on Web site.

Tips ''Please make sure that you have looked at our Web site to see what we publish and read our complete submission guidelines. Manuscripts must meet all four of our stated criteria. We are currently looking for manuscripts about the Rocky Mt. area (animals, etc.) We look for fairly realistic, bright and colorful art—no cartoons.''

TANGLEWOOD BOOKS

P.O. Box 3009, Terre Haute IN 47803. E-mail: ptierney@tanglewoodbooks.com. Web site: www.tanglewoodbooks.com. Estab. 2003. Specializes in trade books. **Writers contact:** Peggy Tierney, publisher. **Illustrators contact:** Peggy Tierney, publisher. Produces 2-3 picture books/year, 1-2 middle readers/year, 1-2 young adult titles/year. 20% of books by first-time authors. ''Tanglewood Press strives to publishh entertaining, kid-centric books.''
Fiction Picture books: adventure, animal, concept, contemporary, fantasy, humor. Average word length: picture books—800. Recently published *Mystery at Blackbeard's Cove*, by Audrey Penn, illustrated by Josh Miller and Phillip Howard (ages 8-12, adventure); *The Mice of Bistrot des Sept Freres*, written and illustrated by Marie Letourneau; *You Can't Milk a Dancing Cow*, by Tom Dunsmuir, illustrated by Brain Jones (ages 4-8, humorous).
How to Contact/Writers Accepts international submissions. Fiction: Query with 3-5 sample chapters. Responds to mss in 6-9 months. Publishes book 2 years after acceptance. Considers simultaneous submissions.
Illustration Accepts material from international illustrators. Works with 3-4 illustrators/year. Uses both color and b&w. Reviews ms/illustration packages. For ms/illustration packages: Send ms with sample illustrations. Submit ms/illustration packages to Peggy Tierney, publisher. If interested in illustrating future titles, query with samples. Submit samples to Peggy Tierney, publisher. Samples returned with SASE. Samples filed.
Terms Illustrators paid by the project for covers and small illustrations; royalty of 3-5% for picture books. Author sees galleys for review. Illustrators see dummies for review. Originals returned to artist at job's completion.
Tips ''Please see lengthy 'Submissions' page on our Web site.''

TILBURY HOUSE, PUBLISHERS

2 Mechanic St., #3, Gardiner ME 04345. (207)582-1899. Fax: (207)582-8227. E-mail: karen@tilburyhouse.com. Web site: www.tilburyhouse.com. **Publisher:** Jennifer Bunting. **Children's Book Editor:** Audrey Maynard. **Associate Children's Book Editor:** Karen Fisk. Publishes 1-3 young readers/year.
Fiction Picture books, young readers, middle readers: multicultural, nature/environment. Special needs include books that teach children about tolerance and honoring diversity. Recently published *Our Friendship Rules*, by Peggy Moss and Dee Dee Tardif; *Opening Day*, by Susan Bartlett; *Keep Your Ear on the Ball*, by Genevieve Petrillo.
Nonfiction Picture books, young readers, middle readers: multicultural, nature/environment. Recently published *Just for Elephants*, by Carol Buckley; *Life Under Ice*, by Mary Cerullo, with photography by Bill Curtsinger.
How to Contact/Writers Fiction/nonfiction: Submit complete ms or outline/synopsis. Responds to queries/mss in 1 month. Publishes a book 1-2 years after acceptance. Will consider simultaneous submissions ''with notification.''
Illustration Works with 2-3 illustrators/year. Illustrations only: Query with samples. Responds in 1 month. Samples returned with SASE. Original artwork returned at job's completion.

Photography Buys photos from freelancers. Works on assignment only.

Terms Pays authors royalty based on wholesale price. Pays illustrators/photographers by the project; royalty based on wholesale price. Sends galleys to authors. Book catalog available for SAE and postage.

Tips "We are always interested in stories that will encourage children to understand the natural world and the environment, as well as stories with social justice themes. We really like stories that engage children to become problem solvers as well as those that promote respect, tolerance and compassion." We do not publish books with personified animal characters; historical fiction; chapter books; fantasy.

Ⓐ MEGAN TINGLEY BOOKS

Imprint of Little, Brown Books for Young Readers, Hachette Book Group USA, 237 Park Ave, New York NY 10017. (212)364-1100. Fax: (212)364-0925. Web sites: www.lb-kids.com; www.lb-teens.com.
- See listing for Little, Brown Books for Young Readers.

TOKYOPOP INC.

5900 Wilshire Blvd., Los Angeles CA 90036. (323)692-6700. Fax: (323)692-6701. Web site: www.tokyopop.com. Estab. 1996. Specializes in trade books, fiction, multicultural material. **Submissions:** Rob Tokar, editor-in-chief. Produces 75 picture books/year; 6 young readers/year; 6 young adult books/year. 25% of books by first-time authors. "We are the leading Asian popculture-influenced publisher in the world. Our product lines include manga, cine-manga™, young adult novels, chapter books, and merchandise."

Fiction Young readers: adventure, contemporary, humor, science fiction, suspense. Middle readers: adventure, contemporary, fantasy, humor, problem novels, science fiction. Young adults/teens: adventure, contemporary, fantasy, humor, problem novels, science fiction, suspense. Average word length: young readers—9,000; middle readers—9,000; young adult—50,000.

Nonfiction Middle readers, young adult/teens: activity books, arts/crafts, hobbies.

How to Contact/Writers Accepts international submissions. Fiction: Submit outline/synopsis and 2 sample chapters. Responds to queries/mss in 6 months. Publishes book 18 months after acceptance.

Illustration Accepts material from international illustrators. Works with 25 illustrators/year. Uses primarily b&w artwork. Reviews ms/illustration packages. Submit ms/illustration packages to Rob Tokar, editor-in-chief. Reviews work for future assignments. If interested in illustrating future titles, query with samples. Submit samples to Rob Tokar, editor-in-chief. Responds in 3 months. Samples not returned.

Terms Pays authors royalty of 8% based on retail price. Pays illustrators by the project (range: $500-5,000). Author sees galleys for review. Illustrators see dummies for review. Originals not returned. Catalog on Web site. See Web site for artist's guidelines.

Tips "Submit cool, innovative, offbeat, cutting-edge material that captures the essence of teen pop culture."

TOR BOOKS

175 Fifth Ave., New York NY 10010-7703. Fax: (212)388-0191. E-mail: Juliet.Pederson@Tor.com. Web site: www.tor-forge.com. **Contact:** Juliet Pederson, assistant to publisher, children's/YA division. Publisher: Kathleen Doherty; Senior Editor: Susan Chang. Imprints: Forge, Orb, Starscape, Tor Teen. Publishes 5-10 middle readers/year; 5-10 young adult titles/year.
- Tor Books is the "world's largest publisher of science fiction and fantasy, with strong category publishing in historical fiction, mystery, western/Americana, thriller, YA."

Fiction Middle readers, young adult titles: adventure, animal, anthology, concept, contemporary, fantasy, history, humor, multicultural, nature/environment, problem novel, science fiction, suspense/mystery. Average word length: middle readers—30,000; young adults—60,000-100,000. Published *Hidden Talents, Flip*, by David Lubar (ages 10 and up, fantasy); *Briar Rose*, by Jane Yolen (ages 12 and up).

Nonfiction Middle readers and young adult: geography, history, how-to, multicultural, nature/environment, science, social issues. Does not want to see religion, cooking. Average word length: middle readers—25,000-35,000; young adults—70,000. Published *Strange Unsolved Mysteries*, by Phyllis Rabin Emert; *Stargazer's Guide (to the Galaxy)*, by Q.L. Pearce (ages 8-12, guide to constellations, illustrated).

How to Contact/Writers Fiction/nonfiction: Submit outline/synopsis and complete ms. Responds to queries in 1 month; mss in 6 months for unsolicited work; 1 month or less for agented submissions. Note: We do not accept electronic submissions, synopsis or querys of any kind. Do not email your inquiries.

Illustration Query with samples. Contact: Irene Gallo, art director. Responds only if interested. Samples kept on file.

Terms Pays authors royalty. Offers advances. Pays illustrators by the project. Book catalog available for 9 × 12 SAE and 3 first-class stamps. See website, www.tor-forge.com for latest submission guidelines.

Tips "Know the house you are submitting to, familiarize yourself with the types of books they are publishing. Get an agent. Allow him/her to direct you to publishers who are most appropriate. It saves time and effort."

TRICYCLE PRESS

Imprint of Ten Speed Press, P.O. Box 7123, Berkeley CA 94707. (510)559-1600. Web site: www.tricyclepress.com. **Acquisitions:** Nicole Geiger, publisher. Publishes 12-14 picture books/year; 2-4 middle readers/year; 3 board books/year. 25% of books by first-time authors. "Tricycle Press looks for something outside the mainstream; books that encourage children to look at the world from a different angle. Tricycle Press, like its parent company, Ten Speed Press, is known for its quirky, offbeat books. We publish high-quality trade books."

Fiction Board books, picture books, young readers: concept. Middle grade: literary fiction, high-quality contemporary, fantasy, history, multicultural, nature, poetry, suspense/mystery; no mass market fiction. Average word length: picture books—800-1,000. Published *Rough, Touch Charley*, by Verla Kay, illustrated by Adam Gustavson (ages 5-7, picture book); *Hey, Little Ant*, by Phillip and Hannah Hoose, illustrated by Debbie Tiley (ages 4-8, picture book); *Hugging the Rock*, by Susan Taylor Brown (ages 9-12, novel).

Nonfiction Picture books, middle readers: animal, arts/crafts, biography, careers, concept, cooking, history, how-to, multicultural, music/dance, nature/environment, science. Recently published *Will Fibonacci*, by Joy N. Hulme, illustrated by Carol Schwartz (ages 7 and up, picture book); *Salad People and More Real Recipes: A New Cookbook for Preschoolers and Up*, by Mollie Katzen; *Why Explore?*, by Susan Lendroth, illustrated by Enrique S. Moreiro (agest 6 and up, nonfiction picture book).

How to Contact/Writers Submit complete ms for picture books. Submit outline/synopsis and 2-3 sample chapters for middle grade, young adult and longer nonfiction. "No queries!" Responds to mss in 4-6 months. Publishes a book 1-2 years after acceptance. Welcomes simultaneous submissions and previously published work. Do not send original artwork; copies only, please. No electronic or faxed submissions.

Illustration Works with 12 illustrators/year. Uses color and some b&w. Reviews ms/illustration dummies from artists. Submit ms with dummy and/or 2-3 pieces of final art. Illustrations only: Query with samples, promo sheet, tearsheets. Responds only if interested. Samples returned with SASE; samples filed. Original artwork returned at job's completion unless work for hire.

Photography Works on assignment only. Uses 35mm transparencies or high resolution electronic files. Submit samples.

Terms Pays authors royalty of 7.5% based on net receipts. Offers advances. Pays illustrators and photographers royalty of 7.5% based on net receipts. Sends galleys of novels to authors. Book catalog for 9 × 12 SASE (3 first-class stamps). Manuscript guidelines for SASE (1 first-class stamp). Guidelines available at Web site.

Tips "We are looking for something a bit outside the mainstream and with lasting appeal (no one-shot-wonders)."

Ⓐ TROPHY/HARPERTEEN/EOS PAPERBACKS

1350 Avenue of the Americas, New York NY 10019. (212)261-6500. Fax: (212)261-6668. Web sites: www.harpercollins.com, www.harperteen.com, www.harpertrophy.com. Book publisher. Imprint of HarperCollins Children's Books. Publishes 15-20 chapter books/year, 55-60 middle grade titles/year, 15-20 reprint picture books/year, 65-70 teen titles/year.

● Trophy is a chapter book and middle grade imprint. HarperTeen is a teen imprint. Eos is a fantasy/science fiction imprint. In addition to paperback reprints, Eos and HarperTeen also publish a number of hardcover and/or paperback originals each year.

How to Contact/Writers Does not accept unsolicited or unagented mss.

TURTLE BOOKS

866 United Nations Plaza, Suite 525, New York NY 10017. (212)644-2020. Web site: www.turtlebooks.com. **Acquisitions:** John Whitman. "Turtle Books publishes only picture books for young readers. Our goal is to publish a small, select list of quality children's books each spring and fall season. As often as possible, we will publish our books in both English and Spanish editions."

● Turtle Books does a small number of books and may be slow in responding to unsolicited manuscripts.

Fiction Picture books: adventure, animal, concept, contemporary, fantasy, folktales, hi-lo, history, humor, multicultural, nature/environment, religion, sports, suspense/mystery. Recently published *The Legend of Mexicatl*, by Jo Harper, illustrated by Robert Casilla (the story of Mexicatl and the origin of the Mexican people); *Vroom, Chugga, Vroom-Vroom*, by Anne Miranda, illustrated by David Murphy (a number identification book in the form of a race car story); *The Crab Man*, by Patricia VanWest, illustrated by Cedric Lucas (the story of a young Jamaican boy who must make the difficult decision between making an income and the ethical treatment of animals); *Prairie Dog Pioneers*, by Jo and Josephine Harper, illustrated by Craig Spearing (the story of a young girl who doesn't want to move, set in 1870s Texas); *Keeper of the Swamp*, by Ann Garrett, illustrated by Karen Chandler (a dramatic coming-of-age story wherein a boy confronts his fears and learns from his ailing grandfather the secrets of the swamp); *The Lady in the Box*, by Ann McGovern, illustrated by Marni Backer (a modern story about a homeless woman named Dorrie told from the point of view of two children); *Alphabet Fiesta*, by Anne Miranda, illustrated by young schoolchildren in Madrid, Spain (an English/Spanish alphabet story).

How to Contact/Writers Send complete ms. "Queries are a waste of time." Response time varies.

Illustrators Works with 6 illustrators/year. Responds to artist's queries/submissions only if interested. Samples returned with SASE only. Do not send original art!
Terms Pays royalty. Offers advances.

TWO LIVES PUBLISHING

P.O. Box 736, Ridley Park PA 19078. (609)502-8147. Fax: (610)717-1460. E-mail: bcombs@twolives.com. Web site: www.twolives.com. **Manuscript Acquisitions:** Bobbie Combs. Publishes 1 picture book/year; 1 middle reader/year. 100% of books by first-time authors. "We create books for children whose parents are lesbian, gay, bisexual or transgender."
Fiction Picture books, young readers, middle readers: contemporary.
How to Contact/Writers Fiction: Query. Responds to queries/mss in 3 months. Publishes book 2-3 years after acceptance. Will consider e-mail submissions, simultaneous submissions, previously published work.
Illustration Works with 2 illustrators/year. Uses color artwork only. Query ms/illustration packages. Contact: Bobbie Combs, publisher. Illustrations only: Send postcard sample with brochure, photocopies. Contact: Bobbie Combs, publisher. Responds only if interested. Samples filed.
Terms Pays authors royalty of 5-10% based on retail price. Offers advances (average amount: $250). Pays illustrators royalty of 5-10% based on retail price. Sends galleys to authors. Originals returned to artist at job's completion. Catalog available on Web site.

VIKING CHILDREN'S BOOKS

Penguin Group Inc., 345 Hudson St., New York NY 10014-3657. (212)414-3600. Fax: (212)414-3399. Web site: www.penguin.com. **Acquisitions:** Catherine Frank, senior editor (picture books, middle grade and young adult fiction); Tracy Gates, executive editor (picture books, middle grade, young adult fiction); Joy Peskin, senior editor (picture books, middle grade, young adult fiction); Anne Gunton, editor (picture books, middle grade, young adult); Kendra Levin, assistant editor. **Art Acquisitions:** Denise Cronin, Viking Children's Books. Publishes hardcover originals. Publishes 60 books/year. Receives 7,500 queries/year. 25% of books from first-time authors; 33% from unagented writers. "Viking Children's Books is known for humorous, quirky picture books, in addition to more traditional fiction and publishes the highest quality trade books for children including fiction, nonfiction, and novelty books for pre-schoolers through young adults." Publishes book 1-2 years after acceptance of artwork. Hesitantly accepts simultaneous submissions.
• Viking Children's Books is not accepting unsolicited submissions at this time.
Fiction All levels: adventure, animal, contemporary, fantasy, hi-lo, history, humor, multicultural, nature/environment, poetry, problem novels, religion, romance, science fiction, sports, suspense/mystery. Recently published *Llama Llama Red Pajama*, by Anna Dewdney (ages 2 up, picture book); *Prom*, by Laurie Halse Anderson (ages 12 and up); *Follow the Line*, by Laura Ljungkvist; *Just Listen*, by Sarah Dessen.
Nonfiction Picture books: animal, biography, concept. Young readers, middle readers, young adult: animal, biography, concept, geography, hi-lo, history, multicultural, music/dance, nature/environment, science, sports. Recently published *John Lennon: All I Want Is the Truth*, by Elizabeth Partridge (ages 11 up, nonfiction).
Illustration Works with 30 illustrators/year. Responds to artist's queries/submissions only if interested. Samples returned with SASE only or samples filed. Originals returned at job's completion.
Terms Pays 2-10% royalty on retail price or flat fee. Advance negotiable.

WALKER & COMPANY

Books for Young Readers, 175 Fifth Ave., New York NY 10010. (646)307-5151. Fax: (212)727-0984. Web site: www.walkeryoungreaders.com. **Manuscript Acquisitions:** Emily Easton, publisher; Stacy Cantor, associate editor. Publishes 20 picture books/year; 5-10 nonfiction books/year; 5-10 middle readers/year; 5-10 young adult titles/year. 5% of books by first-time authors; 65% of books from agented writers.
Fiction Picture books: adventure, history, humor. Middle readers: adventure, contemporary, history, humor, multicultural. Young adults: adventure, contemporary, humor, historical fiction, suspense/mystery. Recently published *Gimme Cracked Corn and I Will Share* written and illustraed by Kevin O'Malley (ages 6-10, picture book); *Revenge of the Cheerleaders*, by Janette Rallison (12 and up, teen/young adult novel). *Skinny* by Ibi Kaslik (ages 14 and up).
Nonfiction Picture book, middle readers: biography, history. Recently published *Blue*, by K.M. Grant (ages 10-14); *I, Matthew Henson*, by Carole Boston Weatherford, illustrated by Eric Velasquez (ages 7-12, picture book history); *101 Things to Do Before You're Old and Boring* , by Richard Horne (ages 12 and up). Multicultural needs include "contemporary, literary fiction and historical fiction written in an authentic voice. Also high interest nonfiction with trade appeal."
How to Contact/Writers Fiction/nonfiction: Submit outline/synopsis and sample chapters; complete ms for picture books. Responds to queries/mss in 3-4 months. Send SASE for writer's guidelines.
Illustration Works with 20-25 illustrators/year. Editorial department reviews ms/illustration packages from

.

artists. Query or submit ms with 4-8 samples. Illustrations only: Tearsheets. "Please do not send original artwork." Responds to art samples only if interested.

Terms Pays authors royalty of 5-10%; pays illustrators royalty or flat fee. Offers advance payment against royalties. Original artwork returned at job's completion. Sends galleys to authors. Book catalog available for 9×12 SASE; ms guidelines for SASE.

Tips Writers: "Make sure you study our catalog before submitting. We are a small house with a tightly focused list. Illustrators: Have a well-rounded portfolio with different styles." Does not want to see folktales, ABC books, paperback series, genre fiction. "Walker and Company is committed to introducing talented new authors and illustrators to the children's book field."

◻ WEIGL PUBLISHERS INC.

350 5th Ave. Suite 3304, New York NY 10118-0069. (866)649-3445. Fax: (866)449-3445. E-mail: linda@weigl.com. Web site: www.weigl.com. **Manuscript/Art Acquisitions:** Heather Hudak. Publishes 25 young readers/year; 40 middle readers/year; 20 young adult titles/year. 15% of books by first-time authors. "Our mission is to provide innovative high-quality learning resources for schools and libraries worldwide at a competitive price."

Nonfiction Young readers: animal, biography, geography, history, multicultural, nature/environment, science. Middle readers: animal, biography, geography, history, multicultural, nature/environment, science, social issues, sports. Young adults: biography, careers, geography, history, multicultural, nature/environment, social issues. Average word length: young readers—100 words/page; middle readers—200 words/page; young adults—300 words/page. Recently published *Prehistoric Life* (ages 8 and up, science series); *Indigenous Peoples* (ages 8 and up, social studies series); *Natural Wonders* (ages 6 and up, social studies series).

How to Contact/Writers Nonfiction: Query. Responds to queries in 3 months. Publishes book 6-9 months after acceptance. Will consider e-mail submissions, simultaneous submissions.

Terms Work purchased outright from authors. Pays illustrators by the project. Pays photographers per photo. Originals returned to artist at job's completion. Book catalog available for 9½×11 SASE. Catalog available on website.

▥ WESTWINDS PRESS/ALASKA NORTHWEST BOOKS

Graphic Arts Center Publishing Company, P.O. Box 10306, Portland OR 97296-0306. (503)226-2402. Fax: (503)223-1410. E-mail: editorial@gacpc.com. Web site: www.gacpc.com. Independent book packager/producer. **Writers contact:** Tim Frew, executive editor. **Illustrators contact:** same. Produces 4 picture books/year, 1-2 young readers/year. 10% of books by first-time authors. "Graphic Arts Center Publishing Company publishes and distributes regional titles through its three imprints: Graphic Arts Books, Alaska Northwest Books and WestWinds Press. GAB is known for its excellence in publishing high-end photo-essay books. Alaska Northwest, established in 1959, is the premier publisher of nonfiction Alaska books on subjects ranging from cooking, Alaska Native culture, memoir, history, natural history, reference, biography, humor and children's books. WestWinds Press, established in 1999, echoes those themes with content that focuses on the Western States."

Fiction Picture books: animal, folktales, nature/environment. Young readers: adventure, animal, folktales, nature/environment. Average word length: picture books—1,100; young readers—9,000. Recently published *Kumak's Fish*, by Michael Bania (folktale, ages 6 and up); *Sweet Dreams, Polar Bear*, by Mindy Dwyer (3 and up); *Seldovia Sam and the Sea Otter Rescue*, by Susan Springer, illustrated by Amy Meissner (adventure, beginning chapter book).

Nonfiction Picture books: animal, nature/environment. Young readers: animal, nature/environment. Middle readers: nature/environment. Average word length: picture books—1,100; young readers—9,000. Recently published *Sharkabet*, by Ray Troll (ages 5 and up); *Winter Is*, by Anne Dixon, illustrated by Mindy Dwyer (environment/nature, ages 3-6).

How to Contact/Writers Accepts international submissions. Fiction/nonfiction: Submit complete ms. Responds to queries in 3 months; mss in 6 months. Publishes book 1-2 years after acceptance. Considers simultaneous submissions, electronic submissions, previously published work. "Please include SASE for response and return of materials."

Illustration Accepts material from international illustrators. Works with 4 illustrators/year. Uses both color and b&w. Reviews ms/illustration packages. For ms/illustration packages: Send ms with dummy. Submit ms/illustration packages to Tricia Brown, acquisitions editor. Reviews work for future assignments. If interested in illustrating future titles, query with samples. Samples returned with SASE. Samples not filed.

Photography Works on assignment only. Submit photos to Tim Frew, executive editor. Photo captions required. For first contact, send cover letter, portfolio, complete proposal, return postage.

Terms Offers advance against royalties. Originals returned to artist at job's completion. All imprints included in single catalog.

WHITE MANE KIDS

Imprint of White Mane Publishing Co., Inc., P.O. Box 708, 73 W. Burd St., Shippensburg PA 17257. (717)532-2237. Fax: (717)532-6110. E-mail: marketing@whitemane.com. Web site: www.whitemane.com. **Acquisitions:** Harold Collier, acquisitions editor. Imprints: White Mane Books, Burd Street Press, White Mane Kids, Ragged Edge Press. Publishes 7 middle readers/year. 50% of books are by first-time authors.

Fiction Middle readers, young adults: history (primarily American Civil War). Average word length: middle readers—30,000. Does not publish picture books. Recently published *The Witness Tree and the Shadow of the Noose: Mystery, Lies, and Spies in Manassas*, by K.E.M. Johnston; and *Drumbeat: The Story of a Civil War Drummer Boy*, by Robert J. Trout (grades 5 and up).

Nonfiction Middle readers, young adults: history. Average word length: middle readers—30,000. Does not publish picture books. Recently published *Hey, History Isn't Boring Anymore! A Creative Approach to Teaching the Civil War*, by Kelly Ann Butterbaugh (young adult).

How to Contact/Writers Fiction: Query. Nonfiction: Submit outline/synopsis and 2-3 sample chapters. Responds to queries in 1 month; mss in 3 months. Publishes a book 18 months after acceptance. Will consider simultaneous submissions.

Illustration Works with 4 illustrators/year. Illustrations used for cover art only. Responds only if interested. Samples returned with SASE.

Photography Buys stock and assigns work. Submit cover letter and portfolio.

Terms Pays authors royalty of 7-10%. Pays illustrators and photographers by the project. Sends galleys for review. Originals returned to artist at job's completion. Book catalog and writer's guidelines available for SASE. All imprints included in a single catalog.

ALBERT WHITMAN & COMPANY

6340 Oakton St, Morton Grove, IL 60053-2723. (847)581-0033. Fax: (847)581-0039. Web site: www.albertwhitman.com. **Manuscript Acquisitions:** Kathleen Tucker, editor-in-chief. Art Acquisitions: Carol Gildar. Publishes 30 books/year. 20% of books by first-time authors; 15% off books from agented authors.

Fiction Picture books, young readers, middle readers: adventure, concept (to help children deal with problems), fantasy, history, humor, multicultural, suspense. Middle readers: problem novels, suspense/mystery. "We are interested in contemporary multicultural stories-stories with holiday themes and exciting distinctive novels. We publish a wide variety of topics and are interested in stories that help children deal with their problems and concerns. Does not want to see, "religion-oriented, ABCs, pop-up, romance, counting." Recently published fiction: *Little Rooster's Diamond Button*, by Margaret Read MacDonald, illustrated by Will Terry; *My Mom's Having a Baby!* by Dori Hillestad Butler, illustrated by Carol Thompson; *The Bully-Blockers Club*, by Teresa Bateman, illustrated by Jackie Urbanovic; *The Truth about Truman School*, by Dori Hillestad Butler.

Nonfiction Picture books, young readers, middle readers: animal, arts/crafts, health, history, hobbies, multicultural, music/dance, nature/environment, science, sports, special needs. Does not want to see, "religion, any books that have to be written in, or fictionalized biographies." Recently published *Shelter Dogs*, by Peg Kehret; *An Apple for Harriet Tubman* by Glennette Tilly Turner; *The Groundhog Day Book of Facts and Fun*, by Wendie Old, illustrated by Paige Billin-Frye.

How to Contact/Writers Fiction/nonfiction: Submit query, outline, and sample chapter. For picture books send entire ms. Include cover letter. Responds to submissions in 4 months. Publishes a book 18 months after acceptance. Will consider simultaneous submissions "if notified."

Illustration "We are not accepting Illustration samples at this time. Submissions will not be returned."

Photography Publishes books illustrated with photos, but not stock photos-desires photos all taken for project. "Our books are for children and cover many topics; photos must be taken to match text. Books often show a child in a particular situation (e.g., kids being home-schooled, a sister whose brother is born prematurely)." Photographers should query with samples; send unsolicited photos by mail.

Terms Pays author's, illustrator's, and photographer's royalties. Book catalog for 8×10 SAE and 3 first-class stamps.

Tips "In both picture books and nonfiction, we are seeking stories showing life in other cultures and the variety of multicultural life in the U.S. We also want fiction and nonfiction about mentally or physically challenged children-some recent topics have been autism, stuttering, and diabetes. Look up some of our books first to be sure your submission is appropriate for Albert Whitman & Co."

◨ JOHN WILEY & SONS, INC.

111 River St., Hoboken NJ 07030. (201)748-6000. Web sites: www.wiley.com, www.josseybass.com. **Senior Editor:** Nana Twumasi. Publishes 18 middle readers/year; 2 young adult titles/year. 10% of books by first-time authors. Publishes educational nonfiction: primarily science and math and some history.

Nonfiction Middle readers: activity books, arts/crafts, biography, geography, health, history, hobbies, how-to, nature/environment, reference, science, self help. Young adults: activity books, arts/crafts, health, hobbies, how-to, nature/environment, reference, science, self help. Average word length: middle readers—20,000-40,000. Recently published The Extreme Animal Series: *Animal Planet Extreme Animals*, by Sherry Gerstein, *Animal Planet Extreme Bugs*, by Catherine Nichols; and *Animal Planet Extreme Predators*, by Mary Packard (ages 8-12, science/nature-based on the popular Animal Planet show *The Most Extreme Animals*); *Speed Math for Kids: The Fast, Fun Way to Do Basic Calculations*, by Bill Handley (ages 8-14, math); and *Janice VanCleave's Super Science Challenges: Hands-On Science Inquiry Projects for School, Science Fair, or Just Plain Fun* (ages 8-12, science/activity).

How to Contact/Writers Query. Submit outline/synopsis, 2 sample chapters and an author bio. Responds to queries in 6-8 weeks; mss in 3 months. Publishes a book 1 year after acceptance. Will consider simultaneous and previously published submissions.

Illustration Works with 6 illustrators/year. Uses primarily b&w artwork. Reviews ms/illustration packages from artists. Query. Illustrations only: Query with samples, résumé, client list. Responds only if interested. Samples filed. Original artwork returned at job's completion. No portfolio reviews.

Photography Buys photos from freelancers.

Terms Pays authors royalty of 10-12% based on wholesale price, or by outright purchase. Offers advances. Pays illustrators by the project. Photographers' pay negotiable. Sends galleys to authors. Book catalog available for SASE.

Tips "We're looking for topics and writers that can really engage kids' interest, plus we're always interested in a new twist on time-tested subjects." Nonfiction submissions only; no picture books.

WILLIAMSON BOOKS

An imprint of Ideals Publications, 535 Metroplex Drive, Suite 250, Nashville TN 37211. Web site: www.idealsbooks.com. **Manuscript and Art Acquisitions:** Williamson Books Submission. Publishes 6-10 titles/year. 50% of books by first-time authors; 10% of books from agented authors. Publishes "very successful nonfiction series (Kids Can!® Series) on subjects such as history, science, arts/crafts, geography, diversity, multiculturalism. Successfully launched *Little Hands*® series for ages 2-6, *Kaleidoscope Kids*® series (age 7 and up) and *Quick Starts for Kids!* ® series (ages 8 and up). "Our goal is to help every child fulfill his/her potential and experience personal growth."

Nonfiction Hands-on active learning books, animals, African-American, arts/crafts, Asian, biography, diversity, careers, geography, health, history, hobbies, how-to, math, multicultural, music/dance, nature/environment, Native American, science, writing and journaling. Does not want to see textbooks, picture books, fiction. "Looking for all things African American, Asian American, Hispanic, Latino, and Native American including crafts and traditions, as well as their history, biographies, and personal retrospectives of growing up in U.S. for grades pre-K-8th. We are looking for books in which learning and doing are inseparable." Recently published *Making Amazing Art*, by Sandi Henry, illustrated by Sarah Cole (ages 7-13); *Kids Care*, by Rebecca Olien, illustrated by Michael Kline (ages 7-12); *Super Science Concoctions*, by Jill Frankel Hauser, illustrated by Michael Kline (ages 6-12).

How to Contact/Writers Query with annotated TOC/synopsis and 1 sample chapter. Responds to queries/mss in 4 months. Publishes book "about 1 year" after acceptance. Writers may send a SASE for guidelines or e-mail.

Illustration Works with at least 6 illustrators and 6 designers/year. "We're interested in expanding our illustrator and design freelancers." Uses primarily b&w artwork and 2-color and 4-color. Responds only if interested. Samples returned with SASE; samples filed.

Photography Buys photos from freelancers; uses archival art and photos.

Terms Pays authors advance against future royalties based on wholesale price or purchases outright. Pays illustrators by the project. Pays photographers per photo. Sends galleys to authors.

Tips "Please do not send any fiction or picture books of any kind—those should go to Ideals Children's Books. Look at our books to see what we do. We're interested in interactive learning books with a creative approach packed with interesting information, written for young readers ages 3-7 and 8-14. In nonfiction children's publishing, we are looking for authors with a depth of knowledge shared with children through a warm, embracing style. Our publishing philosophy is based on the idea that all children can succeed and have positive learning experiences. Children's lasting learning experiences involve their participation."

◻ WINDWARD PUBLISHING

An imprint of the Finney Company, 8075 215th Street West, Lakeville MN 55044. (952)469-6699. Fax: (952)469-1968. E-mail: feedback@finneyco.com. Web site: www.finneyco.com. **Manuscript/Art Acquisitions:** Alan E. Krysan. Publishes 2 picture books/year; 4-6 young readers, middle readers, young adult titles/year. 50% of books by first-time authors.

Fiction Young readers, middle readers, young adults: adventure, animal, nature/environment. Recently published *Storm Codes*, by Tracy Nelson Maurer (ages 6-12, picture book); *Wild Beach*, by Marion Coste (ages 4-8, picture book).

Nonfiction Young readers, middle readers, young adults: activity books, animal, careers, nature/environment, science. Young adults: textbooks. Recently published *My Little Book of Manatees,* by Hope Irvin Marston (ages 4-8, introductions to the wonders of nature); *Space Station Science*, by Marianne Dyson (ages 8-13, science).

How to Contact/Writers Fiction: Query. Nonfiction: Submit outline/synopsis and 3 sample chapters. Responds to queries in 1 month; mss in 2 months. Publishes book 6-12 months after acceptance. Will consider simultaneous submissions and previously published work.

Illustration Reviews ms/illustration packages from artists. Send ms with dummy. Query with samples. Responds in 2 months. Samples returned with SASE; samples filed.

Photography Buys stock and assigns work. Photography needs depend on project—mostly ocean and beach subject matter. Uses color, 4×6, glossy prints. Submit cover letter, résumé, stock photo list.

Terms Author's payment negotiable by project. Offers advances (average amount: $500). Illustrators and photographers payment negotiable by project. Sends galleys to authors; dummies to illustrators. Originals returned to artist at job's completion. Book catalog available for 6×9 SAE and 3 first-class stamps; ms guidelines available for SASE on web site, www.finneyco.com/authoring.html. Catalog mostly available on Web site.

PAULA WISEMAN BOOKS

Imprint of Simon & Schuster, 1230 Sixth Ave., New York NY 10020. (212)698-7272. Fax: (212)698-2796. Web site: www.simonsays.com. Publishes 12 picture books/year; 4 middle readers/year; 2 young adult titles/year. 10% of books by first-time authors.

Fiction Considers all categories. Average word length: picture books—500; others standard length. Recently published President Pennybaker, by Kate Feiffer, illustrated by Diane Goode.

Nonfiction Picture books: animal, biography, concept, history, nature/environment. Young readers: animal, biography, history, multicultural, nature/environment, sports. Average word length: picture books—500; others standard length.

How to Contact/Writers Submit complete ms.

Illustration Works with 15 illustrators/year. Uses color artwork only. Will review ms/illustration packages from artists. Prefers mail for initial contact. Send manuscript with dummy.

WORDSONG

815 Church St., Honesdale PA 18431. Web site: www.wordsongpoetry.com. Estab. 1990. An imprint of Boyds Mills Press, Inc. 5% of books from agented writers. ''We publish fresh voices in contemporary poetry.''

Fiction/Nonfiction All levels: All types of quality children's poetry.

How to Contact/Writers Fiction/ nonfiction: Submit complete ms or submit through agent. Label package ''Manucript Submission'' and include SASE. ''Please send a book-length collection of your owm poems. Do not send an initial query.'' Responds to in 3 months. Reviews ms/illustration packages from artists. Submit complete ms with 1 or 2 pieces of art. Illustrations only: Query with samples best suited to the art (postcard, 8½×11, etc.). Label package ''Art Sample Submission.'' Responds only if interested. Samples returned with SASE. Samples filed. Originals returned at job's completion.

Photography Assigns work.

Terms Authors paid royalty or work purchased outright. Offers advances. Illustrators paid by the project or royalties; varies. Photographers paid by the project, per photo, or royalties; varies. Manuscripts/artist's guidelines available on Web site.

Tips ''Collections of original poetry, not anthologies, are our biggest need at this time. Keep in mind that the strongest collections demonstrate a facility with multiple poetic forms. Check to see what's already on the market and on our Web site before submitting.''

Canadian & International Book Publishers

While the United States is considered the largest market in children's publishing, the children's publishing world is by no means strictly dominated by the U.S. After all, the most prestigious children's book extravaganza in the world occurs each year in Bologna, Italy, at the Bologna Children's Book Fair and some of the world's most beloved characters were born in the United Kingdom (i.e., Winnie-the-Pooh and Mr. Potter).

In this section you'll find book publishers from English-speaking countries around the world from Canada, Australia, New Zealand and the United Kingdom. The listings in this section look just like the U.S. Book Publishers section; and the publishers listed are dedicated to the same goal—publishing great books for children.

Like always, be sure to study each listing and research each publisher carefully before submitting material. Determine whether a publisher is open to U.S. or international submissions, as many publishers accept submissions only from residents of their own country. Some publishers accept illustration samples from foreign artists, but do not accept manuscripts from foreign writers. Illustrators do have a slight edge in this category as many illustrators generate commissions from all around the globe. Visit publishers' Web sites to be certain they publish the sort of work you do. Visit online bookstores to see if publishers' books are available there. Write or e-mail to request catalogs and submission guidelines.

When mailing requests or submissions out of the United States, remember that U.S. postal stamps are useless on your SASE. Always include International Reply Coupons (IRCs) with your SAE. Each IRC is good for postage for one letter. So if you want the publisher to return your manuscript or send a catalog, be sure to enclose enough IRCs to pay the postage. For more help visit the United State Postal Service Web site at www.usps. com/global. Visit www.timeanddate.com/worldclock and American Computer Resources, Inc.'s International Calling Code Directory at www.the-acr.com/codes/cntrycd. htm before calling or faxing internationally to make sure you're calling at a reasonable time and using the correct numbers.

As in the rest of *Children's Writer's & Illustrator's Market*, the maple leaf ❦ symbol identifies Canadian markets. Look for International 🌐 symbol throughout *Children's Writer's & Illustrator's Market* as well. Several of the Society of Children's Book Writers and Illustrator's (SCBWI) international conferences are listed in the Conferences & Workshops section along with other events in locations around the globe. Look for more information about SCBWI's international chapters on the organization's Web site, www.scbwi.org. You'll also find international listings in Magazines and Young Writer's & Illustrator's Markets. See Useful Online Resources on page 367 for sites that offer additional international information.

Information on Canadian and international book publishers listed in the previous edition but not included in this edition of *Children's Writer's & Illustrator's Market* may be found in the General Index.

ANNICK PRESS LTD.

15 Patricia Ave., Toronto ON M2M 1H9 Canada. (416)221-4802. Fax: (416)221-8400. E-mail: annickpress@annic kpress.com. Web site: www.annickpress.com. **Creative Director:** Sheryl Shapiro. Publishes 5 picture books/ year; 6 young readers/year; 8 middle readers/year; 9 young adult titles/year. 25% of books by first-time authors. "Annick Press maintains a commitment to high-quality books that entertain and challenge. Our publications share fantasy and stimulate judgment and abilities."

- Annick Press does not accept unsolicited manuscripts.

Fiction Recently published *Baboon: A Novel*, by David Jones, (ages 10-14); *The Night Wanderer: A Native Gothic Novel*, by Drew Hayden Taylor, (ages 12 and up); *Shoe Shakes*, by Loris Lesynski, illustrated by Michael Martchenko,(picture book, ages 3-5).

Nonfiction Recently published *The Siege: Under Attack in Renaissance Europe*, by Stephen Shapiro, illustrated by John Mantha, (ages 10 and up); *The Inuit Thought of It: Amazing Arctic Innovations*, by Alootook Ipellie with David MacDonald, (ages 9-11); *The Big Book of Pop Culture: A How-To Guide for Young Artists*, by Hal Niedzviecki, illustrated by Marc Ngui, (ages 12 and up).

Illustration Works with 20 illustrators/year. Illustrations only: Query with samples. Contact: Creative Director. Samples cannot be returned. Response sent only if SASE included and submission being kept on file.

Terms Pays authors royalty of 5-12% based on retail price. Offers advances (average amount: $3,000). Pays illustrators royalty of 5% minimum. Originals returned to artist at job's completion. Book catalog available on Web site.

BOARDWALK BOOKS

Imprint of The Dundurn Group, 3 Church St., Suite 500, Toronto ON M5E 1M2 Canada. (416)214-5544. Fax: (416)214-5556. E-mail: info@dundurn.com. Web site: www.dundurn.com. **Manuscript Acquisitions:** Barry Jowett. Boardwalk Books is the YA imprint of The Dundurn Group. Publishes 6 young adult titles/year. 25% of books by first-time authors. "We aim to publish sophisticated literary fiction for youths aged 12 to 16."

Fiction Young adults: contemporary, historical, suspense/mystery. Average word length: young adults—40,000-45,000. Recently published *Three Million Acres of Flame*, by Valerie Sherrard (ages 10-14, fiction), *Fathom Five*, by James Bow (ages 11-15, fiction), *The Third Eye*, by Mahtab Narsimhan (ages 10-13, fiction).

How to Contact/Writers Accepts material from residents of Canada only. Fiction: Submit outline/synopsis and 3 sample chapters (or approximately 50 pages). Responds to queries/mss in 3 months. Publishes book 1 year after acceptance. Will consider simultaneous submissions.

Terms Offers advances. Sends galleys to authors. Book catalog available for 9×12 SAE with sufficient Canadian postage or international coupon. Writer's guidelines available on Web site.

Tips "Be sure your submission suits our list. We do not accept picture books."

COTEAU BOOKS LTD.

2517 Victoria Ave., Regina SK S4P 0T2 Canada. (306)777-0170. E-mail: coteau@coteaubooks.com. Web site: www.coteaubooks.com. **Acquisitions:** Barbara Sapergia, children's editor. Publishes 8-10 juvenile and/or young adult books/year; 18-20 books/year; 40% of books by first-time authors. "Coteau Books publishes the finest Canadian fiction, poetry, drama and children's literature, with an emphasis on western writers."

- Coteau Books publishes Canadian writers and illustrators only; mss from the U.S. are returned unopened.

Fiction Young readers, middle readers, young adults: adventure, contemporary, fantasy, history, humor, multi-cultural, nature/environment, science fiction, suspense/mystery. "No didactic, message pieces, nothing religious, no horror. No picture books. Recently published *New: Terror at Turtle Mountain*, by Penny Draper (ages 9 and up); *The Weathermage: Tales of Three Lands, Book III*, by Linda Smith (ages 10 and up); *Mud Girl*, by by Alison Acheson (ages 13 and up).

Nonfiction Young readers, middle readers, young adult/teen: biography, history, multicultural, nature/environment, social issues.

How to Contact/Writers Fiction: Submit complete ms or sample chapters to acquisitions editor. No e-mail submissions or queries. Include SASE. Responds to queries/mss in 4 months. Publishes a book 1-2 years after acceptance.

Illustration Works with 1-4 illustrators/year. Illustrations only: Submit nonreturnable samples. Responds only if interested. Samples returned with SASE; samples filed.

Photography "Very occasionally buys photos from freelancers." Buys stock and assigns work.

Terms Pays authors royalty based on retail price. Pays illustrators and photographers by the project. Sends galleys to authors; dummies to illustrators. Original artwork returned at job's completion. Book catalog free on request with 9×12 SASE.

Tips "Truthfully, the work speaks for itself! Be bold. Be creative. Be persistent! There is room, at least in the Canadian market, for quality novels for children, and at Coteau, this is a direction we will continue to take."

EMMA TREEHOUSE

Treehouse Children's Books, Little Orchard House, Mill Lane, Beckington, Somerset BA11 6SN United Kingdom. (44)(137)383-1215. Fax: (44)(137)383-1216. E-mail: sales@emmatreehouse.com. Web site: www.emmatreehouse.com. Estab. 1992. Publishes mass market books, trade books. We are an independent book packager/producer. **Manuscript Acquisitions:** David Bailey, director. **Art Acqusitions:** Richard Powell, creative director. Imprints: Treehouse Children's Books. Produces 100 young readers/year.

Fiction Picture books: adventure, animal, concept, folktales, humor.

Nonfiction Picture books: activity books, animal, concept.

How to Contact/Writers Only interested in agented material. Accepts international submissions. Fiction: Submit outline/synopsis. Nonfiction: Submit complete ms. Responds to queries in 3 weeks. No simultaneous, electronic, or previously published submissions.

Illustration Only interested in agented illustration submissions. Accepts material from international illustrators. Works with 10 illustrators/year. Uses color artwork only. Reviews ms/illustration packages. For ms/illustration packages: Send ms with dummy. Submit ms/illustration packages to Richard Powell, creative director. Reviews work for future assignments. If interested in illustrating future titles, arrange personal portfolio review. Submit samples to Richard Powell, creative director. Responds in 3 weeks. Samples returned with SASE. Samples not filed.

Terms Work purchased outright. Pays illustrators by the project. Illustrators see dummies for review. Catalog available for SASE. All imprints included in single catalog.

FENN PUBLISHING CO.

34 Nixon Rd., Bolton ON L7E 1W2 Canada. (905)951-6600. Fax: (905)951-6601. E-mail: fennpubs@hbfenn.com. Web site: www.hbfenn.com. Manuscript/Art Acquisitions: C. Jordan Fenn, publisher. Publishes 35 books/year. Publishes children's and young adult fiction.

Fiction Picture books: adventure, animal, sports. adult sports.

How to Contact/Writers Query or submit complete ms. Responds to queries/mss in 2 months.

Illustration Reviews ms/illustration packages from artists. Responds only if interested. Samples not returned or filed.

DAVID FICKLING BOOKS

31 Beaumont St., Oxford OX1 2NP United Kingdom. (018)65-339000. Fax: (018)65-339009. E-mail: tburgess@randomhouse.co.uk. Web site: www.davidficklingbooks.co.uk/. Publishes 12 titles/year.

Fiction Considers all categories. Recently published *Lyra's Oxford*, by Phillip Pullman; *The Curious Incident of the Dog in the Night-time*, by Mark Haddon; *The Boy in the Striped Pyjamas*, by John Boyne.

How to Contact/Writers Submit 3 sample chapters. Responds to mss in 2-3 months.

Illustration Reviews ms/illustration packages from artists. Illustrations only: query with samples.

Photography Submit cover letter, résumé, promo pieces.

FITZHENRY & WHITESIDE LTD.

195 Allstate Pkwy., Markham ON L3R 4T8 Canada. (905)477-9700. Fax: (905)477-9179. E-mail: godwit@fitzhenry.ca. Web site: www.fitzhenry.ca. Book publisher. **President:** Sharon Fitzhenry; Children's Publisher: Gail Winskill. Publishes 6 picture books/year; 4 middle novels/year; 6 young adult titles/year; 4 juvenile nonfiction titles/year. 10% of books by first-time authors. Publishes fiction and nonfiction—social studies, visual arts, biography, environment. Emphasis on Canadian authors and illustrators, subject or perspective.

How to Contact/Writers Fiction/nonfiction. Publishes a book 12-24 months after acceptance. See full submission guidelines on Web site www.fitzhenry.com.

Illustration Works with approximately 15 illustrators/year. Reviews ms/illustration packages from artists. Submit outline and sample illustration (copy). Illustrations only: Query with samples and promo sheet. Samples not returned unless requested.

Photography Buys photos from freelancers. Buys stock and assigns work. Captions required. Uses b&w 8×10 prints; 35mm and 4×5 transparencies. Submit stock photo list and promo piece.

Terms Pays authors 8-10% royalty with escalations. Offers "respectable" advances for picture books, 50/50 splite between author and illustrator. Pays illustrators by the project and royalty. Pays photographers per photo. Sends galleys to authors; dummies to illustrators.

Tips "We respond to quality."

🇨🇦 Ⓐ KEY PORTER BOOKS

6 Adelaide St. E, Toronto ON M5C 1H6 Canada. (416)862-7777. Fax: (416)862-2304. E-mail: info@keyporter.c om. Web site: www.keyporter.com. Book publisher. Key Porter Books is the largest independent, 100% Canadian-owned trade publisher.

Fiction Picture books: Biographies, memoirs. Middle readers, young adult: adventure, anthology, sports. Recently published *Shooting Water*, by Devyani Saltzman; *Duty: The Life of a Cop*, by Julian Fantino with Jerry Amernic; *Consequences*, by Penelope Lively; *Last Sam's Cage*, by David A. Poulsen; *The Alchemist's Dream* and *Where Soldiers Lie*, by John Wilson; *The Feathered Cloak*, by Sean Dixon; *Rink of Dreams* and *So Long, Jackie Robinson*, by Nancy L.M. Russell; *Past Crimes*, by Carol Matas; *Carew*, by J. C. Mills; *Sundancer*, by Shelley Peterson; *Alligator Tales: Alligator Pie*, by Dennis Lee, illustrated by Nora Hilb (board books)

Nonfiction Picture books: animal, arts/crafts, cooking, geography, nature/environment, reference, science. Middle readers: animal, nature/environment, reference, science. Recently published *Taken by Storm*, by Christopher Essex and Ross McKitrick; *Sharkwater*, by Rob Stewart; *Dancing Elephants & Floating Continents*, by John Wilson; *Being a Girl*, by Kim Cattrall.

How to Contact/Writers Only interested in agented material; no unsolicited mss. ''Although Key Porter Books does not review unsolicited manuscript submissions, we do try and review queries and proposals.'' Responds to queries/proposals in 6 months.

Photography Buys photos from freelancers. Buys stock and assigns work. Captions required. Uses 35mm transparencies. Submit cover letter, résumé, duplicate slides, stock photo list.

Tips ''Please note that all proposals and accompanying materials will be discarded unless sufficient postage has been provided for their return. Please do not send any original artwork or other irreplaceable materials. We do not accept responsibility for any materials you submit.''

🇨🇦 KIDS CAN PRESS

29 Birch Ave., Toronto ON M4V 1E2 Canada. (800)265-0884. E-mail: info@kidscan.com. Web site: www.kidsca npress.com. **Manuscript Acquisitions:** Acquisitions Editor. **Art Acquisitions:** Art Director. Publishes 6-10 picture books/year; 10-15 young readers/year; 2-3 middle readers/year; 2-3 young adult titles/year. 10-15% of books by first-time authors.

• Kids Can Press is currently accepting unsolicited manuscripts from Canadian authors only.

Fiction Picture books, young readers: concept. All levels: adventure, animal, contemporary, fantasy, folktales, history, humor, multicultural, nature/environment, poetry, special needs, sports, suspense/mystery. Average word length: picture books—1,000-2,000; young readers—750-1,500; middle readers—10,000-15,000; young adults—over 15,000. Recently published *Suki's Kimono*, by Chieri Ugaki, illustrated by Stephane Jorisch (picture book); *The Mob*, by Clem Martini (novel); *Stanley's Party*, by Linda Bailey, illustrated by Bill Slavin (picture book).

Nonfiction Picture books: activity books, animal, arts/crafts, biography, careers, concept, health, history, hobbies, how-to, multicultural, nature/environment, science, social issues, special needs, sports. Young readers: activity books, animal, arts/crafts, biography, careers, concept, history, hobbies, how-to, multicultural. Middle readers: cooking, music/dance. Average word length: picture books—500-1,250; young readers—750-2,000; middle readers—5,000-15,000. Recently published *The Kids Book of the Night Sky*, by Jane Drake and Ann Love, illustrated by Heather Collins (informational activity); *Animals at Work*, by Etta Kaner, illustrated by Pat Stephens (animal/nature); *Quilting*, by Biz Storms, illustrated by June Bradford (craft book).

How to Contact/Writers Fiction/nonfiction: Submit outline/synopsis and 2-3 sample chapters. For picture books submit complete ms. Responds in 6 months. Publishes a book 18-24 months after acceptance.

Illustration Works with 40 illustrators/year. Reviews ms/illustration packages from artists. Send color copies of illustration portfolio, cover letter outlining other experience. Contact: Art Director. Illustrations only: Send tearsheets, color photocopies. Contact: Art Director, Kids Can Press, 2250 Military Rd., Tonawanda NY 14150. Responds only if interested. Samples returned with SASE; samples filed.

🌐 KOALA BOOKS

P.O. Box 626, Mascot NSW 1460 Australia. (61)02 9667-2997. Fax: (61)02 9667-2881. E-mail: admin@koalabook s.com.au. Web site: www.koalabooks.com.au. **Manuscript Acquisitions:** Children's Editor. Art Acquisitions: Children's Designer, deb@koalabooks.com.au. ''Koala Books is an independent wholly Australian-owned children's book publishing house. Our strength is providing quality books for children at competitive prices.''

How to Contact/Writers Accepts material from residents of Australia only. Hard copy only. Picture books only: Submit complete ms, blurb, synopsis, brief author biography, list of author's published works. Also SASE large enough for ms return. Responds to mss in 3 months.

Illustration Accepts material from residents of Australia only. Illustrations only: Send cover letter, brief bio, list of published works and samples (color photographs or photocopies) in ''an A4 folder suitable for filing.'' Contact: Children's Designer. Responds only if interested. Samples not returned; samples filed.

Terms Pays authors royalty of 10% based on retail price or work purchased outright occasionally (may be split with illustrator).

Tips "Take a look at our Web site to get an idea of the kinds of books we publish. A few hours research in a quality children's bookshop would be helpful when choosing a publisher."

◨ LOBSTER PRESS

1620 Sherbrooke St. W., Suites C&D, Montreal QC H3H 1C9 Canada. (514)904-1100. Fax: (514)904-1101. E-mail: editorial@lobsterpress.com. Web site: www.lobsterpress.com. **Assistant Editor:** Meghan Nolan. Publishes picture books, young readers and YA fiction and nonfiction. "Driven by a desire to produce quality books that bring families together."

● Lobster Press is currently accepting manuscripts and queries.

Fiction Picture books, young readers, middle readers, young adults: adventure, animal, contemporary, health, history, multicultural, nature/environment, special needs, sports, suspense/mystery, science fiction, historical fiction, teen issues. Average word length: picture books—200-1,000. Average word length: middle, YA readers—40,000-70,000. Recently published *Oliver Has Something to Say!*, by Pamela Edwards, illustrated by Louis Pilon (picture book, 3+); *Zibby Payne & The Drama Trauma*, by Alison Bell (ages 7+); *Dear Jo: The story of losing Leah . . . and searching for hope*, by Christina Kilbourne (novel, 10+).

Nonfiction Young readers, middle readers and adults/teens: animal, biography, Canadian history/culture, careers, geography, hobbies, how-to, multicultural, nature/environment, references, science, self-help, social issues, sports, travel. Recently published *Don't Squash That Bug! The Curious Kid's Guide to Insects*, by Natalie Rompella (ages 3+); *Island of Hope and Sorrow: The Story of Grosse Ile*, by Anne Renaud (ages 8+).

How to Contact/Writers "Please address all submissions to Editorial, Lobster Press and specify the genre of your work on the envelope; e-mailed or faxed submissions will not be considered. No editorial comment will be forthcoming unless Lobster Press feels that a manuscript is publishable."

Illustration Works with 5 illustrators/year. Uses line drawings as well as digital and color artwork. Reviews ms/illustration packages from artists. Query with samples. Illustrations only: query with samples. Samples not returned; samples kept on file.

Terms Pays authors 5-10% royalty based on retail price. Original artwork returned to artist at job's completion. Writer's and artist's guidelines available on Web site.

◉ MANTRA LINGUA

Global House, 303 Ballards Lane, London N12 8NP United Kingdom. (44)(208)445-5123. Web site: www.mantralingua.com. **Manuscript Acquisitions:** Series Editor. Mantra Lingua "connects and transcends national differences in a way that is respectful and appreciative of local cultures."

● Mantra Lingua publishes books in English and more than 42 languages, including sign language. They are currently seeking fables, contemporary stories and folklore for picture books only.

Fiction Picture books, young readers, middle readers: folktales, multicultural, myths. Average word length: picture books—1,000-1,500; young readers—1,000-1,500. Recently published *Little Red Hen and the Grains of Wheat*, retold by Henriette Berkow, illustrated by Jago (ages 3-7); *Ali Baba and the Forty Thieves*, by Enebor Attard, illustrated by Richard Holland (ages 6-10).

How to Contact/Writers Accepts material from residents of United Kingdom only. Fiction: Myths only. Submit outline/synopsis (250 words, describe myth, "where it is from, whether it's famous or unknown, and why it would make a great picture book." Will consider e-mail and mail submissions. Include SASE if you'd like ms returned.

Illustration Uses 2D animations for CD-ROMs. Query with samples. Responds only if interested. Samples not returned; samples filed.

◨ MOOSE ENTERPRISE BOOK & THEATRE PLAY PUBLISHING

Imprint of Moose Hide Books, 684 Walls Rd., Sault Ste. Marie ON P6A 5K6 Canada. E-mail: mooseenterprises@on.aibn.com. Web site: www.moosehidebooks.com. **Manuscript Acquisitions:** Edmond Alcid. Publishes 2 middle readers/year; 2 young adult titles/year. 75% of books by first-time authors. Editorial philosophy: "To assist the new writers of moral standards."

● This publisher does not offer payment for stories published in its anthologies and/or book collections. Be sure to send a SASE for guidelines.

Fiction Middle readers, young adults: adventure, fantasy, humor, suspense/mystery, story poetry. Recently published *Realm of the Golden Feather*, by C.R. Ginter (ages 12 and up, fantasy); *Tell Me a Story*, short story collection by various authors (ages 9-11, humor/adventure); *Spirits of Lost Lake*, by James Walters (ages 12 and up, adventure); *Rusty Butt—Treasure of the Ocean Mist*, by R.E. Forester.

Nonfiction Middle readers, young adults: biography, history, multicultural.

How to Contact/Writers Fiction/nonfiction: Query. Responds to queries in 1 month; mss in 3 months. Publishes book 1 year after acceptance. Will consider simultaneous submissions.

Illustration Uses primarily b&w artwork for interiors, cover artwork in color. Illustrations only: Query with samples. Responds in 1 month, if interested. Samples returned with SASE; samples filed.

Terms Originals returned to artist at job's completion. Manuscript and art guidelines available for SASE.

Tips "Do not copy trends, be yourself, give me something new, something different."

ORCA BOOK PUBLISHERS

1016 Balmoral St., Victoria BC V8T 1A8 Canada. (250)380-1229. Fax: (250)380-1892. Web site: www.orcabook.c om. **Acquisitions:** Maggie deVries, children's book editor (young readers); Andrew Woolridge, editor (Orca Soundings); Bob Tyrrell, editor (teen fiction); Sarah Harvey, editor (juvenile fiction); Melanie Jeffs, editor (Orca Currents). Publishes 7 picture books/year; 16 middle readers/year; 10 young adult titles/year. 25% of books by first-time authors.

• Orca only considers authors who are Canadian or who live in Canada.

Fiction Picture books: animals, contemporary, history, nature/environment. Middle readers: contemporary, history, fantasy, nature/environment, problem novels, graphic novels. Young adults: adventure, contemporary, hi-lo (Orca Soundings), history, multicultural, nature/environment, problem novels, suspense/mystery, graphic novels. Average word length: picture books—500-1,500; middle readers—20,000-35,000; young adult—25,000-45,000; Orca Soundings—13,000-15,000; Orca Currents—13,000-15,000. Published *Tall in the Saddle*, by Anne Carter, illustrated by David McPhail (ages 4-8, picture book); *Me and Mr. Mah*, by Andrea Spalding, illustrated by Janet Wilson (ages 5 and up, picture book); *Alone at Ninety Foot*, by Katherine Holubitsky (young adult).

How to Contact/Writers Fiction: Submit complete ms if picture book; submit outline/synopsis and 3 sample chapters. "All queries or unsolicited submissions should be accompanied by a SASE." Responds to queries in 2 months; mss in 3 months. Publishes a book 18-36 months after acceptance. Submission guidelines available online.

Illustration Works with 8-10 illustrators/year. Reviews ms/illustration packages from artists. Submit ms with 3-4 pieces of final art. "Reproductions only, no original art please." Illustrations only: Query with samples; provide résumé, slides. Responds in 2 months. Samples returned with SASE; samples filed.

Terms Pays authors royalty of 5% for picture books, 10% for novels, based on retail price. Offers advances (average amount: $2,000). Pays illustrators royalty of 5% minimum based on retail price and advance on royalty. Sends galleys to authors. Original artwork returned at job's completion if picture books. Book catalog available for SASE with $2 first-class postage. Manuscript guidelines available for SASE. Art guidelines not available.

Tips "We are not seeking seasonal stories, board books, or 'I Can Read' Books. Orca Sounding/Currents lines offer high interest teen novels aimed at reluctant readers. The story should reflect the universal struggles young people face, but need not be limited to 'gritty' urban tales. Can include adventure, mystery/suspense, fantasy, etc. There's a definite need for humorous stories that appeal to boys and girls. Protagonists are between 14 and 17 years old."

PICCADILLY PRESS

5 Castle Rd., London NW1 8PR United Kingdom. (44)(207)267-4492. Fax: (44)(207)267-4493. E-mail: books@pi ccadillypress.co.uk. Web site: www.piccadillypress.co.uk.

Fiction Picture books: animal, contemporary, fantasy, nature/environment. Young adults: contemporary, humor, problem novels. Average word length: picture books-500-1,000; young adults-25,000-35,000. Recently published *Style Sisters*, by Liz Elwes (young adult); *Cinnamon Girl*, by Cathy Hopkins (young adult); *Hurray Up, Birthday*, by Paeony Lewis and Sarah Gill (picture book).

Nonfiction Young adults: self help (humorous). Average word length: young adults-25,000-35,000. Recently published *Body Blips, Wobbly Bits and Great Big Zits*, by Anita Naik; *Do the Right Thing*, by Jane Goldman.

How to Contact/Writers Fiction: Submit complete ms for picture books or submit outline/synopsis and 2 sample chapters for YA. Enclose a brief cover letter and SASE for reply. Nonfiction: Submit outline/synopsis and 2 sample chapters. Responds to mss in approximately 6 weeks.

Illustration Illustrations only: Query with samples (do not send originals).

Tips "Keep a copy of your manuscript on file."

PLAYNE BOOKS LIMITED

Park Court Barn, Trefin, Haverfordwest, Pembrokeshire SA62 5AU United Kingdom. (44)(134)883-7073. Fax: (44)(134)883-7063. E-mail: playne.books@virgin.net. Web site: www.playnebooks.com. **Manuscript Acquisitions:** Gill Davies. **Art Acquisitions:** David Playne, design and production. Publishes 2 picture books/year; 4 young readers/year.

Fiction Picture books: fantasy, early learning "fun encapsulated in a story—and humorous." Young readers:

early learning "fun encapsulated in a story—and humorous." Recently published *A Bug is Very Little*; *One Happy Hippo*, by Gill Davies (ages 3-5, novelty/educational).

Nonfiction Picture books: activity books. Young readers: activity books, animal, nature/environment. Young adults: animal, history, theatre. Recently published *Create Your Own Stage Make-Up*, by Gill Davies (ages 13 and up, How-to achieve state make-up, step by step).

How to Contact/Writers Fiction/nonfiction: Query or submit outline/synopsis. Responds to queries in 2 weeks. Will consider e-mail submissions, simultaneous submissions.

Illustration Works with 2 illustrators/year. Reviews ms/illustration packages from artists. Query. Contact: Gill Davies, editor. Illustrations only: Query with photocopies. Responds in 2 weeks.

Photography Buys stock and assigns work. Contact: David Playne, art director. Photo captions required. Uses color, 35mm, 60×70 or 4×5 transparencies. Submit cover letter, stock photo list.

Terms Work purchased outright from authors. Pays illustrators and photographers by the project. Sends galleys to authors; dummies to illustrators. Book catalog available. All imprints included in a single catalog. Information available on Web site.

Tips "Be adaptable, persevere—keep optimistic!"

🌐 MATHEW PRICE LTD.

The Old Glove Factory, Bristol Rd., Sherborne Dorset DT94EP United Kingdom. (44)(193)581-6010. Fax: (44)(193)581-6310. E-mail: mathewp@mathewprice.com. Web site: www.mathewprice.com. **Manuscript Acquisitions:** Mathew Price, chairman. Publishes 2 picture books/year; 2 young readers/year; 3 novelties/year; 1 gift book/year. Looking especially for stories for 2- to 4-year-olds. "Mathew Price Ltd. works to bring to market talented authors and artists profitably by publishing books for children that lift the hearts of people young and old all over the world."

Fiction/Nonfiction Will consider any category.

Illustration Accepts material from artists in other countries. Uses color artwork only. Reviews ms/illustration packages from artists. Send ms with dummy or submit ms with 2 pieces of final art. Nothing returned without prepaid envelope. Do not send orginals—please only send PDFs or JPEGs and only by e-mail.

Terms Originals returned to artist at job's completion. Book catalog available. All imprints included in a single catalog. Catalog available on Web site.

Tips "Study the market, keep a copy of all your work, and include a SAE if you want materials returned."

🌐 QED PUBLISHING

Quarto Publishing plc, 226 City Road, London EC1V 2TT United Kingdom. (44)(207)812-8631. Fax: (44)(207)253-4370. E-mail: zetad@quarto.com. Web site: www.qed-publishing.co.uk. Estab. 2003. Specializes in trade books, educational material, multicultural material. **Manuscripts Acquisitions:** Hannah Ray, senior editor. **Art Acquisitions:** Zeta Davies, creative director. Produces 8 picture books/year; 20 nonfiction readers/year. Strives for "editorial excellence with ground-breaking design."

Fiction Average word length: picture books—500; young readers—3,000; middle readers—3,500. Recently published *Said Mouse to Mole*, by Clare Bevan, illustrated by Sanja Rescek (ages 4 and up); *Lenny's Lost Spots*, by Celia Warren, illustrated by Genny Haines (ages 2 and up); *Pet the Cat*, by Wes Magee, illustrated by Pauline Siewert (ages 5 and up, poetry).

Nonfiction Picture books: animal, arts/crafts, biography, geography, reference, science. Young readers: activity books, animal, arts/crafts, biography, geography, reference, science. Middle readers: activity books, animal, arts/crafts, biography, geography, science. Average word length: picture books—500; young readers—3,000; middle readers—3,500. Recently published *You and Your Pet Kitten*, by Jean Coppendale (ages 7 and up, animal); *Travel Through India*, by Elaine Jackson (ages 7 and up, geography); *Cartooning*, by Deri Robins (ages 7 and up, art).

How to Contact/Writers Fiction/nonfiction: Query.

Illustration Accepts material from international illustrators. Works with 25 illustrators/year. For ms/illustration packages: Submit ms with 2 pieces of final art. Submit ms/illustration packages to Zeta Davies, creative director. Reviews work for future assignments. Submit samples to Hannah Ray, senior editor. Responds in 2 weeks. Samples filed.

Photography Buys stock images and assigns work. Submit photos to Zeta Davies, creative director. Uses step-by-step photos. For first contact, send CD of work or online URL.

Tips "Be persistent."

🌐 RANDOM HOUSE CHILDREN'S BOOKS

61-63 Uxbridge Rd., London W5 5SA England. (44)(208)579-2652. Fax: (44)(208)579-5476. E-mail: enquiries@randomhouse.co.uk. Web site: www.kidsatrandomhouse.co.uk. Book publisher. **Manuscript Acquisitions:**

Philippa Dickinson, managing director. Imprints: Doubleday, Corgi, Johnathan Cape, Hutchinson, Bodley Head, Red Fox, David Fickling Books. Publishes 120 picture books/year; 120 fiction titles/year.

Fiction Picture books: adventure, animal, anthology, contemporary, fantasy, folktales, humor, multicultural, nature/environment, poetry, suspense/mystery. Young readers: adventure, animal, anthology, contemporary, fantasy, folktales, humor, multicultural, nature/environment, poetry, sports, suspense/mystery. Middle readers: adventure, animal, anthology, contemporary, fantasy, folktales, humor, multicultural, nature/environment, problem novels, romance, sports, suspense/mystery. Young adults: adventure, contemporary, fantasy, humor, multicultural, nature/environment, problem novels, romance, science fiction, suspense/mystery. Average word length: picture books—800; young readers—1,500-6,000; middle readers—10,000-15,000; young adults—20,000-45,000.

How to Contact/Writers Only interested in agented material. No unsolicited mss or picture books.

Illustration Works with 50 illustrators/year. Reviews ms/illustration packages from artists. Query with samples. Contact: Margaret Hope. Samples are returned with SASE (IRC).

Photography Buys photos from freelancers. Contact: Alison Gadsby. Photo captions required. Uses color or b&w prints. Submit cover letter, published samples.

Terms Pays authors royalty. Offers advances. Pays illustrators by the project or royalty. Pays photographers by the project or per photo.

Tips ''Although Random House is a big publisher, each imprint only publishes a small number of books each year. Our lists for the next few years are already full. Any book we take on from a previously unpublished author has to be truly exceptional. Manuscripts should be sent to us via literary agents.''

⚏ RED DEER PRESS

#1512, 1800 4th Street SW, Calgary AB T2S 2S5 Canada. (403)509-0802. Fax: (403)228-6503. E-mail: rdp@redde erpress.com. Web site: www.reddeerpress.com. **Manuscript/Art Acquisitions:** Peter Carver, children's editor. Publishes 3 picture books/year; 4 young adult titles/year. 20% of books by first-time authors. Red Deer Press is known for their ''high-quality international children's program that tackles risky and/or serious issues for kids.''

• Red Deer only publishes books written and illustrated by Canadians and books that are about or of interest to Canadians.

Fiction Picture books, young readers: adventure, contemporary, fantasy, folktales, history, humor, multicultural, nature/environment, poetry. Middle readers, young adult/teens: adventure, contemporary, fantasy, folktales, hi-lo, history, humor, multicultural, nature/environment, problem novels, suspense/mystery. Recently published *Courage to Fly*, by Troon Harrison, illustrated by Zhong-Yang Huung (ages 4-7, picture book); *Amber Waiting*, by Nan Gregory, illustrated by Macdonald Denton (ages 4-7, picture book); *Tom Finder*, by Martine Leavitt (ages 14 and up).

How to Contact/Writers Fiction/nonfiction: Query or submit outline/synopsis. Responds to queries in 6 months; mss in 8 months. Publishes a book 18 months after acceptance. Will consider simultaneous submissions.

Illustration Works with 4-6 illustrators/year. Illustrations only: Query with samples. Responds only if interested. Samples not returned; samples filed for six months. Canadian illustrators only.

Photography Buys stock and assigns work. Model/property releases required. Submit cover letter, résumé and color promo piece.

Terms Pays authors royalty (negotiated). Occasionally offers advances (negotiated). Pays illustrators and photographers by the project or royalty (depends on the project). Sends galleys to authors. Originals returned to artist at job's completion. Guidelines not available on Web site.

Tips ''Writers, illustrators, and photographers should familiarize themselves with Red Deer Press's children's publishing program, including the kinds of books we do and do not publish.''

⚏ RONSDALE PRESS

3350 W. 21st Ave., Vancouver BC V6S 1G7 Canada. (604)738-4688. Fax: (604)731-4548. E-mail: ronsdale@shaw .ca. Web site: ronsdalepress.com. Estab. 1988. Book publisher. **Manuscript/Art Acquisitions:** Veronica Hatch, children's editor. Publishes 2 children's books/year. 40% of titles by first-time authors. ''Ronsdale Press is a Canadian literary publishing house that publishes 8-10 books each year, two of which are children's titles. Of particular interest are books involving children exploring and discovering new aspects of Canadian history.''

Fiction Young adults: Canadian historical novels. Average word length: middle readers and young adults—50,000. Recently published *Red Goodwin*, by John Wilson (ages 10-14); *Shadows of Disaster*, by Cathy Beveridge (ages 10-14); *Dark Times*, edited by Ann Walsh (anthology of short stories, ages 10 and up); *Rosie's Dream Cape*, by Zelsa Freedman (ages 8-14); *Hurricanes over London*, by Charles Reid (ages 10-14).

Nonfiction Middle readers, young adults: animal, biography, history, multicultural, social issues. Average word length: young readers—90; middle readers—90.

How to Contact/Writers Accepts material from residents of Canada only. Fiction/nonfiction: Submit complete ms. Responds to queries in 2 weeks; mss in 2 months. Publishes a book 1 year after acceptance. Will consider simultaneous submissions.

Illustrations Works with 2 illustrators/year. Reviews ms/illustration packages from artists. Requires only cover art. Responds in 2 weeks. Samples returned with SASE. Originals returned to artist at job's completion.

Terms Pays authors royalty of 10% based on retail price. Pays illustrators by the project $800-1,200. Sends galleys to authors. Book catalog available for 8½×11 SAE and $1 postage; ms and art guidelines available for SASE.

Tips "Ronsdale Press publishes well-written books that have a new slant on things and that can take an age-old story and give it a new spin. We are particularly interested in novels for young adults with a historical component that offers new insights into a part of Canada's history. We publish only Canadian authors."

⊕ SCHOLASTIC AUSTRALIA

Scholastic Press and Scholastic Press, P.O. Box 579, Lindfield NSW 2070 Australia. Omnibus Books, 225 Unley Road, Malvern SA 5061 Australia. Web site: www.scholastic.com.au. "Communicating with children around the world."
- Scholastic Australia accepts material from residents of Australia only. Visit thier Web site for manuscript guidelines (www.scholastic.com.ay/common/about/manuscript.asp).

Fiction Picture books, young readers. Recently published *After Alice*, by Jane Carroll (ages 8-12, fiction); *Amelia Ellicott's Garden*, by Lilianna Stafford, illustrated by Stephen Michael King (ages 5-7, picture book); *An Ordinary Day*, by Libby Gleeson, illustrated by Armin Greder (ages 5-15, picture book).

Nonfiction Omnibus and Scholastic Press will consider nonfiction. Recently published *Bass and Flinders*, by Cathy Dodson, illustrated by Roland Harvey (ages 9-12, history); *The Cartoon Faces Book*, by Robert Ainsworth (ages 7-14, art & craft); *Excuse Me, Captain Cook, Who Did Discover Australia?*, by Michael Salmon (ages 7-12, history).

How to Contact/Writers Fiction/nonfiction: Submit complete ms. For picture books, submit only ms, no art. Responds to mss in 2 months.

Illustration Illustrations only: Send portfolio. Contact appropriate office for more information on what to include with portfolio.

Tips "Scholastic Australia publishes books for children under three publishing imprints—Scholastic Press, Omnibus Books and Margaret Hamilton Books. To get a more specific idea of the flavor of each list, you will need to visit your local bookstore. Don't be too surprised or disappointed if your first attempts are not successful. Children's book publishing is a highly competitive field, and writing children's books is not quite as easy as some might imagine. But we are always ready to find the next Harry Potter or Paddington Bear, so if you believe you can write it, we're ready to hear from you."

⊞ SCHOLASTIC CANADA LTD.

604 King St. West, ON M5V 1E1 Canada. (416)915-3500. Fax: (416)849-7912. Web site: www.scholastic.ca; for ms/artist guidelines: www.scholastic.ca/aboutscholastic/manuscripts.htm. **Acquisitions:** Editor, children's books. Publishes hardcover and trade paperback originals. Imprints: Scholastic Canada; North Winds Press; Les Editions Scholastic. Publishes 30 titles/year; imprint publishes 4 titles/year. 3% of books from first-time authors; 50% from unagented writers. Canadian authors, theme or setting required.
- At presstime Scholastic Canada was not accepting unsolicited manuscripts. For up-to-date information on their current submission policy, call their publishing status line at (905)887-7323, ext. 4308 or view their submission guidelines on their Web site.

Fiction Picture books, young readers, young adult. Average word length: picture books—under 1,000; young readers—7,000-10,000; young adult—25,000-40,000.

Nonfiction Animals, biography, history, hobbies, nature, recreation, science, sports. Reviews artwork/photos as part of ms package. Send photocopies.

How to Contact/Writers Query with synopsis, 3 sample chapters and SASE. Nonfiction: Query with outline, 1-2 sample chapters and SASE (IRC or Canadian stamps only). Responds in 3 months. Publishes book 1 year after acceptance.

Illustration Illustrations only: Query with samples; send résumé. Never send originals. Contact: Ms. Yuksel Hassan.

Terms Pays authors royalty of 5-10% based on retail price. Offers advances (range: $1,000-5,000, Canadian). Book catalog for 8½×11 SAE with $2.05 postage stamps (IRC or Canadian stamps only).

⊕ SCHOLASTIC CHILDREN'S BOOKS UK

Euston House, 24 Eversholt St., London NW1 1DB United Kingdom. Web site: www.scholastic.co.uk. **Submissions:** The Editorial Department.

• Scholastic UK accepts material from residents of United Kingdom only.

Fiction Recently published *A Darkling Plain*, by Philip Reeve; *Storm Thief*, by Chris Wooding; *Looking for JJ*, by Anne Cassidy; *Captain Underpants*.

Nonfiction Recently published *The Horrible Science of Everything*, by Nick Arnold and Tony de Saulles; *Horrible Histories: Horrible Geography, Foul Football*, and *My Story*, by Terry Deary.

Picture Book and Novelty Recently published *Chuckling Ducklings* and *My Little Star*.

How to Contact/Writers Fiction/nonfiction: Query or submit complete ms and SASE. Responds to queries/mss in 6 months. Does not accept electronic submissions.

Tip "Do not be depressed if your work is not accepted. Getting work published can be a frustrating process, and it's often best to be prepared for disappointment."

SECOND STORY PRESS

20 Maud St., Suite 401, Toronto ON M5V 2M5 Canada. (416)537-7850. Fax: (416)537-0588. E-mail: info@second storypress.ca. Web site: www.secondstorypress.ca.

Fiction Considers nonsexist, nonracist, and nonviolent stories, as well as historical fiction, chapter books, picture books. Recently published *Mom and Mum Are Getting Married!*, by Ken Setterington.

Nonfiction Picture books: biography. Recently published *The Underground Reporters: A True Story*, by Kathy Kacer (a new addition to our Holocaust remembrance series for young readers).

How to Contact/Writers Accepts appropriate material from residents of Canada only. Fiction and nonfiction: Submit complete ms or submit outline and sample chapters by postal mail only. No electronic submissions or queries.

TRADEWIND BOOKS

202-1807 Maritime Mews, Vancouver BC V6H 3W7 Canada. (604)662-4405. Fax: (604)730-0454. E-mail: tradewi ndbooks@yahoo.com. Web site: www.tradewindbooks.com. **Manuscript Acquisitions:** Michael Katz, publisher. **Art Acquisitions:** Carol Frank, art director. Senior Editor: R. David Stephens. Publishes 2 picture books; 2 young adult titles/year; 1 book of poetry. 15% of books by first-time authors.

Fiction Picture books: adventure, multicultural, folktales. Average word length: 900 words. Recently published *The Clone Emerald Curse*, by Simon Rose; *Crocodiles Say*, by Robert Heidbreder; *If I had a Million Onions*, by Sheree Fitch.

How to Contact/Writers Picture books: Submit complete ms. YA novels by Canadian authors only. Will consider simultaneous submissions. Do not send query letter. Responds to mss in 6 weeks. Unsolicited submissions accepted only if authors have read a selection of books published by Tradewind Books. Submissions must include a reference to these books.

Illustration Works with 3-4 illustrators/year. Reviews ms/illustration packages from artists. Send ms with dummy. Illustrations only: Query with samples. Responds only if interested. Samples returned with SASE; samples filed.

Terms Royalties negotiable. Offers advances against royalties. Originals returned to artist at job's completion. Catalog available on Web site.

USBORNE PUBLISHING

83-85 Saffron Hill, London EC1N 8RT United Kingdom. Fax: (44)(20)743-1562. Web site: www.usborne.com. **Manuscript Acquisitions:** Fiction Editorial Director. **Art Acquisitions:** Usborne Art Department. "Usborne Publishing is a multiple-award winning, world-wide children's publishing company specializing in superbly researched and produced information books with a unique appeal to young readers."

Fiction Young readers, middle readers: adventure, contemporary, fantasy, history, humor, multicultural, nature/environment, science fiction, suspense/mystery. Average word length: young readers—3,500-8,000; middle readers—10,000-30,000. Recently publshed Oliver Moon series, by Sue Mongredien (ages 6 and up); Fame School series, by Cindy Jefferies (ages 8 and up).

How to Contact/Writers Refer to guidelines on Web site or request from above address. Fiction: Submit 3 sample chapters and a full synopsis with SASE. Does not accept submissions for nonfiction or picture books. Responds to queries in 1 month; mss in 4 months.

Illustration Works with 100 illustrators per year. Illustrations only: Query with samples. Samples not returned; samples filed.

Photography Contact: Usborne Art Department. Submit samples.

Terms Pays authors royalty.

Tips "Do not send any original work and, sorry, but we cannot guarantee a reply."

Magazines

C hildren's magazines are a great place for unpublished writers and illustrators to break into the market. Writers, illustrators and photographers alike may find it easier to get book assignments if they have tearsheets from magazines. Having magazine work under your belt shows you're professional and have experience working with editors and art directors and meeting deadlines.

But magazines aren't merely a breaking-in point. Writing, illustration and photo assignments for magazines let you see your work in print quickly, and the magazine market can offer steady work and regular paychecks (a number of them pay on acceptance). Book authors and illustrators may have to wait a year or two before receiving royalties from a project. The magazine market is also a good place to use research material that didn't make it into a book project you're working on. You may even work on a magazine idea that blossoms into a book project.

TARGETING YOUR SUBMISSIONS

It's important to know the topics typically covered by different children's magazines. To help you match your work with the right publications, we've included several indexes in the back of this book. The **Subject Index** lists both book and magazine publishers by the fiction and nonfiction subjects they're seeking.

If you're a writer, use the Subject Index in conjunction with the **Age-Level Index** to narrow your list of markets. Targeting the correct age group with your submission is an important consideration. Many rejection slips are sent because a writer has not targeted a manuscript to the correct age. Few magazines are aimed at children of all ages, so you must be certain your manuscript is written for the audience level of the particular magazine you're submitting to. Magazines for children (just as magazines for adults) may also target a specific gender.

If you're a poet, refer to the **Poetry Index** to find which magazines publish poems.

Each magazine has a different editorial philosophy. Language usage also varies between periodicals, as does the length of feature articles and the use of artwork and photographs. Reading magazines *before* submitting is the best way to determine if your material is appropriate. Also, because magazines targeted to specific age groups have a natural turnover in readership every few years, old topics (with a new slant) can be recycled.

If you're a photographer, the **Photography Index** lists children's magazines that use photos from freelancers. Using it in combination with the subject index can narrow your search. For instance, if you photograph sports, compare the Magazine list in the Photography Index with the list under Sports in the Subject Index. Highlight the markets that appear on both lists, then read those listings to decide which magazines might be best for your work.

Since many kids' magazines sell subscriptions through direct mail or schools, you may not be able to find a particular publication at bookstores or newsstands. Check your local library, or send for copies of the magazines you're interested in. Most magazines in this section have sample copies available and will send them for a SASE or small fee.

Also, many magazines have submission guidelines and theme lists available for a SASE. Check magazines' Web sites, too. Many offer excerpts of articles, submission guidelines, and theme lists and will give you a feel for the editorial focus of the publication.

Watch for the Canadian 🎴 and International 🌐 symbols. These publications' needs and requirements may differ from their U.S. counterparts.

For some great advice on children's magazine writing, see the Insider Report with author **Barbara Kanninen** on page 254.

Information on magazines listed in the previous edition but not included in this edition of *Children's Writer's & Illustrator's Market* may be found in the General Index.

ADVENTURES

WordAction Publications,, 6401 The Paseo, Kansas City MO 64131.(816)333-7000. Fax: (816)333-4439. E-mail: dfillmore@nazarene.org. **Articles Editor:** Donna Filmore. Weekly magazine. "Adventures is a full-color story paper for first and second graders. It is designed to connect Sunday School learning with the daily living experiences of the early elementary child. The reading level should be beginning. The intent of Adventures is to provide a life-related paper enabling Christian values, encouraging good choices and providing reinforcement for biblical concepts taught in WordAction Sunday School curriculum." Entire publication aimed at juvenile market.

Fiction Picture-Oriented Material: contemporary, inspirational, religious. Young Readers: contemporary, inspirational, religious. . Byline given.

How to Contact/Writers Fiction: Send complete ms. Responds to queries in 6 weeks; to mss in 6 weeks.

Terms Pays on acceptance. Buys all rights. Writer's guidelines free for SASE.

Tips "Send SASE for themes and guidelines or e-mail acallison@nazarene.org. Stories should realistically portray the life experiences of first- and second-grade children from a variety of ethnic and social backgrounds. We also need simple puzzles, easy recipes and easy-to-do craft ideas."

ADVOCATE, PKA'S PUBLICATION

PKA Publication, 1881 Little Westkill Rd., Prattsville NY 12468. (518)299-3103. **Publisher:** Patricia Keller. Bimonthly tabloid. Estab. 1987. Circ. 12,000. "*Advocate* advocates good writers and quality writings. We publish art, fiction, photos and poetry. *Advocate*'s submitters are talented people of all ages who do not earn their livings as writers. We wish to promote the arts and to give those we publish the opportunity to be published."

● Gaited Horse Association newsletter is included in this publication. Horse-oriented stories, poetry, art and photos are currently needed.

Fiction Middle readers, young adults/teens: adventure, animal, contemporary, fantasy, folktales, health, humorous, nature/environment, problem-solving, romance, science fiction, sports, suspense/mystery. Looks for "well written, entertaining work, whether fiction or nonfiction." Buys approximately 42 mss/year. Prose pieces should not exceed 1,500 words. Byline given. Wants to see more humorous material, nature/environment and romantic comedy.

Nonfiction Middle readers, young adults/teens: animal, arts/crafts, biography, careers, concept, cooking, fashion, games/puzzles, geography, history, hobbies, how-to, humorous, interview/profile, nature/environment, problem-solving, science, social issues, sports, travel. Buys 10 mss/year. Prose pieces should not exceed 1,500 words. Byline given.

Poetry Reviews poetry any length.

How to Contact/Writers Fiction/nonfiction: send complete ms. Responds to queries in 6 weeks; mss in 2 months. Publishes ms 2-18 months after acceptance.

Illustration Uses b&w artwork only. Uses cartoons. Reviews ms/illustration packages from artists. Submit a photo print (b&w or color), an excellent copy of work (no larger than 8×10) or original. Illustrations only: "Send previous unpublished art with SASE, please." Responds in 2 months. Samples returned with SASE; samples not filed. Credit line given.

Photography Buys photos from freelancers. Model/property releases required. Uses color and b&w prints (no slides).

Send unsolicited photos by mail with SASE. Responds in 2 months. Wants nature, artistic and humorous photos.
Terms Pays on publication with contributor's copies. Acquires first rights for mss, artwork and photographs. Pays in copies. Sample copies for $4. Writer's/illustrator/photo guidelines with sample copy.
Tips "Please, no simultaneous submissions, work that has appeared on the Internet, po rnography, overt religiousity, anti-environmentalism or gratuitous violence. Artists and photographers should keep in mind that we are a b&w paper. Please do not send postcards. Use envelope with SASE."

AIM MAGAZINE, America's Intercultural Magazine

P.O. Box 390, Milton WA 98354-0390. Web site: www.aimmagazine.org. **Contact:** Ruth Apilado, associate editor. Quarterly magazine. Circ. 8,000. "Readers are high school and college students, teachers, adults interested in helping to purge racism from the human blood stream by the way of the written word—that is our goal!" 15% of material aimed at juvenile audience.
Fiction Young adults/teens: adventure, folktales, humorous, history, multicultural, "stories with social significance." Wants stories that teach children that people are more alike than they are different. Does not want to see religious fiction. Buys 20 mss/year. Average word length: 1,000-4,000. Byline given.
Nonfiction Young adults/teens: biography, interview/profile, multicultural, "stuff with social significance." Does not want to see religious nonfiction. Buys 20 mss/year. Average word length: 500-2,000. Byline given.
How to Contact/Writers Fiction: Send complete ms. Nonfiction: Query with published clips. Responds to queries/mss in 1 month. Will consider simultaneous submissions.
Illustration Buys 6 illustrations/issue. Preferred theme: Overcoming social injustices through nonviolent means. Reviews ms/illustration packages from artists. Query first. Illustrations only: Query with tearsheets. Responds to art samples in 1 month. Samples filed. Original artwork returned at job's completion "if desired." Credit line given.
Photography Wants "photos of activists who are trying to contribute to social improvement."
Terms Pays on acceptance. Buys first North American serial rights. Pays $15-25 for stories/articles. Pays in contributor copies if copies are requested. Pays $25 for b&w cover illustration. Photographers paid by the project. Sample copies for $5.
Tips "Write about what you know."

AMERICAN CAREERS

Career Communications, Inc., 6701 W. 64th St., Overland Park KS 66202. (913)362-7788. Fax: (913)362-4864. Web site: www.carcom.com. **Articles Editor:** Mary Pitchford. **Art Director:** Jerry Kanabel. Published 1 time/year. Estab. 1990. Circ. 400,000. Publishes career and education information for students in grades 6-12.
Nonfiction Buys 10 mss/year. Average word length: 300-800. Byline given.
How to Contact/Writers Nonfiction: Query with résumé and published clips. Acknowledges queries within 30 days. Keeps queries on file up to 2 years. Accepts simultaneous submissions with notification.
Terms Pays on acceptance. Pays writers variable amount.
Tips Send a query in writing with résumé and clips.

AMERICAN CHEERLEADER

Lifestyle Ventures LLC, 250 W. 57th St., Suite 420, New York NY 10107. (212)265-8890. Fax: (212)265-8908. E-mail: editors@americancheerleader.com. Web site: www.americancheerleader.com. **Publisher:** Sheila Noone. **Editor:** Marisa Walker. Bimonthly magazine. Estab. 1995. Circ. 200,000. Special interest teen magazine for kids who cheer.
Nonfiction Young adults: biography, interview/profile (sports personalities), careers, fashion, beauty, health, how-to (cheering techniques, routines, pep songs, etc.), problem-solving, sports, cheerleading specific material. "We're looking for authors who know cheerleading." Buys 20 mss/year. Average word length: 750-2,000. Byline given.
How to Contact/Writers Query with published clips. Responds to queries/mss in 3 months. Publishes ms 3 months after acceptance. Will consider electronic submission via disk or e-mail.
Illustration Buys 2 illustrations/issue; 12-20 illustrations/year. Works on assignment only. Reviews ms/illustration packages from artists. Illustrations only: Query with samples; arrange portfolio review. Responds only if interested. Samples filed. Originals not returned at job's completion. Credit line given.
Photography Buys photos from freelancers. Looking for cheerleading at different sports games, events, etc. Uses 35mm, $2\frac{1}{4} \times 2\frac{1}{4}$ transparencies and 5×7 prints. Query with samples; provide résumé, business card, tearsheets to be kept on file. "After sending query, we'll set up an interview." Responds only if interested.
Terms Pays on publication. Buys all rights for mss, artwork and photographs. Pays $100-500 for stories. Pays illustrators $50-200 for b&w inside, $100-300 for color inside. Pays photographers by the project $300-750; per photo (range: $25-100). Sample copies for $4.
Tips "Authors: We invite proposals from freelance writers who are involved in or have been involved in

cheerleading—i.e. coaches, sponsors or cheerleaders. Our writing style is upbeat, and 'sporty' to catch and hold the attention of our teen readers. Articles should be broken down into lots of sidebars, bulleted lists, etc. Photographers and illustrators must have teen magazine experience or high profile experience.''

AMERICAN GIRL

8400 Fairway Place, Middleton WI 53562-0984. (608)836-4848. Web site: www.americangirl.com. **Contact:** Editorial Dept. Assistant. Bimonthly magazine. Estab. 1992. Circ. 750,000. "For girls ages 8-12. We use fiction and nonfiction."

Fiction Middle readers: contemporary, multicultural, suspense/mystery, good fiction about anything. No romance, science fiction or fantasy. No preachy, moralistic tales or stories with animals as protagonists. Only girl characters—no boys. Buys approximately 2 mss/year. Average word length: 2,300. Byline given.

Nonfiction How-to, interview/profile, history. Any articles aimed at girls ages 8-12. Buys 3-10 mss/year. Average word length: 600. Byline sometimes given. No historical profiles about obvious female heroines—Annie Oakley, Amelia Earhart; no romance or dating.

How to Contact/Writers Fiction: Query with published clips. Nonfiction: Query. Responds to queries/mss in 3 months. Will consider simultaneous submissions.

Illustration Works on assignment only.

Terms Pays on acceptance. Buys first North American serial rights. Pays $500 minimum for stories; $300 minimum for articles. Sample copies for $4.50 and 9×12 SAE with $1.98 in postage (send to Magazine Department Assistant). Writer's guidelines free for SASE.

Tips "Keep (stories and articles) simple but interesting. Kids are discriminating readers, too. They won't read a boring or pretentious story. We're looking for short (maximum 175 words) how-to stories and short profiles of girls for 'Girls Express' section, as well as word games, puzzles and mazes."

APPLESEEDS

Cobblestone Publishing, A Division of Carus Publishing, 30 Grove Street, Peterborough, NH 03458 . E-mail (for writers queries): swbuc@aol.com. Web site: www.cobblestonepub.com. **Editor:** Susan Buckley. Magazine published 9 times annually. *AppleSeeds* is a 36-page, multidisciplinary, nonfiction social studies magazine from Cobblestone Publishing for ages 8-10. Each issue focuses on one theme.

• Requests for sample issues should be mailed to Cobblestone directly. See Web site for current theme list.

How to Contact/Writers Nonfiction: Query only. Send all queries to Susan Buckley. See Web site for submission guidelines and theme list. E-mail queries only. See Web site for editorial guidelines.

Illustration Contact Ann Dillon at Cobblestone. See Web site for illustration guidelines.

Tips "Submit queries specifically focused on the theme of an upcoming issue. We generally work 6 months ahead on themes. We look for unusual perspectives, original ideas, and excellent scholarship. We accept **no unsolicited manuscripts**. Writers should check our Web site at cobblestonepub.com/pages/writersAPPguides/html for current guidelines, topics, and query deadlines. We use very little fiction. Illustrators should not submit unsolicited art."

🌐 AQUILA

New Leaf Publishing, P.O. Box 2518, Eastbourne BN22 8AP United Kingdom. (44)(132)343-1313. Fax: (44)(132)373-1136. E-mail: info@aquila.co.uk. Web site: www.aquila.co.uk. **Submissions Editor:** Jackie Berry and Karen Lutener. Monthly magazine. Estab. 1993. "Aquila is an educational magazine for readers ages 8-13 including factual articles (no pop/celebrity material), arts/crafts and puzzles." Entire publication aimed at juvenile market.

Fiction Young Readers: animal, contemporary, fantasy, folktales, health, history, humorous, multicultural, nature/environment, problem solving, religious, science fiction, sports, suspense/mystery. Middle Readers: animal, contemporary, fantasy, folktales, health, history, humorous, multicultural, nature/environment, problem solving, religious, romance, science fiction, sports, suspense/mystery. Buys 6-8 mss/year. Byline given.

Nonfiction Considers Young Readers: animal, arts/crafts, concept, cooking, games/puzzles, health, history, how-to, interview/profile, math, nature/environment, science, sports. Middle Readers: animal, arts/crafts, concept, cooking, games/puzzles, health, history, interview/profile, math, nature/environment, science, sports. Buys 48 mss/year. Average word length: 350-750.

How To Contact/Writers Fiction: Query with published clips. Nonfiction: Query with published clips. Responds to queries in 6-8 weeks.Publishes ms 1 year after acceptance. Considers electronic submissions via disk or e-mail, previously published work.

Illustration Color artwork only.Works on assignment only. For first contact, query with samples. Submit samples to Jackie Berry, Editor. Responds only if interested. Samples not returned. Samples filed.

Terms Buys exclusive magazine rights. Buys exclusive magazine rights rights for artwork. Pays 150-200 for stories; 50-100 for articles. Additional payment for ms/illustration packages. Additional payment for ms/photo packages. Pays illustrators $130-150 for color cover. Sample copies (€5 sterling) this must be bankers cheque in sterling, not US dollars. Writer's guidelines free for SASE. Publishes work by children.

Tips "We only accept a high level of educational material for children ages 8-13 with a good standard of literacy and ability."

ASK, Arts and Sciences for Kids

Carus Publishing, 70 E. Lake Sreet, Suite 300, Chicago IL 60601. (312)701-1720. E-mail: ask@caruspub.com. Web site: www.cricketmag.com. **Editor:** Lonnie Plecha. **Art Director:** Karen Kohn. Magazine published 9 times/year. Estab. 2002. "*ASK* encourages children between the ages of 7 and 10 to inquire about the world around them."

Nonfiction Young readers, middle readers: animal, history, nature/environment, science. Average word length: 150-1,500. Byline given.

How to Contact/Writers *Ask* does not accept unsolicited mss or queries. All articles are commissioned. To be considered for assignments, experienced science writers may send a résumé and 3 published clips.

Illustration Buys 10 illustrations/issue; 60 illustrations/year. Works on assignment only. Illustrations only: Query with samples.

BABAGANEWZ

Jewish Family & Life, 11141 Georgia Ave. #406, Wheaton MD 20902. (301)962-9636. Fax: (301)962-9635. Web site: www.babaganewz.com. **Articles Editor:** Mark Levine. **Managing Editor:** Jean Max. Monthly magazine. Estab. 2001. Circ. 40,000. "*BabagaNewz* helps middle school students explore Jewish values that are at the core of Jewish beliefs and practices."

Fiction Middle readers: religious, Jewish themes. Buys 1 ms/year. Average word length: 1,000-1,500. Byline given.

Nonfiction Middle readers: arts/crafts, concept, games/puzzles, geography, history, humorous, interview/profile, nature/environment, religion, science, social issues. Most articles are written by assignment. Average word length: 350-1,000. Byline given.

How to Contact/Writers Queries only for fiction; queries preferred for nonfiction. No unsolicited manuscripts.

Illustration Uses color artwork only. Works on assignment only. Illustrations only: Send postcard sample with promo sheet, résumé, URL. Responds only if interested. Credit line given.

Photography Photos by assignment.

Terms Pays on acceptance. Usually buys all rights for mss. Original artwork returned at job's completion only if requested. Sample copies free for SAE 9×12 and 4 first-class stamps.

Tips "Most work is done on assignment. We are looking for freelance writers with experience writing nonfiction for 9- to 13-year-olds, especially on Jewish-related themes. No unsolicited manuscripts."

BABYBUG

Carus Publishing Company, 70 E. Lake St., Suite 300, Chicago IL 60601. **Editor:** Alice Letvin. **Art Director:** Suzanne Beck. Published 10 times/year (monthly except for combined May/June and July/August issues). Estab. 1994. "A listening and looking magazine for infants and toddlers ages 6 to 24 months, *Babybug* is 6×7, 24 pages long, printed in large type on high-quality cardboard stock with rounded corners and no staples."

Fiction Looking for very simple and concrete stories, 4-6 short sentences maximum.

Nonfiction Must use very basic words and concepts, 10 words maximum.

Poetry Maximum length 8 lines. Looking for rhythmic, rhyming poems.

How to Contact/Writers "Please do not query first." Send complete ms with SASE. "Submissions without SASE will be discarded." Responds in 6 months.

Illustration Uses color artwork only. Works on assignment only. Reviews ms/illustration packages from artists. "The manuscripts will be evaluated for quality of concept and text before the art is considered." Contact: Suzanne Beck. Illustrations only: Send tearsheets or photo prints/photocopies with SASE. "Submissions without SASE will be discarded." Responds in 3 months. Samples filed.

Terms Pays on publication for mss; after delivery of completed assignment for illustrators. Rights purchased vary. Original artwork returned at job's completion. Rates vary ($25 minimum for mss; $250 minimum for art). Sample copy for $5. Guidelines free for SASE or available on Web site, FAQ at www.cricketmag.com.

Tips "*Babybug* would like to reach as many children's authors and artists as possible for original contributions, but our standards are very high, and we will accept only top-quality material. Before attempting to write for *Babybug*, be sure to familiarize yourself with this age child."

BOYS' LIFE

Boy Scouts of America, 1325 W. Walnut Hill Lane, Irving TX 75015-2079. (972)580-2366. Fax: (972)580-2079. Web site: www.boyslife.org. **Managing Editor:** Michael Goldman. **Senior Writer:** Aaron Derr. **Fiction Editor:**

Paula Murphey. **Director of Design:** Scott Feaster. Monthly magazine. Estab. 1911. Circ. 1,300,000. *Boys' Life* is "a 4-color general interest magazine for boys 8 to 18 who are members of the Cub Scouts, Boy Scouts or Venturers."

Fiction Young readers, middle readers, young adults: adventure, animal, contemporary, history, humor, multicultural, nature/environment, problem-solving, sports, science fiction, spy/mystery. Does not want to see animals and adult reminiscence." Buys only 12-16 mss/year. Average word length: 1,000-1,500. Byline given.

Nonfiction Young readers, middle readers, young adult: animal, arts/crafts, biography, careers (middle readers and young adults only), cooking, health, history, hobbies, how-to, interview/profile, multicultural, nature/environment, problem-solving, science, sports. Matter is broad. We cover everything from professional sports to American history to how to pack a canoe. A look at a current list of the BSA's more than 100 merit badge pamphlets gives an idea of the wide range of subjects possible. Even better, look at a year's worth of recent issues. Column subjects are science, nature, earth, health, sports, space and aviation, cars, computers, entertainment, pets, history, music and others." Average word length: 500-1,500. Columns 300-750 words. Byline given.

How to Contact/Writers Fiction: Send complete ms with cover letter and SASE to fiction editor. Nonfiction: Major articles query senior editor. Columns query associate editor with SASE for response. Responds to queries/mss in 2 months.

Illustration Buys 10-12 illustrations/issue; 100-125 illustrations/year. Works on assignment only. Reviews ms/illustration packages from artists. "Query first." Illustrations only: Send tearsheets. Responds to art samples only if interested. Samples returned with SASE. Original artwork returned at job's completion. Credit line given.

Terms Pays on acceptance. Buys first rights. Pays $750 and up for fiction; $400-1,500 for major articles; $150-400 for columns; $250-300 for how-to features. Pays illustrators $1,500-3,000 for color cover; $100-1,500 color inside. Pays photographers by the project. Sample copies for $3.95 plus 9×12 SASE. Writer's/illustrator's/photo guidelines available for SASE.

Tips "We strongly urge you to study at least a year's issues to better understand the type of material published. Articles for *Boys' Life* must interest and entertain boys ages 8 to 18. Write for a boy you know who is 12. Our readers demand crisp, punchy writing in relatively short, straightforward sentences. The editors demand well-reported articles that demonstrate high standards of journalism. We follow *The New York Times* manual of style and usage. All submissions must be accompanied by SASE with adequate postage."

BOYS' QUEST

P.O. Box 227, Bluffton OH 45817-0227. (419)358-4610. Fax: (419)358-5027. Web site: www.boysquest.com. **Articles Editor:** Marilyn Edwards. Bimonthly magazine. Estab. 1995. "*Boys' Quest* is a magazine created for boys from 6 to 13 years, with youngsters 8, 9 and 10 the specific target age. Our point of view is that every young boy deserves the right to be a young boy for a number of years before he becomes a young adult. As a result, *Boys' Quest* looks for articles, fiction, nonfiction, and poetry that deal with timeless topics, such as pets, nature, hobbies, science, games, sports, careers, simple cooking, and anything else likely to interest a young boy."

Fiction Picture-oriented material, young readers, middle readers: adventure, animal, history, humorous, multicultural, nature/environment, problem-solving, sports. Does not want to see violence, teenage themes. Buys 30 mss/year. Average word length: 200-500. Byline given.

Nonfiction Picture-oriented material, young readers, middle readers: animal, arts/crafts, cooking, games/puzzles, history, hobbies, how-to, humorous, math, problem-solving, sports. Prefer photo support with nonfiction. Buys 30 mss/year. Average word length: 200-500. Byline given.

Poetry Reviews poetry. Maximum length: 21 lines. Limit submissions to 6 poems.

How to Contact/Writers All writers should consult the theme list before sending in articles. To receive current theme list, send a SASE. Fiction/nonfiction: Query or send complete ms (preferred). Send SASE with correct postage. No faxed or e-mailed material. Responds to queries in 2 weeks; mss in 2 weeks (if rejected); 5 weeks (if scheduled). Publishes ms 3 months-3 years after acceptance. Will consider simultaneous submissions and previously published work.

Illustration Buys 10 illustrations/issue; 60-70 illustrations/year. Uses b&w artwork only. Works on assignment only. Reviews ms/illustration packages from artists. Illustrations only: Query with samples, tearsheets. Responds in 1 month only if interested and a SASE. Samples returned with SASE; samples filed. Credit line given.

Photography Photos used for support of nonfiction. "Excellent photographs included with a nonfiction story is considered very seriously." Model/property releases required. Uses b&w, 5×7 or 3×5 prints. Query with samples; send unsolicited photos by mail. Responds in 3 weeks.

Terms Pays on publication. Buys first North American serial rights for mss. Buys first rights for artwork. Pays 5/word for stories and articles. Additional payment for ms/illustration packages and for photos accompanying articles. Pays $150-200 for color cover; $25-35 for b&w inside. Pays photographers per photo (range: $5-10). Originals returned to artist at job's completion. Sample copies for $6 (includes postage); $7.50 outside U.S. Writer's/illustrator's/photographer's guidelines and theme list are free for SASE.

Tips "First be familiar with our magazines. We are looking for lively writing, most of it from a young boy's point of view—with the boy or boys directly involved in an activity that is both wholesome and unusual. We need nonfiction with photos and fiction stories—around 500 words—puzzles, poems, cooking, carpentry projects, jokes and riddles. Nonfiction pieces that are accompanied by black and white photos are far more likely to be accepted than those that need illustrations. We will entertain simultaneous submissions as long as that fact is noted on the manuscript."

BREAD FOR GOD'S CHILDREN

Bread Ministries, Inc., P.O. Box 1017, Arcadia FL 34265-1017. (863)494-6214. Fax: (863)993-0154. E-mail: bread@breadministries.org. Web site: www.breadministries.org. **Editor:** Judith M. Gibbs. Bimonthly magazine. Estab. 1972. Circ. 10,000 (U.S. and Canada). "*Bread* is designed as a teaching tool for Christian families." 85% of publication aimed at juvenile market.

Fiction Young readers, middle readers, young adult/teen: adventure, religious, problem-solving, sports. Looks for "teaching stories that portray Christian lifestyles without preaching." Buys approximately 20 mss/year. Average word length: 900-1,500 (for teens); 600-900 (for young children). Byline given.

Nonfiction All levels: how-to. "We do not want anything detrimental to solid family values. Most topics will fit if they are slanted to our basic needs." Buys 3-4 mss/year. Average word length: 500-800. Byline given.

Illustration "The only illustrations we purchase are those occasional good ones accompanying an accepted story."

How to Contact/Writers Fiction/nonfiction: Send complete ms. Responds to mss in 6 months "if considered for use." Will consider simultaneous submissions and previously published work.

Terms Pays on publication. Pays $30-50 for stories; $30 for articles. Sample copies free for 9×12 SAE and 5 first-class stamps (for 2 copies).

Tips "We want stories or articles that illustrate overcoming obstacles by faith and living solid, Christian lives. Know our publication and what we have used in the past. Know the readership and publisher's guidelines. Stories should teach the value of morality and honesty without preaching. Edit carefully for content and grammar."

BRILLIANT STAR

National Spiritual Assembly of the Bahá'ís of the U.S., 1233 Central St., Evanston IL 60201. (847)853-2354. Fax: (847)256-1372. E-mail: brilliant@usbnc.org. Web site: www.brilliantstarmagazine.org. **Associate Editor:** Susan Engle. **Art Director:** Amethel Parel-Sewell. Publishes 6 issues/year. Estab. 1969. "Our magazine is designed for children ages 8-12. *Brilliant Star* presents Bahá'í history and principles through fiction, nonfiction, activities, interviews, puzzles, cartoons, games, music, and art. Universal values of good character, such as kindness, courage, creativity, and helpfulness are incorporated into the magazine."

Fiction Middle readers: contemporary, fantasy, folktale, multicultural, nature/environment, problem-solving, religious. Average word length: 700-1,400. Byline given.

Nonfiction Middle readers: arts/crafts, games/puzzles, geography, how-to, humorous, multicultural, nature/environment, religion, social issues. Buys 6 mss/year. Average word length: 300-700. Byline given.

Poetry "We only publish poetry written by children at the moment."

How to Contact/Writers Fiction: Send complete ms. Nonfiction: Query. Responds to queries/mss in 6 weeks. Publishes ms 6 months-1 year after acceptance. Will consider e-mail submissions.

Illustration Works on assignment only. Reviews ms/illustration packages from artists. Illustrations only: Query with samples. Contact: Aaron Kreader, graphic designer. Responds only if interested. Samples kept on file. Credit line given.

Photography Buys photos with accompanying ms only. Model/property release required; captions required. Responds only if interested.

Terms Pays 2 copies of issue. Buys first rights and reprint rights for mss. Buys first rights and reprint rights for artwork; first rights and reprint rights for photos. Sample copies for $3. Writer's/illustrator's/photo guidelines for SASE.

Tips "*Brilliant Star's* content is developed with a focus on children in their 'tween' years, ages 8-12. This is a period of intense emotional, physical, and psychological development. Familiarize yourself with the interests and challenges of children in this age range. Protagonists in our fiction are usually in the upper part of our age-range: 10-12 years old. They solve their problems without adult intervention. We appreciate seeing a sense of humor but not related to bodily functions or put-downs. Keep your language and concepts age-appropriate. Use short words, sentences, and paragraphs. Activities and games may be submitted in rough or final form. Send us a description of your activity along with short, simple instructions. We avoid long, complicated activities that require adult supervision. If you think they will be helpful, please try to provide step-by-step rough sketches of the instructions. You may also submit photographs to illustrate the activity."

CADET QUEST

Calvinist Cadet Corps, P.O. Box 7259, Grand Rapids MI 49510. (616)241-5616. E-mail: submissions@calvinistca dets.org. Web site: www.calvinistcadets.org. **Editor:** G. Richard Broene. Magazine published 7 times/year. Circ. 9,000.'' ur magazine is for members of the Calvinist Cadet Corps—boys aged 9-14. Our purpose is to show how God is at work in their lives and in the world around them. Our magazine offers nonfiction articles and fast-moving fiction—everything to appeal to the interests and concerns of boys and teach Christian values.''

Fiction Middle readers, boys/early teens: adventure, humorous, multicultural, problem-solving, religious, sports. Buys 12 mss/year. Average word length: 900-1,500.

Nonfiction Middle readers, boys/early teens: arts/crafts, games/puzzles, hobbies, how-to, humorous, interview/profile, problem-solving, science, sports. Buys 6 mss/year. Average word length: 400-900.

How to Contact/Writers Fiction/nonfiction: Send complete ms by mail with SASE or by e-mail. Please note: e-mail submissions must have material in the body of the e-mail. Will not open attachments.'' Responds to mss in 2 months. Will consider simultaneous submissions.

Illustration Buys 2 illustration/issue; buys 12 illustrations/year. Works on assignment only. Reviews ms/illustration packages from artists. Responds in 5 weeks. Samples returned with SASE. Originals returned to artist at job's completion. Credit line given.

Photography Buys photos from freelancers. Wants nature photos and photos of boys.

Terms Pays on acceptance. Buys first North American serial rights; reprint rights. Pays 4-5 cent a word for stories/articles. Pays illustrators $50-200 for b&w/color cover or b&w/color inside. Sample copy free with 9 × 12 SAE and 3 first-class stamps.

Tips ''Our publication is mostly open to fiction; look for new themes at our Web site. We use mostly fast-moving fiction from a Christian persepective and based on our themes for each issue. Articles on sports, outdoor activities, science, crafts, etc. should emphasize a Christian perspective. Best time to submit material is February-April. Themes available on our Web site February 1.''

CALLIOPE, Exploring World History

Cobblestone Publishing Company, 30 Grove St., Peterborough NH 03458. (603)924-7209. Fax: (603)924-7380. Web site: www.cobblestonepub.com. **Editorial Director:** Lou Waryncia. **Co-editors:** Rosalie Baker and Charles Baker. **Art Director:** Ann Dillon. Magazine published 9 times/year. ''*Calliope* covers world history (East/West), and lively, original approaches to the subject are the primary concerns of the editors in choosing material.''

- *Calliope* themes for 2005-2006 include the Aztecs, Medieval Japan, the Spice Trade, Rembrandt, the Irish Potato Famine, Charles Dickens. For additional themes and time frames, visit their Web site.

Fiction Middle readers and young adults: adventure, folktales, plays, history, biographical fiction. Material must relate to forthcoming themes. Word length: up to 800.

Nonfiction Middle readers and young adults: arts/crafts, biography, cooking, games/puzzles, history. Material must relate to forthcoming themes. Word length: 300-1,000.

How to Contact/Writers ''A query must consist of the following to be considered (please use nonerasable paper): a brief cover letter stating subject and word length of the proposed article; a detailed one-page outline explaining the information to be presented in the article; an bibliography of materials the author intends to use in preparing the article; a self-addressed stamped envelope. Writers new to *Calliope* should send a writing sample with query. In all correspondence, please include your complete address as well as a telephone number where you can be reached. A writer may send as many queries for one issue as he or she wishes, but each query must have a separate cover letter, outline and bibliography as well as a SASE. Telephone and e-mail queries are not accepted. Handwritten queries will not be considered. Queries may be submitted at any time, but queries sent well in advance of deadline *may not be answered for several months*. Go-aheads requesting material proposed in queries are usually sent five months prior to publication date. Unused queries will be returned approximately three to four months prior to publication date.''

Illustration Illustrations only: Send tearsheets, photocopies. Original work returned upon job's completion (upon written request).

Photography Buys photos from freelancers. Wants photos pertaining to any forthcoming themes. Uses b&w/color prints, 35mm transparencies. Send unsolicited photos by mail (on speculation).

Terms Buys all rights for mss and artwork. Pays 20-25¢/word for stories/articles. Pays on an individual basis for poetry, activities, games/puzzles. ''Covers are assigned and paid on an individual basis.'' Pays photographers per photo ($15-100 for b&w; $25-100 for color). Sample copy for $5.95 and SAE with $2 postage. Writer's/illustrator's/photo guidelines for SASE.

CAMPUS LIFE'S IGNITE YOUR FAITH

Christianity Today, International, 465 Gundersen Dr., Carol Stream IL 60188. (630)260-6200. Fax: (630)260-2004. E-mail: iyf@igniteyourfaith.com. Web site: www.igniteyourfaith.com. **Articles and Fiction Editor:** Chris

Lutes. Magazine published 5 times yearly. Estab. 1944. Circ. 100,000. "Our purpose is to creatively engage and empower Christian teens to become fully devoted followers of Jesus Christ."
Fiction Young adults: humorous, problem-solving with a Christian worldview. Buys 1-3 mss/year. Byline given.
Poetry Reviews poetry.
How to Contact/Writers Fiction/nonfiction: Query only.
Terms Pays on acceptance. Writer's guidelines available on Web site.

CAREER WORLD

Weekly Reader Corp., Publishing Group, 1 Reader's Digest Rd., Pleasantville, NY 10570. E-mail: careerworld@w eeklyreader.com. **Articles Editor:** Anne Flounders. **Art Director:** Kimberly Shake. Monthly (school year) magazine. Estab. 1972. A guide to careers, for students grades 6-12.
Nonfiction Young adults/teens: education, how-to, interview/profile, career awareness and development. Byline given.
How to Contact/Writers Nonfiction: Query with published clips and résumé. Does not accept unsolicited manuscripts. Responds to queries only if interested.
Illustration Buys 5-10 illustrations/year. Works on assignment only. Reviews ms/illustration packages from artists. Manuscript/illustration packages and illustration only: Query; send promo sheet and tearsheets. Credit line given.
Photography Purchases photos from freelancers.
Terms Pays on publication. Buys all rights for mss. Pays $150 and up for articles. Pays illustrators by the project. Writer's guidelines free, but only on assignment.

CAREERS AND COLLEGES

A division of Alloy Education, an Alloy Media + Marketing Company, 10 Abeel Road, Cranbury NJ 08512. (609) 619- 8739. Web site: www.careersandcolleges.com. **SVP/Managing Director:** Jayne Pennington. Editor: Don Rauf. Magazine published 3 times a year (2 issues direct-to-home in July and 1 to 10,000 high schools in December). Circulation: 760,000. Distributed to 760,000 homes of 15- to 17-year-olds and college-bound high school graduates, and 10,000 high schools. *Careers and Colleges* magazine provides juniors and seniors in high school with editorial, tips, trends, and Web sites to assist them in the transition to college, career, young adulthood, and independence.
Nonfiction Young adults/teens: careers, college, health, how-to, humorous, interview/profile, personal development, problem-solving, social issues, sports, travel. Buys 10-20 mss/year. Average word length: 1,000-1,500. Byline given.
How to Contact/Writers Nonfiction: Query. Responds to queries in 6 weeks. Will consider electronic submissions.
Illustration Buys 2 illustrations/issue; buys 8 illustrations/year. Works on assignment only. Reviews samples online. Query first. Credit line given.
Terms Pays on acceptance plus 45 days. Buys all rights. Pays $100-600 for assigned/unsolicited articles. Additional payment for ms/illustration packages "must be negotiated." Pays $300-1,000 for color illustration; $200-700 for b&w/color inside illustration. Pays photographers by the project. Sample copy $5. Contributor' s Guidelines are available electronically.
Tips "Articles with great quotes, good reporting, good writing. Rich with examples and anecdotes. Must tie in with the objective to help teenaged readers plan for their futures. Current trends, policy changes and information regarding college admissions, financial aid, and career opportunities."

CARUS PUBLISHING COMPANY

P.O. Box 300, Peru IL 61354.
  • See listings for *Babybug*, *Cicada*, *Click*, *Cricket*, *Ladybug*, *Muse*, *Spider* and *ASK*. Carus Publishing owns Cobblestone Publishing, publisher of *AppleSeeds*, *Calliope*, *Cobblestone*, *Dig*, *Faces* and *Odyssey*.

CATHOLIC FORESTER

Catholic Order of Foresters, P.O. Box 3012, 355 Shuman Blvd., Naperville IL 60566-7012. (630)983-4900. E-mail: magazine@CatholicForester.com. Web site: www.catholicforester.com. **Articles Editor:** Patricia Baron. **Assistant V.P. Communication:** Mary Ann File. **Art Director:** Keith Halla. Quarterly magazine. Estab. 1883. Circ. 85,000. Targets members of the Catholic Order of Foresters. In addition to the organization's news, it offers general interest pieces on health, finance, family life. Also use inspirational and humorous fiction.
Fiction Buys 6-10 mss/year. Average word length: 500-1,500.
How to Contact/Writers Fiction: Submit complete ms. Responds in 4 months. Will consider previously published work.
Illustration Buys 2-4 illustrations/issue. Uses color artwork only. Works on assignment only.

Photography Buys photos with accompanying ms only.

Terms Pays on acceptance. Buys first North American serial rights, reprint rights, one-time rights. Sample copies for 9×12 SASE with 3 first-class stamps. Writer's guidelines free for SASE.

CELEBRATE

Word Action Publishing Co., Church of the Nazarene, 2923 Troost Ave, Kansas City MO 64109. (816)931-1900, ext. 8228. Fax: (816)412-8306. E-mail: dxb@nph.com. Web site: www.wordaction.com. **Editor:** Abigail L. Takala. **Assistant Editor:** Danielle J. Broadbooks. Weekly publication. Estab. 2001. Circ. 30,000. "This weekly take-home paper connects Sunday School learning to life for preschoolers (age 3 and 4), kindergartners (age 5 and 6) and their families." 75% of publication aimed at juvenile market; 25% parents.

Nonfiction Picture-oriented material: arts/crafts, cooking, poems, action rhymes, piggyback songs (theme based). 50% of mss nonfiction. Byline given.

Poetry Reviews poetry. Maximum length: 4-8 lines. Unlimited submissions.

How to Contact/Writers Nonfiction: query. Responds to queries in 1 month. Responds to mss in 6 weeks. Publishes ms 1 year after acceptance. Will accept electronic submission via e-mail.

Terms Pays on acceptance. Buys all rights, multi-use rights. Pays $15 for activities, crafts, recipes, songs, rhymes, and poems. Compensation includes 2 contributor copies. Sample copy for SASE.

Tips "We are accepting submissions at this time."

CHEMMATTERS

American Chemical Society, 1155 16th Street, NW, Washington DC 20036. (202)872-6164. Fax: (202)833-7732. E-mail: chemmatters@acs.org. Web site: http://www.acs.org/chemmatters.html. **Editor:** Pat Pages. **Art Director:** Cornithia Harris. Quarterly magazine. Estab. 1983. Circ. 35,000. "*ChemMatters* is a magazine for connecting high school readers with the fascinating chemistry of their everyday lives."

- *ChemMatters* only accepts e-mail submissions.

Audience: NonfictionYoung Adults: biography, health, history, nature/environment, problem-solving, science. Must be related to chemistry. Buys 20 manuscripts/year. Average word length: 1,400-2,100. Byline given.

How to Contact: Query with published clips. Only e-mail submissions will be considered. Responds to queries/mss in 2 weeks. Publishes ms 6 months after acceptance. Will consider simultaneous submissions, e-mail submissions.

Illustration: Buys 3 illustrations/issue; 12 illustrations/year. Uses color artwork only. Works on assignment only. Reviews manuscript/illustration packages from artists. Query. Contact: Cornithia Harris, art director *ChemMatters*. Illustrations only: Query with promo sheet, résumé. Responds in 2 weeks. Samples returned with self-addressed stamped envelope; samples not filed. Credit line given.

Photography: Looking for photos of high school students engaged in science-related activities. Model/property release required; captions required. Uses color prints, but prefers high-resolution PDFs. Query with samples. Responds in 2 weeks.

Terms: Pays on acceptance. Minimally buys first North American serial rights, but prefers to buy all rights, reprint rights, electronic rights for manuscripts. Buys all rights for artwork; non-exclusive first rights for photos. Pays $500-$1,000 for article. Additional payment for manuscript/illustration packages and for photos accompanying articles. **Sample copies** free for self-addressed stamped envelope 10 inches × 13 inches and 3 first-class stamps. **Writer's guidelines** free for self-addressed stamped envelope (available as e-mail attachment upon request).

Tips: Be aware of the content covered in a standard high school chemistry textbook. Choose themes and topics that are timely, interesting, fun, *and* that relate to the content and concepts of the first-year chemistry course. Articles should describe real people involved with real science. Best articles feature young people making a difference or solving a problem.

CHILDREN'S BETTER HEALTH INSTITUTE

1100 Waterway Blvd., P.O. Box 567, Indianapolis IN 46206. See listings for *Children's Digest, Children's Playmate, Humpty Dumpty's Magazine, Jack and Jill, Turtle* and *U*S* Kids*.

CHILDREN'S DIGEST

Children's Better Health Institute, 1100 Waterway Blvd., P.O. Box 567, Indianapolis IN 46206. (317)634-1100. Fax: (317)684-8094. Web site: www.childrensdigestmag.org. For children ages 10-12.

- See Web site for submission guidelines.

CHILDREN'S PLAYMATE

Children's Better Health Institute, 1100 Waterway Blvd., Box 567, Indianapolis IN 46206. (317)634-1100. Fax: (317)684-8094. Web site: www.childrensplaymatemag.org. **Editor:** Terry Harshman. **Art Director:** Rob Falco.

Magazine published 6 times/year. Estab. 1929. Circ. 135,000. For children ages 6-8 years; approximately 50% of content is health-related.

Fiction Average word length: 100-300. Byline given. Sample copies $2.95.

Nonfiction Young readers: easy recipes, games/puzzles, health, medicine, safety, science. Buys 16-20 mss/year. Average word length: 300-500. Byline given.

Poetry Maximum length: 20-25 lines.

How to Contact/Writers Fiction/nonfiction: Send complete ms. Responds to mss in 3 months. Do not send queries.

Illustration Works on assignment only. Reviews ms/illustration packages from artists. Query first.

Terms Pays on publication for illustrators and writers. Buys all rights for mss and artwork. Pays 17¢/word for stories. Pays minimum $25 for poems. Pays $275 for color cover illustration; $90 for b&w inside; $70-155 for color inside. Sample copy $3.95. Writer's/illustrator's guidelines for SASE.

CICADA

Carus Publishing Company, P.O. Box 300, 315 Fifth St., Peru IL 61354. (815)224-5803. Fax: (815)224-6615. Submissions address: 70 East Lake Street, Suite 300, Chicago IL 60601. E-mail: cicada@caruspub.com. Web site: www.cricketmag.com. **Editor-in-Chief:** Marianne Carus. **Executive Editor:** Deborah Vetter. **Art Director:** John Sandford. Bimonthly magazine. Estab. 1998. *Cicada* publishes fiction and poetry with a genuine teen sensibility, aimed at the high school and college-age market. The editors are looking for stories and poems that are thought-provoking but entertaining.

Fiction Young adults: adventure, animal, contemporary, fantasy, history, humorous, multicultural, nature/environment, romance, science fiction, sports, suspense/mystery, stories that will adapt themselves to a sophisticated cartoon, or graphic novel format. Buys up to 60 mss/year. Average word length: about 5,000 words for short stories; up to 15,000 for novellas (one novella per issue).

Nonfiction Young adults: first-person, coming-of-age experiences that are relevant to teens and young adults (example: life in the Peace Corps). Buys 6 mss/year. Average word length: about 5,000 words. Byline given.

Poetry Reviews serious, humorous, free verse, rhyming (if done well) poetry. Maximum length: up to 25 lines. Limit submissions to 5 poems.

How to Contact/Writers Fiction/nonfiction: send complete ms. Responds to mss in 3 months. Publishes ms 1-2 years after acceptance. Will consider simultaneous submissions if author lets us know.

Illustration Buys 20 illustrations/issue; 120 illustrations/year. Uses color artwork for cover; b&w for interior. Works on assignment only. Reviews ms/illustration packages from artists. Send ms with 1-2 sketches and samples of other finished art. Illustrations only: Query with samples. Responds in 6 weeks. Samples returned with SASE; samples filed. Credit line given.

Photography Wants documentary photos (clear shots that illustrate specific artifacts, persons, locations, phenomena, etc., cited in the text) and ''art'' shots of teens in photo montage/lighting effects etc. Uses b&w 4×5 glossy prints. Submit portfolio for review. Responds in 6 weeks.

Terms Pays on publication. Rights purchased vary. Pays up to 25¢/word for mss; up to $3/line for poetry. Pays illustrators $750 for color cover; $50-150 for b&w inside. Pays photographers per photo (range: $50-150). Sample copies for $8.50. Writer's/illustrator's/photo guidelines for SASE.

Tips ''Cicada is currently closed to unsolicited submissions. Please see our current issues for submission guidelines for writing and artwork by readers ages 14-23. The Slam, our online microfiction and poetry forum, is also open to young people ages 14-23. Check www.cricket.mag.com for updates on our submissions policy.''

▨ THE CLAREMONT REVIEW

4980 Wesley Road, Victoria BC V8Y 1Y9 Canada. (250)685-5221. Fax: (250)658-5387. E-mail: editor@theClarem ontReview.ca. Web site: www.theClaremontReview.ca. Magazine 2 times/year. Estab. 1992. Circ. 500. ''Publish quality fiction and poetry of emerging writers aged 13 to 19.''

Fiction Young adults: multicultural, problem-solving, social issues, relationships. Average word length: 1,500-3,000.

Poetry Maximum length: 60 lines. No limit on submissions.

How to Contact/Writers Fiction: Send complete ms. Responds to queries in 2 weeks; mss in 2 months. Publishes ms 6 months after acceptance.

Illustration Illustrations only: Send postcard sample with samples, SASE. Contact: Janice McCachen, editor. Responds in 2 months. Samples returned with SASE. Credit line given.

Terms Buys first North American rights for mss. Pays contributor's copies when published. Sample copies for $10. Writer's guidelines for SASE.

Tips ''Looking for good, concrete narratives with credible dialogue and solid use of original detail. It must be unique, honest and have a glimpse of some truth. Send an error-free final draft with a short covering letter and bio. Read our magazine first to familiarize yourself with what we publish.''

CLICK

70 E. Lake St., Suite 300, Chicago IL 60601. (312)701-1720. Fax: (312)701-1728. E-mail: click@caruspub.com. Web site: www.cricketmag.com. **Editor:** Amy Tao. **Art Director:** Deb Porter. 9 issues/year. Estab. 1998. *"Click is a science and exploration magazine for children ages 3 to 7. Designed and written with the idea that it's never too early to encourage a*
child's natural curiosity about the world, *Click*'s 40 full-color pages are filled with amazing photographs, beautiful illustrations, and stories and articles that are both entertaining and thought-provoking."
Nonfiction Young readers: animals, nature/environment, science. Average word length:100-900. Byline given.
How to Contact Writers *Click* does not accept unsolicited manuscripts or queries. All articles are commissioned. To be considered for assignments, experienced science writers may send a résumé and three published clips.
Illustration Buys 10 illustrations/issue; 100 illustrations/year. Works on assignment only. Query with samples. Responds only if interested. Credit line given.

COBBLESTONE: Discover American History

Cobblestone Publishing, 30 Grove St., Suite C, Peterborough NH 03458. (603)924-7209. Fax: (603)924-7380. Web site: www.cobblestonepub.com. **Editor:** Meg Chorlian. **Art Director:** Ann Dillon. **Editorial Director:** Lou Waryncia. Magazine published 9 times/year. Circ. 27,000. *"Cobblestone* is theme-related. Writers should request editorial guidelines which explain procedure and list upcoming themes. Queries must relate to an upcoming theme. It is recommended that writers become familiar with the magazine (sample copies available)."
• *Cobblestone* themes and deadline are available on Web site or with SASE.
Fiction Middle readers, young adults: folktales, history, multicultural.
Nonfiction Middle readers (school ages 9-14): arts/crafts, biography, geography, history (world and American), multicultural, social issues. All articles must relate to the issue's theme. Buys 120 mss/year. Average word length: 600-800. Byline given.
Poetry Up to 100 lines. "Clear, objective imagery. Serious and light verse considered." Pays on an individual basis. Must relate to theme.
How to Contact/Writers Fiction/nonfiction: Query. "A query must consist of all of the following to be considered: a brief cover letter stating the subject and word length of the proposed article, a detailed one-page outline explaining the information to be presented in the article, an extensive bibliography of materials the author intends to use in preparing the article, a SASE. Writers new to *Cobblestone* should send a writing sample with query. If you would like to know if your query has been received, please also include a stamped postcard that requests acknowledgment of receipt. In all correspondence, please include your complete address as well as a telephone number where you can be reached. A writer may send as many queries for one issue as he or she wishes, but each query must have a separate cover letter, outline, bibliography and SASE. Telephone queries are not accepted. Handwritten queries will not be considered. Queries may be submitted at any time, but queries sent well in advance of deadline *may not be answered for several months.* Go-aheads requesting material proposed in queries are usually sent five months prior to publication date. Unused queries will not be returned."
Illustration Buys 5 color illustrations/issue; 45 illustrations/year. Preferred theme or style: Material that is fun, clear and accurate but not too juvenile. Historically accurate sources are a must. Works on assignment only. Reviews ms/illustration packages from artists. Query. Illustrations only: Send photocopies, tearsheets, or other nonreturnable samples. "Illustrators should consult issues of *Cobblestone* to familiarize themselves with our needs." Responds to art samples in 1 month. Samples are not returned; samples filed. Original artwork returned at job's completion (upon written request). Credit line given.
Photography Photos must relate to upcoming themes. Send transparencies and/or color prints. Submit on speculation.
Terms Pays on publication. Buys all rights to articles and artwork. Pays 20-25¢/word for articles/stories. Pays on an individual basis for poetry, activities, games/puzzles. Pays photographers per photo ($50-100 for color). Sample copy $5.95 with 9×12 SAE and 4 first-class stamps; writer's/illustrator's/photo guidelines free with SAE and 1 first-class stamp.
Tips Writers: "Submit detailed queries which show attention to historical accuracy and which offer interesting and entertaining information. Study past issues to know what we look for. All feature articles, recipes, activities, fiction and supplemental nonfiction are freelance contributions." Illustrators: "Submit color samples, not too juvenile. Study past issues to know what we look for. The illustration we use is generally for stories, recipes and activities."

CRICKET

Carus Publishing Company, 70 East Lake, Suite 300, Chicago, IL 60601. (312)701-1270. Web site: www.cricketm ag.com. **Editor-in-Chief:** Marianne Carus. **Executive Editor:** Lonnie Plecha. **Senior Art Director:** Karen Kohn. Monthly magazine. Estab. 1973. Circ. 72,000. Children's literary magazine for ages 9-14.
Fiction Middle readers, young adults/teens: contemporary, fantasy, folk and fairy tales, history, humorous,

science fiction, suspense/mystery. Buys 140 mss/year. Maximum word length: 2,000. Byline given.
Nonfiction Middle readers, young adults/teens: adventure, architecture, archaeology, biography, foreign culture, games/puzzles, geography, natural history, science and technology, social science, sports, travel. Multicultural needs include articles on customs and cultures. Requests bibliography with submissions. Buys 40 mss/year. Average word length: 200-1,500. Byline given.
Poetry Reviews poems, 1-page maximum length. Limit submission to 5 poems or less.
How to Contact/Writers Send complete ms. Do not query first. Responds to mss in 4-6 months. Does not like but will consider simultaneous submissions. SASE required for response, IRCs for international submissions.
Illustration Buys 35 illustrations (14 separate commissions)/issue; 425 illustrations/year. Preferred theme for style: "strong realism; strong people, especially kids; good action illustration; no cartoons. All media, but prefer other than pencil." Reviews ms/illustration packages from artists, "but reserves option to re-illustrate." Send complete ms with sample and query. Illustrations only: Provide tearsheets or good quality photocopies to be kept on file. SASE required for response/return of samples. Responds to art samples in 2 months.
Photography Purchases photos with accompanying ms only. Model/property releases required. Uses color transparencies, b&w glossy prints.
Terms Pays on publication. Rights purchased vary. Do not send original artwork. Pays up to 25¢/word for unsolicited articles; up to $3/line for poetry. Pays $750 for color cover; $75-150 for b&w, $150-250 for color inside. Writer's/illustrator's guidelines for SASE. Sample issue for $5, check made out to Cricket Magazine Group.
Tips Writers: "Read copies of back issues and current issues. Adhere to specified word limits. *Please* do not query." Illustrators: "Edit your samples. Send only your best work and be able to reproduce that quality in assignments. Put name and address on *all* samples. Know a publication before you submitis your style appropriate?"

CURRENT SCIENCE

Weekly Reader Corp.E-mail: science@weeklyreader.com. Web site: www.weeklyreader.com. **Managing Editor:** Hugh Westrup. 16 times/year magazine. Estab. 1927. "*Current Science*uses today's new to make science relevant to students in grades 6-10. Each issue covers every area of the science curriculum—life, earth, and physical science, plus health and technology."
   • *Current Science* is no longer accepting unsolicited submissions.

DANCE MAGAZINE

333 Seventh Ave., 11th Floor, New York NY 10001. (212)979-4803. Fax: (646)674-0102. Web site: www.dancemagazine.com. **Editor-in-Chief:** Wendy Perron. **Art Director:** Ragnar Johnson. Monthly magazine. Estab. 1927. Circ. 45,000. Covers "all things dance—features, news, reviews, calendar."
How to Contact Query with published clips.
Photography Uses dance photos.
Terms Pays on publication. Buys first rights. Additional payment for ms/illustration packages and for photos accompanying articles. Pays photographers per photo. Byline given. Sample copies for $4.95. (Go to Web site and click on subscription services.)
Tips "Study the magazine for style."

DAVEY AND GOLIATH'S DEVOTIONS

Augsburg Fortress Publishers, P.O. Box 1209, Minneapolis MN 55440-1209. E-mail: cllsub@augsburgfortress.org. Web site: www.augsburgfortress.org. **Editor:** Becky Carlson. Quarterly magazine. Circ. approximately 40,000. This is a booklet of interactive conversations and activities related to weekly devotional material. Used primarily by Lutheran families with elementary school-aged children." avey and Goliath's devotions is a magazine with concrete ideas that families can use to build biblical literacy and share faith and serve others. It includes bible stories, family activities, crafts, games, and a section of puzzles, and mazes."
How to Contact/Writers Visit www.augsburgfortress.org/media/company/downloads/FamilyDevotionalSampleBriefing.doc to view sample briefing. Follow instructions in briefing if interested in submitting a sample for the devotional. Published material is 100% assigned.
Terms Pays on acceptance of final ms assignment. Buys all rights. Pays $40/printed page on assignment. Free sample and information for prospective writers. Include 6×9 SAE and postage.
Tips "Pay attention to details in the sample devotional. Follow the process laid out in the information for prospective writers. Ability to interpret Bible texts appropriately for children is required. Content must be doable and fun for families on the go."

DIG

Cobblestone Publishing, 30 Grove St., Suite C, Peterborough NH 03450. (603)924-7209. Fax: (603)924-7380. E-mail: cfbakeriii@meganet.net. Web site: www.digonsite.com. **Editor:** Rosalie Baker. **Editorial Director:** Lou

Barbara Kanninen

Magazine writing offers great experience

Under Barbara Kanninen's name on her Web site, it says "children's author and adventure economist." Indeed, Kanninen can claim both specialties. She's an environmental economist who holds a Bachelor's degree from Ohio University, a Master of Science in Economics from Texas A&M University and a Ph.D. in Agricultural and Resource Economics from the University of California at Berkeley.

She's also written 20 easy readers and other curriculum materials for educational companies such as Macmillan-McGraw-Hill, Core Knowlege Foundation, Kane Press and Kaeden Books and recently had her first picture book published. *A Story with Pictures* (Holiday House) received a starred review from *Publishers Weekly* and was named a "Picture Book We Admire" by the Children's Literature Network.

Before her publishing successes, however, Kanninen had been submitting to book publishers and getting nothing but form rejections, she says, "So I figured I had to change something about what I was doing." She decided to take a writing course. "I learned to tone up my pacing, brighten my language and employ sensory details. That extra 10% can make the difference between a form rejection and a revision request."

After working to improve her craft, Kanninen spent two years submitting solely to magazines. "I promised myself that I wouldn't submit another picture book manuscript until I'd broken into *Highlights* or *Ladybug*," she says. "I sold my first story to *Highlights* in 2002. It was called 'Marvin's Museum of Magnificent Things,' and Marileta Robinson asked for two revisions before I got it right. My decision to focus on magazines carried the wonderful perk that magazine editors were willing to work with me and help me revise. I learned so much from them."

In addition to *Highlights for Children*, Kanninen has done work for *Ladybug* and *Fun for Kids* among others. She's got a second picture book coming out from Holiday House, *Circle Rolls*, set for release in 2010. Below she talks about the value of her magazine writing experience, including advice on impressing editors, and talks about her picture book projects. To learn more about Kanninen, visit www.barbarakanninen.com.

What did you learn from your experience writing for magazines?

My magazine experience taught me that there are very generous editors out there—editors who will take the time to help you improve. Magazine editors need to buy a lot of stories so they're more likely than book editors to request rewrites and offer revision suggestions, especially if you attract their attention with a unique character or story idea. Magazine editors have reminded me of the basics—that a character needs to change over the course of a story, for example—and pushed me on higher-order skills like humor. I truly would not be the writer I am today without the friendly but firm editors at *Highlights*, *Guideposts for Kids* (now defunct) and the Carus Group.

What type of material have you written for children's magazines? Did writing for magazines help you become a better book writer?

I've written about 80% fiction for magazines and 20% nonfiction. I like to experiment with different genres. For example, my sales to *Highlights* have included a mystery, a sports/science fiction story and a story about a restaurant that makes "half-moon" shaped pizzas.

   Did writing for magazines help me become a better book writer? Yes! As I said above, I learned so many fundamental lessons from magazine editors—lessons that we all know in

After writing and submitting solely to magazines for two years, Barbara Kanninen submitted *A Story With Pictures* to Henry Holt and it was plucked from the slush pile. She says writing for magazines made her a better book writer. "I learned so many fundamental lessons from magazine editors."

theory but that we sometimes forget in practice. I also learned that no editor, no matter how modest the magazine, will settle for "OK." Every story, even one that will earn 10 dollars, has to be your very best. And then it has to be even better. And for books, better yet.

How is writing a magazine piece different from writing a picture book? What are the special considerations regarding children's magazine writing that writers should learn?

I think there are two main differences between magazine stories and picture book stories. The first is pacing. Magazine stories should read "fast." In other words, if you were to read a magazine story aloud to a child, you would read it straight through without pausing (except for air). Picture books have pulses to them. There are page turns, of course, but even if you were to read a picture book manuscript without the page turns built in, you would still feel the pulse of the pages. Picture books should be slower reads.

The other difference is the dialogue/narration split. In magazine stories, dialogue is a great way to show the character's personality and move the story along. Dialogue and narration can be balanced about equally. Picture books often use more narration than dialogue. The key in either genre is to keep dialogue relevant and punchy—no wasted words.

My best advice on writing good magazine stories is to make sure that first paragraph gives at least one interesting detail about the setting, gives a snippet of the character's personality, and also—most importantly—jumps right into the character's problem. If you can pull all that off, your story is likely to sail. Oh, and snappy, surprising endings are pure gold.

What advice would you offer in regards to approaching magazines with story ideas? What gets an editor's attention?

Editors read hundreds of stories in their slush piles every week. They're tired of reading about the tooth fairy and the kid who was picked last for the team. Give them something fresh. Look back to your own experiences to offer a unique problem, character or setting. My first major magazine sale was about a boy who couldn't get kids to come to his "Museum of Magnificent Things." I used a bit of economics in that story. My second was about a girl who was dragged along on a wolf howling trip. I had gone wolf howling myself; it's definitely an unusual and funny thing to do. More recently, I attracted a magazine editor's attention with a story about a boy who can't stop accidentally hitting foul balls into the trash can . . . every time. My son once hit a ball that rolled and rolled around the rim of a trash can. It stopped the game for five minutes while everyone cracked up. These are not standard story ideas. They came from my life and they attracted attention because they were different.

My first stories weren't particularly well-constructed. I had to revise "Marvin's Museum of Magnificent Things" twice for *Highlights*. But again, if you capture their attention with something fresh, they'll work with you to get it right.

When I read *A Story with Pictures* I imagine that it's a book other writers would certainly relate to. What sparked this story?

A Story with Pictures started one day when I thought, "What if there was a character on a blank page wondering where the pictures are? What would that character say? How would he or she try to find the pictures?" I didn't start off with the idea of the character being the author. It was just a character. So many elements of this picture book were added bit by bit over the course of about two and a half years. So, although there was a spark that initiated my work on this book, it is more the product of a very low flame burning for a very, very long time.

Your first published picture book could be used as a tool to teach kids about the basic elements of a story, as suggested by *School Library Journal*. Did you write *A Story with Pictures* with that in mind?

Not at all! As I said above, my original idea wasn't about an author or an illustrator. I was just playing with the idea of a pictureless book. When I submitted a draft to my critique group, a member who is also an elementary school teacher suggested that I figure out a way to include the story elements explicitly. It was a great suggestion because teachers and librarians are always looking for curriculum-relevant picture books. But I should point out that a picture book needs many layers to be successful in today's marketplace. *A Story with Pictures* is, first and foremost, funny.

Your Web site says there are a number of projects on your plate, among them a picture book biography, a new Jake book, a new story for the *Highlights* fiction contest and, "either a middle grade sports book or a YA, I can't decide." Did writing for magazines help you become a diverse writer or does being a diverse writer help you win magazine assignment?

Writing is a very personal endeavor, so I would guess most of us writers end up doing what fits best with our personalities. I do have a diverse array of interests, which translates into a need to write on a diverse set of topics and in a diverse set of genres.

I have never gotten a magazine assignment. All of my published magazine pieces were submitted "on spec," meaning that I wrote the pieces and submitted them for consideration without being asked by the editor to do so. When you're not an established author, you have to do it this way. More recently, though, I have gotten several nice work-for-hire jobs with curriculum companies and I strongly believe that my résumé full of diverse magazine stories has helped me land those jobs. So, yes, magazine work will get you more work. The credits show that you're a professional.

You seem very comfortable doing school visits. Any tips on how to plan an effective appearance? What do kids like?

It helps a lot to have a funny book. Kids love craziness and humor. It also helps to have entertaining props. When I pull a tutu out of my backpack, kids really crack up. Then I pull out a rubber duck. And a dragon. By this time, kids—whether kindergarteners or fifth graders—have decided they're having fun.

It helps to have a strong, clear speaking voice. If you don't have one, I highly encourage taking lessons to develop one. Authors sometimes get asked to speak to as many as 200 kids at once.

Finally, it helps a lot to smile and have fun. If you love what you do, it shows.

Tell me about your *Circle Rolls*, your upcoming book with Henry Holt. When will it be available?

I believe *Circle Rolls* will be available in 2010. It's a quirky, rhyming story about shapes: "Circle rolls, oval rocks; square sits like a box," but the circle keeps rolling and rolling and ends up creating all sorts of havoc—kind of like a toddler. The very short story (less than 200 words) has layers, from teaching shapes, to good rhyme, to a sweet ending.

How did you end up with Holt? Tell me about your path to picture book publication.

So far, I've sold picture book manuscripts the old-fashioned way, by submitting them to slush. In the case of *Circle Rolls*, I'd read that the editor I submitted to was interested in books for preschoolers. So it was a well-targeted submission. She e-mailed me two weeks after I submitted it expressing interest.

What's your advice to writers just starting out?

Well, I'm here in the magazine section of this book and my best advice is to start with magazines. I hear so many writers say they're only interested in writing picture books, for example, so they don't want to bother writing magazine stories. But if you're a new writer, you need to focus on craft first. Magazine editors are more likely to pull your work from slush, even if it's imperfect. They will work with you to tone up those rough edges. Little by little, the lessons you will learn by working with magazine editors will bring your writing up to the level you need to get noticed by book editors. It's a process that will—and should—take years.

—Alice Pope

Waryncia. **Art Director:** Ann Dillon. Magazine published 9 times/year. Estab. 1999. Circ. 20,000. An archaeology magazine for kids ages 8-14. Publishes entertaining and educational stories about discoveries, artifacts, archaeologists.

• *Dig* was purchased by Cobblestone Publishing, a division of Carus Publishing.

Nonfiction Middle readers, young adults: biography, games/puzzles, history, science, archaeology. Buys 50 mss/year. Average word length: 400-800. Byline given.

How to Contact/Writers Fiction/nonfiction: Query. "A query must consist of all of the following to be considered: a brief cover letter stating the subject and word length of the proposed article, a detailed one-page outline explaining the information to be presented in the article, a bibliography of materials the author intends to use in preparing the article, and a SASE. Writers new to *Dig* should send a writing sample with query. If you would like to know if a query has been received, include a stamped postcard that requests acknowledgement of receipt." Multiple queries accepted (include separate cover letter, outline, bibliography, SASE) may not be answered for many months. Go-aheads requesting material proposed in queries are usually sent 5 months prior to publication date. Unused queries will be returned approximately 3-4 months prior to publication date.

Illustration Buys 10-15 illustrations/issue; 60-75 illustrations/year. Prefers color artwork. Works on assignment only. Reviews ms/illustration packages from artists. Query. Illustrations only: Query with samples. Arrange portfolio review. Send tearsheets. Responds in 2 months only if interested. Samples not returned; samples filed. Credit line given.

Photography Uses anything related to archaeology, history, artifacts, and current archaeological events that relate to kids. Uses color prints and 35mm transparencies. Provide résumé, promotional literature or tearsheets to be kept on file. Responds only if interested.

Terms Pays on publication. Buys all rights for mss. Buys first North American rights for photos. Original artwork returned at job's completion. Pays 20-25¢/word. Additional payment for ms/illustration packages and for photos accompanying articles. Pays per photo.

Tips "We are looking for writers who can communicate archaeological concepts in a conversational, interesting, informative and *accurate* style for kids. Writers should have some idea where photography can be located to support their articles."

DISCOVERIES

WordAction Publishing Co., 2923 Troost Ave., Kansas City MO 64109. (816)931-1900. Fax: (816)412-8306. E-mail: kdadams@wordaction.com. **Editor:** Virginia L. Folsom. **Senior Editor:** Donna L. Fillmore. **Assistant Editor:** Kimberly Adams. Take-home paper. "*Discoveries* is a leisure-reading piece for third- and fourth-graders. It is published weekly by WordAction Publishing. The major purpose of the magazine is to provide a leisure-reading piece which will build Christian behavior and values and provide reinforcement for Biblical concepts taught in the Sunday School curriculum. The focus of the reinforcement will be life-related, with some historical appreciation. *Discoveries'* target audience is children ages eight to ten in grades three and four. The readability goal is third to fourth grade." Request guidelines and theme list by e-mail or send SASE.

DRAMATICS MAGAZINE

Educational Theatre Association, 2343 Auburn Ave., Cincinnati OH 45219. (513)421-3900. E-mail: dcorathers@ edta.org. Web site: www.edta.org. **Articles Editor:** Don Corathers. **Graphic Design:** Kay Walters. Published monthly September-May. Estab. 1929. Circ. 35,000. "Dramatics is for students (mainly high school age) and teachers of theater. Mix includes how-to (tech theater, acting, directing, etc.), informational, interview, photo feature, humorous, profile, technical. We want our student readers to grow as theater artists and become a more discerning and appreciative audience. Material is directed to both theater students and their teachers, with strong student slant."

Fiction Young adults: drama (one-act and full-length plays). Does not want to see plays that show no understanding of the conventions of the theater. No plays for children, no Christmas or didactic "message" plays. "We prefer unpublished scripts that have been produced at least once." Buys 5-9 plays/year. Emerging playwrights have better chances with résumé of credits. **Nonfiction** Young adults: arts/crafts, careers, how-to, interview/profile, multicultural (all theater-related). "We try to portray the theater community in all its diversity." Does not want to see academic treatises. Buys 50 mss/year. Average word length: 750-3,000. Byline given.

How to Contact/Writers Send complete ms. Responds in 3 months (longer for plays). Published ms 3 months after acceptance. Will consider simultaneous submissions and previously published work occasionally.

Illustration Buys 0-2 illustrations/year. Works on assignment only. Arrange portfolio review; send résumé, promo sheets and tearsheets. Responds only if interested. Samples returned with SASE; sample not filed. Credit line given.

Photography Buys photos with accompanying ms only. Looking for "good-quality production or candid photography to accompany article. We very occasionally publish photo essays." Model/property release and captions required. Prefers hi-res jpg files. Will consider prints or transparencies. Query with résumé of credits. Responds only if interested.

Terms Pays on acceptance. Buys one-time print and short term Web rights. Buys one-time rights for artwork and photos. Original artwork returned at job's completion. Pays $100-500 for plays; $50-500 for articles; up to $100 for illustrations. Pays photographers by the project or per photo. Sometimes offers additional payment for ms/illustration packages and photos accompanying a ms. Sample copy available for $9 × 12$ SAE with 4 ounces first-class postage. Writer's and photo guidelines available for SASE or via Web site.

Tips "Obtain our writer's guidelines and look at recent back issues. The best way to break in is to know our audience—drama students, teachers and others interested in theater—and write for them. Writers who have some practical experience in theater, especially in technical areas, have an advantage, but we'll work with anybody who has a good idea. Some freelancers have become regular contributors."

FACES, People, Places & Cultures

Cobblestone Publishing Company, 30 Grove St., Peterborough NH 03458. (603)924-7209. Fax: (603)924-7380. E-mail: facesmag@yahoo.com. Web site: www.cobblestonepub.com. **Editor:** Elizabeth Crooker Carpentiere. **Editorial Director:** Lou Warnycia. **Art Director:** Ann Dillon. Magazine published 9 times/year (September-May). Circ. 15,000. *Faces* is a theme-related magazine; writers should send for theme list before submitting ideas/queries. Each month a different world culture is featured through the use of feature articles, activities and photographs and illustrations.

• See Web site for 2008-2009 theme list for *Faces*.

Fiction Middle readers, young adults/teens: adventure, folktales, history, multicultural, plays, religious, travel. Does not want to see material that does not relate to a specific upcoming theme. Buys 9 mss/year. Maximum word length: 800. Byline given.

Nonfiction Middle readers and young adults/teens: animal, anthropology, arts/crafts, biography, cooking, fashion, games/puzzles, geography, history, how-to, humorous, interview/profile, nature/environment, religious, social issues, sports, travel. Does not want to see material not related to a specific upcoming theme. Buys 63 mss/year. Average word length: 300-600. Byline given.

How to Contact/Writers Fiction/nonfiction: Query with published clips and 2-3 line biographical sketch. "Ideas should be submitted six to nine months prior to the publication date. Responses to ideas are usually sent approximately four months before the publication date." Guidelines on Web site.

Illustration Buys 3 illustrations/issue; buys 27 illustrations/year. Preferred theme or style: Material that is meticulously researched (most articles are written by professional anthropologists); simple, direct style preferred, but not too juvenile. Works on assignment only. Roughs required. Reviews ms/illustration packages from artists. Illustrations only: Send samples of b&w work. "Illustrators should consult issues of *Faces* to familiarize themselves with our needs." Responds to art samples only if interested. Samples returned with SASE. Original artwork returned at job's completion (upon written request). Credit line given.

Photography Wants photos relating to forthcoming themes.

Terms Pays on publication. Buys all rights for mss and artwork. Pays 20-25¢/word for articles/stories. Pays on an individual basis for poetry. Covers are assigned and paid on an individual basis. Pays illustrators $50-300 for color inside. Pays photographers per photo ($25-100 for color). Sample copy $5.95 with $7\frac{1}{2} × 10\frac{1}{2}$ SAE and 5 first-class stamps. Writer's/illustrator's/photo guidelines via Web site or free with SAE and 1 first-class stamp.

Tips "Writers are encouraged to study past issues of the magazine to become familiar with our style and content. Writers with anthropological and/or travel experience are particularly encouraged; *Faces* is about world cultures. All feature articles, recipes and activities are freelance contributions." Illustrators: "Submit b&w samples, not too juvenile. Study past issues to know what we look for. The illustration we use is generally for retold legends, recipes and activities."

THE FRIEND MAGAZINE

The Church of Jesus Christ of Latter-day Saints, 50 E. North Temple, Salt Lake City UT 84150-3226. (801)240-2210. **Editor:** Vivian Paulsen. **Art Director:** Mark Robison. Monthly magazine for 3-11 year olds. Estab. 1971. Circ. 275,000.

Nonfiction Publishes children's/true stories—adventure, ethnic, some historical, humor, mainstream, religious/inspirational, nature. Length: 1,000 words maximum. Also publishes family- and gospel-oriented puzzles, games and cartoons. Simple recipes and handicraft projects welcome.

Poetry Reviews poetry. Maximum length: 20 lines.

How to Contact/Writers Send complete ms. Responds to mss in 2 months.

Illustration Illustrations only: Query with samples; arrange personal interview to show portfolio; provide résumé and tearsheets for files.

Terms Pays on acceptance. Buys all rights for mss. Pays $100-250 (400 words and up) for stories; $30 for poems; $20 minimum for activities and games. Contributors are encouraged to send for sample copy for $1.50, 9 × 11 envelope and four 37-cent stamps. Free writer's guidelines.

Tips "*The Friend* is published by The Church of Jesus Christ of Latter-day Saints for boys and girls up to eleven years of age. All submissions are carefully read by the *Friend* staff, and those not accepted are returned within two months for SASE. Submit seasonal material at least one year in advance. Query letters and simultaneous submissions are not encouraged. Authors may request rights to have their work reprinted after their manuscript is published."

FUN FOR KIDZ

P.O. Box 227, Bluffton OH 45817-0227. (419)358-4610. Fax: (419)358-5027. Web site: www.funforkidz.com. **Articles Editor:** Marilyn Edwards. Bimonthly magazine. Estab. 2002. "*Fun for Kidz* is a magazine created for boys and girls ages 6-13, with youngsters 8, 9, and 10 the specific target age. The magazine is designed as an activity publication to be enjoyed by both boys and girls on the alternative months of *Hopscotch* and *Boys' Quest* magazines."

● *Fun for Kidz* is theme-oriented. Send SASE for theme list and writer's guidelines.

Fiction Picture-oriented material, young readers, middle readers: adventure, animal, history, humorous, problem-solving, multicultural, nature/environment, sports. Average word length: 300-700.

Nonfiction Picture-oriented material, young readers, middle readers: animal, arts/crafts, cooking, games/puzzles, history, hobbies, how-to, humorous, problem-solving, sports, carpentry projects. Average word length: 300-700. Byline given.

Poetry Reviews poetry.

How to Contact/Writers Fiction/nonfiction: Send complete ms. Responds to queries in 2 weeks; mss in 5 weeks. Will consider simultaneous submissions. "Will not respond to faxed/e-mailed queries, mss, etc."

Illustration Works on assignment mostly. "We are anxious to find artists capable of illustrating stories and features. Our inside art is pen & ink." Query with samples. Samples kept on file.

Photography "We use a number of back & white photos inside the magazine; most support the articles used."

Terms Pays on publication. Buys first American serial rights. Buys first American serial rights and photos for artwork. Pays 5/word; $10/poem or puzzle; $35 for art (full page); $25 for art (partial page). Pays illustrators $5-10 for b&w photos. Sample copies available for $6 (includes postage); $7 outside U.S.

Tips "Our point of view is that every child deserves the right to be a child for a number of years before he or she becomes a young adult. As a result, *Fun for Kidz* looks for activities that deal with timeless topics, such as pets, nature, hobbies, science, games, sports, careers, simple cooking, and anything else likely to interest a child."

GIRLS' LIFE

Monarch, 4529 Harford Rd., Baltimore MD 21214. (410)426-9600. Fax: (410)254-0991. E-mail: mandy@girlslife.com. Web site: www.girlslife.com. **Contact:** Mandy Forr, associate editor. Bimonthly magazine for girls, ages 9-15. Estab.1994. Circ. 400,000.

Fiction "We accept short fiction. They should be stand alone stories and are generally 2,500-3,500 words.

Nonfiction "Features and articles should speak to young women ages 10-15 looking for new ideas about relationships, family, friends, school, etc. with fresh, savvy advice. Front-of-the-book columns and quizzes are a good place to start." Buys 40 mss/year. Length: 700-2,000 words. Pays $350/regular column; $500/feature.

How to Contact/Writers Accepts queries by mail or e-mail. Query with published clips. Submit complete mss on spec only. Responds in 3 months to queries.

Photography State availability with submission if applicable. Reviews contact sheets, negatives, transparencies. Negotiates payment individually. Captions, identification of subjects, model releases required.

Terms Pays on publication. Publishes ms an average of 3 months after acceptance. Byline given. Buys all rights. Editorial lead time 4 months. Submit seasonal material 5 months in advance. Sample copy for $5 or online. Writer's guidelines online.

Tips "Send thought-out queries with published writing samples and detailed résumé. Have fresh ideas and a voice that speaks to our audience—not down to them. And check out a copy of the magazine or visit girlslife.com before submitting."

GUIDE MAGAZINE

Review and Herald Publishing Association, 55 W. Oak Ridge Dr., Hagerstown MD 21740. (301)393-4037. Fax: (301)393-4055. E-mail: guide@rhpa.org. Web site: www.guidemagazine.org. **Editor:** Randy Fishell. **Designer:** Brandon Reese. Weekly magazine. Estab. 1953. Circ. 32,000. "Ours is a weekly Christian journal written for middle readers and young teens (ages 10-14), presenting true stories relevant to the needs of today's young person, emphasizing positive aspects of Christian living."

Nonfiction Middle readers, young adults/teens: adventure, animal, character-building, contemporary, games/puzzles, humorous, multicultural, problem-solving, religious. "We need true, or based on true, happenings, not merely true-to-life. Our stories and puzzles must have a spiritual emphasis." No violence. No articles. "We always need humor and adventure stories." Buys 150 mss/year. Average word length: 500-600 minimum, 1,200-1,300 maximum. Byline given.

How to Contact/Writers Nonfiction: Send complete ms. Responds in 6 weeks. Will consider simultaneous submissions. "We can pay half of the regular amount for reprints." Responds to queries/mss in 6 weeks. Credit line given. "We encourage e-mail submissions."

Terms Pays on acceptance. Buys first world North American serial rights; first rights; one-time rights; second serial (reprint rights); simultaneous rights. Pays 6-12¢/word for stories and articles. "Writer receives three complimentary copies of issue in which work appears." Sample copy free with 6×9 SAE and 2 first-class stamps. Writer's guidelines for SASE.

Tips "Children's magazines want mystery, action, discovery, suspense and humor—no matter what the topic. For us, truth is stronger than fiction."

HIGHLIGHTS FOR CHILDREN

803 Church St., Honesdale PA 18431. (570)253-1080. E-mail: eds@highlights-corp.com. Web site: www.highlights.com. **Contact:** Manuscript Coordinator. **Editor in Cheif:** Christine French Clark. **Art Director:** Cindy Smith. Monthly magazine. Estab. 1946. Circ. 2.5 million. "Our motto is 'Fun With a Purpose.' We are looking for quality fiction and nonfiction that appeals to children, encourages them to read, and reinforces positive values. All art is done on assignment."

Fiction Picture-oriented material, young readers, middle readers: adventure, animal, contemporary, fantasy, folktales, history, humorous, multicultural, problem-solving, sports. Multicultural needs include first person accounts of children from other cultures and first-person accounts of children from other countries. Does not want to see war, crime, violence. "We see too many stories with overt morals." Would like to see more contemporary, multicultural and world culture fiction, mystery stories, action/adventure stories, humorous stories, and fiction for younger readers. Buys 150 mss/year. Average word length: 500-800. Byline given.

Nonfiction Picture-oriented material, young readers, middle readers: animal, arts/crafts, biography, careers, games/puzzles, geography, health, history, hobbies, how-to, interview/profile, multicultural, nature/environment, problem-solving, science, sports. Multicultural needs include articles set in a country *about* the people of the country. Does not want to see trendy topics, fads, personalities who would not be good role models for children, guns, war, crime, violence. "We'd like to see more nonfiction for younger readers—maximum of 500 words. We still need older-reader material, too—500-800 words." Buys 200 mss/year. Maximum word length: 800. Byline given.

How to Contact/Writers Send complete ms. Responds to queries in 1 month; mss in 6 weeks.

Illustration Buys 25-30 illustrations/issue. Preferred theme or style: Realistic, some stylization. Works on assignment only. Reviews ms/illustration packages from artists. Illustrations only: photocopies, promo sheet, tearsheets, or slides. Résumé optional. Portfolio only if requested. Contact: Art Director. Responds to art samples in 2 months. Samples returned with SASE; samples filed. Credit line given.

Terms Pays on acceptance. Buys all rights for mss. Pays $50 and up for unsolicited articles. Pays illustrators $1,000 for color cover; $25-200 for b&w inside, $100-500 for color inside. Sample copies $3.95 and 9×11 SASE with 4 first-class stamps. Writer's/illustrator's guidelines free with SASE and on Web site.

Tips "Know the magazine's style before submitting. Send for guidelines and sample issue if necessary." Writers:

"At *Highlights* we're paying closer attention to acquiring more nonfiction for young readers than we have in the past. We're also looking for more material for kids ages 2-6." Illustrators: "Fresh, imaginative work encouraged. Flexibility in working relationships a plus. Illustrators presenting their work need not confine themselves to just children's illustrations as long as work can translate to our needs. We also use animal illustrations, real and imaginary. We need crafts, puzzles and any activity that will stimulate children mentally and creatively. We are always looking for imaginative cover subjects. Know our publication's standards and content by reading sample issues, not just the guidelines. Avoid tired themes, or put a fresh twist on an old theme so that its style is fun and lively. We'd like to see stories with subtle messages, but the fun of the story should come first. Write what inspires you, not what you think the market needs."

HOPSCOTCH, The Magazine for Girls

The Bluffton News Publishing and Printing Company, P.O. Box 164, Bluffton OH 45817-0164. (419)358-4610. Fax: (419)358-5027. Web site: hopscotchmagazine.com. **Editor:** Marilyn Edwards. Bimonthly magazine. Estab. 1989. Circ. 14,000. For girls from ages 6-12, featuring traditional subjects—pets, games, hobbies, nature, science, sports, etc.—with an emphasis on articles that show girls actively involved in unusual and/or worthwhile activities."

Fiction Picture-oriented material, young readers, middle readers: adventure, animal, history, humorous, nature/environment, sports, suspense/mystery. Does not want to see stories dealing with dating, sex, fashion, hard rock music. Buys 30 mss/year. Average word length: 300-700. Byline given.

Nonfiction Picture-oriented material, young readers, middle readers: animal, arts/crafts, biography, cooking, games/puzzles, geography, hobbies, how-to, humorous, math, nature/environment, science. Does not want to see pieces dealing with dating, sex, fashion, hard rock music. "Need more nonfiction with quality photos about a *Hopscotch*-age girl involved in a worthwhile activity." Buys 46 mss/year. Average word length: 400-700. Byline given.

Poetry Reviews traditional, wholesome, humorous poems. Maximum word length: 300; maximum line length: 20. Will accept 6 submissions/author.

How to Contact/Writers All writers should consult the theme list before sending in articles. To receive a current theme list, send a SASE. Fiction: Send complete ms. Nonfiction: Query or send complete ms. Responds to queries in 2 weeks; mss in 5 weeks. Will consider simultaneous submissions.

Illustration Buys approximately 10 illustrations/issue; buys 60-70 articles/year. "Generally, the illustrations are assigned after we have purchased a piece (usually fiction). Occasionally, we will use a painting—in any given medium—for the cover, and these are usually seasonal." Uses b&w artwork only for inside; color for cover. Reviews ms/illustration packages from artists. Query first or send complete ms with final art. Illustrations only: Send résumé, portfolio, client list and tearsheets. Responds to art samples only if interested and SASE in 1 month. Samples returned with SASE. Credit line given.

Photography Purchases photos separately (cover only) and with accompanying ms only. Looking for photos to accompany article. Model/property releases required. Uses 5×7, b&w prints; 35mm transparencies. Black & white photos should go with ms. Should show girl or girls ages 6-12.

Terms For mss: pays on publication. For mss, artwork and photos, buys first North American serial rights; second serial (reprint rights). Original artwork returned at job's completion. Pays 5¢/word and $5-10/photo. "We always send a copy of the issue to the writer or illustrator." Text and art are treated separately. Pays $200 maximum for color cover; $25-35 for b&w inside. Sample copy for $6 and 8×12 SASE. Writer's/illustrator's/photo guidelines, theme list free for #10 SASE.

Tips "Remember we publish only six issues a year, which means our editorial needs are extremely limited. Please look at our guidelines and our magazine . . . and remember, we use far more nonfiction than fiction. Guidelines and current theme list can be downloaded from our Web site. If decent photos accompany the piece, it stands an even better chance of being accepted. We believe it is the responsibility of the contributor to come up with photos. Please remember, our readers are 6-12 years—most are 8-10—and your text should reflect that. Many magazines try to entertain first and educate second. We try to do the reverse. Our magazine is more simplistic, like a book to be read from cover to cover. We are looking for wholesome, non-dated material."

HORSEPOWER, Magazine for Young Horse Lovers

Horse Publications Group, P.O. Box 670, Aurora ON L4G 4J9 Canada. (800)505-7428. Fax: (905)841-1530. E-mail: info@horse-canada.com. Web site: www.horse-canada.com. **Editor:** Susan Stafford. Bimonthly 16-page magazine, bound into Horse Canada, a bimonthly family horse magazine. Estab. 1988. Circ. 17,000. "*Horsepower* offers how-to articles and stories relating to horse care for kids ages 6-16, with a focus on safety."

• *Horsepower* no longer accepts fiction.

Nonfiction Middle readers, young adults: arts/crafts, biography, careers, fashion, games/puzzles, health, history, hobbies, how-to, humorous, interview/profile, problem-solving, travel. Buys 6-10 mss/year. Average word length: 500-1,200. Byline given.

How to Contact/Writers Fiction: query. Nonfiction: send complete ms. Responds to queries in 6 months; mss in 3 months. Publishes ms 6 months after acceptance. Will consider simultaneous submissions, electronic submission via disk or e-mail, previously published work.

Illustration Buys 3 illustrations/year. Reviews ms/illustration packages from artists. Contact: Editor. Query with samples. Responds only if interested. Samples returned with SASE; samples kept on file. Credit line given.

Photography Look for photos of kids and horses, instructional/educational, relating to riding or horse care. Uses color matte or glossy prints. Query with samples. Responds only if interested. Accepts TIFF or JPEG 300 dpi, disk or e-mail. Children on horseback must be wearing riding helmets or photos cannot be published.

Terms Pays on publication. Buys one-time rights for mss. Original artwork returned at job's completion if SASE provided. Pays $50-75 for stories. Additional payment for ms/illustration packages and for photos accompanying articles. Pays illustrators $25-50 for color inside. Pays photographers per photo (range: $15). Sample copies for $4.50. Writer's/illustrator's/photo guidelines for SASE.

Tips "Articles must be easy to understand, yet detailed and accurate. How-to or other educational features must be written by, or in conjunction with, a riding/teaching professional. Fiction is not encouraged, unless it is outstanding and teaches a moral or practical lesson. Note: preference will be given to Canadian writers and photographers due to Canadian content laws. Non-Canadian contributors accepted on a very limited basis."

HUMPTY DUMPTY'S MAGAZINE

Children's Better Health Institute, 1100 Waterway Blvd., Indianapolis IN 46206. (317)636-8881. Fax: (317)684-8094. Web site: www.humptydumptymag.org. **Editor/Art Director:** Phyllis Lybarger. Magazine published 6 times/year. *HDM* is edited for children ages 4-6. It includes fiction (easy-to-reads; read alouds; rhyming stories; rebus stories), nonfiction articles (some with photo illustrations), poems, crafts, recipes, and puzzles. Content encourages development of better health habits.

- *Humpty Dumpty's* publishes material promoting health and fitness with emphasis on simple activities, poems and fiction.

Fiction Picture-oriented stories: adventure, animal, contemporary, fantasy, folktales, health, humorous, multicultural, nature/environment, problem-solving, science fiction, sports. Also, talking inanimate objects are very difficult to do well. Beginners (and maybe everyone) should avoid these." Buys 8-10 mss/year. Maximum word length: 300. Byline given.

Nonfiction Picture-oriented articles: animal, arts/crafts, concept, games/puzzles, health, how-to, humorous, nature/environment, no-cook recipes, science, social issues, sports. Buys 6-10 mss/year. Prefers very short nonfiction pieces—200 words maximum. Byline given. Send ms with SASE if you want ms returned.

How to Contact/Writers Send complete ms. Nonfiction: Send complete ms with bibliography if applicable. "No queries, please!" Responds to mss in 3 months. Send seasonal material at least 8 months in advance.

Illustration Buys 5-8 illustrations/issue; 30-48 illustrations/year. Preferred theme or style: Realistic or cartoon. Works on assignment only. Illustrations only. Query with slides, printed pieces or photocopies. Samples are not returned; samples filed. Responds to art samples only if interested. Credit line given.

Terms Writers: Pays on publication. Artists: Pays within 2 months. Buys all rights. "One-time book rights may be returned if author can provide name of interested book publisher and tentative date of publication." Pays up to 22¢/word for stories/articles; payment varies for poems and activities. 10 complimentary issues are provided to author with check. Pays $275 for color cover illustration; $35-90 per page b&w inside; $70-155 for color inside. Sample copies for $3.95. Writer's/illustrator's guidelines free with SASE.

INSIGHT

Because Life is Full of Decisions, 55 W. Oak Ridge Dr., Hagerstown MD 21740. (301)393-4038. Fax: (301)393-4055. E-mail: insight@rhpa.org. Web site: www.insightmagazine.org. **Contact:** Dwain Nielson Esmond. Weekly magazine. Estab. 1970. Circ. 14,000. "Our readers crave true stories written by teens or written about teens that convey a strong spiritual point or portray a spiritual truth." 100% of publication aimed at teen market.

Nonfiction Young adults: animal, biography, fashion, health, humorous, interview/profile, multicultural, nature/environment, problem-solving, social issues, sports, travel: first-person accounts preferred. Buys 200 mss/year. Average word length: 500-1,500. Byline given.

Poetry Publishes poems written by teens. Maximum length: 250-500 words.

How to Contact/Writers Nonfiction: Send complete ms. Responds to queries in 2 months. Publishes ms 6-12 months after acceptance. Will consider simultaneous submissions, electronic submission via disk or modem, previously published work.

Illustration Works on assignment only. Reviews ms/illustration packages from artists. Query. Illustrations only: Query with samples. Samples kept on file. Credit line given.

Photography Looking for photos that will catch a young person's eye with unique elements such as juxtaposition. Model/property release required; captions not required but helpful. Uses color prints and 35mm, $2\frac{1}{4} \times 2\frac{1}{4}$,

4×5, 8×10 transparencies. Query with samples; provide business card, promotional literature or tearsheets to be kept on file. Responds only if interested.

Terms Pays on publication. Buys first North American serial rights for mss. Buys one-time rights for artwork and photos. Original artwork returned at job's completion. Pays $10-100 for stories/articles. Pays illustrators $100-300 for b&w (cover), color cover, b&w (inside), or color inside. Pays photographers by the project. Sample copies for 9×14 SAE and 4 first-class stamps.

Tips "Do your best to make your work look 'hip,' 'cool,' appealing to young people."

JACK AND JILL

Children's Better Health Institute, 1100 Waterway Blvd., P.O. Box 567, Indianapolis IN 46202. (317)634-1100. Fax: (317)684-8094. Web site: www.cbhi.org/magazines/jackandjill/index.shtml. **Editor:** Daniel Lee. **Art Director:** Jennifer Webber. Magazine for children ages 7-10, published 6 times/year. Estab. 1938. Circ. 360,000. "Write entertaining and imaginative stories *for* kids, not just *about* them. Writers should understand what is funny to kids, what's important to them, what excites them. Don't write from an adult 'kids are so cute' perspective. We're also looking for health and healthful lifestyle stories and articles, but don't be preachy."

Fiction Young readers and middle readers: adventure, contemporary, folktales, health, history, humorous, nature, sports. Buys 30-35 mss/year. Average word length: 700. Byline given.

Nonfiction Young readers, middle readers: animal, arts/crafts, cooking, games/puzzles, history, hobbies, how-to, humorous, interview/profile, nature, science, sports. Buys 8-10 mss/year. Average word length: 500. Byline given.

Poetry Reviews poetry.

How to Contact/Writers Fiction/nonfiction: Send complete ms. Queries not accepted. Responds to mss in 3 months. Guidelines by request with a #10 SASE.

Illustration Buys 15 illustrations/issue; 90 illustrations/year. Responds only if interested. Samples not returned; samples filed. Credit line given.

Terms Pays on publication; up to 17¢/word. Pays illustrators $275 for color cover; $35-90 for b&w, $70-155 for color inside. Pays photographers negotiated rate. Sample copies $1.25. Buys all rights to mss and one-time rights to photos.

Tips Publishes writing/art/photos by children.

KEYS FOR KIDS

CBH Ministries, Box 1001, Grand Rapids MI 49501-1001. (616)647-4971. Fax: (616)647-4950. E-mail: hazel@cbhministries.org. Web site: www.cbhministries.org. **Fiction Editor:** Hazel Marett. Bimonthly devotional booklet. Estab. 1982. "This is a devotional booklet for children and is also widely used for family devotions."

Fiction Young readers, middle readers: religious. Buys 60 mss/year. Average word length: 400.

How to Contact/Writers Fiction: Send complete ms. Will consider simultaneous submissions, E-mail: submissions, previously published work.

Terms Pays on acceptance. Buys reprint rights or first rights for mss. Pays $25 for stories. Sample copies free for SAE 6×9 and 3 first-class stamps. Writer's guidelines for SASE.

Tips "Be sure to *follow* guidelines after studying sample copy of the publication."

KID ZONE

Scott Publications, LLC, 801 W. Norton Ave., Suite 200, Muskegon, MI 49441. (616)475-0414. Fax: (616)475-0411. E-mail: ahuizenga@scottpublications.com. Web site: www.scottpublications.com. **Articles Editor:** Anne Huizenga. Bi-monthly magazine. Estab. 2000. Circ. 65,000. Kid Zone is a crafts and activities magazine for 4-12 year olds. "We publish projects, trivia, recipes, games, puzzles, and kid-friendly features on a variety of topics."

Nonfiction Picture-oriented material, middle readers: animal, arts/crafts, cooking, how-to, multicultural, nature/environment, science. Buys 20 mss/year. Average word length: 300-700. Byline given.

How to Contact/Writers Nonfiction: Send complete ms. Publishes ms 6-12 months after acceptance. Will consider simultaneous submissions, e-mail submissions.

Illustration Buys 6 illustrations/issue. Uses color artwork only. Works on assignment only. Illustrations only: Send postcard sample. Contact: Anne Huizenga, editor. Responds only if interested. Samples filed. Credit line sometimes given.

Photography Uses photos with accompanying ms only. Model/property release required. Uses color prints or digital images. Responds only if interested.

Terms Pays on publication. Buys world rights for mss. Buys first world rights for artwork. Pays $10-$50 for stories. Sample copies for $4.95 plus SASE. Writer's guidelines for SASE.

Tips "Nonfiction writers who can provide extras to coincide with their submission (photos, games, project ideas, recipes) are more likely to be selected also make sure that you have actually looked at our magazine."

◼ THE KIDS HALL OF FAME NEWS

The Kids Hall of Fame, 3 Ibsen Court, Dix Hills NY 11746. (631)242-9105. Fax: (631)242-8101. E-mail: VictoriaNe snick@TheKidsHallofFame.com. Web site: www.TheKidsHallofFame.com. **Publisher:** Dr. Victoria Nesnick. **Art/Photo Editor:** Amy Gilvary. Online publication. Estab. 1998. "We spotlight and archive extraordinary positive achievements of contemporary and historical kids internationally under age 20. These inspirational stories are intended to provide positive peer role models and empower others to say, 'If that kid can do it, so can I,' or 'I can do better.' Our magazine is the prelude to The Kids Hall of Fame set of books (one volume per age) and museum."

How to Contact/Writers Query with published clips or send complete mss with SASE for response. Go to Web site for sample stories and for The Kids Hall of Fame nomination form.

Tips "Nomination stories must be positive and inspirational, and whenever possible, address the 7 items listed in the 'Your Story and Photo' page of our Web site. Request writers' guidelines and list of suggested nominees. Day and evening telephone queries acceptable."

KIDZ CHAT®

Standard Publishing. Web site: www.standardpub.com. **Editor:** Elaina Meyers. Weekly magazine. Circ. 55,000.
● *Kidz Chat*® has decided to reuse much of the material that was a part of the first publication cycle. They will not be sending out theme lists, sample copies or writers guidelines or accepting any unsolicited material because of this policy.

LADYBUG, The Magazine for Young Children

70 E. Lake St., Suite 300, Chicago IL 60603. (312)701-1720. **Editor:** Alice Letvin. **Art Director:** Suzanne Beck. Monthly magazine. Estab. 1990. Circ. 130,000. Literary magazine for children 2-6, with stories, poems, activities, songs and picture stories.

Fiction Picture-oriented material: adventure, animal, fantasy, folktales, humorous, multicultural, nature/environment, problem-solving, science fiction, sports, suspense/mystery. "Open to any easy fiction stories." Buys 50 mss/year. Story length: limit 800 words. Byline given.

Nonfiction Picture-oriented material: activities, animal, arts/crafts, concept, cooking, humorous, math, nature/ environment, problem-solving, science. Buys 35 mss/year. Story length: limit 800 words.

Poetry Reviews poems, 20-line maximum length; limit submissions to 5 poems. Uses lyrical, humorous, simple language , action rhymes.

How to Contact/Writers Fiction/nonfiction: Send complete ms. Queries not accepted. Responds to mss in 6 months. Publishes ms up to 3 years after acceptance. Will consider simultaneous submissions if informed. Submissions without SASE will be discarded.

Illustration Buys 12 illustrations/issue; 145 illustrations/year. Prefers "bright colors; all media, but use watercolor and acrylics most often; same size as magazine is preferred but not required." To be considered for future assignments: Submit promo sheet, slides, tearsheets, color and b&w photocopies. Responds to art samples in 3 months. Submissions without SASE will be discarded.

Terms Pays on publication for mss; after delivery of completed assignment for illustrators. Rights purchased vary. Original artwork returned at job's completion. Pays 25¢/word for prose; $3/line for poetry. Pays $750 for color (cover) illustration, $50-100 for b&w (inside) illustration, $250/page for color (inside). Sample copy for $5. Writer's/illustrator's guidelines free for SASE or available on Web site, FAQ at www.cricketmag.com.

Tips Writers: "Get to know several young children on an individual basis. Respect your audience. We want less cute, condescending or 'preachy-teachy' material. Less gratuitous anthropomorphism. More rich, evocative language, sense of joy or wonder. Keep in mind that people come in all colors, sizes, physical conditions. Be inclusive in creating characters. Set your manuscript aside for at least a month, then reread critically." Illustrators: "Include examples, where possible, of children, animals, and—most important—action and narrative (i.e., several scenes from a story, showing continuity and an ability to maintain interest)." (See listings for *Babybug*, *Cicada*, *Cricket*, *Muse* and *Spider*.)

LEADING EDGE

4088 JKB, Provo UT 84602. (801)378-3553. E-mail: fiction@leadingedgemagazine.com. Web site: www.leadinge dgemagazine.com. Twice yearly magazine. Estab. 1981. "We strive to encourage developing and established talent and provide high quality speculative fiction to our readers." Does not accept mss with sex, excessive violence, or profanity.

Fiction Young adults: fantasy, science fiction. Buys 16 mss/year. Average word length: up to 15,000. Byline given.

How to Contact/Writers Fiction: Send complete ms ℅ Fiction Director. Responds to queries/mss in 4 months. Publishes ms 2-6 months after acceptance.

Illustration Buys 24 illustrations/issue; 48 illustrations/year. Uses b&w artwork only. Works on assignment only. Send manuscript with dummy. Contact: Art Director. Illustrations only: Send postcard sample with portfolio, samples, URL. Responds only if interested.Samples filed. Credit line given.

Terms Pays on publication. Buys first North American serial rights for mss. Buys first North American serial rights for artwork. Original artwork returned at job's completion. Pays $10-$100 for stories. Additional payment for ms/illustration packages. Pays illustrators $50 for color cover, $30 for b&w inside. Sample copies for $4.95. Writer's/illustrator's guidelines for SASE or visit the web site.

LIVE WIRE®

Standard Publishing. E-mail: Web site: www.standardpub.com. **Editor:** Elaina Meyers. Published quarterly in weekly parts. Circ. 40,000.

- *Live Wire®* has decided to reuse much of the material that was a part of the first publication cycle. They will not be sending out theme lists, sample copies, or writers guidelines or accepting any unsolicited material because of this policy.

MUSE

Carus Publishing, 140 S. Dearborn St., Suite 1450, Chicago IL 60603. (312)701-1720. Fax: (312)701-1728. E-mail: muse@caruspub.com. Web site: www.cricketmag.com. **Editor:** Diana Lutz. **Art Director:** Karen Kohn. **Photo Editor:** Carol Parden. Estab. 1996. Circ. 50,000. "The goal of *Muse* is to give as many children as possible access to the most important ideas and concepts underlying the principal areas of human knowledge. Articles should meet the highest possible standards of clarity and transparency aided, wherever possible, by a tone of skepticism, humor, and irreverence."

Nonfiction Middle readers, young adult: animal, arts, history, math, nature/environment, problem-solving, science, social issues.

How to Contact/Writers *Muse* is not accepting unsolicited mss or queries. All articles are commissioned. To be considered for assignments, experienced science writers may send a résumé and 3 published clips.

Illustration Buys 6 illustrations/issue; 40 illustrations/year. Uses color artwork only. Works on assignment only. Responds only if interested. Samples returned with SASE. Credit line given.

Photography Needs vary. Query with samples to photo editor.

NATIONAL GEOGRAPHIC KIDS

National Geographic Society, 1145 17th St. NW, Washington DC 20036-4688. (202)857-7000. Fax: (202)775-6112. Web site: www.nationalgeographic.com/ngkids. **Editor:** Melina Gerosa Bellows. **Art Director:** Jonathan Halling. **Photo Director:** Jay Sumner. Monthly magazine. Estab. 1975. Circ. 1.3 million.

NATURE FRIEND MAGAZINE

4253 Woodcock Lane, Dayton, VA 22821 (540)867-0764. Fax: (540)867-9516. Web site: www.naturefriendmagazine.com. **Articles Editor:** Kevin Shank. Monthly magazine. Estab. 1983. Circ. 10,000.

Fiction Picture-oriented material, conversational, no talking animal stories.

Nonfiction Picture-oriented material: animal, how-to, nature, photo-essays. No talking animal stories. No evolutionary material. Buys 50 mss/year. Average word length: 500. Byline given.

Photography Submit on CD with a color printout. Photo guidelines free with SASE.

Terms Pays on publication. Buy one-time rights. Pays $75 for front cover photo; $50 for back cover photo, $25 inside photo. Offers sample copy is and writer's/photographer's guidelines for $9.

Tips Needs stories about unique animals or nature phenomena. "Please examine samples and writer's guide before submitting." The best way to learn what we use is to be a subscriber.

NEW MOON: The Magazine for Girls & Their Dreams

New Moon Girl Media, LLC., 2 W. First St., #101, Duluth MN 55802. (218)728-5507. Fax: (218)728-0314. E-mail: girl@newmoongirlmedia.com. Web site: www.newmoonmagazine.org. **Managing Editor:** Melissa Harrison. Bimonthly magazine. Estab. 1992. Circ. 30,000. "*New Moon* is for every girl who wants her voice heard and her dreams taken seriously. *New Moon* portrays strong female role models of all ages, backgrounds and cultures now and in the past."

Fiction Middle readers, young adults: adventure, contemporary, fantasy, folktales, history, humorous, multicultural, nature/environment, problem-solving, religious, science fiction, sports, suspense/mystery, travel. Buys 6 mss/year. Average word length: 1,200-1,600. Byline given.

Nonfiction Middle readers, young adults: animal, arts/crafts, biography, careers, cooking, games/puzzles, health, history, hobbies, humorous, interview/profile, math, multicultural, nature/environment, problem-solving, science, social issues, sports, travel, stories about real girls. Does not want to see how-to stories. Wants more stories about real girls doing real things written *by girls*. Buys 6-12 adult-written mss/year; 30 girl-written mss/year. Average word length: 600. Byline given.

How to Contact/Writers Fiction/Nonfiction: Does not return or acknowledge unsolicited mss. Send copies only. Responds only if interested. Will consider simultaneous and e-mail submissions.

Illustration Buys 6-12 illustrations/year from freelancers. *New Moon* seeks 4-color cover illustrations. Reviews ms/illustrations packages from artists. Query. Submit ms with rough sketches. Illustration only: Query; send portfolio and tearsheets. Samples not returned; samples filed. Responds in 6 months only if interested. Credit line given.

Terms Pays on publication. Buys all rights for mss. Buys one-time rights, reprint rights, for artwork. Original artwork returned at job's completion. Pays 6-12¢/word for stories and articles. Pays in contributor's copies. Pays illustrators $400 for color cover; $50-300 for color inside. Sample copies for $7. Writer's/cover art guidelines for SASE or available on Web site.

Tips "Please refer to a copy of *New Moon* to understand the style and philosophy of the magazine. Writers and artists who understand our goals have the best chance of publication. We're looking for stories about real girls, women's careers, and historical profiles. We publish girl's and women's writing only." Publishes writing/art/photos by girls.

NICK JR. FAMILY MAGAZINE

Nickelodeon Magazine Group, 1515 Broadway, 37th Floor, New York NY 10036. (212)846-4985. Fax: (212)846-1690. Web site: www.nickjr.com/magazine. **Deputy Editor:** Wendy Smolen. **Creative Director:** Don Morris. Published 9 times/year. Estab. 1999. Circ. 1,100,000. A magazine where kids play to learn and parents learn to play. 30% of publication aimed at juvenile market.

Fiction Picture-oriented material: adventure, animal, contemporary, humorous, multicultural, nature/environment, problem-solving, sports. Byline sometimes given.

Nonfiction Picture-oriented material: animal, arts/crafts, concept, cooking, games/puzzles, hobbies, how-to, humorous, math, multicultural, nature/environment, problem-solving, science, social issues, sports. Byline sometimes given.

How to Contact/Writers Fiction/nonfiction: Query or submit complete ms. Responds to queries/mss in 3-12 weeks.

Illustration Only interested in agented material. Works on assignment only. Reviews ms/illustration packages from artists. Query or send ms with dummy. Contact: Don Morris, creative director. Illustrations only: arrange portfolio review; send résumé, promo sheet and portfolio. Responds only if interested. Samples not returned; samples kept on file. Credit line sometimes given.

Tips "Writers should study the magazine before submitting stories. Read-Together Stories must include an interactive element that invited children to participate in telling the story: a repeating line, a fill-in-the-blank rhyme, or rebus pictures."

ODYSSEY, Adventures in Science

Cobblestone Publishing Company, 30 Grove St., Suite C, Peterborough NH 03458. (603)924-7209. Fax: (603)924-7380. E-mail: odyssey@caruspub.com. Web site: www.odysseymagazine.com. **Editor:** Elizabeth E. Lindstrom. **Executive Director:** Lou Waryncia. **Art Director:** Ann Dillon. Magazine published 9 times/year. Estab. 1979. Circ. 22,000. Magazine covers general science and technology for children ages 10-16. All material must relate to the theme of a specific upcoming issue in order to be considered.

• *Odyssey* themes can be found on Web site: www.odysseymagazine.com.

Fiction Middle readers and young adults/teens: science fiction, fiction, science, astronomy. Does not want to see anything not theme-related. Average word length: 900-1,200 words.

Nonfiction Middle readers and young adults/teens: interiors, activities. Don't send anything not theme-related. Average word length: 750-1,200, depending on section article is used in.

How to Contact/Writers Query by mail. "A query must consist of all of the following to be considered (please use nonerasable paper): a brief cover letter stating the subject and word length of the proposed article; a detailed one-page outline explaining the information to be presented in the article; an extensive bibliography of materials/interviews the author intends to use in preparing the article; a SASE. Writers new to *Odyssey* should send a writing sample with query. If you would like to know if your query has been received, please also include a stamped postcard that requests acknowledgment of receipt. In all correspondence, please include your complete address as well as a telephone number and e-mail address where you can be reached. A writer may send as many queries for one issue as he or she wishes, but each query must have a separate cover letter, outline, bibliography, and SASE. Telephone queries are not accepted. Handwritten queries will not be considered. Queries may be submitted at any time ."

Illustration Buys 4 illustrations/issue; 36 illustrations/year. Works on assignment only. Reviews ms/illustration packages from artists. Query. Contact: Beth Lindstrom, editor. Illustration only: Query with samples. Send tearsheets, photocopies. Responds in 2 weeks. Samples returned with SASE; samples not filed. Original artwork returned upon job's completion (upon written request).

Photography Wants photos pertaining to any of our forthcoming themes. Uses color prints; 35mm transparencies, digital images. Photographers should send unsolicited photos by mail on speculation.

Terms Pays on publication. Buys all rights for mss and artwork. Pays 20-25¢/word for stories/articles. Covers are assigned and paid on an individual basis. Pays photographers per photo ($15-100 for b&w; $25-100 for color). Sample copy for $4.95 and SASE with $2 postage. Writer's/illustrator's/photo guidelines for SASE. (See listings for *AppleSeeds, Calliope, Cobblestone, Dig,* and *Faces.*)

ON COURSE, A Magazine for Teens

General Council of the Assemblies of God, 1445 Boonville Ave., Springfield MO 65802-1894. (417)862-2781. Fax: (417)862-1693. E-mail: oncourse@ag.org. Web site: www.oncourse.ag.org. **Editor:** Amber Weigand-Buckley. **Art Director:** Ryan Strong. Bi- annual magazine. Estab. 1991. Circ. 160,000. *On Course* is a magazine to empower students to grow in a real-life relationship with Christ.

• *On Course* no longer uses illustrations, only photos.

Fiction Young adults: Christian discipleship, contemporary, humorous, multicultural, problem-solving, sports. Average word length: 800. Byline given.

Nonfiction Young adults: careers, interview/profile, multicultural, religion, social issues, college life, Christian discipleship.

How to Contact/Writers Works on assignment basis only. Resumes and writing samples will be considered for inclusion in Writer's File to receive story assignments.

Photography Buys photos from freelancers. "Teen life, church life, college life; unposed; often used for illustrative purposes." Model/property releases required. Uses color glossy prints and 35mm or 2¼×2¼ transparencies. Query with samples; send business card, promotional literature, tearsheets or catalog. Responds only if interested.

Terms Pays on acceptance. Buys first or reprint rights for mss. Buys one-time rights for photographs. Pays $30 per assigned stories/articles. Pays illustrators and photographers "as negotiated." Sample copies free for 9×11 SA SE. Writer's guidelines for SASE.

PASSPORT

Sunday School Curriculum, 6401 The Paseo, Kansas City MO 64131-1284. (816)333-7000. Fax: (816)333-4439. E-mail: sweatherwax@nazarene.org. Web site: www.nazarene.org. **Editor:** Ryan R. Pettit. Weekly take-home paper. "*Passport* looks for a casual, witty approach to Christian themes. We want hot topics relevant to preteens."

POCKETS, Devotional Magazine for Children

The Upper Room, 1908 Grand Ave., P.O. Box 340004, Nashville TN 37203-0004. (615)340-7333. Fax: (615)340-7267. E-mail: pockets@upperroom.org. Web site: www.pockets.org. **Articles/Fiction Editor:** Lynn W. Gilliam. **Art Director:** Chris Schechner, 408 Inglewood Dr., Richardson TX 75080. Magazine published 11 times/year. Estab. 1981. Circ. 99,000. "*Pockets* is a Christian devotional magazine for children ages 6-11. Stories should help children experience a Christian lifestyle that is not always a neatly wrapped moral package but is open to the continuing revelation of God's will."

Fiction Picture-oriented, young readers, middle readers: adventure, contemporary, occasional folktales, multicultural, nature/environment, problem-solving, religious. Does not accept violence or talking animal stories. Buys 25-30 mss/year. Average word length: 600-1,400. Byline given. *Pockets* also accepts short-short stories (no more than 600 words) for children 5-7. Buys 11 mss/year.

Nonfiction Picture-oriented, young readers, middle readers: cooking, games/puzzles. "*Pockets* seeks biographical sketches of persons, famous or unknown, whose lives reflect their Christian commitment, written in a way that appeals to children." Does not accept how-to articles. "Nonfiction reads like a story." Multicultural needs include: stories that feature children of various racial/ethnic groups and do so in a way that is true to those depicted. Buys 10 mss/year. Average word length: 400-1,000. Byline given.

How to Contact/Writers Fiction/nonfiction: Send complete ms. "We do not accept queries." Responds to mss in 6 weeks. Will consider simultaneous submissions.

Illustration Buys 25-35 illustrations/issue. Preferred theme or style: varied; both 4-color. Works on assignment only. Illustrations only: Send promo sheet, tearsheets.

RAINBOW RUMPUS, The Magazine for Kids with LGBT Parents,

P.O. Box 6881, Minneapolis MN 55406.(612)721-6442. Fax: (621)729-1420. E-mail: fictionandpoetry@rainbowr umpus.org. Web site: www.rainbowrumpus.org. **Articles Editor:** Laura Matanah. **Fiction Editor:** Beth Wallace. **Art/photo Acquisitions:** Laura Matanah. Monthly online magazine. Estab. 2005. Circ. 100 visits/day. "*Rainbow Rumpus* is an online children's magazine for 4- to 14-year-old children with lesbian, gay, bisexual or transgender parents. We are looking for children's fiction, nonfiction and poetry. *Rainbow Rumpus* publishes and reviews work that is written from the point of view of children with LGBT parents of who are connected to the LGBT community, celebrates the diversity of LGBT-headed families, and is of high quality." 90% of publication aimed at young readers.

Fiction All levels: adventure, animal, contemporary, fantasy, folktales, history, humorous, multicultural, nature/environment, problem solving, science fiction, sports, suspense/mystery. Buys 12 mss/year. Average word length: 800-5,000. Byline given.

Nonfiction All levels: interview/profile, social issues. Buys 12 mss/year. Average word length: 800-5,000. Byline given.

Poetry Maximum of 5 poems per submission.

How To Contact/Writers Send complete ms. Responds to mss in 6 weeks. Considers electronic submission and previously published work.

Illustration Buys 2 illustrations/issue. Uses both b&w and color artwork. Reviews ms/illustration packages from artists: Query. Illustrations only: query with samples. Contact: Laura Matanah, publisher. Samples not returned; samples filed depending on the level of interest. Credit line given.

Terms Pays on publication. Buys first rights for mss; may request print anthology and audio or recording rights. Buys first rights for artwork. Pays $15 or 3¢ a word (whichever is greater) for stories and aritcles. Pays illustrators $100 for b&w; $300 for color. Writer's guidelines available on Web site.

Tips "If you wish to submit nonfiction, please query by e-mail to editor@rainbowrumpus.org."

RANGER RICK

National Wildlife Federation, 11100 Wildlife Center Dr., Reston VA 20190. (703)438-6000. Web site: www.nwf.org/rangerrick. **Editor:** Mary Dalheim. **Design Director:** Donna Miller. Monthly magazine. Circ. 550,000. "Our audience ranges from ages 7 to 12, though we aim the reading level of most material at 9-year-olds or fourth graders."

• Ranger Rick does not accept submissions or queries.

Fiction Middle readers: animal (wildlife), fables, fantasy, humorous, multicultural, plays, science fiction. Average word length: 900. Byline given.

Nonfiction Middle readers: animal (wildlife), conservation, humorous, nature/environment, outdoor adventure, travel. Buys 15-20 mss/year. Average word length: 900. Byline given.

How to Contact/Writers No longer accepting unsolicited queries/mss.

Illustration Buys 5-7 illustrations/issue. Preferred theme: nature, wildlife. Works on assignment only. Illustrations only: Send résumé, tearsheets. Responds to art samples in 2 months.

Terms Pays on acceptance. Buys exclusive first-time worldwide rights and non-exclusive worldwide rights thereafter to reprint, transmit, and distribute the work in any form or medium. Original artwork returned at job's completion. Pays up to $700 for full-length of best quality. For illustrations, buys one-time rights. Pays $150-250 for b&w; $250-1,200 for color (inside, per page) illustration. Sample copies for $2.15 plus a 9×12 SASE.

READ

Weekly Reader Publishing Group, 1 Reader's Digest Rd., Pleasantville, N.Y. 10570. Web site: www.weeklyreader.com.

• READ no longer accepts unsolicited manuscripts. Those that are sent will not be read, responded to, or returned.

SCIENCE WEEKLY

P.O. Box 70638, Chevy Chase MD 20813. (301)680-8804. Fax: (301)680-9240. E-mail: scienceweekly@erols.com. Web site: www.scienceweekly.com. **Publisher:** Dr. Claude Mayberry, CAM Publishing Group, Inc. Magazine published 14 times/year. Estab. 1984. Circ. 200,000.

• Science Weekly uses freelance writers to develop and write an entire issue on a single science topic. Send résumé only, not submissions. Authors must be within the greater D.C., Virginia, Maryland area. Science Weekly works on assignment only.

Nonfiction Young readers, middle readers, (K-6th grade): science/math education, education, problem-solving.

Terms Pays on publication. Prefers people with education, science and children's writing background. Send résumé only. Samples copies free with SAE and 3 first-class stamps. Free samples on Web site www.scienceweekly.com.

SCIENCE WORLD

Scholastic Inc., 557 Broadway, New York NY 10012-3999. (212)343-6100. Fax: (212)343-6945. E-mail: sciencworld@scholastic.com. **Editor:** Patty Janes. **Art Director:** Brenda Jackson. Magazine published biweekly during the school year. Estab. 1959. Circ. 400,000. Publishes articles in Life Science/Health, Physical Science/Technology, Earth Science/Environment/Astronomy for students in grades 7-10. The goal is to make science relevant for teens.

• *Science World* publishes a separate teacher's edition with lesson plans and skills pages to accompany feature articles.

Nonfiction Young adults/teens: animal, concept, geography, health, nature/environment, science. Multicultural needs include: minority scientists as role models. Does not want to see stories without a clear news hook. Buys 20 mss/year. Average word length: 800-1,000. Byline given. Currently does not accept unsolicited mss.

How to Contact/Writers Nonfiction: Query with published clips and/or brief summaries of article ideas. Responds only if interested. No unsolicited mss.

Illustration Buys 2 illustrations/issue; 28 illustrations/year. Works on assignment only. Illustration only: Query with samples, tearsheets. Responds only if interested. Samples returned with SASE; samples filed "if we use them." Credit line given.

Photography Model/property releases required; captions required including background information. Provide résumé, business card, promotional literature or tearsheets to be kept on file. Responds only if interested.

Terms Pays on acceptance. Buys all rights for mss/artwork. Originals returned to artist at job's completion. For stories/articles, pays $200. Pays photographers per photo.

SHARING THE VICTORY, Fellowship of Christian Athletes

8701 Leeds, Kansas City MO 64129. (816)921-0909. Fax: (816)921-8755. Web site: www.sharingthevictory.com. **Articles/Photo Editor:** Jill Ewert. **Art Director:** Mat Casner. Magazine published 9 times a year. Estab. 1982. Circ. 80,000. Purpose is to serve as a ministry tool of the Fellowship of Christian Athletes (FCA) by aligning with its mission to present to athletes and coaches and all whom they influence, the challenge and adventure of receiving Jesus Christ as Savior and Lord.

Nonfiction Young adults/teens: religion, sports. Average word length: 700-1,200. Byline given.

How to Contact/Writers Nonfiction: Query with published clips. Publishes ms 3 months after acceptance. Will consider electronic submissions via e-mail.

Photography Purchases photos separately. Looking for photos of sports action. Uses color prints and high resolution electronic files of 300 dpi or higher.

Terms Pays on publication. Buys first rights and second serial (reprint) rights. Pays $150-400 for assigned and unsolicited articles. Photographers paid per photo. Sample copies for 9×12 SASE and $1. Writer's/photo guidelines for SASE.

Tips "All stories must be tied to FCA ministry."

SHINE BRIGHTLY

GEMS Girls' Clubs, P.O. Box 7259, Grand Rapids MI 49510. (616)241-5616. Fax: (616)241-5558. E-mail: sara@gemsgc.org. Web site: www.gemsgc.gospelcom.net. **Editor:** Jan Boone. **Senior Editor:** Sara Lynne Hilton. Monthly (with combined June/July/August summer issue) magazine. Circ. 1 7,000. "*SHINE brightly* is designed to help girls ages 9-14 see how God is at work in their lives and in the world around them."

Fiction Middle readers: adventure, animal, contemporary, health, history, humorous, multicultural, nature/environment, problem-solving, religious, sports. Does not want to see unrealistic stories and those with trite, easy endings. We are interested in manuscripts that show how girls can change the world. Buys 30 mss/year. Average word length: 400-900. Byline given.

Nonfiction Middle readers: animal, arts/crafts, careers, cooking, fashion, games/puzzles, health, hobbies, how-to, humorous, nature/environment, multicultural, problem-solving, religious, service projects, social issues, sports, travel, also movies, music and musicians, famous people, interacting with family and friends. We are currently looking for inspirational biographies, stories from Zambia, Africa, and articles about living a green lifestyle. Buys 9 mss/year. Average word length: 100- 800. Byline given.

How to Contact/Writers Send for annual update for publication themes. Fiction/nonfiction: Send complete ms. Responds to mss in 1 month. Will consider simultaneous submissions. Guidelines on Web site.

Illustration Buys 3 illustrations/year. Prefers ms/illustration packages. Works on assignment only. Responds to submissions in 1 month. Samples returned with SASE. Credit line given.

Terms Pays on publication. Buys first North American serial rights, first rights, second serial (reprint rights) or simultaneous rights. Original artwork not returned at job's completion. Pays $35 for stories, assigned articles and unsolicited articles. Poetry is $5-15. Games and Puzzles are $5-10. "We send complimentary copies in addition to pay." Pays $25-50 for color inside illustration. Writer's guidelines online at www.gemsgc.org.

Tips Writers: " Please check our website befoe submitting. We have a specific style and theme that deals with how girls can impact the world. The stories should be current, deal with pre-adolescent problems and joys, and help girls see God at work in their lives through humor as well as problem-solving."

SKIPPING STONES

A Multicultural Children's Magazine, P.O. Box 3939, Eugene OR 97403. (541)342-4956. E-mail: editor@skipping stones.org. Web site: www.skippingstones.org. **Articles/Photo/Fiction Editor:** Arun N. Toke. Bimonthly magazine. Estab. 1988. Circ. 2,500. "*Skipping Stones* is an award-winning multicultural, nonprofit magazine designed to encourage cooperation, creativity and celebration of cultural and ecological richness. We encourage submissions by children of color, minorities and under-represented populations."

• Send SASE for *Skipping Stones* guidelines and theme list for detailed descriptions of the topics they want. *Skipping Stones*, now in it's 20th year, has won EDPRESS, National Association for Multicultural Education (N.A.M.E.), Writer Magazine, Newsstand Resources and Parent's Choice Awards.

Fiction Middle readers, young adult/teens: contemporary, meaningful, humorous. All levels: folktales, multicultural, nature/environment. Multicultural needs include: bilingual or multilingual pieces; use of words from other languages; settings in other countries, cultures or multi-ethnic communities.

Nonfiction All levels: animal, biography, cooking, games/puzzles, history, humorous, interview/profile, multicultural, nature/environment, creative problem-solving, religion and cultural celebrations, sports, travel, social and international awareness. Does not want to see preaching, violence or abusive language; no poems by authors over 18 years old; no suspense or romance stories. Average word length: 1,000, max. Byline given.

How to Contact/Writers Fiction: Query. Nonfiction: Send complete ms. Responds to queries in 1 month; mss in 4 months. Will consider simultaneous submissions; reviews artwork for future assignments. Please include your name and address on each page.

Illustration Prefers illustrations by teenagers and young adults. Will consider all illustration packages. Manuscript/illustration packages: Query; submit complete ms with final art; submit tearsheets. Responds in 4 months. Credit line given.

Photography Black & white photos preferred, but color photos with good contrast are welcome. Needs: youth 7-17, international, nature, celebration.

Terms Acquires first and reprint rights for mss and photographs. Pays in copies for authors, photographers and illustrators. Sample copies for $5 with SAE and 4 first-class stamps. Writer's/illustrator's guidelines for 4×9 SASE.

Tips "We want material meant for children and young adults/teenagers with multicultural or ecological awareness themes. Think, live and write as if you were a child, tween or teen." Wants "material that gives insight to cultural celebrations, lifestyle, custom and tradition, glimpse of daily life in other countries and cultures. Photos, songs, artwork are most welcome if they illustrate/highlight the points. Translations are invited if your submission is in a language other than English. Upcoming themes will include cultural celebrations, living abroad, disability, hospitality customs of various cultures, cross-cultural understanding, African, Asian and Latin American cultures, humor, international, turning points and magical moments in life, caring for the earth, spirituality, and Multicutural Awareness."

SPARKLE

GEMS Girls' Clubs, 1333 Alger SE, P,P. Box 7295, Grand Rapids MI 49510. (616)241-5616. Fax: (616)241-5558. E-mail: sara@gemsgc.org. Web site: www.gemsgc.org. **Senior Editor:** Sara Lynn Hilton **Art Director/Photo Editor:** Sara DeRidder. Magazine published 6 times/year. Estab. 2002. Circ. 5,119. "Our mission is to prepare young girls to live out their faith and become world-changers-. We strive to help girls make a difference in the world. We look at the application of scripture to everyday life. We strive to delight the reader and cause the reader to evelute her own life in light of the truth presented. Finally, we strive to teach practical life skills.

Fiction Young readers: adventure, animal, contemporary, fantasy, folktale, health, history, humorous, multicultural, music and musicians, nature/environment, problem-solving, religious, recipes, service projects, sports, suspense/mystery, interacting with family and friends. We currently Looking for sinspirational biographies, stories form Zambia, Africa, and ideas on how to live a green lifestyle. Buys 10 mss/year. Average word length: 100-400. Byline given.

Nonfiction Young readers: animal, arts/crafts, biography, careers, cooking, concept, games/puzzles, geography, health, history, hobbies, how-to, interview/profile, math, multicultural, nature/environment, problem-solving, quizzes, science, social issues, sports, travel, personal experience, inspirational, music/drama/art. Buys 15 mss/year. Average word length: 100-400. Byline given.

Poetry Looks for simple poems about God's creation or traditional Bible truths. Maximum lenth: 15 lines.

How to Contact/Writers Fiction/nonfiction: Send complete ms. Responds to ms in 6 weeks. Publishes ms 6 months after acceptance. Will consider simultaneous submissions, and previously published work.

Illustration Buys 1-2 illustrations/issue; 8-10 illustrations/year. Uses color artwork only. Works on assignment only. Reviews ms/illustration packages from artists. Send ms with dummy. Contact: Sara DeRidder, graphic and web designer. Illustrations only: send promo sheet. Contact: Sara DeRidder. Responds in 3 weeks only if interested. Samples returned with SASE; samples filed. Credit line given.

Terms Pays on publication. Buys first North American serial rights, second serial (reprint rights) or simultaneous rights for mss, artwork and photos. Pays $20 minimum for stories and articles. Pays illustrators $50 for color cover; $25 for color inside. Original artwork not returned at job's completion. Sample copies for $1. Writer's/illustrator/photo guidelines free for SASE or available on Web site.

Tips "Keep it simple. We are writing to 1st-3rd graders. It must be simple yet interesting. Manuscripts should build girls up in Christian character but not be preachy. They are just learning about God and how He wants them to live. Manuscripts should be delightful as well as educational and inspirational."

SPIDER, The Magazine for Children

Carus Publishing Company, 70 E. Lake St., Suite 300, Chicago IL 60601. (312) 701-1720. Web site: www.cricket mag.com and www.spidermagkids.com. **Editor-in-Chief:** Alice Letvin. **Editor:** May-May Sugihara. **Art Director:** Sue Beck. Monthly magazine. Estab. 1994. Circ. 70,000. *Spider* publishes high-quality literature for beginning readers, primarily ages 6-9.

Fiction Young readers: adventure, contemporary, fantasy, folktales, humor, science fiction. "Authentic stories from all cultures are welcome. No didactic, religious, or violent stories, or anything that talks down to children." Average word length: 300-1,000. Byline given.

Nonfiction Young readers: animal, arts/crafts, cooking, games/puzzles, geography, history, human interest, math, multicultural, nature/environment, problem-solving, science. "Well-researched articles on topics are welcome. Would like to see more games, puzzles and activities, especially ones adaptable to *Spider*'s takeout pages. No encyclopedic or overtly educational articles." Average word length: 300-800. Byline given.

Poetry Serious, humorous. Maximum length: 20 lines.

How to Contact/Writers Fiction/nonfiction: Send complete ms with SASE. Do not query. Responds to mss in 6 months. Publishes ms 2-3 years after acceptance. Will consider simultaneous submissions and previously published work.

Illustration Buys 20 illustrations/issue; 240 illustrations/year. Uses color artwork only. "We prefer that you work on flexible or strippable stock, no larger than 20 × 22 (image area 19 × 21). This will allow us to put the art directly on the drum of our separator's laser scanner. Art on disck CMYK, 300 dpi. We use more realism than cartoon-style art." Works on assignment only. Reviews ms/illustration packages from artists. Illustrations only: Send promo sheet and tearsheets. Responds in 3 months. Samples returned with SASE; samples filed. Credit line given.

Photography Buys photos from freelancers. Buys photos with accompanying ms only. Model/property releases and captions required. Uses 35mm, $2\frac{1}{4} \times 2\frac{1}{4}$ transparencies or digital files. Send unsolicited photos by mail; provide résumé and tearsheets. Responds in 3 months.

Terms Pays on publication. Rights purchased vary. Buys first and promotional rights for artwork; one-time rights for photographs. Original artwork returned at job's completion. Pays up to 25¢/word for previously unpublished stories/articles. Authors also receive 6 complimentary copies of the issue in which work appears. Additional payment for ms/illustration packages and for photos accompanying articles. Pays illustrators $750 for color cover; $200-300 for color inside. Pays photographers per photo (range: $25-75). Sample copies for $5. Writer's/illustrator's guidelines online at www.cricketmag.com or for SASE.

Tips Writers: "Read back issues before submitting."

TC MAGAZINE (TEENAGE CHRISTIAN)

Institute for Church & Family, 915 E. Market #10750 Searcy, AR. (501)279-4530. E-mail: editor@tcmagazine.org. Web site: www.tcmagazine.org. **Articles Editor:** Laura Kaiser. Quarterly magazine (published March, June, Sept., Dec.). Estab. 1961. Circ. 5,000. "Music. Movies. Style. Sports. Humor. Friends. Art. Faith. All in one."

Fiction "We are not accepting fiction at this time."

Nonfiction Young adults: interview/profile, first person articles, college, style/fashion, humor. We are especially interested in articles written by teenagers. Buys 2-4 mss/year. Average word length: 500-1,000. Byline sometimes given.

Poetry Maximum length: we are not accepting poetry at this time.

How to Contact/Writers Nonfiction: send complete ms. Responds only if interested. Publishes ms 6 mons after acceptance. Will consider simultaneous submissions, e-mail submissions, no previously published work.

Illustration Works on assignment only. Send ms with dummy. Illustrations only: URL. Responds only if interested.

Photography Buys photos separately. Model/property release required. Uses hi-res color digital photos. E-mail or URL. Responds only if interested.

Terms Pays on publication. Buys one-time rights for mss. Buys all rights for artwork; all rights for photos. Payment varies.

TEEN MAGAZINE

Hearst Magazines, 3000 Ocean Park Blvd., Suite 3048, Santa Monica CA 90405. (310)664-2950. Fax: (310)664-2959. Web site: www.teenmag.com. **Contact:** Jane Fort, editor-in-chief (fashion, beauty, TeenPROM); Kelly

Bryant, deputy editor (entertainment, movies, TV, music, books, covers, photo editor); Heather Hewitt, managing editor (manufacturing, advertising, new products, what's hot, intern coordinator). Quarterly magazine. Estab. 1957. "We are a pure junior high school female (ages 10-15) audience. *TEEN*'s audience is upbeat and wants to be informed."

Fiction Young adults: romance. Does not want to see "that which does not apply to our market , i.e., science fiction, history, religious, adult-oriented."

Nonfiction Young adults: how-to, arts/crafts, fashion, interview/profile, games/puzzles. Does not want to see adult-oriented, adult point of view.

Illustration Buys 50 illustrations/year. Uses various styles. "Light, upbeat." Illustrations only: "Want to see samples whether it be tearsheets, slides, finished pieces showing the style." Responds only if interested. Credit line given. Send illustration/photography samples Attn: Art Department (address above).

Terms Pays on acceptance. Buys all rights. Bylines not guaranteed. Pays $200-800 for fiction; $200-600 for quizzes; $ 500-1,000 for illustrations.

Tips Illustrators: "Present professional finished work. Get familiar with our magazine and send samples that would be compatible with the style of publication." There is a need for artwork with "fiction/specialty articles. Send samples or promotional materials on a regular basis."

TURTLE MAGAZINE, For Preschool Kids

Children's Better Health Institute, 1100 Waterway Blvd., Indianapolis IN 46206-0567. (317)636-8881. Fax: (317)684-8094. Web site: www.turtlemag.org **Editor:** Terry Harshman. **Art Director:** Bart Rivers. Bimonthly magazine published 6 times/year. Circ. 300,000. *Turtle* uses read-aloud stories, especially suitable for bedtime or naptime reading, for children ages 2-5. Also uses poems, simple science experiments, easy recipes and health-related articles.

Fiction Picture-oriented material: health-related, medical, history, humorous, multicultural, nature/environment, problem-solving, sports, recipes, simple science experiments. Avoid stories in which the characters indulge in unhealthy activities. Buys 20 mss/year. Average word length: 150-300. Byline given. Currently accepting submissions for Rebus stories only.

Nonfiction Picture-oriented material: cooking, health, sports, simple science. "We use very simple experiments illustrating basic science concepts. These should be pretested. We also publish simple, healthful recipes." Buys 24 mss/year. Average word length: 100-300. Byline given.

Poetry "We're especially looking for short poems (4-8 lines) and slightly longer action rhymes to foster creative movement in preschoolers. We also use short verse on our inside front cover and back cover."

How to Contact/Writers Fiction/nonfiction: Send complete mss. Queries are not accepted. Responds to mss in 3 months.

Terms Pays on publication. Buys all rights for mss. Pays up to 22¢/word for stories and articles (depending upon length and quality) and 10 complimentary copies. Pays $25 minimum for poems. Sample copy $ 3.95. Writer's guidelines free with SASE and on Web site.

Tips "Our need for health-related material, especially features that encourage fitness, is ongoing. Health subjects must be age-appropriate. When writing about them, think creatively and lighten up! Always keep in mind that in order for a story or article to educate preschoolers, it first must be entertaining—warm and engaging, exciting, or genuinely funny. Here the trend is toward leaner, lighter writing. There will be a growing need for interactive activities. Writers might want to consider developing an activity to accompany their concise manuscripts."

U*S* KIDS

Children's Better Health Institute, 1100 Waterway Blvd., P.O. Box 567, Indianapolis IN 46202. (317)636-8881. Web site: www.uskidsmag.org. **Editor:** Daniel Lee. **Art Director:** Greg Vanzo. Magazine for children ages 6-11, published 6 times a year. Estab. 1987. Circ. 230,000.

Fiction Young readers: adventure, animal, contemporary, health, history, humorous, multicultural, nature/environment, problem-solving, sports, suspense/mystery. Buys limited number of stories/year. Query first. Average word length: 500-800. Byline given.

Nonfiction Young readers: animal, arts/crafts, cooking, games/puzzles, health, history, hobbies, how-to, humorous, interview/profile, multicultural, nature/environment, science, social issues, sports, travel. Wants to see interviews with kids ages 5-10, who have done something unusual or different. Buys 30-40 mss/year. Average word length: 400. Byline given.

Poetry Maximum length: 8-24 lines.

How to Contact/Writers Fiction: Send complete ms. Responds to queries and mss in 3 months.

Illustration Buys 8 illustrations/issue; 70 illustrations/year. Color artwork only. Works on assignment only. Reviews ms/illustration packages from artists. Query. Illustrations only: Send résumé and tearsheets. Responds only if interested. Samples returned with SASE; samples kept on file. Does not return originals. Credit line given.

Photography Purchases photography from freelancers. Looking for photos that pertain to children ages 5-10. Model/property release required. Uses color and b&w prints; 35mm, $2\frac{1}{4} \times 2\frac{1}{4}$, 4×5 and 8×10 transparencies. Photographers should provide résumé, business card, promotional literature or tearsheets to be kept on file. Responds only if interested.

Terms Pays on publication. Buys all rights for mss. Purchases all rights for artwork. Purchases one-time rights for photographs. Pays 17¢/word minimum. Additional payment for ms/illustration packages. Pays illustrators $155/page for color inside. Photographers paid by the project or per photo (negotiable). Sample copies for $3.95. Writer's/illustrator/photo guidelines for #10 SASE.

Tips "Write clearly and concisely without preaching or being obvious."

WHAT IF?, Canada's Fiction Magazine for Teens

What If Publications, 19 Lynwood Place, Guelph ON N1G 2V9 Canada. (519)823-2941. Fax: (519)823-8081. E-mail: editor@whatifmagazine.com. Web site: www.whatifmagazine.com. **Articles/Fiction Editor:** Mike Leslie. **Art Director:** Jean Leslie. Quarterly magazine. Estab. 2003. Circ. 3,000. "The goal of *What If?* is to help young adults get published for the first time in a quality literary setting."

Fiction Young adults: adventure, contemporary, fantasy, folktale, health, humorous, multicultural, nature/environment, problem-solving, science fiction, sports, suspense/mystery. Buys 48 mss/year. Average word length: 500-3,000. Byline given.

Nonfiction Young adults: editorial. "We publish editorial content from young adult writers only—similar to material seen on newspapers op-ed page." Average word length: 500. Byline given.

Poetry Reviews poetry: all styles. Maximum length: 20 lines. Limit submissions to 4 poems.

How to Contact/Writers Fiction/Nonfiction: Send complete ms. Responds to mss in 3 months. Publishes ms 4 months after acceptance. Will consider e-mail submissions, previously published work if the author owns all rights.

Illustration Uses approximately 150 illustrations/year. Reviews ms/illustration packages from young adult artists. Send ms with dummy. Query with samples. Contact: Jean Leslie, production manager. Responds in 2 months. Samples returned with SASE. Credit line given.

Terms Pays on publication. Acquires first rights for mss and artwork. Original artwork returned at job's completion. Pays 3 copies for stories; 1 copy for articles; 3 copies for illustration. Sample copies for $8.00 Writer's/illustrator's guidelines for SASE or available by e-mail.

Tips "Read our magazine. The majority of the material we publish (90%) is by Canadian young adults. Another 10% is staff written. We are currently accepting material from Canadian teens only."

WINNER

The Health Connection, 55 W. Oak Ridge Dr., Hagerstown MD 21740. (301)393-4017. Fax: (301)393- 4055. E-mail: jschleifer@rhpa.org. Web site: www.winnermagazine.org. **Editor:** Jan Schleifer. **Art Director:** Madelyn Gatz. Monthly magazine (September-May). Estab. 1958. Publishes articles that will promote children in grades 4-6 choosing a positive lifestyle and choosing to be drug-free.

Fiction Young readers, middle readers: contemporary, health, nature/environment, problem-solving, anti tobacco, alcohol, and drugs. Byline given.

Nonfiction Young readers, middle readers: positive role model personality features, health. Buys 10-15 mss/year. Average word length: 600-650 (in addition, needs 3 related thought questions and one puzzle/activity). Byline given.

How to Contact/Writers Fiction/nonfiction: Send complete ms; prefers e-mail submissions. Responds in 2 months. Publishes ms 6-12 months after acceptance. Will consider simultaneous.

Illustration Buys up to 3 illustrations/issue; up to 30 illustrations/year. Uses color artwork only. Works on assignment only. Reviews ms/illustration packages from artists ; send ms with dummy. Responds only if interested. Samples returned with SASE.

Terms Pays on acceptance. Buys first rights for mss. Original artwork returned at job's completion. Additional payment for ms/illustration packages. Sometimes additional payment when photos accompany articles. Pays $300 for color inside. Writer's guidelines for SASE. Sample magazine $2; include 9×12 envelope with 3 first-class stamps.

Tips "Keep material upbeat and positive for elementary age children."

YES MAG, Canada's Science Magazine for Kids

Peter Piper Publishing Inc., 3968 Long Gun Place, Victoria BC V8N 3A9 Canada. Fax: (250)477-5390. E-mail: editor@yesmag.ca. Web site: www.yesmag.ca **Publisher:** David Garrison. **Editor:** Shannon Hunt. **Art/Photo Director:** Sam Logan. Managing Editor: Jude Isabella. Bimonthly magazine. Estab. 1996. Circ. 22,000. "*YES Mag* is designed to make science accessible, interesting, exciting, and fun. Written for children ages 9 to 14,

YES Mag covers a range of topics including science and technology news, environmental updates, do-at-home projects and articles about Canadian s cience and scientists.''

Nonfiction Middle readers: all the sciences—math, engineering, biology, physics, chemistry, etc. Buys 70 mss/year. Average word length: 250- 800. Byline given.

How to Contact/Writers Nonfiction: Query with published clips. ''We prefer e-mail queries.'' Responds to queries/mss in 6 weeks. Generally publishes ms 3 months after acceptance.

Illustration Buys 2 illustrations/issue; 10 illustrations/year. Uses color artwork only. Works on assignment only. Reviews ms/illustration packages from artists. Query. Illustration only: Query with samples. Responds in 6 weeks. Samples filed. Credit line given.

Photography ''Looking for science, technology, nature/environment photos based on current editorial needs.'' Photo captions required. Uses color prints. Provide résumé, business card, promotional literature, tearsheets if possible. Will buy if photo is appropriate. Usually uses stock agencies.

Terms Pays on publication. Buys one-time rights for mss. Buys one-time rights for artwork/photos. Original artwork returned at job's completion. Pays $ 70-2 00 for stories and articles. Sample copies for $4 .50. Writer's guidelines available on the website under ''contact'' information.

Tips ''We do not publish fiction or science fiction or poetry. Visit our Web site for more information and sample articles. Articles relating to the physical sciences and mathematics are encouraged.''

YOUNG RIDER, The Magazine for Horse and Pony Lovers

Fancy Publications, P.O. Box 8237, Lexington KY 40533. (859)260-9800. Fax: (859)260-9814. Web site: www.yo ungrider.com. **Editor:** Lesley Ward. Bimonthly magazine. Estab. 1994. ''*Young Rider* magazine teaches young people, in an easy-to-read and entertaining way, how to look after their horses properly, and how to improve their riding skills safely.''

Fiction Young adults: adventure, animal, horses, horse celebrities, famous equestrians. Buys 10 mss/year. Average word length: 1,500 maximum. Byline given.

Nonfiction Young adults: animal, careers, health (horse), sports, riding. Buys 20-30 mss/year. Average word length: 1,000 maximum. Byline given.

How to Contact/Writers Fiction/nonfiction: Query with published clips. Responds to queries in 2 weeks. Publishes ms 6-12 months after acceptance. Will consider simultaneous submissions, electronic submissions via disk or modem, previously published work.

Illustration Buys 2 illustrations/issue; 10 illustrations/year. Works on assignment only. Reviews ms/illustration packages from artists. Query. Contact: Lesley Ward, editor. Illustrations only: Query with samples. Contact: Lesley Ward, editor. Responds in 2 weeks. Samples returned with SASE. Credit line given.

Photography Buys photos with accompanying ms only. Uses color, slides, photos—in focus, good light. Model/property release required; captions required. Uses color 4×6 prints, 35mm transparencies. Query with samples. Responds in 2 weeks. Digital images must be high-res.

Terms Pays on publication. Buys first North American serial rights for mss, artwork, photos. Original artwork returned at job's completion. Pays $150 maximum for stories; $250 maximum for articles. Additional payment for ms/illustration packages and for photos accompanying articles. Pays $70-140 for color inside. Pays photographers per photo (range: $65-155). Sample copies for $3.50. Writer's/illustrator's/photo guidelines for SASE.

Tips ''Fiction must be in third person. Read magazine before sending in a query. No 'true story from when I was a youngster.' No moralistic stories. Fiction must be up-to-date and humorous, teen-oriented. Need horsey interest or celebrity rider features. No practical or how-to articles—all done in-house.''

Young Writer's & Illustrator's Markets

The listings in this section are special because they publish work of young writers and artists (under age 18). Some of the magazines listed exclusively feature the work of young people. Others are adult magazines with special sections for the work of young writers. There are also a few book publishers listed that exclusively publish the work of young writers and artists. Many of the magazines and publishers listed here pay only in copies, meaning authors and illustrators receive one or more free copies of the magazine or book to which they contributed.

As with adult markets, markets for children expect writers to be familiar with their editorial needs before submitting. Many of the markets listed will send guidelines to writers. Guidelines state exactly what a publisher accepts and how to submit it. You can often get these by sending a request with a self-addressed, stamped envelope (SASE) to the magazine or publisher, or by checking a publication's Web site (a number of listings include Web addresses). In addition to obtaining guidelines, read through a few copies of any magazines you'd like to submit to—this is the best way to determine if your work is right for them.

A number of kids' magazines are available on newsstands or in libraries. Others are distributed only through schools, churches or home subscriptions. If you can't find a magazine you'd like to see, most editors will send sample copies for a small fee.

Before you submit your material to editors, take a few minutes to read Before Your First Sale on page 8 for more information on proper submission procedures. You may also want to check out two other sections—Contests, Awards & Grants and Conferences & Workshops. Some listings in these sections are open to students (some exclusively)—look for the phrase **Open to students** in bold. Additional opportunities and advice for young writers can be found in *The Young Writers Guide to Getting Published* (Writer's Digest Books) and *A Teen's Guide to Getting Published: the only writer's guide written by teens for teens*, by Danielle and Jessica Dunn (Prufrock Press). More information on these books are given in the Helpful Books & Publications section in the back of this book.

Information on companies listed in the previous edition but not included in this edition of *Children's Writer's & Illustrator's Market* may be found in the General Index.

CHIXLIT, the literary 'zine by and for chicks ages 7 to 17

P.O. Box 12051, Orange CA 92859. E-mail: chixlit@earthlink.net. Web site: www.chixlit.com. Bimonthly 'zine is a place for girls ages 7-17 to express themselves. "We cultivate talent and confidence; share writing techniques; communicate ideas and feelings; and let each other know we are not alone. Writers must be female and age 7-17,from anywhere in the world as long as writing in English; parent or guardian OK requested. Writer's guidelines on request and on Web site. Always seeking girls for editorial panel.

Magazine 95% written by young people. "We publish poems, short stories, reviews, rants, raves, love letters, song lyrics, journal entries and more. Always looking for regular contributors, critics, editors." Pays 1 free copy of the 'zine. Prizes for contests. Submit complete ms by e-mail (no attachments). Will accept typewritten form but prefer e-mail. Must be in English. "We plan a bilingual-Spanish-language edition for 2009." Responds via e-mail in 4-8 weeks, usually faster; "include your contact info!"

Artwork Publishes artwork and photography by girls ages 7-17 or of girls in that age range. Looks for "iconic images of chix, things chix like, or whatever makes you think of chix. Must be flat and scannable and look decent in b&w." No originals. Pays 1 free issue for artwork used and a small gift if chosen for the cover. "We prefer submission of work (original or a good color or b&w copy) in a flat envelope (not rolled) and sent to our P.O. box (so not too big)."

Tips "We dare you to dare. Our motto is, 'Words are powerful, and they can make you powerful too.' Buy a subscription or back issues to see what we're up to."

CICADA

Carus Publishing Company, 70 East Lake Street, Suite 300, Chicago IL 60601. (312)701-1720. Fax: (312)701-1728. Submissions address: 70 East Lake Street, Suite 300, Chicago IL 60601. E-mail: cicada@caruspub.com. Web site: www.cricketmag.com. **Editor-in-Chief:** Marianne Carus. **Executive Editor:** Deborah Vetter. **Art Director:** John Sandford. Bimonthly magazine.

- *Cicada* publishes work of writers and artists of high-school age and older (must be at least 14 years old). See the *Cicada* listing in the magazines section for more information, or check their Web site or copies of the magazine.

CREATIVE KIDS

P.O. Box 8813, Waco TX 76714-8813. (800)998-2208. Fax: (254)756-3339. E-mail: ck@prufrock.com. Web site: www.prufrock.com. **Editor:** Lacy Elwood. Magazine published 4 times/year. Estab. 1979. "Material is by children, for children." Purpose in publishing works by children: "to create a product that provides children with an authentic experience and to offer an opportunity for children to see their work in print. *Creative Kids* contains the best stories, poetry, opinion, artwork, games and photography by kids ages 8-16." Writers ages 8-16 must have statement by teacher or parent verifying originality. Writer's guidelines available on request with SASE. No adult submissions please.

Magazines Uses fiction and nonfiction stories (800-900 words), poetry, plays, ideas to share (200-750 words) per issue. Pays "free magazine." Submit mss to submissions editor. Will accept typewritten mss. Include SASE. Responds in 1 month.

Artwork/Photography Publishes artwork and photos by children. Looks for "any kind of drawing, cartoon, or painting." Pays "free magazine." Send color copy of the work to submissions editor. Include SASE. Responds in 1 month.

Tips "*Creative Kids* is a magazine by kids, for kids. The work represents children's ideas, questions, fears, concerns and pleasures. The material never contains racist, sexist, or violent expression. A person may submit one piece of work per envelope. Each piece must be labeled with the student's name, birth date, grade, school, home address and school address. Material submitted to *Creative Kids* must not be under consideration by any other publication. Items should be carefully prepared, proofread and double checked (perhaps also by a parent or teacher). All activities requiring solutions must be accompanied by the correct answers. Young writers and artists should always write for guidelines and then follow them. We only publish work creatid by children. Adult submissions will not be considered."

HIGH SCHOOL WRITER

P.O. Box 718, Grand Rapids MN 55744-0718. (218)326-8025. Fax: (218)326-8025. Web site: www.writerpublicatio ns.com. E-mail: writer@mx3.com. **Editor:** Robert Lemen. Magazine published 6 times during the school year. "The *High School Writer* is a magazine written *by* students *for* students. All submissions must exceed contemporary standards of decency." Purpose in publishing works by young people: to provide a real audience for student writers—and text for study. Submissions by junior high and middle school students accepted for our junior edition. Senior high students' works are accepted for our senior high edition. Students attending schools that subscribe to our publication are eligible to submit their work." Writer's guidelines available on request.

Magazines Uses fiction, nonfiction (2,000 words maximum) and poetry. Submit mss to editor. Submit complete ms (teacher must submit). Will accept typewritten, computer-generated (good quality) mss.

Tips "Submissions should not be sent without first obtaining a copy of our guidelines (see page 2 of every issue). Also, submissions will not be considered unless student's school subscribes."

HIGHLIGHTS FOR CHILDREN

803 Church St., Honesdale PA 18431. (570)253-1080. Magazine. Published monthly. "We strive to provide wholesome, stimulating, entertaining material that will encourage children to read. Our audience is children ages 6-12." Purpose in publishing works by young people: to encourage children's creative expression.

Magazines 15-20% of magazine written by children. Uses stories and poems. Also uses jokes, riddles, tongue twisters. Features that occur occasionally: "What Are Your Favorite Books?" (8-10/year), Recipes (8-10/year), "Science Letters" (15-20/year). Special features that invite children's submissions on a specific topic occur several times per year. Recent examples include "Amusement Park Rides," "Funniest Dreams," "Your Dream Vacation, " and "Help the Cartoonists." Pays in copies. Submit complete ms to the editor. Will accept typewritten, legibly handwritten and computer printout mss. Responds in 6 weeks.

Artwork Publishes artwork by children. Pays in copies. No cartoon or comic book characters. No commercial products. Submit b&w or color artwork on unlined paper for "Your Own Pages." Features include "Creatures Nobody Has Ever Seen" (5-8/year) and "You Illustrate the Story" (18-20/year). Responds in 6 weeks.

Tips "Remember to keep a photocopy of your work because we cannot return it. When submitting your work, please include your name, age, and full address."

KWIL KIDS PUBLISHING, The Little Publishing Company That Kwil Built

Kwilville, P.O. Box 98037-135 Davie Street, Vancouver, B.C., Canada V6Z 2Y0. E-mail: kalenmarquis@live.ca. Publishes weekly column in local paper, four quarterly newsletters. "*Kwil Kids* come in all ages, shapes and sizes—from 4-64 and a whole lot more! Kwil does not pay for the creative work of children but provides opportunity/encouragement. We promote literacy, creativity and creative 'connections' through written and artistic expression and publish autobiographical, inspirational, stories of gentleness, compassion, truth and beauty. Our purpose is to foster a sense of pride and enthusiasm in young writers and artists, to celebrate the voice of youth and to encourage growth through joy-filled practice and cheerleading, not criticism." Must include name, age, address and parent signature (if a minor). Will send guidelines upon request."

Books Publishes autobiographical, inspirational, creative stories (alliterative, rhyming refrains, juicy words), short rhyming and nonrhyming poems (creative, fun, original, expressive) and creative nonfiction. Length: 500 words for fiction; 8-16 lines for poetry. No payments; self-published and sold "at cost" only (1 free copy). Submit mss to Kwil or Mr. Marquis. Submit complete ms. Send copy only; expect a reply but will not return ms. Will accept typewritten and legibly handwritten mss and e-mail. Include SASE or enclose IRC or $1 for postage, as US stamps may not be used from Canada. Responds in three months.

Newsletter 95% of newsletter written by young people. Uses 15 short stories, poems (20-100 words). No payment; free newsletters only. Submit complete ms. Will accept typewritten and legibly handwritten mss and e-mail. Kwil answers every letter in verse. Responds in 4 weeks.

Artwork Publishes artwork and photography by children with writing. Looks for black ink sketches to go with writing and photos to go with writing. Submit by postal mail only; white background for sketches. Submit artwork/photos to Kwil publisher. Submit holiday/seasonal work 4 months in advance. Include SASE. Responds in 3 months.

Tips "We love stories that teach a lesson or encourage peace, love and a fresh, new understanding. Just be who you are and do what you do. Then all of life's treasures will come to you."

NEW MOON: THE MAGAZINE FOR GIRLS & THEIR DREAMS

New Moon Girl Media, LLC., 2 W. First St., #101, Duluth MN 55802. (218)728-5507. Fax: (218)728-0314. E-mail: girl@newmoongirlmedia.com. Web site: www.newmoonmagazine.org. **Managing Editor:** Melissa Harrison. Bimonthly magazine. *New Moon*'s primary audience is girls ages 8-12. "We publish a magazine that listens to girls." More than 70% of *New Moon* is written by girls. Purpose in publishing work by children/teens: "We want girls' voices to be heard. *New Moon* wants girls to see that their opinions, dreams, thoughts and ideas count." Writer's guidelines available for SASE or online.

● See *New Moon*'s listing in Magazines section.

Magazine Buys 6 fiction mss/year (1,200-1,600 words); 30 nonfiction mss/year (600 words). Submit to Editorial Department. Submit query or complete mss for nonfiction; complete ms only for fiction. "We do not return or acknowledge unsolicited material. Do not send originals—we will not return any materials." Responds in 6 months if interested.

Artwork/Photography Publishes artwork and photography by girls. "We do not return unsolicited material."

Tips "Read *New Moon* to completely understand our needs."

▶ SKIPPING STONES

Multicultural Children's Magazine, P.O. Box 3939, Eugene OR 97403-0939. (541)342-4956. E-mail: editor@Skipp ingStones.org. Web site: www.SkippingStones.org. **Articles/Poems/Fiction Editor:** Arun N. Toke. 5 issues a year. Estab. 1988. Circulation 2,500. "*Skipping Stones* is a multicultural, nonprofit, children's magazine to encourage cooperation, creativity and celebration of cultural and ecological richness. It offers itself as a creative forum for communication among children from different lands and backgrounds. We prefer work by children under 18 years old. International, minorities and under-represented populations receive priority, multilingual submissions are encouraged." Guidelines for children's work available on request with SASE.

- *Skipping Stones*' theme for the Youth Honor Awards is multicultural/international understanding and nature awareness. Send SASE for guidelines and more information on the awards. *Skipping Stones*, now in it's 20th year, is winner of the N.A.M.E., Parents' Choice, Newsstand Resouces, Writer and EDPRESS awards.

Magazines 70% written by children and teenagers. Uses 5-10 fiction short stories and plays (500-1,000 words); 5-10 nonfiction articles, interviews, letters, history, descriptions of celebrations (500-1,000 words); 15-20 poems, jokes, riddles, proverbs (250 words or less) per issue. Pays in contributor's copies. Submit mss to editor. Submit complete ms for fiction or nonfiction work; teachers and parents can also submit their contributions. Submissions should include "cover letter with name, age, address, school, cultural background, inspiration piece, dreams for future." Will accept typewritten, legibly handwritten and computer/word processor mss. Include SASE. Responds in 4 months. Accepts simultaneous submissions.

Artwork/Photography Publishes artwork and photography for children. Will review all varieties of ms/illustration packages. Wants comics, cartoons, b&w photos, color paintings, drawings (preferably ink & pen or pencil), 8×10, color photos OK. Prints 4-color cover/back cover and b&w inside. Subjects include children, people, celebrations, nature, ecology, multicultural. Pays in contributor's copies.

Terms "*Skipping Stones* is a labor of love. You'll receive complimentary contributor's (up to 4) copies depending on the extent/length of your contribution. 25% discount on additional copies. We may allow others to reprint (including by electronic means) articles and art or photographs." Responds to artists in 4 months. Sample copy for $5 and 4 first-class stamps.

Tips "Let the 'inner child' within you speak out—naturally, uninhibited." Wants "material that gives insight on cultural celebrations, lifestyle, custom and tradition, glimpse of daily life in other countries and cultures. Please, no mystery for the sake of mystery! Photos, songs, artwork are most welcome if they illustrate/highlight the points. Upcoming features: Living abroad, turning points, inspirations and magical moments in life, cultural celebrations around the world, folktales, caring for the earth, endangered species, your dreams and visions, heroes, kid-friendly analysis of current events, resolving conficts, summer experiences, poetry, and minority experiences."

STONE SOUP, The Magazine by Young Writers and Artists

Children's Art Foundation, P.O. Box 83, Santa Cruz CA 95063-0083. (831)426-5557. Fax: (831)426-1161. E-mail: editor@stonesoup.com. Web site: www.stonesoup.com. **Articles/Fiction Editor, Art Director:** Ms. Gerry Mandel. Magazine published 6 times/year. Circ. 20,000. "We publish fiction, poetry and artwork by children through age 13. Our preference is for work based on personal experiences and close observation of the world. Our audience is young people through age 13, as well as parents, teachers, librarians." Purpose in publishing works by young people: to encourage children to read and to express themselves through writing and art. Writer's guidelines available online at stonesoup.com.

Magazines Uses animal, contemporary, fantasy, history, problem-solving, science fiction, sports, spy/mystery/ adventure fiction stories. Uses 5-10 fiction stories (150-2,500 words); 5-10 nonfiction stories (150-2,500 words); 2-4 poems per issue. Does not want to see classroom assignments and formula writing. Buys 65 mss/year. Byline given. Pays on publication. Buys all rights. Pays $40 each for stories and poems, $40 for book reviews. Contributors also receive 2 copies. Sample copy $4. Free writer's guidelines. Writers' guidelines are available online at stonesoup.com.

Artwork/Photography Does not publish artwork other than illustrations. Pays $25 for color illustrations. Contributors receive 2 copies. Sample copy $ 4. Illustrator's guidelines are available online at stonesoup.com. Send color copies, not originals. If you would like to illustrate for *Stone Soup*, send us 2 or 3 samples (color copies) of your work, along with a letter telling us what kinds of stories you would like to illustrate. We are looking for artists who can draw complete scenes, including the background. Send submissions to editor. Include SASE. Responds in 6 weeks. All artwork must be by children through age 13.

Tips "Only work by young people through age 13 is considered. Whether your work is about imaginary situations or real ones, use your own experiences and observations to give your work depth and a sense of reality. Read a few issues of our magazine to get an idea of what we like."

WHOLE NOTES

2305 Turrentine Drive, Las Cruces NM 88005. (505)541-5744. E-mail: rnhastings@zianet.com. **Editor:** Nancy Peters Hastings. Magazine published twice yearly. "We encourage interest in contemporary poetry by showcasing outstanding creative writing. We look for original, fresh perceptions in poems that demonstrate skill in using language effectively, with carefully chosen images and clear ideas. Our audience (general) loves poetry. We try to recognize excellence in creative writing by children as a way to encourage and promote imaginative thinking.'' Writer's guidelines available for SASE.

Magazines Every fourth issue is 100% by children. Writers should be 21 years old or younger. Uses 30 poems/issue (length open). Pays complimentary copy. Submit mss to editor. Submit complete ms. ''No multiple submissions, please.'' Will accept typewritten and legibly handwritten mss. SASE. Responds in 2 months.

Artwork/Photography Publishes artwork and photographs by children. Looks for b&w line drawings which can easily be reproduced; b&w photos. Pays complimentary copy. Send clear photocopies. Submit artwork to Nancy Peters Hastings, editor. SASE. Responds in 2 months.

Tips Sample issue is $3. ''We welcome translations. Send your best work. Don't send your only copy of your poem. Keep a photocopy.''

THE WRITERS' SLATE

The Writing Conference, Inc., P.O. Box 664, Ottawa KS 66067. Phone/fax: (785)242-1995. E-mail: jbushman@writingconference.com. Web site: www.writingconference.com. Magazine. Publishes 3 issues/year online. *The Writers' Slate* accepts original poetry and prose from students enrolled in kindergarten-12th grade. The audience is students, teachers and librarians. Purpose in publishing works by young people: to give students the opportunity to publish and to give students the opportunity *to read* quality literature written by other students. Writer's guidelines are available on Web Site.

Magazines 90% of magazine written by young people. Uses 10-15 fiction, 1-2 nonfiction, 10-15 other mss per issue. Submit mss to Shelley McNerney, editor, 7619 Hemlock St., Overland Park KS 66204. Submit complete ms. Will accept typewritten mss. Responds in 1 month. Include SASE with ms if reply is desired.

Artwork Publishes artwork by young people. Bold, b&w, student artwork may accompany a piece of writing. Submit to Shelley McNerney, editor. Responds in 1 month.

Tips ''Always accompany submission with a letter indicating name, home address, school, grade level and teacher's name. If you want a reply, submit a SASE.''

Agents & Art Reps

This section features listings of literary agents and art reps who either specialize in, or represent a good percentage of, children's writers and/or illustrators. While there are a number of children's publishers who are open to non-agented material, using the services of an agent or rep can be beneficial to a writer or artist. Agents and reps can get your work seen by editors and art directors more quickly. They are familiar with the market and have insights into which editors and art directors would be most interested in your work. Also, they negotiate contracts and will likely be able to get you a better deal than you could get on your own.

Agents and reps make their income by taking a percentage of what writers and illustrators receive from publishers. The standard percentage for agents is 10 to 15 percent; art reps generally take 25 to 30 percent. We have not included any agencies in this section that charge reading fees.

WHAT TO SEND

When putting together a package for an agent or rep, follow the guidelines given in their listings. Most agents open to submissions prefer initially to receive a query letter describing your work. For novels and longer works, some agents ask for an outline and a number of sample chapters, but you should send these only if you're asked to do so. Never fax or e-mail query letters or sample chapters to agents without their permission. Just as with publishers, agents receive a large volume of submissions. It may take them a long time to reply, so you may want to query several agents at one time. It's best, however, to have a complete manuscript considered by only one agent at a time. Always include a self-addressed, stamped envelope (SASE).

For initial contact with art reps, send a brief query letter and self-promo pieces, following the guidelines given in the listings. If you don't have a flier or brochure, send photocopies. Always include a SASE.

For those who both write and illustrate, some agents listed will consider the work of author/illustrators. Read through the listings for details.

As you consider approaching agents and reps with your work, keep in mind that they are very choosy about who they take on to represent. Your work must be high quality and presented professionally to make an impression on them. For more information on approaching agents and additional listings, see *Guide to Literary Agents* (Writer's Digest Books). For additional listings of art reps see *Artist's & Graphic Designer's Market* (Writer's Digest Books).

Information on agents and art reps listed in the previous edition but not included in this edition of *Children's Writer's & Illustrator's Market* may be found in the General Index.

An Organization for Agents

In some listings of agents you'll see references to AAR (The Association of Authors' Representatives). This organization requires its members to meet an established list of professional standards and code of ethics.

The objectives of AAR include keeping agents informed about conditions in publishing and related fields; encouraging cooperation among literary organizations; and assisting agents in representing their author-clients' interests. Officially, members are prohibited from directly or indirectly charging reading fees. They offer writers a list of member agents on their Web site. They also offer a list of recommended questions an author should ask an agent and other FAQs, all found on their Web site. They can be contacted at AAR, 676A 9th Ave. #312, New York NY 10036. (212)840-5777. E-mail: aarinc@mindspring.com. Web site: www.aar-online.org.

AGENTS

ADAMS LITERARY

7845 Colony Rd., #215, Charlotte NC 28226. (704)542-1440. Fax: (704)542-1450. E-mail: info@adamsliterary.com. Web site: www.adamsliterary.com. **Contact:** Tracey Adams, Josh Adams. Estab. 2004. Member of AAR and SCBWI. 20% of clients are new/previously unpublished writers. 100% of material handled is books for young readers.

- Prior to becoming an agent, Tracey Adams worked in the editorial and marketing departments at several children's publishing houses.

Represents Considers fiction, picture books, middle grade, young adult. "We place authors' work based on insight and experience. Adams Literary offers editorial guidance and marketing knowledge."

How to Contact See Web site for updates on submission policy.

Terms Agent receives 15% commission on domestic sales; 20% on foreign sales. Offers written contract.

Writers' Conferences Attends Bologna Book Fair in Bologna, Italy. Other conferences listed on Web site.

Tips "We represent authors, not books, so we enjoy forming long-term relationships with our clients. We work hard to be sure we are submitting work which is ready to be considered, but we respect the role of editors and don't over-edit manuscripts ourselves. Our style is assertive yet collaborative."

⃞N⃞ BOOKS & SUCH

4788 Carissa Ave., Santa Rosa CA 95405. (707)538-4184. Fax: (707)538-4184. E-mail: janet@janetgrant.com. Web site: www.janetgrant.com. **Contact:** Janet Kobobel Grant. Estab. 1996. Associate member of CBA. Represents 50 clients. 1% of clients are new/unpublished writers. Specializes in "the Christian booksellers market but places some projections in the general market."

- Before becoming an agent, Janet Kobobel Grant was an editor for Zondervan and managing editor for *Focus on the Family.*

Represents 8% juvenile books. Considers: nonfiction, fiction, picture books, young adult.

How to Contact Prefers E-mail: queries (no attachments) and queries via postal mail with SASE. Considers simultaneous queries. Responds in 1 month to queries; 6 weeks to mss. Returns material only with SASE.

Recent Sales *Landon Snow and the Auctor's Riddle* (Barbour); *God Called a Girl* (Bethany); *Ten Minutes to Showtime* (Tommy Nelson).

Needs Actively seeking "material that delights and charms the reader. A fresh approach to a perennial topic is always of interest." Obtains new clients through recommendations and conferences.

Terms Agent receives 15% commission on domestic and foreign sales. Offers written contract. 2 months notice must be given to terminate contract. Charges for postage, photocopying, fax and express mail.

Tips "The heart of my motivation is to develop relationships with the authors I serve, to do what I can to shine the light of success on them, and to help be a caretaker of their gifts and time."

BOOKSTOP LITERARY AGENCY

67 Meadow View Rd., Orinda CA 94563. Web site: www.bookstopliterary.com. Seeking both new and established writers. Estab. 1983. 100% of material handled is books of young readers.
Represents Considers fiction, nonfiction, picture books, middle grade, for young adult. "Special interest in Hispanic writers and illustrators for children."
How to Contact Query only with nonfiction; all others send entire ms with SASE. Considers simultaneous submissions. Responds in 6 weeks. Responds with e-mail but returns material only with SASE.
Terms Agent receives 15% commission on domestic sales. Offers written contract, binding for 1 year.

ANDREA BROWN LITERARY AGENCY, INC.

1076 Eagle Dr., Salinas CA 93905. (831)422-5925. Web site: www.andreabrownlit.com. **President:** Andrea Brown. Estab. 1981. Member of SCBWI and WNBA. 20% of clients are new/previously unpublished writers. Specializes in "all kinds of children's books—illustrators and authors."
• Prior to opening her agency, Andrea Brown served as an editorial assistant at Random House and Dell Publishing and as an editor with Alfred A. Knopf.
Member Agents Andrea Brown, president; Laura Rennert, senior agent; Caryn Wiseman, agent; Jennifer Jaeger and Michelle Andelman, Jamie Weiss Chilton, and Jennifer Laughran associate agents. Offices in California and New York City.
Represents 98% juvenile books. Considers: nonfiction (animals, anthropology/archaeology, art/architecture/design, biography/autobiography, current affairs, ethnic/cultural interests, history, how-to, nature/environment, photography, popular culture, science/technology, sociology, sports); fiction (historical, science fiction); picture books, young adult.
How to Contact Query. Responds in 3 months to queries and mss. E-mail queries only.
Needs Mostly obtains new clients through recommendations, editors, clients and agents.
Recent Sales *Fire on Ice*, autobiography of Sasha Cohen (HarperCollins); three book series, by Ellen Hopkins (S&S); *Downside Up*, by Neal Shusterman (Simon & Schuster).
Terms Agent receives 15% commission on domestic sales; 20% on foreign sales. Written contract.
Writers' Conferences Agents at Andrea Brown Literary Agency attend Austin Writers League; SCBWI; Columbus Writers Conference; Willamette Writers Conference; Orange County Conferences; Mills College Childrens Literature Conference (Oakland CA); Asilomar (Pacific Grove CA); Maui Writers Conference; Southwest Writers Conference; San Diego State University Writer's Conference; Big Sur Children's Writing Workshop (Director); BookExpo America/Writer's Digest Books Writing Conference.
Tips Query first. "Taking on very few picture books. Must be unique—no rhyme, no anthropomorphism. Do not call or fax queries or manuscripts. E-mail queries first. Check Web site for details."

CURTIS BROWN, LTD.

Ten Astor Place., New York NY 10003. (212)473-5400. Fax: (212)598-0917. Seeking both new and established writers. Estab. 1914. Members of AAR and SCBWI. Signatory of WGA. **Staff includes:** Ginger Clark, Elizabeth Harding and Ginger Knowlton.
Represents Authors and illustrators of fiction, nonfiction, picture books, middle grade, young adult.
How to Contact Query with SASE. If a picture book, send only one picture book ms. Considers simultaneous queries, "but please tell us." Returns material only with SASE. Obtains clients through recommendations from others, queries/solicitations, conferences.
Terms Agent receives 15% commission on domestic sales; 20% on foreign sales. Offers written contract. 75 days notice must be given to terminate contract.

BROWNE & MILLER LITERARY ASSOCIATES, LLC

410 S. Michigan Ave., Suite 460, Chicago IL 60605. (312)922-3063. Fax: (312)922-1905. E-mail: mail@brownean dmiller.com. Web site: www.browneandmiller.com. **Contact:** Danielle Egan-Miller, president. Prefers to work with established writers. Handles only certain types of work. Estab. 1971. Member of AAR, RWA, MWA. Represents 85+ clients. 5% of clients are new/previously unpublished writers. 15% of material handled is books for young readers.
• Prior to opening the agency, Danielle Egan-Miller worked as an editor.
Represents Considers primarily YA fiction, fiction, young adult. "We love great writing and have a wonderful list of authors writing YA in particular." Not looking for picture books, middle grade.
How to Contact Query with SASE. Accepts queries by e-mail. Considers simultaneous queries. Responds in 2-4 weeks to queries; 4-6 months to mss. Returns material only with SASE. Obtains clients through recommendations from others.
Recent Sales Sold 10 books for young readers in the last year.

Terms Agent receives 15% commission on domestic sales; 20% on foreign sales. Offers written contract. Offers written contract, binding for 2 years. 30 days notice must be given to terminate contract.

Tips "We are very hands-on and do much editorial work with our clients. We are passionate about the books we represent and work hard to help clients reach their publishing goals."

PEMA BROWNE LTD.

11 Tena Place, Valley Cottage NY 10989. (845)268-0029. **Contact:** Pema Browne. Estab. 1966. Represents 2 illustrators. 10% of artwork handled is children's book illustration. Specializes in general commercial. Markets include: all publishing areas; children's picture books. Clients include HarperCollins, Holiday House, Bantam Doubleday Dell, Nelson/Word, Hyperion, Putnam. Client list available upon request.

Handles Fiction, nonfiction, picture books, middle grade, young adult, manuscript/illustration packages. Looking for "professional and unique" talent.

Recent Sales *The Daring Ms. Quimby*, by Suzanne Whitaker (Holiday House).

Terms Rep receives 30% illustration commission; 20% author commission. Exclusive area representation is required. For promotional purposes, talent must provide color mailers to distribute. Representative pays mailing costs on promotion mailings.

How to Contact For first contact, send query letter, direct mail flier/brochure and SASE. If interested will ask to mail appropriate materials for review. Portfolios should include tearsheets and transparencies or good color photocopies, plus SASE. Accepts queries by mail only. Obtains new talent through recommendations and interviews (portfolio review).

Tips "We are doing more publishing—all types—less advertising." Looks for "continuity of illustration and dedication to work."

LIZA DAWSON ASSOCIATES

350 7th Ave, Suite 2003, New York, NY 10001. E-mail: anna@olswanger.com. Web site: www.olswanger.com. **Contact:** Anna Olswanger. Member of SCBWI, WNBA, Authors Guild. Represents 10 clients. 30% of clients are new/unpublished writers. 50% of material handled is books for young readers.

  • Anna Olswanger coordinates the Jewish Childrens's Book Writers' Conference each fall at the 92nd Street Y in New York City and is a children's book author.

Represents Fiction, nonfiction; author-illustrator picture books.

How to Contact Query with first 5 pages. Must include e-mail address for response. Considers simultaneous queries. Responds in 4 weeks to queries; 8 weeks to mss. Obtains most new clients through recommendations and queries.

Terms Agent receives 15% commission on domestic sales; 20% commission on foreign sales. Offers written contract. Charges client for color photocopying and overseas postage.

DUNHAM LITERARY, INC.

156 Fifth Ave., Suite 625, New York NY 10010-7002. Web site: www.dunhamlit.com. **Contact:** Jennie Dunham. Seeking both new and established writers but prefers to work with established writers. Estab. 2000. Member of AAR, signatory of SCBWI. Represents 50 clients. 15% of clients are new/previously unpublished writers. 50% of material handled is books of young readers.

Represents Considers fiction, picture books, middle grade, young adult. Most agents represent children's books or adult books, and this agency represents both. Actively seeking mss with great story and voice. Not looking for activity books, workbooks, educational books, poetry.

How to Contact Query with SASE. Consider simultaneous queries and submissions. Responds in 2 week s to queries; 2 months to mss. Returns material only with SASE. Obtains clients through recommendations from others.

Recent Sales Sold 30 books for young readers in the last year. *Winter's Tale*, by Robert Sabuda (Little Simon); *Clever Beatrice Christmas*, by Margaret Willey, illustrated by Heather Solomon (Atheneum); Adele and Simon, by Barbara McClintock (Farrar, Straus & Giroux); *Sweetgrass Basket*, by Marlene Carvell (Dutton); *How I Found the Strong*, by Margaret McMullan (Houghton Mifflin).

Terms Agent receives 15% commission on domestic sales; 20-25% on foreign sales. Offers written contract. 60 days notice must be given to terminate contract.

Fees The agency takes expenses from the clients' earnings for specific expenses documented during the marketing of a client's work in accordance with the AAR (Association of Authors' Representatives) Canon of Ethics. For example, photocopying, messenger, express mail, UPS, etc. The client is not asked to pay for these fees up front. ·

DWYER & O'GRADY, INC.

P.O. Box 790, Cedar Key FL 32625. (352)543-9307. Fax: (603)375-5373. E-mail: jdwyer@dwyerogrady.com. Web site: www.dwyerogrady.com. **Contact:** Jeff Dwyer. Estab. 1990. Member of Society of Illustrators, Graphic

Artist's Guild, SCBWI, ABA. Represents 15 illustrators. Staff includes Elizabeth O'Grady, Jeff Dwyer. Specializes in children's books (picture books, middle grad and young adult). Markets include: publishing/books, audio/film.

• Dwyer & O'Grady is currently not accepting new clients.

Handles Illustrators and writers of children's books.

Terms Agent receives 15% commission on domestic sales; 20% on foreign sales. Additional fees are negotiable. Exclusive representation is required (world rights). Advertising costs are paid by representative.

How to Contact For first contact, send query letter by postal mail only.

EDUCATIONAL DESIGN SERVICES LLC

5750 Bou Ave, Ste. 1508, N. Bethesda, MD 20852. E-mail: blinder@educationaldesignservices.com. Web site: www.educationaldesignservices.com. **Contact:** B. Linder. Handles only certain types of work. Estab. 1981. 80% of clients are new/previously unpublished writers.

Represents Considers text materials for K-12 market. "We specialize in educational materials to be used in classrooms (in class sets) or in teacher education classes." Actively seeking educational, text materials. Not looking for picture books, story books, fiction; no illustrators.

How to Contact Query with SASE or send outline and 1 sample chapter. Considers simultaneous queries and submissions if so indicated. Responds in 6-8 weeks to queries/mss. Returns material only with SASE. Obtains clients through recommendations from others, queries/solicitations, or through conferences.

Recent Sales *How to Solve Word Problems in Mathematics*, by Wayne (McGraw-Hill); *Reviewing U.S. & New York State History*, by Farran-Paci (Amsco); *Minority Report*, by Gunn-Singh (Scarecrow Education); *No Parent Left Behind*, by Petrosino & Spiegel (Rowman & Littlefield); *Teaching Test-taking Skills* (R&L Education).

Terms Agent receives 15% commission on domestic sales; 25% on foreign sales. Offers written contract, binding until any party opts out. Terminate contract through certified letter.

ETHAN ELLENBERG LITERARY AGENCY

548 Broadway, #5-E, New York NY 10012. (212)431-4554. Fax: (212)941-4652. E-mail: agent@ethanellenberg.com. Web site: EthanEllenberg.com. **Contact:** Ethan Ellenberg. Estab. 1983. Represents 80 clients. 10% of clients are new/previously unpublished writers. "Children's books are an important area for us."

• Prior to opening his agency, Ethan Ellenberg was contracts manager of Berkley/Jove and associate contracts manager for Bantam. Represents 2002 Cladecott Medal winner Eric Rohmann, for *My Friend Rabbit*, adapted by Nelvana and running in an animated series fall 2007 on NBC.

Represents "We do a lot of children's books." Considers: picture books, middle grade, YA and selected.

How to Contact Picture books—send full ms with SASE. Illustrators: Send a representative portfolio with color copies and SASE. No original artwork. Young adults—send outline plus 3 sample chapters with SASE. Accepts queries by e-mail; does not accept attachments to e-mail queries or fax queries. Considers simultaneous queries and submissions. Responds in six weeks to snail mail queries; only responds to e-mail queries if interested.1 month to mss. Returns materials only with SASE. "See Web site for detailed instructions, please follow them carefully." No phone calls.

Terms Agent receives 15% on domestic sales; 20% on foreign sales. Offers written contract, "flexible." Charges for "direct expenses only: photocopying for manuscript submissions, postage for submission and foreign rights sales."

Tips "We do consider new material from unsolicited authors. Write a clear letter with a succinct description of your book. We prefer the first three chapters when we consider fiction, but for children's book submissions, we prefer the full manuscript. For all submissions you must include SASE for return or the material is discarded. It's always hard to break in, but talent will find a home. We continue to seek natural storytellers and nonfiction writers with important books." This agency sold over 100 titles per year in the last 4 years (combining adult and children's books).

FLANNERY LITERARY

1155 South Washington St., Suite 202, Naperville IL 60540-3300. (630)428-2682. Fax: (630)428-2683. **Contact:** Jennifer Flannery. Estab. 1992. Represents 40 clients. 95% of clients are new/previously unpublished writers. Specializes in children's and young adult, juvenile fiction and nonfiction.

• Prior to opening her agency, Jennifer Flannery was an editorial assistant.

Represents 100% juvenile books. Considers: nonfiction, fiction, picture books, middle grade, young adult.

How to Contact Query. "No e-mail or fax queries, please." Responds in 2 weeks to queries; 5 weeks to mss.

Needs Obtains new clients through referrals and queries.

Terms Agent receives 15% commission on domestic sales; 20% on foreign sales. Offers written contract, binding for life of book in print, with 30-day cancellation clause. 100% of business is derived from commissions on sales.

Tips "Write an engrossing succinct query describing your work." Flannery Literary sold 20 titles in the last year.

BARRY GOLDBLATT LITERARY LLC

320 Seventh Ave., #266, Brooklyn NY 11215. (718)832-8787. Fax: (718)832-5558. E-mail: bgliterary@earthlink.n et. Web site: www.bgliterary.com. **Contact:** Barry Goldblatt. Estab. 2000. Member of AAR, SCBWI. Represents 45 clients. 15% of clients are new/previously unpublished writers. 100% of material handled is books for young readers. Staff includes Barry Goldblatt (picture books, middle grade, and young adult novels).

Represents Considers picture books, fiction, middle grade, young adult.

How to Contact Send queries only; no longer accepting unsolicited manuscript submissions. Prefers to read material exclusively. Responds in 3 weeks to queries; 2 months to mss. Returns material only with SASE. Obtains clients through recommendations from others.

Recent Sales Calvin Coconut series, by Graham Salisbury; The Infernal Devices trilogy, by Cassandra Clare; *Rose Sees Red*, by Cecil Castellucci.

Terms Agent receives 15% commission on domestic sales; 20% on foreign and dramatic sales.

Tips "I structure my relationship with each client differently, according to their wants and needs. I'm mostly hands-on, but some want more editorial input, others less. I'm pretty aggressive in selling work, but I'm fairly laid back in how I deal with clients. I'd say I'm quite friendly with most of my clients, and I like it that way. To me this is more than just a simple business relationship."

ASHLEY GRAYSON LITERARY AGENCY

1342 18th St., San Pedro CA 90732. (310)514-0267. Fax: (310)514-1148. Seeking both new and established writers. Estab. 1976. Agency is member of AAR, SCBWI, SFWA, RWA. Represents 75 clients. 5-10% new writers. 25% books for young readers. Staff includes Ashley Grayson, young adult and middle grade; Carolyn Grayson, young adult, middle grade, some picture books; Denise Dumars, young adult.

Represents Handles fiction, middle grade, young adult. "We represent top authors in the field and we market their books to publishers worldwide." Actively seeking fiction of high commercial potential.

How to Contact Query with SASE. Include first 3 pages of manuscript; if querying about a picture books, include entire text. Accepts queries by mail and e-mail. Considers simultaneous queries. Responds 1 month after query, 2-3 months after ms. Returns mss only with SASE. Obtains new clients through recommendations from others, queries/solicitations, conferences.

Recent Sales Sold 25+ books last year. *Juliet Dove, Queen of Love*, by Bruce Coville (Harcourt); *Alosha*, by Christopher Pike (TOR); *Sleeping Freshmen Never Lie*, by David Lubar (Dutton); *Ball Don't Lie*, by Matt de la Peña (Delacorte); *Wiley & Grampa's Creature Features*, by Kirk Scroggs (6-book series, Little Brown); *Street Pharm*, by Allison van Diepen (Simon Pulse). Also represents: J.B. Cheaney (Knopf), Bruce Wetter (Atheneum).

Terms Agent receives 15% on domestic sales, 20% on foreign sales. Offers written contract. Contract binding for 1 year. 30 days notice must be given for termination of contract.

Tips "We do request revisions as they are required. We are long-time agents, professional and known in the business. We perform professionally for our clients and we ask the same of them."

N THE GREENHOUSE LITERARY AGENCY

11308 Lapham Drive, Oakton VA 22124. E-mail: sarahd@greenhouseliterary.com. Web site: www.greenhouselit erary.com. **Contact:** Sarah Davies. New agency actively seeking clients. Seeking both new and established writers. Estab. 2008. Member of SCBWI. Represents 4 clients. 100% new writers. 100% books for young readers. Staff includes Sarah Davies.

• Sarah Davis has had an editorial and management career in children's publishing spanning 25 years; for 5 years prior to launching the Greenhouse she was Publishing Director of Macmillan Children's Books in London, working with and publishing leading authors from both sided of the Atlantic.

Represents Handles fiction, middle grade, young adult. "Sarah Davies (who is British) represents authors personally to both the USA and UK, and the Greenhouse has offices in both countries. Commission structure reflects this as the agency takes the same commission for both the USA and UK, treating both as the 'domestic' market. Foreign rights are sold by Rights People (a separate business but also part of the Greenhouse's parent company), a dedicated team of rights-selling experts with a fast-growing international track record. This means sub-agents are rarely used, giving the agency an exceptionally cohesive presence around the world and a truly global reach. Davies has a strong editorial background and is able, as necessary, to work creatively with authors in a very hands-on way to help them reach submission point." Actively seeking children's and YA fiction of all kinds, from age 5+ (post picture book) through teen and crossover. Does not seek "nonfiction, poetry or picture books (text or illustration). However, if a client diversified from children's fiction into other areas, then the Greenhouse would continue to represent the author, whatever the age group or genre of work. The agency represents authors, not books."

How to Contact Send a one-paragraph outline and biography, plus 3 sample chapters. Accepts queries by e-mail, mail. "Allow 6 weeks for a response to initial material. Check Web site before submitting." Returns mss with SASE only. Obtains new clients through recommendations from other, queries/solicitations, conference.

Terms Receives 15% commission on sales to both US and UK; 25% on foreign sales. Offers written contract.-Sarah Davies attends Bologna Children's Bookfair in Bologna, Italy; SCBWI conferences; BookExpo America; and other conference—see Web site for information.

Tips "It's very important to me to have a strong, long-term relationship with clients. Having been 25 years in the publishing industry, I know the business from the inside and have excellent contacts in both the US and UK. I work hard to find every client the very best publisher and deal for their writing. My editorial background means I can work creatively with authors where necessary; I aim to submit high-quality manuscripts to publishers while respecting the role of the editor who will have their own publishing vision. Before submitting, prospective authors should look at the Greenhouse's 'Top 10 tips for authors of children's fiction', which can be found on our Web site."

BARBARA S. KOUTS, LITERARY AGENT

P.O. Box 560, Bellport NY 11713. (631)286-1278. **Contact:** Barbara Kouts. Currently accepting new clients. Estab. 1980. Member of AAR. Represent 50 clients. 10% of clients are new/previously unpublished writers. Specializes in children's books.

Represents 100% juvenile books. Considers: nonfiction, fiction, picture books, ms/illustration packages, middle grade, young adult.

How to Contact Accepts queries by mail only. Responds in 1 week to queries; 6 weeks to mss.

Needs Obtains new clients through recommendations from others, solicitation, at conferences, etc.

Recent Sales *Code Talker*, by Joseph Bruchac (Dial); *The Penderwicks*, by Jeanne Birdsall (Knopf); *Frogg's Baby Sister*, by Jonathan London (Viking).

Terms Agent receives 10% commission on domestic sales; 20% on foreign sales. Charges for photocopying.

Tips "Write, do not call. Be professional in your writing."

MCINTOSH & OTIS, INC.

353 Lexington Ave., New York NY 10016. (212)687-7400. Fax: (212)687-6894. **Contact:** Edward Necarsulmer IV. Seeking both new and established writers. Estab. 1927. Member of AAR and SCBWI. 30% of clients are new/previously unpublished writers. 90% of material handled is books for young readers.

Represents Considers fiction, middle grade, young adult. "McIntosh & Otis has a long history of representing authors of adult and children's books. The children's department is a separate division." Actively seeking "books with memorable characters, distinctive voice, and a great plot." Not looking for educational, activity books, coloring books.

How to Contact Query with SASE. Exclusive submission only. Responds in 6 -8 weeks. Returns material only with SASE. Obtains clients through recommendations from others , editors, conferences and queries.

Terms Agent receives 15% commission on domestic sales; 20% on foreign sales.

Writers' Conferences Attends Bologna Book Fair, in Bologna Italy in April, SCBWI Conference in New York in February, and regularly attends other conferences and industry conventions.

Tips "No e-mail or phone calls!"

MEWS BOOKS

20 Bluewater Hill, Westport CT 06880. (203)227-1836. Fax: (203)227-1144. E-mail: mewsbooks@aol.com. **Contact:** Sidney B. Kramer. Seeking both new and established writers. Estab. 1974. 50% of material handled is books for young readers. Staff includes Sidney B. Kramer and Fran Pollak.

- Previously Sidney Kramer was Senior Vice President and founder of Bantam Books, President of New American Library, Director and Manager of Corgi Books in London, and attorney.

Represents Considers adult nonfiction, fiction; picture books, middle grade, young adult with outstanding characters and stories. Actively seeking books that have continuity of character and story. Not looking for unedited, poorly written mss by authors seeking learning experience.

How to Contact Query with SASE, send outline and 2 sample chapters by regular mail only. Accepts short e-mail specific queries but not sumbissions or attachments. Prefers to read material exclusively. Responds in a few weeks to queries. Returns material only with SASE. Obtains clients through recommendations from others.

Recent Sales Sold 10 books for young readers in the last year.

Terms Agent receives 15% commission on domestic sales; 20% on foreign sales. Offers written contract, binding for 1-2 years. "We never retain an unhappy author, but we cannot terminate in the middle of activity. If submission is accepted, we ask for $100 against all expenses. We occasionally make referrals to editing services."

ERIN MURPHY LITERARY AGENCY

2700 Woodlands Village, #300-458, Flagstaff AZ 86001-7127. (928)525-2056. **Contact:** Erin Murphy. Closed to unsolicited queries and submissions. Considers both new and established writers, by referral from industry professionals she knows or personal contact (such as conferences) only. Estab. 1999. Member of SCBWI and AAR.

Represents 50 clients. 40% of clients are new/previously unpublished writers. 100% of material handled is books of young readers.

- Prior to opening her agency, Erin Murphy was editor-in-chief at Northland Publishing/Rising Moon. Agency is not currently accepting unsolicited queries or submissions.

Represents Picture books, middle grade, young adult.

Terms Agent receives 15% commission on domestic sales; 20% on foreign sales. Offers written contract. 30 days notice must be given to terminate contract.

Recent sales Sold 17 books for young readers in the last year. Recent releases: *Dogs on The Bed*, by Elizabeth Bluemle (Candlewick); *A Curse Dark As Gold*, by Elizabeth C. Bunce (Levine/ Scholoastic); *Man in the Moon*, by Dotti Enderle (Delacorte); *Summer Camp Secrets Trilogy*, by Katy Grant (Alladdin); *Big Mouth*, by Deborah Halverson (Delacorte); *10 Lucky Things That Have Happened to Me Since I Nearly Got Hit by Lightning*, by Mary Hershey (Lamb/Random House); *Theodocia and the Staff of Osiris*, by R.L. Lafevers (Houghton); *The Last Wish*, by Janeete Rallison (Putnam); *Maybelle Goes to Tea*, by Katie Speck (Holt); *Aurelie: A Faerie Tale*, by Heather Tomlinson (Holt); *When Fala Ran the White House*, by Elizabeth Van Steenwyk (Peachtree); *Big Fat Manifesto*, by Susan Vaught (Bloomsbury).

MUSE LITERARY MANAGEMENT

189 Waverly Place #4, New York NY 10014-3135.(212)925-3721. E-mail: MuseLiteraryMgmt@aol.com. Web site: www.museliterary.com. Seeking both new and established writers. Estab. 1998. Agency is member of SCBWI. Represents 10 clients. 90% new writers. 60% books for young readers. **Contact:** Deborah Carter.

Represents Handles nonfiction, fiction, picture books, middle grade, young adult. As an independent literary agent, Deborah Carter focuses on manuscript development; the sale and administration of print, performance and foreign rights to literary works; and post-publication publicity and appearances. Works in both children's and adult books. Actively seeking literary fiction and nonfiction, poetry collections, mystery/thriller/suspense novels, and sci-fi/fantasy grounded in reality with compelling characters and situations. Looking for picture books and novels that bring something new to their bookselling category. Prefers writers who interact with the age groups they're writing for. Originality and imagination are treasured; derivative work less so. See "Bookshelf" page at www.museliterary.com for links to favorite books. Actively pursuing new writers with formal training and published authors who want to try something new. Those who submit should be receptive to editorial feedback and willing to revise to be competitive. Writers are encouraged to read *Publishers Weekly* to develop an awareness of the marketplace and bookselling categories for their book. Does not want vulgar subject matter or books that copy others. "I'm only interested in intelligent books."

How to Contact Accepts queries by e-mail, mail. Considers simultaneous queries, submissions. Responds in 1-2 weeks to queries; 2-3 weeks to ms.

Recent Sales Sold 1 book for young readers in the last year. *The Adventures of Molly Whuppie and Other Appalachian Folktales*, by Anne Shelby (University of North Carolina Press).

Terms Agent receives 15% commission on domestic sales; 20% on foreign sales. Offers written contract. Contract binding for 1 year. One day's notice must be given for termination of contract.

Writers' Conferences Attending BookExpo America 2009 in New York, May 28-21, 2009; AWP in Chicago, February 11-14, 2009; ThrillerFest, location TBA, in July 2009.

Tips "I give editorial feedback and work on revisions on spec. Agency agreement is offered when the writer and I feel the manuscript is ready for submission to publishers. Writers should also be open to doing revisions with editors who express serious interest in their work, prior to any offer of a publishing contract. All aspects of career strategy are discussed with writers, and all decisions are ultimately theirs. I make multiple and simultaneous submissions when looking for rights opportunities, and share all correspondence. All agreements are signed by the writers. Reimbursement for expenses is subject to client's approval, limited to photocopying (usually press clips) and postage. I always submit fresh manuscripts to publishers printed in my office with no charge to the writer."

JEAN V. NAGGAR LITERARY AGENCY, INC.

216 E. 75th Street, Suite 1E, New York NY 10021.(212)794-1082. Fax: (212)794-3605. E-mail: jregel@jvnla.com (all first initial last name@jvnla.com). Web site: www.jvnla.com. Seeking both new and established writers. Estab. 1978. Member of AAR, SCBWI. Represents 150 clients. Large percentage of clients are new/previously unpublished writers. 25% material handled is books for young readers.

Member Agents Jennifer Weltz (subrights, children's, adults); Jessica Regel (young adult, adult, subrights); Jean Naggar (adult, children's); Alice Tasman (adult, children's); Mollie Glick (adult, fiction and nonfiction, contracts).

Represents Handles nonfiction, fiction, picture books, middle grade, young adult.

How to Contact Query with SASE. Accepts queries by e-mail, mail. Prefers to read materials exclusively. Responds in 2 weeks to queries; response time for ms depends on the agent. Returns mss only with SASE.

Obtains new clients through recommendations from others, queries/solicitations, conferences.
Recent Sales See Web site for information.

ALISON PICARD, LITERARY AGENT

P.O. Box 2000, Cotuit MA 02635. Phone/fax: (508)477-7192. E-mail: ajpicard@aol.com. **Contact:** Alison Picard. Seeking both new and established writers. Estab. 1985. Represents 50 clients. 40% of clients are new/previously unpublished writers. 20% of material handled is books for young readers.

- Prior to opening her agency, Alison Picard was an assistant at a large New York agency before co-founding Kidde, Hoyt & Picard in 1982. She became an independent agent in 1985.

Represents Considers nonfiction, fiction, a very few picture books, middle grade, young adult. "I represent juvenile and YA books. I do not handle short stories, articles, poetry or plays. I am especially interested in commercial nonfiction, romances and mysteries/suspense/thrillers. I work with agencies in Europe and Los Angeles to sell foreign and TV/film rights. "Actively seeking middle grade fiction. Not looking for poetry or plays.

How to Contact Query with SASE. Accepts queries by e-mail with no attachments. Considers simultaneous queries and submissions. Responds in 2 weeks to queries; 4 months to mss. Returns material only with SASE. Obtains clients through queries/solicitations.

Recent Sales *Funerals and Fly Fishing*, by Mary Bartek (Henry Holt & Co.); *Playing Dad's Song*, by Dina Friedman (Farrar Straus & Giroux); *Escaping into the Night*, by Dina Friedman (Simon & Schuster); *Celebritrees* and *The Peace Bell*, by Margi Preus (Henry Holt & Co.)

Terms Receives 15% commission on domestic sales; 20-25% on foreign sales. Offers written contract, binding for 1 year. 1-week notice must be given to terminate contract.

Tips "We currently have a backlog of submissions."

PROSPECT AGENCY

285 5th Ave., PMB 445, Brooklyn NY 11215. (718)788-3217. Fax: (718)788-3217. E-mail: esk@prospectagency.com. Web site: www.prospectagency.com. **Contact:** Emily Sylvan Kim. Seeking both new and established writers. Estab. 2005. Agent is member of SCBWI and RWA. Represents 25 clients. 75% of clients are new/previously unpublished writers. 50% of material handled is books for young readers.

Represents Handles nonfiction, fiction, picture books, middle grade, young adult. "Prospect Agency is a small, personal agency that focuses on helping each client reach maximum success through hands-on editorial assistance and professional contract negitiations. We also strive to be on the cutting edge technologically." Actively seeking middle grade and YA books..

How to Contact Send outline and 3 sample chapters. Accepts queries through Web site. Considers sumultaneous queries, submissions. Responds in 6 weeks to query and mss. Discards unaccepted mss. Obtains new clients through recommendations from others, queries/solicitations, conferences.

Recent Sales Sold 2 books for young readers in the last year. (Also represents adult fiction.) Recent sales include: *God's Own Drunk*, by Tim Tharp (Knopf); *Bewitching Season*, by Marissa Doyle (Holt); *Debbie Harry Sings in French*, by Meagan Brothers (Holt); *Knights of the Hill Country*, by Tim Tharp (Knopf). Clients include: Rose Kent, Meagan Brothers, Catherine Stine.

Terms Agent receives 15% on domestic sales, 20% on foreign sales. Offers written contract.

Writer's Conferences Attends SCBWI Annual Winter Conference in New York (February annually); South Carolina Writers Workshop, Myrtle Beach, SC (October 2007); RWA (Romance Writers of America), location varies (July annually).

Tips "I am a very hands-on agent who spends a lot of time forming personal relationships both with the work and the author him or herself. I try to balance the goals of selling individual product and managing a career."

WENDY SCHMALZ AGENCY

P.O. Box 831, Hudson NY 12534. (518)672-7697. Fax: (518)672-7662. E-mail: wendy@schmalzagency.com. **Contact:** Wendy Schmalz. Seeking both new and established writers. Estab. 2002. Member of AAR. Represents 30 clients. 10% of clients are new/previously unpublished writers. 50% of material handled is books for young readers.

- Prior to opening her agency, Wendy Schmalz was an agent for 23 years at Harold Ober Associates.

Represents Considers nonfiction, fiction, middle grade, young adult. Actively seeking young adult novels, middle grade novels. Not looking for picture books, science fiction or fantasy.

How to Contact Query with SASE. Accepts queries by e-mail. Responds in 2 weeks to queries; 4-6 weeks to mss. Returns material only with SASE. Obtains clients through recommendations from others.

Recent Sales Sold 30 books for young readers in the last year.

Terms Agent receives 15% commission on domestic sales; 20% on foreign sales. Fees for photocopying and FedEx.

SUSAN SCHULMAN LITERARY AGENCY

454 W. 44th, New York NY 10036. (212)713-1633. Fax: (212)581-8830. E-mail: schulman@aol.com. Web site: www.Schulmanagency.com. **Contact:** Susan Schulman. Seeking both new and established writers. Estab. 1980. Member of AAR, WGA, SCBWI, Dramatists Guild. 15% of material handled is books for young readers. Staff includes Emily Uhry, YA; Linda Kiss, picture books.

Represents Handles nonfiction, fiction, picture books, middle grade, young adult. Actively seeking well-written, original stories for any age group.

How to Contact Query with SASE. Accepts queries by e-mail. Considers sumultaneous queries and submissions. Returns mss only with SASE. Obtains new clients through recommendations from others, queries/solicitations, conferences.

Recent Sales Of total agency sales, approximately 20% is children's literature. Recent sales include: 10-book deal to Scholastic for Jim Arnosky; *Remarkable Girl*, by Pamela Lowell (Marshall Cavendish); I Get All Better, by Vickie Cobb (4-book series with Lerner); film rights to *Geography Club*, by Brent Hartinger (East of Doheny); television rights to Louis Sachar's *Sideways Stories from Wayside School* (Nickelodeon).

Terms Agent receives 15% on domestic sales, 20% on foreign sales.

Writers' Conferences Attending IWWG in Geneva, Switzerland and New York and Columbus Writer's Conference. Sridmore Colleg, Antioch Conference.

Tips Schulman decribes her agency as "professional boutique, long-standing, eclectic."

SERENDIPITY LITERARY AGENCY

305 Gates Ave., Brooklyn NY 11216.(718)230-7689. Fax: (718)230-7829. E-mail: rbrooks@serendipitylit.com. Web site: www.serendipitylit.com. **Contact:** Regina Brooks. Estab. 2000. Represents 50 clients. 65% of clients are new/unpublished writers. 50% of material handled is books for young readers.

- Prior to becoming an agent, Regina Brooks was an acquisitions editor for John Wiley & Sons and McGraw-Hill Companies.

Represents Handles all children's books areas from picture books to young adult, both fiction and nonfiction. Actively seeking young adult novels with an urban flair and juvenile books.

How to Contact Prefers to read material exclusively. For nonfiction, submit outline, 1 sample chapter and SASE. Accepts e-mail queries. Responds to queries in 4 weeks; mss in 1 month. Obtains new clients through writer's conferences and referrals.

Recent Sales *A Wreath for Emmitt Till*, by Marilyn Nelson (Houghton Mifflin); *A Song for Present Existence*, by Marilyn Nelson and Tonya Hegamin (Scholastic); *Ruby and the Booker Boys*, by Derrick Barnes (Scholastic); *Brenda Buckley's Universe and Everything In It*, by Sundee Frazier (Delacorte Books for Young Readers); *Wait Until the Black Girl Sings*, by Bil Wright Simon and Schuster (Scholastic); *First Semester*, by Cecil R. Cross II (KimaniTru/ Harlequin).

Terms Agent receives 15% commission on domestic sales; 20% on foreign sales. Offers written contract. Terminations notice—2 months.

Tips "I adore working with first-time authors whose books challenge the readers emotionally; tears and laughter. I also represent award-winning illustrators."

STIMOLA LITERARY STUDIO, LLC

306 Chase Court, Edgewater NJ 07020. Phone/fax: (201)945-9353. E-mail: LtryStudio@aol.com. **Contact:** Rosemary B. Stimola. Seeking both new and established writers. Estab. 1997. Member of AAR, SCBWI, ALA. Represents 45+ clients. 25% of clients are new/previously unpublished writers. 85% of material handled is books for young readers.

- Prior to opening her agency Rosemary Stimola was an independent children's bookseller.

Represents Preschool through young adult, fiction and nonfiction. Agency is owned and operated by a former educator and children's bookseller with a Ph.D. in Linguistics. Actively seeking remarkable young adult fiction and debut picture book author/illustrators. No institutional books.

How to Contact Query via e-mail here listed. No attachments, please! Considers simultaneous queries. Responds in 3 weeks to queries; 6-8 weeks to mss. Returns snail mail material with SASE. While unsolicited queries are welcome, most clients come through editor, agent, client referrals.

Recent Sales Sold 38 books for young readers in the last year. Among these, *Nighty Night, Sleepy Sleep*, by Brian Anderson (Roaring Brook Press); *Steinbeck's Ghost*, by Lewis Buzbee (Feiwel & Friends/Holtzbrinck); *Days of Little Texas*, by R.A Nelson (Knopf/RH); *Road Trip*, by Mary Pearson (Henry Holt/ Holtzbrink; *Sophomore Switch*, by Abby McDonald (Candlewick Press); *Accidentally Fabulous*, by Lisa Papdemetriou (Scholastic); *Sandy's Circus*, by Tanya Stone (Viking/Penguin).

Terms Agent receives 15% commission on domestic sales; 20% on foreign sales (if subagents used). Offers written contract, binding for all children's projects. 60 days notice must be given to terminate contract. Charges

$85 one-time fee per project to cover expenses. Client provides all copies of submission. Fee is taken from first advance payment and is payable *only* if manuscript is sold.''

Writers' Conferences Will attend: ALA Midwinter, BEA, Bologna Book Fair, SCBWI-Illinois regional conference; SCBWI Annual Winter Conference in New York, SCBWI- New York Metro.

Tips Agent is hands-on, no-nonsense. May request revisions. Does not edit but may offer suggestions for improvement. Well-respected by clients and editors. ''A firm but reasonable deal negotiator.''

S©OTT TREIMEL NY

434 Lafayette St., New York NY 10003. (212)505-8353. Fax: (212)505-0664. E-mail: st.ny@verizon.net. **Contact:** Scott Treimel. Estab. 1995. Represents 45 clients. 10% of clients are new/unpublished writers. Specializes in children's books, all genres: tightly focused segments of the trade and institutional markets. Member AAR, Author's Guild, SCBWI.

- Prior to opening his agency, Scott Treimel was an assistant to Marilyn E. Marlow of Curtis Brown; a rights agent for Scholastic, Inc.; a book packager and rights agent for United Feature Syndicate; the founding director of Warner Bros. Worldwide Publishing; a freelance editor; and a rights consultant for HarperCollins Children's Books.

Represents 100% juvenile books. Actively seeking career clients. Not seeking picture book authors, but author/illustrators may submit.

How to Contact Send query/ouline (include word count, number of chapters, and protagonists' ages), SASE, sample chapters of no more than 50 pages. No multiple submission. Queries without SASE will be recycles. No fax. queries.

Recent Sales Sold 29 titles in the last year. *Right Behind You*, by Gail Gailes (Little, Brown); *Comic Guy*, by Timothy Roldand (Scholastic); *Kitchen Dance*, by Maurie Manning (Clarion); *The Ninja Who Wanted to be Noticed* (Viking); *Love is a Good Thing to Feel*, by Barbara Joosse (Philomel); *Kiki*, by Janie Bynum (Sterling); *The Hunchback Chronicles*, by Arthur Slade (Penguin Canada); *Before and After Otis*, illustrations by Cyndy Szekeres (Harcourt); *Grandma Calls Me Beautiful*, by Barbara Joosse (Chronicle).

Terms Agent receives 15-20% commission on domestic sales; 20-25% on foreign sales. Offers verbal or written contract, binding on a ''contract-by-contract basis.'' Charges for photocopying, overnight/express postage, messengers. Offers editorial guidance, if extensive charges higher commission.

Writers' Conferences Speaks at Society of Children's Book Writers & Illustrators Conference, The New School; Southwest Writers Conference; Pikes Peak Writers Conference.

Tips ''Keep cover letters short and do not pitch. Let your work speak for itself.''

WRITERS HOUSE

21 W. 26th St., New York NY 10010. (212)685-2400. Fax: (212)685-1781. Web site: www.writershouse.com. Estab. 1974. Member of AAR. Represents 280 clients. Specializes in all types of popular fiction and nonfiction. No scholarly, professional, poetry or screenplays.

Member Agents Amy Berkower; Merrilee Heifetz (middle grade and YA); Susan Cohen (picture book illustrators as well as children's authors), Jodi Reamer; Steven Malk (middle-grade, YA, and picture book illustrators and authors); Robin Rue; Kenneth Wright; Rebecca Sherman (picture book author/illustrators, middle grade & YA); Daniel Lazar (middle grade & YA).

Represents 35% juvenile books. Considers: nonfiction, fiction, picture books, middle grade, young adult.

How to Contact Query. Please check our Web site for more specific submission guidelines and info about our agents.

Needs Obtains new clients through referrals and query letters.

Terms Agent receives 15% commission on domestic sales; 20% on foreign sales. Offers written contract, binding for 1 year.

Tips ''Do not send manuscripts. Write a compelling letter. If you do, we'll ask to see your work.''

ART REPS

ART FACTORY

925 Elm Grove Rd., Elm Grove WI 53122. (262)785-1940. Fax: (262)785-1611. E-mail: tstocki@artfactoryltd.com. Web site: www.artfactoryltd.com. **Contact:** Tom Stocki. Commercial illustration representative. Estab. 1978. Represents 9 illustrators including: Tom Buchs, Tom Nachreiner, Todd Dakins, Linda Godfrey, Larry Mikec, Bill Scott, Gary Shea, Terry Herman, Troy Allen. 10% of artwork handled is children's book illustration. Currently open to illustrators seeking representation. Open to both new and established illustrators.

Handles Illustration.

Terms Receives 25-30% commission. Offers written contract. Advertising costs are split: 75% paid by illustrators; 25% paid by rep. "We try to mail samples of all our illustrators at one time and we try to update our Web site; so we ask the illustrators to keep up with new samples." Advertises in *Picturebook, Workbook*.

How to Contact For first contact, send query letter, tearsheets. Responds only if interested. Call to schedule an appointment. Portfolio should include tearsheets. Finds illustrators through queries/solicitations.

Tips "Have a unique style."

ASCIUTTO ART REPS., INC.

1712 E. Butler Circle, Chandler AZ 85225. (480)899-0600. Fax: (480)899-3636. E-mail: Aartreps@cox.net. Web site: www.Aatreps.com. **Contact:** Mary Anne Asciutto, art agent. Children's illustration representative since 1980. Specializing in childrens illustrations for childrens educational text books, grades K thru 8, childrens trade books, childrens magazines, posters, packaging, etc.

Recent Sales *Bats, Sharks, Whales, Snakes, Penguins, Alligators and Crocodiles*, illustrated by Meryl Henderson for Boyds Mills Press.

Terms Agency receives 25% commission. Advertising and promotion costs are split: 75% paid by talent; 25% paid by representative. US citizens only.

How to Contact Send samples via email with a cover letter résumé. Submit sample portfolio for review with an SASE for it's return. Responds in 2 to 4 weeks. Portfolio should include at least 12 samples of original art, printed tearsheets, photocopies or color prints of most recent work.

Tips In obtaining representation, "be sure to connect with an agent who handles the kind of work, you (the artist) *want*."

CAROL BANCROFT & FRIENDS

P.O. Box 2030, Danbury, CT 06813 (203)730-8270 or (800)720-7020. Fax: (203)730-8275. E-mail: artists@carolbancroft.com. Web site: www.carolbancroft.com. **Owner:** Joy Elton Tricarico. **Founder:** Carol Bancroft. Estab. 1972. Illustration representative for all aspects of children's publishing and design. Text and trade; any children's related material. Member of Society of Illustrators, Graphic Artists Guild, National Art Education Association, SCBWI. Represents 30 + illustrators. Specializes in illustration for children's publishing—text and trade; any children's-related material. Clients include, but not limited to, Scholastic, Houghton Mifflin, HarperCollins, Dutton, Harcourt, Marshall Cavendish, Mcgraw Hill, Hay House.

Handles Illustration for children of all ages including young adult

Terms Rep receives 25% commission. Advertising costs are split: 75% paid by talent; 25% paid by representative. For promotional purposes, artists must provide "laser copies (not slides), tearsheets, promo pieces, good color photocopies, etc.; 6 pieces or more is best; narrative scenes and children interacting." Advertises in Picture Book, Directory of Illustration.

How to Contact Send either 2-3 samples with your Website address to the e-mail address above or mail 6-10 samples, along with a self Addressed, stamped envelope (SASE) to the above p.o. box."

SHERYL BERANBAUM

(401)737-8591. Fax: (401)739-5189. E-mail: sheryl@beranbaum.com. Web site: www.beranbaum.com. **Contact:** Sheryl Beranbaum. Commercial illustration representative. Estab. 1985. Member of Graphic Artists Guild. Represents 17 illustrators. 75% of artwork handled is children's book illustration. Currently open to illustrators seeking representation. Open to new and established illustrators only. Submission guidelines available by phone.

• Sheryl Beranbaum is currently not taking on new artists.

Handles Illustration. "My illustrators are diversified and their work comes from a variety of the industry's audiences."

Terms Receives 30% commission. Charges marketing-plan fee or Web-only fee. Offers written contract. Advertising costs are split: 75% paid by illustrators; 25% paid by rep. Requires Itoya portfolio; postcards only for promotion.

How to Contact For first contact, send direct mail flier/brochure, tearsheets, photocopies. Responds only if interested. Portfolio should include photocopies.

PEMA BROWNE LTD.

11 Tena Place, Valley Cottage NY 10989. (845)268-0029. **Contact:** Pema Browne. Estab. 1966. Represents 2 illustrators. 10% of artwork handled is children's book illustration. Specializes in general commercial. Markets include: all publishing areas; children's picture books. Clients include HarperCollins, Holiday House, Bantam Doubleday Dell, Nelson/Word, Hyperion, Putnam. Client list available upon request.

Handles Fiction, nonfiction, picture books, middle grade, young adult, manuscript/illustration packages. Looking for "professional and unique" talent.

Recent Sales *The Daring Ms. Quimby*, by Suzanne Whitaker (Holiday House).

Terms Rep receives 30% illustration commission; 20% author commission. Exclusive area representation is required. For promotional purposes, talent must provide color mailers to distribute. Representative pays mailing costs on promotion mailings.

How to Contact For first contact, send query letter, direct mail flier/brochure and SASE. If interested will ask to mail appropriate materials for review. Portfolios should include tearsheets and transparencies or good color photocopies, plus SASE. Accepts queries by mail only. Obtains new talent through recommendations and interviews (portfolio review).

Tips "We are doing more publishing—all types—less advertising." Looks for "continuity of illustration and dedication to work."

CATUGEAU: ARTIST AGENT, LLC

3009 Margaret Jones Lane, Williamsburg VA 23185. (757)221-0666. Fax: (757)221-6669. E-mail: chris@catugea u.com. Web site: www.CATugeau.com. **Owner/Agent:** Chris Tugeau. Children's publishing trade book, mass market, educational. Estab. 1994. Member of SPAR, SCBWI, Graphic Artists Guild. Represents 35 illustrators. 95% of artwork handled is children's book illustration.

  • Accepting limited new artists from North America only.

Handles Illustration ONL Y.

Terms Receives 25% commission. "Artists responsible for providing samples for portfolios, promotional books and mailings." Exclusive representation required in educational. Trade "house accounts" acceptable. Offers written contract. Advertises in *Picturebook*.

How to Contact For first contact, e-mail samples with note. No CDs. Responds ASAP. Finds illustrators through recommendations from others, conferences, personal search.

Tips "Do research, read articles on CAT Web site, study picture books at bookstores, promote yourself a bit to learn the industry. Be professional . . . know what you do best, and be prepared to give rep what they need to present you! Do have e-mail and scanning capabilities, too."

CORNELL & MCCARTHY, LLC

2-D Cross Hwy., Westport CT 06880. (203)454-4210. Fax: (203)454-4258. E-mail: contact@cmartreps.com. Web site: www.cmartreps.com. **Contact:** Merial Cornell. Children's book illustration representatives. Estab. 1989. Member of SCBWI and Graphic Artists Guild. Represents 30 illustrators. Specializes in children's books: trade, mass market, educational.

Handles Illustration.

Terms Agent receives 25% commission. Advertising costs are split: 75% paid by talent; 25% paid by representative. For promotional purposes, talent must provide 10-12 strong portfolio pieces relating to children's publishing.

How to Contact For first contact, send query letter, direct mail flier/brochure, tearsheets, photocopies and SASE or e-mail. Responds in 1 month. Obtains new talent through recommendations, solicitation, conferences.

Tips "Work hard on your portfolio."

CREATIVE FREELANCERS, INC.

4 Greenwich Hills Drive, Greenwich CT 06831 (800)398-9544. Web site: www.illustratorsonline.com; www.freel ancers.com. **Contact:** Marilyn Howard. Commercial illustration representative. Estab. 1988. Represents over 30 illustrators. "Our staff members have art direction, art buying or illustration backgrounds." Specializes in children's books, advertising, architectural, conceptual. Markets include: advertising agencies; corporations/ client direct; design firms; editorial/magazines; paper products/greeting cards; publishing/books; sales/promotion firms.

Handles Illustration. Artists must have published work.

Terms Rep receives 30% commission. Exclusive area representation is preferred. Advertising costs are split: 75% paid by talent; 25% paid by representative. For promotional purposes, talent must provide scans of artwork. Advertises in *American Showcase, Workbook*.

How to Contact For first contact, send tearsheets, low res jpegs or "whatever best shows work." Responds back only if interested.

Tips Looks for experience, professionalism and consistency of style. Obtains new talent through "word of mouth and Web site."

DIMENSION

13420 Morgan Ave. S., Burnsville MN 55337. (952)201-3981. Fax: (952)895-9315. E-mail: jkoltes@dimensioncre ative.com. Web site: www.dimensioncreative.com. **Contact:** Joanne Koltes. Commercial illustration representative. Estab. 1982. Member of MN Book Builder. Represents 12 illustrators. 45% of artwork handled is children's book illustration. Staff includes Joanne Koltes.

Terms Advertises in *Picturebook* and *Minnesota Creative*.
How to Contact Contact via phone or e-mail. Responds only if interested.

DWYER & O'GRADY, INC.

P.O. Box 790, Cedar Key FL 32625-0790. (352)543-9307. Fax: (603)375-5373. E-mail: eogrady@dwyerogrady.com. Web site: www.dwyerogrady.com. **Contact:** Elizabeth O'Grady. Agents for authors and illustrators of children's books artists and writers. Estab. 1990. Member of Society of Illustrators, Author's Guild, SCBWI, Graphic Artis's Guild. Represents 14 illustrators and 15 writers. Staff includes Elizabeth O'Grady, Jeffrey Dwyer. Specializes in children's books (picture books, middle grade and young adult). Markets include: publishing/books, audio/film.
  • Dwyer & O'Grady is currently not accepting new clients.
Handles Illustrators and writers of children's books.
Recent Sales *Alphabet & Tiger & Turtle*, by James Rumford (Roaring Brook); *Pennies for Elephants & Pigeons* (Hyperion); *They Call Him Yellowstone Moran* (Viking); *Born to Be Giants* (Roaring Brook); *D is for Dinosaur*, written and illustrated by Lita Judge (Seeping Bear); *Ordinary Albert*, by Nancy Antle (Penguin: Aust.).
Terms Receives 15% commission domestic, 20% foreign. Additional fees are negotiable. Exclusive representation is required (world rights). Advertising costs are paid by representative.
How to Contact For first contact, send query letter by postal mail only.

PAT HACKETT/ARTIST REP

7014 N. Mercer Way, Mercer Island WA 98040-2130. (206)447-1600. Fax: (206)447-0739. Web site: www.pathackett.com. **Contact:** Pat Hackett. Commercial illustration representative. Estab. 1979. Member of Graphic Artists Guild. Represents 12 illustrators. 10% of artwork handled is children's book illustration. Currently open to illustrators seeking representation. Open to both new and established illustrators.
Handles Illustration. Looking for illustrators with unique, strong, salable style.
Represents Bryan Ballinger, Kooch Campbell, Jonathan Combs, Eldon Doty. Ed Fotheringham, John Fretz, Lilly Lee, Bruce Morser, Dennis Ochsner, Mark Zingarelli
Terms Receives 25-33% commission. Advertising costs are split: 75% paid by illustrators; 25% paid by rep. Illustrator must provide portfolios (2-3) and promotional pieces. Advertises in *Picturebook*, *Workbook*.
How to Contact For first contact, send query letter, tearsheets, SASE, direct mail flier/brochure. Responds only if interested. Wait for response. Portfolio should include tearsheets. Lasers OK. Finds illustrators through recommendations from others, queries/solicitations.
Tips "Send query plus 1-2 samples, either by regular mail or e-mail."

HANNAH REPRESENTS

14431 Ventura Blvd., #108, Sherman Oaks CA 91423. (818)378-1644. E-mail: hannahrepresents@yahoo.com. **Contact:** Hannah Robinson. Literary representative for illustrators. Estab. 1997. 100% of artwork handled is children's book illustration. Looking for established illustrators only.
Handles Manuscript/illustration packages. Looking for illustrators with picture book story and illustration proposal.
Terms Receives 15% commission. Offers written contract.
How to Contact For first contact, send SASE and tearsheets. Responds only if interested. Call to schedule an appointment. Portfolio should include photocopies. Finds illustrators through recommendations from others, conferences, queries/solicitations, international.
Tips "Present a carefully developed range of characterization illustrations that are world-class enough to equal those in the best children's books."

HERMAN AGENCY

350 Central Park West, New York NY 10025. (212)749-4907. Fax: (212)662-5151. E-mail: ronnie@hermanagencyinc.com. Web site: www.hermanagencyinc.com. **Contact:** Ronnie Ann Herman. Literary and artistic agency. Estab. 1999. Member of SCBWI and Graphic Artists Guild. Illustrators include: Joy Allen, Tom Arma, Durga Bernhard, Mary Bono, Jason Chapman, Seymour Chwast, Pascale Constantin, Kathy Couri, Doreen Gay-Kassel, Jan Spivey Gilchrist, Barry Gott, Steve Haskamp, Aleksey Ivanov, Jago, Gideon Kendall, Ana Martin Larranaga, Mike Lester, Bob McMahon, Margie Moore, Alexi Natchev, Jill Newton, John Nez, Betina Ogden, Tamara Petrosino, Michael Rex, Pete Whitehead, David Sheldon, Richard Torrey, Mark Weber, Candace Whitman, Deborah Zemke. Authors include: Deloris Jordan. 90% of artwork handled is children's book illustration and related markets. Currently not accepting new clients unless they have been successfully published by major trade publishing houses.
Terms Receives 25% commission for illustration assignments; 15% for ms assignments. Artists pay 75% of

costs for promotional material, about $300 a year. Exclusive representation usually required. Offers written contract. Advertising costs are split: 75% paid by illustrator; 25% paid by rep.
How to Contact For first contact, send samples, SASE, direct mail flier/brochure, tearsheets, photocopies. Authors should e-mail with a query. Responds in 1 month or less. I will contact you if I like your samples. Portfolio should include tearsheets, photocopies, books, dummies. Finds illustrators and authors through recommendations from others, conferences, queries/solicitations.

LEVY CREATIVE MANAGEMENT

300 E. 46th St., Suite 8E, New York NY 10017. (212)687-6465. Fax: (212)661-4839. E-mail: info@levycreative.com. Web site: www.levycreative.com. **Contact:** Sari Levy. Estab. 1998. Member of Society of Illustrators, Graphic Artists Guild, Art Directors Club. Represents 13 illustrators including: Mike Byers, Alan Dingman, Marcos Chin, Robin Eley, Trip Park, Thomas Fluharty, Max Gafe, Liz Lomax, Oren Sherman, Jason Tharp, Andrea Wicklund, and Denis Zilber. 30% of artwork handled is children's book illustration. Currently open to illustrators seeking representation. Open to both new and established illustrators. Submission guidelines available on Web site.
Handles Illustration, manuscript/illustration packages.
Terms Exclusive representation required. Offers written contract. Advertising costs are split: 75% paid by illustrators; 25% paid by rep. Advertises in *Picturebook*, *American Showcase*, *Workbook*, *Alternative Pick*, *Contact*.
How to Contact For first contact, send tearsheets, photocopies, SASE. "See Web site for submission guidelines." Responds only if interested. Portfolio should include professionally presented materials. Finds illustrators through recommendations from others, word of mouth, competitions.

LINDGREN & SMITH

630 Ninth Ave., New York NY 10036. (212)397-7330. E-mail: representation@lsillustration.com. Web site: www.lindgrensmith.com/kids. **Contact:** Pat Lindgren, Piper Smith. Illustration representative. Estab. 1984. Member of SCBWI. Markets include children's books, advertising agencies; corporations; design firms; editorial; publishing.
Handles Illustration.
Terms Exclusive representation is required. Advertises in *The Workbook*.
How to Contact For first contact, send postcard or e-mail a link to a Web site or send one JPEG file. Responds only if interested via e-mail or phone.
Tips "Check to see if your work seems appropriate for the group."

MARLENA AGENCY, INC.

322 Ewing St., Princeton NJ 08540. (609)252-9405. Fax: (609)252-1949. E-mail: marlena@marlenaagency.com. Web site: www.marlenaagency.com. Commercial illustration representative. Estab. 1990. Member of Society of Illustrators. Represents 30 international illustrators including: Gerard Dubois, Linda Helton, Paul Zwolak, Martin Jarrie, Serge Bloch, Hadley Hooper, Jean-François Martin, Perre Mornet, Pep Montserrat, Tomasz Walenta, Istvan Orosz and Carmen Segovia. Staff includes Marlena Torzecka, Simone Stark, Ella Lupo, Marie Joanne Wimmr, Anna Pluskota. Currently open to illustrators seeking representation. Open to both new and established illustrators. Submission guidelines available for #10 SASE.
Handles Illustration.
Recent Sales *Sees Behind Trees*, by Linda Helton (Harcourt); *Ms. Rubinstein's Beauty*, by Pep Montserrat (Sterling); *ABC USA*, by Martin Jarrie (Sterling); *My Cat*, by Linda Helton (Scholastic); *The McElderry Book of Greek Myths*, by Pep Monserrat (McElderly Books)
Terms Exclusive representation required. Offers written contract. Requires printed portfolios, transparencies, direct mail piece (such as postcards) printed samples. Advertises in *Workbook*.
How to Contact For first contact, send tearsheets, photocopies, or e-mail low resolution samples only. Responds only if interested. Drop off or mail portfolio, photocopies. Portfolio should include tearsheets, photocopies. Finds illustrators through queries/solicitations, magazines and graphic design.
Tips "Be creative and persistent."

MB ARTISTS

(formerly HK Portfolio), 10 E. 29th St., 40G, New York NY 10016. (212)689-7830. E-mail: mela@mbartists.com. Web site: www.mbartists.com. **Contact:** Mela Bolinao. Illustration representative. Estab. 1986. Member of SPAR, Society of Illustrators and Graphic Artists Guild. Represents 45 illustrators. Specializes in illustration for juvenile markets. Markets include: advertising agencies; editorial/magazines; publishing/books, Tos, games boards, stationary, etc.
Handles Illustration.

Recent Sales *Sweet Tooth*, illustrated by Jack E. Davis (Simon & Schuster); *The Perfect Nest*, illustrated by John Manders (Candlewick); *The Goodnight Train*, illustrated by by Laura Huliska Beith (Harcourt); *Ducks Dunk*, illustrated by Hiroe Nakata (Henry Holt); *Here Comes T. Rex Cottontail*, illustrated by Jack E. Davis (HarperCollins).
Terms Rep receives 25% commission. No geographic restrictions. Advertising costs are split: 75% paid by talent; 25% paid by representative. Advertises in *Picturebook*, *Directory of Illustration*, *Play* and *Workbook*.
How to Contact No geographic restrictions. For first contact, send query letter, direct mail flier/brochure, Web site address, tearsheets, slides, photographs or color copies and SASE or send Web site link to mela@hkportfolio. com. Responds in 1 week. Portfolio should include at least 12 images appropriate for the juvenile market.

THE NEIS GROUP

14600 Sawyer Ranch Rd. Dripping Springs TX 78620. (616)450-1533 Fax: (512)-829-4508. E-mail: neisgroup@w mis.net. Web site: www.neisgroup.com. **Contact:** Judy Neis. Commercial illustration representative. Estab. 1982. Represents 45 illustrators including: Lyn Boyer, Pam Thomson, Dan Sharp, Terry Workman, Liz Conrad, Garry Colby, Clint Hansen, Don McLean, Julie Borden, Johnna Bandle, Jack Pennington, Gary Ferster, Erika LeBarre, Joel Spector, John White, Neverne Covington, Ruth Pettis, Matt LeBarre. 60% of artwork handled is children's book illustration. Currently open to illustrators seeking representation. Looking for established illustrators only.
Handles Illustration, photography and calligraphy/manuscript packages.
Terms Receives 25% commission. Advertising costs are split: 75% paid by illustrator; 25% paid by rep. "I prefer portfolios on CD, color printouts and e-mail capabilities whenever possible." Advertises in *Picturebook*, *American Showcase*, *Creative Black Book*.
How to Contact For first contact, send bio, tearsheets, direct mail flier/brochure. Responds only if interested. After initial contact, drop off portfolio of nonreturnables. Portfolio should include tearsheets, photocopies. Obtains new talent through recommendations from others and queries/solicitations.

WANDA NOWAK/CREATIVE ILLUSTRATORS AGENCY

231 E. 76th St., 5D, New York NY 10021. (212)535-0438, ext. 1624. Fax: (212)535-1629. E-mail: wanda@wandanow. com. Web site: www.wandanow.com. **Contact:** Wanda Nowak. Commercial illustration representative. Estab. 1996. Represents 20 illustrators including: Emilie Chollat, Thea Kliros, Pierre Pratt, Frederique Bertrand, Ilja Bereznickas, Boris Kulikov, Yayo, Laurence Cleyet-Merle, E. Kerner, Ellen Usdin, Marie Lafrance, Stephane Jorisch, Oliver Latyk, Benoit Laverdiere, Konald Saaf, Anne-Sophie Lanquetin, Andre Letria. 50% of artwork handled is children's book illustration. Staff includes Wanda Nowak. Open to both new and established illustrators.
Handles Illustration. Looking for "unique, individual style."
Terms Receives 30% commission. Exclusive representation required. Offers written contract. Advertising costs are split: 70% paid by illustrators; 30% paid by rep. Advertises in *Picturebook*, *Workbook*, *The Alternative Pick*, *Black Book*.
How to Contact For first contact, send SASE. Responds only if interested. Drop off portfolio. Portfolio should include tearsheets. Finds illustrators through recommendations from others, sourcebooks like *CA*, *Picture Book*, *Creative Black Book*, exhibitions.
Tips "Develop your own style. Send a little illustrated story, which will prove you can carry a character in different situations with facial expressions, etc."

REMEN-WILLIS DESIGN GROUP—ANN REMEN-WILLIS

2964 Colton Rd., Pebble Beach CA 93953. (831)655-1407. Fax: (831)655-1408. E-mail: remenwillis@comcast.n et. Web sites: www.annremenwillis.com or www.picture-book.com. **Contact:** Ann Remen-Willis. Specializes in childrens' book illustration trade/education. Estab. 1984. Member of SCBWI. Represents 18 illustrators including: Dominic Catalano, Siri Weber Feeney, Doug Roy, Susan Jaekel, Dennis Hockerman, Rosiland Solomon, Meredith Johnson, Renate Lohmann, Robin Kerr, Len Ebert, Gary Undercuffler, Sheila Bailey, John Goodell. 100% of artwork handled is children's book illustration.
Terms Offers written contract. Advertising costs are split: 50% paid by illustrators; 50% paid by rep. Illustrator must provide small precise portfolio for promotion. Advertises in *Picturebook*, *Workbook*.
How to Contact For first contact, send tearsheets, photocopies or e-mail. Responds in 1 week.
Tips "Send samples of only the type of work you are interested in receiving. Check out rep's forte first."

RENAISSANCE HOUSE

9400 Lloydcrest Dr., Beverly Hills CA 90210. (800)547-5113. Fax: (310)860-9902. E-mail: info@renaissancehous e.net. Web site: www.renaissancehouse.net or www.laredopublishing.com. **Contact:** Raquel Benatar. Children's, educational, multicultural, and textbooks, advertising rep. Estab. 1991. Represents 80 illustrators. 95% of artwork handled is children's book illustration and photography. Currently open to illustrators and photographers seeking representation. Open to both new and established illustrators.

Handles Illustration and photography.

Recent Sales Maribel Suarez (Little Brown, Hyperion); Gabriel Pacheco (MacMillan)Ana Lopez (Scholastic); Ruth Araceli (Houghton Mifflin); Vivi Escriva (Albert Whitman); Marie Jara (Sparknotes); Sheli Petersen (McGraw-Hill).

Terms Exclusive and non-exclusive representation. Illustrators must provide scans of illustrations. Advertises in *Picturebook*, *Directory of Illustration*, own Web site and *Catalog of Illustrators*.

How to Contact For first contact send tearsheets. Responds in 2 weeks. Finds illustrators through recommendations from others, conferences, direct contact.

S.I. INTERNATIONAL

43 E. 19th St., New York NY 10003. (212)254-4996. Fax: (212)995-0911. E-mail: information@si-i.com. Web site: www.si-i.com. Commercial illustration representative. Estab. 1983. Member of SPAR, Graphic Artists Guild. Represents 50 illustrators. Specializes in license characters, educational publishing and children's illustration, digital art and design, mass market paperbacks. Markets include design firms; publishing/books; sales/promotion firms; licensing firms; digital art and design firms.

Handles Illustration. Looking for artists "who have the ability to do children's illustration and to do license characters either digitally or reflectively."

Terms Rep receives 25-30% commission. Advertising costs are split: 70% paid by talent; 30% paid by representative. "Contact agency for details. Must have mailer." Advertises in *Picturebook*.

How to Contact For first contact, send query letter, tearsheets. Responds in 3 weeks. After initial contact, write for appointment to show portfolio of tearsheets, slides.

SALZMAN INTERNATIONAL

1751 Charles Ave., Arcate CA 95521. Phone/fax: (707)822-5500. E-mail: rs@salzint.com. Web site: www.salzint .com. Commercial illustration representative. Estab. 1982. Represents 20 illustrators. 20% of artwork is children's book illustration. Staff includes Richard Salzman. Open to illustrators seeking representation. Accepting both new and established illustrators.

Handles Accepts illustration.

Terms Receives 25% commission. Offers written contract. 100% of advertising costs paid by illustrator. Advertises in *Workbook*, ispot.com, altpick.com.

How to Contact For first contact, send link to Web site or printed samples. Portfolio should include tearsheets, photocopies; "best to post samples on Web site and send link." Finds illustrators through queries/solicitations.

LIZ SANDERS AGENCY

2415 E. Hangman Creek Lane, Spokane WA USA 99224-8514. E-mail: liz@lizsanders.com. Web site: www.lizsander s.com. **Contact:** Liz Sanders. Commercial illustration representative. Estab. 1985. Represents Craig Orback, Amy Ning, Tom Pansini, Chris Lensch, Lynn Gesue, Poozie, Susan Synarski, Sudi McCollum, Sue Rama, Suzanne Beaky and more. Currently open to illustrators seeking representation. Open to both new and established illustrators. Handles Illustration. Markets include publishing, licensed properties, entertainment and advertising.

Terms Receives 30% commission against pro bono mailing program. Offers written contract. Advertises in Picturebook and picture-book.com, directory of illustration, childrensillustrators.com, theispot.com, folioplanet. com. No geographic restrictions.

How to Contact For first contact, send tearsheets, direct mail flier/brochure, color copies, non-returnables or e-mail. Responds only if interested. Obtains new talent through recommendations from industry contacts, conferences and queries/solicitations, Literary Market Place.

🌐 THOROGOOD KIDS

E-mail: kids@thorogood.net. Web site: www.thorogood.net/kids. Commercial illustration representative. Estab. 1978. Represents 30 illustrators including: Nicola Slater, Anne Yvonne Gilbert, Olivier Latyk, Sophie Allsopp, Carol Morley, Philip Nicholson, Dan Hambe, Bill Dare, Hannah Cumming, Lisa Zibamanzar, Christiane Engel, Robin Heighway-Bury, Leo Timmers, Kanako & Yuzuru, Shaunna Peterson, Daniel Egneus, Al Sacui, John Woodcock. Staff includes Doreen Thorogood, Steve Thorogood, Tom Thorogood. Open to illustrators seeking representation. Accepting both new and established illustrators. Guidelines not available.

Handles Accepts illustration, illustration/manuscript packages.

Recent Sales Anne Yvonn

How to Contact For first contact, send tearsheets, photocopies, SASE, direct mail flyer/brochure. After initial contact, we will contact the illustrator if we want to see the portfolio. Portfolio should include tearsheets, photocopies. Finds illustrators through queries/solicitations, conferences.

Tips "Be unique and research your market. Talent will win out!"

TUGEAU 2, INC.

2231 Grandview Ave., Cleveland Heights OH 44106. (216)707-0854. Fax: (216)795-8404. E-mail: nicole@tugeau 2.com. Web site: www.tugeau2.com. Children's publishing art/illustration representative. Estab. 2003. Member of SCBWI. Represents 30 illustrators. Staff includes Nicole Tugeau, Jeremy Tugeau and assistant Margaret Bell. Open to illustrators seeking representation. Accepting both new and established illustrators.

Handles Accepts illustration.

Terms Receives 25% commission. Exclusive representation in the children's industry required. Offers written contract. Illustrator must provide digital portfolio (for Web and e-mail proposals) as well as 50-100 tearsheets (postcards or otherwise) with agency name and logo—to be kept inhouse for promotion. Advertises in *Picturebook*.

How to Contact For first contact, e-mail with 4 or 5 digital files of artwork. Responds immediately. Agency will request full portfolio with SASE if interested. Finds illustrators through recommendations from others, queries/ solicitations.

Tips "Do not look for representation until you have a portfolio (12-15 pieces) geared toward the children's market. Hone in on your personal style, consistency, and diversity of scenes and characters. Be ready to articulate your ambitions in the industry and the time you will be able to commit to those ambitions."

GWEN WALTERS ARTIST REPRESENTATIVE

1801 S. Flagler Dr., #1202, W. Palm Beach FL 33401. (561)805-7739. E-mail: artincgw@aol.com. Web site: www.gwenwaltersartrep.com. **Contact:** Gwen Walters. Commercial illustration representative. Estab. 1976. Represents 18 illustrators. 90% of artwork handled is children's book illustration. Currently open to illustrators seeking representation. Looking for established illustrators only.

Handles Illustration.

Recent Sales Sells to "All major book publishers."

Terms Receives 30% commission. Artist needs to supply all promo material. Offers written contract. Advertising costs are split: 70% paid by illustrator; 30% paid by rep. Advertises in *Picturebook*, *RSVP*, *Directory of Illustration*.

How to Contact For first contact, send tearsheets. Responds only if interested. Finds illustrators through recommendations from others.

Tips "Go out and get some first-hand experience. Learn to tell yourself to understand the way the market works."

WENDYLYNN & CO.

504 Wilson Rd., Annapolis MD 21401. (401)224-2729. Fax: (410)224-2183. E-mail: wendy@wendylynn.com. Web site: www.wendylynn.com. **Contact:** Wendy Mays. Children's illustration representative. Estab. 2002. Member of SCBWI. Represents 24 illustrators. 100% of artwork handled is children's illustration. Staff includes Wendy Mays, Janice Onken. Currently open to illustrators seeking representation. Open to both new and established illustrators. Submission guidelines available on Web site.

Handles Illustration.

Terms Receives 25% commission. Exclusive representation required. Offers written contract. Requires 15-20 images submitted on disk. Advertises in *Picturebook* or *Creative Black Book*.

How to Contact For first contact, e-mail or send color photocopies or tearsheets with bio; e-mail is preferred. Responds ASAP. After initial contact mail artwork on CD and send tearsheets. Portfolio should include a minimum of 15 images. Finds illustrators through recommendations from others and from portfolio reviews.

Tips "In this day and age, you should be able to scan your own artwork and send files digitally to publishers. Also, having your own Web site is important, and knowing how to use Photoshop is a plus."

DEBORAH WOLFE LTD.

731 N. 24th St., Philadelphia PA 19130. (215)232-6666. Fax: (215)232-6585. E-mail: inquiry@illustrationonline.c om. Web site: www.illustrationOnline.com. **Contact:** Deborah Wolfe. Commercial illustration representative. Estab. 1978. Member of Graphic Artist Guild. Represents 30 illustrators. Currently open to illustrators seeking representation.

Handles Illustration.

Terms Receives 25% commission. Exclusive representation required. Offers written contract. Advertising costs are split: 75% paid by illustrators; 25% paid by rep. Advertises in *Picturebook*, *Directory of Illustration*, *The Workbook*, *The Black Book*.

How to Contact Responds in 2 weeks. Portfolio should include "anything except originals." Finds illustrators through queries/solicitations.

Clubs & Organizations

C ontacts made through organizations such as the ones listed in this section can be quite beneficial for children's writers and illustrators. Professional organizations provide numerous educational, business, and legal services in the form of newsletters, workshops, or seminars. Organizations can provide tips about how to be a more successful writer or artist, as well as what types of business records to keep, health and life insurance coverage to carry, and competitions to consider.

An added benefit of belonging to an organization is the opportunity to network with those who have similar interests, creating a support system. As in any business, knowing the right people can often help your career, and important contacts can be made through your peers. Membership in a writer's or artist's organization also shows publishers you're serious about your craft. This provides no guarantee your work will be published, but it gives you an added dimension of credibility and professionalism.

Some of the organizations listed here welcome anyone with an interest, while others are only open to published writers and professional artists. Organizations such as the Society of Children's Book Writers and Illustrators (SCBWI, www.scbwi.org) have varying levels of membership. SCBWI offers associate membership to those with no publishing credits, and full membership to those who have had work for children published. International organizations such as SCBWI also have regional chapters throughout the U.S. and the world. Write or call for more information regarding any group that interests you, or check the Web sites of the many organizations that list them. Be sure to get information about local chapters, membership qualifications, and services offered.

Information on organizations listed in the previous edition but not included in this edition of Children's Writer's & Illustrator's Market may be found in the General Index.

AMERICAN ALLIANCE FOR THEATRE & EDUCATION

4811 Saint Elmo Ave, Unit B, Bethesda, MD 20814. (301)951-7977. E-mail: info@aate.com. Web site: www.aate. com. Purpose of organization: to promote standards of excellence in theatre and drama education. "We achieve this by assimilating quality practices in theatre and theatre education, connecting artists, educators, researchers and scholars with each other, and by providing opportunities for our members to learn, exchange and diversify their work, their audiences and their perspectives." Membership cost: $110 annually for individual in U.S. and Canada, $220 annually for organization, $60 annually for students, $70 annually for retired people; add $30 outside Canada and U.S. Holds annual conference (July). Newsletter published quarterly. Contests held for unpublished play reading project and annual awards in various categories. Awards plaque and stickers for published playbooks. Publishes list of unpublished plays deemed worthy of performance and stages readings at conference. Contact national office at number above or see Web site for contact information for Playwriting Network Chairpersons.

AMERICAN SOCIETY OF JOURNALISTS AND AUTHORS

1501 Broadway, Suite 302, New York NY 10036. (212)997-0947 Fax: (212)937-2315 Web site: www.asja.org. **Executive Director:** Alexandra Owens. Qualifications for membership: "Need to be a professional freelancenon-fiction writer. Refer to Web site for further qualifications." Membership cost: Application fee—$50; annual dues—$195. Group sponsors national conferences; Professional Seminars online and inperson around the country. Workshops/conferences open to nonmembers. Publishes a newsletter for members that provides confidential information for nonfiction writers.

ARIZONA AUTHORS ASSOCIATION

6145 West Echo Lane, Glendale AZ 85302. E-mail: info@azauthors.com. Web site: www.azauthors.com. **President:** Toby Heathcotte. Purpose of organization: to offer professional, educational and social opportunities to writers and authors, and serve as a network. Members must be authors, writers working toward publication, agents, publishers, publicists, printers, illustrators, etc. Membership cost: $45/year writers; $30/year students; $60/year other professionals in publishing industry. Holds regular workshops and meetings. Publishes bimonthly newsletter and Arizona Literary Magazine. Sponsors Annual Literary Contest in poetry, essays, short stories, novels, and published books with cash prizes and awards bestowed at a public banquet in Phoenix. Winning entries are also published or advertised in the *Arizona Literary Magazine.* First and second place winners in poetry, essay and short story categories are entered in the Pushcart Prize. Winning novel published and free listings by www.fivestarpublications.com. Send SASE or view Web site for guidelines.

ASSITEJ/USA

1602 Belle View Blvd #810, Alexandria VA 22307. E-mail: info@assitej-usa.org. Web site: www.assitej-usa.org Purpose of organization: to promote theater for children and young people by linking professional theaters and artists together; sponsoring national, international and regional conferences and providing publications and information. Also serves as U.S . Center for International Association of Theatre for Children and Young People. Different levels of membership include: organizations, individuals, students, retirees, libraries. *TYA Today* includes original articles, reviews and works of criticism and theory, all of interest to theater practitioners (included with membership). Publishes journal that focuses on information on field in U.S. and abroad.

THE AUTHORS GUILD

31 East 32nd Street 7th floor; New York, NY 10016. (212)563-5904. Fax: (212)564-5363. E-mail: staff@authorsguild.org. Web site: www.authorsguild.org. **Executive Director:** Paul Aiken. Purpose of organization: to offer services and materials intended to help authors with the business and legal aspects of their work, including contract problems, copyright matters, freedom of expression and taxation. Guild has 8,000 members. Qualifications for membership: Must be book author published by an established American publisher within 7 years or any author who has had 3 works (fiction or nonfiction) published by a magazine or magazines of general circulation in the last 18 months. Associate membership also available. Annual dues: $90. Different levels of membership include: associate membership with all rights except voting available to an author who has a firm contract offer or is currently negotiating a royalty contract from an established American publisher. "The Guild offers free contract reviews to its members. The Guild conducts several symposia each year at which experts provide information, offer advice and answer questions on subjects of interest and concern to authors. Typical subjects have been the rights of privacy and publicity, libel, wills and estates, taxation, copyright, editors and editing, the art of interviewing, standards of criticism and book reviewing. Transcripts of these symposia are published and circulated to members. The Authors Guild Bulletin, a quarterly journal, contains articles on matters of interest to writers, reports of Guild activities, contract surveys, advice on problem clauses in contracts,

transcripts of Guild and League symposia and information on a variety of professional topics. Subscription included in the cost of the annual dues.''

⚑ CANADIAN SOCIETY OF CHILDREN'S AUTHORS, ILLUSTRATORS AND PERFORMERS, (CANSCAIP)

104-40 Orchard View Blvd., Toronto ON M4R 1B9 Canada. (416)515-1559. E-mail: office@canscaip.org. Web site: www.cansaip.org. **Office Manager:** Lena Coakley. Purpose of organization: development of Canadian children's culture and support for authors, illustrators and performers working in this field. Qualifications for membership: Members—professionals who have been published (not self-published) or have paid public performances/records/tapes to their credit. Friends—share interest in field of children's culture. Membership cost: $75 (Members dues), $35 (Friends dues), $45 (Institution dues). Sponsors workshops/conferences. Publishes newsletter: includes profiles of members; news round-up of members' activities countrywide; market news; news on awards, grants, etc; columns related to professional concerns.

LEWIS CARROLL SOCIETY OF NORTH AMERICA

11935 Beltsville Dr., Beltsville MD 20705. E-mail: imholtz99@atlantech.net. Web site: www.lewiscarroll.org/lcsna.html. **Secretary:** Clare Imholtz. ''We are an organization of Carroll admirers of all ages and interests and a center for Carroll studies.'' Qualifications for membership: ''An interest in Lewis Carroll and a simple love for Alice (or the Snark for that matter).'' Membership cost: $35 (regular membership), $100 (sustaining membership). The Society meets twice a year—in spring and in fall; locations vary. Publishes a semiannual journal, *Knight Letter*, and maintains an active publishing program.

THE CHILDREN'S BOOK COUNCIL, INC.

12 W. 37th St., 2nd Floor, New York NY 10018. (212)966-1990. Fax: (212)966-2073. E-mail: info@cbcbooks.org. Web site: www.cbcbooks.org. **Executive Director:** Robin Adelson. Purpose of organization: A nonprofit trade association of children's and young adult publishers and packagers, CBC promotes the enjoyment of books for children and young adults and works with national and international organizations to that end. The CBC has sponsored Children's Book Week since 1945 and Young People's Poetry Week since 1999. Qualifications for membership: trade publishers and packagers of children's and young adult books and related literary materials are eligible for membership. Publishers wishing to join should contact the CBC for dues information. Sponsors workshops and seminars for publishing company personnel. Individuals wishing to receive the CBC semiannual journal, *CBC Features* with articles of interest to people working with children and books and materials brochures, may be placed on CBC's mailing list for a one-time-only fee of $60. Sells reading encouragement posters and graphics and informational materials suitable for libraries, teachers, booksellers, parents, and others working with children.

FLORIDA FREELANCE WRITERS ASSOCIATION

Cassell Network of Writers, P.O. Box A, North Stratford NH 03590. (603)922-8338. E-mail: FFWA@Writers-Editors.com. Web sites:www.ffwamembers.com and www.writers-editors.com. **Executive Director:** Dana K. Cassell. Purpose of organization: To provide a link between Florida writers and buyers of the written word; to help writers run more effective editorial businesses. Qualifications for membership: ''None. We provide a variety of services and information, some for beginners and some for established pros.'' Membership cost: $90/year. Publishes a newsletter focusing on market news, business news, how-to tips for the serious writer. Annual *Directory of Florida Markets* included in FFWA newsletter section and electronic download. Publishes annual *Guide to CNW/Florida Writers*, which is distributed to editors around the country. Sponsors contest: annual deadline March 15. Guidelines on Web site. Categories: juvenile, adult nonfiction, adult fiction and poetry. Awards include cash for top prizes, certificate for others. Contest open to nonmembers.

GRAPHIC ARTISTS GUILD

32 Broadway, Suite 1114, New York NY 10004. (212)791-3400. Fax: (212) 791-0333. E-mail: membership@gag.org. Web site: www.gag.org. **President:** John P. Schmelzer. Purpose of organization: ''To promote and protect the economic interests of member artists. It is committed to improving conditions for all creators of graphic arts and raising standards for the entire industry.'' Qualification for full membership: 50% of income derived from the creation of artwork. Associate members include those in allied fields, students and retirees. Initiation fee: $30. Full memberships: $200; student membership: $75/year. Associate membership: $170/year. Publishes *Graphic Artists Guild Handbook, Pricing and Ethical Guidelines* (free to members, $34.95 retail). ''The Graphic Artists Guild is a national union that embraces all creators of graphic arts intended for presentation as originals or reproductions at all levels of skill and expertise. The long-range goals of the Guild are: to educate graphic artists and their clients about ethical and fair business practices; to educate graphic artists about emerging trends and technologies impacting the industry; to offer programs and services that anticipate and respond to

the needs of our members, helping them prosper and enhancing their health and security; to advocate for the interests of our members in the legislative, judicial and regulatory arenas; to assure that our members are recognized financially and professionally for the value they provide; to be responsible stewards for our members by building an organization that works efficiently on their behalf.''

HORROR WRITERS ASSOCIATION

244 5th Avenue, Suite 2767, New York, NY 10001. E-mail: hwa@horror.org. Web site: www.horror.org. **Office Manager:** Lisa Morton. Purpose of organization: To encourage public interest in horror and dark fantasy and to provide networking and career tools for members. Qualifications for membership: Complete membership rules online at www.horror.org/memrule.htm. At least one low-level sale is required to join as an affiliate. Non-writing professionals who can show income from a horror-related field may join as an associate (booksellers, editors, agents, librarians, etc.). To qualify for full active membership, you must be a published, professional writer of horror. Membership cost: $65 annually. Holds annual Stoker Awards Weekend and HWA Business Meeting. Publishes monthly newsletter focusing on market news, industry news, HWA business for members. Sponsors awards. We give the Bram Stoker Awards for superior achievement in horror annually. Awards include a handmade Stoker trophy designed by sculptor Stephen Kirk. Awards open to nonmembers.

INTERNATIONAL READING ASSOCIATION

800 Barksdale Rd., P.O. Box 8139, Newark DE 19714-8139. (302)731-1600, ext. 293. Fax: (302)731-1057. E-mail: pubinfo@reading.org. Web site: www.reading.org. **Public Information Associate:** Beth Cady. Purpose of organization: ''Formed in 1956, the International Reading Association seeks to promote high levels of literacy for all by improving the quality of reading instruction through studying the reading process and teaching techniques; serving as a clearinghouse for the dissemination of reading research through conferences, journals, and other publications; and actively encouraging the lifetime reading habit. Its goals include professional development, advocacy, partnerships, research, and global literacy development.'' **Open to students.** Basic membership: $36. Sponsors annual convention. Publishes a newsletter called ''Reading Today.'' Sponsors a number of awards and fellowships. Visit the IRA Web site for more information on membership, conventions and awards.

THE INTERNATIONAL WOMEN'S WRITING GUILD

P.O. Box 810, Gracie Station, New York NY 10028. (212)737-7536. Fax: (212) 737-9469. E-mail: dirhahn@iwwg.org. Web site: www.iwwg.org. **Executive Director and Founder:** Hannelore Hahn. IWWG is ''a network for the personal and professional empowerment of women through writing.'' Qualifications: open to any woman connected to the written word regardless of professional portfolio. Membership cost: $45 annually. ''IWWG sponsors several annual conferences a year in all areas of the U.S. The major conference is held in June of each year at Skidmore College in Saratoga Springs, NY. It is a week-long conference attracting over 500 women internationally.'' Also publishes a 32-page newsletter, *Network*, 6 times/year; offers dental and vision insurance at group rates, referrals to literary agents.

▣ LEAGUE OF CANADIAN POETS

920 Yonge St., Suite 608, Toronto ON M4W 3C7 Canada. (416)504-1657. Fax: (416)504-0096. Web site: www.poets.ca. **Acting Executive Director:** Joanna Poblocka. President: Mary Ellen Csamer. Inquiries to Program Manager: Joanna Poblocka. The L.C.P. is a national organization of published Canadian poets. Our constitutional objectives are to advance poetry in Canada and to promote the professional interests of the members. Qualifications for membership: full—publication of at least 1 book of poetry by a professional publisher; associate membership—an active interest in poetry, demonstrated by several magazine/periodical publication credits; student—an active interest in poetry, 12 sample poems required; supporting—any friend of poetry. Membership fees: full—$175/year, associate—$60, student—$20, supporting—$100. Holds an Annual General Meeting every spring; some events open to nonmembers. ''We also organize reading programs in schools and public venues. We publish a newsletter which includes information on poetry/poetics in Canada and beyond. Also publish the books *Poetry Markets for Canadians*; *Who's Who in the League of Canadian Poets*; *Poets in the Classroom* (teaching guide), and online publications. The Gerald Lampert Memorial Award for the best first book of poetry published in Canada in the preceding year and The Pat Lowther Memorial Award for the best book of poetry by a Canadian woman published in the preceding year. Deadline for awards: November 1. Visit www.poets.ca for more details. Sponsors youth poetry competition. Visit www.youngpoets.ca for details.

LITERARY MANAGERS AND DRAMATURGS OF THE AMERICAS

P.O. Box 728 Villiage Station, New York NY 10014. E-mail: lmda@lmda.org or lmdanyc@hotmail.com. Web site: www.lmda.org. LMDA is a not-for-profit service organization for the professions of literary management and dramaturgy. Student Membership: $25/year. Open to students in dramaturgy, performing arts and literature programs, or related disciplines. Proof of student status required. Includes national conference, New Dramaturg activities, local symposia, job phone and select membership meetings. Active Membership: $60/year. Open to full-time and part-time professionals working in the fields of literary management and dramaturgy. All privileges and services including voting rights and eligibility for office. Institutional Membership: $130/year. Open to theaters, universities, and other organizations. Includes all privileges and services except voting rights and eligibility for office. Publishes a newsletter featuring articles on literary management, dramaturgy, LMDA program updates and other articles of interest.

THE NATIONAL LEAGUE OF AMERICAN PEN WOMEN
1300 17th St. N.W., Washington DC 20036-1973. (202)785-1997. E-mail: nlapw1@verizon.net. Web site: www.a mericanpenwomen.org. **President:** Elaine Waidelich. Purpose of organization: to promote professional work in art, letters, and music since 1897. Qualifications for membership: An applicant must show "proof of sale" in each chosen category—art, letters, and music. Levels of membership include: Active, Associate, International Affiliate, Members-at-Large, Honorary Members (in one or more of the following classifications: Art, Letters, and Music). Holds workshops/conferences. Publishes magazine 4 times/year titled *The Pen Woman.* Sponsors various contests in areas of Art, Letters, and Music. Awards made at Biennial Convention. Biannual scholarships awarded to non-Pen Women for mature women. Awards include cash prizes—up to $1,000. Specialized contests open to nonmembers.

NATIONAL WRITERS ASSOCIATION
10940 S. Parker Rd., #508, Parker CO 80138. (303)841-0246. Fax: (303)841-2607. E-mail: anitaedits@aol.com. Web site: www.nationalwriters.com. **Executive Director:** Sandy Whelchel. Purpose of organization: association for freelance writers. Qualifications for membership: associate membership—must be serious about writing; professional membership—must be published and paid writer (cite credentials). Membership cost: $65 associate; $85 professional; $35 student. Sponsors workshops/conferences: TV/screenwriting workshops, NWAF Annual Conferences, Literary Clearinghouse, editing and critiquing services, local chapters, National Writer's School. Open to non-members. Publishes industry news of interest to freelance writers; how-to articles; market information; member news and networking opportunities. Nonmember subscription: $20. Sponsors poetry contest; short story contest; article contest; novel contest. Awards cash for top 3 winners; books and/or certificates for other winners; honorable mention certificate places 5-10. Contests open to nonmembers.

NATIONAL WRITERS UNION
113 University Place, 6th Floor, New York NY 10003. (212)254-0279 Fax: 212-254-0673 . E-mail: nwu@nwu.org. Web site: www.nwu.org. Students welcome. Purpose of organization: Advocacy for freelance writers. Qualifications for membership: "Membership in the NWU is open to all qualified writers, and no one shall be barred or in any manner prejudiced within the Union on account of race, age, sex, sexual orientation, disability, national origin, religion or ideology. You are eligible for membership if you have published a book, a play, three articles, five poems, one short story or an equivalent amount of newsletter, publicity, technical, commercial, government or institutional copy. You are also eligible for membership if you have written an equal amount of unpublished material and you are actively writing and attempting to publish your work." Membership cost: annual writing income less than $4,500—$120/year or $67.50 1/2 year; $4,500-15,000—$195/year or $105 ½ year; $15,001-30,000—$265/year or $140 ½ year; $30,001-$45,000—$315 a year or $165 1/2 year; $45,001-$60,000—$340/year or $177.50 ½ year. Holds workshops throughout the country. Members only section on web site offers rich resources for freelance writers. Skilled contract advice and grievance help for memebers.

PEN AMERICAN CENTER
588 Broadway, Suite 303, New York NY 10012. (212)334-1660. Fax: (212)334-2181. E-mail: pen@pen.org. Web site: www.pen.org. Purpose of organization: "An associate of writers working to advance literature, to defend free expression, and to foster international literary fellowship." Qualifications for membership: "The standard qualification for a writer to become a member of PEN is publication of two or more books of a literary character, or one book generally acclaimed to be of exceptional distinction. Also eligible for membership: editors who have demonstrated commitment to excellence in their profession (usually construed as five years' service in book editing); translators who have published at least two book-length literary translations; playwrights whose works have been produced professionally; and literary essayists whose publications are extensive even if they have not yet been issued as a book. Candidates for membership may be nominated by a PEN member or they may nominate themselves with the support of two references from the literary community or from a current PEN member. Membership dues are $75 per year and many PEN members contribute their time by serving on committees, conducting campaigns and writing letters in connection with freedom-of-expression cases, contributing to the PEN journal, participating in PEN public events, helping to bring literature into underserved communities, and judging PEN literary awards. PEN members receive a subscription to the PEN journal, the PEN Annual Report, and have access to medical insurance at group rates. Members living in the New York

metropolitan and tri-state area, or near the Branches, are invited to PEN events throughout the year. Membership in PEN American Center includes reciprocal privileges in PEN American Center branches and in foreign PEN Centers for those traveling abroad. Application forms are available on the Web at www.pen.org. Associate Membership is open to everyone who supports PEN's mission, and your annual dues ($40; $20 for students) provides crucial support to PEN's programs. When you join as an Associate Member, not only will you receive a subscription to the PEN Journal http://pen.org/page.php/prmID/150 and notices of all PEN events but you are also invited to participate in the work of PEN. PEN American Center is the largest of the 141 centers of International PEN, the world's oldest human rights organization and the oldest international literary organization. International PEN was founded in 1921 to dispel national, ethnic, and racial hatreds and to promote understanding among all countries. PEN American Center, founded a year later, works to advance literature, to defend free expression, and to foster international literary fellowship. The Center has a membership of 2,900 distinguished writers, editors, and translators. In addition to defending writers in prison or in danger of imprisonment for their work, PEN American Center sponsors public literary programs and forums on current issues, sends prominent authors to inner-city schools to encourage reading and writing, administers literary prizes, promotes international literature that might otherwise go unread in the United States, and offers grants and loans to writers facing financial or medical emergencies. In carrying out this work, PEN American Center builds upon the achievements of such dedicated past members as W.H. Auden, James Baldwin, Willa Cather, Robert Frost, Langston Hughes, Thomas Mann, Arthur Miller, Marianne Moore, Susan Sontag, and John Steinbeck. The Children's Book Authors' Committee sponsors annual public events focusing on the art of writing for children and young adults and on the diversity of literature for juvenile readers. The PEN/Phyllis Naylor Working Writer Fellowship was established in 2001 to assist a North American author of fiction for children or young adults (E-mail: awards@pen.org). Visit www.pen.org for complete information. Sponsors several competitions per year. Monetary awards range from $2,000-35,000.

🌐 PLAYMARKET

P.O. Box 9767, Te Aro Wellington New Zealand. (64)4 3828462. Fax: (64)4 3828461. E-mail: info@playmarket.org.nz. Web site: www.playmarket.org.nz. **Director:** Mark Amery. **Script Development**: Jean Betts & Janie Walker. **Administrator:** Michael Daly. **Agency Coordinator:** Katrina Chandra. Purpose of organization: funded by Creative New Zealand, Playmarket serves as New Zealand's script advisory service and playwrights' agency. Playmarket offers script assessment, development and agency services to help New Zealand playwrights secure professional production for their plays. Playmarket runs the NZ Young Playwrights Competition, The Aotearoa Playwrights Conference and the Adam Playreading Series and administers the annual Bruce Mason Playwriting Award. The organization's magazine, *Playmarket News*, is published biannually. Inquiries e-mail info@playmarket.org.nz.

PUPPETEERS OF AMERICA, INC.

Membership Office: 26 Howard Ave, New Haven, CT 06519-2809. (888)568-6235. E-mail: membership@puppeteers.org. Web site: www.puppeteers.org. **Membership Officer:** Fred Thompson. Purpose of organization: to promote the art and appreciation of puppetry as a means of communications and as a performing art. The Pupeteers of America boasts an international membership. Qualifications for membership: interest in the art form. Membership cost: single adult, $50; seniors (65 +) and youth members, $30 (6-17 years of age); full-time college student, $30; family, $70; couple, $60; senior couple, $50. Membership includes a bimonthly newsletter (*Playboard*). Discounts for workshops/conferences, access to the Audio Visual Library & Consultants in many areas of Puppetry. *The Puppetry Journal*, a quarterly periodical, provides a color photo gallery, news about puppeteers, puppet theaters, exhibitions, touring companies, technical tips, new products, new books, films, television, and events sponsored by the Chartered Guilds in each of the 8 P of A regions. Subscription: *Puppetry Journal* only, $40 (libraries only). The Puppeteers of America sponsors an annual National Day of Puppetry the last Saturday in April.

SCIENCE-FICTION AND FANTASY WRITERS OF AMERICA, INC.

P.O. Box 877, Chestertown MD 21620. E-mail: execdir@sfwa.org. Web site: www.sfwa.org. **Executive Director:** Jane Jewell. Purpose of organization: to encourage public interest in science fiction literature and provide organization format for writers/editors/artists within the genre. Qualifications for membership: at least 1 professional sale or other professional involvement within the field. Membership cost: annual active dues—$70; affiliate—$55; one-time installation fee of $10; dues year begins July 1. Different levels of membership include: active—requires 3 professional short stories or 1 novel published; associate—requires 1 professional sale; or affiliate—which requires some other professional involvement such as artist, editor, librarian, bookseller, teacher, etc. Workshops/conferences: annual awards banquet, usually in April or May. Open to nonmembers. Publishes quarterly journal, the SFWA *Bulletin*. Nonmember subscription: $18/year in U.S. Sponsors Nebula Awards for best published science fiction or fantasy in the categories of novel, novella, novelette and short story.

Awards trophy. Also presents the Damon Knight Memorial Grand Master Award for Lifetime Achievement, and, beginning in 2006, the Andre Norton Award for Outstanding Young Adult Science Fiction or Fantasy Book of the Year.

SOCIETY OF CHILDREN'S BOOK WRITERS AND ILLUSTRATORS
8271 Beverly Blvd., Los Angeles CA 90048. (323)782-1010. Fax:(323)782-1892 E-mail: info@scbwi.org (autoresponse). Web site: www.scbwi.org. **President:** Stephen Mooser. Executive Director: Lin Oliver. Chairperson, Board of Advisors: Sue Alexander. Purpose of organization: to assist writers and illustrators working or interested in the field. Qualifications for membership: an interest in children's literature and illustration. Membership cost: $60/year. Plus one time $15 initiation fee. Different levels of membership include: full membership—published authors/illustrators; associate membership—unpublished writers/illustrators. Holds 100 events (workshops/conferences) worldwide each year. National Conference open to nonmembers. Publishes a newsletter focusing on writing and illustrating children's books. Sponsors grants for writers and illustrators who are members.

SOCIETY OF ILLUSTRATORS
128 E. 63rd St., New York NY 10021-7303. (212)838-2560. Fax: (212)838-2561. E-mail: info@societyillustrators. org. Web site: www.societyillustrators.org. **Contact:** Terrence Brown, director. ''Purpose is to promote interest in the art of illustration for working professional illustrators and those in associated fields.'' Cost of membership: Initiation fee is $250. Annual dues for nonresident members (those living more than 125 air miles from SI's headquarters): $287. Dues for Resident Artist Members: $475 per year; Resident Associate Members: $552.'' Artist Members shall include those who make illustration their profession and earn at least 60% of their income from their illustration. Associate Members are those who earn their living in the arts or who have made a substantial contribution to the art of illustration. This includes art directors, art buyers, creative supervisors, instructors, publishers and like categories. The candidate must complete and sign the application form which requires a brief biography, a listing of schools attended, other training and a résumé of his or her professional career. Candidates for Artist membership, in addition to the above requirements, must submit examples of their work.'' Sponsors contest. Sponsors ''The Annual of American Illustration,'' which awards gold and silver medals. Open to nonmembers. Deadline: October 1. Also sponsors ''The Original Art: The Best of Children's Book Illustration.'' Deadline: mid-August. Call for details.

SOCIETY OF MIDLAND AUTHORS
P.O. 10419, Chicago IL 60610-0419. Web site: www.midlandauthors.com. **President:** Thomas Frisbie. Purpose of organization: create closer association among writers of the Middle West; stimulate creative literary effort; maintain collection of members' works; encourage interest in reading and literature by cooperating with other educational and cultural agencies. Qualifications for membership: membership by invitation only. Must be author or co-author of a book demonstrating literary style and published by a recognized publisher and be identified through residence with Illinois, Indiana, Iowa, Kansas, Michigan, Minnesota, Missouri, Nebraska, North Dakota, Ohio, South Dakota or Wisconsin. **Open to students** (if authors). Membership cost: $35/year dues. Different levels of membership include: regular—published book authors; associate, nonvoting—not published as above but having some connection with literature, such as librarians, teachers, publishers and editors. Program meetings held 5 times a year, featuring authors, publishers, editors or the like individually or on panels. Usually second Tuesday of October, November, February, March and April. Also holds annual awards dinner in May. Publishes a newsletter focusing on news of members and general items of interest to writers. Sponsors contests. ''Annual awards in six categories, given at annual dinner in May. Monetary awards for books published which premiered professionally in previous calendar year. Send SASE to contact person for details.'' Categories include adult fiction, adult nonfiction, juvenile fiction, juvenile nonfiction, poetry, biography. No picture books. Contest open to nonmembers. Deadline for contest: February 1.

SOCIETY OF SOUTHWESTERN AUTHORS
P.O. Box 30355, Tucson AZ 85751-0355. Fax: (520)751-7877. E-mail: Information: Penny Porter wporter202@aol.com. Web site: www.ssa-az.org. Purpose of organization: to promote fellowship among professional and associate members of the writing profession, to recognize members' achievements, to stimulate further achievement, and to assist persons seeking to become professional writers. Qualifications for membership: Professional Membership: proof of publication of a book, articles, TV screenplay, etc. Associate Membership: proof of desire to write, and/or become a professional. Self-published authors may receive status of Professional Membership at the discretion of the board of directors. Membership cost: $25 initiation plus $25/year dues. The Society of Southwestern Authors sponsors an annual 2-day Writers' Conference (all genres) held September 15-16, 2007(check Web site for updated information). SSA publishes a bimonthly newsletter, *The Write Word*, promoting members' published works, advice to fellow writers, and up-to-the-minute trends in publishing and market-

ing. Yearly writing contest open to all writers; short story, memoir, poetry, children's stories. Applications available in February—write Mary Ann Hutchinson douglashutchinson@comcast.net; Subject Line: SSA Writer's Contest.

SOUTHWEST WRITERS
3721 Morris NE, Suite A, Albuquerque NM 87111. (505)265-9485. Fax: (505)265-9483. E-mail: swwriters@juno.com. Web site: www.southwestwriters.org. Non-profit organization dedicated to helping members of all levels in their writing. Members enjoy perks such as networking with professional and aspiring writers; substantial discounts on mini-conferences, monthly workshops, writing classes, and annual and monthly SWW writing contest; monthly newsletter; two writing programs per month; critique groups, critique service (also for nonmembers); discounts at bookstores and other businesses; and website linking. Cost of membership: Individual, $60/year, $100/2 years; Two People, $50 each/year; Student, $40/year; Student under 18, $25/year; Outside U.S., $65/year; Lifetime, $750. See Web site for information.

TEXT AND ACADEMIC AUTHORS ASSOCIATION
P.O. Box 76477, St. Petersburg FL 33734-6477. (727)563-0020. Fax: (727)230-2409. E-mail: TEXT@tampabay.rr.com. Web site: www.taaonline.net. **President:** John Wakefield. Purpose of organization: to address the professional concerns of text and academic authors, to protect the interests of creators of intellectual property at all levels, and support efforts to enforce copyright protection. Qualifications for membership: all authors and prospective authors are welcome. Membership cost: $30 first year; $75 per year following years. Workshops/conferences: June each year. Newsletter focuses on all areas of interest to text authors.

VOLUNTEER LAWYERS FOR THE ARTS
1 E. 53rd St., 6th Floor, New York NY 10022-4201. (212)319-ARTS, ext. 1 (the Art Law Line). Fax: (212)752-6575. E-mail: askvla@vlany.org. Web site: www.vlany.org. **Executive Director:** Elena M. Paul. Purpose of organization: Volunteer Lawyers for the Arts is dedicated to providing free arts-related legal assistance to low-income artists and not-for-profit arts organizations in all creative fields. Over 800 attorneys in the New York area donate their time through VLA to artists and arts organizations unable to afford legal counsel. There is no membership required for our services. Everyone is welcome to use VLA's Art Law Line, a legal hotline for any artist or arts organization needing quick answers to arts-related questions. VLA also provides clinics, seminars and publications designed to educate artists on legal issues which affect their careers. Membership is through donations and is not required to use our services. Members receive discounts on publications and seminars as well as other benefits. Some of the many publications we carry are *All You Need to Know About the Music Business*; *Business and Legal Forms for Fine Artists*, *Photographers & Authors & Self-Publishers*; *Contracts for the Film & TV Industry*, plus many more.

WESTERN WRITERS OF AMERICA, INC.
1012 Mesa Vista Hall, MSCO6 3770, 1 University of New Mexico, Albuquerque NM 87131-0001. (505)277-5234. E-mail: wwa@unm.edu; candywwa@aol.com. Web site: www.westernwriters.org. **Executive Director:** Paul Andrew Hutton. Open to students. Purpose of organization: to further all types of literature that pertains to the American West. Membership requirements: must be a published author of Western material. Membership cost: $75/year ($90 foreign). Different levels of membership include: Active and Associate-the two vary upon number of books or articles published. Holds annual conference. The 2007 conference held in Springfield, MO; 2008 in Scottsdale AZ, and 2010 in Oklahoma City. Publishes bimonthly magazine focusing on western literature, market trends, bookreviews, news of members, etc. Nonmembers may subscribe for $30 ($50 foreign). Sponsors youth writing contests. Spur awards given annually for a variety of types of writing. Awards include plaque, certificate, publicity. Contest and Spur Awards open to nonmembers.

WOMEN WRITING THE WEST
8547 E. Arapahoe Rd., #J-541, Greenwood Village CO 80112. (303)773-8349. E-mail: WWWAdmin@lohseworks.com. Web site: www.womenwritingthewest.org. **Contact:** Joyce Lohse, administrator. Purpose of organization: Women writing the West is a nonprofit association of writiers, editors, publishers, agents, booksellers, and other professionals writing and promoting the Women's West. Assuch, Women Writing thier stories in th American West in a way that illuminates them authentically. In addition, the organization provides support, encouragement, and inspiration to all women writing about any facet of the American West. Membership is open to all interested persons worldwide. **Open to students.** Cost of membership: Annual membership dues $50. Publisher dues are $50. In addition to the annual dues, there is an option to become a sustaining member for $100. Sustaining members receive a WWW enamel logo pin, prominent listing in WWW publications, and the knowledge that they are assiting the organzation. Members actively exchange ideas on a listerv e-bulletin board. WWW membership also allows the choice of participation in our marketing marvel, the annual WWW

Catalog of Author's Books. An annual conference is held the third weekend every October. Our WWW newsletter is current WWW activities; features market research, and expereince artcles of interest pertaining to American West literatrue and member news. Sponsors annual WILLA Literary Award, which is given in several categories for outstanding literatrue featuring women's stories, set in the West. The winner of a WILLA literary Award receives a cash award and a trophy at the annual conference. Contest open to non-members.

WRITERS GUILD OF ALBERTA

11759 Groat Rd., Edmonton AB T5M 3K6 Canada. (780)422-8174. Fax: (780)422-2663. E-mail: mail@writersguild.ab.ca. Web site: www.writersguild.ab.ca. Purpose of organization: to provide meeting ground and collective voice for the writers in Alberta. Membership cost: $60/year; $30 for seniors/students. Holds workshops/conferences. Publishes a newsletter focusing on markets, competitions, contemporary issues related to the literary arts (writing, publishing, censorship, royalties etc.). Sponsors annual Literary Awards in six categories (novel, nonfiction, short fiction, children's literature, poetry, drama). Awards include $1,000, leather-bound book, promotion and publicity. Open to nonmembers.

WRITERS OF KERN

P.O. Box 22335, Bakersfield CA 93390. (661)399-0423. E-mail: sm@sandymoffett.com. Web site: http://home.bak.rr.com/writersofkern/. **Membership:** Sandy Moffett. Open to published writers and any person interested in writing. Dues: $45/year, $20 for students; $20 initiation fee. Types of memberships: Active Writers with published work; Associate Writers working toward publication, affiliate—beginners and students. Monthly meetings held on the third Saturday of every month. Annual writers' workshops, with speakers who are authors, agents, etc., on topics pertaining to writing; critique groups for several fiction genres, poetry, children's, nonfiction, journalism and screenwriting which meet bimonthly. Members receive a monthly newsletter from WOK and CWC with marketing tips, conferences and contests.

WRITERS' FEDERATION OF NEW BRUNSWICK

Box 37, Station A, Fredericton E3B 4Y2 Canada. (506)459-7228. E-mail: wfnb@nb.aibn.com. Web site: www.umce.ca/wfnb. **Executive Director:** Mary Hutchman. Purpose of organization: "to promote New Brunswick writing and to help writers at all stages of their development." Qualifications for membership: interest in writing. Membership cost: $40, basic annual membership; $20, high school students; $45, family membership; $50, institutional membership; $100, sustaining member; $250, patron; and $1,000, lifetime member. Holds workshops/conferences. Publishes a newsletter with articles concerning the craft of writing, member news, contests, markets, workshops and conference listings. Sponsors annual literary competition, $15 entry fee for members, $20 for nonmembers. Categories: fiction, nonfiction, poetry, children's literature—3 prizes per category of $150, $75, $50; Alfred Bailey Prize of $400 for poetry ms; The Richards Prize of $400 for short novel, collection of short stories or section of long novel; The Sheree Fitch Prize for writing by young people (14-18 years of age). Contest open to nonmembers (residents of Canada only).

Resources

Conferences & Workshops

Writers and illustrators eager to expand their knowledge of the children's publishing industry should consider attending one of the many conferences and workshops held each year. Whether you're a novice or seasoned professional, conferences and workshops are great places to pick up information on a variety of topics and network with experts in the publishing industry, as well as with your peers.

Listings in this section provide details about what conference and workshop courses are offered, where and when they are held, and the costs. Some of the national writing and art organizations also offer regional workshops throughout the year. Write, call or visit Web sites for information.

Writers can find listings of more than 1,000 conferences (searchable by type, location, and date) at The Writer's Digest/Shaw Guides Directory to Writers' Conferences, Seminars, and Workshop—www.writersdigest.com/conferences.

Members of the Society of Children's Book Writers and Illustrators can find information on conferences in national and local SCBWI newsletters. Nonmembers may attend SCBWI events as well. SCBWI conferences are listed in the beginning of this section under a separate subheading. For information on SCBWI's annual national conferences, contact them at (323)782-1010 or check their Web site for a complete calendar of national and regional events (www.scbwi.org).

CONFERENCES & WORKSHOPS CALENDAR
To help you plan your conference travel, here is a month-by-month calendar of all the conferences, workshops and retreats included in this section. The calendar lists conferences alphabetically by the month in which they occur.

January
Butler University Children's Literature Conference (Indianapolis IN)
Kindling Words East (Burlington VT)
San Diego State University Writers' Conference (San Diego CA)
SCBWI—Florida Regional Conference (Miami FL)
South Coast Writers Conference (Gold Beach OR)
Winter Poetry & Prose Getaway in Cape May (Cape May NJ)

February
San Francisco Writers Conference (San Francisco CA)
SCBWI; Annual Conference on Writing and Illustrating for Children (New York NY)

SCBWI—Norca (San Francisco/South); Retreat at Asilomar (Pacific Grove CA)
SCBWI—Southern Breeze; Spring Mingle (Atlanta GA)
South Coast Writers Conference (Gold Beach OR)

March
Florida Christian Writers Conference (Bradenton FL)
Kentucky Writer's Workshop (Pineville KY)
Perspectives in Children's Literature Conference (Amherst MA)
SCBWI Bologna Biennial Conference & SCBWI Showcase Booth at the
   Bologna Children's Book Fair (Bologna, Italy)
SCBWI—Utah; Forum on Children's Literature (Orem UT)
Virginia Festival of the Book (Charlottesville VA)
Whidbey Island Writers' Conference (Langley WA)
Tennessee Williams/New Orleans Literary Festival (New Orleans LA)

April
AEC Conference on Southern Literature (Chattanooga TN)
Central Ohio Writers of Literature for Children (Columbus OH)
Children's Literature Conference (Hempstead NY)
Festival of Children's Literature (Minneapolis MN)
Festival of Faith and Writing (Grand Rapids MI)
Missouri Writers' Guild Annual State Conference (St. Charles MO)
Mount Hermon Christian Writers Conference (Mount Hermon CA)
SCBWI New Mexico Handsprings: A Conference for Children's Writers and Illustrators (Albu-
   querque NM)

May
Annual Spring Poetry Festival (New York NY)
BookExpo America/Writer's Digest Books Writers Conference (New York NY)
Kindling Words West (Abiquiu NM)
Oklahoma Writers' Federation, Inc. Annual Conference (Oklahoma City OK)
Pima Writers' Workshop (Tucson AZ)

June
Aspen Summer Words Writing Retreat (Aspen CO)
East Texas Christian Writers Conference (Marshall TX)
The Environmental Writers' Conference and Workshop in Honor of Rachel Carson (Boothbay
   Harbor ME)
Great Lakes Writers Conference (Milwaukee WI)
Highland Summer Conference (Radford VA)
International Creative Writing Camp (Minot ND)
Iowa Summer Writing Festival (Iowa City IA)
Manhattanville Summer Writers' Week (Purchase NY)
Outdoor Writers Association of America Annual Conference (Lake Charles LA)
SCBWI—Florida Mid-Year Writing Workshop (Orlando FL)
SCBWI—New Jersey; Annual Spring Conference (Princeton NJ)
Southeastern Writer's Association—Annual Writer's Workshop (Athens GA)
UMKC/Writers Place Writers Workshops (Kansas City MO)
Wesleyan Writers Conference (Middleton CT)
Write! Canada (Guelph ON Canada)

Resources

Write-by-the-Lake Writer's Workshop & Retreat (Madison WI)
Write-to-Publish Conference (Wheaton IL)
Writers Retreat Workshop (Erlanger KY)

July
Children's Book Workshop at Castle Hill (Truro MA)
Conference for Writers & Illustrators of Children's Books (Corte Madera CA)
Highlights Foundation Writers Workshop at Chautauqua (Chautaqua NY)
Hofstra University Summer Workshop (Hempstead NY)
Maritime Writers' Workshop (Fredericton NB Canada)
Midwest Writers Workshop (Muncie IN)
Montrose Christian Writer's Conference (Montrose PA)
Pacific Northwest Children's Book Conference (Portland OR)
Pacific Northwest Writer Assn. Summer Writer's Conference (Seattle WA)
Robert Quackenbush's Children's Book Writing and Illustrating Workshop (New York NY)
Sage Hill Writing Experience (Saskatoon SK Canada)
Saskatchewan Festival of Words and Workshops (Moose Jaw SK Canada)
Steamboat Springs Writers Conference (Steamboat Springs CO)
The Victoria School of Writing (Victoria BC Canada)

August
Cape Cod Writer's Conference (Cape Cod MA)
The Columbus Writers Conference (Columbus OH)
Green Lake Writers Conference (Green Lake WI)
The Manuscript Workshop in Vermont (Londonderry VT)
Moondance International Film Festival (Hollywood CA)
The Pacific Coast Children's Writer's Workshop (Aptos CA)
SCBWI; Annual Conference on Writing and Illustrating for Children (Los Angeles CA)
Willamette Writers Annual Writers Conference (Portland OR)

September
League of Utah Writers' Roundup (Ogden UT)
Maui Writers Conference (Kihei HI)
SCBWI—Carolinas; Annual Fall Conference (Durham NC)
SCBWI—Eastern Pennsylvania; Fall Philly Conference (Exton PA)
SCBWI—Idaho; Editor Day (Boise ID)
SCBWI—Midsouth Fall Conference (Nashville TN)
SCBWI—Northern Ohio; Annual Conference (Cleveland OH)
SCBWI—Rocky Mountain Events (Lakewood CO)
Society of Southwestern Authors' Wrangling with Writing (Tucson AZ)
South Coast Writers Conference (Gold Beach CO)

October
Flathead River Writers Conference (Whitefish MT)
Ozark Creative Writers, Inc. Conference (Eureka Springs AR)
SCBWI—Iowa Conference (Iowa City IA)
SCBWI—Midatlantic; Annual Fall Conference (Arlington VA)
SCBWI—Oregon Conferences (Portland OR)
SCBWI—Southern Breeze; Writing and Illustrating for Kids (Birmingham AL)
SCBWI—Ventura/Santa Barbara; Fall Conference (Thousand Oaks CA)

SCBWI—Wisconsin; Fall Retreat for Working Writers (Milton WI)
Surrey International Writer's Conference (Surrey BC Canada)
Vancouver Internatinoal Writers Festival (Vancouver BC Canada)
Write on the Sound Writers Conference (Edmonds WA)

November
Jewish Children's Book Writers' Conference (New York NY)
LaJolla Writers Conference (LaJolla CA)
North Carolina Writers' Network Fall Conference (Durham NC)
SCBWI—Illinois; Prairie Writers Day
SCBWI—Missouri; Children's Writer's Conference (St. Peters MO)

December
Big Sur Writing Workshop (Big Sur CA)

Multiple or Seasonal Events
The conference listings below include information on multiple or year-round events or events
that are seasonal (held in fall or spring, for example). Please read the listings for more information on the dates and locations of these events and check the conferences' Web sites.

American Christian Writers Conference
Booming Ground Online Writers Studio
Cat Writers' Association Annual Writers Conference
Children's Authors' Bootcamp
Peter Davidson's How to Write a Children's Picture Book Seminar
The DIY Book Festival
Duke University Youth Programs: Creative Writers' Workshop
Duke University Youth Programs: Young Writers' Camp
Gotham Writers' Workshop (New York NY)
Highlights Foundation Founders Workshops (Honesdale PA)
Iowa Summer Writing Festival (Iowa City IA)
The Manuscript Workshop in Vermont (Londonderry VT)
Publishinggame.com Workshop
SCBWI—Arizona; Events
SCBWI—Eastern Canada; Annual Events
SCBWI—Dakotas
SCBWI—Idaho; Editor Day
SCBWI—Iowa Conferences
SCBWI—Los Angeles; Events
SCBWI—Metro New York; Professional Series (New York NY)
SCBWI—New Jersey; First Page Sessions (Princeton NJ)
SCBWI—Oregon Conferences
SCBWI—Pocono Mountains Retreat (Sterling PA)
SCBWI—Taiwan; Events
SCBWI—Ventura/Santa Barbara; Retreat for Children's Authors and Illustrators
   (Santa Barbara CA)
SCBWI—Western Washington State; Retreats & Conference
Southwest Writers Conferences
Split Rock Arts Program (St. Paul MN)
Sydney Children's Writers and Illustrators Network (Woollahra NSW Australia)

UMKC/Writers Place Writers Workshops (Kansas City MO)
Writers' League of Texas Workshop Series (Austin TX)
The Writers' Retreat Writing Workshop at Castle Hill

Information on conferences listed in the previous edition but not this edition of Children's Writer's & Illustrator's Market may be found in the General Index.

SCBWI CONFERENCES

SCBWI; ANNUAL CONFERENCES ON WRITING AND ILLUSTRATING FOR CHILDREN

8271 Beverly Blvd., Los Angeles CA 90048. (323)782-1010. Fax: (323)782-1892. E-mail: scbwi@scbwi.org. Web site: www.scbwi.org. **Conference Director:** Lin Oliver. Writer and illustrator workshops geared toward all levels. **Open to students.** Covers all aspects of children's book and magazine publishing—the novel, illustration techniques, marketing, etc. Annual conferences held in August in Los Angeles and in New York in February. Cost of conference (LA): approximately $390; includes all 4 days and one banquet meal. Write for more information or visit web site.

SCBWI—ARIZONA; EVENTS

P.O. Box 26384, Scottsdale AZ 85255-0123. E-mail: rascbwiaz@aol.com. Web site: www.scbwi-az.org. **Regional Advisor:** Michelle Parker-Rock. SCBWI Arizona will offer a variety of workshops, retreats, intensives, conferences, meetings and other craft and industry-related events throughout 2008-2009. Open to members and nonmembers, published and nonpublished. Registration to major events is usually limited. Pre-registration always required. Visit Web site, write or e-mail for more information.

⊕ SCBWI BOLOGNA BIENNIAL CONFERENCE & SCBWI SHOWCASE BOOTH AT THE BOLOGNA CHILDREN'S BOOK FAIR

(323)782-1010 (PST). E-mail: Bologna@scbwi.org. Web site: www.scbwi.org. Contact: Bologna@scbwi.org. Two-day writer and illustrator conference for children's book professionals held in the spring every two years in association with the largest annual international children's book rights fair in the world, the Bologna Children's Book Fair (www.bookfair.bolognafiere.it. Next conference date: 2010. Please watch SCBWI.org events for exact dates and details. A professional craft-based conference, with talks, panels, and hands-on workshops. A chance to meet editors, art directors and agents and children's book creators, before the rights fair gets going. Registration limited to 100 attendees. Manuscript and illustration critiques available by reservation for additional fee Register at http://www.scbwi.org/events.htm. "Register early and reserve affordable rooms at local bed & breakfast establishments. Illustrators attend the Book Fair for free, if they submit illustrations to the illustration contest; others: often discounts for early registration to the Book Fair." SCBWI showcase at the Bologna Children's Book Fair: published authors and illustrators may send proposals for 2-hour stand-time at the SCBWI Showcase booth at the Book Fair. Send proposals to bologna@scbwi.org only between January 2 and 30 of Conference year (next stand scheduled for 2010). SCBWI Bologna Biennial Conference 2008 program featured: Adams Literary (agents US); Stephen Barbara (agent US); Marc Boutavant (illustrator, ARIOL series and others FR); Val Brathwaite (design director, Bloomsbury UK); Babette Cole (author/illustrator UK, *Princess Smartypants*); Pat Cummings (author/illustrator US, *Squashed in the Middle*); Steven Chudney (agent US); Ginger Clark (agent US/UK); Carmen Diana Dearden (Ekare Venezuela); Kathleen Duey (writer US, NBA-finalist for *A Resurrection of Magic: Skin Hunger*); Susan Fletcher (writer US, *Alphabet of Dreams*); Susanne Gervay (writer AUS,*That's Why I Wrote This Song*); Fiammetta Giorgi (editor, Mondadori IT); Candy Gourlay (author & webmaster, Philippines/UK); Emmanuel Guibert (author of ARIOL series and illustrator FR); Katherine Halligan (editorial director picture books, novelty and gifts, Scholastic UK); Laura Harris (publisher, Penguin Australia); Jana Novotny Hunter (author, editor, teacher Czech Rep/UK); Susanne Koppe (agent Germany); Leonard Marcus (critique, historian, author of *Golden Legacy: How Golden Books Won Children's Hearts, Changed Publishing Forever, and Became an American Icon Along the Way*); Pauline Mermet (editor, Bayard FR); Nancy Miles (agent UK); Sarah Odedina (editorial director, Bloomsbury UK); Martha Rago (art director, HarperCollins US); Davd Saylor (VP, Associate Publisher, Hardcover and Graphix, Scholastic US); John Shelley (illustrator, The Boat in the Tree); Bridget Strevens-Marzo (author/illustrator *UK/FR, How Do You Make a Baby Smile?*); Giselle Tsai (editor, CommonWealth Taiwan); Cecilia Yung (art director and vice-president, Penguin Putnam); Marie Wabbes (author/illustrator *Un Amour de Petit Lapin*, Belgium); Paul O. Zelinsky (author/illustrator; Caldecott winner & creator of The Wheels on the Bus).

SCBWI—CAROLINAS; ANNUAL FALL CONFERENCE
E-mail: scgbooks@aol.com; write_something@earthlink.net; jhackl@wyche.com. Regional Advisor: Stephanie Greene. Sept 19-21 at the Sheraton Imperial Airport Hotel, Durham, NC. Speakers include: Anita Silvey, Martha Mihalick, Greenwillow, Alyssa Eisner Henkin, agent. Friday afternoon manuscript and portfolio critiques, workshops in mystery, fantasy, non-fiction, craft, and more. Visit www.scbwicarolinas.org for more information.

SCBWI—DAKOTAS; SPRING CONFERENCE
100 N. Sanborn Blvd. #210, Mitchell SD 57301.E-mail: jean@santel.net. Web site: www.scbwidakotas.org. **Regional Advisor:** Jean Patrick. Conference for writers of all levels. "In addition to providing the basics about picture books and novels, we strive to offer unique information about other avenues for publication, including magazine writing, craft writing, work-for-hire writing and more. Recent conferences included keynote speakers Marilyn Kratz and Rose Ross Zebiker." Annual event held every spring. Check Web site for details.

SCBWI—DAKOTAS; WRITERS CONFERENCE IN CHILDREN'S LITERATURE
Grand Forks ND 58202-7209. (701)777-3321. E-mail: jean@jeanpatrick.com. Web site: www.und.edu/dept/english/ChildrensLit.html or www.scbwidakotas.org. **Regional Advisor:** Jean Patrick. Conference sessions geared toward all levels. "Although the conference attendees are mostly writers, we encourage & welcome illustrators of every level." Open to students. "Our conference offers 3-4 children's authors, editors, publishers, illustrators, or agents. Past conferences have included Kent Brown (publisher, Boyds Mills Press); Alexandra Penfold (Editor, Simon & Schuster); Jane Kurtz (author); Anastasia Suen (author); and Karen Ritz (illustrator). Conference held each fall. "Please call or e-mail to confirm dates. Writers and illustrators come from throughout the northern plains, including North Dakota, South Dakota, Montana, Minnesota, Iowa, and Canada." Writing facilities available: campus of University of North Dakota. Local art exhibits and/or concerts may coincide with conference. Cost of conference includes Friday evening reception and sessions, Saturday's sessions, and lunch. A manuscript may be submitted 1 month in advance for critique (extra charge). E-mail for more information.

SCBWI—DAKOTAS/UND WRITERS CONFERENCE IN CHILDREN'S LITERATURE
Department. of English, Merrifield Hall, Room 110, 276 Centennial Drive, Stop 7209, Univeristy of North Dakota, Grand Forks ND 58202. (701)777-3321 or (701)777-3984. E-mail: jean@jeanpatrick.com. Web site: www.und.edu or www.scbwidakotas.com. **Regional Advisor:** Jean Patrick. Conference for all levels. "Our conference offers 3-4 chlidren's authors, editors, publishers, illustrators or agents. Past conferences have included Elaine Marie Alphin (author), Jane Kurtz (author), Alexandra Penfold (editor), Kent Brown (publisher), and Karen Ritz (illustrator)." Annual conference held every fall. "Please call or e-mail to confirm dates." Cost of conference to be determined. Cost included Friday evening sessions, Saturday sessions, and Saturday lunch. "We welcome writers, illustrators, and others who are interested in children's literature."

⚡ SCBWI—EASTERN CANADA; ANNUAL EVENTS
E-mail: ara@scbwicanada.org; ra@scbwicanada.org. Web site: www.scbwicanada.org/east. **Regional Advisor:** Lizann Flatt. Writer and illustrator event geared toward all levels. Usually offers one event in spring and another in the fall. Check Web site Events pages for updated information.

SCBWI—EASTERN PENNSYLVANIA; FALL PHILLY CONFERENCE
Whitford Country Club, Exton PA. Web site: www.scbwiepa.org. Conference focuses on writing skills, the publishing market, and finding inspiration. Manuscript and Portfolio critiques with editors available for an additional fee. Conference held in September. Registration is limited to 150. Information will be posted on the Web site in July. Cost: $100. Registration includes buffet lunch.

SCBWI—FLORIDA; MID-YEAR WRITING WORKSHOP
(305)382-2677. E-mail: lindabernfeld@hotmail.com. Web site: www.scbwiflorida.com. **Regional Advisor:** Linda Rodriguez Bernfeld. Annual workshop held in June in Orlando. Workshop is geared toward helping everyone hone their writing skills. Attendees choose one track and spend the day with industry leaders who share valuable information about that area of children's book writing. There are a minimum of 3 tracks, picture book, middle grade and young adult. The 4th and 5th tracks are variable, covering subjects such as poetry, non-fiction, humor or writing for magazines.Speakers in 2008 included Ellen Hopkins, Bruce Hale, Debra Garfinkle, Lisa McCourt, Linda Shulte, Nancy Springer, Nina Hess (senior editor at Mirrorstone), Nancy Siscoe, associate publishing director and executive editor at Knopf and Crown), Krista Marino, (editor at Delacorte), Andrea Tompa, (associate editor at Candlewick) and Nicole Kasprzak (assistant editor at G.P. Putnam). E-mail for more information.

SCBWI—FLORIDA; REGIONAL CONFERENCE

(305)382-2677. E-mail: lindabernfeld@gmail.com. Web site: www.scbwiflorida.com. **Regional Advisor:** Linda Rodriguez Bernfeld. Annual conference held in January in Miami. 2009 conference will be held January 16-18, 2009. Speakers included Linda Sue Park (A Single Shard), Lisa Yee (Millicent Min), Ginger Knowlton (Curtis Brown LTD), and Alexandra Cooper, editor, Simon and Schuster . Cost of conference: approximately $225. The 3-day conference will have workshops Friday afternoon and a field trip to Books and Books Friday evening. There will be a general session all day Saturday covering all aspects of writing for children. There will be hands on workshops Sunday morning led by industry leaders. There is a Saturday only option. Past speakers have included Judy Blume, Paula Danziger, Bruce Coville, Arthur Levine, Libba Bray and Kate DiCamillo. For more information, contact e-mail Linda Rodriguez Bernfeld at lindabernfeld@gmail.com.

SCBWI—IDAHO; EDITOR DAY

Email: neysajensen@msn.com. **Regional Advisor:** Sydney Husseman; **Assistant Regional Advisor:** Neysa Jensen. One day workshop focuses on the craft of writing, as well as getting to know an editor. One-on-one critiques available for an additional fee. Event held in Boise, Idaho every fall.

N SCBWI—ILLINOIS; PRAIRIE WRITERS DAY

Chicago IL 60614. E-mail: esthersh@aol.com. Web site: www.scbwi-illinois.org/events. **Regional Advisor:** Esther Hershenhorn. Workshop held in early November at Dominican University in River Forest. Highlights 3 newly-published members and their editors, along with agents, booksellers and reviewers. Ms critiques and First Page readings are on the program. 2007 speakers included Andrea Beaty and her Abrams Editor Susan Van Metre; Deborah Ruddell and her Margaret McElderry Editor Karen Woytyla; agents Sara Crowe and Rosemary Stimola; and Andersons Book Buyer Jan Dundon; among others. Visit Web site for more information on this and other SCBWI—Illinois events or contact Sara Shacter at sfshacter@gmail.com.

SCBWI—IOWA CONFERENCES

E-mail: hecklit@aol.com. Web site: www.scbwi-iowa.org. **Regional Advisor:** Connie Heckert. Writer and illustrator workshopsin all genres of children writing. The Iowa Region offers conferences of high quality events usually over a three-day period with registration options.. Recent speakers included Jane Yolen, Adam Stemple, Bruce Coville and well-known edtiors from the finest publisheing houses, Holds spring and fall events on a regional level, and network events across that state. Individual critiques and portfolio review offerings vary with the program and presenters. For more information e-mail or visit Web site.

SCBWI—LOS ANGELES; EVENTS

P.O. Box 1728, Pacific Palisades CA 90272. (310)573-7318. Web site: www.scbwisocal.org. **Co-regional Advisors:** Claudia Harrington (claudiascbwi@earthlink.net) and Edie Pagliasotti (ediescbwi@sbcgloablnet). SCBWI—Los Angeles hosts 7 major events each year: **Writer's Workshop** (winter)—half-day workshop featuring speaker demonstrating nuts and bolts techniques on the craft of writing for childrens; **Writer's Day** (spring)—a one-day conference featuring speakers, a professional forum, writing contests and awards; **Critiquenic** (summer)—a free informal critiquing session for writers and illustrators facilitated by published authors/illustrators, held after a picnic lunch; **Writers & Illustrator's Sunday Field Trip** (summer)—hands-on creative field trip for writers and illustrators; **Illustrator's Day** (fall)—a one-day conference featuring speakers, juried art competition, contests, and portfolio review//display;. **Working Writer's Retreat** (winter)—a 3-day, 2-night retreat featuring an editor, speakers, and intensive critiquing. See calendar of events on Web site for more details and dates.

SCBWI—METRO NEW YORK; PROFESSIONAL SERIES

P.O. Box 1475, Cooper Station, New York NY 10276-1475. (212)545-3719. E-mail: scbwi_metrony@yahoo.com. Web site: www.home.nyc.rr.com/scbwimetrony. **Regional Advisor:** Nancy Lewis and Seta Toroyan. Writer and illustrator workshops geared toward all levels. **Open to students.** The Metro New York Professional Series generally meets the second Tuesday of each month, from October to June, 7-9 p.m. Check Web site to confirm location, dates, times and speakers. Cost of workshop: $12 for SCBWI members; $15 for nonmembers. ''We feature an informal, almost intimate evening with coffee, cookies, and top editors, art directors, agents, publicity and marketing people, librarians, reviewers and more.''

N SCBWI—MIDATLANTIC; ANNUAL FALL CONFERENCE

Mid-Atlantic SCBWI, P.O. Box 3215, Reston, VA 20195-1215. E-mail: sydney.dunlap@adelphia.net or midatlanti cscbwi@tidalwave.net. Web site: www.scbwi-midatlantic.org. **Conference Chair:** Sydney Dunlap and Erin Teagan. Regional Advisor: Ellen Braaf. Conference takes place Saturday, October 25, 2008 in Arlington, VA from 8 to 5. Keynote speaker: Jane Yolen. For updates and details visit Web site. Registration limited to 200.

Conference fills quickly. Cost: $95 for SCBWI members; $120 for nonmembers. Includes continental breakfast. Lunch is on your own. (The food Court at the Ballston Common Mall is two blocks away.)

[N] SCBWI—MIDSOUTH FALL CONFERENCE

P.O. Box 120061, Nashville TN 37212.E-mail: expressdog@bellsouth.net or cmoonwriter@aol.com. Web site: www.scbwi-midsouth.org. E-mail: cmoonwritr@aol.com or cameron_s_e@yahoo.com. **Conference Coordinators:** Genetta Adair and Candie Moonshower. Conference for writers and illustrators of all levels. In the past, workshops were offered on Plotting You Novel, Understanding the Language of Editors, Landing an Agent, How to Prepare a Portfolio, Negotiating a Contract, The Basics for Beginners, and many others. Attendees are invited to bring a manuscript and/or art portfolio to share in the optional, no-charge critique group session. Illustrators are invited to bring color copies of their art (*not* originals) to be displayed in the bookstore. For an additional fee, attendees may schedule a 15-minute manuscript critique or portfolio critique by the editor, art director or other expert consultant. Annual conference held in September. Registration limited to 120 attendees. Cost to be determined. The 2008 Midsouth Conference included SCBWI co-founder/executive director and author Lin Oliver; Clarion Books editor Jennifer Wingertzahn; Henry Holt associate art director Laurent Linn; literary agent Ginger Clark (Curtis Brown, Ltd.); author Jaime Adoff; Editor Harold Underdown; award-winning authors Bruce Coville and Alexis O'neill; and more.

SCBWI—MISSOURI; CHILDREN'S WRITER'S CONFERENCE

St. Charles County Community College, P.O. Box 76975, 103 CEAC, St. Peters MO 63376-0975. (314)213-8000, ext. 4108. Web site: www.geocities.com/scbwimo. **Regional Advisor:** Lynnea Annette. Writer and illustrator conference geared toward all levels. **Open to students.** Speakers include editors, writers, and other professionals. Topics vary from year to year, but each conference offers sessions for both writers and illustrators as well as for newcomers and published writers. Previous topics included: "What Happens When Your Manuscript is Accepted" by Dawn Weinstock, editor; "Writing—Hobby or Vocation?" by Chris Kelleher; "Mother Time Gives Advice: Perspectives from a 25 Year Veteran" by Judith Mathews, editor; "Don't Be a Starving Writer" by Vicki Berger Erwin, author; and "Words & Pictures: History in the Making," by author-illustrator Cheryl Harness. Annual conference held in early November. For exact date, see SCBWI Web site: www.scbwi.org or the events page of the Missouri SCBWI Web site. Registration limited to 75-90. Cost of conference includes one-day workshop (8 a.m. to 5 p.m.) plus lunch. Write for more information.

[N] SCBWI—NEW JERSEY; FIRST PAGE SESSIONS

E-mail: njscbwi@newjerseyscbwi.com. Web site: www.newjerseyscbwi.com. Held 4 times a year at the Princeton Theological Seminary in Princeton, NJ. Two editors/agents give their first impression of a first page and let participants know if they would read more. These sessions are held late afternoon during the week and are limited to 30 people. Attendees can choose to have dinner with the editors after the session. Please visit www.newjerseyscbwi.com for more information.

SCBWI—NEW MEXICO; HANDSPRINGS: A CONFERENCE FOR CHILDREN'S WRITERS AND ILLUSTATORS

P.O. Box 1084, Socorro NM. E-mail: handsprings@scbwi-nm.org. Web site: www.scbwi-nm.org. **Registrar:** Lucy Hampson. **Regional Advisor:** Chris Eboch. Conference for beginner and intermediate writers and illustrators. "Each conference features three keynote speakers—editors, agents, and/or art directors. 2008 speakers include Alisha Niehaus, Editor, Dial Books for Young Children; Rebecca Sherman, Literary Agent, Writers House; and Tim Gillner, Art Director, Boyds Mills Press.Writers and illustrators lead breakout sessions. Workshop topics included: Writing Picture Books for the Very Young, Writing Middle Grade and YA Dialogue, and The Essential Elements for a Successful Illustrator." Annual workshop held in April or May. Registration limited to 100. "Offers classroom-style workshops and large-group presentations." Cost: $90-100 for basic Saturday registration; $15-20 for Friday evening party with edtior panel; $30-40 for private critiques (lowest prices are for SCBWI members). "The Friday evening party included social time, a First Page critique panel with our visiting editors, mini book launches and an illustrators' portfolio display. Saturday features a full day of keynote speeches by visiting editors, agents and/or art directors; breakout workshops on the craft and business of writing; and optional one-on-one critiques with the editors or portfolio review by the art director."

SCBWI—NORCA (SAN FRANCISCO/SOUTH); GOLDEN GATE CONFERENCE AT ASILOMAR

Web site: www.scbwisf.org. **Co-Regional Advisors:** Amy Laughlin and Shirley Klock. We welcome published and" not-yet-published" writers and illustrators. Lectures and workshops are geared toward professionals and those striving to become professional. Program topics cover aspects of writing or illustrating picture books to young adult novels. Past speakers include editors, art directors, Newbery Award-winning authors, and Caldecott Award-winning illustrators. Annual conference, generally held last weekend in February; Friday evening through Sunday lunch. Registration limited to approximately 100. Most rooms shared with one other person. Additional charge for single when available. Desks available in most rooms. All rooms have private baths. Conference center is set in wooded campus on Asilomar Beach in Pacific Grove, California. Approximate cost: $395 for SCBWI members, $575 for nonmembers; includes shared room, 6 meals, ice breaker party and all conference activities. Vegetarian meals available. Scholarships available to SCBWI members. Registration opens at the end of September or early October and the conference sells out within one or two days. A waiting list is formed. Coming together for shared meals and activities builds a strong feeling of community among the speakers and conferees. For more information, including exact costs and dates, visit our Web site in September.

SCBWI—NORTHERN OHIO; ANNUAL CONFERENCE

% Blossom Farm, 2946 Lampson Road, Austinburg, Ohio 44010, (440) 275-1638. Email: annettesheldon@alltel. net. Web site: www.nohscbwi.org. **Regional Advisor:** Annette Sheldon. Writer and illustrator conference for all levels. Open to students. "This conference is the premier marketing/networking event of the year for Northern Ohio SCBWI. The emphasis is on current market trends; what the market is publishing; getting manuscripts/portfolios market-ready; staying alive in the market post-publication; and the nuts and bolts of writing and illustrating for children. Additional emphasis is on meeting/networking with peers." Annual event held in September at the Sheraton Cleveland Airport Hotel. Registration limited to 200. Conference costs will be posted on our Web site with registration information. SCBWI members receive a discount. Additional fees apply for late registration, critiques, or portfolio reviews. Cost includes an optional Friday evening Opening Banquet from 6-10 p.m. with keynote speaker; Saturday event from 8:30 a.m. to 5 p.m. which includes breakfast snack, full-day conference with headliner presentations, general sessions, breakout sessions, lunch, panel discussion, bookstore, and autograph session. New For 2008: Half-day track for illustrators. Illustrator Showcase is open to all attendees at no additional cost. Grand door prize, drawn at the end of the day Saturday, is free admission to the following year's conference.

SCBWI—OREGON CONFERENCES

E-mail: robink@scbwior.com. Web site: www.scbwior.com. **Regional Advisor:** Robin Koontz. Writer and illustrator workshops and presentations geared toward all levels. "We invite editors, teachers, agents, attorneys, authors, illustrators and others in the business of writing and illustrating for children. They present lectures, workshops, and on-site critiques on a first-registered basis." Critique group network for local group meetings and regional retreats; see Web site for details. Two main events per year: Writers and Illustrators Retreat: Retreat held near Portland Thursday-Sunday the 2nd weekend in October. Cost of retreat: $335 plus $35.00 critique fee includes double occupancy and all meals; Spring Conference: Held in the Portland area (2 day event the third Fri-Sat in May); cost for presentations and workshops: about $115 includes continental breakfast and lunch on Saturday, critique fee $35.00-attendees only; Friday intensive cost about $65 with writer and illustrator tracks includes snacks and coffee. Registration limited to 300 for the conference and 55 for the retreat. SCBWI Oregon is a regional chapter of the SCBWI. SCBWI Members receive a discount for all events. Oregon and S. Washington members get preference.

SCBWI—POCONO MOUNTAINS RETREAT

Web site: www.scbwiepa.org. Held in the spring at Sterling Inn, Sterling PA. Faculty addresses writing, illustration and publishing. Registration limited to 100. Cost of retreat: tuition $140, room and board averages $200. For information and registration form, visit Web site.

SCBWI—ROCKY MOUNTAIN; EVENTS

E-mail: denise@rmcscbwi.org. or colin@rmcscbwi.org. Web site: www.rmcscbwi.org. **Co-Regional Advisors:** Denise Vega and Colin Murcray. SCBWI Rocky Mountain chapter offers various special events, schmoozes, meetings, and conferences throughout the year. Their 2008 events, Letter and Lines Fall Conference, held September 20-21 in Lakewood, CO, featured editors Joy Neaves (Front Street), John Rudolph (Putnam), and Melissa Manlove (Chronicle); agents Barry Goldblatt and Bernadette Szost; authors Bruce Hall and Lauren Myracle; and more. For more information check Web site.

⒩ SCBWI—SAN DIEGO; CHAPTER MEETINGS & WORKSHOPS

San Diego—SCBWI, San Diego CA. E-mail: ra-sd@sandiego-scbwi.org. Web site: www.sandiego-scbwi.org. **Regional Advisor:**Janice M. Yuwiler. Writer and illustrator meetings and workshops geared toward all levels. Topics vary but emphasize writing and illustrating for children. Check Web site, e-mail or write for more infomation. "The San Diego chapter holds meetings the second Saturday of each month from September-May at the University of San Diego's from 2-4 p.m.; cost $7 (members), $9 (nonmembers). Check web site for room, speaker and directions." 2009 meeting schedule: January 10, February 14, March 14, April 11, May 9 , September 12, October 10, November 14, and December 13. December 2008 meeting: Published members share lessons learned and holiday book sale. 2009 one-day conference to be held the second Saturday of January, February or March—Check Web site for date and faculty. Season tickets include all regular chapter meetings during the season and newsletter issues for one calendar year as well as discounts on workshops/conferences. If interested in taking a class, Inside Children's books through University of San Diego Continuing Education for 2 units college credit. Class in 2009 begins in September 12, 2009 and ends May 8, 2010. See the Web site for conference/workshop dates, times and prices.

SCBWI—SOUTHERN BREEZE; SPRINGMINGLE

P.O. Box 26282, Birmingham AL 35260. E-mail: JSKittinger@bellsouth.net. Web site: www.southern-breeze.org. **Regional Advisors:** Jo Kittinger and Donna Bowman. Writer and illustrator workshops geared toward intermediate, advanced and professional levels. Speakers typically include agents, editors, authors, art directors, illustrators. **Open to SCBWI members, non-members and college students.** Annual conference held in Atlanta, Georgia. Usually held in late February. Registration limited. Cost of conference: approximately $225; includes Friday dinner, Saturday lunch and Saturday banquet. Manuscript critiques and portfolio reviews available for addtional fee. Pre-registration is necessary. Send a SASE to Southern Breeze, P.O. Box 26282, Birmingham AL 35260 for more information or visit Web site: www.southern-breeze.org.

SCBWI—SOUTHERN BREEZE; WRITING AND ILLUSTRATING FOR KIDS

P.O. Box 26282, Birmingham AL 35260. E-mail: jskittinger@bellsouth.net. Web site: www.southern-breeze.org. **Regional Advisors:** Jo Kittinger and Donna Bowman. Writer and illustrator workshops geared toward all levels. Open to SCBWI members, non-members and college students. All sessions pertain specifically to the production and support of quality children's literature. This one-day conference offers about 30 workshops on craft and the business of writing. Picture books, chapter books, novels covered. Entry and professional level topics addressed by published writers and illustrators, editors and agents. Annual conference. Fall conference is held the third weekend in October in the Birmingham, AL metropolitan area. (Museums, shopping, zoo, gardens, universities and colleges are within a short driving distance.) All workshops are limited to 30 or fewer people. Pre-registration is necessary. Some workshops fill quickly. Cost of conference: approximately $110 for members, $135 for nonmembers, $120 for students; program includes keynote speaker, 4 workshops (selected from 30), lunch, and Friday night dessert party. Mss critiques and portfolio reviews are available for an additional fee; mss must be sent early. Registration is by mail ahead of time. Manuscript and portfolio reviews must be pre-paid and scheduled. Send a SASE to: Southern Breeze, P.O. Box 26282, Birmingham AL 35260 or visit Web site. Fall conference is always held in Birmingham, Alabama. Room block at a hotel near conference site (usually a school) is by individual reservation and offers a conference rate. Keynote for WIK08 is Paul Fleischman. Additional speakers include editor Harold Underdown; Laurent Linn, Associate Art Director at Hernry Holt; and Author Sarah Campbell. WIK09 speakers to be announced.

🌐 SCBWI—TAIWAN; EVENTS

Fax: (886)2363-5358. E-mail: scbwi_taiwan@yahoo.com. Web site: www.scbwi.tw. Mailing list: http://groups.yahoo.com/group/scbwi_taiwan. **Regional Advisor:** Kathleen Ahrens. Writer and illustrator workshops geared toward intermediate level. Open to students. Topics emphasized: "We regularly hold critiques for writers and for illustrators, and invite authors and illustrators visiting Taipei to give talks. See our Web site for more information."

SCBWI—VENTURA/SANTA BARBARA; FALL CONFERENCE

Simi Valley CA 93094-1389. (805)581-1906. E-mail: alexisinca@aol.com. Web site: www.scbwisocal.org/calendar. Writers' conference geared toward all levels. Speakers include editors, authors, illustrators and agents. Fiction and nonfiction picture books, middle grade and YA novels, and magazine submissions addressed. Annual writing contest in all genres plus illustration display. Conference held October 25, 2008 at California Lutheran University in Thousand Oaks, California in cooperation with the CLU School of Education. For fees and other information e-mail or go to Web site.

SCBWI—VENTURA/SANTA BARBARA; RETREAT FOR CHILDREN'S AUTHORS AND ILLUSTRATORS

E-mail: alexisinca@aol.com. Web site: www.scbwisocal.org. The Winter Retreat, usually held in Santa Barbara, focuses on craft or business issues. Go to Web site or e-mail for current theme and fee.

SCBWI—WESTERN WASHINGTON STATE; RETREATS & CONFERENCE

P.O. Box 1907, Port Townsend 98368. Email: info@scbwi-washington.org. Web site: www.scbwi-washington.org. **Co-Regional Advisors:** Jolie Stekly and Sara Easterly "The Western Washington region of SCBWI hosts an annual conference in April, as well as a weekend retreat in November. Please visit the Web site for complete details."

Resources

SCBWI—WISCONSIN; FALL RETREAT FOR WORKING WRITERS

3446 Hazelnut Lane, Milton WI 53563. E-mail: pjberes@centurytel.net. Web site: www.scbwi-wi.com. **Regional Advisor:** Pam Beres. Writer and illustrator conference geared toward all levels. All our sessions pertain to children's writing/illustration. Faculty addresses writing/illustrating/publishing. Annual conference held October. Registration limited to 70. Conference center has retreat-style bedrooms with desks that can be used to draw/write. Cost of conference: $375 for SBCWI member; $450 for non-members; includes program, meals, lodging, ms critique. Write or go to our Web site for more information: www.scbwi-wi.com.

OTHER CONFERENCES

Many conferences and workshops included here focus on children's writing or illustrating and related business issues. Others appeal to a broader base of writers or artists, but still provide information that can be useful in creating material for children. Illustrators may be interested in painting and drawing workshops, for example, while writers can learn about techniques and meet editors and agents at general writing conferences. For more information vist the Web sites listed or contact conference coordinator.

AEC CONFERENCE ON SOUTHERN LITERATURE

3069 South Broad Street, Suite 2, Chattanooga TN 37408-3056. (423)267-1218. Fax: (423)267-1018. E-mail: info@artsedcouncil.org. Web site: www.artsedcouncil.org. **Executive Director:** Susan Robinson. **Open to students.** Conference is geared toward readers. Biennial conference held April 2-4, 2009. Cost of conference: $125 for 3 days. Visit Web site for more information. Features panel discussions, readings and commentaries for adults and students by today's foremost Southern writers.

AMERICAN CHRISTIAN WRITERS CONFERENCE

P.O. Box 110390, Nashville TN 37222-0390. 1(800)21-WRITE or (615)834-0450. Fax: (615)834-7736. E-mail: detroitwriters@aol.com. Web site: www.ACWriters.com. **Director:** Reg Forder. Writer and illustrator workshops geared toward beginner, intermediate and advanced levels. Classes offered include: fiction, nonfiction, poetry, photography, music, etc. Workshops held in 3 dozen U.S. cities. Call or write for a complete schedule of conferences. 75 minutes. Maximum class size: 30 (approximate). Cost of conference: $99, 1-day session; $169, 2-day session (discount given if paid 30 days in advance) includes tuition only.

ANNUAL SPRING POETRY FESTIVAL

City College, New York NY 10031. (212)650-6356. E-mail: plaskin@ccny.cuny.edu. **Director, Poetry Outreach Center:** Pam Laskin. Writer workshops geared to all levels. **Open to students.** Annual poetry festival. Festival held May 16, 2008 . Registration limited to 325. Cost of workshops and festival: free. Write for more information.

ASPEN SUMMER WORDS WRITING RETREAT

110 E. Hallam St., No. 116, Aspen CO 81611. (970)925-3122. Fax: (970)920-5700. E-mail: info@aspenwriters.org. Web site: www.aspenwriters.org **Operations Manager:** Natalie Lacy. Annual retreat held in June in Aspen, CO. Intensive writing workshop geared toward beginner, intermediate and advanced levels. Topics include fiction, memoir and essay, poetry, magazine writing, food writing, and writing for young readers. **Open to students.** Registration limited to 12. Writing facilities available: workshop space; computer, Internet, fax and copy machine at festival site; contemplative gardens. Cost of workshop: $475 (2007 tuition); includes workshop, picnic and receptions. Students are responsible for their own lodging and meals; discount housing available. Must include: completed application, tuition payment, cover letter and manuscript. There is an April 1 application deadline. Enrollment is on a space-available basis thereafter.

BIG SUR WRITING WORKSHOP

Henry Miller Library, Highway One, Big Sur CA 93920. Phone/fax: (831)667-2574. E-mail: magnus@henrymiller.org. Web site: www.henrymiller.org/CWW.html. **Contact:** Magnus Toren, executive director. Annual workshop held in December focusing on children's and young adult writing. Workshop held in Big Sur Lodge in Pfeiffer State Park. Cost of workshop: $695; included meals, lodging, workshop, Saturday evening reception; $595 if lodging not needed.

BOOKEXPO AMERICA/WRITER'S DIGEST BOOKS WRITERS CONFERENCE

4700 East Galbraith Rd., Cincinnati OH 45236. (513) 531-2690. Fax: (513) 891-7185. E-mail: publicity@fwpubs.com. Web site: www.writersdigest.com/bea or http://www.bookexpoamerica.com/en-us/writersconference.c

fm. **Contact:** Greg Hatfield, publicity manager. Estab. 2003. Annual. Conference duration: one day, May 27, 2009. Average attendance: 600. "The purpose of the conference is to prepare writers hoping to get their work published. We offer instruction on the craft of writing, as well as advice for submitting their work to publications, publishing houses and agents. We provide breakout sessions on these topics, including expert advice from industry professionals, and offer workshops on fiction and nonfiction, in the various genres (literary, children's, mystery, romance, etc.). We also provide attendees the opportunity to actually pitch their work to agents." Site: The conference facility varies from year to year, as we are part of the BookExpo America trade show. The 2009 conference will take place at the Jacob K. Javits Convention Center, 655 West 34th Street, New York, NY 10001. Themes and panels have included Writing Genre Fiction, Children's Writing, Brutal Truths About the Book Publishing Industry, Crafting a Strong Nonfiction Book Proposal, Crafting Your Novel Pitch, and Secrets to Irresistible Magazine Queries. Past speakers included Jodi Picoult, Jacquelyn Mitchard, Jerry B. Jenkins, Steve Almond, Loren Estelman and Donald Maass. The price in 2008 was $199, which included a free copy of Writer's Market. Information available in February. For brochure, visit Web site. Agents and editors participate in conference.

BOOMING GROUND ONLINE WRITERS STUDIO
Buch E-462, 1866 Main Mall, UBC, Vancouver BC V6T 1Z1 Canada. (604)822-0257. Fax: (604)648-8848. E-mail: apply@boomingground.com. Web site: www.boomingground.com. **Director:** Nancy Lee. Writer mentorships geared toward beginner, intermediate, and advanced levels. **Open to students.** Online mentorship program—students work for 4-8 months with a mentor by e-mail. Program cost: $780 Canadian. Individual manuscript evaluation also available. Apply online; send manuscript sample with application. No art classes offered. Visit Web site for more information.

BUTLER UNIVERSITY CHILDREN'S LITERATURE CONFERENCE
2060 E. 54th Street, Indianapolis IN 46220. (317)254-0830. E-mail: kidsink@indy.net. Web site: www.butler.edu/childlit/about.htm. **Contact:** Rebecca Mullin. Writer and illustrator conference geared toward all levels. **Open to college students.** Annual conference held the last Saturday of the month of January each year featuring top writers in the field of children's literature. Includes sessions such as Nuts and Bolts for Beginning Writers. Registration limited to 350. Cost of conference: $85; includes SCBWI Networking Luncheon, registration, 3 plenary addresses, 2 workshops, book signing, reception and conference bookstore. Cisit the web site for more information. "The conference is geared toward three groups: teachers, librarians and writers/illustrators."

CAPE COD WRITER'S CONFERENCE
Cape Cod Writer's Center, P.O. Box 408, Osterville MA 02655. (508)420-0200. Fax: (508)420-0212. E-mail: writers@capecodwriterscenter.org. Web site: www.capecodwriterscenter.org. Annual conference held third week in August in a rustic retreat center on Nantucket Sound, Cape Cod; 46th annual conference: August 17-22, 2008. Courses and workshops geared toward beginner, intermediate, and professional levels include writing for the young reader, fiction, nonfiction, poetry, jounalism, screenwriting, and a Young Writers Workshop. Evening programs include speakers, a master class, panels, poetry, and prose reading. Manuscript evaluations and personal conferences with faculty, an agent, and an editor available. The Young Writers' Workshop for 12- to 16-year-olds interested in prose and poetry held concurent with the conference. Pricing available on the web page by May 1.

CAT WRITERS' ASSOCIATION ANNUAL WRITERS CONFERENCE
President Nancy Peterson, 3603 Dundee Driveway, Chevy Chase MD 20815. (304) 951-9511. E-mail: cwa-Nancy@starpower.ne. Web site: www.catwriters.org. The Cat Writers' Association holds an annual conference at varying locations around the US. The agenda for the conference is filled with seminars, editor appointments, an autograph party, networking breakfast, reception and annual awards banquet, as well as the annual meeting of the association. See Web site for details.

CHILDREN'S AUTHORS' BOOTCAMP
P.O. Box 231, Allenspark CO 80510. (303)747-1014. E-mail: CABootcamp@msnl.com. Web site: www.WeMakeWriters.com. **Contact:** Linda Arms White. Writer workshops geared toward beginner and intermediate levels. "Children Authors' Bootcamp provides two full, information-packed days on the fundamentals of writing fiction for children. The workshop covers developing strong, unique characters; well-constructed plots; believable dialogue; seamless description and pacing; point of view; editing your own work; marketing your manuscripts to publishers, and more. Each day also includes in-class writing exercises and small group activities." Workshop held 4 times/year at various locations throughout the United States. Bootcamps are generally held in March, April, June, September, October and November. Please check our Web site for upcoming dates and locations. Maximum size is 55; average workshop has 40-50 participants. Cost of workshop varies; see Web site for details.

Cost includes tuition for both Saturday and Sunday (9:00 a.m. to 4:30 p.m.); morning and afternoon snacks; lunch; handout packet. ''Online workshop also available. Check website for details.''

THE COLUMBUS WRITERS CONFERENCE

P.O. Box 20548, Columbus OH 43220-0176. (614)451-3075. Fax: (614)451-0174. E-mail: angelaPL28@aol.com. Web site: www.creativevista.com. **Director:** Angela Palazzolo. ''In addition to consultations with agents and editor, this two-day conference offers a wide variety of topics and has included writing in the following markets: children's, young adult, novel, short story, science fiction, fantasy, humor, mystery, finding and working with a literary agent, book proposals, working with an editor, query writing, screenwriting, magazine writing, travel, humor, and freelance writing. Specific sessions that have pertained to children: fiction, nonfiction, children's writing, children's markets, young adult, pitching children's books to agents and editors, and publishing children's poetry and stories. Annual conference. Conference held in August. Cost of conference is TBA. E-mail or call to request brochure or visit the Web site.

CONFERENCE FOR WRITERS & ILLUSTRATORS OF CHILDREN'S BOOKS

Book Passage, 51 Tamal Vista Blvd., Corte Madera CA 94925. (415)927-0960, ext. 234. Fax: (415)927-3069. E-mail: kathryn@bookpassage.com. Web site: www.bookpassage.com. **Conference Coordinator:** Kathryn Petrocelli . Writer and illustrator conference geared toward beginner and intermediate levels. Sessions cover such topics as the nuts and bolts of writing and illustrating, publisher's spotlight, market trends, developing characters/finding voice in your writing, and the author/agent relationship. Four-day conference held each summer. Includes opening night dinner, 3 lunches and a closing reception.

PETER DAVIDSON'S HOW TO WRITE A CHILDREN'S PICTURE BOOK SEMINAR

982 S. Emerald Hills Dr., Arnolds Park IA 51331-0497. E-mail: Peterdavidson@mchsi.com. **Seminar Presenter:** Peter Davidson. ''This seminar is for anyone interested in writing and/or illustrating children's picture books. Beginners and experienced writers alike are welcome.'' **Open to students.** How to Write a Children's Picture Book is a one-day seminar devoted to principles and techniques of writing and illustrating children's picture books. Topics include Definition of a Picture Book, Picture Book Sizes, Developing an Idea, Plotting the Book, Writing the Book, Illustrating the Book, Formatting Your Manuscript, Copyrighting Your Work, Marketing Your Manuscript and Contract Terms. Seminars are presented year-round at community colleges. Even-numbered years, presents seminars in Minnesota, Iowa, Nebraska, Kansas, Colorado and Wyoming. Odd-numbered years, presents seminars in Illinois, Minnesota, Iowa, South Dakota, Missouri, Arkansas and Tennessee (write for a schedule). One day, 9 a.m.-4 p.m. Cost of workshop: varies from $40-59, depending on location; includes approximately 35 pages of handouts. Write for more information.

THE DIY BOOK FESTIVAL

7095 Hollywood Blvd., Suite 864, Los Angeles CA 90028-0893. (323)665-8080. Fax: (323)372-3883. E-mail: diyconvention@aol.com. Web site: www.diyconvention.com. **Managing Director:** Bruce Haring. Writer and illustrator workshops geared toward beginner and intermediate levels. **Open to students.** Festival focus on getting your book into print, book marketing and promotion. Annual workshop. Workshop held February-October, various cities. Cost of workshop: $50; includes admission to event, entry to prize competition, lunch for some events. Check out our Web site for current dates and locations:www.diyconvention.com.

DUKE UNIVERSITY YOUTH PROGRAMS: CREATIVE WRITERS' WORKSHOP

P.O. Box 90702, Durham NC 27708. (919)684-6259. Fax: (919)681-8235. E-mail: youth@duke.edu. Web site: www.learnmore.duke.edu/youth. **Contact:** Duke Youth Programs. Writer workshops geared toward intermediate to advanced levels. **Open to students.** The Creative Writers' Workshop provides an intensive creative writing experience for advanced high school age writers who want to improve their skills in a community of writers. ''The interactive format gives participants the opportunity to share their work in small groups, one-on-one with instructors, and receive feedback in a supportive environment. The review and critique process helps writers sharpen critical thinking skills and learn how to revise their work.'' Annual workshop. Every summer there is one 2-week residential session. Costs for 2008—$1,655 for residential campers; $1,065 for extended day campers; $825 for day campers. Visit Web site for more information.

DUKE UNIVERSITY YOUTH PROGRAMS: YOUNG WRITERS' CAMP

P.O. Box 90702, Durham NC 27708. (919)684-2827. Fax: (919)681-8235. E-mail: youth@duke.edu. Web site: www.learnmore.duke.edu/youth. **Contact:** Duke Youth Programs (919)684-6259. Beginner and intermediate levels writing workshops for middle and high school students. **Open to students** (grades 6-11). Summer Camp. The Young Writers' Camp offers courses to enhance participants skills in creative and expository writing. ''Through a core curriculum of short fiction, poetry, journalism and playwriting students choose two courses for study to develop creative and analytical processes of writing. Students work on assignments and projects in and out of class, such as newspaper features, short stories, character studies, and journals." Annual workshop. Every summer there are three 2-week sessions with residential and day options. Costs for 2008—$1,655 for residential campers; $1,065 for extended day campers; $825 for day campers. Visit Web site or call for more information.

EAST TEXAS CHRISTIAN WRITERS CONFERENCE

East Texas Baptist University, 1209 North Grove Street, Marshall TX 75670. (903)923-2083. Fax: (903)923-2077. E-mail: jcornish@etbu.edu or jhopkins@etbu.edu. Web site: www.etbu.edu/News/CWC/default.htm. **Humanities Secretary:** Joy Cornish. Writer workshops geared toward beginner, intermediate and advanced levels. **Open to students.** Children's literature, books, stories, plays, art, and general literature. Annual conference. Workshop held first Friday and Saturday in June each year. Cost of workshop: $70/individual; $50/student; includes 5 writing workshops, materials, Friday evening dinner and luncheon; pre-conference workshops extra. Write, e-mail or call for more information.

THE ENVIROMENTAL WRITERS' CONFERENCE AND WORKSHOP IN HONOR OF RACHEL CARSON

The Spruce Point Inn, Boothbay Harbor ME. (845)398-4247. Fax: (845)398-4224. E-mail: info@new-cue.org. Web site: www.new-cue.org. **President:** Barbara Ward Klein. Writer and illustrator workshops geared toward beginner, intermediate, advanced and professional levels. Our conference emphasizes environmental and nature writing for juvenile fiction and non-fiction. Workshop held in June every 2 years on the even numbered year. Registration limited to 100 participants. Writing/art facilities available: Large meeting rooms for featured authors/speakers. Smaller break-out rooms for concurrent sessions. Cost of workshop: $395/returning participants; $445/new-before 5/1/08. Includes all featured and keynote addresses, concurrent sessions, workshops, guided outdoor activities and almost all meals. Submit writing sample, no longer than 3 pages. Write for more information. Additional information about featured speakers, The Spruce Point Inn, and the Boothbay Harbor Area is available on-line at www.new-cue.org.

FESTIVAL OF CHILDREN'S LITERATURE

The Loft Literary Center, Suite 200, Open Book, 1011 Washington Avenue South, Minneapolis MN 55415. (612)379-8999. E-mail: loft@loft.org. Web site: www.loft.org. Writer workshops, small critique gruops with editors, panels with writers, editors publishers, and illustrators of children's literatrue at annual April conference. Registration limited to 185 people; smaller groups for breakout sessions. Writing facilities available with a performance hall, classrooms and writers studios. Cost of conference: approximately $225; includes admission to full and break-out sessions, Saturday lunch. Write for more information, www.loft.org. "We also have a new program for advanced children's writer's called "Loft Master Track," a two-year apprenticeship with writers, editors and agents."

FESTIVAL OF FAITH AND WRITING

Department of English, Calvin College 1795 Knollcrest Circle SE, Grand Rapids MI 49546. (616)526-6770. E-mail: ffw@calvin.edu. Web site: www.calvin.edu/festival. E-mail all inquiries about attendance (for registration brochures, program information, etc.). Geared toward all levels of readers and writers. Open to students. "The Festival of Faith and Writing has talks, panel discussions, and workshops by nearly 100 individuals, many of whom compose, write, illustrate, and publish children's books and books for young adults. Each break-out session will have a session on children's books/young adult books. Conference held in April of the even years. Registration limited to approximately 1,900 people. This conference is geared towards a variety of writers and readers. The Festival brings together writers and readers who wonder about the intersections of faith with words on a page, lyrics in a melody, or images on a screen. Novelists, publishers, musicians, academics, poets, playwrights, editors, screenwriters, agents, journalists, preachers, students, and readers of every sort sit down together for three days of conversation and celebration."

FLATHEAD RIVER WRITERS CONFERENCE

P.O. Box 7711, Kalispell MT 59904. E-mail: slimsmty@montanasky.net. **Director:** Val Smith. Two, 12 person, intense workshops geared toward beginner, intermediate, advanced and professional levels. **Open to students.** Along with our presenters, we periodically feature a children's writer workshop/speaker. Annual conference held early-October at the Flathead Valley Community College. Registration limited to 100. Cost of the weekend conference: $150; includes all lectures and a choice of weekend workshops plus breakfast and lunch. Lodging not included.Write for more information.

FLORIDA CHRISTIAN WRITERS CONFERENCE

2344 Armour Ct., Titusville FL 32780. (321)269-5831. Fax: (321)747-0046. E-mail: billiewilson@cfl.rr.com. Web site: www.flwriters.org. **Conference Director:** Billie Wilson. Writer workshops geared toward all levels. **Open** to students. "We offer 53 one-hour workshops and 7 six-hour classes. Approximately 15 of these are for the children's genre." Annual workshop held in March. "We have 30 publishers and publications represented by editors teaching workshops and reading manuscripts from the conferees. The conference is limited to 200 people. Advanced or professional workshops are by invitation only via submitted application. Cost of workshop: $410; includes tuition and ms critiques and editor review of your ms plus personal appointments with editors. Write or e-mail for more information.

GOTHAM WRITERS' WORKSHOP

New York NY 10018. (877)974-8377. (212)307-6325. E-mail: dana@write.org. Web site: www.WritingClasses.com. **Director, Student Affairs:** Dana Miller. Creative writing workshops taught by professional writers are geared toward beginner, intermediate and advanced levels. **Open to students.** "Workshops cover the fundamentals of plot, structure, voice, description, characterization, and dialogue appropriate to all forms of fiction and nonfiction for pre-schoolers through young adults. Students can work on picture books or begin middle-readers or young adult novels." Annual workshops held 4 times/year (10-week and 1-day workshops). Workshops held January, April, July, September/October. Registration limited to 14 students/in-person (NYC) class; 18 students/online class; 40 students for in-person (NYC) one-day workshops. Cost of workshop: $420 for 10-week workshops; $150 for 1-day workshops; 10-week NYC classes meet once a week for 3 hours; 10-week online classes include 10 week-long, asynchronous "meetings"; 1-day workshops are 7 hours and are held 8 times/year. E-mail for more information.

GREAT LAKES WRITER'S WORKSHOP: Real Writing for Real People

Milwaukee WI 53234-3922. (414)382-6176. Fax: (414)382-6332. E-mail: nancy.krase@alverno.edu. Web site: www.alverno.edu. **Coordinator:** Nancy Krase. Annual writing workshops geared toward beginner and intermediate levels; subjects include publishing, short story writing, novel writing, poetry, writing techniques/focus in character development, techniques for overcoming writers block and children's writing. Workshop held June 28, 2008. Cost of workshop: $115/entire workshop; $99 if you register before June 6. 2008 conference includes continental breakfast, and lunch along with author's keynote followed by choice of 2 workshops. See online brochure. Featured at lunch will be a panel on publishing. Online brochure will be available for viwing March 17 at alverno.edu.

GREEN LAKE CHRISTIAN WRITERS CONFERENCE

Green Lake Conference Center, W2511 State Road 23, Green Lake WI 54941. Web site: www.glcc.org E-mail: janwhite@glcc.org. In 2009: Sunday-Friday, August 23-28. Attendees may be well-published or beginners, may write for secular and/or Christian markets. Leaders are experienced writing teachers. Spend 11½ contact hours in the workshop of your choice: fiction, non-fiction, poetry, inspirational/devotional. Afternoon seminars may include marketing, humor, songwriting, writing for children, self-publishing, writing for churches, interviewing, memoir writing, the magazine market, and more. Evening: panels of experts will answer your questions. Social, leisure and worship opportunities. GLCC is in south central WI, has 1000 acres, 2½ mi of shoreline on WI's deepest lake, and offers a beautiful resort setting. Hotels, lodges and all meeting rooms are a/c. Affordable rates, excellent meals. Writers' contest. Party & writers' showcase. Brochure and scholarship info from website or contact Jan White (920-294-7327). To register, call 920-294-3323.

HIGHLAND SUMMER CONFERENCE

P.O. Box 7014, Radford University, Radford VA 24142-7014. (540)831-5366. Fax: (540)831-5951. E-mail: jasbury@radford.edu. Web site: www.radford.edu/ ~ arsc. **Director:** Grace Toney Edwards. **Assistant to the Director:** Jo Ann Asbury. **Open to students.** Writer workshops geared toward beginner, intermediate and advanced levels. Emphasizes Appalachian literature, culture and heritage. Annual workshop. Workshop held first 2 weeks in June annually. Registration limited to 20. Writing facilities available: computer center. Cost of workshop: Regular tuition (housing/meals extra). Must be registered student or special status student. E-mail, fax or call for more information. Past visiting authors include: Wilma Dykeman, Sue Ellen Bridgers, George Ella Lyon, Lou Kassem.

HIGHLIGHTS FOUNDATION FOUNDERS WORKSHOPS

814 Court St., Honesdale PA 18431. (570)253-1192. Fax: (570)253-0179. E-mail: contact@highlightsfoundation.org. Web site: www.highlightsfoundation.org. **Contact:** Kent Brown, director. Workshops geared toward those interested in writing and illustrating for children, intermediate and advanced levels. Classes offered include: Writing Novels for Young Adults, Biography, Nonfiction Magazine Writing, Writing Historical Fiction, Wordplay: Writing Poetry for Children, Heart of the Novel, Nature Writing for Kids, Visual Art of the Picture Book, The Whole Novel Workshop, and more (see Web site for updated list). Workshops held near Honesdale, PA.

Workshops limited to between 8 and 14 people. Cost of workshops range from $695 and up. Cost of workshop includes tuition, meals, conference supplies and housing. Call for application and more information.

HIGHLIGHTS FOUNDATION WRITERS WORKSHOP AT CHAUTAUQUA
814 Court St., Honesdale PA 18431. (570) 253-1192. Fax: (570) 253-0179. E-mail: contact@highlightsfoundation.org. To view faculty and other details please got to Web site: www.hihglightsfoundation.org. **Contact:** Kent Brown, Director. Writer Workshops geared toward those interested in writing for children; beginner, intermediate and advanced levels. Classes include: Writing Poetry, Book Promotion, Characterization, Developing a Plot, How to Promote Your Book, and many many more. Annual workshop held: July 11-18, 2009, at Chautauqua Institution, Chautauqua, NY. Registration limited to 100. Cost of workshop: $2,485 if registered by February 27, 2009. Includes tuition, meals, conference supplies. Cost does not include housing. Call for availability and pricing. Scholarships are available for first-time attendees. Call for more information or visit the Web site.

HOFSTRA UNIVERSITY SUMMER WRITERS' WORKSHOP
250 Hofstra University, UCCE, Hempstead NY 11549. (516) 463-7200. Fax: (516)463-4833. E-mail: uccelibarts@hofstra.edu. Web site: http://ccepa.hofstra.edu. **Contact:** Richard Pioreck, Summer Writing Workshop Coordinator Workshops geared toward all levels. Classes offered include fiction, nonfiction, poetry, children's literature, stage/screenwriting and other genres. Annual workshop. Workshops held for 2 weeks in mid-July. Each workshop meetss daily for a total of 35 hours. Enrollees may register as noncredit students or credit students. Cost of workshop: noncredit students' enrollment fee is approximately $550; 3-credit student enrollment fee is Hofstra University standard tuition rates. On-campus accommodations for the sessions are available for the 2-weekconference. Accepts inquiries by fax or e-mail. Web site includes details on dates, faculty, general description and tuition.

INTERNATIONAL CREATIVE WRITING CAMP
111-11th Ave Sw, Minot, ND 58701. (701)838-8472. Fax: (701)838-1351. E-mail: info@internationalmusiccamp.com. Web site: www.internationalmusiccamp.com. **Camp Director:** Dr. Timothy Wollenzien. Writer and illustrator workshops geared toward beginner, intermediate and advanced levels. **Open to students.** Sessions offered include those covering poems, plays, mystery stories, essays. Workshop held June 22-28, 2008. Registration limited to 40. The summer camp location at the International Peace Garden on the Border between Manitoba and North Dakota is an ideal site for creative thinking. Excellent food, housing and recreation facilities are available. Cost of workshop: Before May 15th -$295.00; after May 15th - $320.00. Write for more information.

IOWA SUMMER WRITING FESTIVAL
C215 Seashore Hall, Iowa City IA 52242. (319)335-4160. Fax: (319)335-4743. E-mail: iswfestival@uiowa.edu. Web site: www.uiowa.edu/~iswfest. **Director:** Amy Margolis. Writer workshops geared toward beginner, intermediate and advanced levels. Open to writers age 21 and over. "We offer writing workshops across the genres, including workshops for children's writers in picture books, structuring writing for children, the young adult novel, and nonfiction." Annual workshop held June and July. Registration limited to 12/workshop. Workshops meet in university classrooms. Cost of workshop: $500-525/week-long session; $250/weekend. Housing is separate and varies by facility. Write or call for more information.

JEWISH CHILDREN'S BOOK WRITERS' CONFERENCE
New York NY. E-mail: anna@olswanger.com. **Contact:** Anna Olswanger, conference coordinator. The 2007 conference faculty included senior editor Reka Simonsen of Henry Holt Books for Young Readers, editor Jennifer Wingertzahn of Clarion Books, editor-in-chief Lindsey Silken of JVibe/JFL Media, sales manager Sarah Aronson of Jewish Lights Publishing, literary agent Kirsten Wolf of Jill Grinberg Literary Management, and associate art director Einav Aviram of Simon & Schuster Books for Young Readers. Neil Waldman, winner of the National Jewish Book Award, gave opening remarks. And the day included talks on publishing and writing in Israel, the Sydney Taylor Book Award and Manuscript Competition, and new for 2007: a panel on "How I Got My First Book Published." Held in November, the Sunday before Thanksgiving. Cost of workshop: includes Kosher breakfast and lunch. E-mail for more information.

KENTUCKY WRITER'S WORKSHOP
1050 State Park Road, Pineville KY 40977. (606)337-3066. Fax: (606)337-7250. Email: Dean.Henson@ky.gov. Web site: http://parks.ky.gov **Event Coordinator:** Dean Henson. Writer workshops featuring published authors and geared toward beginner and intermediate levels. **Open to students.** Annual workshop. Workshop will next be held March 28-29, 2008. Writing facilities available: classroom setup. An all-inclusive, on-site package is available and includes two nights accommodations, two evening buffet meals, and admission to all sessions. Write or call for more information.

KINDLING WORDS EAST

Web site (for registration and information): www.kindlingwords.org. Annual retreat held in late January near Burlington, Vermont. A retreat with three strands: writer, illustrator and editor; professional level. Intensive workshops for each strand, and an open schedule for conversations and networking. Registration limited to approximately 70. Tuition: $195. Hosted by the 4-star Inn at Essex (room and board extra). Participants must be published by a CBC listed publisher, or if in publishing, occupy a professional position. Registration opens August 1 or as posted on the Web site, and fills quickly. Check Web site to see if spaces are available, to sign up to be notified when registration opens each year, or for more information.

KINDLING WORDS WEST

Web site (for registration and information): www.kindlingwords.org. Annual retreat held in early May at a stunning and sacred location: Ghost Ranch, in Abiquiu, New Mexico, KWW is an artist's colony- style week with workshops by gifted teachers followed by a working retreat. Participants gather just before dinner to have white-space discussions; evenings inculde fireside readings, star gazing and songs. $340 tuition; room/board extra. Participants must be published by CBC-recognized publisher. Go to www.kindlingwords.org to view speakers and register.

LA JOLLA WRITERS CONFERENCE

P.O. Box 178122, San Diego CA 92177. (858)467-1978. Web site: www.lajollawritersconference.com. **Contact:** Jared Kuritz, Director. Established 2001. Annual. 2008 Conference held November 7-9. Conference duration: 3 days. Maximum attendance limited to 200. The La Jolla Writers Conference welcomes writers of all levels of experience. This three-day event, now in its 8th year, always boasts exciting, interactive workshops, lectures, and presentations by an outstanding and freely accessible faculty comprised of best-selling authors, editors from major publishing houses, and literary agents, all of whom value meeting and working with a diverse group of creative people passionate about writing. The LJWC uniquely covers the art, craft, and business of writing for both fiction and non-fiction.

Costs $285 Early, $355 Regular, $400 Late, includes access to all classes, 3 keynotes, Friday night reception, and Saturday Lunch/Saturday Dinner.

Additional Information: Private Read & Critiques for an additional fee.

LEAGUE OF UTAH WRITERS' ANNUAL ROUNDUP

P.O. Box 18430, Kearns UT 84118. (435) 313-4459. E-mail: jayrich@infowest.com. Web site: www.luwrite.com. **President:** Marilyn Richardson **President Elect**: Natalie Pace. **Membership Chairman:** Dorothy Crofts. Writer workshops geared toward beginner, intermediate or advanced. Annual conference. Roundup usually held in Ogden Utah, September 12-13, 2008. Registration limited to 300. Cost is $99 for members/$129 for nonmembers registering before August 19; $120 for members; $150 non-members after August 19. Cost includes 3 meals, all workshops, general sessions, a syllabus, handouts and conference packet. Contact Natalie Pace - natpace@yaho o.com with questions or (435)674-9792 or above e-mail address. Send registration to Dorothy Crofts, Member-ship Chairman, P.O. Box 18430, Kearns, UT 84118. Check Web site for updates and specifics.

MANHATTANVILLE SUMMER WRITERS' WEEK

2900 Purchase Street, Purchase NY 10577-2103. (914)694-3425. Fax: (914)694-3488. E-mail: dowdr@mville.e du. Web site: www.manhattanville.edu. **Dean, School of Graduate & Professional Studies:** Ruth Dowd. Writer workshops geared toward writers and aspiring writers. **Open to students.** Writers' week offers a special work-shop for writers interested in children's/young adult writing. We have featured such workshop leaders as: Patricia Gauch, Richard Peck, Elizabeth Winthrop and Janet Lisle. In 2008, Patricia Gauch will conduct a workshop entitled ''Writing for Middle Grade & Young Adults.'' Annual workshop held in June 23-27. Length of each session: one week. Cost of workshop: $725 (non-credit); includes a full week of writing activities, 5-day workshop on children's literature; lectures; readings; sessions with editors and agents; keynote speaker, Nan Talese; etc. Workshop may be taken for 2 graduate credits. Write or e-mail for more information.

THE MANUSCRIPT WORKSHOP IN VERMONT

P.O. Box 529, Londonderry VT 05148. (802)824-3968 or (212)877-4457. E-mail: aplbrk@earthlink.net. Web site: www.themanuscriptworkshop.com. **Director:** Barbara Seuling. Writer workshop for all levels. Annual workshop estab. 1992. Generally held mid to late July and August and sometimes early September. Intensive workshop spans 5 days, from dinner on Monday evening to lunch on Friday, and is primarily for writers of children's books, but open to illustrators who write. The time is divided among instructive hands-on sessions in the mornings, writing time in the afternoons, and critiquing in the evenings. A guest speaker from the world of children's books appears at each workshop. Registration is limited to 8; smaller workshops are considered for specialized workshops. Cost of workshop: $845 per person; includes a shared room and all meals. Private room available for additional cost. Inquire about smaller, specialized workshops in novel writing and picture books.

◪ MARITIME WRITERS' WORKSHOP

UNB College of Extended Learning, P.O. Box 4400, Fredericton NB E3B 5A3 Canada. E-mail: extend@unb.ca. Web site: unb.ca/extend/writers/ **Coordinator:** Andrew Titus. Week-long workshop on writing for children, general approach, dealing with submitted material, geared to all levels and held in July. Annual workshop. 3 hours/day. Group workshop plus individual conferences, public readings, etc. Registration limited to 10/class. Cost of workshop: $395 tuition; meals and accommodations extra. Room and board on campus is approximately $320 for meals and a single room for the week. 10-20 ms pages due before conference (deadline announced). Limited scholarships available.

MAUI WRITERS CONFERENCE

P.O. Box 1118, Kihei HI 96753. (808)879-0061. Fax: (808)879-6233. E-mail: writers@mauiwriters.com.net. Web site: www.mauiwriters.com. **Director:** Shannon Tullius. Writer workshops geared toward beginner, intermediate, advanced. **Open to students.** "We offer a small children's writing section covering picture books, middle grade and young adult. We invite one *New York Times* Bestselling Author and plus agents and editors, who give consultations to attendees for a fee." Workshop held annually over the Labor Day weekend. Cost includes admittance to all conference sessions and classes only—no airfare, food or consultations.

MIDWEST WRITERS WORKSHOP

Department of Journalism, Ball State University, Muncie IN 47306. (765)282-1055. Fax: (765)285-7997. Web site: www.midwestwriters.org. **Director:** Jama Kehoe Bigger. Writer workshops geared toward intermediate level. Topics include most genres. Past workshop presenters include Joyce Carol Oates, Jeffrey Deaver, James Alexander Thom, Bill Brashler and Richard Lederer. Workshop also includes ms evaluation and a writing contest. Annual workshop held in late July. Registration tentatively limited to 125. Most meals included. Offers scholarships. Write for more information.

MISSOURI WRITERS' GUILD ANNUAL STATE CONFERENCE

(816)361-1281. E-mail: conferenceinfo@missouriwritersguild.org. Web site: www.missouriwritersguild.org. **Contact:** Karen Heywood, vice president and conference chairman. Writer and illustrator workshops geared to all levels. **Open to students.** Annual conference held mid April or early May each year. Cost of conference: $125-175.

MONTROSE CHRISTIAN WRITER'S CONFERENCE

5 Locust St., Montrose PA 18801-1112. (570)278-1001. Fax: (570)278-3061. E-mail: mbc@montrosebible.org. Web site: www.montrosebible.org. **Executive Director:** Jim Fahringer. **Secretary-Registrar:** Donna Kosik. **Open to adults and students.** Writer workshops geared toward beginner, intermediate and advanced levels. Annual workshop held in July. Cost of workshop: $150 tuition, 2007 rate. Brochure available in April.

MOONDANCE INTERNATIONAL FILM FESTIVAL

970 Ninth St., Boulder CO 80302. (303)545-0202. E-mail: info@moondancefilmfestival.com (with MIFF or MOONDANCE in the subject line). Web site: www.moondancefilmfestival.com. **Executive Director:** Elizabeth English. Moondance Film Festival Workshop Sessions include screenwriting, playwriting, short stories, filmmaking (feature, documentary, short, animation), TV and video filmmaking, writing for TV (MOW, sitcoms, drama), writing for animation, adaptation to screenplays (novels and short stories), how to get an agent, what agents want to see, and pitch panels. 2008 workshops and film festival held August, 2008 (exact date and location TBA). Cost of workshops, seminars, panels, pitch session: $50 each. Check website for more information and registration forms. The 2008 competition deadline for entries in the first or second week of April. "The Moondance competition includes special categories for writers and filmmakers who create work for the children's market!" Entry forms and guidelines are on the Web site.

MOUNT HERMON CHRISTIAN WRITERS CONFERENCE

Mount Hermon Christian Conference Center, Mount Hermon CA 95041-0413. (831)335-4466. Fax: (831)335-9413. E-mail: rachelw@mhcamps.org. Web site: www.mounthermon.org/writers. **Writers Conferences Director :** David R. Talbott. Writer workshops geared toward all levels. **Open to students over 16 years** with special teen track. Emphasizes religious writing for children via books, articles; Sunday school curriculum; marketing. 70 workshops offered include: Suitable Style for Children; Everything You Need to Know to Write and Market Your Children's Book; Take-Home Papers for Children. Workshops held annually over Palm Sunday weekend: April 3-7, 2009 and March 26-30, 2010. Length of each session: 5-day residential conferences held annually.

Registration limited 45/class, but most are 20-30. Conference center with hotel-style accommodations. Cost of workshop: $600-1100 variable; includes tuition, resource notebook, refreshment breaks, full room and board for 13 meals and 4 nights. Conference information posted annually on Web site by December 1. Write or e-mail for more information or call toll-free to 1-888-MH-CAMPS.

NORTH CAROLINA WRITERS' NETWORK FALL CONFERENCE

P.O. Box 954, Carrboro NC 27510-0954. (919)967.9540. Fax: (919)929.0535. E-mail: mail@ncwriters.org. Web site: www.ncwriters.org. Writing workshops and services geared toward beginning, intermediate and advanced or published levels. **Open to students.** We offer workshops, keynote, presentations and critique sessions in a variety of genres: fiction, poetry, creative nonfiction, children, youth, etc. Past youth and children writing faculty include Louise Hawes, Jackie Ogburn, Clay Carmichael, Carole Boston Weatherford, Susie Wilde, Stephanie Greene, Joy Neaves, and Frances O'Roark Dowell. Annual Conference to be held next at the Marriott Winston-Salem Twin City Quarter. Date: November 16-18 (Most recent was in RTP, November 10-12). Cost of conference usually $250/members, $350/nonmembers, including all workshops, panels, roundtables, social activities and four meals. Extra costs for accommodations, master classes and critique sessions.

OKLAHOMA WRITERS' FEDERATION, INC. ANNUAL CONFERENCE

P.O. Box 1904, Sherman, TX 75091, (903)868-1022. shojai@verizon.net. **2008 President:** Amy D. Shojai (please see Web site for most current info): www.owfi.org. Writer workshops geared toward all levels. **Open to students.** "The 2008 event celebrates the 40th Anniversary Conference, with J.A. Jance as Keynote Speaker, 40 seminars, plus 27 speakers consisting of 7 New York editors and 5 literary agents and many best-selling authors. Topics include avoiding writing scams; genre writing (romances, horror, thrillers, and nonfiction); all about collaboration; submitting plays for publication; developing characters and pacing; self promotion; publishing poetry; and more." Annual conference. Held first weekend in May each year. Writing facilities available: book room, autograph party, free information room, two lunch workshops. Cost of conference: $125 (early bird); $150 after (early bird date); $60 for single days; $20 for lunch workshops; full tuition includes 2-day conference—all events (except lunch workshops) and includes 2 banquets and one 10-minute appointment with an attending editor or agent of your choice (must be reserved in advance). "If writers would like to participate in the annual writing contest, they must become members of OWFI. You don't have to be a member to attend the conference." Write or e-mail for more information.

OUTDOOR WRITERS ASSOCIATION OF AMERICA ANNUAL CONFERENCE

121 Hickory St., Missoula, MT 59801. (406)728-7434. Fax: (406)728-7445. E-mail: owaa@montana.com. **Meeting Planner:** Robin Giner. Writer workshops geared toward all levels. Annual four-day conference. Craft Improvement seminars; newsmaker sessions. Workshop held in June. 2008 conference to be held in Bismarck, ND. Cost of workshop: $380; includes attendance at all workshops and most meals. Attendees must have prior approval from Executive Director before attendance is permitted. Write for more information.

OZARK CREATIVE WRITERS, INC. CONFERENCE

400 E. Chilhowie Ave., Johnson City TN 37601. (423)439-6024. E-mail: ozarkcreativewriters@earthlink.net. Web site: www.ozarkcreativewriters.org. **Program Chair:** Chrissy Willis. **Open to students.** Writer's workshops geared to all levels. "All forms of the creative process dealing with the literary arts. We sometimes include songwriting. We invite best selling authors, editors and agents. We also promote writing by providing competitions in all genres." Always the second full weekend in October at Inn of the Ozarks in Eureka Springs AR, a resort town in the Ozark Mountains. "Approximately 200 attend the conference yearly. Many others enter the creative writing competition." Cost of registration/contest entry fee approximately $80-100. Includes entrance to all sessions, contest entry fees and continental breakfast. This does not include banquet meals or lodging. For more information contact Chrissy Willis.

THE PACIFIC COAST CHILDREN'S WRITERS WORKSHOP, for Middle Grade and Young Adult Novelists

P.O. Box 244, Aptos CA 95001. (831)684-2042. Web site: www.childrenswritersworkshop.com. **Founding Director:** Nancy Sondel. This seventh annual workshop is geared toward intermediate through professional levels; beginners may attend with some limits in participation. **Open to students.** "As with all enrollees, students must demonstrate competence in story-crafting and/or come prepared to learn from highly skilled writers. (Discount for students age 16-24.) Our keynotes, master-class clinics, and hands-on focus sessions explore topics such as 'How to Craft Scenes Integrating Character, Plot and Theme. We focus on less-commonly discussed (but crucial) aspects of these topics. Some of our enrollees have landed contracts as a direct result of our event." Annual seminar; held August 15-17, 2008 and August 21-23 2009. Registration limited to 30. Venue offers free use of the Hilton Hotel copier, printer, and more; sleeping rooms have DSL Internet access. "We have private veranda/conference rooms available day and night.'' Cost of workshop: $299-599, which includes basic program, most meals, up to 3 faculty critiques per enrollee (written and/or in person); additional fee for optional academic/CEU credits conferred by the University of California. Discounts available. ''Our e-application includes essay questions about each writer's manuscript; sample chapters and synopsis must be submitted with the application, by *mid-April* for the most critique options. Content: We focus on literary, character-driven, realistic novels with protagonists ages 11 and older. Our seminar-style, master-class format is 90 percent hands-on—highly interactive, with continuous dialogues between seasoned faculty and savvy, congenial peers. Manuscript clinics are team-taught by our nationally-known agent, editor, and author. Critiques may address enrollees' opening/midbook chapters and breif synopses. Our pre-workshop prep (personalized manuscript worksheets, peer critiques) maximizes learning and networking with the pros. For more information, please reach us via our Web site's contact form.''

PACIFIC NORTHWEST CHILDREN'S BOOK CONFERENCE
Portland State University School of Extended Studies, P.O. Box 751, Portland OR 97207. (503)725-9786 or (800)547-8887, ext. 9786. Fax: (503)725-5595. E-mail: katagiri@pdx.ed. Web site: www.ceed.pdx.edu/children. Focus on the craft of writing and illustrating for children while working with an outstanding faculty of acclaimed editors, authors, and illustrators. Daily afternoon faculty-led writing and illustration workshops. Acquire specific information on how to become a professional in the field of children's literature. Annual workshop for all levels. Conference held July 14-18 on the campus of Reed College, Portland, Oregon. Cost depends on options selected, including: noncredit or 3 graduate credits; individual ms/portfolio reviews and room and board at Reed campus. E-mail for more information. Linda Zuckerman, editor, coordinates conference and brings together knowledgeable and engaging presenters every year.

PACIFIC NORTHWEST WRITER ASSN. SUMMER WRITER'S CONFERENCE
PMB 2717, 1420 NW Gilman Blvd, Suite 2, Issaquah, WA 98027. (425) 673-BOOK (2665). E-mail: staff@pnwa.org. Web site: www.pnwa.org. Writer conference geared toward beginner, intermediate, advanced and professional levels. Meet agents and editors. Learn craft from renowned authors. Uncover new marketing secrets. PNWA's 53rd Anniversary Conference was held July 17-20, 2008 at the Seattle Airport Hilton, Seattle, WA 98188. Annual conference held every July.

PERSPECTIVES IN CHILDREN'S LITERATURE CONFERENCE
School of Education, 226 Furcolo Hall, Amherst MA 01003-3035. (413)545-4190 or (413)545-1116. Fax: (413)545-2879. E-mail: childlit@educ.umass.edu. Web site: www.umass.edu/childlit. **Conference Coordinator:** Katelyn McLaughlin. Writer and illustrator workshops geared to all levels. Presenters talk about what inspires them, how they bring their stories to life and what their visions are for the future. Conference held in March. For more information contact coordinator by phone, fax or e-mail.''

PIMA WRITERS' WORKSHOP
Pima College, 2202 W. Anklam Rd., Tucson AZ 85709-0170. (520)206-6084. Fax: (520)206-6020. E-mail: mfiles @pima.edu. **Director:** Meg Files. Writer conference geared toward beginner, intermediate and advanced levels. **Open to students.** The conference features presentations and writing exercises on writing and publishing stories for children and young adults, among other genres. Annual conference. Workshop held in May. Cost of workshop: $80; includes tuition, manuscript consultation. Write for more information.

PUBLISHINGGAME.COM WORKSHOP
Newton MA 02459. (617)630-0945. E-mail: Alyza@publishinggame.com. Web site: www.publishinggame.com. **Coordinator:** Alyza Harris. Fern Reiss, author of the popular ''Publishing Game'' book series and CEO of Expertizing.com, will teach this one-day workshop. Writer workshops geared toward beginner, intermediate and advanced levels. **Open to students.** Sessions will include: Find A Literary Agent, Self-Publish Your Children's Book, Book Promotion For Children's Books. September—New York; October—Boston; November—New York; December—Philadelphia; January—Washington, DC; February—New York; March—New York; April—New York; May—Boston; June—Los Angeles, CA; July—San Francisco; August—Boston. Registration limited to 18. Fills quickly! Cost of workshop: $195; included information-packed course binder and light refreshments. E-mail for more information. Workshop now available as a 5-CD audio workshop. For information on getting more media attention for your children's book, see Fern Reiss' complementary Expertizing workshop atwww.expertizingc.om.

ROBERT QUACKENBUSH'S CHILDREN'S BOOK WRITING AND ILLUSTRATING WORKSHOP
Studio address: 223 East 79th St., New York, NY 10075. Mailing address: 460 East 79th St., New York, NY 10075. (212)744-3822. Fax: (212)861-2761. E-mail: Rqstudios@aol.com. Web site: www.rquackenbush.com.

Contact: Robert Quackenbush. A four-day extensive workshop on writing and illustrating books for young readers held annually the second week in July at author/artist Robert Quackenbush's Manhattan studio for beginning and advance writers and illustrators. The focus of this workshop is on creating manuscripts and/or illustrated book dummies from start to finish for picture books and beginning reader chapter books ready to submit to publishers. Also covered is writing fiction and nonfiction for middle grades and young adults, if that is the attendee's interest. In addition, attention is given to review of illustrator's portfolios and new trends in illustration, including animation for films, are explored. During the four days, the workshop meets from 9 a.m-4 p.m. including one hour for lunch. Registration is limited to 10. Some writing and/or art supplies are available at the studio and there is an art store nearby, if needed. There are also electrical outlets for attendee's laptop computers. Cost of workshop is $750. A $100 non-refundable deposit is required tro enroll; balace is due three weeks prior the workshop.Attendees are responsible for arranging for their own hotel and meals. On request, suggestions are given for economical places to stay and eat. Recommended by Foder's *Great American Learning Vacations*, which says, "This unique workshop, held annually since 1982, provides the opportunity to work with Robert Quackenbush, a prolific author and illustrator of children's books with more than 200 fiction and nonfiction books for young readers to his credit, including mysteries, biographies and songbooks. The workshop attracts both professional and beginning writers and artists of different ages from all over the world." Brochure available. Also inquire about fall, winter and spring workshops that meet once a week for ten weeks each that are offered to artists and writers in the New York area.

ℕ ⚡ SAGE HILL WRITING EXPERIENCE, Writing Children's & Young Adult Fiction Workshop
Box 1731, Saskatoon SK S7K 3S1 Canada. Phone/fax: (306) 244-0255. E-mail: sage.hill@sasktel.net. Web site: www.sagehillwriting.ca. **Executive Director:** Steven Ross Smith. Writer conference geared toward intermediate level. This program occurs every 2 or 3 years, but the Sage Hill Conference is annual. Conference held in July. Registration limited to 6 participants for this program, and to 37 for full program. Cost of conference approximately $ 1095; includes instruction, meals, accommodation. Require ms samples prior to registration. Write or visit the Web site for more information and workshop dates.

SAN DIEGO STATE UNIVERSITY WRITERS' CONFERENCE
The College of Extended Studies, San Diego CA 92182-1920. (619)594-2517. Fax: (619)594-8566. E-mail: extended.std@sdsu.edu. Web site: www.ces.sdsu.edu/writers **Conference Facilitator:**Rose Brown. Writer workshops geared toward beginner, intermediate and advanced levels. Emphasizes nonfiction, fiction, screenwriting, advanced novel writing; includes sessions specific to writing and illustrating for children. Workshops offered by children's editors, agents and writers. Annual workshops. Workshops held January 25-27, 2008. Registration limited. Cost of workshops: approximately $300. Call for more information or visit Web site.

SAN FRANCISCO WRITERS CONFERENCE
1029 Jones St., San Francisco CA 94l09 (415)673-0939. Web site: www.sfwriters.org. **Co-founders:** Michael Larsen & Elizabeth Pomada. Writer workshops and panels geared toward beginner, intermediate, advanced and professional levels on the business of publishing, craft, and marketing. Also features a writing contest and attendee/presenter anthology. Annual conference held President's Day Weekend in mid-February. Registration limited to 300. Cost of conference: $495—$695 depending on time of registration; includes party, 2 breakfasts, and 3 lunches. Visit Web site for more information. The preliminary program for the following year's conference will be on the Web site by December.

⚡ SASKATCHEWAN FESTIVAL OF WORDS AND WORKSHOPS
217 Main Street, Moose Jaw SK S6H 0W1 Canada. (306)691-0557. Fax: (306)693-2994. E-mail: word.festival@sasktel.net. Web site: www.festivalofwords.com. **Artistic Coordinator:** Donna Lee Howes. Writer workshops geared toward beginner and intermediate levels. **Open to students.** Readings that include a wide spectrum of genres—fiction, creative non-fiction, poetry, songwriting, screenwriting, playwriting, children's writing, panels, interviews and performances. Annual festival. Workshop held third weekend in July. Cost of workshop: $8/session—$125 for full festival pass. Write, e-mail, or visit Web site for more information.

SOCIETY OF SOUTHWESTERN AUTHORS' WRANGLING WITH WRITING
P.O. Box 30355, Tucson AZ 85751-0355. (520)546-9382. Fax: (520)296-0409. E-mail: wporter202@aol.com. Web site: www.ssa-az.org. **Conference Director:** Penny Porter. 36 Writer workshops geared toward all genres. "Limited scholarships available." Sessions include Writing and Publishing the Young Adult Novel, What Agents Want to See in a Children's Book, Writing Books for Young Children, Writing the Children's Story. One-on-one interviews with agents/editors scheduled prior to conference at an additional cost of $20 for a 15-minute meeting. "We always have several children's book editors and agents interested in meeting with children's writers." Annual workshop held September 27-28, 2008. Registration limited to 400. Hotel rooms have dataports

for internet access. Tentative cost: $350 nonmembers, $275 for SSA members; includes 5 meals and 3 banquets and 2 full continental breakfasts, all workshop sessions—individual appointments with keynoters, author/teachers. Hotel accommodations are not included. Write for more information. SSA has put on this conference for over 36 years now. "It's hands-on, it's friendly, and every year writers sell their manuscripts."

SOUTH COAST WRITERS CONFERENCE
P.O. Box 590, 29392 Ellensburg Ave., Gold Beach OR 97444. (541)247-2741. E-mail: scwc@socc.edu. **Coordinator:** Janet Pretti. Writer workshops geared toward beginner, intermediate levels. **Open to students.** Includes fiction, nonfiction, nuts and bolts, poetry, feature writing, children's writing, publishing. Annual workshop. Workshop held Friday and Saturday of President's day weekend in February. Registration limited to 25-30 students/workshop. Cost of workshop: $55 before January 31, $65 after; includes Friday night author's reading and book signing, Saturday conference, choice of 4 workshop sessions, Saturday evening writers' circle (networking and critique). Write or email for more information. "We also have four six-hour workshops Friday for more intensive writing exercises. The cost is an additional $40."

SOUTHEASTERN WRITERS ASSOCIATION—ANNUAL WRITERS WORKSHOP
161 Woodstone, Athens GA 30605. E-mail: purple@southeasternwriters.com. Web site: www.southeasternwriters.com. CFO: Tim Hudson. **Open to all writers.** Contests with cash prizes. Instruction offered for novel and short fiction, nonfiction, children's books, humor, inspirational writing, and poetry. Manuscript deadline April 1st, includes evaluation conference with instructor(s). Agent and editors in residence. Annual 4-day workshop held in June. Cost of workshop: $359 before April 15; $399 after April 15; $125 daily tuition. Accommodations: Offers overnight accommodations on workshop site. Visit Web site for more information and cost of overnight accommodations. E-mail or send SASE for brochure.

SOUTHWEST WRITERS CONFERENCES
3721 Morris NE, Suite A, Albuquerque NM 87111. (505)265-9485. Fax: (505)265-9483. E-mail: swwriters@juno.com. Web site: www.southwestwriters.org. **Open to adults and students.** Writer workshops geared toward all genres at all levels of writing. Various aspects of writing covered, including children's. Mini-conference, monthly workshops, and writing classes. Examples from mini-conferences: Suzy Capozzi and Delacorte Press Editor Claudia Gable; Pitch, Publish and Promote conference with Literary Agent Katherine Sands, Mundania Press Publisher Bob Sanders and Literary Agent Jerry D. Simmons. Cracking the Code: Secrets of Writing and Selling Compelling Nonfiction conference featured literary agents Michael Larsen, Elizabeth Pomoda and Jeff Herman; Lee Gutkind, publisher; David Fryxell, editor; Lucinda Schroeder, criminologist/writer; and a panel of New Mexico publishers. Making a Good Script Great: All-day seminar with Dr. Linda Seger and other speakers. Dimension in Fiction and Non-fiction: All-day workshop with Sean Murphy. Prices vary, but usually $79-$179. Also offers annual and monthly contests, two monthly programs, writing classes, monthly workshop, monthly newsletter, critique service, Web site linking, e-mail addresses and various discount perks. See Web site for information.

SPLIT ROCK ARTS PROGRAM
University of Minnesota, Twin Cities Campus, 360 Coffey Hall, 1420 Eckles Ave., St. Paul MN 55108-6084. (612)625-8100. Fax: (612)624-6210. E-mail: splitrockarts@umn.edu. Web site: www.cce.umn.edu/splitrockarts. Workshop topics, including poetry, fiction, nonfiction, young-adult literature, and picture books, among others, are taught by renowned writers and illustrators.Past falculty include Marcia Brown, Marion DAne BAur, Jan Spivey Gilchris, David Haynesm Gerald McDermott, Daniel Powers, Ilae Plume, Lauren Stringerm Jane Resh Thomas, and others. Weeklong and three day workshops run June throught Aughst. Registration limited to 16/workshop. Graduate/undergraduate credit, scholarships and on-campus accommodations available. Cost of workshop: $365-550 and up. Printed and online catalogs available in late February.

STEAMBOAT SPRINGS WRITERS CONFERENCE
P.O. Box 774284, Steamboat Springs CO 80477. (970)879-8079. E-mail: sswriters@cs.com. Web site: www.steamboatwriters.com. **Conference Director:** Harriet Freiberger. Writers' workshops geared toward intermediate levels. **Open to students.** Some years offer topics specific to children's writing. Annual conference since 1982. Workshops will be held in July. Registration limited to 35. Cost of workshop: $45; includes 4 seminars and luncheon. Write, e-mail or see website for more information.

⚑ SURREY INTERNATIONAL WRITER'S CONFERENCE
Guildford Continuing Education, 10707 146th St., Surrey BC U3R IT5 Canada. (604)589-2221. Fax: (604)588-9286. E-mail: contest@siwc.ca. Web site: www.siwc.ca. **Coordinator:** kc dyer. Writer and illustrator workshops geared toward beginners, intermediate and advanced levels. Topics include marketing, children's agents and

editors. Annual Conference. Conference held in October. Cost of conference includes all events for 3 days and most meals. Check our website for more information.

⊕ SYDNEY CHILDREN'S WRITERS AND ILLUSTRATORS NETWORK

The Hughenden Boutique Hotel, Woollahra NSW 2025 Australia. (61)(2)363-4863. Fax: (61)(2) 93620398. E-mail: admin@hughendenhotel.com.au. Web site: www.hughendenhotel.com.au. **Contact:** Susanne Gervay. Writer and illustrator network geared toward professionals. Topics emphasized include networking, information and expertise about Australian children's publishing industry. Network held the first Wednesday of every month, except for January, commencing at 10:30 a.m. Registration limited to 30. Writing facilities available: internet and conference facilities. No Cost. As a prerequisite must be published in a commercial or have a book contract. E-mail for more information. "This is a professional meeting which aims at an interchange of ideas and information between professional children's authors and illustrators. Editors and other invited guests speak from time to time."

UMKC/WRITERS PLACE WRITERS WORKSHOPS

5300 Rockhill Rd., Kansas City MO 64110-2450. (816)235-2736. Fax: (816)235-5279. E-mail: seatons@umkc.edu. **Contact:** Kathi Wittfeld. New Letters Writer's Conference and Mark Twain Writer's Workshop geared toward intermediate, advanced and professional levels. Workshops open to students and community. Annual workshops. Workshops held in Summer. Cost of workshop varies. Write for more information.

⊠ VANCOUVER INTERNATIONAL WRITERS FESTIVAL

1398 Cartwright St., Vancouver BC V6H 3R8 Canada. (604)681-6330. Fax: (604)681-8400. E-mail: viwf@writersfest.bc.ca. Web site: www.writersfest.bc.ca. **Artistic Director:** Hal Wake. Annual literary festival. The Vancouver International Writers Festival strives to encourage an appreciation of literature and to promote literacy by providing a forum where writers and readers can interact. The VIWF produces of special events and an annual Festival that feature writers from around the world. The Festival attracts over 12,000 readers of all ages to 60+ events including spreading the word events for grades K-12. Held in late October on Granville Island, laocated in the heart of Vancouver. All writers who participate are invited by the A.D. The events are open to anyone who wishes to purchase tickets. Cost of events ranges from $10-22.

VIRGINIA FESTIVAL OF THE BOOK

145 Ednam Dr., Charlottesville VA 22903. (434)924-6890. Fax: (434)296-4714. E-mail: vabook@virginia.edu. Web site: www.vabook.org. **Program Director:** Nancy Damon. **Open to Students.** Readings, panel discussions, presentations and workshops by author, and book-related professionals for children and adults. Most programs are free and open to the public. Held March 26-30, 2008. See Web site for more information. Applications for 2009 Festival will be accepted beginning in May 2008.

WESLEYAN WRITERS CONFERENCE

Wesleyan University, Middletown CT 06459. (860)685-3604. Fax: (860)685-2441. E-mail: agreene@wesleyan.edu. Web site: www.wesleyan.edu/writers. **Director:** Anne Greene. Seminars, workshops, readings, ms advice; geared toward all levels. "This conference is useful for writers interested in how to structure a story, novel, poem or nonfiction piece, or mixed genre. Although we don't always offer classes in writing for children, the advice about structuring a piece is useful for writers of any sort, no matter who their audience is." One of the nation's best-selling children's authors was a student here. Classes in the novel, short story, fiction techniques, poetry, journalism, literary nonfiction and mixed media work. Guest speakers, readings, lectures, workshops, and panels offer discussion of fiction, poetry, nonfiction, memoir, reviewing, editing and publishing. Individual ms consultations available. Conference held annually the third week in June. Length of each session: 5 days. Usually, there are 100 participants at the Conference. Classrooms, meals, lodging, library and computer word processing facilities available on campus. Cost of conference 2007: tuition—$830, room—$175, meals- $240. "Anyone interested in attending may register; people who want financial aid must submit their work and be selected by scholarship judges." Call for a brochure or check Web site.

WHIDBEY ISLAND WRITERS' CONFERENCE

P.O. Box 1289, Langley WA 98260. (360)331-6714. E-mail: writers@whidbey.com. Web site: www.writeonwhidbey.org. **Writers Contact:** Pam Owen, conference director. Three days focused on the tools you need to become a great writer. Learn from a variety of award-winning children's book authors and very experienced literary agents. Variety of preconference workshops and conference topics. Conference held February 27-March 1, 2009. Registration limited to 290. Cost: $395; early bird and member discounts available. Registration includes workshops, fireside chats, book-signing reception, various activities, and daily luncheons. The conference offers consultation appointments with editors and agents. Preconference workshops available on February 28.

Registrants may reduce the cost of their conference by volunteering. See the Web site for more information. "The uniquely personal and friendly weekend is designed to be highly interactive."

WILLAMETTE WRITERS ANNUAL WRITERS CONFERENCE

9045 SW Barbur Blvd., Suite 5A, Portland OR 97219. (503)452-1592. Fax: (503)452-0372. E-mail: wilwrite@willa mettewriters.com. Web site: www.willamettewriters.com. **Office Manager:** Bill Johnson. Writer workshops geared toward all levels. Emphasizes all areas of writing, including children's and young adult. Opportunities to meet one-on-one with leading literary agents and editors. Workshops held in August. Cost of conference: $230-$430; includes membership.

TENNESSEE WILLIAMS/NEW ORLEANS LITERARY FESTIVAL

938 Lafayette St., Suite 514, New Orleans LA 70113. (504)581-1144. Fax: (504)523-3680. E-mail: info@tennessee williams.net. Web site: www.tennesseewilliams.net. **Executive Director:** Paul J. Willis. Writer workshops geared toward beginner, intermediate, advanced, and professional levels. **Open to students.** Annual workshop. Workshop held around the third week in March (March 26-30, 2008). Master classes are limited in size to 100— all other panels offered have no cap. Cost of workshop: prices range from $15-35. Visit Web site for more information. "We are a literary festival and may occasionally offer panels/classes on children's writing and/ or illustration, but this is not done every year."

N WINTER POETRY & PROSE GETAWAY IN CAPE MAY

18 N. Richards Ave., Ventnor NJ 08406. (609)823-5076. E-mail: info@wintergetaway.com. Web site: www.wint ergetaway.com. **Director:** Peter E. Murphy. Writer workshops geared toward all levels. **Open to students** (18 years and over). "Writing for Children: You will learn to develop character, plot, setting, points of view. There will also be a discussion of genres in juvenile literature, voice, detail and revision. Choose 1 of 2 sections— picture books and younger readers or middle graders and teens." Annual workshop held in January. Registration limited to 8 writers in each workshop. Writing/art facilities available in hotel meeting and ballrooms. Cost of workshop: $345, includes lunches and evening receptions. Single and shared rooms, which include breakfast, are available for an additional cost. Prices will be posted on the Web site in September, 2006. "The Winter Poetry & Prose Getaway, held in Cape May NJ, is well known for its challenging and supportive atmosphere which encourages imaginative risk taking and promotes freedom and transformation in each participant's creative work."

WRITE ON THE SOUND WRITERS CONFERENCE

700 Main St., Edmonds WA 98020-3032. (425)771-0228. Fax: (425)771-0253. E-mail: wots@ci.edmonds.wa.us. Web site: www.ci.edmonds.wa.us/ArtsCommission/wots.stem. **Conference Coordinator:** Kris Gillespie. Writer workshops geared toward beginner, intermediate, advanced and professional levels with some sessions on writing for children. Annual conference held in Edmonds, on Puget Sound, on the first weekend in October with 2.5 full days of workshops. Registration limited to 200. Cost of conference: approximately $108 for early registration, $130 for late registration; includes two days of workshops plus one ticket to keynote lecture. Brochures are mailed in August. Attendees must pre-register. Write, e-mail or call for brochure. Writing contest and critiques for conference participants.

WRITE! CANADA

698A Highpoint Ave, Waterloo, ON N2V 1G9 Canada. (519)886-4196. Fax: (905)471-6912. E-mail: info@thewor dguild.com. Web site: www.thewordguild.com. Estab. 1984. Annual conference for writers who are Christian. Hosted by The Word Guild, an association of Canadian writers and editors who are Christian. The Word Guild seeks to connect, develop, and promote its members. Keynote speaker, continuing classes, workshops, panels, editor appointments, reading times, critiques, and more. For all levels of writers from beginner to professional. Held at a retreat center in Guelph ON in mid-June.

WRITE-BY-THE-LAKE WRITER'S WORKSHOP & RETREAT

610 Langdon St., Room 621, Madison WI 53703. (608)262-3447. E-mail: cdesmet@dcs.wisc.edu. Web site: www.dcs.wisc.edu/lsa/writing **Coordinator:** Christine DeSmet. Writer workshops geared toward beginner , intermediate , and andvanced levels. **Open to students** (1-3 graduate credits available in English). "One week-long session is devoted to writitng for children." Annual workshop. Workshop held the third week of June. Registration limited to 15. Writing facilities available: computer labs. Cost of workshop: $325 before May 2 1; $355 after May 2 1. Cost includes instruction, reception, and continental breakfast each day. E-mail for more information. "Brochure goes online every January for the following June."

WRITE-TO-PUBLISH CONFERENCE

9118 W. Elmwood Dr., #1G, Niles IL 60714-5820. (847)296-3964. Fax: (847)296-0754. E-mail: lin@writetopublish.com. Web site: www.writetopublish.com. **Director:** Lin Johnson. Writer workshops geared toward all levels. **Open to students.** Conference is focused for the Christian market and includes classes on writing for children. Annual conference held in June. Cost of conference approximately: $425; includes conference and banquet. For information e-mail brochure@writetopublish.com. Conference takes place at Wheaton College in the Chicago area.

WRITERS RETREAT WORKSHOP

E-mail: wrw04@netscape.net (brochure and other information). Web site: www.writersretreatworkshop.com. **Director:** Jason Sitzes. Intensive workshops geared toward beginner, intermediate and advanced levels. Workshops are appropriate for writers of full length novels for children/YA. Also, for writers of all novels or narrative nonfiction. Annual workshop held in Marydale Retreat Center, Erlanger KY in late May early June. Registration limited to 32: beginners and advanced. Writing facilities available: private rooms with desks. Cost includes tuition, food and lodging for nine nights, daily classes, writing space, time and assignments, consultation and instruction. One annual scholarship available: February deadline. Requirements: short synopsis required to determine appropriateness of novel for our nuts and bolts approach to getting the work in shape for publication. Write for more information. For complete updated details, visit www.writersretreatworkshop.com.

WRITERS' LEAGUE OF TEXAS WORKSHOP SERIES

611 S. Congress Ave., Suite 130, Austin TX 78704. (512)499-8914. Fax: (512)499-0441. E-mail: wlt@writersleague.org. Web site: www.writersleague.org. **Contact:** Kristy Bordine. Writer workshops and conferences geared toward adults. Annual agents and editors conferences. Classes are held during weekend and retreats/workshops are held throughout the year. Annual Teddy Children's Book Award of $1,000 presented each fall to book published the previous year.

⚫ THE WRITERS' RETREAT

15 Canusa St., Stanstead QC J0B 3E5 Canada. (819)876-2065. E-mail: info@writersretreat.com. Web site: www.writersretreat.com. **Contact:** Micheline Cote. Residency and workshops for beginners to advanced writers. Residential retreats located in Canada, Costa Rica, Mexico and the United States are open year-round. The Writers' Retreat caters to writers of all genres and offer on-site support such as mentoring, workshops, editing, and lodging. Residency rates vary between $575 and $1,200 per week depending on the location; workshop tuition varies from $65-$1,500 depending on the format. There's no application process to stay at the writers retreat, first reserved basis.

WRITING WORKSHOP AT CASTLE HILL

1 Depot Road, P.O. Box 756, Truro MA 02666-0756. (508)349-7511. Fax: (508)349-7513. E-mail: castlehill@gis.net. Web site: www.castlehill.org. **Director:** Cherie Mittenthal. Poetry, Fiction, Memoir workshops geared toward intermediate and advanced levels. **Open to students.** Workshops by Espada, Doty, Hoagland, Feldman, Unger, Lerman, Laux, Seligson, Loomis, Campion, Millar, Lisicky, Bernays, Kaplan and more! Workshop are week-long and begin June 23 through August 28th. Registration limited to 10-12. Writing/art facilities available: classroom space. Cost of workshop: $325; includes week long workshop and one-on-one conference with teacher. Write for more information.

Contests, Awards & Grants

P ublication is not the only way to get your work recognized. Contests and awards can also be great ways to gain recognition in the industry. Grants, offered by organizations like SCBWI, offer monetary recognition to writers, giving them more financial freedom as they work on projects.

When considering contests or applying for grants, be sure to study guidelines and requirements. Regard entry deadlines as gospel and follow the rules to the letter.

Note that some contests require nominations. For published authors and illustrators, competitions provide an excellent way to promote your work. Your publisher may not be aware of local competitions such as state-sponsored awards—if your book is eligible, have the appropriate person at your publishing company nominate or enter your work for consideration.

To select potential contests and grants, read through the listings that interest you, then send for more information about the types of written or illustrated material considered and other important details. A number of contests offer information through Web sites given in their listings.

If you are interested in knowing who has received certain awards in the past, check your local library or bookstores or consult *Children's Books: Awards & Honors*, compiled and edited by the Children's Book Council (www.cbcbooks.org). Many bookstores have special sections for books that are Caldecott and Newbery Medal winners. Visit the American Library Association Web site, www.ala.org, for information on the Caldecott, Newbery, Coretta Scott King and Printz Awards. Visit www.hbook.com for information on The Boston Globe-Horn Book Award. Visit www.scbwi.org/awards.htm for information on The Golden Kite Award.

For a contest success story see the Insider Report with **Jay Asher**, author and award and grant recipient, on page 348.

Information on contests listed in the previous edition but not included in this edition of *Children's Writer's & Illustrator's Market* may be found in the General Index.

🌐 ACADEMY OF CHILDREN'S WRITERS' WRITING FOR CHILDREN COMPETITION

Academy of Children's Writers, P.O. Box 95, Huntington Cambridgeshire PE28 5RL England. 01487 832752. Fax: 01487 832752. E-mail: enquiries@childrens-writers.co.uk **Contact:** Roger Dewar, contest director. Annual contest for the best unpublished short story writer for children. **Deadline:** March 31. Visit Web site for guidelines: www.chidrens-writers.co.uk. **Charges $10 (US) Bill;** Prize: 1st Prize: $4,000; 2nd Prize: $600; 3rd Prize: $400. Judged by a panel appointed by the Academy of Children's Writers. Open to any writer.

JANE ADDAMS CHILDREN'S BOOK AWARDS

Jane Addams Peace Association, Inc./Women's International League for Peace and Freedom, 777 United Nations Plaza 6th floor. New York NY 10017. (212)682-8830. Fax: (212)286-8211. E-mail: japa@igc.org. Web site: www.janeaddamspeace.org. **Contact:** Linda Belle. "Two copies of published books the previous year only." Annual award. Estab. 1953. Previously published submissions only. Submissions made by author, author's agent, person, group or publisher, submitted by the publisher. Must be published January 1-December 31 of preceding year. Deadline for entries: December 31. Check Web site for all submission information. Cash awards and certificate, $1,000 to winners (winning book) and $500 each to Honor Book winners (split between author and illustrator, if necessary). Judging by national committee from various N.S. regions (all are members of W.I.L.P.F.). The award ceremony is held in New York the third Friday October annually.

AIM MAGAZINE SHORT STORY CONTEST

P. O. Box 390, Milton, WA 98354-0390. (773)874-6184. **Contest Director:** Ruth Apilado, associate editor. Annual contest. **Open to students.** Estab. 1983. Purpose of contest: "We solicit stories with lasting social significance proving that people from different racial/ethnic backgrounds are more alike than they are different." Unpublished submissions only. Deadline for entries: August 15. SASE for contest rules and entry forms. SASE for return of work. No entry fee. Awards $100. Judging by editors. Contest open to everyone. Winning entry published in fall issue of *AIM*. Subscription rate: $20/year. Single copy: $5.

🍁 ALCUIN CITATION AWARD

The Alcuin Society, P.O. Box 3216, Vancouver BC V6B 3X8 Canada. (604)732-5403. E-mail: awards@alcuinsociety.com. Web site: www.alcuinsociety.com /awards. Annual award. Estab. 1981. Purpose of contest: Alcuin Citations are awarded annually for excellence in Canadian book design. Previously published submissions from the year prior to the Award's Call for Entries (i.e., 2005 awards went to books published in 2004). Submissions made by the publisher, author or designer. Deadline for entries: mid-March. Entry fee is $25/book for Society members; $30/book for non-members; include cheque and entry form with book; downloadable entry form available at web site. Awards certificate. Winning books are exhibited nationally, and internationally at the Frankfurt and Leipzig Book Fairs, and are Canada's entries in the international competition in Leipzig, "Book Design from all over the World" in the following Spring. Judging by professionals and those experienced in the field of book design. Requirements for entrants: Winners are selected from books designed and published in Canada. Awards are presented annually at an appropriate ceremonies held in early June each year.

AMERICA & ME ESSAY CONTEST

Farm Bureau Insurance, P.O. Box 30400, 7373 W. Saginaw, Lansing MI 48909-7900. (517)323-7000. Fax: (517)323-6615. E-mail: lfedewa@fbinsmi.com. Web site: www.farmbureauinsurance-mi.co. **Contest Coordinator:** Lisa Fedewa. Annual contest. **Open to students only.** Estab. 1968. Purpose of the contest: to give Michigan 8th graders the opportunity to express their thoughts/feelings on America and their roles in America. Unpublished submissions only. Deadline for entries: mid-November. SASE for contest rules and entry forms. "We have a school mailing list. Any school located in Michigan is eligible to participate." Entries not returned. No entry fee. Awards savings bonds and plaques for state top ten ($500-1,000), certificates and plaques for top 3 winners from each school. Each school may submit up to 10 essays for judging. Judging by home office employee volunteers. Requirements for entrants: "Participants must work through their schools or our agents' sponsoring schools. No individual submissions will be accepted. Top ten essays and excerpts from other essays are published in booklet form following the contest. State capitol/schools receive copies."

AMERICAN ASSOCIATION OF UNIVERSITY WOMEN, NORTH CAROLINA DIVISION, AWARD IN JUVENILE LITERATURE

North Carolina Literary and Historical Association, 4610 Mail Service Center, Raleigh NC 27699-4610. (919)807-7290. Fax: (919)733-8807. E-mail: michael.hill@ncmail.net. **Award Coordinator:** Mr. Michael Hill. Annual award. Purpose of award: to recognize the year's best work of juvenile literature by a North Carolina resident. Book must be published during the year ending June 30. Submissions made by author, author's agent or publisher. Deadline for entries: July 15. SASE for contest rules. Awards a cup to the winner and winner's name inscribed on a plaque displayed within the North Carolina Office of Archives and History. Judging by Board of Award selected by sponsoring organization. Requirements for entrants: Author must have maintained either legal residence or actual physical residence, or a combination of both, in the state of North Carolina for three years immediately preceding the close of the contest period. Only published work (books) eligible.

AMERICAS AWARD

CLASP Committee on Teaching and Outreach, % Center for Latin American and Caribbean Studies, P.O. Box 413, Milwaukee WI 53201. (414)229-5986. Fax: (414)229-2879. E-mail: jkline@uwm.edu. Web site: www.uwm.edu/Dept/CLACS/outreach/americas.html. **Coordinator:** Julie Kline. Annual award. Estab. 1993. Purpose of contest: Up to two awards are given each spring in recognition of U.S. published works (from the previous year) of fiction, poetry, folklore or selected nonfiction (from picture books to works for young adults) in English or Spanish which authentically and engagingly relate to Latin America, the Caribbean, or to Latinos in the United States. By combining both and linking the "Americas," the intent is to reach beyond geographic borders, as well as multicultural-international boundaries, focusing instead upon cultural heritages within the hemisphere. Previously published submissions only. Submissions open to anyone with an interest in the theme of the award. Deadline for entries: January 15. Visit Web site or send SASE for contest rules and any committee changes. Awards $500 cash prize, plaque and a formal presentation at the Library of Congress, Washington DC. Judging by a review committee consisting of individuals in teaching, library work, outreach and children's literature specialists.

⊕ HANS CHRISTIAN ANDERSEN AWARD

IBBY International Board on Books for Young People, Nonnenweg 12, Postfach CH-4003 Basel Switzerland. (004161)272 29 17. Fax: (004161)272 27 57. E-mail: ibby@ibby.org. Web site: www.ibby.org. **Director:** Liz Page; Director Member Services, Communications and New Projects: Liz Page. Award offered every two years. Purpose of award: A Hans Christian Andersen Medal shall be awarded every two years by the International Board on Books for Young People (IBBY) to an author and to an illustrator, living at the time of the nomination, who by the outstanding value of their work are judged to have made a lasting contribution to literature for children and young people. The complete works of the author and of the illustrator will be taken into consideration in awarding the medal, which will be accompanied by a diploma. Published work only. Submissions are nominated by National Sections of IBBY in good standing. The National Sections select the candidates. The Hans Christian Andersen Award, named after Denmark's famous storyteller, is the highest international recognition given to an author and an illustrator of children's books. The Author's Award has been given since 1956, the Illustrator's Award since 1966. Her Majesty Queen Margrethe of Denmark is the Patron of the Hans Christian Andersen Awards. The Hans Christian Andersen Jury judges the books submitted for medals according to literary and artistic criteria. The awards are presented at the biennial congresses of IBBY.

THE ASPCA HENRY BERGH CHILDREN'S BOOK AWARD

The American Society For the Prevention of Cruelty to Animals, 424 E. 92nd St., New York NY 10128-6804. (212)876-7700, ext. 4400. Fax: (212)860-3435. E-mail: education@aspca.org. Web site: www.aspca.org/bookaward. **Award Manager:** Kristen Limbert, Coordinator, Humane Education. Competition open to authors, illustrators, and publishers. Annual award. Estab. 2000. Purpose of contest: To honor outstanding children's literature that fosters empathy and compassion for all living things. Awards presented to authors. Previously published submissions only. Submissions made by author or author's agent. Must be published between January 2008-December 2008. Deadline for entries: October 31, 2008. Awards foil seals and plaque. Judging by professionals in animal welfare and children's literature. Requirements for entrants: Open to children's literature about animals and/or the environment published in 2008. Includes fiction, nonfiction and poetry in 5 categories: Companion Animals, Ecology and Environment and Ecology, Humane Heroes, Illustration, and Young Adult.

⚡ ASTED/GRAND PRIX DE LITTERATURE JEUNESSE DU QUEBEC-ALVINE-BELISLE

Association pour l'avancement des sciences et des techniques de la documentation, 3414 Avenue du Parc, Bureau 202, Montreal QC H2X 2H5 Canada. (514)281-5012. Fax: (514)281-8219. E-mail: info@asted.org. Web site: www.asted.org. **Contact:** Olivia Marleau or Brigitte Moreay, co-presidents. "Prize granted for the best work in youth literature edited in French in the Quebec Province. Authors and editors can participate in the contest." Offered annually for books published during the preceding year. **Deadline: June 1.** Prize: $1,000.

⚡ ATLANTIC WRITING COMPETITION

Writer's Federation of Nova Scotia, 1113 Marginal Rd., Halifax NS B3H 4P7 Canada. (902)423-8116. Fax: (902)422-0881. E-mail: talk@writers.ns.ca. Web site: www.writers.ns.ca/competitions.html. Annual contest. Purpose is to encourage emerging writers in Atlantic Canada to explore their talents by sending unpublished work to any of six categories: novel, short story, poetry, writing for younger children, writing for juvenile/

young adult or essay/magazine article. Unpublished submissions only. Only open to residents of Atlantic Canada who are unpublished in category they enter. Visit Web site for more information.

BAKER'S PLAYS HIGH SCHOOL PLAYWRITING CONTEST

Baker's Plays, 45 W. 25th St., New York NY 10010. E-mail: publications@bakersplays.com Web site: www.bake rsplays.com. **Contest Director:** Roxanne Heinze-Bradshaw. **Open to any high school students.** Annual contest. Estab. 1990. Purpose of the contest: to encourage playwrights at the high school level and to ensure the future of American theater. Unpublished submissions only. Postmark deadline: January 31. Notification: May. SASE for contest rules and entry forms. No entry fee. Awards $500 to the first place playwright with publication by Baker's Plays; $250 to the second place playwright with an honorable mention; and $100 to the third place playwright with an honorable mention in the series. Judged anonymously. Plays must be accompanied by the signature of a sponsoring high school drama or English teacher, and it is recommended that the play receive a production or a public reading prior to the submission. To ensure return of manuscripts, please include SASE. Teachers must not submit student's work. The winning work will be listed in the Baker's Plays Catalogue, which is distributed to 50,000 prospective producing organizations.

 • Baker's Plays is now encouraging submission via e-mail at publications@bakersplay.com.

JOHN AND PATRICIA BEATTY AWARD

California Library Association, 717 20th Street, Suite 200, Sacramento CA 95811. (916)447-8541. Fax: (916)447-8394. E-mail: info@cla-net.org. Web site: www.cla-net.org. **Executive Director:** Susan Negreen. Annual award. Estab. 1987. Purpose of award: "The purpose of the John and Patricia Beatty Award is to encourage the writing of quality children's books highlighting California, its culture, heritage and/or future." Previously published submissions only. Submissions made by the author, author's agent or review copies sent by publisher. The award is given to the author of a children's book published the preceding year. Deadline for entries: Submissions may be made January-December. Contact CLA Executive Director who will liaison with Beatty Award Committee. Awards cash prize of $500 and an engraved plaque. Judging by a 5-member selection committee appointed by the president of the California Library Association. Requirements for entrants: "Any children's or young adult book set in California and published in the U.S. during the calendar year preceding the presentation of the award is eligible for consideration. This includes works of fiction as well as nonfiction for children and young people of all ages. Reprints and compilations are not eligible. The California setting must be depicted authentically and must serve as an integral focus for the book." Winning selection is announced through press release during National Library Week in April. Author is presented with award at annual California Library Association Conference in November.

▧ THE GEOFFREY BILSON AWARD FOR HISTORICAL FICTION FOR YOUNG PEOPLE

The Canadian Children's Book Centre, 40 Orchard View Blvd., Suite 101, Toronto ON M4R 1B9 Canada. (416)975-0010. Fax: (416)975-8970. E-mail: naseem@bookcentre.ca. Web site: www.bookcentre.ca. **Contact:** Naseem Hrab, librarian. Created in Geoffrey Bilson's memory in 1988. Offered annually for a previously published "outstanding work of historical fiction for young people by a Canadian author." Open to Canadian citizens and residents of Canada for at least 2 years. Deadline: January 15. Prize: $1,000. Judged by a jury selected by the Canadian Children's Book Centre.

THE IRMA S. AND JAMES H. BLACK BOOK AWARD

Bank Street College of Education, New York NY 10025-1898. (212)875-4450. Fax: (212)875-4558. E-mail: lindag @bnkst.edu. Web site: http://streetcat.bnkst.edu/html/isb.html. **Contact:** Linda Greengrass. Annual award. Estab. 1972. Purpose of award: "The award is given each spring for a book for young children, published in the previous year, for excellence of both text and illustrations." Entries must have been published during the previous calendar year (between January '08 and December '08 for 2009 award). Deadline for entries: mid-December. "Publishers submit books to us by sending them here to me at the Bank Street Library. Authors may ask their publishers to submit their books. Out of these, three to five books are chosen by a committee of older children and children's literature professionals. These books are then presented to children in selected first, second, and third grade classes here and at a number of other cooperating schools. These children are the final judges who pick the actual award winner. A scroll (one each for the author and illustrator, if they're different) with the recipient's name and a gold seal designed by Maurice Sendak are awarded in May."

WALDO M. AND GRACE C. BONDERMAN/IUPUI NATIONAL YOUTH THEATRE PLAYWRITING COMPETITION AND DEVELOPMENT WORKSHOP AND SYMPOSIUM

Bonderman Youth Theatre Playwriting Workshop, 1114 Red Oak Drive, Avon, IN 46123. E-mail: bonderma@iup ui.edu. Web site: www.liberalarts.iupui.edu/bonderman. **Director:** Dorothy Webb. **Open to students.** Chairperson, Canadian Association of Children's Librarians. Annual award. Estab. 1947. "The main purpose of the award is to encourage writing and publishing in Canada of good books for children up to and including age 14. If, in any year, no book is deemed to be of award calibe r, the award shall not be given that year. To merit consideration, the book must have been published in Canada and its author must be a Canadian citizen or a permanent resident of Canada." Previously published submissions only; must be published between January 1 and December 1 of the previous year. Deadline for entries: January 1. SASE for award rules. Entries not returned. No entry fee. Judging by committee of members of the Canadian Association of Children's Librarians. Requirements for entrants: Contest open only to Canadian authors or residents of Canada.

BOOKTRUST EARLY YEARS AWARDS

Booktrust, Book House, 45 E. Hill, Wandsworth, London SW18 2QZ United Kingdom. Fax: (00 44)20 8516 2978. E-mail: tarryn@booktrust.org.uk; megan@booktrust.org.uk. Web site: www.booktrust.org.uk. **Contact:** Tarryn McKay, and Megan Farr. The Booktrust Early Years Awards were initially established in 1999 and are awarded annually. The awards are given to the best books, published between September 1 and the following August 31, in the opinion of the judges in each category. The categories are: Baby Book Award, Pre-School Award, and Best Emerging New Illustrator Award. Authors and illustrators must be of British nationality, or other nationals who have been residents in the British Isles for at least 10 years. Books can be any format. Deadline: June. Prize: £2,000 and a crystal award to each winner (to be split between author/illustrator if necessary). In addition, the publisher receives a crystal award naming them as "The Booktrust Early Years Awards Publisher of the Year."

THE BOSTON GLOBE-HORN BOOK AWARDS

The Boston Globe & The Horn Book, Inc., The Horn Book, 56 Roland St., Suite 200, Boston MA 02129. (617)628-0225. Fax: (617)628-0882. E-mail: info@hbook.com. Web site: www.hbook.com/awards/bghb/submissions_b ghb.asp. Annual award. Estab. 1967. Purpose of award: To reward literary excellence in children's and young adult books. Awards are for picture books, nonfiction, fiction and poetry. Up to two honor books may be chosen for each category. Books must be published between June 1, 2005 and May 31, 2006. Deadline for entries: May 2005. Textboks, e-books, and audiobooks will not be considered, nor will manuscripts. Books should be submitted by publishers, although the judges reserve the right to honor any eligible book. Award winners receive $500 and silver engraved bowl, honor book winners receive a silver engraved plate. Judging by 3 judges involved in children's book field. *The Horn Book Magazine* publishes speeches given at awards ceremonies. The book must have been published in the U.S.

ANN ARLYS BOWLER POETRY CONTEST

Bowler Poetry Contest, Read Magazine, Weekly Reader Corporation, 1 Reader's Digest Rd., Pleasantville, NY 10570. Contest infromation and entry forms at: www.weeklyreader.com/read. **Open to students.** Annual contest. Estab. 1988. Purpose of the contest: to reward young-adult poets (grades 6-12). Unpublished submissions only. Submissions. Entry form must include signature of teacher, parent or guardian, and student verifying originality. Maximum number of submissions per student: 3 poems. Deadline for entries: mid-January. No entry fee. Awards 6 winners $100 each, medal of honor and publication in *Read*. Judging by *Read* and *Weekly Reader* editors and the Bowler family.

ANN CONNOR BRIMER AWARD

Nova Scotia Library Association, P.O. Box 36036, Halifax NS B3J 3S9 Canada. (902)490-5875. Fax: (902)490-5893. Web site: http://nsla.ns.ca/aboutnsla/brimeraward.html. **Award Director:** Heather MacKenzie. Annual award. Estab. 1991. Purpose of the contest: to recognize excellence in writing. Given to an author of a children's book who resides in Atlantic Canada. Previously published submissions only. Submissions made by the author's agent or nominated by a person or group of people. Must be published in previous year. Deadline for entries: October 15. SASE for contest rules and entry forms. No entry fee. Awards $1,000 and framed certificate. Judging by a selection committee. Requirements for entrants: Book must be intended for use up to age 15; in print and readily available; fiction or nonfiction except textbooks.

BUCKEYE CHILDREN'S BOOK AWARD

Kent State School of Library and Information Science, P.O.Box 5190, Kent, OH 44242-0001. Web site: www.bcbo okaward.info. **President:** Christine Watters. Correspondence should be sent to Christine Watters via the Web site. **Open to students.** Award offered every year. Estab. 1981. Purpose of the award: The Buckeye Childerens Book Award Program was designed to encourage children to read literatrue critically, to promote teacher and librarian involvement in children's literature programs, and to commend authors of such literature, as well as to promote the use of libraries. Nominees are submitted by students between Dec. 1 and March 1, and votes are cast between October 1 and December 1.

BYLINE MAGAZINE CONTESTS

P.O. Box 111, Albion, NY 14411. E-mail: robbi@bylinemag.com. Web site: www.bylinemag.com. **Contest Director:** Robbi Hess. Purpose of contest: *ByLine* runs 4 contests a month on many topics to encourage and motivate writers. Past topics include first chapter of a novel, new talent short story, juvenile fiction, nonfiction, personal essay, general short stories, various poetry contests, etc. Send SASE for contest flier with topic list and rules, or see Web site. Unpublished submissions only. Submissions made by the author. "On occasion we will print winning submissions." Entry fee is $3-5. Awards cash prizes for first, second and third place. Amounts vary. Judging by qualified writers or editors. List of winners will appear in magazine.

BYLINE MAGAZINE STUDENT PAGE

P.O. Box 111, Albion NY 14411. (585)355-8172. E-mail: robbi@bylinemag.com. Web site: www.bylinemag.com. **Contest Directors:** Robbi Hess and Donna Marbach, editor/poetry editor. **Open to students.** Estab. 1981. "We offer writing contests for students in grades 1-12 on a monthly basis, September through May, with cash prizes and publication of top entries." Previously unpublished submissions only. "This is not a market for illustration." Deadline for entries varies. "Entry fee usually $2." Awards cash and publication. Judging by qualified editors and writers. "We publish top entries in student contests. Winners' list published in magazine dated 3 months past deadline." Send SASE for details.

RANDOLPH CALDECOTT MEDAL

Association for Library Service to Children, Division of the American Library Association, 50 E. Huron, Chicago IL 60611. (312)280-2163. E-mail: alsc@ala.org. Web site: www.ala.org. **Executive Director:** Diane Foote. Annual award. Estab. 1938. Purpose of the award: to honor the artist of the most outstanding picture book for children published in the U.S. (Illustrator must be U.S. citizen or resident.) Must be published year preceding award. Deadline for entries: December 31. SASE for award rules. Entries not returned. No entry fee. "Medal given at ALA Annual Conference during the Newbery/Caldecott Banquet."

CALIFORNIA YOUNG PLAYWRIGHTS CONTEST

Playwrights Project, 2356 Moore Street, #204, San Diego CA 92110. (619)239-8222. Fax: (619)239-8225. E-mail: write@playwrightsproject.org. Web site: www.playwrightsproject.org. **Director:** Deborah Salzer. **Open to Californians under age 19.** Annual contest. Estab. 1985. "Our organization and the contest is designed to nurture promising young writers. We hope to develop playwrights and audiences for live theater. We also teach playwriting." Submissions required to be unpublished and not produced professionally. Submissions made by the author. Deadline for entries: June 1. SASE for contest rules and entry form. No entry fee. Award is professional productions of 3-5 short plays each year, participation of the writers in the entire production process, with a royalty awarded. Judging by professionals in the theater community, a committee of 5-7; changes somewhat each year. Works performed in San Diego at a professional theatre. Writers submitting scripts of 10 or more pages receive a detailed script evaluation letter upon request.

CALLIOPE FICTION CONTEST

Writers' Specialized Interest Group (SIG) of American Mensa, Ltd., 2506 SE Bitterbrush Dr., Madras, OR 97741. E-mail: cynthia@theriver.com. Web site: www.us.mensa.org. **Fiction Editor:** Sandy Raschke. **Open to students.** Annual contest. Estab. 1991. Purpose of contest: "To promote good writing and opportunities for getting published. To give our member/subscribers and others an entertaining and fun exercise in writing." Unpublished submissions only (all genres, no violence, profanity or extreme horror). Submissions made by author. Deadline for entries: changes annually but usually around September 15. Entry fee is $2 for nonsubscribers; subscribers get first entry fee. Awards small amount of cash (up to $75 for 1st place, to $10 for 3rd), certificates, full or mini-subscriptions to *Calliope* and various premiums and books, depending on donations. All winners are published in subsequent issues of *Calliope*. Judging by fiction editor, with concurrence of other editors, if needed. Requirements for entrants: winners must retain sufficient rights to have their stories published in the January/February issue, or their entries will be disqualified; one-time rights. Open to all writers. No special considerations—other than following the guidelines. Contest theme, due dates and sometimes entry fees change annually. Always send SASE for complete rules; available after April 15 each year. Sample copies with prior winners are available for $3.

◪ CANADA COUNCIL GOVERNOR GENERAL'S LITERARY AWARDS

350 Albert St., Ottawa ON K1P 5V8 Canada. (613)566-4410, ext. 4582. Fax: (613)566-4410. E-mail: joanne.laroc que-poirier@canadacouncil.ca. **Program Officer, Writing and Publishing Section:** TBA. Annual award. Estab. 1937. Purpose of award: given to the best English-language and the best French-language work in each of the seven categories of Fiction, Literary Non-fiction, Poetry, Drama, Children's Literature (text), Children's Literature (illustration) and Translation. Books must be first-edition trade books that have been written, translated

or illustrated by Canadian citizens or permanent residents of Canada. In the case of Translation, the original work written in English or French, must also be a Canadian-authored title. English titles must be published between September 1, 2007 and September 1, 2008. Books must be submitted by publishers. Books must reach the Canada Council for the Arts no later than August 7, 2008. The deadlines are final; no bound proofs or books that miss the applicable deadlines will be given to the peer assessment committees. The awards ceremony is scheduled mid-November. Amount of award: $25,000 to winning authors; $1,000 to non-winning finalists.

SANDRA CARON YOUNG ADULT POETRY PRIZE

National League of American Pen Women, Nob Hill, San Francisco Branch, 1544 Sweetwood Dr.Broadmoor Vlg., Colma CA 94015-2029. E-mail: pennobhill@aol.com. Web site: www.soulmakingcontest.us. **Contact:** Eileen Malone. **Open to students.** Three poems/entry; one poem/page; one-page poems only from poets in grades 9-12 or equivalent. Annually. Deadline:November 30. Guidelines for SASE. Charges $5/entry (make checks payable to NLAPW, Nob Hill Branch). Prize: 1st Place: $100; 2nd Place: $50; 3rd Place: $25. Open to any writer in grade 9-12.

CHILDREN'S AFRICANA BOOK AWARD

Outreach Council of the African Studies Association, ℅ Rutgers University, 132 George St., New Brunswick NJ 08901. (732)932-8173. Fax: (732)932-3394. Web site: www.africanstudies.org. Administered by Africa Access, P.O. Box 8028, Silver Spring MD 20910. (301)587-3040. Fax: (301)562-5244. E-mail: africaaccess@aol.com. Web site: www.africaaccessreview.org. **Chairperson**: Brenda Randolph. Annually. Estab. 1991. Purpose of contest: "The Children's Africana Book Awards are presented annually to the authors and illustrators of the best books on Africa for children and young people published or republished in the U.S. The awards were created by the Outreach Council of the African Studies Association (ASA) to dispel stereotypes and encourage the publication and use of accurate, balanced children's materials about Africa. The awards are presented in 2 categories: Young Children and Older Readers. Since 1991, 51 books have been recognized." Entries must have been published in the calendar year previous to the award. No entry fee. Awards plaque, announcement each spring, reviews published at Africa Access Review website and in *Sankofa: Journal of African Children's & Young Adult Literature*. Judging by Outreach Council of ASA and children's literature scholars. "Work submitted for awards must be suitable for children ages 4-18; a significant portion of books' content must be about Africa; must by copyrighted in the calendar year prior to award year; must be published or republished in the US."

CHILDREN'S WRITER WRITING CONTESTS

93 Long Ridge Rd., West Redding CT 06896-1124. (203)792-8600. Fax: (203)792-8406. Web site: www.childrens writer.com. Contest offered twice per year by *Children's Writer*, the monthly newsletter of writing and publishing trends. Purpose of the award: To promote higher quality children's literature. "Each contest has its own theme. Any original unpublished piece, not accepted by any publisher at the time of submission, is eligible." Submissions made by the author. Deadline for entries: Last weekday in February and October. "We charge a $10 entry fee for nonsubscribers only, which is applicable against a subscription to *Children's Writer* Awards: 1st place—$250 or $500, a certificate and publication in *Children's Writer*; 2nd place—$100 or $250, and certificate; 3rd-5th places—$50 or $100 and certificates. To obtain the rules and theme for the current contest go to the website and click on "Writing Contests," or send a SASE to *Children's Writer* at the above address. Put "Contest Request" in the lower left of your envelope. Judging by a panel of 4 selected from the staff of the Institute of Children's Literature. "We acquire First North American Serial Rights (to print the winner in *Children's Writer*), after which all rights revert to author." Open to any writer. Entries are judged on age targeting, originality, quality of writing and, for nonfiction, how well the information is conveyed and accuracy. "Submit clear photocopies only, not originals; submission will *not* be returned. Manuscripts should be typed double-spaced. No pieces containing violence or derogatory, racist or sexist language or situations will be accepted, at the sole discretion of the judges."

CHILDREN'S WRITERS FICTION CONTEST

Stepping Stones, P.O. Box 601721, Miami Beach FL 33160. (305)944-6491. E-mail: williams872@earthlink.net. **Director:** V.R. Williams. Annual contest. Estab. 1993. Purpose of contest: to promote writing for children by giving children's writers an opportunity to submit work in competition. Unpublished submissions only. Submissions made by the author. Deadline for entries: August 31. SASE for contest rules and entry forms. Entry fee is $10. Awards cash prize, certificate; certificates for Honorable Mention. Judging by Williams, Walters & Associates. First rights to winning material acquired or purchased. Requirements for entrants: Work must be suitable for children and no longer than 1,500 words. Send SASE for list of winners. "Stories should have believable characters. Work submitted on colored paper, in book format, illustrated, or with photograph attached is not acceptable."

CHRISTIAN BOOK AWARDS

Evangelical Christian Publishers Assocation, 9633 South 48th Street, Suite 140, Phoenix, AZ 85044. (480)966-3998. Fax: (480)966-1944. E-mail: info@ecpa.org. Web site: www.ecpa.org. **President:** Mark W. Kuyper. Annual award. Established 1978. Categories include Children & Youth. "All entries must be evangelical in nature and cannot be contrary to ECPA's Statement of Faith (stated in official rules)." Deadline for entry: January (see Web site for specific date). Guidelines available on Web site in October. "The work must be submitted by an ECPA member publisher." Awards a Christian Book Award plaque.

COLORADO BOOK AWARDS

1490 Lafayette Street, Suite 101, Denver CO 80218. (303)894-7951, ext. 21. Fax: (303) 864-9361, E-mail: bookawardinfo@coloradohumanities.org. Web site: www.ceh.org. Annual award established 1993. Previously published submissions only. Submissions are made by the author, author's agent, nominated by a person or group of people. Requires Colorado residency by author, illustrator, photographer, editor, or other major contributor. Deadline for entries: March 15. Entry fee is $50. Awards $250 and plaque. Judging by a panel of literary agents, booksellers and librarians. See Web site for complete contest guidelines and entry form.

THE COMMONWEALTH CLUB'S BOOK AWARDS CONTEST

The Commonwealth Club of California, 595 Market St., San Francisco CA 94105. (415)597-6703. Fax: (415)597-6729. E-mail: bookawards@commonwealthclub.org. Web site: www.commonwealthclub.org/features/cabook awards. **Contact:** Gina Baleria. Annual contest. Estab. 1932. Purpose of contest: the encouragement and production of literature in California. Juvenile and Young Adult categories included. Previously published submissions; must be published from January 1 to December 31, previous to contest year. Deadline for entries: December 21. SASE for contest rules and entry forms. No entry fee. Awards gold and silver medals. Judging by the Book Awards Jury. The contest is only open to California writers/illustrators (must have been resident of California when ms was accepted for publication). The award winners will be honored at the Annual Book Awards Program on June 5, 2008 at 6pm. Winning entries are displayed at awards program and advertised in newsletter.

CRICKET LEAGUE

Cricket magazine, P.O. Box 300, 315 Fifth St., Peru IL 61354. (815)224-5803 ext 633. Web site: www.cricketmag.com/cricketleague.htm Address entries to: Cricket League. **Open to students.** Monthly contest. Estab. 1973. "The purpose of Cricket League contests is to encourage creativity and give young people an opportunity to express themselves in writing, drawing, painting or photography. There is a contest each month. Possible categories include story, poetry, or art. Each contest relates to a *specific theme* described on each *Cricket* issue's Cricket League page. Signature verifying originality, age and address of entrant and permission to publish required. Entries which do not relate to the current month's theme cannot be considered." Unpublished submissions only. Deadline for entries: the 25th of each month. Cricket League rules, contest theme, and submission deadline information can be found in the current issue of *Cricket* and via Web site. "We prefer that children who enter the contests subscribe to the magazine or that they read *Cricket* in their school or library." No entry fee. Awards certificate suitable for framing and children's books or art/writing supplies. Judging by *Cricket* editors. Obtains right to print prizewinning entries in magazine. Refer to contest rules in current *Cricket* issue. Winning entries are published on the Cricket League pages in the *Cricket* magazine 3 months subsequent to the issue in which the contest was announced. Current theme, rules, and prizewinning entries also posted on the Web site.

DELACORTE DELL YEARLING CONTEST FOR A FIRST MIDDLE-GRADE NOVEL

Delacorte Press, Random House, Inc., 1745 Broadway, 9th Floor, New York NY 10019. Estab. 1992. (212)782-9000 Web site: www.randomhouse.com. Annual award. Purpose of the award: to encourage the writing of fiction for children ages 9-12, either contemporary or historical; to encourage unpublished writers in the field of middle grade fiction. Unpublished submissions only. No simultaneous submissions. Length: between 96-160 pages. Submissions made by author only. Must not be out with an agent. Entries should be postmarked between April 1 and June 30. Letter sized SASE for notification. Because of new postal regulations no manuscripts can be returned. No entry fee. Awards a $1,500 cash prize plus a hardcover and paperback book contract with a $7,500 advance against a royalties to be negotiated. Judging by Delacorte Press Books for Young Readers editorial staff. Open to U.S. and Canadian writers who have not previously published a novel for middle-grade readers (ages 9-12).

DELACORTE PRESS CONTEST FOR A FIRST YOUNG ADULT NOVEL

Delacorte Press, Books for Young Readers Department, 1745 Broadway, 9th Floor, New York NY 10019. Web site: www.randomhouse.com/kids/writingcontests. Annual award. Estab. 1982. Purpose of award: to encourage the writing of contemporary young adult fiction (for readers ages 12-18). Previously unpublished submissions only. Manuscripts sent to Delacorte Press may not be submitted to other publishers while under consideration for the prize. Entries must be submitted between October 1 and December 31. Length: between 100-224 pages. No entry fee. Awards a $1,500 cash prize and a $7,500 advance against royalties for world rights on a hardcover and paperback book contract. Works published in an upcoming Delacorte Press, an imprint of Random House, Inc., Books for Young Readers list. Judged by the editors of the Books for Young Readers Department of Delacorte Press. Requirements for entrants: The writer must be American or Canadian and must not have previously published a young adult novel but may have published anything else. Foreign-language mss and translations and mss submitted to a previous Delacorte Press are not eligible. Send SASE for notification. Guidelines are also available on our Web site.

MARGARET A. EDWARDS AWARD

50 East Huron St., Chicago IL 60611-2795. (312)280-4390 or (800)545-2433. Fax: (312)280-5276. E-mail: yalsa@ala.org. Web site: www.ala.org/yalsa/edwards. Annual award administered by the Young Adult Library Services Association (YALSA) of the American Library Association (ALA) and sponsored by *School Library Journal* magazine. Purpose of award: "ALA's Young Adult Library Services Association (YALSA), on behalf of librarians who work with young adults in all types of libraries, will give recognition to those authors whose book or books have provided young adults with a window through which they can view their world and which will help them to grow and to understand themselves and their role in relationships, society and the world." Previously published submissions only. Nomination form is available on the YALSA Web site. No entry fee. Judging by members of the Young Adult Library Services Association. Deadline for entry: December 1. "The award will be given annually to an author whose book or books, over a period of time, have been accepted by young adults as an authentic voice that continues to illuminate their experiences and emotions, giving insight into their lives. The book or books should enable them to understand themselves, the world in which they live, and their relationship with others and with society. The book or books must be in print at the time of the nomination."

DOROTHY CANFIELD FISHER CHILDREN'S BOOK AWARD

Vermont Department of Libraries, Northeast Regional Library, 109 State St.,Montpelier VT 05609. (802)828-6954. Fax: (802)828-2199. E-mail: grace.greene@dol.state.vt.us. Web site: www.dcfaward.org. **Chair:** Steve Madden. Annual award. Estab. 1957. Purpose of the award: to encourage Vermont children to become enthusiastic and discriminating readers by providing them with books of good quality by living American or Canadian authors published in the current year. Deadline for entries: December of year book was published. SASE for award rules and entry forms or e-mail. No entry fee. Awards a scroll presented to the winning author at an award ceremony. Judging is by the children grades 4-8. They vote for their favorite book. Requirements for entrants: "Titles must be original work, published in the United States, and be appropriate to children in grades 4 through 8. The book must be copyrighted in the current year. It must be written by an American author living in the U.S. or Canda, or a Canadian author living in Canada or the U.S."

⚡ THE NORMA FLECK AWARD FOR CANADIAN CHILDREN'S NONFICTION

The Canadian Children's Book Centre, 40 Orchard View Blvd., Suite 101, Toronto ON M4R 1B9 Canada. (416)975-0010. Fax: (416)975-8970. E-mail: info@bookcentre.ca. Web site: www.bookcentre.ca. **Contact:** Shannon Howe, program coordinator. The Norma Fleck Award was established by the Fleck Family Foundation in May 1999 to honor the life of Norma Marie Fleck, and to recognize exceptional Canadian nonfiction books for young people. Publishers are welcome to nominate books using the online form. Offered annually for books published between May 1, 2006, and April 30, 2007. Open to Canadian citizens or landed immigrants. The jury will always include at least 3 of the following: a teacher, a librarian, a bookseller, and a reviewer. A juror will have a deep understanding of, and some involvement with, Canadian children's books. The Canadian Children's Book Centre will select the jury members. **Deadline: March 31 (annually).** Prize: $10,000 goes to the author (unless 40% or more of the text area is composed of original illustrations, in which case the award will be divided equally between the author and the artist).

FLICKER TALE CHILDREN'S BOOK AWARD

Flicker Tale Award Committee, North Dakota Library Association, Mandan Public Library, 609 West Main St., Mandan ND 58554. Web site: www.ndla.info/ftaward.htm. **Contact:** Kelly Loftis. Estab. 1979. Purpose of award: to give children across the state of North Dakota a chance to vote for their book of choice from a nominated list of 20: 4 in the picture book category; 4 in the intermediate category; 4 in the juvenile category (for more advanced readers); 4 in the upper grage level non-fiction category. Also, to promote awareness of quality literature for children. Previously published submissions only. Submissions nominated by librarians and teachers across the state of North Dakota. Awards a plaque from North Dakota Library Association and banquet dinner. Judging by children in North Dakota. Entry deadline in June.

FLORIDA STATE WRITING COMPETITION

Florida Freelance Writers Association, P.O. Box A, North Stratford NH 03590. (603)922-8338. Fax: (603)922-8339. E-mail: contest@writers-editors.com. Web site: www.writers-editors.com. **Executive Director:** Dana K. Cassell. Annual contest. Estab. 1984. Categories include children's literature (length appropriate to age category). Entry fee is $5 (members), $10 (nonmembers) or $10-20 for entries longer than 3,000 words. Awards $100 first prize, $75 second prize, $50 third prize, certificates for honorable mentions. Judging by teachers, editors and published authors. Judging criteria: interest and readability within age group, writing style and mechanics, originality, salability. Deadline: March 15. For copy of official entry form, send #10 SASE or visit Web site. List of winners on Web site.

DON FREEMAN MEMORIAL GRANT-IN-AID

Society of Children's Book Writers and Illustrators, 8271 Beverly Blvd., Los Angeles CA 90048.(323)782-1010 Fax: (323) 782-1892 E-mail: scbwi@scbwi.org. Web site: www.scbwi.org. Estab. 1974. Purpose of award: to "enable picture book artists to further their understanding, training and work in the picture book genre." Applications and prepared materials are available in October and must be postmarked between February 1 and March 1. Grant awarded and announced in August. SASE for award rules and entry forms. SASE for return of entries. No entry fee. Annually awards one grant of $1,500 and one runner-up grant of $500. "The grant-in-aid is available to both full and associate members of the SCBWI who, as artists, seriously intend to make picture books their chief contribution to the field of children's literature."

FRIENDS OF THE AUSTIN PUBLIC LIBRARY AWARD FOR BEST CHILDREN'S AND BEST YOUNG ADULT'S BOOK

Web site: www.smu.edu/english/creativewriting/The_Texas_Institute_of_Letters.htm. Offered annually for work published January 1-December 31 of previous year to recognize the best book for children and young people. Writer must have been born in Texas or have lived in the state for at least 2 consecutive years at one time, or the subject matter must be associated with the state. See Web site for information on eligibility, deadlines, and the judges names and addresses to whom the books should be sent. Prize: $500 for each award winner.

THEODOR SEUSS GEISEL AWARD

Association for Library Service to Children, Division of the American Library Association, 50 E. Huron, Chicago IL 60611.1(800)-545-2433. E-mail: alsc@ala.org. Web site: www.ala.org The Theodor Seuss Geisel Award, established in 2004, is given annually beginning in 2006 to the author(s) and illustrator(s) of the most distinguished contribution to the body of American children's literature known as beginning reader books published in the United States during the preceding year. The award is to recognize the author(s) and illustrator(s) of a beginning reader book who demonstrate great creativity and imagination in his/her/their literary and artistic achievements to engage children in reading. The award is named for the world-renowned children's author, Theodor Geisel. "A person's a person no matter how small," Theodor Geisel, a.k.a. Dr. Seuss, would say. "Children want the same things we want: to laugh, to be challenged, to be entertained and delighted." Brilliant, playful and always respectful of children, Dr. Seuss charmed his way into the consciousness of four generations of youngsters and parents. In the process, he helped them to read.

☑ AMELIA FRANCES HOWARD GIBBON AWARD FOR ILLUSTRATION

Canadian Library Association, 328 Frank St., Ottawa ON K2P 0X8 Canada. (613)232-9625; Fax: (613)563-9895. Web site: www.cla.ca. **Contact:** Chairperson, Canadian Association of Children's Librarians. Annual award. Estab. 1971. Purpose of the award: "to honor excellence in the illustration of children's book(s) in Canada. To merit consideration the book must have been published in Canada and its illustrator must be a Canadian citizen or a permanent resident of Canada." Previously published submissions only; must be published between January 1 and December 31 of the previous year. Deadline for entries: December 31. SASE for award rules. Entries not returned. No entry fee. Judging by selection committee of members of Canadian Association of Children's Librarians. Requirements for entrants: illustrator must be Canadian or Canadian resident.

GOLDEN KITE AWARDS

Society of Children's Book Writers and Illustrators, 8271 Beverly Blvd., Los Angeles CA 90048. (323)782-1010. E-mail: scbwi@scbwi.org. Web site: www.scbwi.org. **Contact:** SCBWI Golden Kite Coordinator. Annual award. Estab. 1973. "The works chosen will be those that the judges feel exhibit excellence in writing, and in the case of the picture-illustrated books—in illustration, and genuinely appeal to the interests and concerns of children. For the fiction and nonfiction awards, original works and single-author collections of stories or poems of which at least half are new and never before published in book form are eligible—anthologies and translations are not. For the picture-illustration awards, the art or photographs must be original works (the texts—which may

Resources

be fiction or nonfiction—may be original, public domain or previously published). Deadline for entries: December 15. SASE for award rules. No entry fee. Awards, in addition to statuettes and plaques, the four winners receive $2,500 cash award plus trip to LA SCBWI Conference. Editors of four winning books receive $1,000 cash award. The panel of judges will consist of professional authors, illustrators, editors or agents." Requirements for entrants: "must be a member of SCBWI and books must be published in that year." Winning books will be displayed at national conference in August. Books to be entered, as well as further inquiries, should be submitted to: The Society of Children's Book Writers and Illustrators, above address.

GOVERNOR GERERAL'S LITERARY AWARD FOR CHILDREN'S LITERATURE
Canada Council for the Arts, 350 Albert St., P.O. Box 1047, Ottawa ON K1P 5V8 Canada. (613)566-4414, ext. 5576. Fax: (613)566-4410. E-mail: caroline.lecours@canadacouncil.ca. Web site: www.canadacouncil.ca/prizes/ggla. Offered for work published September 1-September 30. Submissions in English must be published between September 1, 2005 and September 30, 2006; submissions in French between July 1, 2005 and June 30, 2006. Publishers submit titles for consideration. Deadline: March 15, June 1 and August 7, depending on the book's publication date. Prize: Each laureate receives $15,000; nonwinning finalists receive $1,000.

GUIDEPOSTS YOUNG WRITERS CONTEST
Guideposts, 16 E. 34th St., New York NY 10016. (212)251-8100. E-mail: ywcontest@guideposts.org. Web site: gp4teens.com. Offered annually for unpublished high school juniors and seniors. Stories "needn't be about a highly dramatic situation, but it should record an experience that affected you and deeply changed you. Remember, *Guideposts* stories are true, not fiction, and they show how faith in God has made a specific difference in a person's life. We accept submissions after announcement is placed in the October issue each year. If the manuscript is place, we require all rights to the story in that version." Open only to high school juniors or seniors. Deadline: November 24. Prize: 1st Place: $10,000; 2nd Place: $8,000; 3rd Place: $6,000; 4th Place: $4,000; 5th Place: $3,000; 6th-10th Place: $1,000; 11th-20th Place: $250 gift certificate for college supplies.

THE MARILYN HALL AWARDS FOR YOUTH THEATRE
Beverly Hills Theatre Guild, P.O. Box 148, Beverly CA 90213. Web site: www.beverlyhillstheatreguild.org. **Contact:** Dick Dotterer. **Open to students.** Annual contest. Estab. 1998/99. Purpose of contest: "To encourage the creation and development of new plays for youth theatre." Unpublished submissions only. Authors must be U.S. citizens or legal residents and must sign entry form personally. Deadline for entries: between January 15 and last day of February each year (postmark accepted). Playwrights may submit up to two scripts. One nonprofessional production acceptable for eligibility. SASE for contest rules and entry forms. No entry fee. Awards: $500, 1st prize; $300, 2nd prize; $200, 3rd prize. Judging by theatre professionals cognizant of youth theatre and writing/producing.

HIGHLIGHTS FOR CHILDREN FICTION CONTEST
803 Church St., Honesdale PA 18431-1895. (570)253-1080. Fax: (570)251-7847. Web site: www.highlights.com. **Fiction Contest Editor:** Christine French Clark. Annual contest. Estab. 1980. Purpose of the contest: to stimulate interest in writing for children and reward and recognize excellence. Unpublished submissions only. Deadline for entries: January 31; entries accepted after January 1 only. SASE for contest rules and return of entries. No entry fee. Awards 3 prizes of $1,000 each in cash and a pewter bowl (or, at the winner's election, attendance at the Highlights Foundation Writers Workshop at Chautauqua) and a pewter bowl. Judging by a panel of *Highlights* editors and outside judges. Winning pieces are purchased for the cash prize of $1,000 and published in *Highlights*; other entries are considered for purchase at regular rates. Requirements for entrants: open to any writer 16 years of age or older. Winners announced in May. Length up to 800 words. Stories for beginning readers should not exceed 500 words. Stories should be consistent with *Highlights* editorial requirements. No violence, crime or derogatory humor. Send SASE or visit Web site for guidelines and current theme.

THE MARILYN HOLINSHEAD VISITING SCHOLARS FELLOWSHIP
Kerlan Grant-in-Aid, University of Minnesota, 113 Anderson Library, 222 21st Ave. South, Minneapolis MN 55455.E-mail: circ@umn.edu. Web site: http://special.lib.umn.edu/clrc/kerlan/index.php. This fellowship provides grants-in-aid for travel to the Kerlan Collection. These grants will be available for research study in 2007. The Kerlan Collection is one of the world's finest research collections in children's literature and contains over 100,000 books and original art and manuscript material for approximately 16,000 titles. For more information about our holdings, please visit the Kerlan Collection's Web site. Applicants may request up to $1,500. Send a letter with the proposed purpose, a plan to use specific research materials (manuscripts and art), dates, and budget (including airfare and per diem) to above address. The deadline for receipt of all materials is December 30, 2007. Travel and a written report on the project must be completed and submitted in 2008.

HRC SHOWCASE THEATRE

Hudson River Classics, Inc., P.O. Box 940, Hudson NY 12534. "(518)851 7244." Fax: "none" . E-mail: jangrice20 02@yahoo.com. **President:** Jan M. Grice. Annual contest. Estab. 1992. HRCs Showcase Theatre is a not-for-profit professional theater company dedicated to the advancement of performing in the Hudson River Valley area through reading of plays and providing opportunities for new playwrights. Unpublished submissions only. Submissions made by author and by the author's agent. Deadlines for entries: May 1st. SASE for contest rules and entry forms. Entry fee is $5. Awards $500 cash plus concert reading by professional actors. Judging by panel selected by Board of Directors. Requirements for entrants: Entrants must live in the northeastern U.S.

IMPRINT OF MIDLAND COMMUNITY THEATRE

Midland Community Theatre, 2000 W. Wadley, Midland TX 79705. (432)682-2544. Fax: (432)682-6136. E-mail: mclaren@mctmidland.org. Web site: www.mctmidland.org. **Chair :** William Payne. Estab. 1989. Open to students. Annual contest. Purpose of conference: "The McLaren Memorial Comedy Play Writing Competition was established in 1989 to honor long-time MCT volunteer Mike McLaren who loved a good comedy, whether he was on stage or in the front row." Unpublished submissions only. Submissions made by author. Deadline for entries: January 31st (scripts are accepted from December 1st through January 31st each year). SASE for contest rules and entry forms. Entry fee is $10 per script. Awards $400 for full-length winner and $200 for one-act winner as well as staged readings for 3 finalists in each category. Judging by the audience present at the McLaren festival when the staged readings are performed. Rights to winning material acquired or purchased. 1st right of production or refusal is acquired by MCT. Requirements for entrants: "Yes, the contest is open to *any* playwright, but the play submitted must be unpublished and never produced in a for-profit setting. One previous production in a *nonprofit* theatre is acceptable. 'Readings' do not count as productions."

INSIGHT WRITING CONTEST

Insight Magazine, 55 W. Oak Ridge Dr., Hagerstown MD 21740-7390. (301) 393-4038;Web site: www.insightmag azine.org. **Open to students.** Annual contest. Unpublished submissions only. Submissions made by author. Deadline for entries: June. SASE for contest rules and entry forms. Awards first prizes, $ 100-250; second prizes, $75-200; third prizes, $50-150. Winning entries will be published in *Insight*. Contest includes three catagories: Student Short Story, General Short Story and Student Poetry. You must be age 22 or under to enter the student catagories. Entries must include cover sheet form available with SASE or on Web site.

IRA CHILDREN'S BOOK AWARDS

International Reading Association, 800 Barksdale Rd., P.O. Box 8139, Newark DE 19714-8139. (302)731-1600. Fax: (302)731-1057. E-mail: exec@reading.org. Web site: www.reading.org. Annual award. Awards are given for an author's first or second published book for fiction and nonfiction in three categories: primary (ages preschool-8), intermediate (ages 9-13), and young adult (ages 14-17). This award is intended for newly published authors who show unusual promise in the children's book field. Deadline for entries: November 1. Awards $1000. For guidelines write or e-mail exec@reading.org.

JOSEPH HENRY JACKSON AND JAMES D. PHELAN LITERARY AWARDS

Sponsored by The San Francisco Foundation. Administered by Intersection for the Arts, 446 Valencia St., San Francisco CA 94103. (415)626-2787. Fax: (415)626-1636. Web site: www.theintersection.org/resource_awards. php. Submit entries to Awards Coordinator. **Open to Students.** Annual award. Estab. 1937. Purpose of award: to encourage young writers for an unpublished manuscript-in-progress. Submissions must be unpublished. Submissions made by author. Deadline for entry: March 31. SASE for contest rules and entry forms. Judging by established peers. All applicants must be 20-35 years of age. Applicants for the Henry Jackson Award must be residents of northern California or Nevada for 3 consecutive years immediately prior to the January 31 deadline. Applicants for the James D. Phelan awards must have been born in California but need not be current residents.

THE EZRA JACK KEATS NEW WRITER AND NEW ILLUSTRATOR AWARDS

Ezra Jack Keats Foundation/Administered by The Office of Children's Services, The New York Public Library, 450 14th St., Brooklyn NY 11215. E-mail: mtice@nypl.org. Web site: www.ezra-jack-keats.org. **Program Coordinator:** Margaret Tice. Annual awards. Purpose of the awards: "The awards will be given to a promising new writer of picture books for children and a promising new illustrator of picture books for children. Selection criteria include books for children (ages 9 and under) that reflect the tradition of Ezra Jack Keats. These books portray: the universal qualities of childhood, strong and supportive family and adult relationships, the multicultural nature of our world." Submissions made by the publisher. Must be published in the preceding year. Deadline for entries: mid-December. SASE for contest rules and entry forms or email Margaret Tice at mtice@nypl.org. No entry fee. Awards $1,000 coupled with Ezra Jack Keats Bronze Medal. Judging by a panel of experts. "The author or illustrator should have published no more than 3 children's books. Entries are judged on the outstanding features of the text, complemented by illustrations. Candidates need not be both author and illustrator. Entries should carry a 2006 copyright (for the 2007 award)." Winning books and authors to be presented at reception at The New York Public Library.

EZRA JACK KEATS/KERLAN COLLECTION MEMORIAL FELLOWSHIP

Ezra Jack Keats/Kerlan Collection, Memorial Fellowship Committee, 113 Andersen Library, 222 21st Avenue South, University of Minnesota, Minneapolis, MN 55455. Web site: http://special.lib.umn.edu/clrc/kerlan/awards.php. This fellowship from the Ezra Jack Keats Foundation will provide $1,500 to a "talented writer and/or illustrator of children's books who wishes to use the Kerlan Collection for the furtherance of his or her artistic development." Special consideration will be given to someone who would find it difficult to finance a visit to the Kerlan Collection. The Ezra Jack Keats Fellowship recipient will receive transportation costs and a per diem allotment. Applications for 2007 must be postmarked by December 30, 2006. For digital application materials, please visit Web site. For paper copies of the application send a large (6×9 or 9×12) self- addressed envelope with 87¢ postage envelope to above address.

KENTUCKY BLUEGRASS AWARD

Kentucky Reading Association, % Melissa Schutt, Eastern Kentucky University Libraries, 521 Lancaster Ave, Richmond KY 40475. (859)622- 1778. Fax: (859)622-1174. E-mail: melissa.schutt@eku.edu. Web site: www.kyreading.org **Award Director:** Melissa Schutt. Submit entries to: Melissa Schutt. Annual award. Estab. 1983. Purpose of award: to promote readership among young children and young adolescents. Also to recognize exceptional creative efforts of authors and illustrators. Previously published submissions only. Submissions made by author, made by author's agent, nominated by teachers or librarians. Must be published no more than 3 years prior to the award year. Deadline for entries: March 15. Contest rules and entry forms are available from the Web site. No entry fee. Awards a framed certificate and invitation to be recognized at the annual luncheon of the Kentucky Bluegrass Award. Judging by children who participate through their schools or libraries. "Books are reviewed by a panel of teachers and librarians before they are placed on a Master List for the year. These books must have been published within a three year period prior to the review. Winners are chosen from this list of preselected books. Books are divided into four divisions, K-2, 3-5, 6-8, 9-12 grades. Winners are chosen by children who either read the books or have the books read to them. Children from the entire state of Kentucky are involved in the selection of the annual winners for each of the divisions."

CORETTA SCOTT KING AWARD

Coretta Scott King Committee, Ethnic and Multicultural Information Exchange Round Table, American Library Association, 50 E. Huron St., Chicago IL 60611. (800)545-2433. Fax: (312)280-3256. E-mail: olos@ala.org. Web site: www.ala.org/csk. "The Coretta Scott King Award is an annual award for books (1 for text and 1 for illustration) that convey the spirit of brotherhood espoused by Martin Luther King, Jr.—and also speak to the Black experience—for young people. There is an award jury of children's librarians that judges the books— reviewing over the year—and making a decision in January. A copy of an entry must be sent to each juror by December 1 of the juried year. A copy of the jury list can be found on Web site. Call or e-mail ALA Office for Literary Services for jury list. Awards breakfast held on Tuesday morning during A.L.A. Annual Conference. See schedule at Web site.

LA BELLE LETTRE SHORT STORY CONTEST

La Belle Lettre, P.O. Box 2009, Longview WA 98632. E-mail: admin@labellelettre.com. Web site: www.labellelettre.com. **Executive Director:** Jennifer Hill. Contest offered seasonally—spring, summer, fall and winter. "La Bell Lettre's mission in sponsoring these contests is to provide encouragement and support to writers. We aim to be a bridge to authors' literary accomplishments. Therefore (in addition to monetary awards for 1st, 2nd, and 3rd place) The 1st, 2nd, and 3rd place entries, three Honorable Mentions, and three submssions drawn at random will all receive critiques." Unpublished submissions only. Deadlines remain the same from year to year: May 1, August 1, November 1, February 1. Themes changes yearly. 2007 themes were: May1—Children's Short Story; August 1—Memoir/Personal Essay; November 1—Holiday Fiction/Nonfiction; February 1—Romance. Guidelines available on Web site. "Writers may also contact us vis "Contact Us" on our Web site." Entry fee is $6. Awards (in 2007): 1st place—$150 plus critique; 2nd place—$75 plus critique; 3rd place—$50 plus critique. Judging by Jennifer Hill, executive director and Mary Stone, assistant director. "Future judges may include other published authors. Writers retain all rights to submitted material. Contest are open to any/all writers. International writers may entry fees via PayPal, although entries must be submitted by mail."

LONGMEADOW JOURNAL LITERARY COMPETITION

% Rita and Robert Morton, 6750 N. Longmeadow, Lincolnwood IL 60712. (312)726-9789. Fax: (312)726-9772. **Contest Directors:** Rita and Robert Morton. Competition **open to students** (anyone age 10-19). Held annually

Resources

and published every year. Estab. 1986. Purpose of contest: to encourage the young to write. Submissions are made by the author, nominated by a person or group of people, by teachers, librarians or parents. Deadline for entries: June 30. SASE. No entry fee. Awards first place, $175; second place, $100; and five prizes of $50. Judging by Rita Morton and Robert Morton. Works are published every year and are distributed to teachers and librarians and interested parties at no charge.

LOUISE LOUIS/EMILY F. BOURNE STUDENT POETRY AWARD

Poetry Society of America, 15 Gramercy Park South, New York NY 10003-1705. (212)254-9628. Fax: (212)673-2352. E-mail: eve@poetrysociety.org. Web site: www.poetrysociety.org. **Contact:** Program Director. **Open to students.** Annual award. Purpose of the award: award is for the best unpublished poem by a high or preparatory school student (grades 9-12) from the U.S. and its territories. Unpublished submissions only. Deadline for entries: Oct. 1 to Dec. 22. SASE for award rules and entry forms. Entries not returned. "High schools can send an unlimited number of submissions with one entry per individual student for a flat fee of $20. (High school students may send a single entry for $5.)" Award: $250. Judging by a professional poet. Requirements for entrants: Award open to all high school and preparatory students from the U.S. and its territories. School attended, as well as name and address, should be noted. PSA submission guidelines must be followed. These are printed in our fall calendar on our Web site and are readily available if those interested send us a SASE. Line limit: none. "The award-winning poem will be included in a sheaf of poems that will be part of the program at the award ceremony and sent to all PSA members."

MCLAREN MEMORIAL COMEDY PLAY WRITING COMPETITION

Midland Community Theatre, Inc., 2000 W. Wadley, Midland TX 79705. (432)682-2554. Web site: www.mctmidl and.org. **Contact:** William Payne. Annual competition. Accepts submissions in 2 division: one-act and full-length. Accepts submissions January 1, through the last day of Februrary for 2008 competition. Entries must be comedies for adults, teens or children; musical comedies not accepted. Work must never have been produced professionally or published. See Web site for competitions guidelines and required brochure with entry form. Entry fee: $15/script. Awards $400 for winning full-length play; $200 for winning one-act play; staged reading for full-length finalists. Winning one-act play will be presented in workshop format.

⚡ THE VICKY METCALF AWARD FOR CHILDREN'S LITERATURE

The Writers' Trust of Canada, 90 Richmond St. E., Suite 200, Toronto ON M5C 1P1 Canada. (416)504-8222. Fax: (416)504-9090. E-mail: info@writerstrust.com. Web site: www.writerstrust.com. **Contact:** James Davies. The Vicky Metcalf Award is presented each spring to a Canadian writer for a body of work in children's literature at The Writers' Trust Awards event in Toronto. Prize: $15,000. Open to Canadian residents only.

MILKWEED PRIZE FOR CHILDREN'S LITERATURE

Milkweed Editions, 1011 Washington Ave. S., Suite 300, Minneapolis MN 55415-1246. (612)332-3192. Fax: (612)215-2550. E-mail: editor@milkweed.org. Web site: www.milkweed.org. **Award Director:** Daniel Slager, Publisher, editor-in-chief. Annual award. Estab. 1993. Purpose of the award: to recognize an outstanding literary novel for readers ages 8-13 and encourage writers to turn their attention to readers in this age group. Unpublished submissions only "in book form." Please send SASE or visit Web site for award guidelines. The prize is awarded to the best work for children ages 8-13 that Milkweed agrees to publish in a calendar year by a writer not previously published by Milkweed. The Prize consists of a $10,000 advance against royalties agreed to at the time of acceptance. Submissions must follow our usual children's guidelines.

MINNESOTA BOOK AWARDS

The Friends of the Saint Paul Public Library, 325 Cedar Street, Suite 555, Saint Paul, MN 55101. (651)366-6497. Fax: (651)222-1988. E-mail: mnbookawards@thefriends.org. Web site: www.thefriends.org. Contact: Ann Nelson. Annual award, established 1988. Purpose of contest: To recognize and honor achievement by members of Minnesota's book community.

NATIONAL CHILDREN'S THEATRE FESTIVAL

Actors' Playhouse at the Miracle Theatre, 280 Miracle Mile, Coral Gables FL 33134. (305)444-9293, ext. 615. Fax: (305)444-4181. E-mail: maulding@actorsplayhouse.org. Web site: www.actorsplayhouse.org. **Director:** Earl Maulding. **Open to students.** Annual contest. Estab. 1994. Purpose of contest: to bring together the excitement of the theater arts and the magic of young audiences through the creation of new musical works and to create a venue for playwrights/composers to showcase their artistic products. Submissions must be unpublished. Submissions are made by author or author's agent. Deadline for entries: May 1 annually. Visit Web site or send SASE for contest rules and entry forms. Entry fee is $10. Awards: first prize of $500, full production, and transportation to Festival weekend based on availability. Final judges are of national reputation. Past judges include Joseph Robinette, Moses Goldberg and Luis Santeiro.

NATIONAL FOUNDATION FOR ADVANCEMENT IN THE ARTS

youngARTS, 444 Brickell Ave., P-14, Miami FL 33131. (305)377-1140. Fax: (305)377-1149. E-mail: info@nfaa. org. Web site: www.youngARTS.org. **Contact:** Carla Hill. **Open to students/high school seniors or other 17- and 18-year-olds.** Created to recognize and reward outstanding accomplishment in *cinematic arts, dance, jazz, music, photography, theater, voice, visual arts and/or writing.* youngARTS is an innovative national program of the National Foundation for Advancement in the Arts (NFAA). Established in 1981, youngARTS touches the lives of gifted young people across the country, providing financial support, scholarships and goal-oriented artistic, educational and career opportunities. Each year, from a pool of more than 8,000 applicants, an average of 800 youngARTS winners are chosen for NFAA support by panels of distinguished artists and educators. Deadline for registration: June 1 (early) and October 1. Deadline for submission of work: Nov. 3. Entry fee is $35(online)/40(paper). Fee waivers available based on need. Awards $100-10,000—unrestricted cash grants. Judging by a panel of artists and educators recognized in the field. Rights to submitted/ winning material: NFAA/youngARTS retains the right to duplicate work in an anthology or in Foundation literature unless otherwise specified by the artist. Requirements for entrants: Artists must be high school seniors or, if not enrolled in high school, must be 17 or 18 years old. Applicants must be U.S. citizens or residents, unless applying in jazz. Literary and Visual works will be published in an anthology distributed during youngARTS Week in Miami when the final adjudication takes place. NFAA invites up to 150 finalists to participate in youngARTS Week in January in Miami-Dade County, Florida. youngARTS Week is a once-in-a-lifetime experience consisting of performances, master classes, workshops, readings, exhibits, and enrichment activities with renowned artists and arts educators. All expenses are paid by NFAA, including airfare, hotel, meals and ground transportation.

NATIONAL PEACE ESSAY CONTEST

United States Institute of Peace, 1200 17th St. NW, Washington DC 20036. (202)457-1700. Fax: (202)429-6063. E-mail: education@usip.org. Web site: www.usip.org. **Open to high school students.** Annual contest. Estab. 1987. "The contest gives students the opportunity to do valuable research, writing and thinking on a topic of importance to international peace and conflict resolution. Teaching guides are available for teachers who allow the contest to be used as a classroom assignment." Deadline for entries is February 1, 2007. "Interested students, teachers and others may write or call to receive free contest kits. Please do not include SASE." Guidelines and rules on Web site. No entry fee. State Level Awards are $1,000 college scholarships. National winners are selected from among the 1st place state winners. National winners receive scholarships in the following amounts: first place $10,000; second $5,000; third $2,500. National amount includes State Award. First place state winners invited to an expenses-paid awards program in Washington, DC in June. Judging is conducted by education professionals from across the country and by the Board of Directors of the United States Institute of Peace. "All submissions become property of the U.S. Institute of Peace to use at its discretion and without royalty or any limitation. Students grades 9-12 in the U.S., its territories and overseas schools may submit essays for review by completing the application process. U.S. citizenship required for students attending overseas schools. National winning essays will be published by the U.S. Institute of Peace."

NATIONAL WRITERS ASSOCIATION NONFICTION CONTEST

10940 S. Parker Rd., #508, Parker CO 80134. (303)841-0246. **Executive Director:** Sandy Whelchel. Annual contest. Estab. 1971. Purpose of contest: "to encourage and recognize those who excel in nonfiction writing." Submissions made by author. Deadline for entries: December 31. SASE for contest rules and entry forms. Entry fee is $18. Awards 3 cash prizes; choice of books; Honorable Mention Certificate. "Two people read each entry; third party picks three top winners from top five." Judging sheets sent if entry accompanied by SASE. Condensed version of 1st place may be published in *Authorship.*

NATIONAL WRITERS ASSOCIATION SHORT STORY CONTEST

10940 S. Parker Rd., #508, Parker CO 80134. (303)841-0246. **Executive Director:** Sandy Whelchel. Annual contest. Estab. 1971. Purpose of contest: "To encourage writers in this creative form and to recognize those who excel in fiction writing." Submissions made by the author. Deadline for entries: July 1. SASE for contest rules and entry forms. Entry fee is $15. Awards 3 cash prizes, choice of books and certificates for Honorable Mentions. Judging by "two people read each entry; third person picks top three winners." Judging sheet copies available for SASE.

THE NENE AWARD

Hawaii State Library, Honolulu HI 96813. (808)586-3510. Fax: (808)586-3584. E-mail: hslear@netra.lib.state. hi.us. Estab. 1964. "The Nene Award was designed to help the children of Hawaii become acquainted with

Jay Asher

Contests & grant wins—two reasons
why this YA author got published

Photo © Jayson Mellom

As I write this, Jay Asher's debut novel *Thirteen Reason's Why* enjoys its first week on the *New York Times* Best Seller List (just four spots below the Caldecott-winning novel *The Invention of Hugo Cabret*). No doubt that's quite satisfying for an author who spent 12 years working toward publication. "I went through three agents, two middle grade novels, a chapter book series, and too many picture books before I struck gold," says Asher.

What kept him going all those years? "My critique group," he says. "For several years, I met every two weeks with S.L.O.W. for Children (San Luis Obispo Writers for Children). Not only did they help me improve my storytelling, but they were my refuge when people in the 'adult world' saw writing for children or teens as a cute little hobby."

Asher's path to publication took a turn in the right direction after he entered—and won—two competitions. *Thirteen Reasons Why* won the 2003 SCBWI Work-in-Progress Grant for Unpublished Authors and the Smartwriters.com Write-It-Now Award. One of the judges for the SCBWI grant later took part in a three-house auction for Asher's book. Novelist Chris Crutcher, who judged the YA category of the SmartWriters.com contest later offered a blurb for the book's a cover. Says Crutcher: "*Very* clever premise, strong voice, perfect suspense. This one will keep you reading. Jay Asher is a *fine* storyteller."

Besides its place on the NYT Best Seller list, Asher's debut novel landed on three lists by the Young Adult Library Services Association (YALSA)—Best Books for Young Adults, Quick Picks for Reluctant Young Adult Readers, and Selected Audiobooks for Young Adults.

Asher has a two-book contract with Razorbill, so another YA work will be forthcoming. Below he talks about working on his debut novel, entering and winning contests, blogging and self-promotion. To learn more about Asher, visit Disco Mermaids, his blog with writer friends Robin Mellom and Eve Porinchak, www.discomermaids.blogspot.com; his book's site, www.thirteenreasonswhy.com; and his MySpace page, www.myspace.com/jay_asher.

How would you describe *Thirteen Reasons Why* to someone who knows nothing about it?

A boy comes home from high school to find an anonymous box of cassette tapes on his doorstep. He eventually finds a cassette player, pops in the first tape, hits play, and out comes the voice of Hannah Baker—his classmate and crush—who, two weeks earlier, committed suicide. She says there are 13 reasons why she took her life, with each side of each tape explaining one of those reasons. And if you received the box of tapes, you're one of the reasons why.

Resources

I used to start by saying, "It's a book for teens about suicide," but by then, people perceive the book as a traditional problem novel. By focusing on the element of suspense, they always ask to hear more. And I think it's a unique reading experience because you literally get two first-person narratives simultaneously.

What sparked your novel? What led you to YA?

A close relative of mine attempted suicide when she was about the same age as the main female character in my book. For years, we discussed her frame of mind at the time. The idea that small things can have a snowball effect in a person's life intrigued me. There were definitely serious issues I wanted to explore within the book, and I figured that writing it as a suspense novel would keep it from getting too heavy. But I never wanted to write a serious novel, or even a novel for teens, until this idea hit me. I wanted to write humorous books for younger readers. But when the idea hit, I just couldn't let it go. Before I started writing it, though, I was a huge fan of teen literature. The first YA novel I read was *Stotan*, by Chris Crutcher. I heard him speak at my first national SCBWI conference and bought his book simply because of his philosophy on the teen years. And seven years later, my first book has a blurb from him on the cover!

Jacket design: Christian Fünfhausen. Cover photo: Getty Images/Ryan McVay. Reprinted with permission.

Jay Asher created interest in his manuscript for *Thirteen Reasons Why* after two contest wins. After hooking up with an agent who set up a three-house auction, Asher's engrossing first novel was published by Razorbill.

What led you to apply for the SCBWI W-I-P grant and enter the Smartwriters.com's W.I.N. competition? Any tips for capturing judges' attention?

When you realize how many writers are currently trying to get published, it can seem impossible. So I aimed to make my manuscript stand out within the first sentence of my cover letter. I'm sure a lot of great manuscripts are rejected because of the frame of mind an editor's in when they read it. If you read 20 horrible manuscripts in a row, it's going to be hard to get excited about that next manuscript . . . or even keep a completely open mind. So I entered every contest around so I could highlight the manuscript as an award-winner from the beginning.

I don't think there's anything an author can do differently with a contest that they shouldn't be doing while seeking publication. It's all about keeping the reader reading.

How did you end up with Razorbill? Why is it good place for you? Do you have an agent or did you get published on your own?

I didn't think I needed an agent to sell this book, because editors were already expressing interest in it because of the SCBWI grant and SmartWriters.com. It was tempting, especially after 12 years of rejections, to jump at the slightest hint of interest. But I wanted to make sure I found the perfect editor, and I knew an agent would help me do that. Because of that decision, the book ended up in an auction involving three houses. After the bids were solidified, my agent set up three phone calls between myself and the editors. After talking with Kristen Pettit at Razorbill, I probably would've forgiven the advance just to work with her. (But I didn't!) There were two reasons I went with Razorbill. First, Kristen and I had identical visions for the book. She knew exactly what I was trying to say with the book, and she knew how to direct my fine-tuning of the story to get it there. Second, the marketing department at Penguin had some extremely creative ideas for marketing the book. So it came down to Kristen's connection to the book and Penguin's excitement.

You've done a lot in the way of promotion for your book—Class of 2k7, blogging, Web site, conference appearances, reading groups, podcasts, etc. How much of a presence had you created for yourself even before your first book was under contract? Can a writer make it if he's not putting himself out there online?

I don't think an online presence is a necessity; it's just another promotional tool on top of what authors have been doing for years. But yes, it's definitely helped me out. We started the Disco Mermaid blog less than a year before my book sold. Our whole point was to have fun within the writing community while we struggled to sell that first book. One series of posts we did, *The dePaola Code* (a spoof of *The DaVinci Code*), really helped raise our profile. We were three unpublished writers gaining a readership among librarians—which was weird. Tomie dePaola even posted the entire thing on his Web site! So when my book sold—and we had a lot of fun with that on our blog—more people were aware of it than if I didn't have a blog.

Your site thirteenreasonswhy.com is easy to navigate and cool to look at. What was your philosophy when you began planning your Web site?

Actually, that was put together by the Penguin marketing department. They're amazing. All I did was pick out bits of dialogue for them to record as clips from Hannah's audiotapes and get myself into a studio to record the podcasts.

I love the interactive map feature on your site—it's a great way for readers to experience the book. What was involved in pulling that off?

Penguin actually hired someone to design that map. They even had tangible maps printed up, which they sent out with the galleys. When I wrote the book, the map was actually a late addition to the story. I just felt Clay, the person we follow as we listen to the tapes, needed to be coaxed out of the house (primarily to keep his half of the story interesting). So that's why Hannah left maps for everyone on the tapes. And I thought, if the publisher wanted to run with that idea, it would be an interesting interactive element for the readers.

Recently *Thirteen Reasons Why* book clubs had formed, modeled after what Holtville Middle School did. How have these come about? What kind of questions are you answering on cassette?

Less than a month after HMS held their book club, we had six more schools and libraries lined up, and it's just kept building. I was impressed by how well organized Holtville was, and how they turned my novel into such a positive experience for their students. So I contacted some of the bookstores and school libraries I met on MySpace and told them what HMS was doing, and got some started that way. I also spoke about it on my blog and had more schools contact me through that.

Mostly, they want to know how I came up with the idea, if any of the 13 reasons were inspired by actual events, and what advice I can offer other budding writers.

Your blog posts are so engaging. Have you found certain types of posts elicit more response from your readers? And what's the story behind the Disco Mermaids?

The posts that are done purely to entertain our readers get the most response because they're often talked about on other blogs and discussion boards. For example, our design based on the Newbery scrotum controversy was huge. Magazines contacted us about reprinting it, and Susan Patron (the author of *Higher Power of Lucky*) even referenced it in her acceptance speech. But it's the lighthearted takes on the frustrations of being a writer that seem to connect the most. The great thing about that is it forces us to look for the fun twists in things that happen to us, even if they're not entirely pleasant when they happen.

We started the Disco Mermaids after we won two costume contests in a row at the national SCBWI conferences. The first year we dressed as disco dancers and the next year we went as mermaids. For three unpublished writers (at the time), we saw those wins as a fun way to stand out a little bit, so we started the blog. And because I'm so closely connected to the other Mermaids, my book sale brought even more attention to them. One Mermaid found her agent when she was contacted by an agent who liked the voice in her blog posts. And both Mermaids have been asked by editors to see manuscripts they spoke about on the blog.

Do you have any upcoming projects to tell us about?

I'm working on my next novel for teens, which is odd because I never would've seen myself as a YA author before working on *Thirteen Reasons Why*. But after my first school visit, I felt so energized to keep moving in this direction. Eventually, though, I'd love to pull out some of my middle-grade novels and bring them up to my current writing level.

Any advice you'd like to pass along?

It took me 12 years to sell my first book—but I wouldn't change a thing. I've had so much fun along the way and made lifelong friends by taking full advantage of things like SCBWI conferences and working on my blog. This is a business, but it's also an art. So have fun!

—Alice Pope

Resources

the best contemporary writers of fiction, become aware of the qualities that make a good book and choose the best rather than the mediocre.'' Previously published submissions only. Books must have been copyrighted not more than 6 years prior to presentation of award. Work is nominated by students, teachers and librarians in Hawaii. Nominations by publishers or authors are not accepted. Ballots are usually due around the middle of March. Awards plaque to the winning author who is invited to an awards ceremony in Honolulu. Judging by the children of Hawaii in grades 4-6. Requirements for entrants: books must be fiction, written by a living author, copyrighted not more than 6 years ago and suitable for children in grades 4, 5 and 6. Current and past winners are displayed in all participating school and public libraries. The award winner is announced in May.

NESTLÉ CHILDREN'S BOOK PRIZE

Booktrust, Book House, 45 East Hill, Wandsworth London SW18 2QZ United Kingdom. Fax: (00 44)20 8516 2978. E-mail: hannah@booktrust.org.uk. Web site: www.booktrusted.com. **Contact:** Rosa Anderson. ''The Nestlé Children's Book Prize was established in 1985 to encourage high standards and stimulate interest in children's books. The prize is split into 3 age categories: 5 and under, 6-8, 9-11. The books are judged by our adult panel, who shortlist 3 outstanding books in each category, and the final decision of who gets Gold, Silver and Bronze is left to the young judges. The young judges are chosen from classes of school children who complete a task for their age category; the best 50 from each category go on to judge the 3 books in their age category. From the 150 classes who judge the books, 1 class from each category is invited to present the award at the ceremony in London. The children are chosen from projects they submit with their votes.'' Open to works of fiction or poetry for children written in English by a citizen of the UK, or an author residing in the UK. All work must be submitted by a UK publisher. Deadline: June. Prize: Gold Award winners in each age category: £2,500; Silver Award winners in each age category: £1,500; Bronze Award winners in each age category: £500.

NEW ENGLAND BOOK AWARDS

New England Independent Booksellers Association, 297 Broadway, #212, Arlington MA 02474. (781)316-8894. Fax: (781)316-2605. E-mail: nan@neba.org. Web site: www.newenglandbooks.org/NE_awards.html. **Assistant Executive Director:** Nan Sorenson. Annual award. Estab. 1990. Purpose of award: ''to promote New England authors who have produced a body of work that stands as a significant contribution to New England's culture.'' Previously published submissions only. Submissions made by New England booksellers; publishers. ''Award given to authors 'body of work' not a specific book.'' Entries must be still in print and available. No entry fee. Judging by NEIBA membership. Requirements for entrants: Author/illustrator must live in New England. Submit written nominations only; actual books should not be sent. Member bookstores receive materials to display winners' books. Submission deadline: March 1.

NEW VOICES AWARD

Lee & Low Books, 95 Madison Ave., New York NY 10016. (212)779-4400. Fax: (212)532-6035. E-mail: general@l eeandlow.com. Web site: www.leeandlow.com/editorial/voices.html. **Editor-in-chief:** Louise May. **Open to students.** Annual award. Estab. 2000. Purpose of contest: Lee & Low Books is one of the few publishing companies owned by people of color. We have published more than 75 first-time writers and illustrators. Titles include *In Daddy's Arms I Am Tall: African Americans Celebrating Fathers*, winner of the Coretta Scott King Illustrator Award; *Passage to Freedom: The Sugihara Story*, an American Library Association Notable Book; and *Crazy Horse's Vision*, a Bank Street College Children's Book of the Year. Submissions made by author. Deadline for entries: October 31. SASE for contest rules or visit Web site. No entry fee. Awards New Voices Award— $1,000 prize and standard publication contract (regardless of whether or not writer has an agent) along with an advance on royalties; New Voices Honor Award—$500 prize. Judging by Lee & Low editors. Restrictions of media for illustrators: The author must be a writer of color who is a resident of the U.S. and who has not previously published a children's picture book. For additional information, send SASE or visit Lee & Low's Web site, (www.leeandlow.com/editorial/voices8.html).

JOHN NEWBERY MEDAL

Association for Library Service to Children, Division of the American Library Association, 50 E. Huron, Chicago IL 60611. (800)545-2433 ext.2162; Fax: (312)280-5271 E-mail: alsc@ala.org. Web site: www.ala.org. **Executive Director, ALSC:** Diane Foote. Annual award. Estab. 1922. Purpose of award: to recognize the most distinguished contribution to American children's literature published in the U.S. Previously published submissions only; must be published prior to year award is given. Deadline for entries: December 31. SASE for award rules. Entries not returned. No entry fee. Medal awarded at Caldecott/Newbery banquet during ALA annual conference. Judging by Newbery Award Selection Committee.

NORTH AMERICAN INTERNATIONAL AUTO SHOW HIGH SCHOOL POSTER CONTEST

Detroit Auto Dealers Association, 1900 W. Big Beaver Rd., Troy MI 48084-3531. (248)643-0250. Fax: (248)637-0784. E-mail: sherp@dada.org. Web site: www.naias.com. **Contact:** Sandy Herp. **Open to students.** Annual contest. Submissions made by the author and illustrator. Contact D.A.D.A. for contest rules and entry forms or retrieve rules from Web site. No entry fee. Awards in the High School Poster Contest are as follows: Chairman's Award—$1,000; Designer's Best of Show (Digital and Traditional)—$500; Best Theme—$250; Best Use of Color—$250; Most Creative—$250. A winner will be chosen in each category from grades 10, 11 and 12. Prizes: 1st place in 10, 11, 12—$500; 2nd place—$250; 3rd place—$100. The winners of the Designer's Best of Show Digital and Traditional will each receive $500. The winner of the Chairman's Award will receive $1,000. Entries will be judged by an independent panel of recognized representatives of the art community. Entrants must be Michigan high school students enrolled in grades 10-12. Winning posters may be displayed at the NAIAS 2006 and reproduced in the official NAIAI program, which is available to the public, international media, corporate executives and automotive suppliers. Winning posters may also be displayed on the official NAIAS Web site at the sole discretion of the NAIAS.

NORTHERN CALIFORNIA BOOK REVIEWERS (NCBR)

% *Poetry Flash*, Berkeley CA 94710. (510)525-5476. Fax: (510)525-6752. E-mail: babra@poetryflash.org. Web site: www.poetryflash.org **Contact:** Joyce Jenkins. Annual Northern California Book Award for outstanding book in literature, open to books published in the current calendar year by Northern California authors. Annual award. Estab. 1981. NCBR presents annual awards to Bay Area (northern California) authors annually in fiction, nonfiction, poetry and children's literature. Purpose is to encourage writers and stimulate interest in books and reading.'' Previously published books only. Must be published the calendar year prior to spring awards ceremony. Submissions nominated by publishers; author or agent could also nominate published work. Deadline for entries: December. No entry forms. Send 3 copies of the book to attention: NCBR . No entry fee. Awards $100 honorarium and award certificate. Judging by voting members of the Northern California Book Reviewers. Books that reach the "finals" (usually 3-5 per category) displayed at annual award ceremonies (spring). Nominated books are displayed and sold at the Northern California Book Awards in the spring of each year; the winner is asked to read at the San Francisco Public Library's Main Branch.

OHIOANA BOOK AWARDS

Ohioana Library Association, 2323 W. 5th Ave., Suite 130, Columbus OH 4320 4. (614) 728- 5252. Fax: (614)728-5256. E-mail: support@oplin.org. Web site: www oplin.org. **Director:** Linda R. Hengst. Annual award. ''The Ohioana Book Awards are given to books of outstanding literary quality. Purpose of contest: to provide recognition and encouragement to Ohio writers and to promote the work of Ohio writers. Up to six are given each year. Awards may be given in the following categories: fiction, nonfiction, children's/juvenile, poetry and books about Ohio or an Ohioan. Books must be received by the Ohioana Library during the calendar year prior to the year the award is given and must have a copyright date within the last two calendar years.'' Deadline for entries: December 31. SASE for award rules and entry forms (or downloaded from Ohioana's website at www.oh ioana.org/awards/books.asp). No entry fee. Winners receive citation and glass sculpture. ''Any book that has been written or edited by a person born in Ohio or who has lived in Ohio for at least five years is eligible.''

OKLAHOMA BOOK AWARDS

Oklahoma Center for the Book, 200 NE 18th, Oklahoma City OK 73105. (405)521-2502. Fax: (405)525-7804. E-mail: gcarlile@oltn.odl.state.ok.us. Web site: www.odl.state.ok.us/ocb. **Executive Director:** Glenda Carlile. Annual award. Estab. 1989. Purpose of award: ''to honor Oklahoma writers and books about our state.'' Previously published submissions only. Submissions made by the author, author's agent, or entered by a person or group of people, including the publisher. Must be published during the calendar year preceding the award. Awards are presented to best books in fiction, nonfiction, children's, design and illustration, and poetry books about Oklahoma or books written by an author who was born, is living or has lived in Oklahoma. Deadline for entries: early January. SASE for award rules and entry forms. Entry fee $25. Awards a medal—no cash prize. Judging by a panel of 5 people for each category—a librarian, a working writer in the genre, booksellers, editors, etc. Requirements for entrants: author must be an Oklahoma native, resident, former resident or have written a book with Oklahoma theme. Winner will be announced at banquet in Oklahoma City. The Arrell Gibson Lifetime Achievement Award is also presented each year for a body of work.

ONCE UPON A WORLD CHILDREN'S BOOK AWARD

Simon Wiesenthal Center's Museum of Tolerance Library and Archives, 1399 S. Roxbury Dr., Los Angeles CA 90035-4709. (310)772-7605. Fax: (310)772-7628. E-mail: bookaward@wiesenthal.net. Web site: www.wiesenth al.com/library. **Award Director:** Adaire J. Klein. Submit 4 copies of each entry to: Adaire J. Klein, Director of Library and Archival Services. Annual award. Estab. 1996. Submissions made by publishers, author or by author's agent. Suggestions from educators, libraries, and others accepted. Must be published January-December of previous year. Deadline for entries: March 30. SASE for contest rules and entry forms. Awards $1,000 and recognition of Honor Books. Judging by 3 independent judges familiar with children's literature. Award open to any writer with work in English language on subjects of tolerance, diversity, human understanding, and social justice for children 6-10 years old. The next award will be presented on October 28, 2007. Book Seals available from the Library.

ORBIS PICTUS AWARD FOR OUTSTANDING NONFICTION FOR CHILDREN

The National Council of Teachers of English, 1111 W. Kenyon Rd., Urbana IL 61801-1096. (217)328-3870. Fax: (217)328-0977. E-mail: dzagorski@ncte.org. Web site: www.ncte.org/elem/awards/orbispictus. **Chair , NCTE Committee on the Orbis Pictus Award for Outstanding Nonfiction for Children:** Kim Ford, Memphis TN. Annual award. Estab. 1989. Purpose of award: To promote and recognize excellence in the writing of nonfiction for children. Previously published submissions only. Submissions made by author, author's agent, by a person or group of people. Must be published January 1-December 31 of contest year. Deadline for entries: November 30. Call for award information. No entry fee. Awards a plaque given at the NCTE Elementary Section Luncheon at the NCTE Annual Convention in November. Judging by a committee. "The name Orbis Pictus commemorates the work of Johannes Amos Comenius, 'Orbis Pictus—The World in Pictures' (1657), considered to be the first book actually planned for children.''

THE ORIGINAL ART

Museum of American Illustration at the Society of Illustrators, 128 E. 63rd St., New York NY 10021-7303. (212)838-2560. Fax: (212)838-2561. E-mail: dir@societyillustrators.org. Web site: www.societyillustrators.org. **Publicity and Awards Coordinator:** Kim Sall. Annual contest. Estab. 1981. Purpose of contest: to celebrate the fine art of children's book illustration. Previously published submissions only. Deadline for entries: August 20. Request "call for entries" to receive contest rules and entry forms. Entry fee is $20/book. Judging by seven professional artists and editors. Works will be displayed at the Society of Illustrators Museum of American Illustration in New York City October-November annually. Medals awarded; catalog published.

HELEN KEATING OTT AWARD FOR OUTSTANDING CONTRIBUTION TO CHILDREN'S LITERATURE

Church and Synagogue Library Association, 2920 SW Dolph Ct Ste 3A, Portland OR 97219. (503)244-6919. Fax: (503)977-3734. E-mail: csla@worldaccessnet.com. Web site: www.cslainfo.org. **Chair of Committee:** Kay Mowery. Annual award. Estab. 1980. "This award is given to a person or organization that has made a significant contribution to promoting high moral and ethical values through children's literature." Deadline for entries: April 1. "Recipient is honored in July during the conference." Awards certificate of recognition and a conference package consisting of all meals, day of awards banquet, two nights' housing and a complimentary 1 year membership. "A nomination for an award may be made by anyone. It should include the name, address and telephone number of the nominee, plus the church or synagogue relationship where appropriate. Nominations of an organization should include the name of a contact person. A detailed description of the reasons for the nomination should be given, accompanied by documentary evidence of accomplishment. The person(s) making the nomination should give his/her name, address and telephone number and a brief explanation of his/her knowledge of the nominee's accomplishments. Elements of creativity and innovation will be given high priority by the judges.''

PATERSON PRIZE FOR BOOKS FOR YOUNG PEOPLE

Poetry Center at Passaic County Community College, One College Blvd., Paterson NJ 07505-1179. (973)684-6555. Fax: (973)523-6085. E-mail: mgillan@pccc.edu. Web site: www.pccc.edu/poetry. **Director:** Maria Mazziotti Gillan. Estab. 1996. Part of the Poetry Center's mission is "to recognize excellence in books for young people." Published submissions only. Submissions made by author, author's agent or publisher. Must be published between January 1-December 31 of year previous to award year. Deadline for entries: March 15. SASE for contest rules and entry forms or visit Web site. Awards $500 for the author in either of 3 categories: PreK-Grade 3; Grades 4-6, Grades 7-12. Judging by a professional writer selected by the Poetry Center. Contest is open to any writer/illustrator.

PEN/PHYLLIS NAYLOR WORKING WRITER FELLOWSHIP

PEN, 588 Broadway, New York NY 10012. (212)334-1660, ext. 108. Fax: (212)334-2181. E-mail: awards@pen.org. Web site: www.pen.org. Submit entries to: awards coordinator. Must have published 2 books to be eligible but no more than five. Annual contest. Estab. 2001. To support writers with a financial need and recognize work of high literary caliber. Unpublished submissions only. Submissions nominated. Deadline for entries: mid-January. Awards $5,000. Upon nomination by an editor or fellow writer, a panel of judges will select the winning book. Open to a writer of children's or young adult fiction in financial need, who has published at least two books, and no more than five during the past ten years. Please visit our Web site for full guidelines.

PENNSYLVANIA YOUNG READERS' CHOICE AWARDS PROGRAM

Pennsylvania School Librarians Association, 148 S. Bethelehem Pike, Ambler PA 19002-5822. (215)643-5048. Fax: (215)646-7250. E-mail: bellavance@verizon.net. Web site: www.psla.org. **Coordinator:** Jean B. Bellavance. Annual award. Estab. 1991. Submissions nominated by a person or group. Must be published within 5 years of the award for example, books published in 2003 to present are eligible for the 2007-2008 award. Deadline for entries: September 1. SASE for contest rules and entry forms. No entry fee. Framed certificate to winning authors. Judging by children of Pennsylvania (they vote). Requirements for entrants: currently living in North America. Reader's Choice Award is to promote reading of quality books by young people in the Commonwealth of Pennsylvania, to promote teacher and librarian involvement in children's literature, and to honor authors whose work has been recognized by the children of Pennsylvania. Four awards are given, one for each of the following grade level divisions: K-3, 3-6, 6-8, YA. View information at the Pennsylvania School Librarians Web site.

JAMES D. PHELAN AWARD

Intersection for the Arts, 446 Valencia Street, San Francisco CA 94103. (415)626-2787. Fax: (415)626-1636. E-mail: info@theintersection.org. Web site: www.theintersection.org. **Contest Director:** Kevin B. Chen. Submit entries to: Awards Coordinator. Annual contest. Estab. 1935. Purpose of contest: "To support unpublished manuscripts in progress." Unpublished submissions only. Submissions made by author. Deadline for entries: March 31. SASE for contest rules and entry forms. No entry fee. Awards: $2,000. Judging by 3 independent judges to be determined. "Must be born in California and must be between ages 20-35."

PLEASE TOUCH MUSEUM® BOOK AWARD

Please Touch Museum, 210 N. 21st St., Philadelphia PA 19103-1001. (215)963-0667. Fax: (215)963-0424. E-mail: kmiller@pleasetouchmuseum.org. Web site: www.pleasetouchmuseum.org. **Contact:** Frank Luzi. Annual award. Estab. 1985. Purpose of the award: "to recognize and encourage the publication of high-quality books for young children. The award is given to books that are imaginative, exceptionally illustrated and help foster a child's life-long love of reading. Each year we select one winner in two age categories—ages 3 and under and ages 4 to 7. These age categories reflect the age of the children Please Touch Museum serves. To be eligible for consideration, a book must: (1) Be distinguished in text, illustration, and ability to explore and clarify an idea for young children (ages 7 and under). (2) Be published within the last year by an American publisher. (3) Be by an American author and/or illustrator." SASE for award rules and entry forms. No entry fee. Publishing date deadlines apply. Judging by selected jury of children's literature experts, librarians and early childhood educators. Education store purchases books for selling at Book Award Ceremony and throughout the year. Autographing sessions may be held at Please Touch Museum, and at Philadelphia's Early Childhood Education Conference.

PNWA ANNUAL LITERARY CONTEST

Pacific Northwest Writers Association, PMB 2717-1420 NW Gilman Blvd, Ste 2, Issaquah, WA 98027. (425)673-2665. E-mail: staff@pnwa.org. Web site: www.pnwa.org. **Open to students.** Annual contest. Purpose of contest: "Valuable tool for writers as contest submissions are critiqued (2 critiques)." Unpublished submissions only. Submissions made by author. Deadline for entries: February 20, 2007. SASE for contest rules and entry forms. Entry fee is $35/entry for members, $50/entry for nonmembers. Awards $600-1st; $300-2nd; $150-3rd. Awards in all 12 categories.

POCKETS MAGAZINE FICTION CONTEST

Pockets Magazine, The Upper Room, P.O. Box 340004, Nashville TN 37203-0004. (615)340-7333. Fax: (615)340-7267. E-mail: pockets@upperroom.org. Web site: www.pockets.org. **Contact:** Lynn W. Gilliam, senior editor. The purpose of the contest is to find new freelance writers for the magazine therefore previous winners are not eligible. Annual competition for short stories. Award: $1,000 and publication in *Pockets*. Competition receives 400 submissions. Judged by *Pockets* editors and editors of other Upper Room publications. Guidelines available on website or upon request and SASE. No entry fee. No entry form. Note on envelope and first sheet: Fiction Contest. Submissions must be postmarked between March 1 and August 15 of the current year. **Unpublished submissions only.** Word length: 1,000-1,600 words. Winner notified November 1. Submissions returned after November 1 if accompanied by SASE.

EDGAR ALLAN POE AWARD

Mystery Writers of America, Inc., 6th Floor, 17 E. 47th St., New York NY 10017. (212)888-8171. Fax: (212)888-8107. E-mail: mwa@mysterywriters.org. Web site: www.mysterywriters.org. **Administrative Manager:** Margery Flax. Annual award. Estab. 1945. Purpose of the award: to honor authors of distinguished works in the mystery field. Previously published submissions only. Submissions made by the author, author's agent; "normally by the publisher." Work must be published/produced the year of the contest. Deadline for entries: Must be recieved by November 30. Submission infromation can be found at:www.mysterywriters.org. No entry fee. Awards ceramic bust of "Edgar" for winner; scrolls for all nominees. Judging by professional members of Mystery Writers of America (writers). Nominee press release sent in mid January. Winner announced at the Edgar® Banquet, held in late April/early May.

MICHAEL L. PRINTZ AWARD

Young Adult Library Services Association, Division of the American Library Association, 50 E. Huron, Chicago IL 60611. Fax: (312)280-5276. E-mail: yalsa@ala.org. Web site: www.ala.org/yalsa. Annual award. The Michael L. Printz Award is an award for a book that exemplifies literary excellence in young adult literature. It is named for a Topeka, Kansas school librarian who was a long-time active member of the Young Adult Library Services Association. It will be selected annually by an award committee that can also name as many as 4 honor books. The award-winning book can be fiction, nonfiction, poetry or an anthology, and can be a work of joint authorship or editorship. The books must be published between January 1 and December 31 of the preceding year and be designated by its publisher as being either a young adult book or one published for the age range that YALSA defines as young adult, e.g. ages 12 through 18. The deadline for both committee and field nominations will be December 1.

▟ PRIX ALVINE-BELISLE

Association pour l'avancement des sciences et des techniques de la documentation (ASTED) Inc., 3414 Avenue Du Parc, Bureau 202, Montreal QC H2X 2H5 Canada. (514)281-5012. Fax: (514)281-8219. E-mail: info@asted.o rg. **Executive Director:**Louis Cabral. Award open to children's book editors. Annual award. Estab. 1974. Purpose of contest: To recognize the best children's book published in French in Canada. Previously published submissions only. Submissions made by publishing house. Must be published the year before award. Deadline for entries: June 1. Awards $1,000. Judging by librarians jury.

QUILL AND SCROLL INTERNATIONAL WRITING/PHOTO CONTEST

Quill and Scroll, School of Journalism and Mass Communication, University of Iowa, Iowa City IA 52242-1528. (319)335-3457. Fax: (319)335-3989. E-mail: quill-scroll@uiowa.edu. Web site: www.uiowa.edu/ ~ quill-sc **Contest Director:** Vanessa Shelton. **Open to students.** Annual contest. Previously published submissions only. Submissions made by the author or school newspaper adviser. Must be published within the last year. Deadline for entries: February 5. SASE for contest rules and entry forms. Entry fee is $2/entry. Awards engraved plaque to junior high level sweepstakes winners. Judging by various judges. *Quill and Scroll* acquires the right to publish submitted material in the magazine if it is chosen as a winning entry. Requirements for entrants: must be students in grades 9-12 for high school division. Entry form available on Web site.

▦ REDHOUSE CHILDREN'S BOOK AWARD

Federation of Children's Book Groups, 2 Bridge Wood View, Horsforth, Leeds LS18 5PE England. (44)(113)258-8910. E-mail: marianneadey@aol.com. Web site: www.redhousechildrensbookawards.co.uk. **Coordinator:** Marianne Adey. Purpose of the award: "The R.H.B.A. is an annual prize for the best children's book of the year judged by the children themselves." Categories: (I) books for younger children, (II) books for younger readers, (III) books for older readers. Estab. 1980. Works must be published in the United Kingdom. Deadline for entries: December 31. SASE for rules and entry forms. Entries not returned. Awards "a magnificent silver and oak trophy worth over $6,000 and a portfolio of children's work." Silver dishes to each category winner. Judging by children. Requirements for entrants: Work must be fiction and published in the UK during the current year (poetry is ineligible). Work will be published in current "Pick of the Year" publication.

TOMAS RIVERA MEXICAN AMERICAN CHILDREN'S BOOK AWARD

Texas State University-San Marcos, EDU, 601 University Dr., San Marcos TX 78666-4613. (512)245-3839. Fax: (512)245-7911. E-mail: jb23@txstate.edu. Web site: www.education.txstate.edu **Award Director:** Dr. Jennifer Battle. Competition open to adults. Annual contest. Estab. 1995. Purpose of award: "To encourage authors, illustrators and publishers to produce books that authentically reflect the lives of Mexican American appropriate for children and young adults in the United States." Unpublished mss not accepted. Submissions made by "any interested individual or publishing company." Must be published the year prior to the year of consideration. Deadline for entries: November 1 of publication year. Contact Dr. Jennifer Battle for nomination forms, or send copy of book. No entry fee. Awards $3,000 per book. Judging of nominations by a regional committee, national committee judges finalists. Annual ceremony honoring the book and author/illustrator is held during Hispanic Heritage Month at Texas State University-San Marcos and a selected city.

▓ ROCKY MOUNTAIN BOOK AWARD: ALBERTA CHILDREN'S CHOICE BOOK AWARD

Rocky Mountain Book Award Committee, Box 42, Lethbridge AB T1J 3Y3 Canada. (403)381-0855. E-mail: rockymountainbookaward@shaw.ca. Web site: http://rmba.lethsd.ab.ca. **Contest Director:** Michelle Dimnik. Submit entries to: Richard Chase, board member. Open to students. Annual contest. Estab. 2001. Purpose of contest: "Reading motivation for students, promotion of Canadian authors, illustrators and publishers." Previously unpublished submissions only. Submissions made by author's agent or nominated by a person or group. Must be published between 2005-2007. Deadline for entries: January 17, 2008. SASE for contest rules and entry forms. No entry fee. Awards: Gold medal and author tour of selected Alberta schools. Judging by students. Requirements for entrants: Canadian authors and illustrators only.

▓ SASKATCHEWAN BOOK AWARDS: CHILDREN'S LITERATURE

Saskatchewan Book Awards, 205B-2314 11th Avenue, Regina SK S4P 0K1 Canada. (306)569-1585. Fax: (306)569-4187. E-mail: director@bookawards.sk.ca. Web site: www.bookawards.sk.ca. **Award Director:** Glenda James. Open to Saskatchewan authors only. Annual award. Estab. 1995. Purpose of contest: to celebrate Saskatchewan books and authors and to promote their work. Previously published submissions only. Submissions made by author, author's agent or publisher by September 15. SASE for contest rules and entry forms. Entry fee is $20 (Canadian). Awards $2,000 (Canadian). Judging by two children's literature authors outside of Saskatchewan. Requirements for entrants: Must be Saskatchewan resident; book must have ISBN number; book must have been published within the last year. Award-winning book will appear on TV talk shows and be pictured on bookmarks distributed to libraries, schools and bookstores in Saskatchewan.

SCBWI MAGAZINE MERIT AWARDS

Society of Children's Book Writers and Illustrators, 8271 Beverly Blvd., Los Angeles CA 90048. Fax: (323)782-1010. E-mail: scbwi@scbwi.org. Web site: www.scbwi.org. **Award Coordinator:** Dorothy Leon. Annual award. Estab. 1988. Purpose of the award: "to recognize outstanding original magazine work for young people published during that year and having been written or illustrated by members of SCBWI." Previously published submissions only. Entries must be submitted between January 1 and December 15 of the year of publication. For rules and procedures see Web site. No entry fee. Must be a SCBWI member. Awards plaques and honor certificates for each of 4 categories (fiction, nonfiction, illustration, poetry). Judging by a magazine editor and two "full" SCBWI members. "All magazine work for young people by an SCBWI member—writer, artist or photographer—is eligible during the year of original publication. In the case of co-authored work, both authors must be SCBWI members. Members must submit their own work." Requirements for entrants: 4 copies each of the published work and proof of publication (may be contents page) showing the name of the magazine and the date of issue. The SCBWI is a professional organization of writers and illustrators and others interested in children's literature. Membership is open to the general public at large.

SCBWI WORK-IN-PROGRESS GRANTS

Society of Children's Book Writers and Illustrators, 8271 Beverly Blvd., Los Angeles CA 90048. (323)782-1010. Fax: (323)782-1892. E-mail: scbwi@scbwi.org. Web site: www.scbwi.org. Annual award. "The SCBWI Work-in-Progress Grants have been established to assist children's book writers in the completion of a specific project." Four categories: (1) General Work-in-Progress Grant. (2) Grant for a Contemporary Novel for Young People. (3) Nonfiction Research Grant. (4) Grant for a Work Whose Author Has Never Had a Book Published. Requests for applications may be made beginning October 1. Completed applications accepted February 1-April 1 of each year. SASE for applications for grants. In any year, an applicant may apply for any of the grants except the one awarded for a work whose author has never had a book published. (The recipient of this grant will be chosen from entries in all categories.) Five grants of $1,500 will be awarded annually. Runner-up grants of $500 (one in each category) will also be awarded. "The grants are available to both full and associate members of the SCBWI. They are not available for projects on which there are already contracts." Previous recipients not eligible to apply.

SHUBERT FENDRICH MEMORIAL PLAYWRITING CONTEST

Pioneer Drama Service, Inc., P.O. Box 4267, Englewood CO 80155-4267. Fax: (303)779-4315. E-mail: submissions@pioneerdrama.com. Web site: www.pioneerdrama.com. **Director:** Lori Conary. Annual contest. Estab. 1990. Purpose of the contest: "To encourage the development of quality theatrical material for educational and family theater." Previously unpublished submissions only. Open to all writers not currently published by Pioneer Drama Service. Deadline for entries: December 31. SASE for contest rules and guidelines. No entry fee. Cover letter, SASE for return of ms, and proof of production or staged reading must accompany all submissions. Awards $1,000 royalty advance and publication. Upon receipt of signed contracts, plays will be published and made available in our next catalog. Judging by editors. All rights acquired with acceptance of contract for publication. Restrictions for entrants: Any writers currently published by Pioneer Drama Service are not eligible.

SKIPPING STONES BOOK AWARDS

Skipping Stones, P.O. Box 3939, Eugene OR 97403-0939. (541)342-4956. E-mail: info@skippingstones.org. Web site: www.skippingstones.org. Open to published books, magazines, educational videos, and DVDs. Annual awards. Purpose of contest: To recognize contributions to children's literature, teaching resources and educational audio/video resources in the areas of multicultural awareness, nature and ecology, social issues, peace and nonviolence. Submissions made by the author or publishers and/or producers. Deadline for entries: February 1. Send request for contest rules and entry forms or visit Web site. Entry fee is $50; 50% discount for small/nonprofit publishers. Each year, about 15-20 books and A/V resources are selected by a multicultural selection committee of editors, students, parents, teachers and librarians. Winners receive gold honor award seals, certificates and publicity via multiple outlets. Many educational publications announce the winners of our book awards. The reviews of winning books and educational videos/DVDs are published in the May-August issue of *Skipping Stones*, now in 19th year.

SKIPPING STONES YOUTH HONOR AWARDS

Skipping Stones, P.O. Box 3939, Eugene OR 97403-0939. (541)342-4956. E-mail: editor@SkippingStones.org. Web site: www.SkippingStones.org **Open to students.** Annual awards. Purpose of contest: "to recognize youth, 7 to 17, for their contributions to multicultural awareness, nature and ecology, social issues, peace and nonviolence. Also to promote creativity, self-esteem and writing skills and to recognize important work being done by youth organizations." Submissions made by the author. Deadline for entries: June 25. SASE for contest rules. Entries must include certificate of originality by a parent and/or teacher and a cover letter that included cultural background information on the author. Entry fee is $3. Everyone who enters the contest receives the September-October issue featuring Youth Awards. Judging by *Skipping Stones*' staff. "Up to ten awards are given in three categories: (1) Compositions—(essays, poems, short stories, songs, travelogues, etc.) should be typed (double-spaced) or neatly handwritten. Fiction or nonfiction should be limited to 1,000 words; poems to 30 lines. Non-English writings are also welcome. (2) Artwork—(drawings, cartoons, paintings or photo essays with captions) should have the artist's name, age and address on the back of each page. Send the originals with SASE. Black & white photos are especially welcome. Limit: 8 pieces. (3) Youth Organizations—Tell us how your club or group works to: (a) preserve the nature and ecology in your area, (b) enhance the quality of life for low-income, minority or disabled or (c) improve racial or cultural harmony in your school or community. Use the same format as for compositions." The winners are published in the September-October issue of *Skipping Stones*. Now in it's 20th year, *Skipping Stones* is a winner of N.A.M.E., EDPRESS and Parent's Choice Awards.

KAY SNOW WRITERS' CONTEST

Williamette Writers, 9045 SW Barbur Blvd. #5A, Portland OR 97219-4027. (503)452-1592. Fax: (503)452-0372. E-mail: wilwrite@willamettewriters.com. Web site: www.willamettewriters.com. **Contest Director:** Patricia MacAodha. Annual contest. **Open to students.** Purpose of contest: "to encourage beginning and established writers to continue the craft." Unpublished, original submissions only. Submissions made by the author. Deadline for entries: April 23rd. SASE for contest rules and entry forms. Entry fee is $10, Williamette Writers' members; $15, nonmembers; free for student writers grades 1-12. Awards cash prize of $300 per category (fiction, nonfiction, juvenile, poetry, script writing), $50 for students in three divisions: 1-5, 6-8, 9-12. Judges are anonymous.

SOCIETY OF MIDLAND AUTHORS AWARDS

Society of Midland Authors, P.O. Box 10419, Chicago IL 60610-0419. E-mail: writercc@aol.com. Web site: www.midlandauthors.com.

Annual award. Society estab. 1915. Purpose of award: "to stimulate creative literary effort," one of the goals of the Society. There are six categories, including children's fiction and nonfiction, adult fiction and nonfiction, biography and poetry. Previously published submissions only. Submissions made by the author or publisher. Must be published during calendar year previous to deadline. Deadline for entries: February 1st. SASE for award rules and entry forms or check Web site. No entry fee. Awards plaque given at annual dinner, cash ($300). Judging by panel (reviewers, university faculty, writers, librarians) of 3 per category. Author must be currently residing in, born in, or have strong connections to the Midlands, i.e., Illinois, Indiana, Iowa, Kansas, Michigan, Minnesota, Missouri, Nebraska, North Dakota, South Dakota, Ohio or Wisconsin.

SOUTHWEST WRITERS ANNUAL CONTEST

SouthWest Writers, 3721 Morris NE, Suite A, Albuquerque NM 87111. (505)265-9485. Fax: (505)265-9483. E-mail: swwriters@juno.com. Web site: www.southwestwriters.org. Submit entries to: Contest Chair. **Open to adults and students.** Annual contest. Estab. 1982. Purpose of contest: to encourage writers of all genres. Also offers mini-conferences, critique groups (for $60/year, offers 2 monthly programs, monthly newsletter, annual writing and monthly writing contests, other workshops, various discount perks, Web site linking, e-mail addresses and critique service (open to nonmembers). See Web site for more information or call or write.

GEORGE G. STONE CENTER FOR CHILDREN'S BOOKS RECOGNITION OF MERIT AWARD
George G. Stone Center for Children's Books, Claremont Graduate University, 740 N. College Ave., Claremont CA 91711-6188. (909)607-3670. **Award Director:** Carolyn Angus. Annual award. Estab. 1965. Purpose of the award: to recognize an author or illustrator of a children's book or a body of work exhibiting the "power to please and expand the awareness of children and teachers as they have shared the book in their classrooms." Previously published submissions only. SASE for award rules and entry forms. Entries not returned. No entry fee. Awards a scroll. Judging by a committee of teachers, professors of children's literature and librarians. Requirements for entrants: Nominations are made by students, teachers, professors and librarians. Award given in April.

THE JOAN G. SUGARMAN CHILDREN'S BOOK AWARD
Washington Independent Writers Legal and Educational Fund, Inc., P.O. Box 70437, Washington DC 20024-8437. (202)466-1344. E-mail: sugarman@Lefund.org. Web site: www.Lefund.org/sugarman.html. **Award Director:** Rob Anderson. Submit entries to: Rob Anderson. Award offered annually. Estab. 1987. Previously published submissions only during the two-year time frame specified for each award. Submissions made by author. No entry fee. Awards $1,000 cash prize for book judged best overall. Three honorable mentions in the categories of early readers, middle readers, and young adult readers are also recognized. Judging by a committee drawn from selected fields of children's literature, such as library science, editing, teaching, and psychology. Books eligible for the award must be written by an author residing in Virginia, Maryland or the District of Columbia and be published works with the copyright of 2002 or 2003. The books must be geared for children 15 years or younger, be original and have universal appeal. Since the books are judged on the basis of their written content, picture books without text are not eligible.

SYDNEY TAYLOR BOOK AWARD
Association of Jewish Libraries, P.O. Box 1118, Teaneck, NJ 07666. (212)725-5359. E-mail: chair@sydneytaylorbookaward.org. Web site: www.sydneytaylorbookaward.org. **Contact:** Kathe Pinchuck, chair. Offered annually for work published during the current year. "Given to distinguished contributions to Jewish literature for children. One award for younder readers, one for older readers, and one for teens." Publishers submit books.-Deadline: December 31, but we cannot guarantee that books received after December 1 will be considered.Guidelines on Web site. Awards certificate, cash award, and gold or silver seals for cover of winning book.

SYDNEY TAYLOR MANUSCRIPT COMPETITION
Association of Jewish Libraries, 204 Park St., Montclair NJ 07042. E-mail: stmacajl@aol.com. Web site: www.jewishlibraries.org. **Coordinator:** Aileen Grossberg. **Open to students** and any unpublished writer of fiction.Annual contest. Estab. 1985. Purpose of the contest: "This competition is for unpublished writers of fiction. Material should be for readers ages 8-11, with universal appeal that will serve to deepen the understanding of Judaism for all children, revealing positive aspects of Jewish life." Unpublished submissions only. Deadline for entries: December 15. Download rules and forms from website or send SASE for contest rules and entry forms. No entry fee. Awards $1,000. Award winner will be notified in April, and the award will be presented at the convention in June. Judging by qualified judges from within the Association of Jewish Libraries. Requirements for entrants: must be an unpublished fiction writer; also, books must range from 64-200 pages in length. "AJL assumes no responsibility for publication, but hopes this cash incentive will serve to encourage new writers of children's stories with Jewish themes for all children."

TEDDY AWARD FOR BEST CHILDREN'S BOOK
Writers' League of Texas, 611 S. Congress Ave., Suite 130, Austin TX 78704. (512)499-8914. Fax: (512)499-0441. E-mail: wlt@writersleague.org. Web site: www.writersleague.org. **Contact:** Kristy Bordine, membership administrator. Offered annually for work published June 1-May 31 in the previous year. Honors 2 outstanding books for children published by members of the Writers' League of Texas. Awards and recognition presented at the Texas Book Festival in Austin, Texas. Writer's League of Texas dues may accompany entry fee. Deadline: May 31. Charges $25 fee. Prize: Two prizes of $1,000, and teddy bears.

☕ THE TORONTO BOOK AWARDS
City of Toronto, 100 Queen St. W, 2nd Floor, West Tower, Toronto ON M5H 2N2 Canada. (416)392-8191. Fax: (416)392-1247. E-mail: bkurmey@toronto.ca. **Submit entries to:** Bev Kurmey, Protocol Officer. Annual award. Estab. 1974. Recognizes books of literary or artistic merit that are evocative of Toronto. Submissions made by

author, author's agent or nominated by a person or group. Must be published the calendar year prior to the award year. Deadline for entries: last week day of February annually. Awards $15,000 in prize money. Judging by committee.

MUNICIPAL CHAPTER OF TORONTO IODE JEAN THROOP BOOK AWARD

Toronto Municipal IODE, 40 St. Clair Ave. E., Suite 205, Toronto ON M4T 1M9 Canada. (416)925-5078. Fax: (416)925-5127. E-mail: iodetoronto@bellnet.ca; www.bookcentere.ca/awards/award_ind/awards.php?aw ard = iode **Contest Director:** Jennifer Werry. Submit entries to: Theo Heras, Lillian Smith Library, 239 College St., Toronto. Annual contest. Estab. 1974. Previously published submissions only. Submissions made by author. Deadline for entries: November 1. No entry fee. Awards: $1,000. If the illustrator is different from the author, the prize money is divided. Judging by Book Award Committee comprised of members of Toronto Municipal Chapter IODE. Requirements for entrants: Authors and illustrators must be Canadian and live within the GTA.

VEGETARIAN ESSAY CONTEST

The Vegetarian Resource Group, P.O. Box 1463, Baltimore MD 21203. (410)366-VEGE. Fax: (410)366-8804. E-mail: vrg@vrg.org. Web site: www.vrg.org. Annual contest. **Open to students.** Estab. 1985. Purpose of contest: to promote vegetarianism in young people. Unpublished submissions only. Deadline for entries: May 1 of each year. SASE for contest rules and entry forms. No entry fee. Awards $50 savings bond. Judging by awards committee. Acquires right for The Vegetarian Resource Group to reprint essays. Requirements for entrants: age 18 and under. Winning works may be published in *Vegetarian Journal*, instructional materials for students. Submit 2-3 page essay on any aspect of vegetarianism, which is the abstinence of meat, fish and fowl. Entrants can base paper on interviewing, research or personal opinion. Need not be vegetarian to enter.

VFW VOICE OF DEMOCRACY

Veterans of Foreign Wars of the U.S., 406 W. 34th St., Kansas City MO 64111. (816)968-1117. Fax: (816)968-1149. Web site: www.vfw.org. **Open to high school students.** Annual contest. Estab. 1960. Purpose of contest: to give high school students the opportunity to voice their opinions about their responsibility to our country and to convey those opinions via the broadcast media to all of America. Deadline for entries: November 1. No entry fee. Winners receive awards ranging from $1,000-25,000. Requirements for entrants: "Ninth-twelfth grade students in public, parochial, private and home schools are eligible to compete. Former first place state winners are not eligible to compete again. Contact your participating high school teacher, counselor, our Web site www.vfw.org or your local VFW Post to enter."

VIRGINIA LIBRARY ASSOCIATION/JEFFERSON CUP

Virginia Library Association, P.O. Box 8277, Norfolk, VA 23503-0277. (757)583-0041; Fax: (757)583-5041. E-mail lhahne@coastalnet.com. Web site: www.vla.org. **Executive Director:** Linda Hahne. Award director changes year to year. 2007 Jefferson Cup Director: Audrey Mitchell, e-mail amitchell@kwcps.k12.va.us. Annual award. Estab. 1983. Purpose of award "The Jefferson Cup honors a distinguished biography, historical fiction or American history book for young people. Presented since 1983, the Jefferson Cup Committee's goal is to promote reading about America's past; to encourage the quality writing of United States history, biography and historical fiction for young people and to recognize authors in these disciplines." Entries must be published in the year prior to selection. Deadline for entries, January 31st. Additional information on the Jefferson Cup and criteria on making submissions is available on the VLA Web site at http://www.vla.org/demo/Youth-Serv/JC-How-To.html. Judging by committee. The book must be about US history or an American person, 1492 to present, or fiction that highlights the US past; author must reside in the US. The book must be published especially for young people.

WASHINGTON CHILDREN'S CHOICE PICTURE BOOK AWARD

Washington Library Media Association, 10924 Mukilteo Speedway PMB 142, Mukilteo WA 98275. E-mail: wlma@earthlink.net. Web site: www.wlma.org/wccpba.htm. **Award Directors:** Dave Sonnen and Karen Heubschman. Submit nominations to: Kristin Galante, chairman; mail to Kristin Galante, WCCPBA, Lynndale Elementary School, 7200 191st SW, Lynnwood WA 98036. Annual award. Estab. 1982. Previously published submissions only. Submissions nominated by a person or group. Must be published within 2-3 years prior to year of award. Deadline for entries: January 15. SASE for contest rules and entry forms. Awards pewter plate, recognition. Judging by WCCPBA committee.

WASHINGTON POST/CHILDREN'S BOOK GUILD AWARD FOR NONFICTION

E-mail: theguild@childrensbookguild.org. Web site: www.childrensbookguild.org. **President:** changes yearly. Annual award. Estab. 1977. Purpose of award: "to honor an author or illustrator whose total work has contributed significantly to the quality of nonfiction for children." Award includes a cash prize and an engraved crystal paperweight. Judging by a jury of Children's Book Guild specialists, authors, illustrators and a *Washington Post* book critic. "One doesn't enter. One is selected. Our jury annually selects one author for the award."

WE ARE WRITERS, TOO!

Creative With Words Publications, Carmel CA 93922. Fax: (831)655-8627. E-mail: cwwpub@usa.net. Web site: members.tripod.com/CreativeWithWords. **Contest Director:** Brigitta Geltrich. **Open to students** (up to 19 years of age). Twice a year (January, August). Estab. 1975. Purpose of award: to further creative writing in children. Unpublished submissions only. Can submit year round on any theme (theme list available upon request and SASE). Deadlines for entries: year round. SASE for contest rules and entry forms. SASE for return of entries "if not accepted." No entry fee. Awards publication in an anthology. Judging by selected guest editors and educators. Contest open to children only (up to and including 19 years old). Writer should request contest rules. Include SASE with all correspondence. Age of child and home address must be stated and ms must be verified of its authenticity. Each story or poem must have a title. Creative with Words Publications (CWW) publishes the top 50-100 mss submitted to the contest. CWW also publishes anthologies on various themes throughout the year to which writers of all ages may submit.Focus is on Nature, Seasons, Animals, School/Education, and on Folklore.

WESTERN HERITAGE AWARDS

National Cowboy & Western Heritage Museum, 1700 NE 63rd St., Oklahoma City OK 73111-7997. (405)478-2250. Fax: (405)478-4714. E-mail: editor@nationalcowboymuseum.org. Web site: www.nationalcowboymuseu m.org. **Director of Publications:** M.J. Van deventer. Annual award. Estab. 1961. Purpose of award: The WHA are presented annually to encourage the accurate and artistic telling of great stories of the West through 13 categories of western literature, television, film and music; including fiction, nonfiction, children's books and poetry. Previously published submissions only; must be published the calendar year before the awards are presented. Deadline for literary entries: November 30. Deadline for film, music and television entries: December 31. Entries not returned. Entry fee is $45/entry. Awards a Wrangler bronze sculpture designed by famed western artist, John Free. Judging by a panel of judges selected each year with distinction in various fields of western art and heritage. Requirements for entrants: The material must pertain to the development or preservation of the West, either from a historical or contemporary viewpoint. Literary entries must have been published between December 1 and November 30 of calendar year. Film, music or television entries must have been released or aired between January 1 and December 31 of calendar year of entry. Works recognized during special awards ceremonies held annually at the museum. There is an autograph party preceding the awards. Awards ceremonies are sometimes broadcast.

JACKIE WHITE MEMORIAL NATIONAL CHILDREN'S PLAY WRITING CONTEST

Columbia Entertainment Company, 1800 Nelwood., Columbia MO 65202-1447. (573)874-5628. E-mail: bybetsy @yahoo.com. Web site: www.cectheatre.org. **Contest Director:** Betsy Phillips.Annual contest. Estab. 1988. Purpose of contest: "To encourage writing of family-friendly scripts." Previously unpublished submissions only. Submissions made by author. Deadline for entries: June 1. SASE for contest rules and entry forms. Entry fee is $10. Awards $500 with production possible. Judging by current and past board members of CEC and at least one theater school parent. Play may be performed during the following season. 2006 winner may be presented during CEC's 2006-07 season. We reserve the right to award 1st place and prize monies without a production. All submissions will be read by at least three readers. Author will receive a written evaluation of the script.

LAURA INGALLS WILDER METAL

Association for Library Service to Children, Division of the American Library Association, 50 E. Huron, Chicago IL 60611. (800)545-2433; Fax:(312)280-5271. E-mail: alsc@ala.org. Web site: www.ala.org/ala/alsc/awardssch olarships/literaryawds/wildermedal/wildermedal.htm. **Executive Director:** Diane Foote. Award offered every 2 years. Purpose of the award: to recognize an author or illustrator whose books, published in the U.S., have over a period of years made a substantial and lasting contribution to children's literature. The candidates must be nominated by ALSC members. Medal presented at Newbery/Caldecott banquet during annual conference. Judging by Wilder Award Selection Committee.

RITA WILLIAMS YOUNG ADULT PROSE PRIZE

National League of American Pen Women, Nob Hill, San Francisco Branch, 1544 Sweetwood Dr., Broadmoor Vlg., CA 94015-2029. E-mail: pennobhill@aol.com. Web site: www.soulmakingcontest.us. **Contact:** Eileen Malone. **Open to students.** Up to 3,000 words in story, essay, journal entry, creative nonfiction, or memoir by writers in grades 9-12. Annual prize. Deadline: November 30. Guidelines for SASE or atwww.soulmakingcontest

.us. Charges $5/entry (make checks payable to NLAPW, Nob Hill Branch). Prize: 1st Place: $100; 2nd Place: $50; 3rd Place: $25. Open to any writer in grade 9-12.or equivalent.

PAUL A. WITTY OUTSTANDING LITERATURE AWARD

International Reading Association, Special Interest Group, Reading for Gifted and Creative Learning, School of Education, TCU Box 297900, Fort Worth TX 76129. (817)257-6938. Fax: (817)257-7480. Web site: www.reading. org/association/awards/sig_witty.html. **Award Director:** Dr. Cathy Collins Block. **Open to students.** Annual award. Estab. 1979. Categories of entries: poetry/prose at elementary, junior high and senior high levels. Unpublished submissions only. Deadline for entries: February 1. SASE for award rules and entry forms. SASE for return of entries. No entry fee. Awards $25 and plaque, also certificates of merit. Judging by 2 committees for screening and awarding. "The elementary students' entries must be legible and may not exceed 1,000 words. Secondary students' prose entries should be typed and may exceed 1,000 words if necessary. At both elementary and secondary levels, if poetry is entered, a set of five poems must be submitted. All entries and requests for applications must include a self-addressed, stamped envelope."

PAUL A. WITTY SHORT STORY AWARD

International Reading Association, P.O. Box 8139, 800 Barksdale Rd., Newark DE 19714-8139. (302)731-1600. E-mail: exec@reading.org. Web site: www.reading.org. "The entry must be an original short story appearing in a young children's periodical for the first time. The short story should serve as a literary standard that encourages young readers to read periodicals." Deadline for entries: The entry must have been published for the first time in the eligibility year; the short story must be submitted during the calendar year of publication. Anyone wishing to nominate a short story should send it to the designated Paul A. Witty Short Award Subcommittee Chair by December 1. Award is $1,000 and recognition at the annual IRA Convention.

JOHN WOOD COMMUNITY COLLEGE CREATIVE WRITING CONTEST

Business Office—Writing Conference, John Wood Community College, 1301 S. 48th Street, Quincy IL 62305. (217)641-4940. Fax: (217)641-4900. E-mail: jmcgovern@jwcc.edu. Web site: www.jwcc.edu. **Contact:** Janet McGovern, education specialist . The college sponsors a writing contest for poetry, fiction and nonfiction. Entries for the contest are accpeted March-April of each year. Please see the JWCC Web site for more details or e-mail. jmcgovern@jwcc.edu for more information. In addition, the college sponsors writing workshops, readings, speakers, a humanities series, a photography show in spring, and an art competition in the fall.

ALICE WOOD MEMORIAL OHIOANA AWARD FOR CHILDREN'S LITERATURE

Ohioana Library Association, 274 E. First Ave., Suite 300, Columbus OH 43201. (614)466-3831. Fax: (614)728-6974. E-mail: ohioana@sloma.state.oh.us. Web site: www.ohioana.org. **Contact:** Linda R. Hengst. Offered to an author whose body of work has made, and continues to make, a significant contribution to literature for children or young adults and through their work as a writer, teacher, administrator, and community member, interest in children's literature has been encouraged and children have become involved with reading. Nomination forms for SASE. Recipient must have been born in Ohio or lived in Ohio at least 5 years. Deadline: December 31. Awards $1,000 cash prize.

WRITE IT NOW!

SmartWriters.com, 10823 Worthing Ave., San Diego CA 92126-2665. (858)689-2665. E-mail: editor@smartwrite rs.com. Web site: www.SmartWriters.com. **Editorial Director:** Roxyanne Young. Estab. 1994. Annual contest. "Our purpose is to encourage new writers and help get their manuscripts into the hands of people who can help further their careers." Unpublished submissions only. Submissions made by author. Deadline for entries: May 1. SASE for contest rules and entry forms; also see Web site. Entry fee is $15 for initial entry, $10 for additional entries. Awards a cash prize, books about writing, and an editorial review of the winning manuscripts. 2007's cash prize was $250, plus $100 cash prizes for category winners. Judging by published writers and editors. Requirement for entrants: "This contest is open to all writers age 18 and older. There are 5 categories: Young Adult, Mid-grade, Picture Book, Nonfiction, and Illustration." See Web site for more details, FAQ, and rules updates.

WRITING CONFERENCE WRITING CONTESTS

The Writing Conference, Inc., P.O. Box 664, Ottawa KS 66067. Phone/fax: (785)242-1995. E-mail: jbushman@w ritingconference.com. Web site: www.writingconference.com. **Contest Director:** John H. Bushman. **Open to students.** Annual contest. Estab. 1988. Purpose of contest: to further writing by students with awards for narration, exposition and poetry at the elementary, middle school and high school levels. Unpublished submissions only. Submissions made by the author or teacher. Deadline for entries: January 8. Consult Web site for guidelines and entry form. No entry fee. Awards plaque and publication of winning entry in *The Writers' Slate* online, April issue. Judging by a panel of teachers. Requirements for entrants: must be enrolled in school—K-12th grade.

⚎ WRITING FOR CHILDREN COMPETITION

90 Richmond St. E, Suite 200, Toronto ON M5C 1P1 Canada. (416)703-8982, ext. 226. Fax: (416)504-9090. E-mail: competitions@writersunion.ca. Web site: www.writersunion.ca. **Open to students** and Canadian citizens or landed immigrants who have not had a book published. Annual contest. Estab. 1997. Purpose of contest: to discover, encourage and promote new writers of children's literature. Unpublished submissions only. Submissions made by author. Deadline for entries: April 24. Entry fee is $15. Awards $1,500 and submission of winner and finalists to 3 publishers of children's books. Word limit: 1,500. Judging by members of the Writers Union of Canada (published book authors). Requirements for entrants: Open only to unpublished writers. Please do not send illustrations.

YEARBOOK EXCELLENCE CONTEST

Quill and Scroll Society, School of Journalism and Mass Communication, 100 Adler Building, Room E346, Iowa City IA 52242- 2004. (319)335-3457. Fax: (319)335-3989. E-mail: quill-scroll@uiowa.edu. Web site: www.uiowa .edu/ ~ quill-sc. **Executive Director:** Vanessa Shelton. **Open to students whose schools have Quill and Scroll charters.** Annual contest. Estab. 1987. Purpose of contest: to recognize and reward student journalists for their work in yearbooks and to provide student winners an opportunity to apply for a scholarship to be used freshman year in college for students planning to major in journalism. Previously published submissions only. Submissions made by the author or school yearbook adviser. Must be published between in the 12-month span prior to contest deadline. Deadline for entries: November 1. SASE for contest rules and entry form. Entry fee is $2 per entry. Awards National Gold Key; sweepstakes winners receive plaque; seniors eligible for scholarships. Judging by various judges. Winning entries may be published in *Quill and Scroll* magazine.

⚎ YOUNG ADULT CANADIAN BOOK AWARD

The Canadian Library Association, 328 Frank St., Ottawa ON K2P 0X8 Canada. (613)232-9625. Fax: (613)563-9895. Web site: www.cla.ca. **Contact:** Committee Chair. Annual award. Estab. 1981. Purpose of award: "to recognize the author of an outstanding English-language Canadian book which appeals to young adults between the ages of 13 and 18 that was published the preceding calendar year. Information is available upon request. We approach publishers. Entries are not returned. No entry fee. Awards a leather-bound book. Requirement for entrants: must be a work of fiction (novel or short stories), the title must be a Canadian publication in either hardcover or paperback, and the author must be a Canadian citizen or landed immigrant. Award given at the Canadian Library Association Conference.

THE YOUTH HONOR AWARD PROGRAM

Skipping Stones, P.O. Box 3939, Eugene OR 97403. (514)342-4956. E-mail: info@skippingstones.org. Web site: www.skippingstones.org. **Director of Public Relations:** Arun N. Toke. **Open to students.** Annual contest. Estab. 1994. Purpose of contest: "To recognize creative and artistic works by young people that promote multicultural awareness and nature appreciation." Unpublished submissions only. Submissions made by author. Deadline for entries: June 25. SASE for contest rules and entry forms. Entry fee is $3; low-income entrants, free. "Ten winners will be published in our fall issue. Winners will also receive an Honor Award Certificate, a subscription to *Skipping Stones* and five nature and/or multicultural books." Requirements for entrants: Original writing (essays, interviews, poems, plays, short stories, etc.) and art (photos, paintings, cartoons, etc.) are accepted from youth ages 7 to 17. Non-English and bilingual writings are welcome. Also, you must include a certificate of originality signed by a parent or teacher. "Include a cover letter telling about yourself and your submissions, your age, and contact information. Every student who enters will receive a copy of *Skipping Stones* featuring the ten winning entries."

THE ANNA ZORNIO MEMORIAL CHILDREN'S THEATRE PLAYWRITING AWARD

University of New Hampshire, Department of Theatre and Dance, Paul Creative Arts Center, 30 College Rd., Durham NH 03824-3538. (603)862-3038. Fax: (603)862-0298. E-mail: mike.wood@unh.edu. Web site: www.un h.edu/theatre-dance/zornio.html. **Contact:** Michael Wood. Contest every 4 years; next contest is November 2008 for 2009-2010 season. Estab. 1979. Purpose of the award: "to honor the late Anna Zornio, an alumna of The University of New Hampshire, for dedication to and inspiration of playwriting for young people, K-12th grade. Open to playwrights who are residents of the U.S. and Canada. Plays or musicals should run about 45 minutes." Unpublished submissions only. Submissions made by the author. Deadline for entries: March 3, 2008. SASE for award rules and entry forms. No entry fee. Awards $1,000 plus guaranteed production. Judging by faculty committee. Acquires rights to campus production. For more information visit Web site.

Helpful Books & Publications

The editors of *Children's Writer's & Illustrator's Market* suggest the following books and periodicals to keep you informed on writing and illustrating techniques, trends in the field, business issues, industry news and changes, and additional markets.

BOOKS

An Author's Guide to Children's Book Promotion, Ninth edition, by Susan Salzman Raab, 345 Millwood Rd., Chappaqua NY 10514. (914)241-2117. E-mail: info@raabassociates.com. Web site: www.raabassociates.com/authors.htm.

The Business of Writing for Children, by Aaron Shepard, Shepard Publications. Available on www.amazon.com.

Children's Writer Guide, (annual), The Institute of Children's Literature, 93 Long Ridge Rd., West Redding CT 06896-0811. (800)443-6078. Web site: www.writersbookstore.com.

The Children's Writer's Reference, by Berthe Amoss and Eric Suben, Writer's Digest Books, 4700 E. Galbraith Rd., Cincinnati OH 45236. (800)448-0915. Web site: www.writersdigest.com.

Children's Writer's Word Book, Second edition, by Alijandra Mogilner & Tayopa Mogilner, Writer's Digest Books, 4700 E. Galbraith Rd., Cincinnati OH 45236. (800)448-0915. Web site: www.writersdigest.com.

The Complete Idiot's Guide® to Publishing Children's Books, Second Edition, by Harold D. Underdown, Alpha Books, 201 W. 103rd St., Indianapolis IN 46290. Web site: www.underdown.org/cig.htm.

Creating Characters Kids Will Love, by Elaine Marie Alphin, Writer's Digest Books, 4700 E. Galbraith Rd., Cincinnati OH 45236. (800)448-0915. Web site: www.writersdigest.com.

Formatting & Submitting Your Manuscript, Second Edition, by Cynthia Laufenberg and the editors of Writer's Market, Writer's Digest Books, 4700 E. Galbraith Rd., Cincinnati OH 45236. (800)448-0915. Web site: www.writersdigest.com.

Guide to Literary Agents, edited by Chuck Sambuchino, Writer's Digest Books, 4700 E. Galbraith Rd., Cincinnati OH 45236. (800)448-0915. Web site: www.writersdigest.com.

How to Write a Children's Book and Get It Published, Third Edition, by Barbara Seuling, John Wiley & Sons, 111 River St., Hoboken NJ 07030. (201)748-6000. Web site: www.wiley.com.

How to Write and Illustrate Children's Books and Get Them Published, edited by Treld Pelkey Bicknell and Felicity Trottman, Writer's Digest Books, 4700 E. Galbraith Rd., Cincinnati OH 45236. (800)448-0915. Web site: www.writersdigest.com.

How to Write Attention-Grabbing Query & Cover Letters, by John Wood, Writer's Digest Books, 4700 E. Galbraith Rd., Cincinnati OH 45236. (800)448-0915. Web site: www.writers digest.com.

Illustrating Children's Books: Creating Pictures for Publication, by Martin Salisbury, Barron's Educational Series, 250 Wireless Blvd., Hauppauge NY 11788. (800)645-3476. Web site: www.barronseduc.com.

It's a Bunny-Eat-Bunny World: A Writer's Guide to Surviving and Thriving in Today's Competitive Children's Book Market, by Olga Litowinsky, Walker & Company, 104 Fifth Ave., New York NY 10011. (212)727-8300. Web site: www.walkerbooks.com.

Page After Page: discover the confidence & passion you need to start writing & keep writing (no matter what), by Heather Sellers, Writer's Digest Books, 4700 E. Galbraith Rd., Cincinnati OH 45236. (800)448-0915. Web site: www.writersdigest.com.

Picture Writing: A New Approach to Writing for Kids and Teens, by Anastasia Suen, Writer's Digest Books, 4700 E. Galbraith Rd., Cincinnati OH 45236. (800)448-0915. Web site: www.writersdigest.com.

Story Sparkers: A Creativity Guide for Children's Writers, by Marcia Thornton Jones and Debbie Dadey, Writer's Digest Books, 4700 E. Galbraith Rd., Cincinnati OH 45236. (800)448-0915. Web site: www.writersdigest.com.

Take Joy: A Writer's Guide to Loving the Craft, by Jane Yolen, Writer's Digest Books, 4700 E. Galbraith Rd., Cincinnati OH 45236. (800)448-0915. Web site: www.writersdigest.com.

A Teen's Guide to Getting Published; Publishing for Profit, Recognition and Academic Success, Second edition, by Jessica Dunn & Danielle Dunn, Prufrock Press, P.O. Box 8813, Waco TX 76714-8813. (800)998-2208. Web site: www.prufrock.com.

The Writer's Guide to Crafting Stories for Children, by Nancy Lamb, Writer's Digest Books, 4700 E. Galbraith Rd., Cincinnati OH 45236. (800)448-0915. Web site: www.writers digest.com.

Writing and Illustrating Children's Books for Publication: Two Perspectives, Revised Edition, by Berthe Amoss and Eric Suben, Writer's Digest Books, 4700 E. Galbraith Rd., Cincinnati OH 45236. (800)448-0915. Web site: www.writersdigest.com.

N Writing & Selling the YA Novel, by K.L. Going, Writer's Digest Books, 4700 E. Galbraith Rd., Cincinnati OH 45236. (800)448-0915. Web site: www.writersdigest.com.

Writing for Young Adults, by Sherry Garland, Writer's Digest Books, 4700 E. Galbraith Rd., Cincinnati OH 45236. (800)448-0915. Web site: www.writersdigest.com.

Writing With Pictures: How to Write and Illustrate Children's Books, by Uri Shulevitz, Watson-Guptill Publications, 770 Broadway, New York NY 10003. (800)278-8477. Web site: www.watsonguptill.com/products.html.

You Can Write Children's Books, by Tracey E. Dils, Writer's Digest Books, 4700 E. Galbraith Rd., Cincinnati OH 45236. (800)448-0915. Web site: www.writersdigest.com.

You Can Write Children's Books Workbook, by Tracey E. Dils, Writer's Digest Books, 4700 E. Galbraith Rd., Cincinnati OH 45236. (800)448-0915. Web site: www.writersdigest.com.

Resources

PUBLICATIONS

Book Links: Connecting Books, Libraries and Classrooms, editor Laura Tillotson, American Library Association, 50 E. Huron St., Chicago IL 60611. (800)545-2433. Web site: www. ala.org/BookLinks. *Magazine published 6 times a year (September-July) for the purpose of connecting books, libraries and classrooms. Features articles on specific topics followed by bibliographies recommending books for further information. Subscription: $39.95/year.*

Children's Book Insider, editor Laura Backes, 901 Columbia Rd., Ft. Collins CO 80525-1838. (970)495-0056 or (800)807-1916. E-mail: mail@write4kids.com. Web site: www.write4ki ds.com. *Monthly newsletter covering markets, techniques and trends in children's publishing. Subscription: $29.95/year; electronic version $26.95/year.*

Children's Writer, editor Susan Tierney, The Institute of Children's Literature, 93 Long Ridge Rd., West Redding CT 06896-0811. (800)443-6078. Web site: www.childrenswriter.com. *Monthly newsletter of writing and publishing trends in the children's field. Subscription: $24/year; special introductory rate: $19.*

The Five Owls, editor Dr. Mark West, P.O. Box 235, Marathon TX 79842. (432)386-4257. Web site: www.fiveowls.com. *Quarterly online newsletter for readers personally and professionally involved in children's literature. Subscription: $35/year.*

The Horn Book Magazine, editor-in-chief Roger Sutton, The Horn Book Inc., 56 Roland St., Suite 200, Boston MA 02129. (800)325-1170. E-mail: info@hbook.com or cgross@hbook.c om. Web site: www.hbook.com. *Bimonthly guide to the children's book world including views on the industry and reviews of the latest books. Subscription: $34.95/year for new subscriptions; $49/year for renewals.*

The Lion and the Unicorn: A Critical Journal of Children's Literature, editors George Bodmer, Lisa Paul and Sandra Beckett, The Johns Hopkins University Press, P.O. Box 19966, Baltimore MD 21211-0966. (800)548-1784 or (410)516-6987 (outside the U.S. and Canada). E-mail: jrlncirc@press.jhu.edu. Web site: www.press.jhu.edu/journals/lion_an d_the_unicorn/. *Magazine published 3 times a year serving as a forum for discussion of children's literature featuring interviews with authors, editors and experts in the field. Subscription: $33/year.*

Once Upon a Time, editor Audrey Baird, 553 Winston Court, St. Paul MN 55118. (651)457-6223. E-mail: audreyouat@comcast.net. Web site: www.onceuponatimemag.com. *Quarterly support magazine for children's writers and illustrators and those interested in children's literature. Subscription: $27/year.*

Publishers Weekly, editor-in-chief Sara Nelson, Reed Business Information, a division of Reed Elsevier Inc., 360 Park Ave. S., New York NY 10010. (800)278-2991. Web site: www.publishersweekly.com. *Weekly trade publication covering all aspects of the publishing industry; includes coverage of the children's field and spring and fall issues devoted solely to children's books. Subscription: $239.99/year. Available on newsstands for $8/ issue. (Special issues are higher in price.)*

Society of Children's Book Writers and Illustrators Bulletin, editors Stephen Mooser and Lin Oliver, SCBWI, 8271 Beverly Blvd., Los Angeles CA 90048. (323)782-1010. E-mail: bulletin@scbwi.org. Web site: www.scbwi.org/pubs.htm. *Bimonthly newsletter of SCBWI covering news of interest to members. Subscription with $60/year membership.*

Resources

Useful Online Resources

The editors of *Children's Writer's & Illustrator's Market* suggest the following Web sites to keep you informed on writing and illustrating techniques, trends in the field, business issues, industry news and changes, and additional markets.

Amazon.com: www.amazon.com
Calling itself "A bookstore too big for the physical world," Amazon.com has more than 3 million books available on their Web site at discounted prices, plus a personal notification service of new releases, reader reviews, bestseller and suggested book information.

America Writes for Kids: http://usawrites4kids.drury.edu
Lists book authors by state along with interviews, profiles and writing tips.

Artlex Art Dictionary: www.artlex.com
Art dictionary with more than 3,200 terms

Association for Library Service to Children: www.ala.org
This site provides links to information about Newbery, Caldecott, Coretta Scott King, Michael L. Printz and Theodor Seuss Geisel Awards as well as a host of other awards for notable children's books.

Association of Authors' Representatives: www.aar-online.org
The Web site of the AAR offers a list of agent members, links, and frequently asked questions including useful advice for authors seeking representation.

Association of Illustrators: www.theaoi.com
This U.K.-based organization has been working since 1973 to promote illustration, illustrators' rights and standards. The Web site has discussion boards, artists' directories, events, links to agents and much more.

Authors and Illustrators for Children Webring: www.geocities.com/heartland/shores/2084/
Here you'll find a list of links of sites of interest to children's writers and illustrators or created by them.

The Authors Guild Online: www.authorsguild.org
The Web site of The Authors Guild offers articles and columns dealing with contract issues, copyright, electronic rights and other legal issues of concern to writers.

Barnes & Noble Online: www.barnesandnoble.com
The world's largest bookstore chain's Web site contains 600,000 in-stock titles at discount

prices as well as personalized recommendations, online events with authors and book forum access for members.

The Book Report Network: includes www.bookreporter.com; www.readinggroupguides.com; www.authorsontheweb.com; www.teenreads.com and www.kidsreads.com.
All the sites feature giveaways, book reviews, author and editor interviews, and recommended reads. A great way to stay connected.

Bookwire: www.bookwire.com
A gateway to finding information about publishers, booksellers, libraries, authors, reviews and awards. Also offers frequently asked publishing questions and answers, a calendar of events, a mailing list and other helpful resources.

Canadian Children's Book Centre: www.bookcentre.ca
The site for the CCBC includes profiles of illustrators and authors, information on recent books, a calendar of upcoming events, information on CCBC publications, and tips from Canadian children's authors.

Canadian Society of Children's Authors, Illustrators and Performers: www.canscaip.org
This organization promotes all aspects of children's writing, illustration and performance.

The Children's Book Council: www.cbcbooks.org
This site includes a complete list of CBC members with addresses, names and descriptions of what each publishes, and links to publishers' Web sites. Also offers previews of upcoming titles from members; articles from *CBC Features*, the Council's newsletter; and their catalog.

Children's Literature: www.childrenslit.com
Offers book reviews, lists of conferences, searchable database, links to over 1,000 author/illustrator Web sites and much more.

Children's Literature Web Guide: www.ucalgary.ca/ ~ dkbrown
This site includes stories, poetry, resource lists, lists of conferences, links to book reviews, lists of awards (international), and information on books from classic to contemporary.

Children's Writer's & Illustrator's Market Web Page: www.cwim.com
Visit the new web page for market updates and sign up for a free e-newsletter.

Children's Writing Supersite: www.write4kids.com
This site (formerly Children's Writers Resource Center) includes highlights from the newsletter *Children's Book Insider*; definitions of publishing terms; answers to frequently asked questions; information on trends; information on small presses; a research center for Web information; and a catalog of material available from *CBI*.

The Colossal Directory of Children's Publishers Online: www.signaleader.com/
This site features links to Web sites of children's publishers and magazines and includes information on which publishers offer submission guidelines online.

Cynthia Leitich Smith's Web site: www.cynthialeitichsmith.com
In addition to information about her books and appearances and a blog, Cynthia Leitich Smith has assembled a site chock full of great useful and inspiring information including interviews with writers and illustrators, favorite reads, awards, bibliographies, and tons of helpful links, many to help writers explore diversity.

Database of Award-Winning Children's Literature: www.dawcl.com
A compilation of over 4,000 records of award-winning books throughout the U.S., Canada,

Australia, New Zealand and the U.K. You can search by age level, format, genre, setting, historical period, ethnicity or nationality of the protagonist, gender of protagonist, publication year, award name, or even by keyword. Begin here to compile your reading list of award-winners.

The Drawing Board: http://thedrawingboardforillustrators.blogspot.com
This site for illustrators features articles, interviews, links and resources for illustrators from all fields.

Editor & Publisher: www.editorandpublisher.com
The Internet source for *Editor & Publisher*, this site provides up-to-date industry news, with other opportunities such as a research area and bookstore, a calendar of events and classifieds.

International Board on Books for Young People: www.ibby.org
Founded in Switzerland in 1953, IBBY is a nonprofit that seeks to encourage the creation and distribution of quality children's literature. They cooperate with children's organizations and children's book institutions around the world.

International Reading Association: www.reading.org
This Web site includes articles; book lists; event, conference and convention information; and an online bookstore.

Kid Magazine Writers: www.kidmagwriters.com
Writer Jan Fields created this site to offer support and information to the often-neglected children's magazine writer. The Web site features editor interviews, articles on technique, special reports, an A to Z magazine market guide, and archives of monthly features.

National Association for the Education of Young Children: www.naeyc.org.
This organization is comprised of over 100,000 early childhood educators and others interested in the development and education of young children. Their Web site makes a great introduction and research resource for authors and illustrators of picture books.

National Writers Union: www.nwu.org
The union for freelance writers in U.S. Markets. The NWU offers contract advice, greviance assistance, health and liability insurance and much more.

Once Upon a Time: www.onceuponatimemag.com
This companion site to *Once Upon A Time* magazine offers excerpts from recent articles, notes for prospective contributors, and information about *OUAT*'s 11 regular columnists.

Picturebook: www.picture-book.com
This site brought to you by *Picturebook* sourcebook offers tons of links for illustrators, portfolio searching, and news, and offers a listserv, bulletin board and chatroom.

Planet Esmé: A Wonderful World of Children's Literature: www.planetesme.com
This site run by author Esmé Raji Codell, offers extensive lists of children's book recommendations, including the latest titles of note for various age groups, a great list of links, and more. Be sure to click on "join the club" to receive Codell's delightful e-mail newsletter.

Publishers' Catalogues Home Page: www.lights.ca/publisher
A mammoth link collection of more than 6,000 publishers around the world arranged geographically. This site is one of the most comprehensive directories of publishers on the Internet.

The Purple Crayon: www.underdown.org
Editor Harold Underdown's site includes articles on trends, business, and cover letters

and queries as well as interviews with editors and answers to frequently asked questions. He also includes links to a number of other sites helpful to writers and excerpts from his book *The Complete Idiot's Guide to Publishing Children's Books*.

Slantville: www.slantville.com
An online artists community, this site includes a yellow pages for artists, frequently asked questions and a library offering information on a number of issues of interest to illustrators. This is a great site to visit to view artists' portfolios.

Smartwriters.com: www.smartwriters.com
Writer, novelist, photographer, graphic designer, and co-founder of 2-Tier Software, Inc., Roxyanne Young, runs this online magazine, which is absolutely stuffed with resources for children's writers, teachers and young writers. It's also got contests, interviews, free books, advice and well—you just have to go there.

Society of Children's Book Writers and Illustrators: www.scbwi.org
This site includes information on awards and grants available to SCBWI members, a calendar of events listed by date and region, a list of publications available to members, and a site map for easy navigation. Follow the Regional Chapters link to find the SCBWI chapter in your area.

The Society of Illustrators: www.societyillustrators.org
Since 1901, this organization has been working to promote the interest of professional illustrators. Information on exhibitions, career advice, and many other links provided.

U.K. Children's Books: www.ukchildrensbooks.co.uk
Filled with links to author sites, illustrator sites, publishers, booksellers, and organizations—not to mention help with Web site design and other technicalities—visit this site no matter which side of the Atlantic you rest your head.

United States Board on Books for Young People: www.usbby.org
Serves as the U.S. national section of the International Board on Books for Young People.

United States Postal Service: www.usps.com
Offers domestic and International postage rate calculator, stamp ordering, zip code look up, express mail tracking and more.

Verla Kay's Web site: www.verlakay.com
Author Verla Kay's Web site features writer's tips, articles, a schedules of online workshops (with transcripts of past workshops), a good news board and helpful links.

Writersdigest.com: www.writersdigest.com
Brought to you by *Writer's Digest* magazine, this site features articles, resources, links, writing prompts, a bookstore, and more.

Writersmarket.com: www.writersmarket.com
This gateway to the *Writer's Market* online edition offers market news, FAQs, tips, featured markets and web resources, a free newsletter, and more.

Writing-world.com: www.writing-world.com/children/
Site features reams of advice, links and offers a free bi-weekly newsletter.

Glossary

AAR. Association of Authors' Representatives.

ABA. American Booksellers Association.

ABC. Association of Booksellers for Children.

Advance. A sum of money a publisher pays a writer or illustrator prior to the publication of a book. It is usually paid in installments, such as one half on signing the contract, one half on delivery of a complete and satisfactory manuscript. The advance is paid against the royalty money that will be earned by the book.

ALA. American Library Association.

All rights. The rights contracted to a publisher permitting the use of material anywhere and in any form, including movie and book club sales, without additional payment to the creator.

Anthology. A collection of selected writings by various authors or gatherings of works by one author.

Anthropomorphization. The act of attributing human form and personality to things not human (such as animals).

ASAP. As soon as possible.

Assignment. An editor or art director asks a writer, illustrator or photographer to produce a specific piece for an agreed-upon fee.

B&W. Black and white.

Backlist. A publisher's list of books not published during the current season but still in print.

BEA. BookExpo America.

Biennially. Occurring once every 2 years.

Bimonthly. Occurring once every 2 months.

Biweekly. Occurring once every 2 weeks.

Book packager. A company that draws all elements of a book together, from the initial concept to writing and marketing strategies, then sells the book package to a book publisher and/or movie producer. Also known as book producer or book developer.

Book proposal. Package submitted to a publisher for consideration usually consisting of a synopsis, outline and sample chapters. (See Before Your First Sale, page 8.)

Business-size envelope. Also known as a #10 envelope. The standard size used in sending business correspondence.

Camera-ready. Refers to art that is completely prepared for copy camera platemaking.

Caption. A description of the subject matter of an illustration or photograph; photo captions include persons' names where appropriate. Also called cutline.

CBC. Children's Book Council.

Clean-copy. A manuscript free of errors and needing no editing; it is ready for typesetting.

Clips. Samples, usually from newspapers or magazines, of a writer's published work.

Concept books. Books that deal with ideas, concepts and large-scale problems, promoting an understanding of what's happening in a child's world. Most prevalent are alphabet and counting books, but also includes books dealing with specific concerns facing young people (such as divorce, birth of a sibling, friendship or moving).

Contract. A written agreement stating the rights to be purchased by an editor, art director or producer and the amount of payment the writer, illustrator or photographer will receive for that sale. (See Running Your Business, page 13.)

Contributor's copies. The magazine issues sent to an author, illustrator or photographer in which her work appears.

Co-op publisher. A publisher that shares production costs with an author, but, unlike subsidy publishers, handles all marketing and distribution. An author receives a high percentage of royalties until her initial investment is recouped, then standard royalties. (*Children's Writer's & Illustrator's Market* does not include co-op publishers.)

Copy. The actual written material of a manuscript.

Copyediting. Editing a manuscript for grammar usage, spelling, punctuation and general style.

Copyright. A means to legally protect an author's/illustrator's/photographer's work. This can be shown by writing ©, the creator's name, and year of work's creation. (See Running Your Business, page 13.)

Cover letter. A brief letter, accompanying a complete manuscript, especially useful if responding to an editor's request for a manuscript. May also accompany a book proposal. (See Before Your First Sale, page 8.)

Cutline. See caption.

Division. An unincorporated branch of a company.

Dummy. A loose mock-up of a book showing placement of text and artwork.

Electronic submission. A submission of material by modem or on computer disk.

Final draft. The last version of a polished manuscript ready for submission to an editor.

First North American serial rights. The right to publish material in a periodical for the first time, in the United States or Canada. (See Running Your Business, page 13.)

F&Gs. Folded and gathered sheets. An early, not-yet-bound copy of a picture book.

Flat fee. A one-time payment.

Galleys. The first typeset version of a manuscript that has not yet been divided into pages.

Genre. A formulaic type of fiction, such as horror, mystery, romance, science fiction or western.

Glossy. A photograph with a shiny surface as opposed to one with a non-shiny matte finish.

Gouache. Opaque watercolor with an appreciable film thickness and an actual paint layer.

Halftone. Reproduction of a continuous tone illustration with the image formed by dots produced by a camera lens screen.

Hard copy. The printed copy of a computer's output.

Hardware. All the mechanically-integrated components of a computer that are not software—circuit boards, transistors and the machines that are the actual computer.

Hi-Lo. High interest, low reading level.

Home page. The first page of a Web site.

IBBY. International Board on Books for Young People.

Imprint. Name applied to a publisher's specific line of books.

Internet. A worldwide network of computers that offers access to a wide variety of electronic resources.

IRA. International Reading Association.

IRC. International Reply Coupon. Sold at the post office to enclose with text or artwork sent to a recipient outside your own country to cover postage costs when replying or returning work.

Keyline. Identification of the positions of illustrations and copy for the printer.

Layout. Arrangement of illustrations, photographs, text and headlines for printed material.

Line drawing. Illustration done with pencil or ink using no wash or other shading.

Mass market books. Paperback books directed toward an extremely large audience sold in supermarkets, drugstores, airports, newsstands, online retailers, and bookstores.

Mechanicals. Paste-up or preparation of work for printing.

Middle grade or mid-grade. See middle reader.

Middle reader. The general classification of books written for readers approximately ages 9-11. Often called middle grade or mid-grade.

Ms (mss). Manuscript(s).

Multiple submissions. See simultaneous submissions.

NCTE. National Council of Teachers of English.

One-time rights. Permission to publish a story in periodical or book form one time only. (See Running Your Business, page 13.)

Outline. A summary of a book's contents; often in the form of chapter headings with a descriptive sentence or two under each heading to show the scope of the book.

Package sale. The sale of a manuscript and illustrations/photos as a "package" paid for with one check.

Payment on acceptance. The writer, artist or photographer is paid for her work at the time the editor or art director decides to buy it.

Payment on publication. The writer, artist or photographer is paid for her work when it is published.

Picture book. A type of book aimed at preschoolers to 8-year-olds that tells a story using a combination of text and artwork, or artwork only.

Print. An impression pulled from an original plate, stone, block, screen or negative; also a positive made from a photographic negative.

Proofreading. Reading text to correct typographical errors.

Query. A letter to an editor or agent designed to capture interest in an article or book you have written or propose to write. (See Before Your First Sale, page 8.)

Reading fee. Money charged by some agents and publishers to read a submitted manuscript. (*Children's Writer's & Illustrator's Market* does not include agencies that charge reading fees.)

Reprint rights. Permission to print an already published work whose first rights have been sold to another magazine or book publisher. (See Running Your Business, page 13.)

Response time. The average length of time it takes an editor or art director to accept or reject a query or submission and inform the creator of the decision.

Rights. The bundle of permissions offered to an editor or art director in exchange for printing a manuscript, artwork or photographs. (See Running Your Business, page 13.)

Rough draft. A manuscript that has not been checked for errors in grammar, punctuation, spelling or content.

Roughs. Preliminary sketches or drawings.

Royalty. An agreed percentage paid by a publisher to a writer, illustrator or photographer for each copy of her work sold.

SAE. Self-addressed envelope.

SASE. Self-addressed, stamped envelope.

SCBWI. The Society of Children's Book Writers and Illustrators. (See listing in Clubs & Organizations section.)

Second serial rights. Permission for the reprinting of a work in another periodical after its first publication in book or magazine form. (See Running Your Business, page 13.)

Semiannual. Occurring every 6 months or twice a year.

Semimonthly. Occurring twice a month.

Semiweekly. Occurring twice a week.

Serial rights. The rights given by an author to a publisher to print a piece in one or more periodicals. (See Running Your Business, page 13.)

Simultaneous submissions. Queries or proposals sent to several publishers at the same time. Also called multiple submissions. (See Before Your First Sale, page 8.)

Slant. The approach to a story or piece of artwork that will appeal to readers of a particular publication.

Slush pile. Editors' term for their collections of unsolicited manuscripts.

Software. Programs and related documentation for use with a computer.

Solicited manuscript. Material that an editor has asked for or agreed to consider before being sent by a writer.

SPAR. Society of Photographers and Artists Representatives.

Speculation (spec). Creating a piece with no assurance from an editor or art director that it will be purchased or any reimbursements for material or labor paid.

Subsidiary rights. All rights other than book publishing rights included in a book contract, such as paperback, book club and movie rights. (See Running Your Business, page 13.)

Subsidy publisher. A book publisher that charges the author for the cost of typesetting, printing and promoting a book. Also called a vanity publisher. (*Children's Writer's & Illustrator's Market* does not include subsidy publishers.)

Synopsis. A brief summary of a story or novel. Usually a page to a page and a half, single-spaced, if part of a book proposal.

Tabloid. Publication printed on an ordinary newspaper page turned sideways and folded in half.

Tearsheet. Page from a magazine or newspaper containing your printed art, story, article, poem or photo.

Thumbnail. A rough layout in miniature.

Trade books. Books sold in bookstores and through online retailers, aimed at a smaller audience than mass market books, and printed in smaller quantities by publishers.

Transparencies. Positive color slides; not color prints.

Unsolicited manuscript. Material sent without an editor's, art director's or agent's request.

Vanity publisher. See subsidy publisher.

Work-for-hire. An arrangement between a writer, illustrator or photographer and a company under which the company retains complete control of the work's copyright. (See Running Your Business, page 13.)

YA. See young adult.

Young adult. The general classification of books written for readers approximately ages 12-18. Often referred to as YA.

Young reader. The general classification of books written for readers approximately ages 5-8.

Names Index

This index lists the editors, art directors, agents and art reps listed in *Children's Writer's & Illustrator's Market*, along with the publisher, publication or company for which they work. Names were culled from Book Publishers, Canadian & International Books Publishers, Magazines, Young Writer's & Illustrator's Markets, and Agents & Art Reps.

D

Dahl, Michael (Stone Arch) 222

Dalheim, Mary (Ranger Rick) 269

Damkoehler, Katrina (Philomel) 207

Dandino, Jessica (Dial) 167

Darmstadt, Frank (Facts on File) 173

Dateno, Sr. Maria Grace (Pauline Books) 205

Davenport, May (May Davenport, Publishers) 167

Davies, Gill (Playne Books) 236

Davies, Sarah (The Greenhouse) 286

Davies, Zeta (QED Publishing) 237

Day, Alyson (Joanna Cotler Books) 165

Dean, Tanya (Darby Creek) 166

DeFabis, Sue (Five Star) 174

DeRidder, Sara (Sparkle) 271

Derr, Aaron (Boys' Life) 245

deVries, Maggie (Orca) 236

Dickinson, Philippa (Random House UK) 237

Diebel, Ann (Hyperion) 182

Dietsche, Meghan (Blooming Tree) 155

Dillon, Ann (Calliope, Cobblestone, Dig, Faces, Odyssey) 248, 252, 253, 259, 267

Dloughy, Caitlyn (Atheneum) 152

Doherty, Kathleen (Tor) 224

Donovan, Mary Lee (Candlewick) 160

Doobinin, Gail (Little, Brown) 192

Doorasamy, Sharon F. (Morgan Reynolds) 197

Dorfman, Debra (Grosset & Dunlap, Price Stern Sloan) 178, 210

Dryden, Emma D. (Atheneum, Margaret K. McElderry) 152, 194

Dubruiel, Michael (Our Sunday Visitor) 199

Dumars, Denise (Ashley Grayson Literary) 286

Duncan, Virginia (Greenwillow) 178

Dunham, Jennie (Dunham Literary) 284

Dwyer, Jeff (Dwyer & O'Grady) 284

E

Eagan, Cynthia (Little, Brown) 192

Easton, Emily (Walker) 226

Edwards, Marilyn (Boys' Quest, Fun for Kidz, Hopscotch) 246, 260, 262

Egan-Miller, Danielle (Brown & Miller) 283

Eisenhardt, Gae (Azro) 152

Ellenberg, Ethan (Ethan Ellenberg Literary) 285

Elwood, Lacy (Creative Kids) 277

Engle, Susan (Brilliant Star) 247

Esmond, Dwain Neilson (Insight) 263

Ewert, Jill (Sharing the Victory) 270

F

Falco, Rob (Children's Playmate) 250

Farrell, Kate (Henry Holt) 181

Feaster, Scott (Boys' Life) 245

Felus, Allison (Chicago Review Press) 162

Ferguson, Margaret (Farrar) 174

Field, Nancy (Dog-Eared) 168

File, Mary Ann (Catholic Forester) 249

Fillmore, Donna L. (Adventures, Discoveries) 242, 258

Fishell, Randy (Guide) 261

Fisk, Karen (Tilbury) 223

Fitzsimmons, Barbara (HarperCollins) 180

Flannery, Jennifer (Flannery Literary) 285

Fletcher, Kate (Candlewick) 160

Flounders, Anne (Career World) 249

Age-Level Index

This index lists book and magazine publishers by the age-groups for which they publish. Use it to locate appropriate markets for your work, then carefully read the listings and follow the guidelines of each publisher. Use this index in conjunction with the Subject Index to further narrow your list of markets. **Picture Books** and **Picture-Oriented Material** are for preschoolers to 8-year-olds; **Young Readers** are for 5- to 8-year-olds; **Middle Readers** are for 9- to 11-year-olds; and **Young Adults** are for ages 12 and up.

BOOK PUBLISHERS

Picture Books

Middle Readers

Young Adult/Teen

Subject Index

This index lists book and magazine publishers by the fiction and nonfiction subject areas in which they publish. Use it to locate appropriate markets for your work, then carefully read the listings and follow the guidelines of each publisher. Use this index in conjunction with Age-Level Index to further narrow your list of markets.

BOOK PUBLISHERS: FICTION

Adventure

Animal

Fantasy

Folktales

Humor

Subject Index

Suspense/Mystery

Subject Index

Pitspopany Press 208
Price Ltd., Mathew 237
Sterling Publishing Co., Inc. 222
Tricycle Press 225

Geography

Azro Press 152
Blooming Tree Press 155
Candlewick Press 160
Capstone Press Inc. 161
Carolrhoda Books, Inc. 161
Charlesbridge 162
Creative Education 166
Facts on File 173
Farrar, Straus & Giroux Inc. 174
Fenn Publishing Co. 233
Holiday House Inc. 181
Holt & Company, Henry 181
Houghton Mifflin Co. 182
Kaeden Books 189
Key Porter Books 234
Lerner Publishing Group 192
Lobster Press 235
NorthWord Books for Young
   Readers 198
Owen Publishers, Inc., Richard C.
   200
Pineapple Press, Inc. 208
Pitspopany Press 208
Price Ltd., Mathew 237
QED Publishing 237
Scholastic Library Publishing 214
Tor Books 224
Viking Children's Books 226
Weigl Publishers Inc. 227
Wiley & Sons, Inc., John 228
Williamson Books 229

Health

Bancroft Press 153
Capstone Press Inc. 161
Charlesbridge 162
Creative Education 166
Facts on File 173

Farrar, Straus & Giroux Inc. 174
Fenn Publishing Co. 233
Freestone/Peachtree, Jr. 175
Health Press NA Inc 180
Houghton Mifflin Co. 182
Hunter House Publishers 182
Kids Can Press 234
Lucent Books 193
Magination Press 194
Parenting Press, Inc. 201
Pitspopany Press 208
Price Ltd., Mathew 237
Scholastic Library Publishing 214
Whitman & Company, Albert 228
Wiley & Sons, Inc., John 228
Williamson Books 229

Hi-Lo

Azro Press 152
Barrons Educational Series 154
Farrar, Straus & Giroux Inc. 174
Houghton Mifflin Co. 182
Milet Publishing Ltd. 195
Owen Publishers, Inc., Richard C.
   200
Philomel Books 207
Place in the Woods, The 209
Price Ltd., Mathew 237
Viking Children's Books 226

History

Alaska Northwest Books 150
All About Kids Publishing 150
American Girl Publications 151
Azro Press 152
Bancroft Press 153
Blooming Tree Press 155
Calkins Creek Books 160
Capstone Press Inc. 161
Carolrhoda Books, Inc. 161
Cartwheel Books 161
Charlesbridge 162
Chicago Review Press 162
Coteau Books Ltd. 232

Hobbies

Music/Dance

Nature/Environment

Photography Index

This index lists markets that buy photos from freelancers and is divided into Book Publishers and Magazines. It's important to carefully read the listings and follow the guidelines of each publisher to which you submit.

BOOK PUBLISHERS

General Index

Market listings that appeared in the 2008 edition of *Children's Writer's & Illustrator's Market* but do not appear in this edition are identified with a two-letter code explaining why the listing was omitted: **(NR)**—no response to our requests for updated information; **(NS)**—not currently accepting submissions; **(RR)**—removed by request; **(RP)**—business restructured or purchased.